More Bad News From Israel

By the same authors

ISRAEL AND PALESTINE
Mike Berry and Greg Philo
(Pluto Press, 2006)

MORE BAD NEWS
FROM ISRAEL

Greg Philo and Mike Berry

THE RESEARCH GROUP
Greg Philo, Mike Berry, Alison Gilmour, Maureen Gilmour,
Suzanna Rust, Lucy West, John Brophy, Nicola Marshall,
Nicola Moat, Cairistiona Russell, Daniela Latina,
Colin Macpherson and Stevie Docherty

PlutoPress
www.plutobooks.com

First published 2004 as *Bad News From Israel*
This expanded and updated edition first published 2011 by Pluto Press
345 Archway Road, London N6 5AA

www.plutobooks.com

Distributed in the United States of America exclusively by
Palgrave Macmillan, a division of St. Martin's Press LLC,
175 Fifth Avenue, New York, NY 10010

British Library Cataloguing in Publication Data
A catalogue record for this book is available from the British Library

ISBN   978 0 7453 2979 6   Hardback
ISBN   978 0 7453 2978 9   Paperback

Library of Congress Cataloging in Publication Data applied for

This book is printed on paper suitable for recycling and made from fully managed
and sustained forest sources. Logging, pulping and manufacturing processes are
expected to conform to the environmental standards of the country of origin.

10   9   8   7   6   5   4   3   2   1

Designed and produced for Pluto Press by Chase Publishing Services Ltd
Typeset from disk by Stanford DTP Services, Northampton, England
Simultaneously printed digitally by CPI Antony Rowe, Chippenham, UK
and Edwards Bros in the USA

Contents

Acknowledgements

We would like to thank other members of the Glasgow University Media Group who helped us and gave advice and encouragement: John Eldridge, David Miller, Jacquie Reilly and Emma Miller. Thanks especially to Ruth Moore and Etta Gaskill who gave a great deal of time and energy to data preparation on the project. Thanks to Bernard Glancy for filming and also to Aidan Warner and Michelle Tonge for their help in preparing press reports. Thanks to others in the Department of Sociology: Andy Furlong, Giuliana Tiripelli, Chen Li, Emma Briant, Adrian Quinn, Yue Li, Ruth Madigan, Kathleen Ward, Lynn Campbell, Olive Kearns and Maureen McQuillan. Thanks also for help and advice to Avi Shlaim, Nachman Shai, David Ruben, Joy Wolfe, Ghada Karmi, Justin Lewis, Frank Webster, Lucretia Chauvel, David Morley, James Curran, Daya Kishan Thussu, Georgina Sykes, Mary Philo, David Anderson, David McLennan, Norman Finkelstein, Ian Lustick, Baruch Kimmering, Roane Carey, Gershon Shafir, Shaul Mishal and Geoffrey Aronson. For help in transcription, preparation of manuscripts and organising interviews, thanks also to Daniela Latina, Daniela Dudysova, Luke Nicholas, Scott Gordon and Anna Terje.

Many people helped in the development and setting up of interviews and focus groups. Thanks especially to Ursula Grimberg and to Lyndall O'Brien. Special thanks also to Anna and Iain Semple, Margaret and Andrew Dunn, Phillip Radcliffe, Claire Wood, Daniel Green, Phoebe Maine, Adele Cowie, Margaret and Keith Bradly, Gregor Mill, Mike Phillips, Jenny Owen and Sarah and John Philo.

Thanks also to all the journalists and media practitioners who spoke with us and who gave help and advice: George Alagiah, Brian Hanrahan, Tim Llewellyn, Lindsey Hilsum, Ken Loach, Adrian Monck, Gaye Flashman, John Humphrys, Sian Kevill, Chris Shaw, Gary Rogers, Fran Unsworth, Sue Inglish, Evan Davis, Paul Adams, Nik Gowing, John Underwood, Alex Graham, Sandy Ross, Paul McKinney, John Pilger, David Cowling, Robin Lustig, Marie Colvin, Rodrigo Va'zquez, Alan Hayling, Leon Barkho, Jack Enright, Colin Brierly and Donald McLeod, and the staff at Pluto Press: Anne Beech, Robert Webb and other members of the production team. Finally thanks again to all those people who took part in producing this work and who gave so much of their time and energy so freely and with such good grace.

East Jerusalem,
annexed by Israel, 1980

Settlement area (in
land to be annexed)

○ Other Settlements

1949 armistice line

Rehan
Jenin
Kadim
Ganim
Mevo Dotan
Sanur
Mehola
Tulkarem
Ayne Hefez
Enav
Shave Shomron
Sal'it
Elon Moreh
Zofin
Kedumim
Nablus
Qalqilya
Yizhar
Afa Menashe
Brakha
Itamar
Emanuel
Shomron Settlements
Oranit
Biddia
Elkana
Ariel
Ma'ale Efraim
Shilo
Rantis
Bet Arye
Ofarim
Halamish
Ni'lin
Talmon
Ofra
Modiin Illit
Bet El
Saffa
Ramallah
Deir Dibwan
Giv'at Ze'ev
Jib
Jericho

No Man's Land
under 1949
armistice

N.B.
Pockets of the Palestinian
Autonomous Area falling
within zones to be annexed
by Israel were not to come
under Palestinian
sovereignty

Ma'ale Adumim
Abu Dis
Kalia
Betar
Betlehem
K. Etzion
Efrat
Tekoa
to Gaza
Halhul

DEAD
SEA

Hebron
K. Arba
Dhahiriya
Eshkolot
Shim'a
Mezadot Yehuda

Offered by Israel in
exchange of annexed
part of West Bank

Palestinian Autonomous Area
(Zones A+B), 2001

Israeli offer at Taba as described subsequently
by members of the Palestinian Delegation:

to come under Palestinian sovereignty

to be annexed by Israel

ISRAEL

JORDAN

R.Jordan

Final Status Map – Taba, January 2001 (Andras Bereznay, adapted from
Jan de Jong and the Foundation for Middle East Peace, 2001)

Introduction

This is the second edition of our study, originally published as *Bad News from Israel*. It includes our earlier findings plus a new study of the Israeli attack on Gaza, from December 2008 to January 2009, and new analysis of audience understanding and responses. The first edition began with a history of the conflict which we have now updated to include other major events such as the Palestinian elections and the Lebanon war of 2006 and the recent history of Gaza. We wrestled with the idea of simply bringing out a new book with the new material. But it was obvious that we couldn't divide the history section and simply start where we had left off. We also wanted to cross reference our analyses of news content between different periods of the conflict and to compare the full range of audience samples. In the end we decided it was more useful to keep all of the results together. So this is a new introduction for both the original material and for the new studies included in this volume. We also include here a discussion of the public debate about media coverage, which has developed since the publication of the first study.

It need hardly be said that the Israeli-Palestinian conflict is one of the most problematic with which journalists have to deal. After our first publications in this area, many commented to us on the pressures which they felt in reporting it. They were working in a political climate in which the British government was closely allied to the US, which in turn had Israel as a key ally. The Israeli state had developed a very extensive lobbying and public relations capacity in both the US and the UK. Politicians from the US speaking on television in Britain have routinely voiced their support for Israel, as have significant parts of the British press. Tony Blair, after being prime minister of the UK, was appointed in 2007 as Middle East envoy in the search for peace. Yet his lack of neutrality is sometimes manifest. Consider this interview which was filmed during the Israeli attack on Gaza, in January 2009. The ITN correspondent begins by stating that:

Correspondent: Mr. Blair believes that the key to a ceasefire lies in stopping Hamas smuggling weapons through these tunnels into Gaza.

1

Blair then gives his very critical view of Hamas, noting how Gaza can be used as a base for directing rockets at civilians in Israel:

> *Tony Blair*: Either Hamas agree to be part of the solution, or alternatively Hamas stay in Gaza, using Gaza as a base for operations, directing rockets at civilians in Israel, in which case they are not part of the solution, they are part of the problem.

He is then repeatedly asked if he will also condemn Israel's use of force on Gaza as 'disproportionate'. To which he first replies:

> *Tony Blair*: The most important thing for me to do as international community representative is to try and get this thing stopped.

And then:

> *Tony Blair*: Look there is nothing that can take away the fact that when military action of this sort happens there are innocent civilians that suffer and the people of Gaza are suffering badly. The most important thing for me to do, rather than condemning one side or the other, is actually get the thing sorted and that's what I am trying to do. (ITV early evening News, 6 January 2009)

So when Hamas fires rockets and 13 Israelis are killed, they are part of the problem, but when Israel attacks Gaza and over 1,000 Palestinians are killed, then this is the sort of thing that happens when military action takes place. It can be seen that journalists who do try to feature both sides of the conflict are facing something of an uphill task. There is less to fear in criticising the Palestinians, but to criticise Israel can create major problems. Journalists spoke to us of the extraordinary number of complaints which they receive. We have presented our findings to many groups of media practitioners. After one such meeting a senior editor from a major BBC news programme told us: 'we wait in fear for the phone call from the Israelis'. He then said that the main issues they would face were from how high up had the call come (e.g., a monitoring group, or the Israeli embassy), and then how high up the BBC had the complaint gone (e.g. to the duty editor or the director general). He described how journalists had checked with him minutes before a programme was broadcast on which words to describe the conflict, should now be used. On another occasion, the journalist and filmmaker John Pilger told us of the storm of criticism which followed the broadcast of his film, *Palestine is Still the Issue* in 2002. The film was attacked by supporters of Israel and by Michael Green, the chairman of Carlton Television. At the time, Pilger wrote in the *Guardian*:

> What is disquieting is that Green had actually seen the film before it went to air and had not alerted the programme makers to his concerns, waiting until the Jewish Board of Deputies, the Conservative Friends of Israel and the Israeli embassy expressed their outrage. (23 September 2002)

He told us how he had received 20,000 emails and letters and many of the most critical were sent to the governing body of Independent Television. Pilger had then to stop other projects, and to spend six weeks writing a defence of the programme. In this he was able to show that many of the critical emails had come from the US where the programme had not actually been shown. His work was cleared, but the point is that many journalists when faced with such a climate are likely to be cautious. The simplest approach is to avoid areas which will attract criticism. This does not mean that they will all be pro-Israeli, but there is a tendency, as we show here, to focus critical commentary in the areas where they are on the strongest ground such as the discussion of civilian casualties. This means that issues which are likely to attract the most critical response, such as the Palestinian view of the causes of the conflict, tend to be neglected.

In recent years, the public debate on the quality of news and its influence has if anything intensified. The continuing conflict produced a flurry of claims and counter arguments on 'bias' in media coverage. In April 2006 a report was published, commissioned by the BBC governors, on the impartiality of BBC coverage. It was produced by an independent panel headed by Quentin Thomas. The report supported many of the findings in our work, noting for example that there was 'an absence of historical background and deficiencies in the provision of other contexts', and 'there was little reporting of the difficulties faced by the Palestinians in their daily lives'. It commented on the 'incomprehension of viewers and listeners' and that:

> One important feature of this is the failure to convey adequately the disparity in the Israeli and Palestinian experience, reflecting the fact that one side is in control and the other lives under occupation. (Thomas, 2006: 6–7)

The report concluded:

> In short, we found that BBC output does not consistently give
> a full and fair account of the conflict. In some ways the picture
> is incomplete and, in that sense, misleading. (Thomas, 2006: 4)

The arguments over the quality of output continued, and in
January 2009 the BBC refused to broadcast a charity appeal for
the people of Gaza, which was seen as some of further evidence of
BBC partiality towards Israel. Meanwhile supporters of different
sides continued to search for individual instances where journalists
have supposedly made 'biased' references. Where these are found
they often relate to journalists making generalisations which are
difficult to sustain. For example, the BBC correspondent Jeremy
Bowen was criticised for two pieces of journalism in a ruling by
the BBC Trust in April 2009. Among the phrases cited was one
in which he had referred to 'Zionism's innate instinct to push out
the frontier' (BBC Trust, 2009). Now some might argue that this
is logically true since a philosophy which is about initiating and
developing a new state where it did not exist before, could be seen
as inherently expansionary. But as we argue in this book, almost any
account of history in this area is subject to competing explanations
and others may find grounds to contest what is said – in this case
for example they might argue that Israel has not always expanded.

In our own studies we have also found generalisations made by
journalists which are difficult to sustain and which could be seen as
favouring one side or the other. For example an ITV correspondent
interviewing an Israeli spokesman about the Gaza attack stated:
'Major Leibovitch, *the world understands* why you are attacking
Hamas' (ITV early evening News, 6 January 2009 – our italics).
Critics of Israel might immediately reject this, saying they neither
understood nor approved of the Israeli attack. But on the following
night another ITV correspondent interviews president Shimon
Peres and states, 'The *world is aghast* at the civilian deaths'. He
is interrupted by Peres who comments, 'You don't speak for the
world – what you call the world is a certain mood in Great Britain'
(ITV early evening News, 7 January 2009 – our italics).

In our view, to focus on such individual instances does very little
to explain the overall structure of news coverage and how it works
to influence audience understanding. Some academics have tried
to produce more systematic studies examining, for example, the
range of speakers who appear and issues which are covered. A

study by Loughborough University as part of the BBC Impartiality Enquiry, analysed the content of BBC news coverage between August 2005 and January 2006. They noted for example that the Israeli withdrawals from Gaza and elsewhere 'were seen by the BBC as the single most newsworthy event of the sample period'. Twenty-seven per cent of reports had included this theme. But in contrast the continuing annexation of land by Israel in the West Bank was included in only 0.4 per cent of reports (Loughborough University, 2006: 30).

Other academics such as Leon Barkho have employed discourse analysis to show how the legitimacy of action is conveyed by different use of language and phrasing. He compared the BBC and Al Jazeera and their respective use of words such as 'militants' (BBC) and 'resistance fighters' (Barkho, 2010: 115). Such techniques can also reveal differences in the status given to different accounts – where for example one side is reported as 'claiming' that something has occurred while the statements of the other side may be treated as merely factual. This difference is also explored by Yonatan Mendel who wrote of his experience as a journalist in Israel:

> In most of the articles on the conflict two sides battle it out: *Israel defence forces*, on the one hand, and the *Palestinians* on the other. When a violent incident is reported, the IDF *confirms* or the army *says* but the Palestinians *claimed:* 'that a baby was severely injured in IDF shootings'. (italics in original)

He also discusses the different uses of the words 'kidnap' and 'arrest':

> In June 2006, four days after the Israeli soldier Gilad Shalit was *kidnapped* from the Israeli side of the Gazan *security fence*, Israel, according to the Israeli media, *arrested* some 60 members of Hamas, of whom 30 were elected members of parliament and 8 ministers in the Palestinian government … that these officials were taken from their beds late at night and transferred to Israeli territory probably to serve (like Gilad Shalit) as future bargaining-chips did not make this operation a kidnapping. Israel never *kidnaps*: it *arrests*. (Mendel, 2008 – italics in original)

These analyses can provide very important insights. But the use of words and phrasing is itself a function of the much broader explanatory themes and assumptions which underpin news accounts. These relate to the reasons why events are assumed to occur and to the legitimacy given to the motives and actions of different sides. The political status of Israel plus its extensive public relations activity means in practice that its explanations and rationales are much more likely than those of the Palestinians to underpin the thematic structures of the news. As we have argued in this book and elsewhere, news is organised around coherent ways of understanding. Key themes relating to issues of cause, effect and consequence can be systematically reported and developed in news. This does not mean that there is a single, coherent meaning in media reporting. Different thematic explanations may compete and be present in news accounts. But it is crucial to understand their role since they can operate as organising principles in the development of a news story. So in the Gaza conflict, an argument on its cause put forward by Israel was that Hamas and the Palestinians fired rockets into Israeli towns. In this explanatory theme, the cause of the conflict is Palestinian action and the effect is the Israeli response. Different strands of the news story can then be organised to unpack this account, by for example, journalists going to Israeli towns such as Sderot to show the impact of rockets on Israeli communities. In contrast, a Palestinian explanation of cause was that Israel had maintained a blockade of Gaza which produced a crippling impact on its economy and left much of its population in poverty. But this explanation and its relationship to the firing of rockets was much less evident in news accounts at the time of the Gaza attack in December 2008. It was unpacked or developed in the manner of the Israeli view. In other words, it was not developed in news as a coherent explanatory theme.

This analysis of the manner in which news is organised to convey meaning raises a series of important theoretical issues in mass communications, on for example the relation between texts and audiences, on the power of media and the capacity of people to resist or reject dominant messages. The main focus in this book is on giving a clear exposition of our methods and results, but the theoretical concerns are latent and there is a more detailed discussion of them in other publications by the Media Group.[1] Overall in this volume we have tried as far as possible to preserve the structure of the first edition. We begin with a history of the conflict which we have now updated, and as before it illustrates the range of conflicting beliefs and opinions which exist in this area. The second chapter is the study of news content which originally appeared in the first edition. For this we had analysed large samples of news from September to October 2000, at the outbreak of the intifada and then later samples from October to December 2001 and March to April 2002. Chapter 3 is our original study of processes of audience reception and how television viewers responded to news about the conflict. We had questioned large groups of students from Britain, the US and Germany and also engaged in detailed discussions in focus groups. There were 14 of these groups whose participants were drawn from the population as a whole and 100 people took part in this way. This part of our work raised a number of issues such as the relation between viewers' understanding of news and their level of interest in it. We also looked at the role of television in informing mass audiences and asked the young people in our samples a range of questions on international issues in order to assess their levels of knowledge. In Chapter 4 we discuss the key factors which affect the production of news about the Israeli-Palestinian conflict including the impact of lobbying and public relations. The conclusions to this early work are given in Chapter 5. The bulk of our new research on content and reception is in Chapters 6 and 7. The first of these is a new content analysis of TV news on the Israeli attack on Gaza between December 2008 and January 2009. Chapter 7 focuses on public understanding of the Israeli-Palestinian conflict and the Gaza attack.

Since our original study we have questioned additional large groups of young people in Britain. We did this in successive years in 2004, 2005, 2008 and 2009 and 2010 (total of 641 people). For this part of the study, we modified the original questionnaire to take account of new developments and in 2009 we also conducted a further six focus groups to ask 40 people specific questions about the Gaza attack and to investigate their understanding of this. As we were finishing this volume in May 2010, the Israelis launched an assault on an aid flotilla to Gaza, in which nine activists were killed and there were many injuries. We analysed a further 21 news programmes which covered this and include the results in Chapter 8. These are very substantial samples and we have now analysed in total 298 news items on this conflict. In Chapter 9 we give our conclusions.

In bringing together the processes of production, news content and audience reception, this research has developed into one of the most extensive studies ever undertaken in this area. We were given invaluable help in it by a large number of journalists and media practitioners, whom we interviewed and who gave us comments and sometimes detailed accounts of stories on which they had worked.

Some also took part in the research for the book by sitting in on focus groups and playing an active role in the discussions. Since then we have had many other contacts and meetings with journalists in which we have presented and discussed our findings. It is not our role as academics to take sides in the conflict. But we have argued very strongly that a better informed and more open public debate should replace the public relations and propaganda wars which currently rage alongside the actual violence. We know that there are many journalists who feel the same and we hope that our work helps in achieving this.

1
Histories of the Conflict

INTRODUCTION

The Israeli-Palestinian conflict is deep and long-standing. In all such conflicts the origins and history of particular events are contested by the different parties involved. Participants tell the story from their own point of view and often to legitimise their own actions. In the course of this study we interviewed a large number of journalists who had worked in this area. Several commented on the difficulties of reporting when the causes of the conflict are subject to constant debate, as one very experienced correspondent noted:

> Even describing the physical reasons why things happened or what happened in the Middle East you are on very tricky territory. The Israelis will say the '67 war, that they were threatened, that it was a pre-emptive strike and the Arabs say there was no question of attacking Israel, that they were too feeble, too disorganised that the Israelis had always wanted this territory. So there are two schools of thought always about the reasons. (Focus group interview, November 2002)

This makes the journalist's task very difficult. If there is no single account of what happened which everyone accepts, then the journalist has to rely on the concept of balance and attempt to represent the range of views which do exist. This is made more complex because there are not simply two sides in the conflict but there are actually divisions of opinion within each 'side'. Journalists therefore have to pick their way through the competing opinions and versions of events and to make clear if possible what is established as fact. In the Israeli-Palestinian conflict there is some agreed information but much is still disputed. In the following histories we will illustrate this range of views and we will begin with the period leading up to the creation of the State of Israel in 1948.

ZIONIST ROOTS AND THE FIRST WAVE OF JEWISH IMMIGRATION INTO PALESTINE

The American historian Howard Sachar (1977) traces the contemporary emergence of Zionist thought to the European Rabbis, Judah Alkalai and Zvi Hirsh Kalischer, who from the 1830s onwards stressed the need for Jews to return to the Holy Land as a necessary prelude to the Redemption and the coming of the Messiah. Sachar argues that such messianic exhortations did not immediately or widely take root amongst European Jews. However, he suggests that by the 1870s societies generally known as Chovevei Zion – 'Lovers of Zion' – had formed across Russia, which viewed Palestine as a site for national renewal and a refuge from anti-Semitism.

In 1881, following the assassination of Tsar Alexander II, large numbers of Jews were killed in a series of Russian pogroms. By 1914 up to 2 million Jews had fled Russia to escape persecution. The vast majority sought sanctuary in the United States but 25,000 arrived in Palestine in two waves of immigration in 1882–84 and 1890–91. At the time the Jewish population in Palestine was small. The official Ottoman census of 1878 had put the total at 15,011 living amongst a combined Muslim/Christian population of 447,454 (McCarthy, 1990). The newcomers, backed with Jewish capital from prominent families such as the Rothschilds, saw themselves as agricultural pioneers, who were working to establish the foundations of Jewish self-determination in Palestine. A letter dated 21 September 1882 from Vladimir Dubnow, a worker at the Mikveh Israel agricultural settlement, to his brother Simon, captures the sentiments and hopes of the early Jewish settlers:

> My ultimate aim, like that of many others, is greater, broader, incomprehensible but not unattainable. The final goal is eventually to gain control of Palestine and to restore to the Jewish people the political independence of which it has been deprived for two thousand years. Don't laugh this is no illusion. The means for realising this goal is at hand: the founding of settlements in the country based on agriculture and crafts, the establishment and gradual expansion of all sorts of factories, in brief – to make an effort so that all the land, all the industry will be in Jewish hands. In addition, it will be necessary to instruct young people and the future generation in the use of firearms (in free, wild Turkey anything can be done), and then – here I too am plunging into

conjecture – then the glorious day will dawn of which Isaiah prophesised in his burning and poetic utterances. The Jews will proclaim in a loud voice and if necessary with arms in their hands that they are the masters of their ancient homeland. (cited in Gilbert, 1999: 5–6)

Relations between the new Jewish immigrants and the native population were mixed. Jewish settlements were built on land that was purchased from absentee *effendi* landlords. Often the locals who had tended the land were evicted with the help of Turkish police and this led to resentment and violence. Some Zionists such as Ahad Aham were very critical of the way the settlers gained control of the land and treated the local population. In 1891 he argued that the settlers 'treat the Arabs with hostility and cruelty and, unscrupulously deprive them of their rights, insult them without cause and even boast of such deeds; and none opposes this despicable and dangerous inclination' (1923: 107, cited in Hirst, 1977: 24). There was also evidence that the two groups were able partially to accommodate each other because the settlers also brought benefits. They provided employment opportunities, access to medical care, the loan of modern equipment, and a market for produce. Sachar (1977) reports that in the 1890s the agricultural settlement of Zichron Ya'akov employed more than a thousand Arabs working for 200 Jews. The former *Guardian* Middle East correspondent David Hirst (1977) argues that the beginning of the twentieth century saw the arrival of a more militant type of settler to Palestine, inspired by the ideas of Theodor Herzl and determined to take control of the land and exclude non-Jews from the labour market. The Jewish National Fund, set up to manage Jewish land purchases, decreed in 1901 that all land it purchased could never be resold or leased to gentiles, and settlers began to boycott Arab labour (Hirst, 1977; Shafir, 1999).

THEODOR HERZL AND THE EMERGENCE OF POLITICAL ZIONISM

Theodor Herzl, who is commonly regarded as the father of political Zionism, was a Jewish Austro-Hungarian journalist and playwright. He had been deeply affected by the virulent anti-Semitism sweeping across Europe, and as a journalist for the Vienna newspaper *Neue Freie Presse* had covered the notorious Dreyfus trial in Paris, where a Jewish officer was falsely charged with passing secrets to the Germans. He had also been alarmed by the election of Karl Lueger as mayor of Vienna at the head of an openly anti-Semitic party. Herzl felt that a central issue for Jews was their dispersal across the Diaspora and their existence as a minority in each country they inhabited. This, Herzl argued, led to a dependence on the host culture and a suppression of self-determination. Furthermore, Herzl believed that widespread anti-Semitism meant that complete assimilation into European society was an impossibility for most Jews. His solution as laid out in the 1896 *Der Judenstaat* or *The Jewish State* was for Jews to create their own state, in which they would constitute a majority and be able to exercise national self-determination. In contrast to the 'practical Zionism' of the Jewish settlers who began to arrive in Palestine from 1882, Herzl adopted a political orientation, cultivating links with prominent imperial statesmen in an attempt to gain a charter for Jewish land settlement.

Herzl had two potential locations in mind for the prospective Jewish state – Argentina and Palestine. His diaries show that he was greatly influenced by the British imperialist Cecil Rhodes, and in particular the manner in which Rhodes had gained control of Mashonaland and Matabeleland from its inhabitants (Hirst, 1977). In his diaries he suggests that the settlers should follow Rhodes' example and 'gently' expropriate the native population's land and 'try to spirit the penniless population across the border by procuring employment for it in the transit countries, while denying it any employment in our own country' but that 'the process of expropriation and the removal of the poor must be carried out discreetly and circumspectly' (Herzl, 1960: 88, cited in Hirst, 1977: 18). In order to further this aim Herzl sought out an imperial sponsor prepared to grant a settlement charter. He canvassed Germany's Kaiser, the Ottoman Sultan and Britain's Joseph Chamberlain, stressing to each the benefits that a Jewish state and Jewish capital could bring. In 1901 Herzl travelled to Constantinople and met the Sultan. Herzl offered capital to re-finance the Ottoman public debt in what turned out to be a failed attempt to gain a charter for the establishment of a Jewish Ottoman Colonisation Association in Palestine. Bohm (1935) claims that the third article of the proposed charter would have given the Jewish administration the right to deport the native population from Palestine. Herzl subsequently switched his attention to lobbying British politicians. Hirst (1977) suggests that Herzl linked Zionist ambitions to British imperial interests, and tried to play on the anti-Semitism of certain British politicians by arguing that a Jewish homeland would lessen the flow of Jewish refugees, who were fleeing pogroms, into Britain. During this period there was a fear amongst some members of the British establishment that Jews were agents of Bolshevism. Herzl lobbied Lord Rothschild for the creation of Jewish colonies in Cyprus, the Sinai Peninsula and Egyptian Palestine, but the plans met with resistance from the Egyptian authorities. In April 1903 Neville Chamberlain proposed to Herzl that the Zionists set up a homeland in Uganda under the sovereignty of the British crown. Chamberlain offered a territory under the control of a Jewish governor into which a million Jews could immigrate and settle (Gilbert, 1999). Herzl accepted the plan. Martin Gilbert suggests that Herzl 'was determined to take up the first offer presented to the Jews by a great power, and to provide at least a place of temporary asylum for the Jews of Russia' (1999: 21). The proposal did not receive universal endorsement from Zionists, but at the sixth Zionist conference in Basle in 1903 Herzl succeeded in securing a majority in favour of the Uganda scheme: 295 voted for the proposal, 175 voted against and 99 abstained. However, shortly afterwards in July 1903 Herzl died at the age of 44 and with him the Uganda project, which was rejected by the 1905 Zionist conference. The task of forwarding political Zionism passed to the British chemist, Chaim Weizmann.

THE SECOND WAVE OF JEWISH IMMIGRATION INTO PALESTINE

1904 saw the beginning of another wave of Jewish immigration into Palestine, again as a result of Russian pogroms. Over the next ten years between 35,000 and 40,000 Jewish immigrants arrived. Amongst this group was a 20-year-old Russian Jew, David Gruen (later changed to Ben-Gurion, or son of Gruen) who arrived in Jaffa in September 1906 and was later to play a pivotal role in the creation and development of the Israeli state. The new immigrants mostly worked as labourers on the agricultural settlements established by the previous wave of Jewish immigrants, or in the towns. They also established the first Jewish political parties, a Hebrew language press, collective farms (*kibbutzim*) and in 1909 the first Jewish self-defence militia, Ha-Shomer (The Watchman). Its motto was 'By blood and fire Judaea fell; by blood and fire Judaea shall rise' (Gilbert, 1999: 27). The Israeli sociologist Gershon Shafir argues that the struggle to create an all-Jewish labour force transformed Jewish workers into 'militant nationalists' who 'sought to establish a homogenous Jewish society' (1999: 88). Palestine became the site for two emerging and competing nationalisms: (1) the native Muslim and Christian population keen to throw off Ottoman rule, and (2) the Jewish newcomers determined to create their own homeland. Some Zionists began to stress the importance of armed force. Israel Zangwill, who had coined the Zionist slogan 'a land without people for a people without land', informed a meeting of Zionists in Manchester in 1905 that '[We] must be prepared either to drive out by the sword the [Arab] tribes in possession as our forefathers did or to grapple with the problem of a large alien population' (Zwangill, cited in Morris, 2001: 140).

The Palestinians, as a subject population under Ottoman rule, were initially deferential in their protests. During the 1890s members of the Palestinian elite repeatedly and unsuccessfully petitioned their imperial overlords in Constantinople to limit Jewish immigration. The late nineteenth century had been a period of growing pan-Arab awareness which had seen a renaissance, in the appreciation of Arab literature and culture. Ovendale argues that both the Ottoman Empire and the spread of Zionism were seen as a threat to Arab development. He suggests that 'between 1909 and 1914 nationalist opposition in Palestine to Zionism grew: there were fears that if the Jews conquered Palestine the territorial unity of the Arab world would be shattered and the Arab cause weakened' (Ovendale, 1999: 12). By 1914 the Muslim intellectual Rashid Rida argued that the Palestinians faced a decisive choice. They could either come to an accommodation with the Zionists in which the Zionists, in return for concessions, would put a limit on their ambitions, or they could oppose them with arms:

> It is incumbent upon the leaders of the Arabs – the local population – to do one of two things. Either they must reach an agreement with the leaders of the Zionists to settle the differences between the interests of both parties ... or they must gather all their forces to oppose the Zionists in every way, first by forming societies and companies, and finally by forming armed gangs which oppose them by force. (Rida, cited in Hirst, 1977: 32–3)

THE BALFOUR DECLARATION AND THE BRITISH MANDATE

During the First World War the dissolution of the Ottoman Empire was widely anticipated and the Entente Powers began negotiating over their territorial ambitions. In 1916 negotiations between Britain, France and Russia (later to include Italy) led to the secretive Sykes-Picot agreement which sought to establish 'spheres of influence' for the European Powers within the region. However, the agreement also accepted the realities of emergent Arab nationalism, and specified the recognition of 'an independent Arab State' or 'confederation of Arab States' within the region. British assurances of Arab independence after the defeat of the Central Powers (which had been pledged as a reward for Arab support during the First World War) can be found in the correspondence between Sir Henry McMahon, British High Commissioner in Egypt and Sharif Hussein, Emir of Mecca, who was recognised as the Keeper of Islam's most holy places.[1] However, these pledges by European Powers to strive for the recognition of Arab independence conflicted with British assurances also given at the time to Zionist leaders, that Britain would seek the establishment of a Jewish homeland in Palestine. Zionist leaders established close links with prominent British politicians including Lloyd George, Arthur Balfour, Herbert Samuel and Mark Sykes. In 1915, in a memorandum entitled 'The Future of Palestine' Samuel proposed 'the British annexation of Palestine [where] we might plant three or four million European Jews' (Weisgal, 1944: 131, cited in United Nations, 1990). British support for a Jewish homeland was made explicit in the Balfour Declaration of November 1917:

> His Majesty's Government view with favour the establishment in Palestine of a national home for the Jewish people, and will use their best endeavours to facilitate the achievement of this object, it being clearly understood that nothing shall be done which may prejudice the civil and religious rights of existing non-Jewish communities in Palestine or the rights and political status enjoyed by Jews in any other country.

The 'non-Jewish communities', which comprised the 89 per cent of the population who were Arab, Muslim and Christian, were angered by the declaration.[2] They noted that it only spoke of their 'civil and religious rights' making no mention of political rights. They also questioned the right of the British to give away a country which did not belong to them. Conversely for the Zionists the declaration was regarded as a triumph. The Israeli historian Avi Shlaim, paraphrasing Chaim Weizmann, argues that it 'handed the Jews a golden key to unlock the doors of Palestine and make themselves the masters of the country' (2000: 7). The legality of the Balfour Declaration has since been questioned by some experts (Linowitz, 1957; Cattan, 1973).

After the First World War Britain was assigned control of Palestine, through the Mandates system governing the dismemberment of the Ottoman Empire. In 1921 the British divided the area in two with the sector east of the Jordan river becoming Transjordan and the area west of the river becoming the Palestinian Mandate. In July 1922 the League of Nations Council ratified the Palestinian Mandate, Article 4 of which stated that 'an appropriate Jewish agency shall be recognized as a public body for the purpose of advising and co-operating with the administration of Palestine in such economic, social and other matters as may affect the establishment of the Jewish National Home' (Gilbert, 1999: 50). For many supporters of the Israeli state the inclusion of the terms of the Balfour Declaration into the League of Nations mandate provide a legal justification for the creation of the Israeli state in Palestine. The view of Palestinians is that such agreements were essentially colonialist in nature and the Jewish presence no more legitimate than the French settler colonies in Algeria which were evacuated after independence.

The indigenous population of mandated Palestine feared mass Jewish immigration would lead to the further colonisation of their country, and that this would be followed by their own subjugation. The view was shared by some prominent British politicians such as Lord Curzon who, on 26 January 1919, commented to Lord Balfour: 'I feel tolerably sure therefore that while Weizmann may say one thing to you, or while you may mean one thing by a national home, he is out for something quite different. He contemplates a Jewish State, a Jewish nation, a subordinate population of Arabs, etc. ruled by Jews; the Jews in possession of the fat of the land, and directing the Administration ... He is trying to effect this behind the screen and under the shelter of British trusteeship' (British Government, Foreign Office, 1919a, cited in Ingrams, 1972: 58). Some members of the British establishment believed that by supporting the Jewish national home they were directly violating the terms of the Mandate.[3] Others seemed less concerned about the opinions of the Arab population. A senior British official was cited as telling Chaim Weizmann that in Palestine 'there are a few hundred thousand Negroes but that is a matter of no significance' (Heller, 1985, cited in Chomsky, 1992: 435). Some historians, however, have disputed the notion that the Jewish immigrants intended to dominate or supplant the native Arab population. Martin Gilbert, for instance, has claimed that the Jewish immigrants intended to develop the country for the mutual benefit of both peoples and were very concerned about the impact of Jewish immigration on the indigenous population:

> Ben-Gurion sought to combine the dynamic of Jewish settlement with the basically humane ideals of Judaism as it had evolved over the centuries. The rights of the inhabitants of the land – not always respected in biblical times – were for him of great importance. Co-existence with the Arabs would, as he saw it, benefit the Arabs considerably, without in any way dispossessing them. (1999: 38)

Other commentators such as ex-prime minister Binyamin Netanyahu have argued that the Jewish settlers had more of a right to the land than the native population because more than 2,000 years earlier Jews had lived there, and in the intervening years had never relinquished their claim over the land. Netanyahu also argues that Jewish claims to the land were superior to those of the native population because the land had allegedly not been fully developed:

> In many ways the argument between Jews and Arabs over their respective historic rights to a national home resembles an argument over the rights of an individual owner to his house. If the original owner is tossed out of his home but never relinquishes his right to return and re-occupy his premises, he may press his claim. But suppose a new occupant has fixed up the place and made a home of it while the original claimant is still around but prevented from pressing his claim? In such a case even if the new occupant has resided there for a considerable period of time and improved the premises, his claim to the place is considered inferior to that of the original owner. Yet in the meantime no one has set up house and the place has become a shambles, there can be no rival claim, and the original owner is clearly entitled to have his property back. (Netanyahu, 2000: 27–8)

Between 1919 and 1926 the Jewish presence in Palestine swelled with the arrival of a further 90,000 immigrants (Bregman, 2003). Gilbert claims that anti-Semitic violence in the Ukraine, in which 100,000 Jews were killed in the aftermath of the First World War, as well as increasing persecution in Poland acted as a 'powerful catalyst for immigration' (1999: 49). The Jewish community in Palestine also became increasingly militarised, with the creation of what Shlaim describes as an 'iron wall' of impregnable strength designed to protect Jewish settlements from Arab attacks. The concept of the 'iron wall' had first been deployed by Vladimar Jabotinsky, the leader of the Revisionist movement.[4] Jabotinsky was convinced that the indigenous Arabs would not accept the Zionist project voluntarily and advocated the creation of an 'iron wall' that the local population would be unable to breach:

> If you wish to colonise a land in which people are already living, you must provide a garrison for the land, or find a benefactor who will maintain the garrison on your behalf. Zionism is a colonising adventure and therefore it stands or falls by the question of armed forces. (Jabotinsky, cited in Masalha, 1992: 45)

The Zionists also substantially increased their land holdings. Agricultural land was purchased from absentee Arab landlords. The peasants who tended and lived on it were evicted. The 1919 American King-Crane Commission, which had been sent to Palestine to assess local opinion, reported in their discussions with Jewish representatives, that 'the Zionists looked forward to a practically complete dispossession of the present non-Jewish inhabitants of Palestine, by various forms of purchase' (British Government, 1947: 3, cited in Laqueur and Rubin, 1984: 29). The Zionists also increasingly boycotted Arab labour. The British Hope-Simpson Commission had criticised the Zionist Keren ha-Yesod employment agreements as discriminatory and pointed to Article 7 which stipulated that 'The settler hereby undertakes that ... if and whenever he may be obliged to hire help, he will hire Jewish workmen only' and Article 11 which stated that 'the settler undertakes ... not to hire any outside labour except Jewish labourers' (British Government, Cmd. 3686: 52–3, cited in United Nations, 1990). The tensions created by this labour exclusivism, the Commission reported, constituted 'a constant and increasing source of danger to the country' (British Government, Cmd. 3686: 55, cited in United Nations, 1990).

Throughout the 1920s Arab hostility to the Zionist project manifested itself in increasingly prolonged outbreaks of violence. In 1921 Arabs attacked Jews at Jaffa during a May Day parade and the violence spread to other towns and the countryside. By the time the British Army brought the situation under control nearly 200 Jews and 120 Arabs were dead or wounded. Britain set up a commission of inquiry to investigate the violence. The Haycraft Commission reported that the violence was spontaneous and anti-Zionist rather than anti-Jewish. The report blamed the Arabs for the violence, but also pointed to Arab fears that the mass influx of Jewish immigrants would lead to their subjugation. General William Congreve, the commander of British forces in the Middle East, criticised Herbert Samuel's policy of trying to establish a Jewish National home in Palestine in the face of the opposition from most of the population (Ovendale, 1999). Shortly afterwards the Arabs sent a petition to the League of Nations asking for democratic elections and independence for Palestine (Segev, 2001). In 1922 the British government published a White Paper which was intended to mollify Arab fears. It denied that the Balfour Declaration paved the way for a Jewish state, and that the Arab population, culture and language would be subordinated. It also proposed a legislative council made up of Jewish, Muslim and Christian representatives, a suggestion that was rejected by the Arabs. Hirst (1977) alleges that a large proportion of the council would have been directly appointed by Britain. This would have been likely to give the Jewish representatives a majority. The Palestinians therefore feared that Zionist policies might be legitimised under a constitutional façade.

THE ARAB REVOLT

The 1920s and 1930s saw more violent disturbances followed on each occasion by Commissions of Inquiry dispatched by Britain to examine causes. After 1921 there was a period of relative calm before the next major outbreak of violence in 1929. The flashpoint for the violence was a dispute over sovereignty of an area containing important Jewish and Muslim religious sites. Tension had been brewing for some months over this issue, fermented by inflammatory rhetoric in the Arab and Hebrew press. In late August 1929 a group of armed Arabs attacked Jewish worshippers in Jerusalem and in a week of rioting and violence 113 Jews and 116 Arabs were killed. In Hebron Arab rioters killed more than 60 members of a long-standing community of non-Zionist religious Jews. In response the British set up the Shaw Commission of Inquiry, which concluded that the trigger for the violence was Jewish demonstrations at the Wailing Wall but that the underlying causes were economic and political grievances against the Mandate. It found that the effects of mass Jewish immigration had been 'to arouse among Arabs the apprehension that they will in time be deprived of their livelihood and pass under the political domination of the Jews' (cited in Gilbert, 1999: 64). An Arab delegation including the Mufti of Jerusalem met with British officials in London requesting a prohibition on the sale of lands from Arabs to non-Arabs, an end to Jewish immigration and the formation of a national parliament. The Hope-Simpson Commission dispatched by Britain shortly afterwards highlighted the problem of a growing population of landless Arabs and recommended controls on Jewish immigration and land purchase. These recommendations were carried through in the 1930 Passfield White Paper. However, these developments were regarded as a serious setback by Zionists who managed through lobbying to reverse the terms of the White Paper. Gilbert suggests that there were two reasons the Zionists were strongly opposed to the recommendations of the Commission. Firstly they wanted to keep open Palestine as a site for mass immigration especially in view of the increased persecution of Jews throughout Europe, and secondly they feared that without mass immigration they would remain a minority within Palestine subject to the control of the Arab majority. He cites a letter dated 3 December 1931 from Arthur Ruppin, a prominent Zionist, which captures this sentiment:

> At most, the Arabs would agree to grant national rights to the Jews in an Arab state, on the pattern of national rights in Eastern Europe. But we know only too well from conditions in Eastern Europe how little a majority with executive power can be moved to grant real and complete national equality to a minority. The fate of the Jewish minority in Palestine would always be dependent upon the goodwill of the Arab majority, which would steer the state. (cited in Gilbert, 1999: 66)

Sporadic violence ignited into a full scale Arab rebellion in the years between 1936 and 1939. Part of the revolt involved peaceful resistance, including a nationwide six-month strike and widespread non-payment of taxes. It also involved extensive violence in which Palestinians formed into bands and destroyed crops and trees, mined roads and sabotaged infrastructure and oil pipelines. They attacked and killed Jews, and also targeted Arabs who failed to offer support or who were suspected of collaboration. Gilbert claims that during this period 'most acts of Arab terror were met with, often within a few hours, by equally savage acts of reprisal by the Revisionists' military arm, the Irgun' (1999: 92). The Arabs demanded democratic elections and an end to immigration. The British dispatched another commission of inquiry which in 1937 stated that the Mandate was unworkable and recommended partition. The Peel Commission proposed that the north-west part of Palestine accounting for 20 per cent of the country though containing its most fertile land would become a Jewish state, and the remaining 80 per cent would become an Arab state linked to Transjordan. A corridor to the sea would remain under British control as would Jerusalem and Bethlehem. The proposal received a mixed reception amongst Jews. One group centred around Jabotinsky's revisionists argued that a Jewish state should only be set up in the whole of Palestine and Transjordan. Another which included Weizmann and David Ben-Gurion, argued that this was a historic opportunity to create the Jewish state. The Israeli historian Simha Flapan suggests that Ben-Gurion accepted the plan as a stepping stone to Zionist control of all of Palestine, and points to comments he made before the Zionist executive in 1937 that: 'after the formation of a large army in the wake of the establishment of the [Jewish] state, we shall abolish partition and expand to the whole of the Palestine' (Ben-Gurion, cited in Flapan, 1987: 22). The Israeli historian and *Ha'aretz* columnist Tom Segev (2001) suggests that for Ben-Gurion the proposal (inherent in the Peel recommendations) for the 'forced transfer' of the Arab inhabitants out of the proposed Jewish state, and the creation therefore of a 'really Jewish' state, outweighed all the drawbacks of the proposal. The partition plan was eventually put before the Twentieth Zionist Congress, convening in Zurich, who approved it by 299 votes to 160. The Arabs categorically rejected the partition scheme, arguing that all of Palestine was part of the Arabian homeland and it should not be broken up. The partition plans were never carried through and the rebellion continued until the British finally quelled it. The rudimentary weapons of the Arab guerrillas were overwhelmed by vastly superior British military power. Hirst (1977) claims that during this period British forces took part in extensive acts of revenge and 'collective punishment'. British soldiers descended on Arab villages, undertook summary executions and destroyed possessions and dwellings. Segev (2001) claims that torture was also employed by the British authorities. The rebellion had cost the lives of 101 Britons and 463 Jews (*The Times*, 21 July 1938, cited in Hirst, 1977: 93). Palestinian losses were harder to gauge but Palestinian historian Walid Khalidi estimates upwards of 5,000 killed and approximately 14,000 injured (Hirst, 1977). The reasons for these increasingly serious outbreaks of hostility between the communities are contested. Some Israelis argue that the Zionist project was essentially beneficial to the Arabs of Palestine, and it was only Arab intransigence and xenophobia which prevented mutual accommodation. Cohn-Sherbok (2001), for instance, stresses the legal basis for settlement in the Balfour Declaration which was incorporated into the Mandate, and points to the Arab rejection of partition in 1937. He argues that Arab violence directed against the Jews was 'incomprehensible' and that the Arabs were never prepared to compromise:

> Throughout this period the Arab community was unwilling to negotiate over any of the issues facing those living in the Holy Land. Jews, on the other hand, continually sought to find a solution to the problems confronting the native population while retaining their conviction that a Jewish national home must be established. (2001: 179)

Martin Gilbert also argues in this vein maintaining that 'the efforts of the Zionist leaders to come to some agreement with the Arabs of Palestine during the early 1930s were continuous'. He claims that the 'most important' of these occurred on 18 July 1934 when Ben-Gurion met Auni Abdul Hadi, the leader of the Palestinian independence movement. He cites comments made to Hadi by Ben-Gurion:

> Our ultimate goal is the independence of the Jewish people in Palestine, on both sides of the Jordan, not as a minority but as a community of several millions. In my opinion, it is possible to create over a period of forty years, if Transjordan was included, a community of four million Jews in addition to an Arab community of two million ... The Arabs of Palestine would remain where they were, their lot would improve, and even politically they would not be dependent on us, even after we came to constitute the vast majority of the population. (Gilbert, 1999: 74)

Similarly, Sachar (1977) argues that the Zionist enterprise developed the country, improved the material living standards of the Arab population and provided employment opportunities. The attacks on Jews, Sachar argues, were the result of incitement by allegedly xenophobic leaders such as the Mufti of Jerusalem and agitation by fascist infiltration from Italy and Germany. Joan Peters (1984) has claimed that the Zionist project was so beneficial to the Arab population that large numbers were drawn in from outside Palestine. She attributes the large rise in the Arab population during the mandatory period to illegal immigration from other Arab countries and argues that because of this the Jewish population in

1948 had as least as much right to the land as the Arab 'newcomers'. However, a number of British and Israeli reviewers have denounced Peters' thesis as dishonest, and most demographers attribute the bulk of the Arab population rise to decreased mortality rates, due to improvements in sanitation and infrastructure.[5] Others provide different explanations for the revolt. Hirst points to economic resentment generated by peasant land evictions and the boycott of Arab labour:

> Driven from the land the peasants flocked to the rapidly growing cities in search of work. Many of them ended up as labourers building houses for the immigrants they loathed and feared. They lived in squalor. In old Haifa there were 11,000 crammed into hovels built of petrol-tins, which had neither water-supply or rudimentary sanitation. Others, without families, slept in the open. Such conditions contrasted humiliatingly with the handsome dwellings the peasants were putting up for the well-to-do newcomers, or even with the Jewish working men's quarters furnished by Jewish building societies. They earned half or just a quarter the wage of their Jewish counterparts and Hebrew Labour exclusivism was gradually depriving them of even that. (1977: 75)

Some Israeli academics, such as Gershon Shafir (1999), have characterised twentieth-century Zionist settlement as similar to a form of European colonialism – the 'pure settlement colony' model which was imposed on societies in North America and Australia. This model 'established an economy based on white labour which together with the forced removal or the destruction of the native population allowed the settlers to regain the sense of cultural and ethnic homogeneity that is identified with a European concept of nationality' (Shafir, 1999: 84). Segev argues that '"disappearing" the Arabs lay at the heart of the Zionist dream and was also a necessary condition of its realization' (2001: 405). He also maintains, in direct contrast with Gilbert, that prominent Zionists such as David Ben-Gurion believed that the Arab revolt was a nationalist struggle designed to prevent their dispossession:

> The rebellion cast the Arabs in a new light. Instead of a 'wild and fractured mob, aspiring to robbery and looting,' Ben-Gurion said, they emerged as an organized and disciplined community, demonstrating its national will with political maturity and

a capacity for self-evaluation. Were he an Arab, he wrote, he would also rebel, with even greater intensity and with greater bitterness and despair. Few Zionists understood the Arab feeling, and Ben-Gurion found it necessary to warn them: the rebellion was not just terror, he said; terror was a means to an end. Nor was it just politics, Nashashibi against the Mufti. The Arabs had launched a national war. They were battling the expropriation of their homeland. While their movement may have been primitive, Ben-Gurion said, it did not lack devotion, idealism and self-sacrifice. (2001: 370–1)

In the wake of the revolt the British dispatched a further commission of inquiry, the result of which was the 1939 MacDonald White Paper. It proposed that 75,000 Jewish immigrants plus 25,000 emergency refugees, be admitted over the next five years, after which any further immigration would require Arab consent.[6] The White Paper also proposed that land sales be strictly regulated and that an independent Palestine state should come about within ten years. The Zionists saw the White Paper as a betrayal that seriously threatened the creation of a Jewish majority state in Palestine, especially in the light of the increased persecution of Jews throughout Europe. Some Israelis such as Binyamin Netanyahu have argued that by failing to allow unrestricted Jewish immigration into Palestine, Britain was complicit in the Nazi genocide:

The extent of the British betrayal of the Jews can be understood only in the context of what was happening in Europe and the 1930s and thereafter. Responding to pressures from the Arabs, the British restriction of Jewish immigration (there was no analogous restriction on Arab immigration) cut off the routes of escape for Jews trying to flee a burning Europe. Thus, while Gestapo was conniving to send boatloads of German Jews out onto the high seas to prove that no country wanted them any more than Germany did, the British dutifully turned back every leaking barge that reached Palestine, even firing on several ... For over ten years the British shut the doors of the Jewish National Home to Jews fleeing their deaths. In doing so they not only worked to destroy the Jewish National Home, which no one believed could survive without immigrants, but made themselves accomplices in the destruction of European Jewry. (2000: 75–6)

The Jewish response to the 1939 MacDonald White Paper was three-pronged. One element involved maintaining a flow of illegal Jewish immigration into Palestine. Another, which gathered pace from 1945 onwards, saw Zionist paramilitary groups launch attacks on the British using sabotage, bombings and assassinations. The third involved switching imperial sponsors from Britain to the United States. Zionists forged close links with American political leaders and used the Jewish vote to pressurise for policies that supported the continuation of immigration and the establishment of the Jewish state in Palestine.

AMERICAN POLITICS AND THE SETTLEMENT OF THE HOLOCAUST SURVIVORS

In May 1942 Zionists meeting in New York for the American Zionist Conference issued the Biltmore Resolution demanding the creation of a 'Jewish commonwealth' in the whole of Palestine, and began to pressurise American political leaders to support its terms. In 1941 Zionists had formed the American Palestine Committee. It included within its membership two-thirds of the Senate, 200 members of the House of Representatives and the leaders of the two main political parties and labour organisations (Ovendale, 1999). Unsuccessful resolutions were put before the House of Representatives and the Senate demanding free Jewish entry into Palestine and its reconstitution as a Jewish commonwealth. Zionist representatives also directly lobbied the two major political parties. The 1944 presidential election was a very close contest and because of this, Ovendale (1999) suggests, Zionist political leverage was considerable. America's 4.5 million Jews were concentrated in three key states (New York, Pennsylvania and Illinois) which could swing the election. The Republican Party adopted a platform calling for unrestricted Jewish immigration into Palestine, no restrictions on land ownership and the conversion of Palestine into a free and independent Jewish commonwealth. Roosevelt was under pressure to match this and in a private letter to Zionist leaders promised if re-elected to seek the 'establishment of Palestine as a free and democratic Jewish commonwealth' (Ovendale, 1999: 87).

The politics surrounding the settlement of Jewish refugees at the end of the Second World War are still highly contentious. The debate concerns whether the Holocaust survivors wished to settle in Palestine voluntarily, or were influenced by Zionist propaganda and left with little option. The reason for this, it is suggested, is because other potential refuges such as the United States were closed to them, and that this was with at least the tacit support of Zionist leaders. The debate remains emotive because tens of thousands of Holocaust survivors died in displaced-persons (DP) camps in Europe at the end of the war. At the same time, US congressional legislation gave priority to accepting refugees from the Russian occupied states, but these included many Nazi sympathisers and ex-SS soldiers (Chomsky, 1999). Zionist leaders stressed the vital importance of Palestine as a sanctuary for the Jewish refugees in Europe who had survived the Nazi Holocaust. It was argued that only Palestine could provide a haven where Jewish refugees could rebuild their lives and avoid future anti-Semitism:

> They (the Holocaust survivors) want to regain their human dignity, their homeland, they want a reunion with their kin in Palestine after having lost their dearest relations. To them the countries of their birth are a graveyard of their people. They do not wish to return and they cannot. They want to go back to their national home, and they use Dunkirk boats. (Ben-Gurion, cited in Gilbert, 1999: 147)

Gilbert (1999) points to attempts by Holocaust survivors aboard ships such as the *Exodus* to reach Palestine as proof that most of the refugees were desperate to get there, and he estimates that 40,000 Jews made their way to Palestine clandestinely between August 1945 and May 1948. Gilbert also cites comments from the British Labour MP Richard Crossman, a strong supporter of Zionism, regarding the true wishes of the Jewish refugees languishing in the DP camps who he claimed were not merely being swayed by Zionist propaganda:

> Even if there had not been a single foreign Zionist or a trace of Zionist propaganda in the camps these people would have opted for Palestine ... For nine months, huddled together, these Jews had had nothing to do but discuss the future. They knew that they were not wanted by the Western democracies, and they had heard Mr Atlee's plan that they should stay and help rebuild their countries. This sounded to them pure hypocrisy. They were not Poles any more; but, as Hitler had taught them, members of the Jewish nation, despised and rejected by 'civilized Europe'. They knew that far away in Palestine there was a National Home willing and eager to receive them and to give them a chance

of rebuilding their lives, not as aliens in a foreign state but as Hebrews in their own country. How absurd to attribute to their longing for Palestine to organized propaganda! Judged by sober realities, their only hope of any early release was Palestine. (cited in Gilbert, 1999: 128)

The Israeli historian Yehuda Bauer (1970) also agues that most refugees were keen to settle in Palestine, citing a 1946 Hebrew investigative commission which reported that 96.8 per cent of Jewish refugees languishing in European displaced-persons camps at the end of the war wanted to settle in Palestine. Avi Shlaim argues that 'few people disputed the right of the Jews to a home after the trauma' of the Holocaust and that the moral case for it became 'unassailable' (2000: 23–4). But other Israeli historians suggest a different picture. Segev argues that:

There is ... no basis for the frequent assertion that the state was established as a result of the Holocaust. Clearly the shock, horror and sense of guilt felt by many generated profound sympathy for the Jews in general and the Zionist movement in particular. The sympathy helped the Zionists advance their diplomatic campaign and their propaganda, and shaped their strategy to focus effort on the survivors, those Jews in displaced-persons camps demanding they be sent to Palestine. All the survivors were Zionists, the Jewish Agency claimed, and they all wanted to come to Palestine. The assertion was not true. The displaced were given the choice of returning to their homes in Eastern Europe or settling in Palestine. Few were able or willing to return to countries then in the grip of various degrees of hunger, anti-Semitism or communism, and they were never given the option of choosing between Palestine and, say the United States. In effect their options were narrowed to Palestine or the DP camps. (2001: 491)

Others such as Feingold (1970) and Shonfeld (1977) have been very critical of the conduct of the Zionist movement in Palestine and America at the end of the Second World War. They argue that the Zionist movement should have mobilised to pressure the US administration to take in the Holocaust survivors, which would have saved the lives of many Jews who died in displaced-persons camps in Europe. Segev argues that the Ben-Gurion and the Labour leadership in Palestine saw the Nazi ascension in the 1930s as potentially 'a fertile force for Zionism' because it created the potential for mass Jewish immigration into Palestine (1993: 18). He alleges that during the 1930s and 1940s the Labour leadership entered into *haavara* (transporting) agreements with the Nazis whereby Jews were permitted to emigrate to Palestine with limited quantities of capital. He claims that Ben-Gurion's political rivals in the Revisionist movement opposed these agreements, and argued that rather than negotiate with Germany it should be boycotted. Segev also suggests that after the *Kristallnacht* pogroms Ben-Gurion was concerned that the 'human conscience' might cause other countries to open their doors to Jewish refugees, a move which he saw as a threat to Zionism:

> If I knew that it was possible to save all the children of Germany by transporting them to England, but only half of them by transporting them to Palestine, I would choose the second – because we face not only the reckoning of those children, but the historical reckoning of the Jewish people. (Ben-Gurion, cited in Segev, 1993: 28)

The view that Jewish refugees were used as political leverage to create the Jewish state in Palestine was also shared by some prominent British and US State Department officials,[7] who feared the effects on stability in Palestine and potential Russian penetration.[8] Roosevelt's successor, Harry Truman decided to press on with a policy supporting the settlement of Jewish refugees in Palestine. Ovendale (1999) suggests that this was primarily because of the 1945 New York election, in which the Jewish vote might be decisive. The American State Department official William Eddy claims that Truman had informed American ambassadors to the Arab world that 'I am sorry, gentlemen, but I have to answer to hundreds of thousands who are anxious for the success of Zionism; I do not have hundreds of thousands of Arabs among my constituents' (1954: 36).

THE END OF THE MANDATE

In Palestine, Zionist paramilitary groups were gradually wearing down British morale. Towards the end of the Arab revolt Jewish groups had launched attacks against the Arabs. In July 1938 more than 100 Arabs were killed when six bombs were planted in Arab public places. The last of these, detonated in the Arab Melon market in Haifa, killed 53 Arabs and a Jew (*Palestine Post*, 26 July 1938). After the publication of the 1939 White Paper, Zionist paramilitary groups commenced operations against the British authorities. However the outbreak of the Second World War saw the main Zionist paramilitary group, the Irgun, call off the revolt, precipitating a split within the organisation. The more militant splinter group, the Stern Gang, continued operations against the British. Following the end of the Second World War in October 1945 the Zionist paramilitaries joined forces with the main Zionist fighting force the Haganah in attacking the British authorities in what became known as the 'movement of the Hebrew revolt'. Roads, bridges, trains and patrol boats were destroyed. British army barracks were attacked and banks and armouries were looted. On a single day in 1946 Zionist forces launched 16 separate attacks on the British Army, destroying many armoured vehicles and leaving 80 dead and wounded (Hirst, 1977). Lord Moyne was assassinated by the Stern Gang, British officers were captured, flogged and killed and in the most well-known attack of all, the centre of British mandatory power in Palestine, the King David Hotel, was destroyed by 500 lb of explosives leaving 88 dead including 15 Jews. Funding for the attacks was provided by sympathetic sources in the United States. The Hollywood scriptwriter Ben Hecht produced an article for the *New York Herald Tribune*, entitled 'Letter to the Terrorists of Palestine', in which he wrote: 'every time you blow up a British arsenal, or wreck a British jail, or send a British railway train sky high, or rob a British bank, or let go with your guns and bombs at the British betrayers and invaders of your homeland, the Jews of America make a little holiday in their hearts ... Brave friends we are working to help you. We are raising funds for you' (15 May 1947, cited in Hirst, 1977: 119). The violence became so widespread that by early 1947 all non-essential British civilians and military families were evacuated from Palestine. Weakened by the Second World War, and demoralised by the attritional warfare, the British were rapidly losing their enthusiasm for maintaining order in Palestine. Gilbert (1999) suggests they were also wary of alienating Arab opinion because they were concerned to protect their oil interests in the region. The Foreign Secretary, Ernest Bevin, perhaps with this in mind indicated that he favoured 'an independent unitary State in Palestine, with special rights for the Jewish minority, but incorporating as much as possible of the Arab plan' (cited in Gilbert, 1999: 142). Bevin also argued that a Zionist government in Palestine would not accept any partition as final but would sooner or later seek to expand its borders. Arab hostility to the Zionist project, he predicted, might lead to long-term instability in the region: 'If Jewish irredentism is likely to develop after an interval, Arab irredentism is certain from the outset. Thus the existence of a Jewish State might prove a constant factor of unrest in the Middle East' (cited in Gilbert, 1999: 142). In February 1947 the British decided to end the Mandate and hand the question of Palestine to the United Nations.

THE UNITED NATIONS DEBATES THE FUTURE OF PALESTINE

The UN dispatched a Special Committee to the region which then recommended partition. Attention then switched to the diplomatic manoeuvring at the United Nations in New York. Arab representatives, called before the UN, questioned whether the Mandate was ever legal and whether the UN had the legal right to decide on the sovereignty of Palestine. They wished to see the issue referred to the International Court of Justice, and ultimately they argued it was the people of Palestine who should decide on the fate of the country rather than an outside body.[9] The Iraqi representative, Dr Fadhil Jamail, argued that Palestinians should not 'suffer for the crimes of Hitler' (cited in Gilbert, 1999: 144). Zionist representatives were more sympathetic to the partition plan being debated by member states and lobbied to maximise the area that might be allotted to a Jewish state. On 29 November 1947 the Partition Plan secured the required two-thirds majority after a last minute change of policy by several nations,[10] with a number complaining over the political and economic pressure that had been exerted on them.[11] The Arab states as well as a number of others indicated that they did not consider themselves bound by the Resolution as they argued it violated the terms of the UN Charter (United Nations, 1990). Some representatives argued that partition could create further strife and instability. The Pakistani representative, Sir Choudhri Mohammed Zafrullah Khan, stated that 'we much fear that the beneficence, if any, to which partition may lead will be small in comparison to the mischief it might inaugurate' (United Nations, 1992). Resolution 181 recommended the division of Palestine, with the Jewish state allotted 5,700 square miles including the fertile coastal areas, whilst the Arab state was allotted 4,300 square miles comprised mostly of the hilly areas. The proposed settlement would mean that each state would have a majority of its own population although many Jews would fall into the Arab state and vice-versa. The proposed Jewish state would, for instance, contain 500,000 Jews and 400,000 Arabs. Jerusalem and Bethlehem were to come under UN control.

For the Arabs the partition plan was a major blow. They believed it was unfair that the Jewish immigrants, most of whom had been in Palestine less than 30 years, and who owned less than 10 per cent of the land, should be given more than half of Palestine including the best arable land. The response amongst many ordinary Jews in Palestine and across the Diaspora was one of celebration and jubilation. The reaction of the Zionist leadership is more contested. Some historians such as Bregman (2003) argue that the partition resolution was seen as a triumph because it allowed for the creation of a Jewish state in an area three times that recommended by the Peel plan ten years earlier. Shlaim claims that the reaction was more ambivalent. He suggests that it was accepted by most Zionist leaders with a 'heavy heart' because they 'did not like the idea of an independent Palestinian state, they were disappointed with the exclusion of Jerusalem, and they had grave doubts about the viability of the State within the UN borders' (2000: 25). He notes that it was dismissed out of hand by Jewish paramilitary groups who demanded all of Palestine for the Jewish state. Gilbert suggests that the Zionist leadership realised that war was inevitable and that Ben-Gurion 'contemplated the possibility of fighting to extend the area allotted to the Jews' (1999: 149). Gilbert cites orders from Ben-Gurion that Jewish forces should 'safeguard the entire Yishuv [Jewish community in Palestine] and settlements (wherever they may be), to conquer the whole country or most of it, and to maintain its occupation until the attainment of an authoritative political settlement' (Ben-Gurion, cited in Gilbert, 1999: 149). Hirst (1977) suggests that the partition plan was accepted by the Zionists because they anticipated they would quickly be able militarily to overwhelm the Arabs, and unilaterally expand the borders of the Jewish state. This position on the relative balance of forces is contested by Netanyahu who argues that after the partition vote the 'consensus in the governing circles of the West, friendly and unfriendly alike, was that the pinhead-sized [Jewish] state would instantly be overrun by the Arabs, and Western military strategists concurred' (2000: 83–4). But Hirst points to comments made at the time by the commander of British forces in Palestine, General J.C. Darcy, who stated that 'if you were to withdraw British troops, the Haganah [Jewish fighting forces] would take over all Palestine tomorrow' and 'could hold it against the entire Arab world' (Crum, 1947: 220, cited in Hirst, 1977: 134).

THE UNOFFICIAL WAR

The UN partition plan did not solve the problems in Palestine. The Arab Higher Committee rejected it outright and called a three-day strike. The Mufti of Jerusalem announced a jihad or struggle for Jerusalem. Fighting between the two communities broke out in early December 1947 and the situation quickly deteriorated into a civil war in which both sides attacked civilian as well as military targets (Gilbert, 1999). The British, unwilling and unable to restore order, announced they would terminate the Mandate on 15 May 1948. In the first stage of the conflict lasting up until Israel's Declaration of Independence on 14 May 1948, Jewish forces fought against Arab forces marshalled by three commanders. Fawzi el-Qawuqji led the Arab Liberation Army (backed by the Arab League, an organisation representing the Arab states), Sir John Bagot Glubb and his 45 British officers led the Transjordanian Arab Legion, and Abdul Qader al-Husseini led the Mufti's Arab forces in Jerusalem (Bregman, 2003). In the early part of this 'unofficial war' the Arab forces won some minor victories and for a time al-Husseini's forces cut the road between Jerusalem and Tel Aviv. In early April Zionist forces launched a major offensive codenamed Plan Dalet. According to Avi Shlaim the aim of Plan Dalet was 'to secure all the areas allocated to the Israeli state under the UN partition resolution as well as Jewish settlements outside these areas and corridors leading to them' (2000: 31). Arab towns and cities were captured and their populations removed so as 'to clear the interior of the country of hostile and potentially hostile Arab elements' in anticipation of an attack by the combined armies of the neighbouring Arab states (2000: 31). Shlaim notes that the Zionist offensive led to the disintegration of Palestinian society:

> The novelty and audacity of this plan lay in the order to capture Arab villages and cities, something [they] had never attempted before ... Palestinian society disintegrated under the impact of the Jewish military offensive that got underway in April, and the exodus of the Palestinians was set in motion ... by ordering the capture of Arab cities and the destruction of cities, it both permitted and justified the forcible expulsion of Arab civilians. (2000: 30)

The operation involved the application of military and psychological pressure on the Arab population, who were reluctant to leave their homes. The Haganah, together with paramilitary forces, sprung surprise attacks on towns and villages, launching rockets, mortars and the Davidka, a device which lobbed 60 lb of TNT 300 yards into densely populated areas (Hirst, 1977). Psychological pressure was also exerted by spreading rumours via clandestine Zionist radio stations and loudspeakers mounted on army vehicles that Jewish forces were planning to burn villages and kill Arabs. An Israeli reserve officer recounts that:

> An uncontrolled panic spread through all the Arab quarters, the Israelis brought up jeeps with loudspeakers which broadcast recorded 'horror sounds'. These included shrieks, wails and the anguished moans of Arab women, the wail of sirens and the clang of fire-alarm bells, interrupted by a sepulchral voice crying out in Arabic: 'Save your souls, all ye faithful: The Jews are using poison gas and atomic weapons. Run for your lives in the name of Allah'. (Childers, 1976: 252, cited in Hirst, 1977: 141)

In April and early May 1948 a number of Arab towns and cities fell before the Zionist offensive, creating many refugees. The aims of Plan Dalet remain highly contested amongst historians. Some, such as Ilan Pappe, Norman Finkelstein, Nur Masalha, Walid Khalidi and David Hirst, place the operation in the context of long-held Zionist plans to 'transfer' the native population out of Palestine.[12] They argue that the notion of transfer had been inherent in Theodore Herzl's plans for Palestine some 50 years earlier and had remained an integral element of Labour and Revisionist strategy. Proponents of this perspective also point to the writings of Joseph Weitz, who was appointed by the Jewish Agency to head 'transfer committees' which encouraged the 1948 exodus by various forms of intimidation. In 1940 he confided in his diary that:

> Between ourselves it must be clear that there is no room for both peoples together in this country ... We shall not achieve our goal of being an independent people with the Arabs in this small country. The only solution is a Palestine, at least western Palestine [west of the Jordan river] without Arabs ... And there is no other way than to transfer the Arabs from here to the neighbouring countries, to transfer all of them; not one village, not one tribe, should be left ... Only after this transfer will the country be able to absorb the millions of our own brethren. There is no other way out. (*Davar*, 29 September 1967, cited in Hirst, 1977: 130)

This perspective is contested by Israeli historians such as Benny Morris and Avi Shlaim who contend that the April expulsions were 'born of war not design', being part of military expediency rather than political planning. For these historians the expulsions were carried out as part of a military strategy that was spontaneous and instigated on an ad hoc basis by local commanders. Morris' conclusions have been subjected to a detailed critique by Finkelstein (2001), who argues that the evidence that Morris presents shows the expulsions to be more systematic and pre-meditated than his conclusions suggest. A third explanation, that the Palestinians left voluntarily in response to radio broadcasts from their leaders, was propagated by some Israeli historians after the 1948 war. However, although this version of events still has some currency across Israel's political spectrum (Pappe, 1999), it has become discredited amongst many historians.[13]

THE FIRST ARAB-ISRAELI WAR

On 14 May 1948, as the United Nations debated a truce and trusteeship arrangement for Palestine and the British were evacuating their troops, David Ben-Gurion declared the birth of the State of Israel in Tel Aviv, under a portrait of Theodor Herzl. The proclamation of statehood pledged that Israel would 'be based on the principles of liberty, justice and peace as conceived by the prophets of Israel; would uphold the full social and political equality of all its citizens, without distinction of religion, race or sex; and would loyally uphold the principles of the UN charter' (Shlaim, 2000: 33). The declaration did not specify the borders of the new state, because Ben-Gurion wanted to keep open the possibility of expansion beyond the UN borders. Eleven minutes later, despite objections from the State Department and US diplomatic staff, America became the first country to recognise the new Israeli state, followed soon afterwards by the Soviet Union. The following day the armies of five Arab nations entered Palestine and engaged Israeli forces. The motives of the various Arab armies and the military balance of power between Jewish and Arab forces are contested. The former head of Israeli military intelligence, Yehoshafat Harkabi, has argued that the combined Arab attack on the newly formed Israeli state had essentially two aims, to destroy the Israeli political entity (what Harkabi describes as 'politicide') and to commit genocide against the Jewish population (Schlaim, 2001). Netanyahu (2000) suggests that both alleged aims were likely because the Israeli forces were outmanned and outgunned by the Arab armies:

> The common belief was that it was only a matter of time before the Jewish state, hardly in its infancy, would be terminated. Israel was coming into its War of Independence with severe handicaps imposed on it by the British ... The result was that Israel's ragtag forces were overwhelmingly outnumbered and outgunned, possessing virtually no tanks, no artillery, and no planes. As the Arab armies invaded, Israel's life hung in the balance. (2000: 84)

Other historians such as Avi Shlaim have questioned these assumptions. He argues that Israeli forces actually outnumbered the Arab forces during all stages of the conflict, primarily because Egypt, Transjordan, Syria, Lebanon and Iraq only sent expeditionary forces leaving the bulk of their armies at home:

> In mid-May 1948 the total number of Arab troops, both regular and irregular, operating in the Palestine theater was under 25,000, whereas the Israel Defense Force (IDF) fielded over 35,000 troops. By mid-July the IDF mobilized 65,000 men under arms, and by December its numbers had reached a peak of 96,441. The Arab states also reinforced their armies, but they could not match this rate of increase. Thus, at each stage of the war, the IDF outnumbered all the Arab forces arrayed against it, and, after the first round of fighting, it outgunned them too. The final outcome of the war was therefore not a miracle but a faithful reflection of the underlying military balance in the Palestine theater. In this war, as in most wars, the stronger side prevailed. (Shlaim, 2001: 80)

The picture of a monolithic Arab force determined to destroy Israel is also contested. Flapan (1987) suggests that the primary objective of King Abdullah of Transjordan (who had nominal control of all the Arab forces) was not to prevent the emergence of a Jewish state but simply to take the Arab part of Palestine, as part of a secret pact that he had made with the future Israeli prime minister Golda Meir in November 1947. Five days before the invasion of the Arab armies on 10 May 1948 Meir had made a second secret visit to Abdullah in Amman. Alarmed that Abdullah might be backtracking on his commitment to allow the emergence of a Jewish state in exchange for annexing the Arab part of Palestine,

Meir sought reassurances. However, the huge number of Palestinian refugees flooding into Transjordan as a result of Plan Dalet had created enormous popular pressure for the Arab states to intervene and halt the Jewish offensive, and Abdullah informed Meir that the situation had changed and he would be unable to keep out of the conflict. Shlaim suggests that Abdullah was dragged reluctantly into the conflict by circumstances beyond his control, but nevertheless his overarching aim remained the capture of the Arab part of Palestine rather than the destruction of the Israeli state:

> His objective in ordering his army across the River Jordan was not to prevent the establishment of a Jewish state but to make himself master of the Arab part of Palestine. Abdullah never wanted the other Arab armies to intervene in Palestine. Their plan was to prevent partition; his plan was to effect partition. His plan assumed and even required a Jewish presence in Palestine although his preference was for Jewish autonomy under his crown. By concentrating his forces on the West Bank, 'Abdullah intended to eliminate once and for all any possibility of an independent Palestinian state and to present his Arab partners with annexation as a *fait accompli*. (2001: 88)

Ovendale (1999) further suggests that the other Arab states involved were riven by competing territorial and political ambitions, in contrast to the Jewish forces that mostly fought with a united front, and this was a decisive factor in their comprehensive defeat.[14] In the first stage of fighting, the armies of Syria, Lebanon and Iraq made initial territorial gains, though almost all the fighting was conducted inside the area of Palestine that had been allocated by the UN to the Arab state. However, despite a serious shortage of armaments the Israeli forces managed to quickly reverse the early Arab gains, and consolidated their hold on a number of mixed Arab-Jewish towns, the eastern and western Galilee and parts of the Negev. Although Jerusalem saw very fierce fighting between Israeli and Transjordanian forces with many casualties, Ben-Gurion was soon contemplating an offensive which would deal a decisive blow to much of the Arab coalition. On 24 May, less than ten days after Israel's Declaration of Independence, he asked the Army General Staff to prepare a plan to go on the offensive. In his war diary he wrote:

> The weak link in the Arab coalition is Lebanon. Muslim rule is artificial and easy to undermine. A Christian state should be

established whose southern border would be the Litani. We shall sign a treaty with it. By breaking the power of the Legion and bombing Amman, we shall also finish off Transjordan and then Syria will fall. If Egypt still dares to fight – we shall bomb Port Said, Alexandria and Cairo. (cited in Shlaim, 2005)

However, such plans proved overoptimistic and by the first week of June a military stalemate had ensued on all fronts. The first truce declared on 11 June came as a relief to the Israeli forces who had been heavily stretched. It also allowed the Israelis to train new recruits and arrange large shipments of armaments from Czechoslovakia in contravention of the UN arms embargo. The Arab armies did not take the opportunity to prepare themselves for another round of fighting by re-arming or reorganising their forces.

During the first truce the UN appointed a mediator, the Swedish Count Bernadotte, who put forward a proposal for ending the conflict. This involved the creation of two states, one Jewish and one Arab. The Arab state would be linked politically to Transjordan, and would contain Jerusalem. Although Abdullah was keen to end hostilities the other members of the Arab League together with Israel rejected the UN plan. Bernadotte then proposed extending the truce but this again was rejected by the Arab League with the exception of Transjordan. King Abdullah summoned Bernadotte to a meeting in Amman to express his worry that a further round of fighting could break out and recommended that the UN do all they could to prevent this. However, his efforts were undermined by Egypt who on 8 July launched an attack ending the truce and committing the Arab forces to another round of fighting. In nine days leading up to a second truce the Israelis took the initiative capturing the Arab towns of Nazareth, Lydda and Ramleh. Then during the truce which followed, Israel mobilised and trained more fighters, many of whom were newly arrived immigrants, and arranged the shipment of more weapons. They also consolidated their hold on the captured territories and, according to Bregman, razed 'Arab villages to the ground so that their previous inhabitants who took what they believed to be a temporary refuge elsewhere would have nowhere to return to' (2003: 57). On 6 September the Arab League led by Egypt decided to create an Arab government for Palestine based in Gaza with a small military force under its control. Shlaim (2000) suggests that this was undertaken for a number of reasons: to placate Arab popular opinion critical of Arab failures to protect the Palestinians, to provide a vehicle for challenging Abdullah's move to absorb the Arab part of Palestine, and to minimise the public outcry as the armies of the Arab League withdrew from the conflict. The government in Gaza was in essence a chimera with no political or military power which was not taken seriously by any of the parties to the conflict. Also during the second truce Count Bernadotte put forward another proposal for settling the conflict. Territorially it was similar to his previous proposal, although Jerusalem would fall under United Nations control, and the Palestinians would decide their own political fate in consultation with other Arab states. The proposal was due to be debated by the United Nations General Assembly on 21 September, but on 17 September Count Bernadotte was assassinated in Jerusalem by members of the Israeli paramilitary group the Stern Gang, under orders from a triumvirate that included Yitzak Shamir, who later became prime minister of Israel (Bregman, 2003). During the second truce Ben-Gurion proposed to the Israeli cabinet the launching of a major offensive to capture much of the West Bank, but failed to gain majority approval and switched his attention to a plan to push Egyptian forces back across the Negev into Egypt. Shlaim (2000) claims that at this time Israel received a peace proposal from the Egyptian government offering de facto recognition of Israel in exchange for Egypt's annexation of a portion of land in the Negev. He argues that Ben-Gurion ignored Egypt's proposals, and persuaded the cabinet to authorise a series of military offensives designed to capture the Negev. Over the next four months Israel picked off the Arab armies one by one, making large territorial gains. This began on 15 October when Israel broke the truce and launched Operation Yoav. In a week it captured Beersheba and Bayt Jibrin, with neither Transjordan nor the Arab legion intervening to support Egypt. On 29 October Israel launched a major offensive in the north codenamed Operation Hiram, which captured central Galilee. Shlaim (2000) claims that during the operation the IDF expelled large numbers of Arabs from the Galilee in line with recommendations made on 26 September by Ben-Gurion that should fighting resume in the north the Galilee should become 'clean' and 'empty' of Arabs. A third UN truce came into effect on 31 October which lasted until 22 December when Israel again broke the truce by launching Operation Horev. This was highly successful with the Israeli army driving the Egyptians out of the Negev and following their army into Egypt proper. Eventually Britain intervened on the Egyptian side under the terms of the 1936 Anglo-Egyptian Treaty, and after forceful pressure from President Truman Ben-Gurion agreed to withdraw his troops from the Sinai and accept a new truce.

POST-WAR NEGOTIATIONS: PEACE TREATIES, BORDERS AND REFUGEES

The war ended on 7 January 1949. It had extracted a high price on all parties. Israel had lost more than 6,000 lives or 1 per cent of its population. It had, however, made huge territorial gains. UN Resolution 181 had recommended the Jewish state be established in 57 per cent of mandatory Palestine. By the end of 1948 the Israeli state had control of 78 per cent.

After the war the Israelis engaged in immediate nation-building. Elections were held in January 1949 based on a system of proportional party lists. The Mapai Party won the most seats, with its leader Ben-Gurion becoming the nation's first prime minister, whilst Chaim Weizmann was installed as president. The Palestinians view the events of 1948 as so traumatic they are simply known as *Al Nakba*, 'The Catastrophe'. The refugees created prior to the start of the 'official war' on 15 May swelled during the conflict. The Israeli historian Illan Pappe, citing evidence from Benny Morris, writes that towards the end of the war 'several massacres were committed' by Israeli forces in the villages of 'Ilabun, Sa'sa'a, Dawamiyya, Sfsa and Zurief' and that these added 'an incentive to the flight of the population'. Pappe also notes that in the final stages of the conflict 'expulsion was even more systematic' (1999: 51–2). The war ended with 520,000 Palestinian refugees according to Israel, 726,000 as estimated by the UN, and 810,000 as estimated by the British government (Gilbert, 1999). The 150,000 Palestinians who were left in the new Israeli state were, according to Bregman, regarded by Israel as a 'dangerous and not-to-be-trusted potential fifth column' and were therefore placed under military rule:

> The military government operated in areas where Arabs were concentrated and its main task was to exercise governmental policies in these areas. It was a most powerful body hated by the Arabs, for it effectively controlled all spheres of their lives imposing on them severe restrictions: it banned the Arabs from leaving their villages and travel to other parts of the country without obtaining special permission; it detained suspects without trial and it also, frequently, in the name of security, closed whole areas, thus preventing Arab peasants access to their fields and plantations which was devastating for them for they were dependent on their crops for their livelihood. The military government also imposed curfews on whole villages and on one occasion, when the village

of Kfar Qassem, unaware of the curfew, returned to their homes, the Israelis opened fire killing 47. (2003: 74)

During 1949 Israel, under the auspices of the UN, negotiated separate armistice agreements with all Arab states involved in the conflict. Jordan moved to annex the West Bank whilst Egypt moved to occupy the Gaza Strip, but unlike Jordan it made no effort to annex the territory. The name 'Palestine' had disappeared from the map, its territory having been absorbed into the Israeli and Jordanian states. In late April 1949 Israel met with delegations from Egypt, Jordan, Syria, Lebanon and the Arab Higher Committee in Lausanne to try to hammer out a peace deal. The two central sticking points were borders and refugees. The Arab delegation wanted to see borders based on the 1947 UN partition resolution that they had previously rejected. The Israelis argued that the permanent borders should be based on the ceasefire lines with only minor modifications. No agreement was reached. On 11 December 1948 the United Nations General Assembly had passed Resolution 194 which resolved 'that the refugees wishing to return to their homes and live at peace with their neighbours should be permitted to do so at the earliest practicable date, and that compensation should be paid for the property of those choosing not to return and for loss of or damage to property'. This position on the repatriation of refugees, Pappe (1999) notes, was shared by the UN, Europe and the US. Israel rejected the return of refugees and the payment of compensation, arguing that the Arab states had created the refugee problem by attacking Israel and they should therefore settle the refugees in their own countries:

> We did not want the war. Tel Aviv did not attack Jaffa. It was Jaffa which attacked Tel Aviv and this will not occur again. Jaffa will be a Jewish town. The repatriation of the Arabs is not justice, but folly. Those who declared war against us will have to bear the result after they have been defeated. (David Ben-Gurion, cited in Gabbay, 1959: 109)

From June 1949 onwards Pappe argues that Israeli leaders were committed to 'creating a fait accompli that would render repatriation impossible' (1999: 52). In that month Joseph Weitz wrote in a memorandum that there was a consensus among Israeli leaders that the best way to deal with the abandoned Palestinian villages was by 'destruction, renovation and settlement by Jews'

(Weitz, cited in Pappe, 1999: 52). This plan, which Pappe claims Israel carried out 'to the letter', required the state 'to demolish what was left of abandoned Palestinian villages, almost 350 in all, so that the term repatriation itself, would become meaningless' (1999: 52). Pappe suggests that for Israelis the subject of the Palestinian refugees raises difficult questions about the nature of the Israeli state:

> Israelis – leaders and people alike – have a genuine psychological problem when faced with the refugee issue. This is indeed for them the 'original sin'. It puts a huge question mark over the Israeli self-image of moral superiority and human sensitivity. It ridicules Israel's oxymorons, such as the 'purity of arms' or misnomers, such as the 'Israeli Defence Forces', and raises doubts over the religious notion of the 'chosen people' and the political pretension of being the only democracy in the Middle East which should be wholeheartedly supported by the West. In the past it has produced a series of repressions and self denials as well as the promotion of unrealistic political solutions … It was accompanied by an intellectual struggle against the Palestinians, epitomised by the official Israeli fabrication of the history of the land and the conflict. (1999: 58)

Although the armistice agreements had ended the military conflict, there were no formal peace treaties signed between Israel and its Arab neighbours, setting the scene for further sporadic clashes. This failure to negotiate comprehensive peace treaties is a contentious issue. Sachar for instance, blames Arab intransigence, claiming that Israel repeatedly attempted to make peace but its efforts were rebuffed by Arab states: '[The] Arab purpose was single minded and all-absorptive. It was flatly committed to the destruction of Israel as an independent state' (1977: 430). Some historians suggest the opposite. Shlaim notes that 'the files of the Israeli Foreign Ministry … burst at the seams with evidence of Arab peace feelers and Arab readiness to negotiate with Israel from September 1948 on' (2000: 49).

In the years after 1948 the Arab world instituted an economic boycott against Israel, shut its borders and refused its aircraft permission to use their airspace. This period also saw a radical demographic shift in the Jewish population throughout the Middle East. In the nine years following the 1948 war 567,000 Jews left Muslim countries and most settled in Israel, so that the population swelled from 1,174,000 in 1949 to 1,873,000 in 1956

(Ovendale, 1999). Sachar (1977) claims that in many of these societies, particularly Iraq and Egypt, the Jewish population had 'prospered mightily', but argues that in the 1940s they were subject to increasing levels of harassment and persecution. He writes that in Libya anti-Jewish riots in 1945 had left several hundred dead or wounded, and in Syria the Jewish population saw its property and employment rights curtailed. Gilbert (1999) maintains that Israeli officials were instrumental in facilitating these population transfers from Muslim countries, known in Israel as 'the ingathering of the exiles', because there was a shortage of manpower in Israel after 1948. It has been claimed that the methods employed were controversial. Gilbert (1999) and Hirst (1977) write that in Iraq, Israeli agents planted bombs in synagogues and Jewish businesses in an attempt to stimulate immigration to Israel.

Despite the stabilisation of the political and military situation following the 1948 war clashes along the armistice lines were a constant source of friction between Israel and its Arab neighbours. Displaced Palestinians in Arab states began to engage in what was known as 'infiltration'. Shlaim comments that '90 per cent or more of all infiltrations were motivated by social and economic concerns involving persons crossing the ceasefire lines to retrieve property, see relatives or tend their land' (2000: 82). Many of the refugees had been separated from their homes and land and so had no employment and went hungry. The other 10 per cent involved acts of sabotage and violence directed against Israelis. Shlaim writes that the Israelis adopted a 'free fire' policy towards infiltrators which encouraged the Arabs to organise into groups and respond in kind. The British Major John Glubb argued that 'the original infiltrator was harmless and unarmed seeking lost property or relatives. Yet Jewish terrorism [i.e. shoot to kill and reprisals raids] made the infiltrator into a gunman' (cited in Morris, 1997: 51). Between the end of the 1948 war and the 1956 Suez War, the Israeli authorities estimated that 294 civilians had been killed by infiltrators from Jordan, Lebanon and Egypt (Morris, 1997: 97–8). Shlaim writes that in this period between 2,700 and 5,000 infiltrators were killed by 'trigger happy' Israeli soldiers 'the great majority of them unarmed' (2000: 82). Some Israeli historians argue that Arab leaders encouraged infiltration as an attempt to weaken and destroy the Israeli state. In contrast Shlaim claims that 'there is strong evidence from Arab, British, American, UN and even Israeli sources to suggest that for the first six years after the war, the Arab governments were opposed to infiltration and tried to curb it' (2000:

84). Israel adopted a policy of reprisals directed against villages in Gaza and Jordan. Shlaim notes that 'all of these raids were aimed at civilian targets' and 'greatly inflamed Arab hatred of Israel and met with mounting criticism from the international community' (2000: 83). A specialist reprisal brigade, Unit 101 was created, under the command of Ariel Sharon. It first major operation involved an attack on the village of Quibya in 1953, following the killing of an Israeli mother and two children by a hand grenade in Yahuda. Unit 101 reduced Quibya 'to a pile of rubble: forty five houses had been blown up and sixty-nine civilians, two-thirds of them women and children' were killed (Shlaim, 2000: 91). A UN report found that 'the inhabitants had been forced by heavy fire to stay inside, until their homes were blown up over them' (Shlaim, 2000: 91). Shlaim also writes that such acts were carried out against Arab villages within the State of Israel:

> Periodic search operations were also mounted in Arab villages inside Israel to weed out infiltrators. From time to time the soldiers who carried out these operations committed atrocities, among them gang rape, murder and on one occasion, the dumping of 120 infiltrators in the Arava desert without water. The atrocities were committed not in the heat of battle but for the most part against innocent civilians, including women and children. Coping with day to day security had a brutalising effect on the IDF. Soldiers in an army which prided itself on the precept of 'the purity of arms' showed growing disregard for human lives and carried out some barbaric acts that can only be described as war crimes. (2000: 83)

It was against this backdrop of border tensions that Israel became involved in a broader struggle between Britain, France and Egypt over control of the Suez Canal.

1956: THE SUEZ CONFLICT

In Egypt in 1952, Gamal Abd al-Nassar and his 'free officers' took power, following a bloodless coup, and turned the state into a republic. In 1954 Nasser became president and attempted to make himself the champion of a pan-Arabic renaissance, and the leader of the de-colonisation movement across the Middle East and Africa. Ovendale (1999) notes that the European colonial powers feared the effects of Nasser's Arab nationalism on their oil interests and geostrategic control of the Middle East and Africa. France was also hostile because of Nasser's support for Algerians fighting for independence. In July 1956 he nationalised the Suez Canal after the US and Britain refused to fund the Aswan Dam Project, which Nasser saw as a means to develop Egypt as a modern nation. Britain and France, who were shareholders in the Canal, decided he had to be removed from power. Israel also wanted to see Nasser deposed and between 22 and 24 October 1956, British, French and Israeli representatives met at Sèvres on the outskirts of Paris to devise a military plan to achieve that end (Shlaim, 2000). At this meeting the Israeli delegation also secured final approval for the supply of a nuclear reactor from France which was delivered the following year and soon used to develop nuclear weapons.[15]

On 29 October 1956 the IDF launched an attack on Egyptian forces in the Sinai peninsula. The next day Britain and France issued an ultimatum to Egypt and Israel to withdraw their forces to a distance of ten miles from the Suez Canal. Israel complied, Egypt refused and the following day Britain and France began an aerial bombardment of the Egyptian airfields. Israel quickly secured an overwhelming military victory, capturing Gaza on the 2 November and the whole Sinai peninsula three days later. On 7 November Ben-Gurion delivered a speech to the Knesset where 'he hinted that Israel planned to annex the entire Sinai peninsula as well as the Straits of Tiran' (Shlaim, 2000: 179). However, under strong pressure from the USA and USSR, and threats of United Nations sanctions, Israel was eventually forced to withdraw from all of the Sinai after six months. Israel's motivations have been the subject of much controversy. One version maintains that Israel was driven to attack Egypt for three main reasons. First it is argued the Egyptian leader Nasser was planning to lead a combined Arab force (Egypt, Jordan, Syria) in an attempt to destroy Israel, and the Suez conflict was necessary as a pre-emptive military strike to prevent this. Sachar (1977) points to belligerent speeches made by Arab leaders in the months preceding the war, which he argues were proof of imminent Arab plans to destroy Israel. He also suggests that Egypt's acquisition of a large shipment of arms from Czecho-slovakia in 1955 had shifted the balance of power against Israel. Sachar also claims that Israel wanted to break Egypt's blockade of the Suez Canal, and stop Palestinian guerrilla attacks on Israel. This perspective on Israeli motivations sees the attack on Egypt as defensive in orientation and concerned only with strengthening the country's security situation.

Other historians have pointed to different reasons for the attack. Shlaim (2000) argues that Israel's military establishment led by Ben-Gurion and Moshe Dayan were determined to goad Nasser into a war by carrying out provocative raids against Egyptian forces, despite Egyptian attempts to curb infiltration. The most serious of these raids occurred in February 1955 when an Israeli unit led by Ariel Sharon attacked the Egyptian army headquarters on the outskirts of Gaza, killing 37 Egyptian soldiers. Hirst claims that Nasser had consistently tried to avoid military confrontation with Israel, and had only 'unleashed the *fedayeen* [Palestinian guerrillas] under pressure from his own public opinion in the wake of further provocations from Israel' (1977: 200). Both Hirst (1977) and Shlaim argue that there was no credible evidence that Nasser was planning a war with Israel, nor that the balance of power had shifted in Egypt's favour. They suggest that the war was undertaken to expand the borders of Israel and overthrow Nasser's regime. Shlaim maintains that Israel hoped to absorb the whole of the Sinai peninsula, the West Bank and part of the Lebanon. He argues that Ben-Gurion 'exposed an appetite for territorial expansion at the expense of the Arabs and expansion in every possible direction: north, east and south' as well as 'a cavalier attitude toward the independence, sovereignty and territorial integrity of the neighbouring Arab states' (2000: 178).

1967: THE SIX DAY WAR

During the 1960s the Middle East became a site of Cold War rivalry between America and the Soviet Union, both of whom were supplying the region's states with weapons. In spring 1967 the Soviet Union informed the Syrian government that Israel was massing troops on its northern border in preparation for an attack on Syria. Whether such troop movements had actually taken place is a matter of dispute amongst historians (see Shlaim, 2000 and Hirst, 1977 for conflicting views). However, the previous year had seen a number of border clashes between the two nations and tensions had been running high. Israel had threatened publicly to overthrow the Syrian regime unless it stopped Palestinian guerrilla attacks launched from Syrian territory. Syria, alarmed by the Soviet reports, turned to Egypt with whom it had a mutual defence pact. Egypt then sent a number of troops into the Sinai, bordering Israel, and asked the United Nations troops, who formed a buffer between the two countries, to evacuate their positions. The Egyptian troops then moved into Sharm el-Sheikh and proclaimed a blockade of the Israeli port of Eilat, which was accessible only through Egyptian waters. Two weeks later, at 7.45 a.m. on 5 June 1967, Israel launched an aerial attack on Egyptian airfields destroying 298 warplanes, the bulk of the Egyptian air force, in a single day. Israeli ground forces also launched an almost simultaneous land invasion of Egyptian territory, forcing their way to the Suez Canal and capturing the Sinai peninsula in two days. At noon on 5 June, as part of a defence pact with Egypt, Syrian, Jordanian and Iraqi forces attacked targets inside Israel. Within two hours the air forces of all three were destroyed by the Israeli air force, as well as an Iraqi military base near the Jordanian border. Jordanian land forces also intervened in support of Egypt. Jordanian artillery shelled Israeli towns and moved troops into Arab East Jerusalem. Israel then drove the Jordanian army out of the West Bank and East Jerusalem, occupying them both by 7 June. The following day Israeli warplanes attacked the American spy ship, the USS *Liberty*, with cannon, missiles and napalm, killing 34 US service personnel and injuring 171.[16] On 9 June Israel attacked Syria, despite strong UN pressure, and occupied the Golan Heights. There have been allegations in the Israeli press that about a thousand unresisting Egyptian soldiers, as well as dozens of unarmed Palestinian refugees, were killed by the Israeli army during the war (*Ha'aretz*, 17 August 1995, cited in *Washington Report on Middle East Affairs*, February/March 1996).

The war was an overwhelming military success for Israel. In six days it destroyed three Arab armies and made large territorial gains, capturing the Sinai peninsula, the Golan Heights, the West Bank, Gaza Strip and Arab East Jerusalem. The reasons behind Israel's decision to launch it are disputed. The official Israeli cabinet documents stated that the 'Government [of Israel] ascertained that the armies of Egypt, Syria and Jordan are deployed for immediate multi-front aggression, threatening the very existence of the state' (cited in Finkelstein, 2001: 130). Three years previously Arab leaders had declared in an official document their intention to achieve 'collective military preparations' for the 'final liquidation of Israel' (Shlaim, 2000: 230). Sachar points to Nasser's decision to replace United Nations peacekeeping troops in the Sinai with Egyptian troops, and military preparations by other Arab nations as evidence that 'the garrote ... was rapidly tightening around Israel' (1977: 632). He also points to Israeli motivations to stop Syrian shelling of Israeli settlements in the demilitarised zone between Israel and Syria, and guerrilla raids into Israeli territory.

Another justification given for Israel's attack was Egypt's decision to blockade the Straits of Tiran which prevented access to the Israeli port of Eilat. This, according to the Israeli foreign minister Abba Eban, was an 'attempt at strangulation' which constituted an 'act of war' (Eban, 1992: 334, cited in Finkelstein, 2001: 137). Some other historians have questioned these explanations and pointed to an alternative set of motivations. The assertions that the Arab states were planning an imminent attack and that they had the military strength to threaten Israel's existence are both disputed. Finkelstein notes that an 'exhaustive US intelligence at the end of the month [May 1967] could find no evidence that Egypt was planning to attack' (2001: 134). Menachem Begin and Yitzak Rabin later argued that the Arab states had not been planning an attack and that the Israeli government had been aware of this at the time.[17] The claim that the combined Arab armies posed a mortal threat to the State of Israel is also disputed. The CIA produced a report in May 1967 forecasting, with remarkable prescience, that Israel would win a war against one or all of the Arab states combined, whoever attacked first, in about a week. British intelligence had reached the identical conclusion (Finkelstein, 2001). Menachem Begin and Ezer Weizman have also argued that Israel's existence was never threatened.[18] Five years after the war, in an Israeli newspaper article, a senior military planner, General Mattityahu Peled, was dismissive of the Arab threat in 1967:

There is no reason to hide the fact that since 1949 no one dared, or more precisely, no one was able to threaten the very existence of Israel. In spite of that, we have continued to foster a sense of our own inferiority, as if we were a weak and insignificant people, which, in the midst of an anguished struggle for its existence, could be exterminated at any moment … it is notorious that the Arab leaders themselves, thoroughly aware of their own impotence, did not believe in their own threats … I am sure that our General Staff never told the government that the Egyptian military threat represented any threat to Israel or that we were unable to crush Nasser's army, which with unheard of foolishness, had exposed itself to the devastating might of our army … To claim that the Egyptian forces concentrated on our borders were capable of threatening Israel's existence not only insults the intelligence of anyone capable of analysing this kind of situation, but is an insult to the Zahal [the Israeli army]. (Ma'ariv, 24 March 1972, cited in Hirst, 1977: 211)

Other posited explanations for Israel's decision to attack its Arab neighbours include a desire to safeguard the deterrent image of the IDF. Shlaim (2000) suggests that the Egyptian blockade represented a threat to Israel's 'iron wall' of militarised strength. Others suggest different motivations. Neff writes that on the eve of the 1967 war the CIA had identified three Israeli objectives: 'the destruction of the centre of power of the radical Arab socialist movements' (i.e. Nasser's regime), 'the destruction of the arms of the radical Arabs', and the 'destruction of both Jordan and Syria as modern States' (Neff, 1985: 230, cited in Finkelstein, 2001: 143). Hirst (1977) argues that Israeli military planners had been preparing the attack since they were forced to leave the Sinai in 1956, and cites comments from General Burns, the chief of staff of the United Nations Truce Supervision Organisation (UNTSO) in the early 1960s that Israel would probably seek to go to war again soon to break the Arab economic blockade and overcome its own economic difficulties. Another explanation that has been cited as a motivation for Israel's decision involved a desire to expand the boundaries of Israel. Proponents of this view, point to comments made by the Israeli commander Yigal Allon on the eve of the 1967 war that 'in the case of a new war' Israel must seek as a central aim 'the territorial fulfilment of the land of Israel' (cited in Finkelstein, 2001: 143). There is evidence since the 1950s in the writings of David Ben-Gurion and other Israeli leaders that there had been a desire to expand Israel to incorporate all of Jerusalem and the West Bank. The Israeli historian Benny Morris notes:

A strong expansionist current ran through both Zionist ideology and Israeli society. There was a general feeling shared by prominent figures as Dayan and Ben-Gurion, that the territorial gains of the 1948 war had fallen short of the envisioned promised land. Bechiya Le Dorot – literally a cause for lamentation for future generations – was how Ben-Gurion described the failure to conquer Arab East Jerusalem; leading groups in Israeli society regarded the Jordanian controlled West Bank with the same feeling. (Morris, 1989: 410–11, cited in Finkelstein, 2001: 221)

The conflict triggered a second mass exodus of Palestinians, many of whom became refugees for a second time, as they had sought refuge in the West Bank and Gaza after having to abandon their homes in 1948–49. Nur Masalha, senior lecturer at the Holy Land Research Project at the University of Surrey, argues that 'there is no evidence to suggest that there were wholesale or blanket expulsion orders adopted or carried out by the Israeli army in June 1967, although the policy of selective eviction, demolition and encouragement of "transfer" continued for several weeks after the Israeli army occupied the West Bank and Gaza Strip' (Masalha, 1999: 100). Masalha maintains that in 1967 'evictions and demolitions were evident in numerous geographical locations in the West Bank' and that 'young men from several cities and refugee camps were also targeted for deportation' (1999: 101). Peter Dodd and Halim Barakat, in their study of the 1967 exodus, *River without Bridges*, provide similar explanations for the exodus:

> The exodus was a response to the severe situational pressures existing at the time. The situational pressures were generated by the aerial attacks upon a defenceless country, including the extensive use of napalm, the occupation of the West Bank villages by the Israeli army, and the actions of the occupying forces. Certainly the most dramatic of these was the eviction of civilians, and the deliberate destruction of a number of villages [Imwas, Yalu, Bayt Nuba, Bayt Marsam, Bayt Awa, Habla, al-Burj and Jiftlik]. Other action, such as threats and the mass detention of male civilians, also created situational pressures. (Dodd and Barakat, 1968: 54, cited in Masalha, 1999: 96)

William Wilson Harris (1980), who reached similar conclusions in his analysis of the exodus, estimates that 250,000 residents of the West Bank, 70,000 residents of the Gaza Strip and 90,000 residents of the Golan Heights were forced to flee their homes during 1967. The displaced residents of the West Bank were prevented from returning to the area by harsh measures. Testimony in the Israeli press, from an unnamed soldier serving in the 5th Reserve Division on the Jordan river, details the fate of displaced Palestinians attempting to return to their homes:

> We fired such shots every night on men, women and children. Even during moonlit nights when we could identify the people, that is distinguish between men, women and children. In the mornings we searched the area and, by explicit order from the officer on the spot, shot the living, including those who hid or were wounded, again including the women and children. (*Haolam Haze*, 10 October 1967, cited in Masalha, 1999: 99)

There were reports that after the war Israel began destroying Palestinian homes in the newly occupied territories. The American historian Alfred Lilienthal claims that

> according to UN figures, the Israelis destroyed during the period between 11 June 1967 and 15 November 1969 some 7,554 Palestinian Arab homes in the territories seized during that war; this figure excluded 35 villages in the occupied Golan Heights that were razed to the ground. In the two years between September 1969 and 1971 the figure was estimated to have reached 16,312 homes. (1978: 160)

On 19 June 1967 Israeli leaders formulated an offer to hand back the Golan Heights, the Sinai and the Gaza Strip in return for demilitarisation agreements, peace treaties and assurance of navigation rights from Egypt, Syria and Jordan. Bergman (2003) suggests that the decision, taken two months later, by Arab leaders meeting in Khartoum to issue the famous 'three nos' to peace, recognition and negotiations with Israel led to the Israeli decision taken on 30 October to officially withdraw the offer, and harden its attitude. Shlaim (2000) disagrees, arguing that there was no evidence that the conditional offer of withdrawal was ever presented to the Arab states, and that the offer was almost immediately killed by political and military leaders in Israel who wanted to retain a large part of the captured territories, and who began in mid July to approve plans for constructing settlements on the occupied Golan Heights. He maintains that the 'three nos' at Khartoum referred to 'no formal peace *treaty*, but not a rejection of a state of peace; no *direct* negotiations, but not a refusal to talk through third parties; and no *de jure* recognition of Israel, but acceptance of its existence as a state' (Shlaim, 2000: 258). He suggests the conference was 'a victory for Arab moderates who argued for trying to obtain the withdrawal of Israeli forces by political rather than military means' (2000: 258). There have also been claims that Israel turned down a peace treaty with Egypt and Jordan at the conference.[19]

Shlaim notes that there was no Israeli debate about handing back East Jerusalem, but that Israeli leaders were split on how much of the West Bank they wanted to retain. He suggests outright annexation was favoured by only a few, because it would mean absorbing large numbers of Arabs into the Jewish state. Most of these leaders favoured one of two options. The 'Allon Plan', put forward by the Israeli deputy prime minister Yigal Allon, proposed limited autonomy for Palestinians in parts of the West Bank (Israel would still own the land and control security in the autonomy area), with Israel taking control of a large strip of the Jordan valley, much of the area around Jerusalem and the Judean desert. These parts of the West Bank would then be colonised with Jewish settlements and army bases. The second option involved handing back to Jordan part of the West Bank with Israel keeping approximately a third of the area. Neither proposal was acceptable to King Hussein or the Palestinians.

RESOLUTION 242 AND THE WAR OF ATTRITION

The 1967 war was followed by the UN Security Council unanimously adopting Resolution 242, which has become the framework document for successive attempts to resolve the conflict. The resolution called for the 'withdrawal of Israeli armed forces from territories occupied in the recent conflict' in line with the principle 'emphasise[d]' in the preambular paragraph of the 'inadmissibility of the acquisition of territory by war'. It also 'emphasised' the 'need to work for a just and lasting peace in which every State in the area can live in security' as well as a 'just settlement of the refugee problem' and the establishment of navigation rights. Egypt and Jordan agreed to Resolution 242 whilst Syria rejected it. The Palestinians also rejected it on the grounds that it only spoke of their plight as a refugee problem, making no mention of their rights to self-determination and national sovereignty. Israel accepted the resolution in 1970. The meaning of the withdrawal clause has been contested. Israel has argued that because the definite article 'the' was not included in the English version of the resolution ('from territories occupied' rather than 'from the territories occupied') it means that the scope of withdrawal was left vague and that Israel did not have to withdraw from all the territories it occupied in the conflict. Israel has also argued that many of the nations who endorsed the resolution, including the United States, United Kingdom, USSR and Brazil, agreed that Israel did not have to withdraw from all the territories (Israeli Ministry of Foreign Affairs, 1999). Finkelstein (2001) disputes this. He points to statements made by the president of the United Nations General Assembly that 'there is virtual unanimity in upholding the principle that conquest of territory by war is inadmissible in our time under the Charter' (UN General Assembly, 1967, cited in Finkelstein, 2001: 145). This affirmation, the president continued, was 'made in virtually all statements' and that 'virtually all speakers laid down the corollary that withdrawal of forces to their original position is expected' (UN General Assembly, 1967, cited in Finkelstein, 2001: 145). The debates at the UN Security Council, Finkelstein argues, were similarly unambiguous with almost all representatives stressing both the inadmissibility clause and the need for a complete Israeli withdrawal.[20] He also argues that the American position was for a full Israeli withdrawal.[21]

Having failed to secure such a withdrawal from the occupied territories Egypt fought the 'War of Attrition' against Israel between 1967 and 1970. Shlaim argues that President Nasser's immediate purpose was to 'prevent the conversion of the Suez Canal into a de facto border, while his ultimate goal was to force Israel to withdraw to the pre-war border' (2000: 289). Egypt bombed Israeli troop concentrations in the occupied Sinai, and Palestinian guerrillas launched cross-border attacks against Israel. Israel then attacked military and civilian targets within Egypt and Jordan. Numerous Egyptian coastal towns and cities were heavily damaged by Israeli air attacks. The Israeli commander Ezer Weizman recalled the fate of an Egyptian border city Ismailia which the Israeli army bombarded 'incessantly, devastating it from the air as well as with land-based artillery' so that aerial photographs 'showed its western portions resembling the cities at the end of World War II' (Weizman, cited in Gilbert, 1999: 410). Moshe Dayan was later to claim that Israeli attacks during the War of Attrition had created 1.5 million Egyptian refugees as well as emptying the entire Jordan valley of its inhabitants (*Al Hamishar*, 10 May 1978). The war was finally brought to a halt in August 1970 when both sides agreed to a US-sponsored ceasefire. Morris (1992) estimates that in the three years of conflict, 367 Israeli soldiers and more than 10,000 Egyptian soldiers and civilians were killed.

SETTLEMENT BUILDING, ECONOMIC INTEGRATION AND THE OCCUPATION

In the aftermath of the 1967 war Israel established settlements on the newly captured territories and placed the Palestinian residents under military rule. Two major reasons were given for the creation of settlements. One stressed their security value:

> There was also a strategic justification for not wanting to give up the occupied West Bank and that was that it turned Israel's

'narrow waist' into something wider. Before seizing the West Bank Israel's width at some parts measured scarcely nine miles from the Jordan bulge to the Mediterranean, and by clinging to the occupied territories west of the Jordan river Israel made it more difficult for a potential Arab invasion force coming from the east to cut in two. (Bregman, 2003: 126–7)

Some Israelis were dismissive of the security argument, alleging it was a pretext to satisfy international public opinion. One official writing in the Israeli press claimed that 'we have to use the pretext of security needs and the authority of the military governor as there is no way of driving out the Arabs from their land so long as they refuse to go and accept our compensation' (*Ha'aretz*, 23 November 1969, cited in Hirst, 1977: 241). A second strand of thought justified settlement building and retention of the occupied territories, on the basis of divine rights. Victory in the Six Day War was seen by many religious Jews as a sign of support from God and evidence that the messianic era was at hand, leading to a surge in support for religious nationalism. A number of new parties and organisations were formed who advocated permanent control and settlement of the West Bank and Gaza Strip because, it was argued, these areas were a central component of the biblical land of Israel. Harold Fisch, the former rector of Israel's Bar-Ilan University, argues that God promised Abraham the land of Israel as an eternal possession, and this provides justification for sovereignty over the West Bank and Gaza Strip:

The covenant between the people of Israel and its God, which includes the promised land as an integral part, is an important objective within the entire scheme of creation. It is from this fact that the linkage between the people of Israel and its land is rooted-in the transcendental will of God who created all in his honor. (Fisch, 1982: 189)

These arguments are echoed in more contemporary comments. In an interview in the *Observer*, Ariel Sharon, the Israeli prime minister, was quoted as saying 'Israel is the promised land – promised to Jews and no-one else' (13 July 2003). The viewpoint also gained ground in the US via the Christian fundamentalist movement, who were key supporters of George W. Bush and the Republicans. In a 2002 programme the BBC interviewed the pastor of a major church in Texas who explained his view that:

Well you understand that the Jewish state was something that's born in the mind of God and we are a people who believe the scripture and the scripture says very clearly that God created Israel, that God is the protector and defender of Israel. If God created Israel, if God defends Israel, is it not logical to say that those who fight with Israel are fighting with God? (BBC Radio 4, *A Lobby to be Reckoned With*, 7 May 2002)

Other arguments for Israel's rights to keep and settle the lands captured in 1967 included the position that since the land has changed sovereignty many times over the last 2,000 years, the Jews have as much claim as any others who had controlled it since they were exiled.[22] Some Israelis have also argued that because the Palestinians rejected partition in 1947 they have given up their rights to a share of mandatory Palestine. Others point to the legal status of the Balfour Declaration or argue that since Israel won the territories in a 'war of self-defence' they have a right to keep them. Binyamin Netanyahu argues that to prevent Jews from building settlements in the occupied territories is a form of apartheid:

Careful manipulation of the media by the Arabs has left many Westerners with the indelible impression that Arab paupers are being kicked off their hovels in droves to make way for Jewish suburbs in the 'densely populated West Bank' ... For what is manifestly occurring is that the West, which so sharply condemned anti-black apartheid in South Africa, is being used by the Arabs as an enforcer of anti-Jewish apartheid that pertains in the Arabs' own countries. (2000: 189–92)

In a review of Israel's settlement building programmes, Israel Shahak and Norton Mezvinsky (1999) note that until 1974, Moshe Dayan oversaw settlement activity. His policy was to limit settlements primarily to Hebron, northern Sinai and the Jordan valley, as part of a bargain he made with the Palestinian feudal notables who controlled the villages. Shahak and Mezvinsky note that, after 1974, religious settler groups, primarily Gush Emunim, and their political allies in the Knesset, came to the fore in determining settlement policy, with the support of both Labour and particularly the Likud Party. In 1973 Israel introduced the Galili Plan, which Shafir suggests transformed the Allon Plan's '*military frontier* to a combination of a *messianic frontier* and a *suburban frontier*' (1999: 92). Some commentators have pointed to the extreme ideological views of many religious settlers which justify attacks on Palestinians and attempts to expel them from their homes and land in what is seen as a process of 'purification' or 'sanctification' of the land.[23] Hirst has suggested that even prior to 1974, the creation of settlements was at the expense of Palestinians:

> Sometimes it was necessary to uproot an entire village – though not necessarily all at once. For years the impoverished inhabitants of Beit Askariyah watched in impotent dismay as the great cantonments of the Kfar Etzion settlement went up around them, relentlessly encroaching on their agricultural and grazing land before swallowing up their homes too. In January 1972, the army expelled 6,000 Bedouins from Rafah in north-east Sinai. It demolished their houses, poisoned their wells, and kept them at bay with a barbed wire fence. The Bedouins were eventually employed as night watchmen or labourers – on their own property and in the service of those who had taken it from them. (1977: 242)

In 1981 the Likud administration introduced the Drobless Plan. Shafir suggests that its purpose was to 'scatter Jewish settlements among Arab towns and villages in order to ensure that no homogenous Palestinian inhabited area, the potential core of a Palestinian state would remain' (1999: 92). In a more recent study Amnesty International (1999c) examined how settlement building and Palestinian house demolitions are 'inextricably linked with Israeli policy to control and colonize areas of the West Bank', a policy that has been 'energetically followed for over 30 years by all administrations from 1967 until the present time'. The process of colonisation, the report continues, depends 'not just on finding land that is physically "suitable", but on alienating it from the Palestinians, defending it against Palestinian use, and ensuring through such processes as registration and leasing that Palestinians are disqualified from having any future benefit from that land'. Amnesty International argue that the damage to the 'tight knit pattern of Palestinian villages' has been 'pervasive'. Settlement building is prohibited by the Fourth Geneva Convention, Article 49 of which stipulates that 'the occupying power shall not deport or transfer parts of its own population into the territory it occupies'. The Israeli government has disputed this, arguing that the area is 'administered' rather than 'occupied' and that Article 49 of the Conventions has 'no bearing' on the Israeli settlements because the

Convention was intended to cover forced transfers during the Second World War, whilst 'the movement of individuals to these areas is entirely voluntary, while the settlements themselves are not intended to displace Arab inhabitants, nor do they do so in practice' (Israeli Ministry of Foreign Affairs, 1996). The practice has, however, been repeatedly condemned by the European Union and United Nations who have deemed the settlements illegal and in need of removal in multiple resolutions. The practice was condemned in December 2000 (United Nations Resolution 55/132) by 152 votes to 4 (Israel, United States, Micronesia, Marshall Islands).

In Jerusalem, Israel initiated a policy of 'Judaisation' in an attempt to change the demographic, physical, cultural, legal and economic status of the city. It appropriated Arab land in the city and demolished Arab housing. In the Jewish Quarter prior to 1948, approximately 20 per cent of the property was Jewish owned. After 1967, Hirst writes that Israelis 'relentlessly forced out the 5,500 [Arab] inhabitants who lived there' (1977: 235). The demolitions and evictions occurred all over the city, with the victims of land expropriations receiving either inadequate levels of compensation or sometimes none. Moves to change the legal and demographic structure of Jerusalem have drawn criticism from the international community. In 1999 the United Nations condemned such actions by 139 votes to 1 (Israel).[24] Hirst also notes that Arab culture was suppressed or denigrated especially in schools.[25] The Israeli state quickly moved to integrate the Arabs living in the occupied territories into the Israeli economy. Some historians such as Sachar suggest that for Palestinians this was a generally beneficial process creating 'unprecedented affluence' as part of a 'comparatively painless' occupation (1977: 688–9). Other Israelis were critical of this process, arguing that Israel was instituting colonial policies in which a powerful Israeli minority was exploiting a captive Arab population for the use of its cheap labour and its role as a market for Israeli products:

> Better men than I have enlarged on the grim paradox that threatens the Zionist vision, the social and moral failure of that vision, which are to be expected from the transformation of the Jews into employers, managers and supervisors of Arab hewers of wood and drawers of water, and all of it plus the slogan of 'Integration' … There is an inescapable process in a population that is divided into two peoples, one dominant, the other dominated. No! The

State of Israel will not be such a monstrosity. (Ya'akov Talmon, cited in Sachar, 1977: 713)

There has also been commentary in the Israeli press suggesting the conditions under which the Palestinians were obliged to work for Israelis were exploitative and humiliating. Palestinians with jobs in Israel were not legally allowed to spend the night there so that many had to be bussed in over long distances from the occupied territories. This sometimes extended their working day to 17 hours. The Israeli magazine *Haolam Haze* reported on those that were permitted to sleep illegally on Israeli farms: 'Too far away for the eye to see, hidden in the orchards, there are the sheep pens for the servants, of a sort that even a state like South Africa would be ashamed of' (22 December 1982, cited in Chomsky, 1999: 141). In a *Jerusalem Post* interview, the Israeli journalist Aryeh Rubinstein asks Amos Hadar, Secretary General of the Moshav (agricultural) movement whether he agrees with the use of Arab labour 'but only on condition that they will live in subhuman conditions, degraded, and not under human conditions, more or less?' 'Correct', replies Hadar, stressing that 'there is a difficult question here'. 'There is no choice but to employ Arabs' but they must be bussed in and out of Israel every day. 'It is hard, it is costly, it is problematic from an economic standpoint but there is no other solution' (26 December 1982, cited in Chomsky, 1999: 141). There has also been criticism of Israeli use of Arab child labour. Israel's Arabic language communist newspaper *Al-Ittihad* described a child labour market at Jaffa:

In this market foremen get rich by exploiting the labour of children and young men from the occupied areas. Every morning at 4 a.m. cars from Gaza and the Strip start arriving there, bringing dozens of Arab workers who line up in the street in a long queue. A little later at 4:30 a.m. Arab boys who work in restaurants in the town begin to arrive. These boys work in restaurants for a month on end, including Saturdays ... Dozens, indeed hundreds of boys, who should be at school come from Gaza to work in Israel. The cars can be seen coming and going from earliest dawn. At about 6 a.m. Israeli labour brokers start arriving to choose 'working donkeys' as they call them. They take great care over their choice, actually feeling the 'donkeys' muscles. (30 April 1973, cited in Hirst, 1977: 246)

MILITARY OCCUPATION/ADMINISTRATION

Israel imposed a military administration on the occupied territories, which seriously restricted the social and political rights of its residents. According to the United Nations and human rights groups, it also involved extensive human rights violations. Israel argued that the policies were necessary to protect the state from attacks by infiltrators or Palestinians in the occupied territory, who they claimed were susceptible to Palestine Liberation Organisation (PLO) incitement. Morris suggests that severe repression coupled with 'massive use' of informers and collaborators by the Israeli security service Shin Bet meant that armed activity by the PLO in the occupied territories was 'virtually eradicated' by 1971 (1992: 279). Some commentators such as Chomsky have suggested that the imposition of such policies had another objective. This was to make life difficult for the Palestinians in the occupied territories, so that they would emigrate and allow Israel to absorb the parts of the occupied territories that it wanted, without having to worry about a large Arab population that would 'dilute' the Jewish character of the Israeli state. Chomsky points to the official government records of a meeting at the start of the Israeli occupation in September 1967, when Moshe Dayan urged government ministers to tell the Palestinian residents of the occupied territories that 'we have no solution, that you shall continue to live like dogs, and whoever wants to can leave – and we will see where this process leads ... In five years we may have 200,000 less people – and that is a matter of enormous importance' (Beilin, 1985, cited in Chomsky, 1992: 434). Professor Ian Lustick suggests that Israel also wanted to break up the territorial continuity of Israeli Arab villages in the Galilee and points to the 1976 Koenig memorandum in which the Israeli Minister of the Interior recommended the 'coordination of a smear campaign against Rakah activists ...' the harassment of 'all negative personalities at all levels and at all institutions' and the employment of techniques for 'encouraging the emigration of Arab intellectuals, and for downgrading the effectiveness of Arab university student organizations' (1980: 256). It is widely argued that the policies Israel instituted breached international law. They also led to it being frequently condemned at the United Nations General Assembly and Security Council by near unanimous votes.[26] These policies included the systematic torture of prisoners,[27] imprisonment without trial,[28] collective punishments,[29] the taking of natural resources, curfews and searches,[30] house demolitions and deportations. The practices have also attracted criticism from human rights groups:

> Amnesty International has for many years documented and condemned violations of international human rights and humanitarian law by Israel directed against the Palestinian population of the Occupied Territories. They include unlawful killings; torture and ill-treatment; arbitrary detention; unfair trials; collective punishments such as punitive closures of areas and destruction of homes; extensive and wanton destruction of property; deportations; and discriminatory treatment as compared to Israeli settlers. Most of these violations are grave breaches of the Fourth Geneva Convention and are therefore war crimes. Many have also been committed in a widespread and systematic manner, and in pursuit of government policy; such violations meet the definition of crimes against humanity under international law. (Amnesty International, 2002a)

NATIONALISM AND THE RISE OF THE OPPOSITION MOVEMENTS

In the aftermath of 1948 the refugees who were displaced had begun to formulate a vision of 'the return'. Initially it was hoped that the United Nations or the Arab states themselves would help the refugees to achieve this objective. However, as the years passed the lack of concrete progress began to frustrate the refugees and they became increasingly disillusioned by the leaders of the Arab states. By 1964 Yasser Arafat had established a small guerrilla organisation, which was granted a secure base by Syria's radical Baathist regime. Fatah's philosophy from the outset was to mobilise popular Arab support behind guerrilla operations of increasing scale and intensity conducted against Israel. Prior to the 1967 war, Hirst (1977) alleges that Egypt, Jordan and Lebanon had all tried to prevent guerrilla incursions into Israel, but that after the war this became more difficult as popular support for guerrilla operations increased. By February 1968 Fatah members had taken control of the National Council of the PLO and Arafat became chairman. The aftermath of the war also saw the formation of Dr George Habash's PFLP (Popular Front for the Liberation of Palestine) begin to build a strong base of support in the refugee camps of the Gaza Strip.

In March 1968 Israeli forces launched an attack on the Karameh refugee camp in Jordan. Israel claimed the attack was in retaliation for attacks which had killed six people and wounded 44. Fifteen

thousand troops backed by tanks attacked the camp. Rather
than retreat to the hills the guerrilla forces stayed and fought and
suffered huge losses. Half the Palestinian guerrillas, 150 in all,
were killed, together with 128 members of the Jordanian army
and 29 Israeli soldiers (Hirst, 1977). Although the guerrillas had
lost many fighters it was considered a significant victory because
the Israelis had suffered unusually high casualties and met fierce
resistance. The battle of Karameh led to an influx of volunteers
from across the Arab world to join the guerrilla movements. In
the years after 1967, as well as engaging in a guerrilla war, the
Palestinians began to formulate a vision of what a future Palestinian
entity would look like. The result of this was the vision of the
'Democratic State of Palestine' put forward by the PLO planner
and negotiator Nabil Shaath in 1969. The new state, it was hoped,
would involve the dismantling of the Israeli state and its replacement
with a non-sectarian Palestine in which Christian, Muslim and Jew
would live together in equality (Hirst, 1977). It would include the
Jews already residing there and the Palestinians who had been
displaced in 1948 and 1967. These proposals were not immediately
or universally accepted by Palestinians. Hirst (1977) suggests that
some saw them as capitulation to the enemy or at best premature
considering that Israel was still militarily dominant. Others feared
that the more technologically advanced Israelis would dominate
them, whilst some considered it a tactical propaganda move aimed
at international opinion.[31] The concept was a complete non-starter
for almost all the Jewish population of Israel. The country had been
constructed out of Palestine with huge military and diplomatic effort
and there was no desire to dilute its Jewish character. Furthermore,
Israelis were fearful of the extreme anti-Jewish rhetoric emanating
from its Arab neighbours and worried that any returning refugees
might want to take revenge for being displaced from their lands.
The former head of Israeli military intelligence, Yehoshafat Harkabi,
argued that the concept was a propaganda device designed to
mask a struggle which was still 'genocidal' in intent. The idea was
eventually dropped after 1974 when the PLO moved towards a
two-state solution.

In the two years after the 1967 war the forces of Fatah and the
other guerrilla movements had gone from 300 to more than 30,000
and substantial funding was coming in from the Arab world. The
number of operations also increased dramatically. Fatah records
claim that 98 per cent of these occurred outside the State of Israel
with two-thirds of them occurring in the West Bank. Fatah regularly

insisted that the army and 'Zionist institutions' were its real targets, not civilians especially women and children, and if these were attacked it was in response to attacks on Palestinian civilians, and was selectively done. However, Hirst (1977) points out that although the 'great bulk' of attacks were aimed at military targets, civilians were unquestionably targeted. Bombs were planted in supermarkets in Jerusalem and bus stops in Tel Aviv and rockets were fired on settlements in Kiryat Shmoneh and Eilat. Whilst Fatah confined its actions to historic Palestine, the PFLP did not. It attacked targets all over the world. It hijacked foreign airliners. It firebombed branches of Marks and Spencer because of their fundraising for Israel. It blew up an Arab oil pipeline because the extraction was by an American oil company on behalf of a 'feudal' Arab monarchy. The main purpose of these actions, George Habash maintained, was publicity:

> When we hijack a plane it had more effect than if we killed a hundred Israelis in battle. For decades world public opinion has been neither for nor against the Palestinians. It simply ignored us. At least the world is talking about us now. (*Der Stern*, 19 September 1970, cited in Hirst, 1977: 304)

However, the opposition movements were to suffer a major blow in 1970. The PLO had formed a state-within-a-state in Jordan, openly threatening the rule of the Hashemite monarchy. Following an assassination attempt on King Hussein and a series of hijackings carried out by the PFLP, the king set his army upon the guerrillas. In ten days of bloody struggle thousands of guerrillas were killed, and within a year most of the fighters and political elements of the Palestinian movement were expelled and ended up in Lebanon. 'Black September', as it became known amongst Palestinians, produced an organisation bearing the same name. Its most well-known operation was the taking of Israeli athletes as hostages at the 1972 Munich Olympics. Eight members of Black September took eleven Israelis hostage at the Olympic village in Munich demanding the release of 200 Palestinians imprisoned in Israel. In the German rescue operation four of the Palestinians and all eleven Israeli hostages were killed. Three days later Israel launched attacks on Syria and Lebanon. There were reports that up to 500 people, many of them women and children, were killed in nine separate simultaneous Israeli air attacks (*Al-Nahar Arab Report*, 18 September 1972):

The Phantoms and Skyhawks swooped on the suburban Damascus resort of al-Hama; the bombs fell indiscriminately on Palestinians in their hillside dwellings and on Syrians, in their cars or strolling by the river Barada on their weekend outing. Survivors recounted how they were machine-gunned as they ran for cover. (Hirst, 1977: 251)

In 1973 there were further hijackings by militant Arab groups. In that year Israel had also shot down a Libyan airliner which had strayed over the occupied Sinai peninsula, killing all 106 passengers. Later, Black September militants took over the Saudi Embassy in the Sudanese capital demanding the release of Palestinian militants held in Jordanian jails. The authorities refused and a Jordanian together with an American and a Belgian diplomat were killed. There followed, in quick succession, hijackings of Japanese, American, and Dutch airliners. The worst loss of life occurred at Rome airport in December 1973 when Palestinian militants killed 34, mainly American, civilians. Eleven months later a British Airways VC10 was hijacked by the Martyr Abu Mahmud Group, who called on the British government to 'declare its responsibility for the greatest crime in history, which was the establishment of the Zionist entity, and foreswear the accursed Balfour Declaration, which brought tragedies and calamities to our region' (cited in Hirst, 1977: 321–2). In the wake of this hijacking Yasser Arafat very publicly attempted to rein in the militants by arresting a number and amending the PLO criminal code to make hijacking that resulted in loss of life a capital offence.

The early 1970s had also seen the PLO begin to make diplomatic headway at the United Nations in its quest for institutional legitimacy and support for Palestinian nationalism. It received support at the UN from the Arab, non-aligned and newly de-colonised states who tended to vote as a block in support of Palestinian rights. In 1970 a General Assembly resolution was passed recognising the need for Palestinian self-determination. General Assembly Resolution 2649 'condemns those Governments that deny the right to self-determination of peoples recognised as being entitled to it, especially of the peoples of southern Africa and Palestine'. In 1974 UN Resolution 3246 was passed which again stressed the need for Palestinian self-determination and added as a corollary that it was legitimate to 'struggle for liberation from colonial and foreign domination and alien subjugation by all available means, including armed struggle'. In November 1974 the UN adopted Resolution

3236 which established UN support for the creation of a Palestinian state: 'The General Assembly ... reaffirms the inalienable rights of the Palestinian people in Palestine, including (a) the right to self-determination without external interference (b) the right to national independence and sovereignty.'

Many Israelis, especially those on the political right, disputed the whole notion of Palestinian nationalism. They argued that it was a post-1967 invention created by the Arab states in order to wage a surrogate war against Israel. In 1969 the Israeli prime minister Golda Meir stated that 'It was not as though there was a Palestinian people in Palestine considering itself as a Palestinian people and we came and threw them out and took their country away from them. They did not exist' (*The Sunday Times*, 15 June 1969, cited Shlaim, 2000: 311). Similarly, Netanyahu has argued that both Palestinian Nationalism and Palestinian refugees are post-1967 fabrications:

> Indeed, most Palestinian Arabs have homes. Many of them, in fact, live as full citizens in Eastern Palestine – today called the Hashemite Kingdom of Jordan. Similarly, most of the Arabs of Judea-Samaria are not homeless refugees; they live in the same homes they occupied before the establishment of Israel. The number of actual refugees is close to nil. (2000: 156–8)

This is disputed by multilateral bodies such as the United Nations, who have explicitly recognised in many resolutions the existence of a distinct Palestinian people, their rights to national self-determination, and the existence of over 3.5 million refugees.

1973: THE OCTOBER WAR/THE YOM KIPPUR WAR

The War of Attrition had failed to secure the return of the occupied Sinai for Egypt but had instead left many of the Suez coastal cities devastated by Israeli raids. Shlaim claims that in the early 1970s Egypt made numerous attempts to regain the occupied Sinai through diplomacy but her peace overtures were rejected by Israel.[32] Shlaim suggests Israel's 'diplomacy of attrition' together with statements indicating that it intended to annex the Sinai left Sadat with no diplomatic option and made war inevitable.

On 6 October 1973 Egyptian and Syrian forces attacked Israeli troop concentrations in the occupied Sinai peninsula and Golan Heights. The Arab armies achieved early successes with the Egyptian army crossing the Suez Canal and advancing into the Sinai, and the Syrian army forcing back the Israelis on the Golan Heights. Eventually the Israeli army turned the tables and regained the territorial losses it initially sustained. The war cost the lives of 2,832 Jews and 8,528 Arabs (Shlaim, 2000). There have been suggestions that the conflict nearly precipitated both a nuclear exchange between the superpowers and an Israeli nuclear strike on Egypt.[33]

The nature of the attack and the motivations of Syria and Egypt are contested. Netanyahu argues that the Arab forces had 'enormous advantages' over the Israelis, and the Israeli army had fought a 'pulverizing battle to keep the front from collapsing in the face of overwhelming numbers' (2000: 282). He claims that 'Israel's army was able, albeit by a hair's breadth, to prevent defeat in the face of a surprise attack' and that having 'so little to show for an onslaught stacked so decisively in their favour' was what brought Sadat to the negotiating table to sign a peace treaty with Israel at Camp David in 1979 (2000: 282). In contrast, Shlaim suggests that the Egyptian/Syrian attack was a limited venture designed to bring Israel to the negotiating table and force a political settlement in which the lands captured in 1967 would be returned. In an exact reversal of Netanyahu's thesis, Finkelstein (2001) argues that it was Israel who finally agreed to come to the negotiating table at Camp David after Egypt and Syria demonstrated that they possessed a 'military option'.

Following the Yom Kippur War the Arab world led by Saudi Arabia instituted an oil embargo on the West leading to a sharp rise in oil prices, which it is argued precipitated a major global recession. This again had the effect of focusing international attention on the need to resolve the conflict, or at least to neutralise some of its more dangerous elements.

CONFLICT IN LEBANON

Having been forced out of Jordan in 1970, the PLO relocated to Lebanon from where it fought a guerrilla war against the Israeli state, attacking both military and civilian targets. Sachar (1977) lists numerous deadly attacks by Palestinian infiltrators on Israelis and argues that during the mid 1970s the 'violence continued almost without respite' (1977: 810). Netanyahu notes that the PLO was using Lebanon as a base from which to fire Katyusha missiles across the border into Israel, which he maintains had a very damaging effect on the lives of those in Israel's northern settlements:

The PLO used the territory of its de facto state to shell Israeli cities and towns. For years, the entire population of the northern border towns and villages were regularly driven into underground bomb shelters by barrages of PLO launched Katyusha missiles, the little brothers of the Scud missiles that Iraq launched against Israel in 1991. By 1982, the population levels of Kiryat Shemona and Nahariya had fallen ominously; factories, schools and beaches were being closed repeatedly to avoid mass casualties during the shellings; and fear of economic ruin and depopulation had spread. (2000: 218–19)

During this period Israel bombed PLO positions, Lebanese villages and Palestinian refugee camps. The Israeli military analyst Ze'ev Schiff justified attacks on civilians on the basis that guerrillas used the villages and refugee camps for shelter:

In south Lebanon we struck the civilian population consciously because they deserved it ... the importance of [Mordechai] Gur's [Israeli chief of staff] remarks is the admission that the Israeli army has always struck civilian populations, purposely and consciously ... the army, he said, has never distinguished civilian [from military] targets ... [but] purposely attacked civilian targets even when Israeli settlements had not been struck. (*Ha'aretz*, 15 May 1978, cited in Chomsky, 1999: 181)

The Israeli Foreign Minister Abba Eban argued that 'there was a rational prospect ultimately fulfilled that affected populations would exert pressure for the cessation of hostilities' (*Jerusalem Post*, 16 August 1981, cited in Chomsky, 1999: 182). The Lebanese villagers, however, were unarmed and in practice could do little to stop the armed guerrillas. The Lebanese army was too weak to remove the Palestinians, who had virtually formed a state-within-a-state. Official government casualty statistics suggest that the scale of Israeli raids was disproportionate to the Palestinian attacks. The Israeli authorities estimated that 106 Israeli civilians were killed by Palestinian guerrillas on Israel's northern border in the period between 1967 and 1982, at a rate of approximately seven a year (*Ha'aretz*, 22 June 1982, cited in Chomsky, 1999: 74). The American journalist Judith Coburn reported that diplomats in Beirut and UN officials estimated 3,500 Lebanese citizens were killed between 1967 and 1975 and at least twice as many Palestinian civilians, giving a rate of more than a thousand per year. Touring Southern Lebanon in the mid 1970s, Coburn found many villages 'attacked almost daily in recent months ... by airplane, artillery, tanks and gunboats' with the Israelis employing 'shells, bombs, phosphorous, incendiary bombs, CBUs [cluster bombs] and napalm' against Lebanese villages and refugee camps as part of what she claimed was a 'scorched earth' policy to remove the population and create a de-militarised zone (*New Times*, 7 March 1975, cited in Chomsky, 1977: 190). By 1977 it was estimated that 300,000 Lebanese Muslims had been turned into refugees by the Israeli attacks (*New York Times*, 2 October 1977, cited in Chomsky, 1999: 191).

The PLO continued its diplomatic offensive at the United Nations. In November 1974, the United Nations officially granted the PLO observer status. Later that month Yasser Arafat addressed the UN General Assembly for the first time, giving his 'gun and olive branch' address. The leadership of the PLO argued for the ending of the armed struggle, in return for the creation of a mini Palestinian state in the West Bank and Gaza Strip and a settlement of the refugee issue. This move was not accepted by all factions within the organisation, the PFLP leading the rejectionist wing which was against the concept of the mini-state and the recognition of Israel. These moves did not impress the Israelis. Israel's Foreign Minister claimed that 'the voice of Arafat was, and remains the voice of indiscriminate terror, the voice of the gun, with nothing in it of the olive branch of peace' (cited in Hirst, 1977: 335). The call for the creation of a Palestinian mini-state between Israel and Jordan was similarly dismissed as a platform from which the PLO would attempt to destroy Israel. The Israeli daily *Yediot Ahronot* argued that 'no reasonable person ... can ask us to hand over these regions to the PLO, unless it expects Israel to commit suicide' (14 November 1974, cited in Hirst, 1977: 336).

In the mid 1970s both sides as well as Syria became involved in the Lebanese civil war. The 1943 power-sharing National Pact broke down in the mid 1970s, culminating in the all-out civil war of 1975–76. The conflict broadly concerned two rival groupings. First the right-wing Christian-Maronite-Phalangist alliance backed by Israel, which was economically dominant in the country, and second the predominately poor majority which consisted of leftist Muslim-Lebanese and Palestinian groupings. In mid 1976, with the leftist Muslim coalition gaining the upper hand in the conflict, the Syrians intervened on the side of the Christians occupying most of Lebanon apart from a southern strip bordering Israel. The intervention of the Syrian army at the behest of the Christians (and with the tacit support of Israel) brought a truce and relative calm to all but Southern Lebanon. The 18 months of civil war had devastated Beirut, which became partitioned, and killed tens of thousands of Palestinians and Lebanese. In April 1976 Israel and Syria reached a secret agreement with American mediation, splitting the area into 'spheres of influence'. Syria agreed to keep its troops north of the Litani river and not to install surface-to-air missiles there, recognising Southern Lebanon as Israel's security buffer.

In the mid 1970s Israel began supplying the two major Christian Maronite militias, the Phalangists and Chamouns with weapons. Jonathan Randal (1983), the former senior foreign correspondent of the *Washington Post*, suggests the conflict was strategically useful for Israel because it tied down two enemies, the Syrians and Palestinians, both of whom had come into conflict with the Christians by 1977. Israel was also backing General Haddad's South Lebanon Army (SLA) which was acting as its proxy force in South Lebanon. Randal (1983) notes that this was controversial because Haddad's forces had been involved in serious abuses including many instances of large-scale killings of civilians and were accused of involvement in the unlawful deaths of UN personnel. In 1978 Israel mounted a large-scale invasion of Southern Lebanon claiming that it was in response to a Palestinian attack in Israel which had left 37 Israelis and nine Palestinians dead. The scale and effects of the invasion are disputed. Gilbert claims that 'several dozen PLO soldiers were killed or captured' and 'all PLO installations were systematically destroyed' (1999: 490). Randal claims it was civilians rather than guerrillas who bore the brunt of the attack:

> The destruction was on a scale well known in Vietnam. Aping the prodigal use of American firepower in Indo-China, the Israelis sought to keep their own casualties to a minimum – and succeeded. But they failed to wipe out the Palestinian commandoes, who had plenty of time to scamper to safety north of the Litani River. Piling mattresses, clothes and families in taxis and overloaded pickup trucks, more than two hundred thousand Lebanese also fled north out of harm's way. They became exiles in their own country, squatters seizing unoccupied apartments, the source of yet more tension in West Beirut. The Israelis did succeed in massive killing: almost all the victims were Lebanese civilians – some one thousand according to the International Committee of the Red Cross. More than six thousand homes were badly damaged or

destroyed. Half a dozen villages were all but levelled in a frenzy of violence in which Israeli troops committed atrocities. (1983: 209)

After three months, under pressure from the United Nations who condemned the attack, the IDF withdrew from Southern Lebanon and were replaced by a United Nations force. Most of the positions abandoned by the IDF were taken by the SLA. In January 1979 Ezer Weizman, the Israeli Defence Secretary, announced a controversial pre-emptive policy against Palestinian guerrillas in Southern Lebanon. He declared that Israel would not only strike in retaliation but 'at any time and any place that Israel deemed desirable' (cited in Randal, 1983: 220). In 1981 hostilities escalated in Lebanon. On 17 July Israel launched a major bombing raid on Southern Lebanon hitting refugee camps, ports, Lebanon's main oil refinery and all but one of the bridges over the Litani and Zahrani rivers (Randal, 1983). The Israelis claimed that the raids were necessary to deal with a PLO arms build-up in Southern Lebanon. The Palestinians held fire for three days and then began shelling and rocketing northern Israel. On 17 July Israel bombed the Fakhani district in West Beirut, home to the PLO offices. More than 120 Palestinian and Lebanese civilians were killed, leading to international condemnation of the raid. The Palestinians then launched artillery attacks on 28 Israeli towns and settlements, damaging crops and orchards, whilst tens of thousands of Israelis were temporarily forced to flee their homes in northern Israel (Randal, 1983). In the wake of this exchange both sides agreed to an American-brokered ceasefire.

DIPLOMACY AND THE CAMP DAVID ACCORDS

A number of attempts had been made by the Palestinians to push for a peace settlement. Palestinian representatives put forward a United Nations Security Council resolution in January 1976 which called for a two-state solution on the 1967 borders 'with appropriate arrangements ... to guarantee ... the sovereignty, territorial integrity and political independence of all states in the area and their right to live in peace within secure and recognised boundaries' (UN Security Council Resolution S/11940). The resolution received nine votes in favour, including France and the Soviet Union, but was blocked by a single vote against from the United States. Chomsky (1999) points to PLO acceptance of the Soviet-American peace plan of October 1977, the Soviet peace plan of 1981 and the Saudi 1982 peace plan as well as a number of public statements by PLO representatives in the late 1970s that the Palestinians were proposing to end the armed struggle in exchange for the creation of a mini-state in Gaza and the West Bank.[34] He notes that all such overtures were rejected by Israel. But some Israelis such as Binyamin Netanyahu have dismissed all such Palestinian peace overtures. They are seen as part of an attempt to force Israel to accept a PLO 'Trojan horse', whose purpose is to destroy the Israeli state. He argues that after the 1973 war the Palestinians realised that they couldn't destroy Israel with a 'frontal military assault' but were planning 'an interim phase in which Israel would be reduced to dimensions that made it more convenient for the coup de grace'. This would be achieved in two phases: 'first create a Palestinian state on any territory vacated by Israel' and 'second mobilize from that state a general Arab military assault to destroy a shrunken and indefensible Israel' (Netanyahu, 2000: 239). Netanyahu claims that the Arabs have been deceiving the Western nations with a moderate front:

> For the PLO is a Pan-Arab Trojan Horse, a gift that the Arabs have been trying to coax the West into accepting for over twenty years, so that the West in turn can force Israel to let it in at the gates. The Arabs paint their gift up prettily with legitimacy with the pathos of its plight, with expressions for the cherished ideas of freedom, justice, and peace. Yet no matter how it is dressed up to conceal the fact, the ultimate aim of the gift remains: to be allowed within Israel's defensive wall, to be parked on the hills overlooking Tel-Aviv, where it can perform its grisly task. Every inch of Western acceptance – the cover stories, the banquets, the observer status, the embassies, and any territory the PLO has been able to get its hands on – it uses to push ever closer to its goal. (2000: 256)

In March 1978, 350 Israeli reservists sent a letter to Menachem Begin which accused the government of preferring to build settlements and create a 'Greater Israel' rather than make peace with the Arab world. This was partly in response to Prime Minister Begin's decision to support the creation of a number of new Gush Emunim settlements deep in the occupied territories. The letter marked the creation of the 'Peace Now' movement which in September 1978 organised a mass rally of 100,000 Israelis in Tel Aviv, the largest political demonstration in the state's history. The European Economic Community also pushed for a solution to the conflict during 1979. Leaders of the EEC meeting in Venice

in June issued statements supportive of Palestinian statehood and
the president-elect of the European Commission, Gaston Thorn,
travelled to the Middle East and met Yasser Arafat. The PLO
was recognised by Ireland and Austria while the French President
Giscard d'Estaing recommended the group be accepted as a partner
in peace negotiations. The Europeans also attempted to widen
Resolution 242 to include Palestinian self-determination. Ovendale
(1999) claims that the United States made it clear that it would veto
any European resolution in the Security Council which supported
Palestinian rights.

In March 1979 Israel signed a peace agreement with Egypt in
Washington, on terms very similar to the ones rejected by Israel
in 1972. The progress to the final settlement had been long and
tortuous, involving diplomacy stretching over several continents
and many years. Israel agreed to hand back the Sinai peninsula in
exchange for a comprehensive peace treaty, and demilitarisation of
most of the Sinai. Both parties had compromised. Israelis agreed
to remove the settlements and airfields. Egypt dropped the issue
of Jerusalem, and the two sides agreed on only a vague autonomy
plan for the Palestinians that would be implemented in stages over a
number of years. The two signatories were subject to a great deal of
criticism over the conclusion of the peace treaty. Begin was attacked
by the right and religious parties for returning the Sinai. Sadat was
criticised for breaking Arab unity by signing a peace treaty with
Israel, without having achieved a deal on the key issues of Jerusalem,
Palestinian statehood or a full Israeli withdrawal from Arab territory.
Finkelstein (2001) suggests that the Israeli government agreed to
peace with Egypt because this would neutralise the most powerful
Arab military force threatening it, and subsequently allow it to
break the core of the Palestinian national movement in Lebanon.
On 30 July 1980 the Israeli government formally annexed all of
Jerusalem, and the following year the Golan Heights were annexed
in violation of the Israel–Egypt peace agreement and Resolution
242. Both annexations drew immediate condemnation from the UN
Security Council (Resolutions 478 and 497) who declared them to
be illegal, and demanded their reversal. The plans for Palestinian
autonomy were not developed and Shlaim suggests that the Begin
administration deliberately sabotaged the autonomy negotiations.
It expanded expropriations of Palestinian land and settlement
building, because it wanted to retain control over the West Bank
and Gaza Strip:

Begin managed the autonomy talks in such a way that nothing could possibly be achieved. The first sign was Begin's appointment of Dr. Yosef Burg, the minister of the interior, to head Israel's six-man negotiating team. Burg was the leader of the National Religious Party, which saw Israel's right to Judea and Samaria as embedded in Scripture and supported the settlement activities of Gush Emunim. (Shlaim, 2000: 381–2)

1982: THE INVASION OF LEBANON

On 6 June 1982 Israel invaded Lebanon and attacked PLO forces. It also engaged the Syrian army in its drive towards Beirut. In the early days of the conflict the *Economist* correspondent G.H. Jansen reported that the Israeli policy was to surround towns and cities 'so swiftly that civilian inhabitants were trapped inside, and then to pound them from land, sea and air. After a couple of days there would be a timid probing attack: if there was resistance the pounding would resume' (*Middle East International*, 2 July 1982, cited in Chomsky, 1999: 219). By the time an American-sponsored ceasefire came into effect on 11 June the Israeli army had reached the southern outskirts of Beirut. Shlaim (2000) suggests that Israel was expecting their Christian allies in Lebanon, led by Bashir Gemayel, to attack the PLO forces, who by this time were trapped in West Beirut. However, Gemayel was reluctant to take on the Palestinians and the Israelis did not want to get involved in potentially costly street-fighting. By 13 June the Israelis had surrounded Beirut and for the next two months they laid siege to the city and bombarded it with heavy weaponry. The Israeli commander Ariel Sharon, who led the Israeli attack, claimed that 'no army in the history of modern warfare ever took such pains to prevent civilian casualties as did the Israeli Defence Forces' and that the 'Jewish doctrine' of *tohar haneshek* (purity of arms) was adhered to 'scrupulously' with the Israeli army 'attacking only predetermined PLO positions and in bombing and shelling buildings only when they served as PLO strongholds' (*New York Times*, 29 August 1982, cited in Chomsky, 1999: 243–4). Gilbert (1999) also stresses that the Israelis concentrated their attacks on PLO strongholds, although he notes that on one occasion a hospital was seriously damaged. Other reports from journalists in Beirut suggested that the Israelis were bombing civilian areas indiscriminately. The *Independent* journalist Robert Fisk wrote that the Israelis were employing 'time-on target salvoes' which 'laid 50 shells at a time' across residential areas 'slaughtering everyone within a 500 yard radius of the explosions' (2001: 284). He also reported that the Israelis used cluster bombs, and phosphorous bombs, which were designed to create fires and cause untreatable burns. The Israeli daily *Ha'aretz* also noted the use of vacuum bombs, which ignite aviation fuel in such a way as to create immense pressure and literally implode large buildings. These were reportedly dropped on residential areas (11 August 1982). A Canadian surgeon Chris Giannou, who had been working in a Palestinian hospital, testified before the US Congress that he had witnessed the 'total, utter devastation of residential areas, and the blind, savage, indiscriminate destruction of refugee camps by simultaneous shelling and carpet bombing from aircraft, gunboats, tanks and artillery'. He testified that cluster bombs and phosphorous bombs had been used widely in residential areas and that he had seen 'savage and indiscriminate beatings' of prisoners, which were sometimes fatal, as well as frequent use of torture.[35] The bombing intensified during July and August and Hirsh Goodman reported that it continued even after an agreement had been reached in principle for the PLO to leave (*Jerusalem Post*, 1 October 1982, cited in Chomsky, 1999: 241). In July, Yitzak Rabin ordered all supplies of food, water, medicines and fuel to be cut from the city. By 4 August Elaine Carey reported that eight of the nine orphanages in Beirut had been destroyed by cluster and phosphorous bombs, despite clear markings and Israeli assurances that they would be spared (*Christian Science Monitor*, 4 August 1982, cited in Chomsky, 1999: 225). On 12 August the bombing reached a peak. The American journalist Charles Powers wrote that:

> To many the siege of Beirut seemed gratuitous brutality ... The arsenal of weapons unleashed in a way that has not been seen since the Vietnam war, clearly horrified those who saw the results firsthand and through film and news reports at a distance. The use of cluster bombs and white phosphorous shells, a vicious weapon, was widespread ... In the last hours of the last air attack on Beirut, Israeli planes carpet bombed Borg el Brajne [a refugee camp]. There were no fighting men left there, only the damaged homes of Palestinian families, who once again would have to leave and find another place to live. (*Los Angeles Times*, 29 August 1982, cited in Chomsky, 1999: 242)

Eventually at the end of August the PLO forces were evacuated from Beirut to Tunis. Outside Beirut there were reports of widespread destruction of refugee camps and Lebanese villages. In Sidon, Fisk noted that over 2,000 Lebanese civilians were killed in air attacks which he described as 'the most ferocious ever delivered upon a Lebanese city' (2001: 204). The head of the UN refugee agency that administered the camps, Olof Rydbeck, said that 32 years of work had been 'wiped out' with 'practically all of the schools, clinics and installations of the agency in ruins' (*New York Times*, 19 August 1982, cited in Chomsky, 1999: 223). The scale of civilian and PLO casualties during the war are contested. Gilbert (1999) claims that 460 Lebanese civilians and 6,000 PLO fighters were killed. The Lebanese police estimated 19,085 killed through to August with 6,775 killed in Beirut, 84 per cent of whom were civilians (*Christian Science Monitor*, 21 December 1982, cited in Chomsky, 1999: 221). The United Nations estimated 13,500 houses severely damaged in West Beirut, thousands more in other parts of the country, not taking into account damage to the refugee camps which were towns themselves (*Christian Science Monitor*, 18 November 1982, cited in Chomsky, 1999: 223). There were also reports that large numbers of teenage and adult Lebanese and Palestinian males were taken to camps where they were humiliated and tortured.[36] Chomsky cites testimony from the IDF Lieutenant Colonel Dov Yirmiah which appeared in the Israeli daily *Yediot Ahronot* on the fate of Palestinian and Lebanese detainees:

> He tells story after story of prisoners savagely and endlessly beaten in captivity, of torture and humiliation of prisoners, and of the many who died of beatings and thirst in Israeli prisons or concentration camps in Lebanon ... The long and repeated inter-rogations were accompanied by constant beatings, or attacks by dogs on leashes, or the use of air rifles that cause intense pain but do not kill ... New loads of clubs had to be brought into the camps to replace those broken under interrogation. The torturers were 'experts in their work,' the prisoners report, and knew how to make blows most painful, including blows to the genitals, until the prisoners confessed that they were 'terrorists'. (8 November 1982, cited in Chomsky, 1999: 240)

Other reports in the Israeli press claimed that members of Israel's proxy militia the South Lebanon Army were allowed in the camps to torture prisoners and that some gang-raped women and attempted to force them to have sex with dogs (*Koteret Rashit*, 16 March 1983, cited in Chomsky, 1999: 236). After the PLO had agreed to leave Lebanon, one of the war's most notorious incidents occurred at the refugee camps at Shatila and Sabra. After the departure of the PLO from Lebanon, the Israeli forces sealed off these camps on 16 September and allowed in between 100 and 130 Phalangist and Haddadist troops. Ariel Sharon claimed that the camps contained 2,000 well-armed Palestinian fighters and the Christian forces had been sent in to clear them out. However, Edward Walsh argues that 'no one has publicly explained how the Israelis expected 100 to 130 Phalangists to defeat such a force of Palestinians' (*Washington Post*, 26 December 1982, cited in Chomsky, 1999: 369), and in a visit to the camp a few days before the killings journalists reported finding no military presence (*Time*, 4 October 1982). Once in the camps the Phalangist forces raped and killed many of the camps' inhabitants who were primarily women, children and the elderly. The death toll is disputed. The official Israeli Kahan Commission estimated 700–800 killed, the Lebanese authorities put the figure at approximately 2,000, whilst the Israeli journalist Amnon Kapeliouk (1984), citing evidence from the International Committee of the Red Cross, estimated 3,000–3,500. Responsibility for the killings has also been partly attributed to the United States who gave explicit assurances that the Muslim civilian population of West Beirut would be protected as part of the PLO deal to evacuate Beirut (Ovendale, 1999). The massacres were condemned by the United Nations by 147 votes to 2 (Israel, United States), and international lawyers in Belgium have since attempted to indict the Israel commanders Ariel Sharon and Amos Yaron for war crimes.

The Lebanon war appeared to split Israeli society. Some questioned whether the scale of death and destruction inflicted on Southern Lebanon was proportionate to the threat posed by Palestinian militants. In 1982 a debate on Zionism was held at Tel Aviv University where Aluf Hareven of the Van Leer Institute commented:

> According to the figures provided by the Ministry of the Interior Yosef Burg, in 1980, 10 Jews were killed by terrorists and in 1981 – 8. In contrast we have killed about a thousand terrorists in 1982, and caused the loss of life of thousands of inhabitants of an enemy country. If so, it results that for every 6–8 Jews sacrificed, we kill in return thousands of Gentiles. This is undoubtedly, a spectacular situation, an uncommon success of Zionism. I might even dare to say-exaggerated. (*Migvan*, October/November 1982, cited in Chomsky, 1999: 74)

The massacres at Sabra and Shatila also led to the largest protests in Israel's history. On 25 September 1982 more than 400,000 Israelis joined a Peace Now demonstration in Tel Aviv. Others suggested that a large part of the population was unconcerned if not approving of the events at the refugee camps:

> In the matter of Sabra and Shatila – a large part of the community, perhaps the majority, is not at all troubled by the massacre itself. Killing of Arabs in general, and Palestinians in particular, is quite popular, or at least 'doesn't bother anyone' in the words of youth these days. Ever since the massacre I have been surprised to hear from educated, enlightened people, 'the conscience of Tel Aviv', the view that the massacre itself, as a step towards removing the remaining Palestinians from Lebanon is not terrible. It is just too bad that we were in the neighbourhood. (*Ha'aretz*, 19 November 1982, cited in Chomsky, 1999: 395)

Israel's motives for launching the attack are contested. Mitchell Bard (2003), the director of the American-Israeli Cooperative Enterprise, points to three reasons for Israel's decision to attack Lebanon. Firstly, he claims that the PLO was repeatedly breaching the ceasefire negotiated by the Americans in July 1981 and attacking Israelis across the Lebanese border. Secondly, he alleges that 15,000–18,000 PLO members were encamped in Southern Lebanon and were equipping themselves with a huge arsenal including rockets, surface-to-air missiles, mortars, tanks and enough weapons to arm five brigades. He suggests that Israeli strikes and commando raids could not prevent the emergence of this 'PLO army'. Finally, Bard points to the attempt on the life of the Israeli ambassador to London, Shlomo Argov, by the Abu Nidal group. All of these explanations have been disputed.[37] Shlaim suggests that Israel had two objectives: to create a new political order in Lebanon, and to 'destroy the PLO's military infrastructure in Lebanon and undermine it as a political organisation' (2000: 396). Former IDF education officer Mordechai Bar-on argued that 'there is no doubt that the [war's] central aim was to deal a crushing blow to the national aspirations of the Palestinians and to their very existence as a nation endeavouring to define itself and gain the right to self-determination' (*New Outlook*, October 1982, cited in Chomsky, 1999: 203). With the PLO infrastructure destroyed and the refugees dispersed, some commentators suggest that the organisation might revert to hijacking and therefore undermine its growing political status:

If the PLO were now thrown out of Lebanon – or, better yet, reduced to mad dog terrorism that would destroy its growing political and diplomatic legitimacy – then Israel stood a better chance of annexing the West Bank and Gaza strip still thoroughly loyal to Arafat's leadership despite his many errors. (Randal, 1983: 250)

Shlaim (2000) suggests that another aspect of Sharon's 'big plan' was to install Israel's Christian ally Bashir Gemayel in power in Lebanon, and force the Palestinian refugees out of Lebanon to Jordan, leading to the overthrow of the Hashemite monarchy and its conversion to a Palestinian state. This would weaken international pressure on Israel to vacate the West Bank and allowing Israel to annex this territory. Neither of the suggested geostrategic aims were achieved. Bashir Gemayel was assassinated shortly after the war whilst the Hashemite monarchy remained intact in Jordan.

In the aftermath of the Sabra and Shatila killings, American marines returned to Lebanon as part of a multinational force. They, however, soon came into conflict with Shia and Druze forces opposed to Israel's occupation of Southern Lebanon. When US warships shelled Druze positions, it appeared that the US had entered the civil war in support of the Christian-Israeli alliance. On 23 October a suicide bomber killed 256 American and 58 French troops in Lebanon, leading to the withdrawal of American and European forces. A Shiite group with links to Iran later claimed responsibility for the attack. Ovendale (1999) claims that after the 1982 war Israel and the United States strengthened their political and military ties by embarking on joint weapons projects. In 1986 the Israeli nuclear technician Mordechai Vanunu revealed in the *Sunday Times* the existence of Israel's substantial nuclear weapons capability. He was subsequently drugged and kidnapped in Rome by the Israeli secret service. After being taken back to Israel he received an 18-year prison term. Recent newspaper reports suggest that the Israeli nuclear arsenal has increased to approximately 200 warheads, many of which are fitted to American-supplied Harpoon cruise missiles capable of hitting any of Israel's Arab neighbours (*Observer*, 12 October 2003).

In the mid 1980s further attempts were also made to find a negotiated solution to the conflict. In February 1985 Yasser Arafat and King Hussein of Jordan issued the Amman Declaration which proposed Palestinian self-determination within a Palestinian-Jordanian confederation. The composition of the negotiating team proved a problem, with Israel refusing to negotiate with any PLO members. Margaret Thatcher attempted to push the plan and proposed a peace conference to include PLO members. However, the plans were derailed by a series of events. Firstly, Abu Nidal, backed by Syria, threatened to assassinate any PLO members who accepted Thatcher's invitation. Then on 25 September 1985 three Israelis were killed on a boat in Larnaca. The Israeli government blamed the PLO. The PLO claimed the three were Mossad agents. Israel then dispatched a number of American-made F-16 fighters to bomb the PLO headquarters in Tunis. In the attack, 58 Palestinians and 15 Tunisians were killed. The attack was supported by the US but condemned by the European Community and United Nations. Soon afterwards a small Palestinian group, the Palestine Liberation Front, hijacked the *Achille Lauro* and killed an elderly disabled Jewish passenger before surrendering. Following the hijacking the US pressurised Britain to cancel a scheduled meeting between the Foreign Secretary and PLO members. Britain then insisted that the PLO members sign a statement denouncing all forms of political violence. They refused, arguing that this would cover armed resistance to the Israeli occupation of the West Bank and Gaza Strip. The meeting was then cancelled. Soon afterwards King Hussein of Jordan announced the end of his collaboration with the PLO leadership, blaming Arafat's refusal to accept Resolutions 242 and 338. In the wake of this rupture between the PLO and Jordan, King Hussein and Shimon Peres kept close diplomatic links and considered ways of restarting peace talks whilst excluding any members of the PLO from negotiations (Shlaim, 2000). Israel's pursuance of the 'Jordanian option', Shlaim suggests, was blocked by the Israeli premier Yitzak Shamir who was opposed to any international conference which might involve pressure from outside mediators.

1987: THE FIRST INTIFADA

On 9 December 1987, following the death of four Gazans in a road traffic incident, Palestinians from the Jebalya refugee camp began throwing stones at an Israeli army compound. Within days unrest spread to the West Bank. Unarmed Palestinian men, women, and children attacked Israeli soldiers and armoured personnel carriers. Benny Morris notes that the intifada was 'not an armed rebellion but a massive, persistent campaign of civil resistance, with strikes and commercial shutdowns accompanied by violent (though unarmed) demonstrations against the occupying forces' (1992: 561). The intifada lasted six years until it was called off by the Palestinian leadership in the wake of the Oslo agreements. The factors behind it are contested. Netanyahu has argued that the Israeli administration in the occupied territories had instituted a 'liberal policy aimed at radically improving the lives of the Palestinians' and that material and educational prosperity had gone hand in hand with political rights including 'a press consisting of newspapers representing various factions (some openly sympathetic to the PLO) and the right to directly appeal all decisions to the democratic court system' (2000: 176). He argues that the impetus for the intifada was 'virulent PLO agitation' that led the population in the occupied territories to adopt 'ever more extreme and implacable positions' (2000: 177). He also claims that the PLO had forced children out of their schools to take part in confrontations with Israeli forces. Gilbert blames Jordan for not integrating the Palestinians living in the West Bank into Jordanian society before 1967, and argues that the impetus for the intifada came from a 'bitter hard core of extremists who were prepared to face Israeli bullets in order to defy the occupiers and assert their national identity' (1999: 525). Some Israelis blamed outside agitation for the intifada. Yitzak Rabin accused Iran and Syria of fermenting unrest. Others have questioned whether Israeli policy in the occupied territories was really liberal and suggest that the intifada was the result of severe and persistent human rights abuses. This is made clear in a report by the Israeli Committee for Solidarity with Bir Zeit (the West Bank University periodically closed by the Israeli authorities). It described the Israeli administration in the occupied territories as an 'attempt to revive an old well-known colonial method in a new "original" Israeli form' in order to create 'an Israeli Bantustan, which imposes on the Palestinians the role of hewers of wood and drawers of water for Israeli society'. To achieve this the report suggested that there was widespread and violent suppression of all forms of political activity, and that 'quislings from the Village Leagues' together with settler groups inflicted 'humiliation, harassment and terror' on the local population.[38] The United Nations also produced a number of reports in the mid 1980s which were critical of Israeli human rights abuses in the occupied territories and pointed to widespread acts of violence committed against Palestinians by armed settlers.[39] Israel Shahak argues that such abuses were the main factor behind the intifada and cites examples from the Israeli press:

In fact, before the intifada, the daily oppression, humiliations, land confiscations and arbitrariness of the Israeli regime were steadily increasing. This increase, duly recorded by the Hebrew press, was the chief reason for the outbreak of the intifada. Readers of Israel's Hebrew-language press are aware of how outrageously the Israeli armed forces were behaving before the intifada. On June 19, 1987, Eyal Ehrlich reported in an article in *Ha'aretz* headlined, 'An occupier against his will,' the testimony of a young Israeli soldier assigned to serve in the border guards. Whenever a Palestinian is accosted to show his I.D., the soldier wrote, its checking is always accompanied by 'a slap, a punch, a kick.' 'The border guards usually enjoy beating the Arabs,' the account continues. 'They derive pleasure from it ... Sometimes I feel like a Nazi when I watch my friends in action. I try hard to stay away from one of my commanders ... He always behaves very badly toward the locals: with violence, beatings, and the like ... The soldiers spit in the faces of the Arabs, or they kick them in the testicles. And there is always that slap in the face.' An article in *Hadashot* of July 7, 1987 by Menahem Shizaf was headlined, 'Border guards order the Arabs to masturbate and to lick the floor.' It described the treatment meted out to Palestinian workers from the occupied territories who were found spending the night in shacks in Israel rather than returning to their homes. (*Washington Report on Middle East Affairs*, March 1991)

The Israeli Minister of Defence Yitzak Rabin explained that the Israeli response to the intifada would consist of 'force, might, beatings' (*New York Times*, 23 January 1988, cited in the *New York Review of Books*, 17 March 1988), whilst Prime Minister Shamir was reported in the Israeli publication *Hadashot* as warning those protesting the occupation that they would be crushed 'like grasshoppers' with their heads 'smashed against the boulders and walls' and that 'we say to them from the heights of this mountain and from the perspective of thousands of years of history that they are like grasshoppers compared to us' (6 January 1988, cited in Chomsky, 1999: 482). By February 1988 the intifada became formalised with the establishment of the United National Leadership of the Uprising. The organisation encouraged strikes amongst those who worked in Israel and attacks on the Israeli administrative structure. Taxes were withheld, those who worked as administrators and tax collectors resigned and Israeli goods were boycotted (Ovendale, 1999). Roadblocks were set up to keep out the Israeli army and Palestinians tried to create an alternative system of local self-government independent of the military authority.

In February 1988 the United States attempted to put forward a peace plan based on Palestinian autonomy in the occupied territories. The plan was rejected by Israel and the PLO who noted that it made no mention of statehood. In April Abu Jihad, the PLO second-in-command, was assassinated by Israel in Tunis. The Tunisian government complained to the United Nations Security Council. The Israeli daily *Ma'ariv* later reported that the future prime minister, Ehud Barak, had directed the assassination from a navy ship off Tunis (4 July 1988). In July King Hussein of Jordan announced that his country was severing its links with the West Bank, effectively killing the 'Jordanian option' that had long been favoured by the US and some Israeli leaders. In September Yasser Arafat told the European Parliament in Strasbourg that the PLO would accept Israel's right to security if Israel recognised a Palestinian mini-state. In November the Palestinian National Council meeting in Algiers agreed to recognise Israel, as well as all UN resolutions dating back to 1947 and to foreswear its claim to all of mandatory Palestine. It also proclaimed the establishment of the state of Palestine with East Jerusalem as its capital. The Israeli prime minister, Shamir, dismissed the resolutions as a 'deceptive propaganda exercise, intended to create the impression of moderation and of achievements for those carrying out violent acts in the territories of Judea and Samaria' (cited in Shlaim, 2000: 466). Yasser Arafat wanted to appeal to the UN General Assembly, but despite being recognised by more than 60 nations the United States refused him an entry visa (Ovendale, 1999). The General Assembly then voted to hold its plenary session in Geneva. Arafat, under strong pressure from the American Secretary of State George Shultz, announced that the PLO accepted Resolutions 242 and 338, as well as Israel's right to exist, and renounced 'terrorism'.

Meanwhile, Israel's response to the intifada was attracting widespread international criticism. By January 1989 the US State Department reported that the unrest had claimed the lives of eleven Israelis and 366 Palestinians. Some on the Israeli right argued that the criticism of Israel and media coverage of the intifada was biased and unfair, and that the Israeli response was restrained and proportionate. Netanyahu, for instance, commented that:

Ignoring the Arab reign of terror in the Palestinian streets, the media created for themselves nightly instalments of a popular romance drama: heroic underdog in search of self-determination taking on a terrifying Israeli tyrant ... Since viewers were being told this was an 'army of occupation' – that is, it had no right to be there in the first place – the media managed to transform even the most necessary aspects of maintaining law and order into unforgivable crimes. Utterly lost from the images on the screen was the organised nature of the rioting, the internecine violence, and the terrorised lives of the innocent Arabs (and Jews) who were ground under the intifada's heel. Similarly lost were the restrictive firing orders that stayed the hand of every Israeli soldier, and the swift trial of the 208 Israelis who in any way disobeyed these orders – as against the tens of thousands of Israeli soldiers and reservists who followed the regulations with impeccable restraint. (2000: 181–2)

The United Nations, NGOs, human rights groups and some Israeli soldiers disputed this. In December 1988 the United Nations General Assembly passed a resolution by 106 to 2 (Israel, United States) which condemned the conduct of the IDF and settlers during the intifada. The resolution 'declare[d] once more that Israel's grave breaches of that Convention are war crimes and an affront to humanity'. Amongst many criticisms the resolution 'strongly condemned' the 'implementation of an "iron-fist" policy against the Palestinian people ... the escalation of Israeli brutality since the beginning of the uprising ... the ill-treatment and torture of children and minors under detention and/or imprisonment ... the killing and wounding of defenceless demonstrators ... the breaking of bones and limbs of thousands of civilians ... the usage of toxic gas, which resulted, inter alia, in the killing of many Palestinians' (United Nations, 1988). Israel was particularly criticised for its treatment of children during the intifada. A 1,000-page Save the Children study documented the 'indiscriminate beating, tear-gassing, and shooting of children'. The report found that the average age of the victims was ten years old and that the majority of those who were shot were not participating in stone-throwing. The report also alleged that in 80 per cent of cases where children were shot the Israeli army prevented the victims from receiving medical attention. The report concluded that more than 50,000 children required medical attention for injuries including gun-shot wounds, tear gas inhalation and multiple fractures (report cited in Finkelstein, 1996: 47). The August 1989 bulletin from the Israeli League for Human and Civil Rights was entitled 'Deliberate Murder' and reported on the targeting of Palestinian children in leadership roles. It found that the Israeli army and snipers from 'special units' had 'carefully chosen' the children who were shot in the head or heart and died instantaneously (report cited in Finkelstein, 1996: 47). Other reports from Israeli human rights groups and articles in the Israeli press also allege that torture, including severe beating and electric shocks, was used extensively against detainees, including children.[40]

The intifada also saw the birth of Hamas, the Islamic opposition movement formed by Sheik Yassin in February 1988. The organisation, which emerged out of the Muslim Brotherhood, stressed a return to conservative Islamic values and provided a network of health and social services for Palestinians in the occupied territories. For many years the organisation received extensive funding from Israel (Shlaim, 2000; Chomsky, 1999; Mishal and Sela, 2000). Shlaim claims that this was done 'in the hope of weakening the secular nationalism of the PLO' (2000: 459). Chomsky (1999) suggests such a weakening would be beneficial to Israel because it would allow them to evade a political solution to the conflict which might involve returning the occupied territories. The Hamas charter issued in August 1988 argued that all of Palestine belonged to the Muslim nation as a religious endowment and that it was each Muslim's duty to engage in jihad ('struggle') to 'liberate' Palestine. The degree to which its intentions match its rhetoric is disputed. Most Israelis regard the organisation as fundamentalist and uncompromising, dedicated to killing Jews and destroying the Israeli state. But two Israeli academics, Shaul Mishal and Avraham Sela, suggest that the organisation is more complex and pragmatic than this. They suggest that Hamas utilises 'controlled violence' as a 'means rather than an end' to mobilise political support and is 'cognizant of power relations and political feasibility' (2000: viii). They argue that its main purpose has been to establish itself as the major force in Palestinian political life and that in the future it 'may find it can accept a workable formula of co-existence with Israel in place of armed struggle' (2000: ix). In 1989 the group's founder, Sheik Yassin, was arrested by Israel, and in the occupied territories the Israelis increased their use of deportations and curfews in an attempt to suppress the intifada. They also outlawed the committees administering the uprising. This was a serious problem for Palestinians as they saw the committees as the nucleus of the self-governing institutions they hoped to build, once the occupation ended.

In 1989 Yitzak Shamir put forward an initiative which proposed elections and expanded Palestinian autonomy in exchange for the ending of the intifada. Shamir set down certain preconditions: there would be no Palestinian state, no PLO involvement (even if its representatives triumphed in the elections) and no participation in the elections for the inhabitants of East Jerusalem. The plans were eventually derailed by members of Shamir's own cabinet, principally Ariel Sharon, David Levy and Yitzhak Moda'i, who argued that Israel was giving too much away, and was adopting too liberal an attitude to the intifada (Shlaim, 2000). Egypt and the United States then put forward their own peace initiatives. These precipitated a split in what was then a National Unity government in Israel, which led to its downfall. One part of the government, the Labour Alignment, unsuccessfully urged Shamir to accept the American initiative, whilst some members of the right-wing Likud Party felt Israel was making too many concessions and not cracking down sufficiently hard on the intifada. For six weeks the Labour Party's Shimon Peres tried unsuccessfully to form a new coalition and eventually Yitzhak Shamir formed one in which his Likud Party linked up with ultra-nationalist and religious parties. This new coalition, which Shlaim suggests was the most right-wing and hard-line (in its attitudes to the Arabs) in Israel's history, immediately announced that it would end the intifada, create new settlements and expand existing ones (Shlaim, 2000). It also insisted there would be no Palestinian state, no negotiation with the PLO and no sharing of Jerusalem.

The intifada, which continued to smoulder during this period, was re-ignited in October 1990 when Israeli troops killed 21 Palestinians on the Temple Mount in Jerusalem. The Israelis claimed they had responded to acts of stone-throwing directed at Israeli worshippers. The Palestinians claimed that the stone-throwing only began after the Israelis started shooting. The United Nations Security Council condemned the killings, but Israel managed to prevent the United Nations from acting on Palestinian demands to replace the Israeli military government in the occupied territories with a UN force (Ovendale, 1999).

In August 1990 the Iraq war intervened when Saddam Hussein invaded Kuwait and occupied the country. Five months later an American-led coalition attacked Iraq, forcing its withdrawal from Kuwait. Both the Palestinians in the occupied territories and the PLO leadership allied themselves with Saddam Hussein because of the Iraqi dictator's attempt to make a 'linkage' between Iraqi withdrawal from Kuwait and Israeli withdrawal from the occupied territories, and because he struck at the Israeli state with scud missiles. In doing so the Palestinian leadership effectively lost much of the political capital it had built up over many years, whilst Israel benefited internationally by not responding to the Iraqi attacks. In the aftermath of the war the US moved to bring Israel and its Arab adversaries together in an international peace conference.

THE BEGINNING OF THE OSLO PROCESS

In Madrid at the end of October 1991 an Israeli delegation met Palestinian and other representatives from Israel's 'confrontation states' (Syria, Jordan, Lebanon). Although the Palestinian representatives were pro-PLO, they were not publicly stated as being members of the organisation, as to do so would have subjected them to imprisonment under Israeli law. The Americans who set up the conference insisted that it be based around UN Resolutions 242 and 338 and the principle of 'land for peace'. This premise was accepted by the Palestinians but rejected by the Israelis (Shlaim, 2000). In the run-up to the conference, the Likud administration announced a new wave of settlement building designed to double the settler population in the occupied territories in four years. Little progress was made in negotiations, either at Madrid or in the five rounds of bilateral talks which took place in Washington. Shlaim argues that an 'immense gap' separated the parties:

> The Palestinians started with the assumption that they were a people with national rights and that the interim arrangements under discussion were the precursor to independence and should be shaped accordingly. The Israeli government started with the assumption that the Palestinians were the inhabitants of the territories with no national rights of any kind and certainly no rights to independence, not even after the end of the transitional period. (2000: 493)

In June 1992 the Israeli population went to the polls to elect a new administration. The Likud Party pledged to continue the peace process whilst retaining all the occupied territories and expanding settlement building. The Labour Party vowed to conclude a deal on Palestinian autonomy, allow residents of East Jerusalem to take part in negotiations and freeze the construction of the 'political settlements' deep in the occupied territory. Labour won the election under Yitzak Rabin in a major political swing which ended 15 years of Likud rule. In an Israeli newspaper interview just after his election defeat Shamir declared that 'I would have carried on autonomy talks for ten years, and meanwhile we would have reached half a million people in Judea and Samaria' (*Ma'ariv*, 26 June 1992).

Over the next 20 months Israelis and Palestinians engaged in ten rounds of negotiations in Washington that produced no tangible results. In the middle of those negotiations Rabin deported 416 Hamas activists to Lebanon following the killing of an Israeli border policeman. The deportations, which were condemned by the UN as a breach of international law, were intended to curb Hamas' influence but actually had the opposite effect. Mishal and Sela argue that the deportations were a 'milestone in Hamas's decision to use car bombs and suicide attacks as a major modus operandi against Israel', because they came into contact with Hezbullah guerrillas who provided training in such techniques (2000: 65–6). They note that Hamas first used suicide attacks shortly after the return of the deportees to the occupied territories.[41]

THE DECLARATION OF PRINCIPLES

While the official negotiations continued, the Israelis decided to open up a second and secret channel of diplomacy in Oslo. For the first time they agreed to negotiate with a section of the PLO. These talks by-passed the bulk of the PLO and Fatah, with negotiations directed only towards Yasser Arafat and a few close associates. In September 1993 the Declaration of Principles between the Palestinians and Israel was finally brought into the open and signed by both parties on the White House lawn. The declaration was an agenda for negotiations which stipulated that within four months of signing the agreement Israel had to withdraw completely from Gaza and Jericho, with a Palestinian police force taking over internal security in those areas. Israel would still maintain overall responsibility for external security and foreign affairs. Elsewhere in the West Bank, Palestinians were to take control of five spheres: education, health, social welfare, direct taxation and tourism. Within nine months elections were to be held for a Palestinian Authority which was to assume responsibilities for those municipal affairs. Final status negotiations were scheduled to start within two years and were due to be completed within five years. All of the most serious issues affecting the two parties, including possible Palestinian statehood, borders, refugees, settlements and Jerusalem, were postponed to the final settlement talks. The PLO agreed to accept UN Resolutions 242 and 338, to end the armed struggle against Israel and amend the parts of the Palestinian National Charter which called for the destruction of the Israeli state. Israel agreed to recognise the PLO as the representative of the Palestinian people. The Declaration of Principles brought to an end the first intifada which, according to the Israeli human rights group B'Tselem, had resulted in the deaths of 160 Israelis and 1,162 Palestinians (B'Tselem, 2003a).

The treaty met with opposition on both Israeli and Palestinian sides. Likud and the right-wing nationalist and religious parties denounced the agreement as a betrayal of the settlers in the occupied territories, an end to Biblical Greater Israel, and a mortal threat to the security of the state. They argued that the occupied territories could not be ceded by politicians as they had been eternally promised to the Jews by God. Binyamin Netanyahu, the Likud leader, completely rejected the accord and pledged to cancel it if he became prime minister. He compared the agreement to the appeasement of Hitler, and told Peres, 'You are even worse than Chamberlain. He imperilled the safety of another people, but you are doing it to your own people' (cited in Shlaim, 2000: 521). The accord was eventually approved by the Knesset by a margin of 61 votes to 50. Israeli public opinion on the accords was generally favourable with 65 per cent saying they approved of the agreement and only 13 per cent declaring themselves 'very much against' it (Shlaim, 2000). In an analysis of Palestinian reaction to the Oslo Accords, Mouin Rabbani identified four distinct positions and argued that 'contrary to most press reports the fault line ... within the Palestinian body politic is not an ideological one separating peace-loving moderates from violent extremists' but rather one which revolves 'primarily around issues of substance and procedure' (*Middle East International*, 24 September 1993). He claimed that only a few Palestinians were 'enthusiastic supporters', while a majority, whom he characterised as 'optimistic and desperate in equal measure', had serious doubts but were prepared to give the agreement a chance. He suggested that this large group could quickly turn against the agreement if the human rights situation did not improve, and the settlement activity and occupation continued. The third group he identified comprised senior political and cultural figures[42] such as Edward Said, who, although supporting a peaceful resolution of the conflict, nevertheless regarded the Accords as 'deeply flawed' and 'potentially fatal to Palestinian national aspirations'. They objected to Arafat signing the document without public debate or consultation and believed it was a bad deal. They pointed out that the Palestinians were agreeing to end the intifada and renounce their rights to 78 per cent of historic Palestine without any guarantee of statehood or agreement to remove settlements (or even stop settlement building). Neither were there any commitments to improve the human rights situation, or to resolve the refugee issue and status of Jerusalem. For this group the agreement undermined the internationally recognised rights of Palestinians and 'foreshadows permanent dispossession of the majority of Palestinians' as well as creating the potential conditions for a civil war. The fourth position that Rabbani identifies is that of the rejectionists who comprise both the radical Islamic and secular movements such as Hamas and the PFLP, and their supporters in the occupied territories. These groups, argues Rabbani, regarded the agreement as a 'textbook case of Bantustanisation' in which the principal Palestinian weapon, the intifada, was being liquidated so that Palestinians could become the joint administrators of the occupation, in a weak subservient statelet or series of statelets. Rabbani suggests that had the agreement involved moves towards real statehood and been reached in 'conformity with the Palestinian national consensus and properly ratified' then much of the rejectionist camp would at least have tacitly accepted the deal. Although the exceptions to this would still have included Islamic Jihad and some sections of Hamas.

The 1993 Declaration of Principles was followed in February 1994 by the signing of the new set of documents in Cairo. The IDF agreed to redeploy its forces from urban centres to rural areas allowing it to maintain control of overall security and land crossings. On 25 February Dr Baruch Goldstein, an American-born settler and member of the Kach Party, opened fire with an IDF-issued Galil assault rifle on Muslim worshippers at the Tomb of the Patriarchs in Hebron, killing 29 people before he himself was killed. Rachelle Marshall, a journalist and member of the Jewish Peace Union, writes that the killings were followed by a five-week round-the-clock curfew imposed on more than a million Palestinians, during which the IDF killed a further 76 Palestinians, mostly stone-throwing youths (*Washington Report on Middle East Affairs*, June 1994). The Israeli journalist Danny Rubinstein was later to argue that the Hebron killings 'directly and immediately created the chain of suicide bombings and the appalling upward spiral composed of Israeli responses and Palestinian counter-responses' (*Ha'aretz*, 28 September 1998). In the wake of these events the Israeli government, under pressure from the Palestinians and sections of Israeli public opinion, moved to outlaw the overtly racist Kach Party, but refused Palestinian demands to remove the few hundred heavily armed and guarded settlers who lived among more than 100,000 Palestinians in Hebron. The Israeli government also refused PLO requests to put the issue of settlements on the negotiating table, arguing that under the Declaration of Principles it was not obliged to do so until the third year of the interim period. Hamas vowed revenge for the Hebron killings, and shortly before the signing of the next stage of the interim agreements in Cairo in May 1994 it carried out a car bombing in Afula which killed eight and the first ever suicide bombing in Israel which killed five people. Suicide bombings involved individuals strapping explosives, nails, and ball bearings to their bodies which were then detonated in densely packed areas such as markets or buses. This new and indiscriminate weapon left those who survived permanently scarred or disabled and significantly intensified security fears amongst Israelis. A report from a BBC1 news bulletin describes the aftermath of a suicide attack on a crowded Israeli market:

> The two explosions came within seconds of each other cutting down scores of people in the heart of the crowded market. It was just after one o'clock and the market was full of shoppers. Streams of ambulances came to carry away the dead and the injured. It was a place of appalling suffering ... Those who escaped injury were led away from the devastation and others arrived desperate to see if their friends and relatives had escaped the carnage. (BBC1 evening news, 30 July 1997)

Some Palestinians have tried to justify such attacks by arguing that they are in response to the killing of Palestinian civilians by Israelis. Others have argued that they are resisting an illegal occupation, or that it is the only effective weapon against a much more powerful adversary. Dr Eyad El-Sarraj, a psychiatrist and winner of the 1998 Martin Ennals human rights award, has noted that most suicide bombers had suffered a severe trauma when young, 'often the torture of a close relative' and that 'children grow up wanting to take revenge for their trauma. Torture is an integral part of that cycle of violence' (*Guardian*, 24 January 2003). Whatever the motivations or factors behind suicide bombings, human rights groups have unequivocally condemned such attacks and demanded that those involved in planning attacks be brought to justice. In a report entitled 'Without Distinction: Attacks on Civilians by Palestinian

Armed Groups', Amnesty International argue that indiscriminate attacks on civilians cannot be justified whatever the circumstances or provocation:

> The obligation to protect civilians is absolute and cannot be set aside because Israel has failed to respect its obligations. The attacks against civilians by Palestinian armed groups are widespread, systematic and in pursuit of an explicit policy to attack civilians. They therefore constitute crimes against humanity under international law. They may also constitute war crimes, depending on the legal characterisation of the hostilities and interpretation of the status of Palestinian armed groups and fighters under international humanitarian law. (Amnesty International, 2002a)

THE CAIRO AGREEMENT, OSLO II AND THE ISRAEL–JORDAN PEACE TREATY

The agreement signed in Cairo on 4 May 1994 concluded the Gaza and Jericho phase of the redeployment and set the terms for expanding Palestinian autonomy in the West Bank. This had three stages. Firstly, the Palestinian National Authority was to take charge of a number of municipal functions; secondly, the IDF would withdraw from population centres; and finally, there would be Palestinian elections for a new authority. However, Palestinian negotiators were disappointed with the new agreement. They had hoped that Israel would replace the complex system of military ordinances and occupation laws with the Fourth Geneva Convention and international law within the occupied territories, but this was not forthcoming (Shlaim, 2000). The United Nations Commission on Human Rights continued to be critical of Israeli human rights abuses in the territories. In 1994 it issued a resolution 'condemning' settler and IDF killings, torture, imprisonment without trial, house demolitions and land expropriations, curfews, collective punishments, restrictions on movement and settlement building (United Nations, 1994).

The construction of illegal Jewish settlements had accelerated following the election of the Rabin administration in 1992. Between 1992 and 1995 the settler population in the occupied territories (excluding East Jerusalem) rose from 74,800 to 136,000 (Foundation for Middle East Peace, 1997). Palestinians believed that increased settlement building and expropriations of Palestinian land was a violation of the spirit if not the letter of the Oslo Accords, and would ultimately prejudice the possibility of a viable Palestinian state. The American historian and Middle East commentator Geoffrey Aronson argued that 'there is no missing the fact that Rabin's settlement drive is aimed at putting the future of the city [Jerusalem] and its West Bank environs beyond the reach of diplomacy' (*Report on Israeli Settlement in the Occupied Territory*, May 1995). He also cited statements from the Israeli commentator Ze'ev Schiff that 'when we come to the final stage [of negotiations] nothing will be left [in Jerusalem] for the Palestinians to negotiate, apart from the Islamic holy places'. Rabin's administration also embarked on a process of building bypass roads linking settlements which could only be used by Jewish settlers and the IDF. This plan, Israel Shahak (1995) claimed, was originally conceived by Ariel Sharon in 1977 but was finally implemented by Rabin directly after the Declaration of Principles. He argued that its purpose was to create a matrix of control whereby all the Arab population centres were split into enclaves criss-crossed by the roads and settlement blocks so that the Israeli army will be able to control the discontinuous cantons 'from outside'. Tel Aviv University professor Tanya Reinhart argued that Rabin's policies 'resemble[d] the beginning of Apartheid rather than its end' and were 'almost identical' to the South African Bantustan model (*Ha'aretz*, 27 May 1994). The construction of the bypass road network also allowed the Israeli government to enforce closures on the Palestinian areas which restricted Palestinian movement and access to employment. Israel justified such measures by arguing that it was necessary to prevent attacks by Palestinians against Israelis. It did, however, have very serious effects on the Palestinian economy. The Israeli journalist Nadav Ha'etzni reported that by May 1995 curfews and closures had 'devastated the Palestinian economy and destroyed 100,000 families in Gaza alone' (*Ma'ariv*, 5 May 1995, cited in Chomsky, 1999: 548). The deteriorating economic situation for Palestinians was compounded by Israeli moves to achieve 'separation' by replacing Palestinian workers with migrant labour from Thailand, the Philippines, Romania and other parts of Eastern Europe. Such factors, Shlaim suggests, 'actually worsened the situation in the occupied territories and confounded Palestinian aspirations for a state of their own' (2000: 530). Furthermore, there was no halt to the bloodshed on both sides. Between the signing of the Declaration of Principles in September 1993 and the end of 1994, 93 Israelis and 194 Palestinians were killed in violent incidents (B'Tselem, 2003a).

In September 1994 Israel and Jordan concluded a peace treaty which normalised relations between the two countries. The agreement set the international border between Israel and Jordan and settled water disputes relating to the Yarmouk and Jordan rivers. The treaty marked the second comprehensive accord which Israel had signed with its Arab neighbours.

In late September 1995 Yasser Arafat and Yitzak Rabin concluded the next stage of the interim agreement under which the West Bank was divided into three areas. Area A (3 per cent of the West Bank incorporating Nablus, Jenin, Tulkarem, Qalqilya, Ramallah, Bethlehem and subsequently, in January 1997, 80 per cent of Hebron) would have its civilian administration and internal security controlled by the Palestinian Authority. Area B (23 per cent of the West Bank comprising 440 villages and surrounding lands) was to have certain municipal functions administered by the Palestinian Authority whilst security would be dealt with by joint Palestinian-Israeli patrols. Area C (comprising 74 per cent of the West Bank, including all of the 145 Jewish settlements including those in and around East Jerusalem) would remain under complete Israeli control.

On 4 November 1995, Yitzak Rabin was assassinated by a 25-year-old settler, Yigal Amir. After the killing the unrepentant Amir accused Rabin of selling out the settlers and preparing to give away the occupied territories to the Palestinians. Rabin was succeeded as prime minister by Shimon Peres who pledged to maintain the momentum of the peace process. No Israelis had been killed in suicide attacks since the 21 August bombing in Jerusalem which had killed three Israelis and an American. Mishal and Sela (2000) suggest that both Hamas and Islamic Jihad were under pressure from both the Palestinian Authority and Israel, and did not want to antagonise Palestinian public opinion by precipitating a halt to the scheduled Israeli redeployments. Mishal and Sela also note that militant groups had been pushing for 'a conditional cease-fire with Israel to stop the bloodshed of innocents on both sides' (2000: 71). In early 1996 Peres ordered the killing of Yahya Ayyash, a Hamas leader who had previously masterminded several suicide attacks which had killed approximately 60 Israelis. Shlaim claims that the Israeli media had exaggerated his status, presenting him as 'public enemy number one' whilst 'omitting to mention that the attacks he organized came as a response to the [Hebron] massacre' (2000: 556). The assassination of Ayyash using a booby-trapped phone led to Hamas vowing revenge and there followed six suicide bombings in February and March 1996 which left 62 Israelis dead (Israeli Ministry of Foreign Affairs, 1999). Peres' popularity declined under attacks from the right, and he moved to suspend talks with the newly elected Palestinian Authority and closed the borders to all workers from the occupied territories.

Shortly afterwards Peres launched a major offensive against Hezbullah in Southern Lebanon where Israel had been fighting a long guerrilla war. Hezbullah claimed they were trying to end the illegal Israeli occupation of Southern Lebanon, which had been ongoing since 1978, in violation of United Security Council Resolution 425.[43] Israel claimed that Hezbullah were intent on the destruction of the Israeli state. Casualty statistics suggest that Palestinian and Lebanese civilians had suffered disproportionately in the conflict. In the period between 1985 and 1996 the Israeli army estimate that Hezbullah guerrilla and rocket attacks had killed six Israeli civilians (Israeli Defence Forces, 2003). Amnesty International (1996a) reported that in a single operation in 1993 Israel killed 118 Lebanese civilians and that 300,000 people were displaced. The journalist and former chief inspector of the US Information Agency, Richard Curtiss, suggests that after this operation, unwritten rules of engagement were crafted by the US State Department's Warren Christopher with both sides agreeing to confine attacks to combatants in South Lebanon (*Washington Report on Middle East Affairs*, May/June 1996). On 11 April 1996 Peres launched Operation 'Grapes of Wrath'. This was claimed to be in retaliation for rocket strikes on Israeli settlements which had injured 34 civilians and other attacks which had killed eight members of the IDF in Southern Lebanon. Hezbullah's view was that they had a right to resist the Israeli troops illegally occupying Southern Lebanon, and that the rockets fired on Israeli settlements were retaliation for the killing by Israel of three Lebanese civilians. The Israeli operation involved more than a thousand air sorties and 16,000 shells against less than 500 Hezbullah fighters (*Ha'aretz*, 21 May 1996). Curtiss claims that many of the attacks were 'targeted at electric power plants and relay stations, bridges, and other parts of Lebanon's war-battered basic infrastructure' (*Washington Report on Middle East Affairs*, May/June 1996). The Israeli journalist Avi Shavit alleges that 400,000 civilians were forced to flee their homes in eight hours, after which the Israeli air force treated the abandoned properties as military targets and shelled them (*Ha'aretz*, 21 May 1996). On 18 April Israel bombed the United Nations Compound at Qana, killing 106 refugees who had sought sanctuary there. Israel stated that the bombing, which involved anti-personnel munitions, was a mistake and that the real target was an area nearby where Hezbullah fighters had been operating. Both a UN (1996) and Amnesty International (1996b) report found that the attack on the UN compound was unlikely to have been accidental and also condemned Israeli missile attacks on ambulances and residential areas which killed many civilians. Shlaim suggests that the operation was an attempt by Shimon Peres to revive his flagging political fortunes and recast himself 'as the hard man of Israeli politics ahead of the crucial general elections' (2000: 560). However it did nothing to revive his political fortunes and the following month he was beaten in the general election by the Likud candidate Binyamin Netanyahu.

THE NETANYAHU ADMINISTRATION

Netanyahu's attitude towards the peace process before his election had been one of undisguised antipathy. He had campaigned publicly against its implementation in speeches and in print, and had been accused by Rabin's widow of inciting his assassination by making inflammatory public speeches, which likened Rabin to an SS officer. His coalition included the far right and settler groups who called for the forced deportation of all Palestinians from the occupied territories. Netanyahu's central argument was that the peace process had illustrated Israel's weakness, reduced the deterrent power of the IDF and damaged the nation's security. He argued that Israel had adhered to the Oslo formula whilst the Palestinians had failed to keep their side of the bargain, by failing to dismantle militant organisations, collecting their weapons or extraditing their members to Israel. Netanyahu's alternative was to renegotiate the redeployments that had been agreed in principle. He argued that these threatened Israel's security and that 'whatever the officials of the previous Labor administration had whispered in Palestinian ears was irrelevant' (Netanyahu, 2000: 343). He was also against full statehood for the Palestinians, arguing that Israel had to control the exit and entry points to the Palestinian entity as well as its airspace, plus much of the Jordan valley and the West Bank water supply. He also suggested that Arab nations should resettle the Palestinian refugees. Shlaim claims that as soon as he took power Netanyahu began to renege on Israel's Oslo obligations:

> Serious deterioration occurred in Israel's relations with the Palestinians as a result of Netanyahu's backtracking. He adopted a

'work-to-rule' approach designed to undermine the Oslo process. There was no Israeli pullout from Hebron, no 'opening of the safe passage' route from Gaza to the West Bank, and no discussion of the further West Bank redeployment that Israel had pledged to carry out in early September. Instead Palestinian homes without an Israeli permit were demolished in east Jerusalem, and plans were approved for the construction of new Israeli settlements. The quality of life for the Palestinians deteriorated progressively, and hopes for a better future were all but extinguished. (2000: 576)

In October 1996, violence erupted in Jerusalem when Netanyahu ordered the blasting open of an archaeological tunnel close to the Al-Aqsa mosque. This was taken by Palestinians as a statement of sovereignty over Islamic holy sites and triggered disturbances in which 15 Israeli soldiers and 80 Palestinians were killed, and a further 1,500 Palestinians wounded. Under pressure from the Americans Netanyahu agreed to the delayed redeployment of Israeli troops from Hebron in January 1997 by signing the Hebron protocol, which also committed Israel to three further redeployments in the West bank over the next 18 months. Under the agreement Hebron was split into Jewish and Arab zones. The Jewish zone reserved for the 450 settlers constituted 20 per cent of the city, including its best commercial areas. The remaining 80 per cent of the city was reserved for the 130,000 Palestinian residents of Hebron who were subject to frequent curfews and restrictions on movement.

After the signing of the Hebron protocol Netanyahu approved a number of new settlements. In February 1997 he announced plans for 6,500 new dwellings for 30,000 settlers at Jabal Ghneim (Har Homa) on the outskirts of annexed East Jerusalem. Har Homa would complete the chain of concentric settlements around Jerusalem and cut off Arab East Jerusalem from the rest of the West Bank. The move was met with anger from Palestinians and condemned by the United Nations (1997) General Assembly by 130 votes to 2 (Israel, United States). Palestinians were unhappy with more expropriation of their land and called a general strike in protest. The US twice vetoed Security Council resolutions condemning the project, whilst the General Assembly passed further resolutions calling for a halt to the Har Homa project, the removal of settlements in the occupied territories, and the application of the Fourth Geneva Convention within the territories. None of these moves stopped the construction of the new settlements. In June 1997 the Israeli journalist Jay Bushinsky reported that Netanyahu had outlined his 'Allon Plus' plan for a possible settlement with the Palestinians. The plan involved Israel annexing approximately 60 per cent of the West Bank that would include Greater Jerusalem, the hills east of Jerusalem, the Jordan valley, the settlements and all the bypass roads connecting them, plus permanent Israeli control of the West Bank water supply (*Jerusalem Post*, 5 June 1997). The proposals were met with dismay by Palestinian leaders who accused Israel of violating the Oslo Accords and trying to destroy the peace process.

Although the conflict between Palestinian militants and the IDF and settlers in the occupied territories continued to claim more lives, there were no suicide attacks in Israel between March 1996 and March 1997. Between 21 March 1997 and 4 September 1997 militants carried out three suicide attacks killing 24 Israelis. Hamas representatives argued that the attacks were the only way to stop the expropriation of more Palestinian land for settlement building and the 'Judaisation' of the holy places. On 23 September 1997 the Hamas leadership sent a letter to Netanyahu, delivered by King Hussein of Jordan, in which Hamas suggested setting up an indirect dialogue with the Israeli government that would be mediated by King Hussein. The purpose of the dialogue would be to achieve a cessation of violence as well as a 'discussion of all matters' (*Ha'aretz*, 9 October 1997, cited in Mishal and Sela, 2000: 72). Two days later Netanyahu ordered the killing of the head of Hamas' Political Bureau, Khalid Mash'al, in Jordan. The attempted assassination by two Mossad agents was botched and Mash'al's bodyguard captured the two assassins who were later traded for the imprisoned Hamas spiritual leader Sheik Ahmed Yassin. The attempted killing soured relations with King Hussein, Israel's closest ally in the Arab world, and ended this opportunity for a ceasefire. The release of Yassin followed by his return to Gaza strengthened Hamas' support.

In March 1998, 1,500 Israeli reservists, including twelve retired major-generals, called on Netanyahu to stop settlement building and try to end the conflict and normalise relations (Shlaim, 2000). However, Netanyahu cancelled the scheduled Israeli redeployments, citing security concerns. Despite efforts by both Britain and the US to revive the process it ground to a halt. Both sides in the conflict accused the other of bad faith in reneging on their Oslo obligations. Netanyahu reiterated his claims that the PLO had failed to disarm or arrest militant groups, prevent attacks against Israelis and amend the PLO charter. Others contested this. Tanya Reinhart, writing in the Israeli publication *Tikkun*, claimed that Arafat had taken strong action against Hamas and that this was recognised by Israel's security services:

> Arafat's security services carried out this job [maintaining Israeli security] faithfully, by assassinating Hamas terrorists (disguised as 'accidents'), and arresting Hamas political leaders ... Ample information was published in the Israeli media regarding these activities, and 'security sources' were full of praises for Arafat's achievements. For example, Ami Ayalon, then head of the Israeli secret service (Shabak), announced, in a government meeting on April 5, 1998 that 'Arafat is doing his job – he is fighting terror and puts all his weight against the Hamas' (*Ha'aretz*, April 6 1998). The rate of success of the Israeli security services in containing terror was never higher than that of Arafat; in fact, it was probably much lower. (*Tikkun*, March/April 2002)

In a 1998 report, the Israeli peace group Gush Shalom (1998) blamed the Netanyahu administration for the breakdown in the peace process and accused the government of 19 separate violations of the Oslo Accords. These included settlement and bypass road building, use of closures, failure to release Palestinian prisoners, torture and other human rights abuses, failure to undertake scheduled military withdrawals or move towards final status negotiations. During this period support for organisations such as Islamic Jihad and Hamas grew whilst the PLO and particularly Yasser Arafat lost popularity. Partly this was because of corruption scandals that engulfed the PLO leadership which was accused of nepotism and siphoning off funds meant for the Palestinian Authority. It was also because of Arafat's autocratic style and the serious human rights abuses committed by the Palestinian security forces who were using torture and engaging in extra-judicial killings against suspected militants. There was also widespread anger that Arafat had failed to stop settlement building. Geoffrey Aronson claimed that Arafat and the other PLO 'outsiders' (those from outside the occupied territories) failed to appreciate the significance of the settlements:

> PA chairman Yasser Arafat is briefed infrequently on Israel's settlement policy, and his response is generally stunned silence as he looks at the maps depicting the dimensions of the enterprise. Palestinian Authority negotiators Mahmoud Abbas (Abu Mazen)

and Ahmad Quray (Abu Ala) have never been on a 'settlement tour.' If one is to judge by their negotiating priorities, they have no concept of the role of settlements in the history of Israel's policies in the occupied territories, nor do they believe that such an understanding is required. (*Report on Israeli Settlement in the Occupied Territories*, July/August 1998)

In October 1998 Israel and Palestinian negotiators concluded the next phase of the peace process signing the Wye Accords in Maryland. Israel undertook to redeploy its troops from a further 13 per cent of the West Bank in three stages. The Palestinians agreed to amend the parts of the Palestinian National Charter calling for Israel's destruction and to work with Israeli security services and the CIA to improve Israel's security. The security component of the agreement was heavily criticised by human rights groups both before and after the signing, who argued it was likely to increase human rights abuses such as torture and imprisonment without trial.[44] The Wye Accords passed in the Knesset by a large majority, though Netanyahu received virtually no support for the agreement amongst his right-wing/religious coalition. Although both parties to the agreement had agreed not to undertake 'unilateral actions' to change the status of the occupied territories, members of Netanyahu's coalition publicly called on settler groups to take as much land as possible to keep it out of Palestinian hands. Ariel Sharon, the infrastructure minister, told a Tsomet Party gathering on the 15 November that 'Everyone should take action, should run, should grab more hills ... We'll expand the area. Whatever is seized will be ours. Whatever isn't seized will end up in their hands' (BBC News Online, 16 November 1998). Netanyahu promoted the same policies, though less overtly: 'There is no such thing as a freeze [on construction] ... Our policy is to grow and expand ... This issue must be coordinated behind closed doors with the army and not in front of the media' (*Ha'aretz*, 24 November 1998). On 20 December 1998 the Israeli government suspended the second redeployment stipulated in the Wye Agreement unless the Palestinian Authority met five conditions, most of which were new. Netanyahu claimed that it was necessary to suspend the redeployments to safeguard Israel's security. Shlaim suggests the move was intended to 'torpedo the peace process and put the blame on the Palestinians' (2000: 605). Three days later the Knesset voted to dissolve itself and schedule new elections for May 1999.

THE BARAK ADMINISTRATION

The May elections brought Labour's Ehud Barak to power. Three months into Barak's tenure the American journalist Deborah Sontag reported that his administration had 'authorized new construction in the West Bank's Jewish settlements at a pace exceeding that of the right-wing administration of Benjamin Netanyahu' (*New York Times*, 28 September 1999). Barak also moved to initiate negotiations with Syria rather than with the Palestinians, which the Palestinians took as a snub and an attempt to pressurise them. Barak argued that he pursued the Syrian track first because this problem was considered less intractable, and secondly because Syria with its large army and non-conventional weapons was considered an 'existential threat' (*New York Review of Books*, 9 August 2001). After four months of negotiations the peace talks between Israel and Syria collapsed without a settlement. Both parties blamed the other.[45] In May 2000 Barak took the decision to withdraw the Israeli army and its proxy forces from South Lebanon. The occupying Israeli army had been taking increasingly heavy casualties from Hezbullah guerrilla raids and the losses were politically unpopular. Rachelle Marshall suggests that the withdrawal allowed hundreds of thousands of Lebanese refugees to return to their devastated villages, and Hezbullah to set up medical facilities and begin rebuilding the civilian infrastructure (*Washington Report on Middle East Affairs*, July 2000).

Following the failure of the Syrian track Barak turned his attention to the Palestinians. Barak's tenure (up until the outbreak of the second intifada) had seen a decline in attacks by Palestinian militants and no suicide attacks (B'Tselem, 2003a). In early 2000, Marshall claims that Barak suspended a number of Israel's Oslo commitments. These included the scheduled release of 1,650 Palestinian prisoners arrested before the Oslo process began and the scheduled handover to Palestinian control of three small villages bordering Jerusalem: Abu Dis, Al Ezzariyye and Swarah (*Washington Report on Middle East Affairs*, July 2000). Instead, she notes that Barak authorised the seizure of 162 acres from these villages for the construction of a new bypass road linking settlement blocks to Jerusalem and the construction of 200 Jewish housing units in Abu Dis. Barak also decided to renegotiate the agreements that the PLO had signed with Netanyahu and cancelled the third partial redeployment of Israeli troops. The Oslo Accords had specified that by the time that final status talks began, Israel should have withdrawn from approximately 90 per cent of the occupied territories, but by the end of May 2000 the figure was only 18 per cent. In March 2000, as preparatory talks between Israeli and Palestinian delegations on final status issues were beginning, 120 Palestinian intellectuals and cultural figures sent an open letter to the 'Israeli and Jewish Public' calling for a just solution to be based on either the 1967 borders or a bi-national state. It argued that 'one side believes the present balance of power to be in its favour and that it can impose a humiliating agreement on the other side, forcing it to accept virtually anything it chooses to enforce' (*Ha'aretz*, 13 March 2000). The Israeli commentator Danny Rabinowitz argued that the letter revealed the deep chasm between Israeli and Palestinian evaluations of the peace process:

> One view, which is accepted by the majority of Israelis, considers Oslo a positive, symmetric process: an elected government in Israel is conducting peace negotiations with a Palestinian leadership that reflects the true interests of the Palestinian people. Pursuing this joint path will ultimately lead to a durable peace between the two peoples. The second view, which is asserted by the signatories to the letter, considers Oslo an inherently asymmetric process whose foregone conclusion is not only unfair, but also dangerous. The gist here is that Israel, which is strong, big, rich and backed by a superpower, is conducting negotiations of a coercive nature with a weak Palestinian leadership that has sold out. Arafat, his aides and the few thousand families that are close to his government are mere puppets with no will of their own and without the ability to engage in true diplomatic manoeuvring. The corruption and despotism constantly being exposed in the economy, judicial system, human rights record and other areas of the Palestinian Authority demonstrate that the thrust of the leadership in the West Bank and Gaza is to preserve its own rule and to divvy up the financial and symbolic spoils flowing in from donor nations. This view of the process sees the true national interest of millions of Palestinians in the territories and the Diaspora ground into the dust. (*Ha'aretz*, 19 March 2000)

In the run-up to the final status talks in May 2000 Israel released maps of a projected final settlement indicating that Palestinian self-rule would be limited to three or four discontinuous pieces of territory.

THE CAMP DAVID FINAL STATUS TALKS

On 11 July 2000 Yasser Arafat and Ehud Barak met for final status negotiations at Camp David in the United States. After two weeks the talks broke down amid bitter recriminations. Israel argued that they had made a 'generous offer' to return 97 per cent of the occupied territories which the other party spurned, turning to violence to force concessions it could not achieve at the negotiating table. The Palestinians argued that the offer was vague and unacceptable, 'less than a Bantustan' in Arafat's words (*New York Times*, 26 July 2001). Analysing the conference is difficult because all of Israel's offers were made orally, with no maps or written proposals presented.

In an interview with Israeli historian Benny Morris, Ehud Barak laid out the Israeli perspective on the failure of the talks (*New York Review of Books*, 9 August 2001). Barak claimed that he had offered Arafat 92 per cent of the West Bank and 100 per cent of the Gaza Strip, together with some territorial compensation from pre-1976 Israel. He denied that the state would consist of Bantustans. Instead he argued that although the West Bank would be sliced in two by a 'razor thin Israeli wedge' running from the settlement of Maale Adumin to the Jordan river, 'Palestinian territorial continuity would have been assured by a tunnel or bridge'. He also claimed to have offered to dismantle most of the settlements and concentrate the bulk of the settlers in the 8 per cent of the West Bank that was to be annexed to Israel. A Palestinian capital would be set up in East Jerusalem with some neighbourhoods to become Palestinian territory and others to enjoy 'functional autonomy'. The Palestinians, it is claimed, were offered custodianship though not sovereignty over the Temple Mount. Barak also alleged that Israel offered a right of return for Palestinian refugees to the prospective Palestinian state, though no admission of Israeli responsibility for the creation of the refugee problem and no return of any refugees to Israel. Barak accused Arafat of saying no to every proposal and offering no counter-proposals. Barak also claimed that Arafat believed that Israel 'has no right to exist and he seeks its demise'. This, argued Barak, would be achieved by using the Palestinian refugees as a demographic tool to subvert the Israeli state. He also accused Arabs in general, and Arafat in particular, of being 'a product of a culture in which to tell a lie ... creates no dissonance', because Arabs 'don't suffer from the problem of telling lies that exists in Judeo-Christian culture'. In Arab societies, he stated, 'there is no such thing as "the truth"'. In making this charge, Barak had perhaps overlooked the comments of Yitzak Shamir, when responding to a charge of dishonesty. He was quoted in *Ha'aretz* as saying that 'for the sake of the land of Israel, it is permissible to lie' (14 February 1992, cited in Shlaim, 2000: 496). Barak also suggested that it would probably take 80 years from 1948 before the Palestinians were ready to make the necessary compromises for peace, because of what Barak described as a 'salmon syndrome' amongst Palestinians. Eighty years after 1948 the Palestinians who experienced displacement at first hand will have largely died, so there will be 'very few "salmons" around who will still want to return to their birthplaces to die'.

Robert Malley, a special advisor to President Clinton, and Hussein Agha, the Oxford historian, have criticised Barak's analysis as 'remarkably shallow' (*New York Review of Books*, 9 August 2001). They suggest that all the protagonists share some responsibility for the failure of the talks. Malley and Agha argue that Barak's decision to renege on Israel's interim commitments such as troop withdrawals and prisoner releases whilst expanding settlements, was designed to reduce political friction from the Israeli right in the lead up to the talks and husband political capital. He could then present 'all concessions and all rewards in one comprehensive package that the Israeli public would be asked to accept in a national referendum'. This 'all or nothing' approach, Malley and Agha allege, put Arafat under tremendous pressure from powerful Palestinian constituencies such as the security establishment, intellectuals, civil servants and the business community who had lost faith in Barak. They also suggest that Barak's refusal to withdraw from territory scheduled in the interim agreements directly affected the perceived balance of power, because the Palestinians believed that they would also have to negotiate over that land in the final status talks. Malley and Agha maintain that all of these factors left Arafat with the impression that the Israelis and Americans were trying to 'dupe' him into accepting a humiliating deal and led him to adopt a siege mentality, unamenable to fluid negotiations and the presentation of counter-proposals. They also suggest that not enough time had gone into laying the groundwork with preparatory negotiations prior to the summit, and that a month prior to the talks Arafat had warned US Secretary of State Madeleine Albright that because of all these factors the talks were very likely to fail.

Other commentators, such as the Israeli human rights group Gush Shalom (2003), have questioned whether a 'generous deal' was offered to Palestinians. They argue that Palestinians made their historic compromise at Oslo in agreeing to cede to Israel 78 per cent of mandatory Palestine, and that they were never offered 95 per cent of the occupied territories at Camp David in July 2000. Gush Shalom allege that Barak insisted on annexing 10 per cent of the West Bank comprised of settlements blocks which they note would 'create impossible borders which severely disrupt Palestinian life in the West bank'. They also suggest that Barak wanted 'temporary Israeli control' of another 10 per cent of the West Bank for an unspecified duration. They argue that 'what appears to be territorial continuity is actually split up by settlement blocs, bypass roads and roadblocks' and that 'the Palestinians have to relinquish land reserves essential for their development and absorption of refugees' as well as accepting 'Israeli supervision of border crossings together with many other restrictions'. They suggest that nobody would accept foreign control of domestic border crossings or travelling 50 miles between areas when the real distance was only five miles. Jeff Halper, an anthropology professor at Ben-Gurion University and coordinator of the Israeli Committee against House Demolitions, argues that the focus on whether the Palestinians were offered 81 per cent or 91 per cent or 95 per cent or 96 per cent is misplaced because even if Israel agreed to hand back 96 per cent of the occupied territories it would still possess a 'matrix of control' which would completely undermine Palestinian sovereignty and independent development:

> What is the matrix of control? It is an interlocking series of mechanisms, only a few of which require physical occupation of territory, that allow Israel to control every aspect of Palestinian life in the Occupied Territories. The matrix works like the Japanese game of Go. Instead of defeating your opponent as in chess, in Go you win by immobilizing your opponent, by gaining control of key points of a matrix so that every time s/he moves s/he encounters an obstacle of some kind ... The matrix imposed by Israel in the West Bank, Gaza and East Jerusalem, similar in appearance to a Go board, has virtually paralysed the Palestinian population without 'defeating' it or even conquering much territory. (*Middle East Report*, Fall 2000)

Part of this matrix, argues Halper, involves the expansion of 'Metropolitan' Jerusalem, which he suggests, stretches almost all the way to the Jordan river and incorporates 40 per cent of the West Bank, including Ramallah and Bethlehem. Halper suggests that Israeli control of this area, which cuts off Palestinians in East Jerusalem from the rest of the West Bank, 'renders the sovereignty of a future Palestinian state meaningless'. Halper also points to the grid of bypass roads criss-crossing the West Bank, linking settlements, which would also require a substantial permanent Israeli military presence across the Palestinian state. All of these factors, suggests Halper, meant that even if Yasser Arafat had agreed to Barak's proposals at Camp David, the agreement would not have held:

> The issue in the Israeli-Palestinian negotiations, then, is not simply territory – it revolves around questions of control, viability and justice. A Palestinian state carved into small, disconnected enclaves, surrounded and indeed truncated by massive Israeli settlement blocs, subject to Israeli military and economic closures, unable to offer justice to its dispersed people and without its most sacred symbols of religion and identity, can hardly be called a viable state. 'Peace' may be imposed, but unless it is just it will not be lasting. (*Middle East Report*, Fall 2000)

The breakdown of the Camp David talks was followed by months of secret negotiations between Palestinian and Israeli officials. Then on 28 September 2000 another decisive event was precipitated by a key figure on the Israeli right. Ariel Sharon and other members of the Likud leadership together with 1,000 armed police visited Islam's third holiest site, the Al-Haram al-Sharif. Palestinians considered this visit to be a statement of sovereignty over one of the Muslim world's holiest sites and a provocative gesture from an Israeli leader notorious for his role in the Sabra and Shatila massacres. It was followed by riots and fighting, from which developed the second intifada.

SEPTEMBER 2000: THE SECOND INTIFADA

The factors behind this outbreak are, as usual, contested. The conservative commentator Charles Krauthammer suggested that Yasser Arafat himself planned and orchestrated the intifada in order to win concessions he couldn't secure at the Camp David negotiating table:

> The plain fact is that Yasser Arafat, thrown on the diplomatic defensive by rejecting Barak's offer (to the astonishment and dismay of the American mediators), has done what he has

always done: resort to violence to regain the initiative and, most important, mint new underage martyrs – on world television – to regain the international sympathy he had forfeited by turning down peace at Camp David … The war that followed was as spontaneous as a Havana demonstration. The preacher at the al-Aqsa mosque called at Friday prayers to 'eradicate the Jews from Palestine.' Official Palestinian television began playing over and over archival footage of the Palestinian intifada of 1987–1993 showing young people out in the streets throwing stones. In case one still didn't get the message, Voice of Palestine radio began playing patriotic war songs. Arafat then closed the schools and declared a general strike, causing everyone to go out into the street. With Arafat's chief political lieutenant on the West Bank orchestrating the militias, war then 'broke out.' (*Jewish World Review*, 6 October 2000)

Others suggested that the intifada was a spontaneous people's uprising triggered by Sharon's visit and inflamed by Israel's decision to use live ammunition against predominately unarmed demonstrators. The situation was especially serious as Arafat's police ended up firing at the Israeli security forces. The Israeli journalist Amira Hass argues that the intifada represented the explosion of seven years of Palestinian frustration at the failures of the Oslo process to end the military occupation, and that Arafat was powerless to stand in its way:

Seven years after the Oslo accord, all Palestinians feel betrayed, because they are still living under occupation … When six Palestinians were killed by close-range bullets at the mosque by Israeli police, the anger which swept everybody contained all other angers, of seven years and longer. This time Arafat could not dream of checking the spreading anger with his security forces. After all, it was about Al Aqsa. All his credibility would have been lost, so he ordered the policemen to stop. Even without an order, his policemen were unable to restrain their fire, while watching Palestinian youngsters being shot in their eyes and heads by the hundreds. Even if the clashes are subdued, the Palestinians now demand a change in the rules of the game. And their message is meant not only for Israel but for Arafat too. (*Guardian*, 3 October 2005).

The Israeli academic and journalist Tanya Reinhart suggests that the intifada was deliberately provoked by prominent Israeli military leaders because they wanted to launch a war against the Palestinians in order to destroy the Palestinian Authority and topple Arafat (*Tikkun*, March 2002). Their ultimate aim, according to Reinhart, was to prevent the emergence of a Palestinian state and retain the occupied territories. She suggests that the subsequent invasion by Israel of Ramallah, Jenin and other West Bank cities in 2003 and the almost complete destruction of the infrastructure of the nascent Palestinian National Authority during these attacks appear to correlate very closely with the 'Fields of Thorns' plan which had been circulating amongst Israeli military and political leaders from 1996 onwards:

Already in October 2000, at the outset of the Palestinian uprising, military circles were ready with detailed operative plans to topple Arafat and the Palestinian Authority. This was before the Palestinian terror attacks started. A document prepared by the security services, at the request of then PM Barak, stated on October 15, 2000 that 'Arafat, the person, is a severe threat to the security of the state [of Israel] and the damage which will result from his disappearance is less than the damage caused by his existence.' (Details of the document were published in *Ma'ariv*, 6 July, 2001.) The operative plan, known as 'Fields of Thorns' had been prepared back in 1996, and was then updated during the Intifada. (Amir Oren, *Ha'aretz*, Nov. 23, 2001) The political echelon for its part (Barak's circles), worked on preparing public opinion to the toppling of Arafat ... *The Foreign Report* (Jane's Defense Information publication) of July 12, 2001 disclosed that the Israeli army (under Sharon's government) has updated its plans for an 'all-out assault to smash the Palestinian authority, force out leader Yasser Arafat and kill or detain its army.' The blueprint, titled 'The Destruction of the Palestinian Authority and Disarmament of All Armed Forces,' was presented to the Israeli government by chief of staff Shaul Mofaz, on July 8 [2001]. The assault would be launched, at the government's discretion, after a big suicide bomb attack in Israel, causing widespread deaths and injuries, citing the bloodshed as justification. (*Tikkun*, March 2002)

On 7 October 2000 the UN Security Council passed Resolution 1322 condemning both Ariel Sharon's visit to the Al-Haram al-Sharif, and Israel's 'excessive use of force against Palestinians'. There was also criticism of the Israeli response to Palestinian demonstrations from human rights groups such as Amnesty International, Human Rights Watch and B'Tselem. An investigation by Amnesty International had found that the 'majority of [Palestinian] people killed were taking part in demonstrations where stones were the only weapon used'. Amnesty also reported that groups of civilians including children appeared, 'on many occasions, to have been deliberately targeted' (Amnesty International, 2000b). Accusations that Israeli soldiers deliberately shot and killed unarmed civilians including children have also been made by Israeli soldiers themselves, some of whom have refused to serve in the occupied territories because they do not want to take part in such alleged activities.[46]

Throughout the remainder of 2000, Palestinian residents of the occupied territories clashed with the IDF. By the end of the year, 279 Palestinians including 82 minors and 41 Israelis (no minors) had been killed in the unrest (B'Tselem, 2003b).

On 21 January 2001 Palestinian and Israeli delegates met with President Clinton at Taba for further peace talks. Israel put forward an improved offer, but after a week Ehud Barak broke off the talks without an agreement, citing the nearness of the Israeli general election. Arafat condemned the decision to call off the talks, and accused Israel of waging 'a savage and barbaric war against the Palestinians'. Nevertheless both sides issued a statement stating that they had made progress and were closer to a deal than ever (*Guardian*, 29 January 2001). In an analysis of the talks, Aronson claims that both sides moved closer on the territorial dimensions of a settlement. Israel dropped its demand for indefinite control of the Jordan valley, southern West Bank perimeter and area around Kiryat Arba, which comprised about 10 per cent of the West Bank (*Report on Israeli Settlements in the Occupied Territories*, March/ April 2001). Instead, their security concerns would have been met by 'the creation of discreet, limited security points in the Jordan valley, arrangements which would have no territorial or settlement dimension and which would not be conditioned on Israeli control of principal transport routes'. There was also a reduction in Israeli demands for the annexation of the settlement corridors which protrude deeply into the prospective Palestinian state, breaking up territorial continuity, controlling roads and cantonising the territory. Aronson claimed that there still remained 'defects impacting upon both territorial continuity and transport corridors in crucial locations near Jerusalem, Ramallah, Bethlehem, Kalkilya and

Nablus'. The Palestinian negotiator Abu Ala put forward a map designed to overcome these. The map fulfilled three Palestinian territorial objectives: 1) 'reducing the area to be annexed by Israel to twice the settlements' current built-up areas; 2) minimizing the number of West Bank Palestinians in areas to be annexed by Israel from more than 20,000 projected by Israel's Taba map to practically zero; 3) rejecting the annexation of any part of the Jerusalem area settlements of Ma'ale Adumim or Givat Ze'ev'. Aronson noted that the plan represented a 'historical and diplomatic landmark' in that it was the first official Palestinian proposal to accept Israeli annexation of part of the occupied territories. Dr Ron Pundak, director of the Peres Centre for Peace in Tel Aviv and a central figure in the Oslo process, claims that 'on the delicate issue of the Palestinian refugees and the right of return, the negotiators reached a draft determining the parameters and procedures for a solution, along with a clear emphasis that its implementation would not threaten the Jewish character of the State of Israel' (2001: 44). Pundak maintains that the talks had seen 'dramatic progress on all the most important issues' (2001: 44).

THE SHARON ADMINISTRATION

On 6 February 2001 Ariel Sharon won the Israeli election, pledging no negotiations with the Palestinians until the intifada ended. Exactly a week later Massoud Ayad, a member of Arafat's Force of 17 bodyguards, was assassinated by an Israeli helicopter gunship, the first official killed since the assassination of the Fatah secretary and director-general of the Palestinian Health Ministry Thabet Thabet on New's Year's Eve. This killing had led to international condemnation because of Thabet's close association with Israeli peace activists (*Guardian*, 14 February 2001). On 19 February Mahmud al-Madani, a young Hamas leader, was assassinated in Nablus. Shortly afterwards Israel's Labour Party voted to join forces with Likud in a government of national unity with Ariel Sharon as prime minister and Shimon Peres as foreign secretary. In early March, a Palestinian blew himself up in the coastal town of Netanya killing three Israeli civilians and injuring 60 others, the first suicide attack within Israel since the beginning of the intifada. The increasing violence led outside parties to try to intervene and stabilise the situation. On 27 March the Non-Aligned states put forward a resolution (SC/7040) at the Security Council calling for a UN observer force to be dispatched to the occupied territories to protect Palestinian civilians. The resolution was vetoed by the United States which cast the sole negative vote. The European Union also criticised the Israeli government for its 'disproportionate' use of force and called for it to end its illegal settlement of the occupied territories (*Guardian*, 22 May 2001). Such complaints were echoed by human rights groups who criticised Israel's use of helicopter gunships against civilians. Throughout the summer of 2001 the violence continued. The Israelis launched a number of attacks on Palestinian towns and villages and continued to kill Palestinian political and military leaders with 40 dying over the summer by rocket attacks from helicopter gunships. Palestinians and armed members of the Palestinian security services fought battles with the Israeli army. There was also a series of suicide bombings within Israel, the most deadly of which killed 19 young Israelis at the Dolphinarium Disco in Tel Aviv on 1 June. This attack was immediately condemned by Amnesty International who described the killing of the teenagers as 'shocking and reprehensible', adding that 'there can never be any justification for the targeting of civilians' (Amnesty International, 2001e). By the end of August 2001, 154 Israelis (28 minors) and 495 Palestinians (123 minors) had been killed in the intifada (B'Tselem, 2003b).

After the 11 September 2001 attacks on America, Yasser Arafat met with Shimon Peres on 26 September to reach a truce, but it failed to halt the bloodshed. Through the last months of 2001 the killings, suicide bombings, and Israeli attacks on Palestinian towns continued with heavy loss of life particularly on the Palestinian side. On 16 October 2001 members of the Popular Front for the Liberation of Palestine killed the far-right-wing Israeli minister Rehavam Ze'evi in a Jerusalem hotel room. The group claimed that this was in revenge for the killing of its leader by Israel on 27 August in a helicopter gunship attack. The killing of the Israeli minister who favoured the forced removal of all Palestinians from the West Bank and Gaza led to a strong rebuke from the White House, who stated that 'It is time for the Palestinian Authority to take vigorous action against terrorists, words are not enough' (Ari Fleisher, cited in *Guardian*, 17 October 2005). The IDF then killed a number of Palestinian leaders and invaded Bethlehem, Ramallah, Nablus and Jenin where a large numbers of Palestinian fighters and civilians, including many children, lost their lives. They also launched a number of air strikes on Palestinian cities using F-16 jet fighters. Between September and December 2001, 13 Israeli soldiers,

61 Israeli civilians (eight minors) and 241 Palestinian fighters and civilians (42 minors) were killed in the intifada.

The same pattern of violence continued throughout early 2002, reaching a peak in fatalities in March and April, with a number of suicide bombings inside Israel and the Israeli re-occupation of a number of West Bank towns including Nabulus, Ramallah, Jenin, and Bethlehem where Palestinians had sought refuge in the Church of the Nativity after being pursued by the IDF. Yasser Arafat's compound in Ramallah was largely destroyed by tanks and bulldozers and the Palestinian leader was trapped under siege for four weeks. In March and April alone 66 Israeli soldiers, 100 Israeli civilians (13 minors) and 495 Palestinians (47 minors) were killed in the conflict. The invasion of Jenin proved extremely controversial, with initial Palestinian claims that a 'massacre' had taken place involving hundreds of civilians being subsequently criticised. Nevertheless the loss of life was very high: 23 Israeli soldiers and 57 Palestinians, of whom half were civilians, were killed and much of the Jenin refugee camp was destroyed. Amnesty International produced a report on the Jenin and Nablus invasions which examined allegations that the Israeli army indulged in 'unlawful killings', 'torture', the use of Palestinians as 'human shields' during military operations and the 'blocking of medical assistance, food and water; and the destruction of property', and concluded that:

> The IDF carried out actions which violated international human rights and humanitarian law, and that some of the actions amounted to grave breaches of the Fourth Geneva Convention relative to the Protection of Civilian Persons in Time of War of 1949 (the Fourth Geneva Convention) and were war crimes. (Amnesty International, 2002b)

The UN reported that the civilian death toll in the Israeli re-occupation of Nablus was twice as high as Jenin and that in total 497 Palestinians were killed and 1,500 wounded between 1 March and 7 May 2002 (*Guardian*, 2 August 2002). July 2002 saw a particularly controversial incident when Israeli jets bombed a residential apartment block in Gaza city killing Salah Shehada, the founder of Hamas' military wing, as well as 15 other Palestinians including nine children. The Israeli prime minister Ariel Sharon described it a 'great success' but the action was 'strongly condemned' by EU foreign policy chief Javier Solano. Criticism from the US was much milder with White House spokesperson Ari Fleisher describing it as 'heavy-handed' (*Ha'aretz*, 23 July 2002).

In 2002, a group of Israeli combat officers and soldiers released a public statement detailing their unwillingness to serve in the occupied territories. The statement said that the 'price of the occupation' was 'the loss of IDF's human character and the corruption of the entire Israeli society' and that they would 'not continue to fight beyond the 1967 borders in order to dominate, expel, starve and humiliate an entire people' (*Ha'aretz*, 25 January 2002). This marked the establishment of the Seruv (Refuse) movement opposed to settlement building and serving in the occupation of the Palestinian territories. They were to be followed in September 2003 by a group of 27 elite combat pilots, who, in a separate letter, stated that they would no longer carry out missions in the occupied territories: 'We, who have been educated to love the state of Israel refuse to take part in airforce attacks in civilian population centres. We refuse to continue harming innocent civilians' (*Guardian*, 25 September 2003).

In June 2002 Israel began construction of a wall which cut through the occupied territories. The Israeli government argued that the wall was necessary to stop the entry of suicide bombers into Israel. But Aronson suggests that the purpose of the wall is to create de facto borders in which Israel will absorb approximately 50 per cent of the West Bank, whilst Palestinians will be 'separated from each other and from Palestinian citizens of Israel by borders based upon settlement blocs' (*Report on Israeli Settlements in the Occupied Territories*, July/August 2003). The Israeli human rights organisation B'Tselem (2003) has condemned the wall which it projects will cause 'direct harm' to 210,000 Palestinians, turning some villages into 'isolated enclaves' and separating Palestinians from their farmlands, villages and livelihoods.

THE 'ROAD MAP' TO PEACE

In June 2002 the US issued statements insisting that the Palestinians must replace their leader and reform their institutions before they would be granted a state. Speaking from Washington, President Bush stated that, 'When the Palestinian people have new leaders, new institutions and new security arrangements with their neighbors, the United States of America will support the creation of a Palestinian state.' He added that 'Peace requires a new and different Palestinian leadership so that a Palestinian state can be born.' This angered Palestinian negotiators who questioned the right of the US to decide who the Palestinians could elect as their leader. The Palestinian negotiator Saeb Erekat argued that 'Palestinian leaders don't drop from parachutes from Washington or anywhere else. Palestinian leaders are chosen by the Palestinian people' (*Guardian*, 25 June 2002). The American statement effectively stated that the US administration would not publish its long-awaited 'road map' for peace until Arafat appointed a prime minister and delegated many of his powers. Finally, after further pressure, Yasser Arafat announced the make-up of a new cabinet in April 2003, with Mahmoud Abbas installed as Palestinian prime minister. Shortly afterwards the Americans unveiled the 'Road Map', drawn up with input from the US, EU, UN and Russia. It called for the setting up of a Palestinian state in the West Bank and Gaza Strip by 2005. The plan had three stages. In the first the following should happen: all Palestinian violence must stop, Palestinian political structures must be reformed, Israel must dismantle the settlement outposts built since March 2001, and there must be a phased Israeli withdrawal from parts of the occupied territories. In the second stage, an international peace conference would take place and a provisional Palestinian state would come into being. The final stage would involve a solution to the most intractable issues such as borders, refugees and the status of Jerusalem. Arab states would also sign peace deals with Israel. Shortly afterwards at the end of June 2003 Hamas, Islamic Jihad and Fatah called a three-month ceasefire to allow space for negotiation. However, the ceasefire did not hold in the face of further killings of Palestinian fighters and civilians by the IDF and a resumption of suicide bombings in Israel. As the killings on both sides escalated again, Mahmoud Abbas resigned as prime minister on 6 September after a brief and decisive power struggle with Yasser Arafat. His replacement, Ahmed Qureia, was sworn in the following day. The suicide bombings and killings of Palestinian leaders continued and Israeli deputy Ehud Olmert publicly threatened to kill Yasser Arafat. This threat was condemned by the British government and some sections of the Israeli Knesset. The left-wing party Meretz argued that the Likud Party was considering this as a strategy to prevent a two-state solution: 'If you deport Arafat you leave the ground only for Hamas, that's not something the government is doing out of stupidity. It's a strategy to keep things as they are, to prevent the solution of two states' (*Guardian*, 15 September 2003).

In October 2003, left-wing Israeli politicians and Palestinian leaders met to sign the 'Geneva Accords', an alternative vision for peace which specifies in detail the parameters for a settlement of the conflict. This included a Palestinian state in almost all the West Bank and Gaza, the removal of the settlements, a right of return of Palestinian refugees to the future Palestinian state but not Israel, and the division of Jerusalem. The agreement received support from international leaders including Bill Clinton but was condemned by the Israeli government. As 2003 drew to a close the construction of the West Bank wall was condemned by the European Union, United Nations General Assembly and UN Secretary-General Koffi Annan. Between September and the end of January 2004 a further 25 Israeli soldiers, 36 Israeli civilians (five minors) and 169 Palestinians (42 minors) were killed in violent incidents.

In early February 2004, in the midst of a corruption probe, Ariel Sharon shocked even members of his cabinet by announcing a plan to remove all the Jewish settlements from the Gaza Strip, on the basis that they were a security liability. The following month Israel killed the blind, quadriplegic spiritual leader of Hamas, Sheik Ahmed Yassin and three bystanders with a multiple missile strike as he was taken to morning prayers at his local mosque in Gaza. Less than a month later his replacement as Hamas leader, the paediatrician Abdel Aziz Rantissi, was killed together with two aides by an Israeli missile strike on his car in Gaza. The attack was condemned by the European Union and UN, but not the US who stated that Israel had a right to defend itself. Shortly afterwards Ariel Sharon suggested that Israel might also kill Yasser Arafat. Meanwhile the suicide bombings and Israeli attacks on Palestinian towns and villages continued. Between March and May a further 16 Israeli soldiers, 17 Israeli civilians (four minors) and 245 Palestinians (69 minors) were killed. Some of the worst loss of life occurred after the IDF invaded the Rafah refugee camp and caused extensive damage to properties. Eventually the IDF withdrew at the end of May 2004 after facing international criticism.

April 2004 also saw a seismic change in the official American approach to the conflict. For decades the official US approach had been to stick to the parameters of UN Resolution 242. The expectation was that Israel would withdraw to its pre-1967 borders and that a negotiated settlement would resolve the Palestinian 'right of return'. It was assumed that Israeli settlements in the occupied territories were 'an obstacle to peace'. However on 14 April 2004, President Bush, flanked by the Israeli Premier Ariel Sharon, announced a radical change in official policy by stating that 'in light of new realities on the ground, including already existing major Israeli population centers, it is unrealistic to expect that the outcome of final status negotiations will be a full and complete return to the armistice lines of 1949' (*Washington Post*, 15 April 2004). President Bush also rejected the right of return of Palestinians to Israel, stating that they should be re-settled in a future Palestinian state. The US move to legitimise Israel's key settlement blocks in the occupied territories and annul the 'right of return' for Palestinian refugees to Israel drew condemnation from Palestinian and European leaders. The French president Jacques Chirac said that Bush's move had set an 'unfortunate and dangerous precedent' and rejected this change of policy. Similarly the Irish foreign minister, Brian Cowen, stated that 'the EU will not recognise any change to the pre-1967 borders other than those arrived at by agreement between the parties' (*Guardian*, 16 April 2004). The BBC's Washington correspondent Jon Leyne suggested that it had angered the Palestinians because Washington had effectively 'pull[ed] the rug from under any future Palestinian negotiators by denying their demands before they have even begun talking'. He added that 'what concessions could a Palestinian negotiator now hope to get in return for renouncing the right of return, for example, when he knows Washington is already committed to opposing that principle?' Leyne suggested that Bush's change of policy was strongly influenced by America's pro-Israel lobby which includes large numbers of Christian fundamentalists who are important backers of the Republican Party:

> It looks as if he was flattened by 'The Bulldozer', as Mr Sharon is known. How could he be seen to be opposing the Israel lobby in this election year, after all? Yet the Israeli leader was pushing at an open door. In President Bush's black and white world, the Israelis are the good guys, the Palestinians, at least their leadership, are the villains ... Certainly Wednesday's announcement will be popular for Mr Bush back home as well, not just in the Jewish lobby, but also the Christian fundamentalists who make up a crucial part of his base, amongst hard line Republicans, and of course, amongst the Democrats, who won 90% of the Jewish vote in the last elections. (BBC Online report, 14 April 2004)

Although the change in official US policy was condemned by many European leaders it was endorsed by Tony Blair, leading to an unprecedented condemnation by a coalition of 52 former British diplomats who in an open letter argued that 'our dismay at this backward step is heightened by the fact that you yourself seem to have endorsed it, abandoning the principles which for nearly four decades have guided international efforts to restore peace in the Holy Land'. They added that 'there is no case for supporting policies which are doomed to failure' (*The Times*, 26 April 2004).

THE INTERNATIONAL COURT OF JUSTICE AND THE WALL

In July 2004 the International Court of Justice delivered its long-awaited verdict on the wall that Israel had been building into the occupied territories. The court ruled by 14 votes to 1 that the wall violated international law, with the American judge casting the sole dissenting vote. The ruling stated that the Court was 'not convinced that the specific course Israel has chosen for the wall was necessary to attain its security objectives' and that its construction had led to the confiscation and destruction of large quantities of Palestinian property in contravention of the Fourth Geneva Convention. The ruling also re-affirmed the illegality of the Israeli settlements in the occupied territories and stated that there was a danger that construction of the wall 'would be tantamount to *de facto* [original emphasis] annexation' of parts of the occupied territories. The Court stated that Israel should dismantle the wall and that it was 'under an obligation to make reparation for all damage caused by the construction of the wall in the Occupied Palestinian Territory'. The Court also recommended that the UN General Assembly and Security Council should consider what action was required to force Israel to comply with the ruling. The ruling was supported by the European Union but rejected by the Americans who argued that disagreements about the wall should be resolved in bilateral negotiations between the Palestinians and Israelis. The Israelis argued that the International Court of Justice had no jurisdiction over the wall, that the ruling was unbalanced and failed to consider Israel's security concerns. The Israeli spokesperson Raanan Gissin stated that 'I believe that after all the rancour dies, this resolution will find its place in the garbage can of history. The court has made an unjust ruling denying Israel its right of self-defence' (*Guardian*, 10 July 2004).

In early October 2004 a storm of controversy erupted after one of Prime Minister Sharon's closest aides, Dov Weisglass, gave an interview with *Ha'aretz* journalist Ari Shavit. In the interview Weisglass stated that at the end of 2003 the Israeli government had been worried about a series of current and future political developments. These included broad public support for the Geneva Accords, a stagnant economy, increasing numbers of high profile 'refuseniks' and the possibility of future international pressure to reach a negotiated settlement with the Palestinians. Weisglass stated that the disengagement from Gaza would act as 'formaldehyde' by putting the onus on the Palestinians to demonstrate that they could manage Gaza without terrorism. If they could not then the roadmap would become stalled at the first stage which stipulated that Palestinians must cease all violence. This would then ensure that 'there will not be a political process with the Palestinians':

> I found a device, in cooperation with the management of the world [the United States], to ensure that there will be no stopwatch here. That there will be no timetable to implement the settlers' nightmare. I have postponed that nightmare indefinitely. Because what I effectively agreed to with the Americans was that part of the settlements would not be dealt with at all, and the rest will not be dealt with until the Palestinians turn into Finns. That is the significance of what we did. The significance is the freezing of the political process. And when you freeze that process you prevent the establishment of a Palestinian state and you prevent a discussion about the refugees, the borders and Jerusalem. Effectively, this whole package that is called the Palestinian state, with all that it entails, has been removed from our agenda indefinitely. And all this with authority and permission. All with a presidential blessing and the ratification of both houses of Congress. What more could have been anticipated? What more could have been given to the settlers? (*Ha'aretz* Magazine, 8 October 2004)

THE DEATH OF ARAFAT

On 29 October 2004 Yasser Arafat was suddenly taken ill and airlifted to a hospital in France, where he died two weeks later. The significance of the death and legacy of Arafat who led the Palestinians for nearly four decades was disputed by politicians and commentators. Many in Israel were highly critical. Shimon Peres, with whom Arafat had shared the Nobel Peace Prize in 1994, stated that it is 'good that the world is rid of him ... the sun is shining in the Middle East' (BBC Online, 11 November 2004). The Israeli historian Michael Oren in a *Washington Post* article headlined 'Arafat Without Tears: The Terrorist Statesman Took Peace Nowhere' accused him of poisoning his own people's attitudes towards Israel and destroying the peace process:

The arc of Arafat's image – from terrorist to Nobel Prize-winning peacemaker and back to terrorist – had been inscribed in the Israeli public's consciousness. Much of that public is now convinced that Arafat never intended to make peace, but merely used Oslo as a means of implementing the Palestinian Liberation Organization's 1974 'Phased Plan,' which called for Israel's gradual destruction through combined violence and diplomacy. Indeed, a solid majority of Israelis have come to believe that Arafat so poisoned his own people that, with or without him, there is little chance to renew negotiations, and that Israel's only option was to hunker down behind a fence separating Israelis from Palestinians until such time as the Palestinians produce a legitimate leadership capable of making peace. (*Washington Post*, 14 November 2004)

Alan Dershowitz, writing in the *Jerusalem Post*, offered an even harsher judgement on the Palestinian leader. He described Arafat as the 'godfather of international terrorism who dashed his people's hopes for statehood' and 'and indoctrinated [Palestinian] children with so much hatred that they willingly turned themselves into human bombs'.

Arafat was personally responsible for the murders of thousands of innocent Israelis, hundreds of innocent Americans, and countless others. Like other ethnically motivated butchers before him, he delighted in killing Jewish children, as he did in several well-planned attacks on Israeli schools and nurseries. He also personally ordered the murder of hundreds of his own people who disagreed with him or collaborated with Israel. Never a man to tolerate dissent, he employed bullets rather than arguments to respond to his critics. Arafat was the inspiration for Osama bin Laden, because he proved to his eager student that terrorism works and that terrorists can be praised and rewarded by a craven world, as Arafat was by so many for so long. Arafat was not one of those leaders who could, a la Nelson Mandela, make the transition from terrorist to peacemaker. He never learned how to take 'yes' for an answer and he never missed an opportunity to miss an opportunity. (*Jerusalem Post*, 12 November 2004)

However, not all Israelis offered such a damning critique of Arafat. Uri Avnery suggested that the Palestinian leader represented for most Israelis the personification of all the violence of the conflict and for this reason they were unable to recognise the concessions and compromises he had made in trying to end the conflict:

> Every conflict generates massive amounts of stereotypes, prejudice, hate, and fear. All of the hate, fear and maybe the guilt, that we erected our national factory on the ruin of the Palestinian people. All of it focused on the character of Arafat. Millions of words condemning him have been written. I don't remember 100 words praising Arafat. It cannot be that there does not exist any words of praise at all for a man. He was the initiator of Oslo, he recognized Israel. The man who gave up 77% of what was Palestine before 1948, and settled for 22% – there has to be something good in him. He was not portrayed as an enemy, but as a monster. He was portrayed as a great enemy and he could have been a great partner. (*Jerusalem Post*, 11 November 2004)

Some other commentators and political leaders offered positive evaluations of Arafat's life. The Malaysian prime minister, Abdullah Ahmad Badawi, described him as a 'great leader' who would be remembered 'by people from all parts of the world for his courage and determination against all odds in championing and protecting the inalienable rights of the people of Palestine' (BBC Online, 11 November 2004). Former South African president Nelson Mandela described him as 'one of the outstanding freedom fighters of this generation, one who gave his entire life to the cause of the Palestinian people' (BBC Online, 11 November 2004). David Hirst writing in the *Guardian* offered a nuanced verdict on his life and legacy. He argued that Arafat had been vital in pulling the Palestinians together after the defeats of 1948 and 1967, but that his leadership after 1990 had been poor. Hirst criticised him for instituting torture and maltreatment in the Palestinian Authority and allowing his economic advisors to throw 'up a ramshackle, nepotistic edifice of monopoly, racketeering and naked extortion which enriched them as it further impoverished society at large'. Hirst however, like Edward Said, reserved his strongest criticism for Arafat's decision to accept the parameters of the Oslo Accords which he suggests were strongly weighted in Israel's favour and served to undermine Palestinian rights enshrined in international jurisprudence:

> He came as collaborator as much as liberator. Oslo provided for a series of 'interim' agreements leading to 'final-status' talks. An Israeli commentator said of the first of them: 'when one looks

through all the lofty phraseology, all the deliberate disinformation, the hundreds of pettifogging sections, sub-sections, appendices and protocols, one clearly recognises that the Israeli victory was absolute and Palestine defeat abject'. It went on like this for six years, long after it had become obvious that his 'momentum' was working against, not for him. It had been bound to do so, because, in this dispensation that outlawed violence, spurned UN jurisprudence on the conflict, and consecrated a congenitally pro-Israeli US as sole arbiter of the peace process, the balance of power was more overwhelmingly in Israel's favour than ever. The 'interim' agreements which should have advanced his conception of 'final status' only advanced the Israelis' conception. (*Guardian*, 11 November 2004)

On 9 January 2005 the Palestinians in the occupied territories went to the polls and elected the Fatah candidate Mahmoud Abbas as president. Two weeks later, on 23 January, Hamas and Islamic Jihad agreed to suspend attacks on Israel in order to give Abbas time to negotiate a ceasefire with the Israelis. This was eventually concluded on 8 February at Sharm el-Sheikh in Egypt, when Abbas met with Ariel Sharon and agreed a ceasefire and terms for the Israelis to release Palestinian prisoners and move their troops out of Palestinian population centres. Hamas protested after the summit that they hadn't been properly consulted about the ceasefire but also declared that they wouldn't breach it without provocation. Despite the ceasefire the killings continued, albeit at a lower rate. Between the ceasefire being signed in February and the Gaza disengagement in August a further 18 Israelis (four minors) and 60 Palestinians (17 minors) were killed (B'Tselem, 2010a).

THE WITHDRAWAL OF SETTLERS FROM GAZA

In early August 2005, Israeli troops moved in to Gaza to remove the Israeli settlers who had refused to accept the government's compensation package and relocate voluntarily. Despite predictions of widespread violence and resistance all Israeli settlers were removed from the Gaza Strip within a matter of days without serious bloodshed. The reasons behind the disengagement from Gaza were the subject of much controversy. The British and American governments spoke of it as a step towards peace. The Israeli cabinet resolution that had authorised the disengagement stated that there was 'no reliable Palestinian partner with which it can make progress in a two-sided peace process' and that it would disengage from Gaza to achieve a 'a better security, political, economic and demographic situation' (Israeli Ministry of Foreign Affairs, 2004). The demographic situation was considered to be particularly pressing. Haifa University geographer Arnon Soffer, who was widely seen as the originator of Ariel Sharon's separation plan, explained the nature of the demographic threat in a 2004 *Jerusalem Post* interview. He suggested that the deal the Israelis were offering to the Palestinians was so unacceptable that they would probably seek to wait until they comprised a majority in the area under Israeli control (Israel and the occupied territories) and then demand equal voting rights, a move which would threaten Israel's existence as a Jewish state. Removing the 1.3 million Palestinians from Israeli control in Gaza would put off that possibility for a number of years:

> Let's view it from a Palestinian perspective. Let's pretend you and I are Arafat and Yasser Abed Rabbo looking at the map. Look at what the Jews are going to leave us for a state. They're going to leave us the Gaza Strip – which is no more than a crowded 'prison.' Then there's another 'prison' called Hebron, and another, larger one called Samaria. Here there are 1.6 million, here 1 million, and here 1.5 million (soon to be 3 million). Each of these 'prisons' is cut off from the rest. The Jews won't permit us to have an army, while their own powerful army will surround us. They won't permit us to have an air force, while their own air force will fly over us. They won't allow us the Right of Return. Why should we make a deal with them? Why should we accept a state from them? Let's wait patiently for another 10 years, when the Jews will comprise a mere 40 percent of the country, while we will be 60 percent. The world won't allow a minority to rule over a majority, so Palestine will be ours. (*Jerusalem Post*, 10 May 2004)

Soffer predicted a bleak and violent future after the disengagement from Gaza, although he also suggested that Israel's demographic and security situation would improve and a 'voluntary transfer' of Palestinians from the occupied territories might be achieved:

> Instead of entering Gaza, the way we did last week, we will tell the Palestinians that if a single missile is fired over the fence, we will fire 10 in response. And women and children will be killed, and houses will be destroyed. After the fifth such incident, Palestinian

mothers won't allow their husbands to shoot Kassams, because they will know what's waiting for them. Second of all, when 2.5 million people live in a closed-off Gaza, it's going to be a human catastrophe. Those people will become even bigger animals than they are today, with the aid of an insane fundamentalist Islam. The pressure at the border will be awful. It's going to be a terrible war. So, if we want to remain alive, we will have to kill and kill and kill. All day, every day. If we don't kill, we will cease to exist.

He also commented on the impact of those policies on Israeli society and the long-term effect on Palestinians:

The only thing that concerns me is how to ensure that the boys and men who are going to have to do the killing will be able to return home to their families and be normal human beings. The Palestinians will be forced to realize that demography is no longer significant, because we're here and they're there. And then they will begin to ask for 'conflict management' talks – not that dirty word 'peace.' ... Unilateral separation doesn't guarantee 'peace' – it guarantees a Zionist-Jewish state with an overwhelming majority of Jews; it guarantees the kind of safety that will return tourists to the country; and it guarantees one other important thing. Between 1948 and 1967, the fence was a fence, and 400,000 people left the West Bank voluntarily. This is what will happen after separation. If a Palestinian cannot come into Tel Aviv for work, he will look in Iraq, or Kuwait, or London. I believe that there will be movement out of the area. (*Jerusalem Post*, 10 May 2004)

Graham Usher also notes what he sees as the key role of demography both in the withdrawal from Gaza and in Israel's naturalisation policies.

Its only logic is demographic: the desperate fear that somehow without ending its presence in Gaza, Israel will one day find itself responsible for 1.3 million Palestinian residents. Demography is also the rationale behind Israel's new naturalisation policies. These grant citizenship to any Jew on the planet, but place draconian restrictions on citizenship on any Palestinians, in the occupied territories or elsewhere, who marry (in some cases, literally) their cousins inside Israel. In Kimmerling's phrase, this is '*herrenvolk*' law that is utterly unabashed about making ethnic discrimination and racial superiority the cornerstone of citizenship. Plans are already in place to expel thousands of 'illegal' Palestinians now in Israel 'across the border' once the border (that is, the wall) is built. (Usher, 2006: 20)

The Israeli withdrawal from Gaza was followed by a series of political earthquakes in the latter months of 2005. On 10 November, Shimon Peres was unexpectedly defeated for the leadership of the Labour Party by Amir Peretz, a trade union leader who immediately indicated that he would pull Labour out of its National Unity coalition with Likud and trigger a general election. Peretz's victory was particularly surprising given that he was the first Sephardic Jew elected as leader of what is widely seen as an Ashkenazi-dominated party. Some in the party hoped that this might increase Labour's share of the vote amongst Middle Eastern Jews who traditionally favoured Likud. On 22 November a second major upheaval occurred when Ariel Sharon resigned from the Likud Party and formed a new party, Kadima ('Forward'), which immediately attracted defections from both Likud and Labour, including senior figures such as Shimon Peres, Ehud Olmert and Shaul Mofaz. Early opinion polls suggested that Kadima would become the largest party in the general election scheduled for 28 March 2006. On 18 December Ariel Sharon suffered a minor stroke, but was released from hospital soon afterwards. Two days later Binyamin Netanyahu was elected the new Likud leader, pledging not to give back any more Palestinian territory unless such moves were first approved by Israelis in a referendum. On 4 January 2006 Ariel Sharon suffered a second and much more devastating stroke which left him in a coma. His place as leader of the newly formed Kadima was taken up by his deputy, Ehud Olmert.

HAMAS WINS THE PALESTINIAN LEGISLATIVE ELECTIONS

At the end of January 2006 the Palestinians went to the polls in what was predicted to be closely fought parliamentary elections. In a surprise result Hamas not only triumphed over Fatah for the first time but actually gained a majority of seats creating the possibility that it might form a government without coalition partners. The result was attributed by some to being a protest against the corruption of Fatah, or as a reaction to the failure of the international community to respond to legal ways of dealing with the conflict. This included most notably the absence of any international action on the ruling by the Court of Justice on the separation barrier. The reaction of Europe and the US to the election result was negative. They demanded that Hamas agree to three pre-conditions before they could be accepted as a negotiating partner. These were that the organisation agree to recognise the state of Israel, renounce violence and accept all previous agreements signed by the Palestinian Authority. Hamas officials including Mahmoud al-Zahar and Khaled Meshall rejected the call to abandon violence. Meshall stated that 'as long as we are under occupation then resistance is our right' (BBC Online, 28 January 2006). Al-Zahar stated that Hamas did not believe Israel intended to allow the creation of an independent Palestinian state and that the organisation would not say whether it would recognise Israel until Israel specified what its borders actually were: 'If Israel is ready to tell the people what is the official border, after that we are going to answer this question' (Benhorin, 2006). Hamas officials also reiterated their longstanding offer of a long-term ceasefire in exchange for a Palestinian state in the pre-1967 borders, the release of prisoners and the return of refugees.

After the elections America and the EU moved to block direct aid to the Hamas administration in Gaza and diplomatically isolate the organisation. According to a report by Stephen Erlanger in the *New York Times*, even before Hamas was sworn in as the new government a plan was being 'discussed at the highest levels of the [US State] Department and the Israeli government' to 'destabilize the Palestinian government so that newly elected Hamas officials will fail and elections will be called again' (14 February 2006). According to Erlanger the intention was 'to starve the Palestinian Authority of money and international connections to the point where, some months from now, its president, Mahmoud Abbas, is compelled to call a new election'. 'The hope', argued Erlanger, was 'that Palestinians will be so unhappy with life under Hamas that they will return to office a reformed and chastened Fatah movement' (14 February 2006). However, this strategy did not achieve its objectives of ousting Hamas but instead set the scene for a violent schism between the Islamist movement and its Fatah rival in the Gaza Strip.

In 2006 there were also Israeli elections in which Kadima, fronted by Ehud Olmert, emerged as the largest single party, with 29 representatives in the 120-seat Knesset. Olmert then moved to form a coalition with Labour, Shas and the Pensioner's Party. The new political situation in Israel did not create momentum towards substantive talks between the Palestinians and Israelis and the peace process did not progress as stipulated under President Bush's 'Road Map for Peace'. Violence continued to claim further victims particularly on the Palestinian side through the early months of 2006. Although Hamas had officially been maintaining a truce with Israel since February 2005, and in April 2006 it stated that it would no longer use suicide bombings, other groups in Gaza continued to fire rockets into Israel (*Observer*, 9 April 2006). The unguided projectiles killed an average of four Israelis per year between 2004 and the end of 2009, with the majority of the rockets falling on the town of Sderot close to the border with Gaza (B'Tselem, 2010b). During the same period Israeli attacks killed an average of 662 Palestinians per year (B'Tselem, 2010a). According to the Israel Centre for Victims of Terror and War the rocket attacks by the Palestinians have taken a heavy psychological toll on the residents of Sderot. A study conducted by the group in 2008 found that 28 per cent of adults and 30 per cent of children were suffering from post-traumatic stress disorder and that a far higher proportion of children (between 75 and 94 per cent) showed symptoms of post-traumatic stress (*Ha'aretz*, 17 January 2008). Palestinian groups have attempted to justify the use of rocket attacks by arguing that they are a response to the Israeli blockade of Gaza or are retaliation for the killing of Palestinians. However, the firing of rockets by groups in Gaza has been condemned by human rights groups as a violation of international law which may constitute a war crime.[47] For instance, Human Rights Watch (2007) have stated that:

> The Palestinian rocket attacks violate international humanitarian law [IHL], also known as the laws of war, which governs the conduct of the parties during armed conflict. Where an attack on a military target is intended and that target is in or near a civilian area, the Palestinian rocket attacks are indiscriminate because they cannot distinguish between military targets and civilians. Where there is no intended military target and the rockets are launched into a civilian area, they constitute deliberate attacks against civilians. Given that the rocket attacks have inflicted very little damage on Israeli military assets, their primary purpose seems to be to kill civilians or at least to spread terror among the Israeli civilian population, both of which IHL prohibits.

During this period Israel continued to kill members of Palestinian armed groups and bystanders in missile strikes and via artillery barrages. In June 2006 the violence in Gaza began to escalate still further. Two particular incidents sparked international concern. On 9 June 2006 Israeli shelling killed seven Palestinians picnicking on the beach in Gaza, and on 13 June 2006 an Israeli missile strike on two members of Islamic Jihad driving through a busy street in Gaza city also killed nine bystanders, including two ambulance workers and two young children. The day after the Gaza beach killings Hamas declared an end to its 16-month ceasefire and stated that it would start firing rockets into Israel (BBC Online, 10 June 2006).

On 25 June 2006, Palestinian fighters emerged from tunnels built below the fence separating Israel from Gaza. Once on the Israeli side they attacked Israeli armoured vehicles killing two soldiers and captured an Israeli corporal, Gilad Shalit, who they took across the border into Gaza. Israel leaders then demanded the immediate release of Shalit, and when this was not forthcoming Israel detained 64 Hamas officials including eight ministers and 20 other parliamentarians. Although Israel denied it, many suspected that the timing of the seizure, only three days after the capture of Shalit, indicated that the elected Palestinians were being used as bargaining chips for the release of the corporal. Israel also escalated its bombing attacks on Gaza and launched a ground invasion of the territory. Israel claimed that the invasion and bomb attacks were intended to free corporal Shalit and prevent rocket attacks, but Palestinian groups argued that the real intention was to topple the Hamas administration in Gaza (*Guardian*, 30 June 2006). Over the following two months Israeli forces killed 225 Palestinians, including 50 children (B'Tselem, 2010c). According to B'Tselem (2010c) approximately half of those killed were not involved in fighting when they were killed by the Israeli military. During the operation Israeli forces also targeted the civilian infrastructure in Gaza including bridges, roads, water networks and the only power station. These attacks were condemned as 'war crimes' by Amnesty International (2006a).

THE 2006 LEBANON WAR

During this period Israel also came into conflict with Hezbullah guerrillas in Lebanon. On 12 July 2006, using a barrage of rocket attacks on Israeli border villages and military outposts as a diversion, a group of Hezbullah fighters crossed the Israeli border and attacked an IDF convoy. They killed three Israeli soldiers and abducted two others who were taken across the border into Southern Lebanon. An Israeli tank which crossed into Lebanon in pursuit of the Hezbullah fighters was destroyed killing a further four IDF members, and a fifth soldier died in a firefight whilst trying to retrieve the tank. According to a report by the *Ha'aretz* correspondent Ze'ev Schiff, the Hezbullah operation was the fifth attempt by the Lebanese group to abduct soldiers over the course of the previous eight months (*Ha'aretz*, 19 September 2006). On the day that the abductions took place the Hezbullah leader Hassan Nasrallah (2006) gave a speech in which he laid out the group's motivations for the attack. Nasrallah argued that the abductions were the only way to secure the release of Lebanese prisoners, some of whom had been held for decades in Israeli prisons. Nasrallah also claimed that Israel had reneged on previous commitments to free the prisoners and the operation was also intended to draw international attention to the 10,000 'Lebanese, Palestinian, and Arab detainees' in Israeli prisons. Nicholas Noe, an expert on the Shiite organisation, suggests that the issue of Lebanese prisoners was one of four unresolved grievances or 'bleeding wounds' that remained after Israel's withdrawal from Lebanon, and which Hezbullah focused on in order to maintain support. The other grievances were the refusal of Israel to hand over all maps detailing the hundreds of thousands of landmines it left in Southern Lebanon, the near daily violation of Lebanese airspace by Israeli reconnaissance aircraft and the retention by Israel of the 'water rich' Sheba Farms 'in addition to several other disputed parcels of land' (*Guardian*, 5 October 2007).

Following the abduction of the two IDF soldiers, Prime Minister Olmert accused the Lebanese government of committing an 'act of war' and warned of a 'painful and far reaching response' (*Guardian*, 13 July 2006). The Israeli army chief of staff, General Halutz, went further in an interview with Israeli Channel 10 and said that his military would target infrastructure and 'turn the clock back in Lebanon by twenty years' if the soldiers were not returned (*Guardian*, 13 July 2006). Israeli leaders argued that the Lebanese government was responsible for Hezbullah's actions because the organisation was a member of the Lebanese government and the government allowed 'Hizbullah to operate freely against Israel from within its sovereign territory' (Ynetnews.com, 12 July 2006). The Lebanese prime minister Fouad Siniora, who was widely seen as pro-Western, attempted to distance himself from the Hezbullah cross-border attack stating that the Lebanese government had no prior knowledge of the attack and did not condone it (*Lebanon Daily Star*, 13 July 2006). Hezbullah themselves refused to return the soldiers except in the context of a prisoner swap.

On the day of the abductions Israeli forces bombed Lebanese infrastructure, hitting numerous bridges. The next day Israel intensified its aerial bombardment, striking targets across Lebanon including Beirut's international airport. It also enforced a land, sea and air closure of the country and members of the IDF invaded Southern Lebanon. Over the course of 34 days Hezbullah and Israel fought what became known as the July or the Second Lebanon War. Hezbullah took part in guerrilla attacks on IDF units that crossed into Lebanon, and the organisation launched more than 4,200 rockets at northern Israel of which 23 per cent landed in urban areas (Rubin, 2006). The great bulk of rockets used by Hezbullah were small unguided Katyusha missiles most likely sourced from old Soviet or Chinese stock, supplemented with a much smaller number of longer range Iranian-manufactured Fajr-3 or Fajr-5 rockets (BBC Online, 18 July 2006). Hasan Nasrallah argued that it was the Israelis who had widened the conflict by attacking infrastructure and civilian targets and that Hezbullah's decision to use its rocket arsenal against Israeli towns was a response to this escalation (*Lebanon Daily Star*, 17 July 2006). The Hezbullah rocket attacks spread panic across northern Israel and an estimated 250,000 Israelis fled the area (Rubin, 2006). Those who remained were confined to bomb shelters for much of the conflict. According to Israel's Ministry of Housing, Hezbullah attacks damaged 12,000 buildings, although according to Amnesty International (2006b) only 'a small percentage' of these were 'badly damaged'. Israeli air and sea attacks were much more extensive and caused widespread damage to Lebanon's infrastructure. According to figures obtained from the Lebanon authorities Israeli attacks completely or partially destroyed 31 'vital points' including airports, ports, water and sewage treatment centres, power stations as well as 80 bridges and 94 roads (Amnesty International, 2006a). Israel's attack on the Jiyyeh power plant 19 miles south of Beirut led to an estimated 4 million gallons of oil being released into the Eastern Mediterranean, creating a 105-mile oil slick the effects of which Lebanese authorities estimated could take up to ten years to recover from (BBC Online, 16 August 2006). More than 25 fuel stations and 900 businesses including supermarkets and food stores were also bombed often with precision-guided munitions (Amnesty International, 2006a). The number of residential properties, shops and offices completely destroyed exceeded 30,000, with a further 70,000 partially destroyed. Two government hospitals were completely destroyed and a further three partially destroyed (Amnesty International,

2006a). An estimated 970,000 Lebanese fled Southern Lebanon during the conflict (Amnesty International, 2006a). The reason why Israel inflicted such extensive damage on Lebanon is contested. Official statements from the Israeli Foreign Ministry, as well as those from some Israeli leaders, argued that Israel was only targeting Hezbullah positions and support facilities and that any damage to the civilian infrastructure was either incidental to these military objectives or a result of Hezbullah using the civilian population as 'human shields'.[48] However, these statements appeared to be at odds with other statements made by Israeli officials which suggested that Lebanese infrastructure was being attacked either as direct reprisals for Hezbullah rocket attacks or in order to place pressure on the Lebanese government to disarm and disband Hezbullah.[49] This latter perspective was clearly expressed in a statement from retired Israeli army colonel Gal Luft which appeared in the American media:

> Israel is attempting to create a rift between the Lebanese population and Hezbullah supporters by exacting a heavy price from the elite in Beirut. The message is: If you want your air conditioning to work and if you want to be able to fly to Paris for shopping, you must pull your head out of the sand and take action toward shutting down Hezbullah-land. (*Washington Post*, 19 July 2006)

As well as suffering more damage to its infrastructure Lebanon also experienced more casualties than Israel. According to official Israeli casualty figures, 44 civilians (seven children) and 117 soldiers were killed during the conflict (Israeli Ministry of Foreign Affairs, 2006b). Human Rights Watch estimated that there had been 'at least 1,109 Lebanese deaths, the vast majority of whom were civilians' and a further 4,399 people were injured (Human Rights Watch, 2007b). About a third of those killed were children, according to a UNICEF (2006) report. There were conflicting accounts of the number of Hezbullah fighters killed. The organisation finally put their losses at 'around 250' after previously putting forward a much lower figure (Associated Press, 15 December 2006). Israel initially claimed that 800 Hezbullah fighters had been killed but later lowered their estimate to around 600 (Associated Press, 28 December 2006).

International reactions to the conflict were varied with most countries, at least, decrying the violence and demanding from an early stage that a ceasefire be implemented. However there were important exceptions. The United States, Australia, Canada, Germany and Great Britain backed Israel's 'right to defend itself' and explicitly blamed Hezbullah for the conflict. The United States went further and expedited a shipment of precision-guided bombs after a request from Israel during the first days of the conflict (*New York Times*, 22 July 2006). A report shortly afterwards in the Saudi press alleged that the United States was also about to supply Israel with 100 'bunker buster' bombs in order to kill the Hezbullah leader Hasan Nasrallah (*Asharq al-Awsat*, 24 July 2006). The United States together with the United Kingdom also tried to block diplomatic efforts towards an early ceasefire.[50] Avi Shlaim argued that both President Bush and Prime Minister Blair pursued this strategy because they 'wanted to give Israel an opportunity to destroy Hezbullah' (*Guardian*, 3 February 2010). This, Shlaim suggested, was unrealistic because in Lebanon the organisation was 'seen not as a terrorist organization but as an authentic Islamic resistance movement' which 'empowers the poor and underprivileged Shiite community' and that 'to destroy Hezbullah, Israel would have to kill all the Shiite population' (*New York Times*, 4 August 2006). Syria and Iran, two of Hezbullah's key weapons providers, issued statements supportive of Hezbullah and there were reports at the beginning of August 2006 that Iran had agreed to supply Hezbullah with more weapons 'for the next stage of the confrontation' (Jane's Defence Weekly, 30 July 2006, cited in Associated Press, 5 August 2006). A wide body of countries and multilateral institutions were sharply critical of Israel's behaviour whilst also condemning Hezbullah's cross-border raid and abductions. The EU described the Israeli attacks as 'disproportionate' and stated that its decision to enforce a sea and air blockade of Lebanon 'could not be justified' (*Ha'aretz*, 13 July 2006). The UN secretary-general Kofi Annan described the Hezbullah abductions as 'deplorable' whilst also condemning Israel's 'excessive use of force' (BBC Online, 20 July 2006).

A number of human rights groups issued reports which were highly critical of the conduct of the war. Human Rights Watch (2007c) and Amnesty International (2006b) issued reports which condemned Hezbullah's strategy of sending thousands of unguided missiles into Israel. Both organisations dismissed attempts by Hezbullah leaders to justify such attacks as reprisals or deterrent, and argued that they constituted deliberate or indiscriminate attacks upon the Israeli civilian population and were thus a violation of international law, and were war crimes. However, human rights groups directed the bulk of their criticism at Israel's behaviour during the war. Both Amnesty International (2006c) and Human Rights Watch (2007b) argued that Israeli actions were 'disproportionate' and primarily directed against the civilian population and infrastructure rather than against military targets:

> The widespread destruction of apartments, houses, electricity and water services, roads, bridges, factories and ports, in addition to several statements by Israeli officials, suggests a policy of punishing both the Lebanese government and the civilian population in an effort to get them to turn against Hizbullah. (Amnesty International, 2006c)

Human Rights Watch (2007b) also questioned whether after warning the Lebanese population to move north of the Litani river, Israel's decision to treat anyone remaining in that part of Southern Lebanon as a 'combatant', constituted a 'war crime'. This decision to widen the scope of what Israel considered a legitimate target, the organisation argued, was a crucial factor in the large number of civilians killed (Human Rights Watch, 2007b). Israel's decision to 'flood' a '1,400 square kilometer area' of South Lebanon with approximately 4 million cluster bombs in the final stages of the conflict, when a ceasefire was imminent, was severely criticised.[51] Both organisations also disputed Israeli claims that the large number of civilian casualties and widespread destruction of civilian infrastructure was a direct consequence of Hezbullah using the population as 'human shields'[52] (Amnesty International, 2006c; Human Rights Watch, 2007b).

The conflict was brought to a close with the passing of UN Security Council Resolution 1701 which stipulated that Hezbullah be disarmed and that only troops from the Lebanese army together with an expanded UN inspection force should be permitted south of the Litani river. However, subsequent media reports have suggested that neither objective has been met, with Hezbullah substantially increasing their rocket stocks and continuing to operate in South Lebanon (*The Times*, 5 August 2009).

HAMAS TAKES CONTROL OF GAZA

In this period there was also an escalation of factional fighting between Palestinian groups. Although Hamas' election victory had initially led to attempts to forge a national coalition between the party and its secular Fatah rival, a violent struggle for control had broken out between the two groups in Gaza, with both sides committing widespread atrocities including murder and torture (Amnesty International, 2007a). Attempts at reconciliation involved an effort by prisoners from the leading Palestinian factions, who were being held in Israeli jails, to create an agreed-upon framework for discussions with Israel. The so-called 'Prisoners' Document' called for a government of national unity that would negotiate with Israel according to a set of agreed parameters. These included the central demand that a Palestinian state be set up in the West Bank and Gaza Strip with its capital in East Jerusalem. It was eventually accepted by Hamas and led to direct negotiations between Ismail Haniyeh and Mahmoud Abbas in order to try to create a government of national unity (*Guardian*, 22 June 2006). This move appeared to precipitate a rift between the members of the quartet of international mediators (US, EU, UN, Russia) with the United States opposing the development and the other members supporting it. Stephen Farrell writing in the *Sunday Times* cited Western officials as stating that non-American quartet members were convinced that the Americans wanted Abbas to dissolve the Hamas government and use his Fatah forces to 'confront Hamas politically and militarily' (18 November 2006). But the official said the non-American quartet members opposed US plans to 'back one side in an emerging civil war' between Hamas and Fatah and instead wanted to support the national unity government and broker a ceasefire.

The decision by Israel and America to shun negotiations and attempt to topple the Hamas administration also appeared to arouse disquiet amongst some members of Israel's former and current intelligence services. A report by Orly Halpern cited a number who were critical of the strategy and argued that at the very least Israel should begin talking to the organisation:

> Growing numbers of Israeli security experts are urging Jerusalem to overcome its misgivings and open a channel to Hamas. Retired Major General Shlomo Gazit, a former chief of military intelligence, called the three conditions laid down by Israel and its Western allies 'ridiculous, or an excuse not to negotiate ... Why should Palestinians stop fighting against us until they know we are willing to make an agreement?' ... Some believe that Hamas's ultimate goal is to destroy Israel, making talks with the Islamist movement a no-go even if it recognized Israel ... [but others] argue that reaching out to Hamas may be the best of bad alternatives available to Israel. 'It may not work, but aren't

we strong enough to be able to try it?' said onetime Mossad chief Ephraim Halevy, who was a top adviser to former prime ministers Yitzhak Shamir and Ariel Sharon. According to Halevy, Israel should take up Hamas's offer of a long-term truce and try negotiating, because the Islamic movement is respected by Palestinians and generally keeps its word. He pointed to the cease-fire in attacks on Israel that Hamas declared two years ago and has largely honored. 'They're not very pleasant people, but they are very, very credible,' Halevy said ... Gazit, however, believes the real reason Israel won't talk to Hamas is because it is still not willing to make the sacrifices necessary to make peace with the Palestinians. 'Why are we not negotiating with [Syrian President Bashar] Assad?' asked Gazit. 'Because we know the price and we aren't willing to pay. The same goes for the Palestinians.' (*The Forward*, 9 February 2007)

Despite the signing of a power-sharing agreement between Fatah and Hamas in February 2007 violence between the two groups continued to increase. It finally came to a head in June 2007 when after eight days of prolonged fighting, Fatah forces were comprehensively defeated and Hamas took complete control of Gaza. The previous 18 months of internecine warfare had left 349 Palestinians dead (B'Tselem, 2010d). There are competing accounts of the events surrounding Hamas' takeover of Gaza. The British foreign secretary Margaret Beckett accused Hamas of conducting a 'coup d'état', a condemnation echoed by others including Palestinian president Mahmoud Abbas (*Daily Telegraph*, 15 June 2007). A different perspective on the events is offered by David Rose in an extended article in *Vanity Fair* (April 2008). Based on confidential documents corroborated by 'former and current U.S. officials' Rose reported that during 2006 senior American officials such as Condoleezza Rice had repeatedly pressurised Mahmoud Abbas to give Hamas an ultimatum: either accept the quartet's preconditions for negotiations or the government would be dissolved. The Americans also pledged to funnel arms and finance training to a Fatah force under the control of the militia leader Muhammad Dahlan. The hope was that Dahlan's forces would be able to defeat any Hamas backlash in the event of the dissolution of their rule. In the months that followed the Americans tried to secure funding from Congress for the training and armament of Dahlan's forces, but this was blocked by the House Subcommittee on the Middle East and South Asia whose members feared that any weapons transferred to Palestinian security forces might later be used against Israel. In the end Congress was only willing to fund a reduced package for non-lethal aid. Following this setback the American administration attempted to secure covert funding and approached the leaders of Jordan, Egypt, Saudi Arabia and the United Arab Emirates. Some money was forthcoming, most of it from the United Arab Emirates, but it was not sufficient to provide Dahlan's forces with the manpower and armaments they needed. Meanwhile in Gaza Dahlan's forces stormed the Islamic University, a Hamas stronghold, and set several buildings on fire. The following day Hamas members attacked police stations manned by Fatah forces. With the prospect of a civil war looming President Abbas decided to change course. King Abdullah of Saudi Arabia had for weeks been trying to persuade him to go to Mecca and negotiate a national unity government with Hamas. On 6 February 2007 Abbas flew to Saudi Arabia with Dahlan and two days later a deal was struck where the Hamas leader Ismail Haniyeh would remain prime minister with Fatah representatives taking several important positions in the new national unity government. This move left the American Foreign Secretary 'apoplectic', and rather than accept the formation of the national unity government the Americans resorted to 'Plan B' which involved increasing the pressure on Abbas to dissolve the government and providing further military aid and training to Dahlan's forces. However, news of the plan leaked out to the Jordanian newspaper *Al-Majd* (30 April 2007). The following month 500 newly trained Fatah security personnel crossed from Egypt into Gaza. They were equipped with new vehicles and weapons and were immediately attacked by Hamas forces. In early June 2007 another leaked report, this time in *Ha'aretz*, alleged that Abbas and the American Lieutenant General Dayton had asked Israel to authorise a large arms shipment to Dahlan's force which included 'dozens of armoured cars, hundreds of armour piercing rockets, thousands of hand grenades and millions of rounds of ammunition' (*Vanity Fair*, April 2008). Hamas spokesman Fawzi Barhoum stated that the leaked report in *Al-Majd* convinced the organisation that 'there was a plan approved by the Americans to destroy the political choice' and that rather than instituting a coup the organisation actually pre-empted one (*Vanity Fair*, April 2008).

Following Hamas' takeover of Gaza, Mahmoud Abbas declared a state of emergency, dissolved the unity government and in its place instituted a twelve-man cabinet comprised primarily of technocrats and political independents (*New York Times*, 17 June 2007). The office of prime minister was handed to Saalam Fayyad, an American educated ex-World Bank economist. Abbas also issued decrees outlawing Hamas' military wing and suspended clauses in the Palestinian basic law which required Parliamentary approval of any new government (*New York Times*, 17 June 2007). Hamas dismissed the new government as illegitimate and accused Abbas of taking part in a 'conspiracy against the Palestinian people' that 'serves Israel and the United States' (*New York Times*, 17 June 2007).

In the days following the Hamas takeover of Gaza, Israel and Egypt tightened their blockade of the territory by closing the main crossing points. A United Nations (2007) report released six months later revealed that the increased restrictions had led to 'unprecedented poverty' with the closure of 90 per cent of all industrial establishments, and that the proportion of Gazans reliant on humanitarian aid had risen to 80 per cent of the population. The report also highlighted severe food, fuel, and water shortages and a rapid deterioration in medical care as hospitals were unable to import spare parts for diagnostic equipment and patients were prevented from leaving Gaza in order to receive treatment for life-threatening illnesses. Amnesty International (2008b) later reported that more than 50 Palestinians had died in the following year, after being refused permission to leave the territory for medical treatment. Israel has argued that it no longer occupies Gaza and has designated the area a 'hostile territory' (*New York Times*, 19 September 2007). Israel further argued that the blockade was legal under international law,[53] was necessary to prevent the smuggling of weapons which are used by Hamas to attack Israeli towns, and carried out with respect to its obligations under international humanitarian law:

> Israel had hoped that the disengagement plan would serve as a springboard towards more positive relations with its neighbors in Gaza. Unfortunately, the opposite happened and the Hamas regime, a terrorist regime, seized control of Gaza and stepped up its attacks on civilian targets in Israel proper, in communities and towns adjacent to the Gaza Strip. So Israel, in response to these attacks on its civilians, undertook a number of measures. And one of these measures was the imposition of economic sanctions against the Hamas regime in Gaza ... Basically this is a tool to exert economic pressure on a problematic regime. This is not an act of collective punishment. Rather, again, this is a legitimate tool that is used under international law to exert pressure on a regime such as the Hamas regime, which is a terrorist regime. (Israeli Ministry of Foreign Affairs, 2010)

However Conal Urquhart, citing remarks from Dov Weisglass, an advisor to Prime Minister Olmert, suggested that the blockade had a different purpose in that it was designed to either force Hamas to accept Israeli preconditions for negotiations or lead to the implosion of their administration in Gaza:

> Israel's policy was summed up by Dov Weisglass, an adviser to Ehud Olmert, the Israeli Prime Minister, earlier this year. 'The idea is to put the Palestinians on a diet, but not to make them die of hunger,' he said. The hunger pangs are supposed to encourage the Palestinians to force Hamas to change its attitude towards Israel or force Hamas out of government. (*Observer*, 16 April 2006)

International human rights groups have contested many of the Israeli arguments regarding the blockade. Organisations such as Amnesty International (2008a) and Human Rights Watch (2008b) have argued that Israel is still the occupying power in Gaza and that its blockade constitutes collective punishment and is therefore also a violation of international law.

Meanwhile the peace process, which had appeared moribund with the failure to move ahead with the timetable laid out in President Bush's 'Road Map', was seemingly revived once more when the American leader invited representatives from more than 40 countries to a peace conference in Annapolis on 27 November 2007. Whilst delegates from Japan and the Vatican City were present, notable in their absence were the winners of the 2006 Palestinian legislative elections, Hamas, who were shunned by the Americans. The organisation itself dismissed the talks, with spokesman Fawzi Barhoum stating: 'President Abbas went there alone; there is no mandate from the Palestinians inside or outside Palestine' (BBC Online, 28 November 2007). Barhoum's comment pointed to a key problem with the conference in that two of the key participants (Olmert and Abbas) lacked the support base and political capital to achieve a deal, even if they had been determined to, which many doubted. Olmert's approval ratings were very low, partly as a result of the criticism he received from the Winograd Report into the conduct of the 2006 Lebanon War, and because of a series of corruption scandals. Abbas could not be seen as a credible figure who could deliver the entire Palestinian polity. The talks themselves failed to produce anything beyond a succession of photo calls and a vaguely worded statement committing the two parties to seeking a two-state solution based on the 'Road Map'.

Progress on the key final status issues was non-existent. This was seen as very problematic by Palestinians because reports in the Israeli press suggested that illegal settlement building was continuing across the occupied West Bank in contravention of promises made to American officials.[54] For Palestinians the concept of negotiating 'land for peace' whilst the Israelis continue to appropriate more of their land for settlement building is fundamentally contradictory. Or as Avi Shlaim has put it, 'It's like two men negotiating the division of a pizza while one continues to gobble it up' (*Guardian*, 3 February 2010).

THE ISRAEL–HAMAS CEASEFIRE

Meanwhile, throughout 2007 and into 2008 Israelis and many more Palestinians continued to die as the violence between the two sides ground on. Israel continued to blockade and bombard Gaza with heavy artillery and missile strikes whilst Palestinian groups continued to launch rockets into Israel. In the West Bank the violence was less pronounced but nevertheless an average of seven Palestinians a month were killed by IDF forces during 2007 (B'Tselem, 2010a). Eventually, on 19 June 2008, a six-month Egyptian-mediated ceasefire was agreed between Israel and Hamas. The two years between the capture of Gilad Shalit in June 2006 and the 2008 ceasefire saw 47 Israelis (four minors) and 1,288 Palestinians (239 minors) die in violent incidents (B'Tselem, 2010a). During the period the humanitarian conditions in Gaza had deteriorated markedly, with a UN official allegedly claiming that acute malnutrition in Gaza was now at a level seen in the poorest nations in the southern Sahara, with more than half of all Palestinian families eating only one meal a day (*Washington Post*, 8 January 2009). Conditions in Gaza would have been even more severe had it not been for the establishment of hundreds of tunnels beneath the border between Gaza and Egypt. These were reportedly used to bring in food, fuel, white goods, livestock and weapons.

The exact terms of the ceasefire were difficult to confirm because no text was produced and no enforcement mechanism was put in place. However, the International Crisis Group reported after interviews with the Egyptian interlocutors that the key terms included a cessation of rocket fire from Gaza in exchange for an ending of Israeli attacks on Gaza and the lifting of the blockade:

According to Egyptian sources involved in the process, it provided for an immediate cessation of hostile activities; a limited increase in the amount of goods entering Gaza after three days; and, after ten days, the opening of the crossings for all products except materials used in the manufacture of projectiles and explosives. After three weeks, the two sides were to commence negotiations for a prisoner exchange and the opening of the Rafah crossing. (International Crisis Group, 2009: 3)

The former American president Jimmy Carter, who had been party to the negotiations, stated that Hamas had originally wanted 'a comprehensive cease-fire in both the West Bank and Gaza' but 'the Israelis refused to discuss anything other than Gaza' (*Washington Post*, 8 January 2009). The ceasefire was opposed by senior political figures in Israel, including Binyamin Netanyahu who argued 'This is not a relaxation, it's an Israeli agreement to the rearming of Hamas' (*Washington Times*, 20 June 2008). A later report in the Israeli press also claimed that during the ceasefire negotiations the Israeli defence minister, Ehud Barak, began an intensive phase of intelligence gathering in order to prepare the 'blueprint' for what became Operation Cast Lead, the attack on Gaza between December 2008 and January 2009 (*Ha'aretz*, 27 December 2008).

Figures from the Israeli Intelligence and Terrorism Information Center (2009), which is close to Israeli intelligence, indicated that between July and the end of October the incidence of rocket and mortar fire from Gaza decreased by 98.4 per cent, from an average of 414 attacks a month in the first six months of 2008 to an average of just over seven a month. The Center (2008) also noted that the Palestinian attacks which continued were not carried out by Hamas but by Palestinian Islamic Jihad and Fatah. The Israeli Ministry of Foreign Affairs (2008) stated that some of these attacks were 'in response' to the killing of Palestinian faction members in the West Bank. The Ministry (2008) also claimed that 'on several occasions, Hamas members ... arrested Fatah operatives who were involved in firing at Israel and confiscated their arms'. According to former US president Carter, Israel increased the amount of goods let into Gaza but only to about 20 per cent of pre-blockade levels. This led to complaints from Hamas leaders in Gaza that Israel was not keeping its side of the bargain. In July 2008 Hamas spokesman Fawzi Barhoum stated that 'easing restrictions on Gaza crossings is going very slow and the population doesn't feel that there is basically a real truce and a normal life' (Xinhua News Agency, 20 July 2008).

According to the International Crisis Group (2009) Israeli officials accused Hamas of continuing to import arms into Gaza which they claimed was a breach of the ceasefire agreements, though this was contested by the Egyptian mediators who denied that this formed part of the terms of the truce (International Crisis Group, 2009). Israeli officials also admitted that they had no intention of opening the crossings fully and that they anticipated that this would create a bone of contention with Hamas (International Crisis Group, 2009). Another area of dispute concerned the captured Israeli soldier Gilad Shalit. Israeli officials argued that opening the crossings was conditional on the return of Shalit, though Hamas argued that this had not been part of the ceasefire agreement (International Crisis Group, 2009). The latter view appeared to be supported by the fact that Gilad Shalit's parents had complained that the Israeli government had not made the soldier's return part of the ceasefire agreement (*Ha'aretz*, 21 June 2008). In November the truce came under strain when Israel killed six members of Hamas' military wing and injured several others during an incursion into Gaza. Israel claimed that the Hamas members were digging a tunnel that was intended to reach across the border in order to abduct more Israeli soldiers. This was denied by Hamas who claimed that the tunnel was purely defensive. According to Dr Robert Pastor, a professor at American University and senior advisor to the Carter Center, an IDF official had also confirmed that the tunnel was defensive (*Huffington Post*, 9 January 2009). The killings were seen by Hamas as a 'massive breach of the truce' and were almost immediately followed by the organisation firing 35 rockets into southern Israel (*Guardian*, 5 November 2008). Following this rupture in the ceasefire Israel moved to close all of the crossings into Gaza preventing goods entering or leaving the territory including UN food and medical aid and forcing Gaza's sole power plant to shut down (Al Jazeera, 17 November 2008). Palestinian groups in Gaza resumed periodic exchanges of fire with Israeli troops across the border and restarted firing rockets into Israel, whilst the IDF resumed rocket and artillery attacks on Gaza killing a further eleven Palestinians in the period leading up to the official end of the ceasefire on 19 December 2008.

Meanwhile, in Israel the corruption scandals that had been dogging Ehud Olmert for months finally forced him to announce his resignation at the end of July 2008. Seven weeks later his Kadima Party voted to replace him with the former foreign minister Tzipi Livni. Under Israeli law Livni had six weeks to try to form a new coalition but was unable to piece together a working majority.

Livni's aides claimed talks with her potential coalition partners, the right-wing religious parties, floundered on two issues – her refusal to rule out possible negotiations on East Jerusalem and her unwillingness to agree to large increases in state funding to ultra-orthodox Jewish families (*The Times*, 27 October 2008). Livni's failure to form a coalition meant that Olmert stayed on as a caretaker prime minister until new national elections which were scheduled for 10 February 2010. The United States also saw a political upheaval in late 2004 with the election of the Democratic candidate Barack Obama. The Palestinians welcomed the end of the Bush administration, which was widely seen as the most pro-Israel in American history, and hoped that the Obama adminis-tration would be more even-handed in its dealing with the conflict. However they were not overly optimistic since in the pre-election period Obama had stated that his 'position on Hamas is indistin-guishable from the position of Hillary Clinton or John McCain' and that he favoured boycotting the organisation until they agreed to the three pre-conditions set by Israel (*The Atlantic*, 12 May 2008).

As the clock ticked down to the expiring of the truce on 19 December 2008 a number of attempts were made to renew the ceasefire. Jimmy Carter travelled to Damascus to meet Hamas officials who indicated that they would be willing to renew the ceasefire provided the crossings were opened. Carter claims that these terms were put to Israeli officials who counter-proposed that '15 percent of normal supplies might be possible if Hamas first stopped all rocket fire for 48 hours'. These terms were rejected by Hamas (*Washington Post*, 8 January 2009). Omar Suleiman, the Egyptian mediator who negotiated the 19 June ceasefire, was also involved in trying to extend the truce. According to the American historian and journalist, Gareth Porter, the interlocutor met with Hamas officials who put forward a new proposal on 14 December 2008:

> Contrary to Israel's argument that it was forced to launch its air and ground offensive against Gaza in order to stop the firing of rockets into its territory, Hamas proposed in mid-December to return to the original Hamas-Israel ceasefire arrangement, according to a U.S.-based source who has been briefed on the proposal. The proposal to renew the ceasefire was presented by a high-level Hamas delegation to Egyptian Minister of Intelligence Omar Suleiman at a meeting in Cairo Dec. 14. The delegation, said to have included Moussa Abu Marzouk, the second-ranking

official in the Hamas political bureau in Damascus, told Suleiman that Hamas was prepared to stop all rocket attacks against Israel if the Israelis would open up the Gaza border crossings and pledge not to launch attacks in Gaza. The Hamas officials insisted that Israel not be allowed to close or reduce commercial traffic through border crossings for political purposes, as it had done during the six-month lull, according to the source. They asked Suleiman, who had served as mediator between Israel and Hamas in negotiating the original six-month Gaza ceasefire last spring, to 'put pressure' on Israel to take the ceasefire proposal seriously. Suleiman said he could not pressure Israel but could only make the suggestion to Israeli officials. It could not be learned, however, whether Israel explicitly rejected the Hamas proposal or simply refused to respond to Egypt. (Inter Press Service, 9 January 2009)

A report from the International Crisis Group (2009) suggested that a deep divide separated Israeli and Palestinian expectations of any renewed ceasefire. It also stated that Hamas were under pressure both from the civilian population in Gaza and other Palestinian armed factions for having achieved so little in exchange for suspending armed 'resistance':

In the run-up to 19 December, both parties expressed interest in prolonging the ceasefire, albeit each on its preferred terms. For Israel, this implied a definitive and unconditional cessation of rocket fire and a means to halt weapons smuggling; for Hamas, it meant opening the crossings with Israel and Egypt. As the date approached, senior Hamas leaders increasingly made clear that, faced with the alternative between 'starvation and fighting', they would choose the latter, an unsubtle indication that they would intensify rocket fire in an attempt to force Israel to relax the siege. Politically, they appear to have surmised that they had more to gain by military escalation than by facing the anger of ordinary, impoverished Gazans, and a substantial constituency believed the Islamist movement had gained nothing in return for stepping back from its raison d'être, resistance. Hamas was not the only party to make this calculation; a consensus among factions – including Islamic Jihad, Popular Front for the Liberation of Palestine and the Al-Aqsa Martyrs' Brigades – opposed extending the ceasefire. (International Crisis Group, 2009: 3–4)

On 19 December 2008 Hamas indicated that they would not be renewing the ceasefire and accused Israel of not honouring its key commitments under the truce – opening the crossings and refraining from military actions in Gaza (*Ha'aretz*, 19 December 2008). According to Palestinian sources quoted in the Israeli press the organisation was still keen to renew the truce but only on the condition that the crossings were opened and Israel refrained from further attacks on Gaza (*Ha'aretz*, 19 December 2008). The source also claimed that the organisation wanted to extend the truce to Gaza (*Ha'aretz*, 19 December 2008). Israel rejected these terms, and the two candidates in the upcoming national elections, Binyamin Netanyahu and Tzipi Livni, both vowed to 'topple' Hamas if elected in February (BBC Online, 22 December 2008).

On 23 December Hamas again stated that they would return to the truce if the crossings were opened and Israel refrained from military action in Gaza (Ynetnews.com, 23 December 2008). On the same day, the Associated Press reported that Israeli leaders had approved 'a large-scale military operation to stop the rocket fire' but had 'not set a date, concerned about heavy casualties on both sides' (23 December 2008). Whilst the Israeli government didn't want to agree to Hamas' terms for a ceasefire, dissenting opinions which challenged this approach did appear in the Israeli press. Writing in the *Jerusalem Post* Larry Derfner argued that Israel's strategy of blockading the territory had been a 'huge mistake borne of arrogance and blindness' which had been designed to 'make life for Gazan civilians so miserable that they turn Hamas out and bring in new leaders who will agree to leave Sderot alone'. He stated that if Israel rejected Hamas' ceasefire offer then the 'principal blame for the [coming] war will lie with us':

Hamas is offering Israel a cease-fire if Israel lifts the siege on Gaza – and Israel should take it. It would have been nice if we had been the ones to make the offer. Then we, not Hamas, would have been the ones calling the shots. But apparently we're too full of ourselves to admit that we, too, are up a tree, so it's Hamas, not us, that's putting out the ladder for us both to climb down and avoid a new, terrible Middle East war. The way out of such a war is for Israel to lift the blockade – to let trucks, ships and planes pass to and from Gaza – and, in return, for Hamas and the other Gazan factions to stop firing rockets at Israeli border towns. They don't bother us, we don't bother them – that's the idea. (*Jerusalem Post*, 24 December 2008)

On 25 December the Israeli prime minister Ehud Olmert warned Hamas via the Arabic-language satellite channel Al Arabiya that unless it stopped rocket attacks from Gaza it would face a broad military offensive: 'I am telling them now, it may be the last minute, I'm telling them stop it. We are stronger. I didn't come here to declare war, but Hamas must be stopped – that is the way it is going to be. I will not hesitate to use Israel's might to strike Hamas and [Islamic] jihad' (*Scotsman*, 26 December 2008). The news report also claimed that the foreign minister Tzipi Livni, who had been in Cairo to discuss a possible re-instatement of the ceasefire, had now 'dismissed that option in favour of military tactics'. Livni had pointed to the continued rocket fire from Gaza, which had increased to average of 21 missiles a day in the period after the end of the ceasefire on the 19th (Intelligence and Terrorism Information Center, 2009), and stated that 'enough is enough. When there's shooting, there's a response. Any state would react that way' (*Scotsman*, 26 December 2008).

THE 2008/09 GAZA WAR

On 27 December 2008 at 11.30 a.m. Israel launched a series of attacks across Gaza using F-16 fighter jets, apache helicopters and unmanned drones. The timing was severely criticised as its most intense phase coincided with the time that children were released from school and the streets were inevitably very busy (Amnesty International, 2008b). Israel also sealed off the entry points to Gaza preventing access for journalists, humanitarian aid workers and human rights monitors. On the first day alone at least 225 Gazans were killed and more than 700 injured, with reports indicating that 'children on their way home from school and policemen parading for a graduation ceremony were the principal victims' (*The Times*, 28 December 2010). The attacks, which according to Al Arabiya (27 December 2008) produced the highest one day death toll in 60 years of conflict between Israelis and Palestinians, led to immediate calls for a ceasefire from the European Union and a condemnation of Israel for its use of 'disproportionate force'. The EU also urged the 'reopening of all checkpoints and the immediate resumption of fuel and humanitarian aid deliveries' (*European Jewish Press*, 28 December 2008). However, both the United States and Great Britain refused to call for a ceasefire and condemned Hamas whilst urging Israel to try to avoid civilian casualties (*The Times*, 28 December 2008). Over the next 21 days Israel attacked large areas of Gaza, targeting the parliament building, the ministries of Foreign Affairs, Labour, Housing and Construction, Finance and Justice, UN food and medicine compounds, civilian apartment blocks, a university, television stations, newspaper offices, a prison, police stations, mosques, schools, kindergartens, hospitals, ambulances, water treatment plants, water wells, sewage works, factories, markets, workshops, food processing plants, orchards, a fish farm, agricultural crops, farm animals and greenhouses (Amnesty International, 2009; United Nations, 2009a). On 5 January, two days after Israeli troops began a ground invasion, the head of the UN relief agency in Gaza, John Ging, described the situation in Gaza as 'inhuman' and stated that 'the whole infrastructure of the future state of Palestine is being destroyed' (*Guardian*, 5 January 2009). A report in the Israeli media later claimed that 15 per cent of all the buildings in Gaza had either 'collapsed or were completely destroyed' during the war (Ynet.com, 18 January 2009). Other media accounts gave differing accounts of the scale of destruction. Patrick Coburn writing in the *Independent* (20 January 2009) gave an estimate of 20,000 homes 'somewhat damaged' and 4,000 destroyed, whilst a later report from Amnesty International (2009) gave a figure of 3,000 homes destroyed and 20,000 damaged. During the war, armed Palestinian groups including Hamas continued to fire rockets into Israel. According to the Israeli authorities 571 rockets and 205 mortars landed in Israel (Israeli Ministry of Foreign Affairs, 2009a). The rockets which struck Israel included the Chinese-manufactured WS-1E which has a range of more than 40 km and allowed Palestinian groups to hit cities such as Ashdod, Beersheba and Gedera for the first time (Globalsecurity, 2009). Damage in Israel was much less extensive than that seen in Gaza, with reports indicating that 'several civilian homes and other structures' were 'damaged' and one was completely destroyed (Amnesty International, 2009: 66).

There was also a great imbalance in the scale of casualties experienced by both sides. Figures supplied by the Israeli authorities indicated that during the 22-day conflict three civilians were killed and four were 'severely wounded' (Israeli Ministry of Foreign Affairs, 2009a). Ten Israeli soldiers were also killed, four of whom died in 'friendly fire' incidents, whilst 'more than a hundred' were wounded, one critically and 20 'moderately to seriously' (B'Tselem, 2009b). The scale, and particularly the composition of Palestinian casualties, was subject to competing accounts. The total number of Palestinian dead was variously estimated at 1,166 by the IDF (*Jerusalem Post*, 26 March 2009), 1,385 by B'Tselem (2009b) and

1,415 by the Palestinian Centre for Human Rights (2009). Child
fatalities (under 18 years) were estimated by B'Tselem (2009b) as 318
whilst the Palestinian Centre for Human Rights (2009) put forward
a figure of 313. The IDF claimed that 89 non-combatants under the
age of 16 were killed (*Jerusalem Post*, 26 March 2009). B'Tselem
(2009c) has taken issue with the IDF's low estimate for children and
civilians killed in the conflict and has noted that the IDF has refused
to provide lists of dead. In contrast the organisation claims to have
both birth and death certificates for the 'vast majority' of those it
has classified as dead minors (B'Tselem, 2009c). The proportion of
Palestinians killed who should be classified as non-combatants is
also contested. The IDF has claimed that only 295 of the 1,166 it
alleges died were protected civilians, and that 709 were identified
as 'Hamas terror operatives' with a further 162 males aged 16–50
whose status could not be determined (*Jerusalem Post*, 26 March
2009). The Palestinian Centre for Human Rights (2009) claimed
that of its estimate of 1,415 total dead, 1,185 were civilians and 230
were combatants. B'Tselem has claimed that out of its estimate of
1,385 dead, 762 were civilians, 330 were combatants, 36 had a role
which could not be identified and 248 were police officers whose
status under international law could not be determined. The legal
standing of the 248 police officers who were killed in a matter of
minutes in near simultaneous strikes on the first day of the war has
aroused great controversy. Israel has argued that the police officers
had forfeited their protected status under international law based on
three factors. Firstly, that the 'overwhelming majority' of the police
officers were also members of the Hamas armed wing. Secondly,
that the police force had been incorporated into the armed forces
of the Gaza authority and were thus not 'solely' a civilian force;
and thirdly, that they 'fulfilled combat functions in the course of
the armed conflict':

> There is evidence that an overwhelming majority of the police
> forces were also members of the Hamas military wing or activists
> of Hamas or other terrorist organizations. More than nine out of
> every ten alleged 'civilian police' were found to be armed terrorist
> activists and combatants directly engaged in hostilities against
> Israel. The internal security services have been and continue to
> be a cadre of terrorist operatives armed with a variety of heavy
> weapons including anti-tank missile launchers, with standing
> orders to fight Israeli forces. Under the Law of Armed Conflict,

Israel is permitted to target such forces and their bases of operation. (Israeli Ministry of Foreign Affairs, 2009b)

However, all three parts of this argument have been challenged in the 575-page United Nations report on the conflict which was produced by the South African judge Richard Goldstone, who had previously served as the chief prosecutor of the United Nations International Criminal Tribunals for the former Yugoslavia and Rwanda. The Goldstone report stated that there was 'insufficient information to conclude that the Gaza police as a whole had been "incorporated" into the armed forces of the Gaza authorities' (United Nations, 2009a: 108). It also argued that the policemen killed on 27 December 2008 'cannot be said to have been taking a direct part in hostilities' and thus they 'did not lose their civilian immunity from direct attack as civilians on this ground' (United Nations, 2009a: 110). Finally Judge Goldstone argued that although there may have been individual members of the police force who were also members of Hamas' military wing, and Israel had failed to establish that large numbers were, 'this did not deprive the whole police force of its status as a civilian law-enforcement agency' and that to target the police force as a whole on this basis failed to strike a balance between military necessity and protecting civilian life and was therefore a breach of international law (United Nations, 2009a: 111).

Israel has argued that it only undertook military operations after exhausting all other avenues for stopping the rocket attacks on its civilian population. However, Avi Shlaim has suggested that the decision to go to war, and its timing, was driven by a different set of strategic calculations:

The declared aim of the war is to weaken Hamas and to intensify the pressure until its leaders agreed to a new ceasefire on Israel's terms. The undeclared aim is to ensure that the Palestinians in Gaza are seen by the world simply as a humanitarian problem and thus to derail their struggle for independence and statehood. The timing of the war was determined by political expediency. A general election in Israel is scheduled for 10 February 2009; as it approaches, all the main contenders are looking for an opportunity to prove their toughness. The army's commanders had been eager to deliver a crushing blow to Hamas in order to remove the stain left on their reputation by the failure of the war against Hizbollah in Lebanon in July-August 2006. Israel's cynical leaders could also count on the apathy and impotence of the pro-western Arab regimes and on blind support from President Bush in the twilight of his term in the White House. Bush readily obliged by putting all the blame for the crisis on Hamas, vetoing proposals at the United Nations Security Council for an immediate ceasefire, and issuing Israel with a free pass to mount a ground invasion of Gaza. (Shlaim, 2009)

Israel has maintained that its forces obeyed international law during the 2008/09 Gaza war. It has also argued that it was entitled to attack Gaza based on Article 51 of the UN Charter, the right to self-defence, and that an attack against the 'Hamas terror organisation' was 'urgent' because it was importing increasingly sophisticated weapons to use against Israeli civilians (Israeli Ministry of Foreign Affairs, 2009b). Israel argued that its key aim was to prevent rocket attacks on Israeli civilians and that it only launched the war 'after exhausting all other alternatives'. During the conflict Israel insisted that 'it made extensive efforts to comply' with international law particularly in relation to issues of proportionality and distinction (between military targets and civilians) and that wherever possible it employed 'pinpoint surgical aerial strikes using precision guided munitions'. In order to comply with international law the IDF claimed to have 'carefully checked and cross-checked targets to make sure they were being used for combat or terrorist activities and not solely for civilian use'. Israel also stated that they made extensive efforts to warn civilians of impending attacks so that they could evacuate out of harm's way:

> The IDF not only implemented a range of precautions related to targeting and munitions, but also used an extensive system of graduated warnings to civilians, including both general advance warnings through media broadcasts and widespread leafleting, regional warnings to alert civilians to leave specific areas before IDF operations commenced, and specific warnings to civilians in or near military targets, through telephone calls and warning shots with light weapons. These warnings were frequently effective, as aerial surveillance was often able to confirm the resulting evacuation of numerous civilians prior to an attack by the IDF. (Israeli Ministry of Foreign Affairs, 2009b)

Although Israel admitted using white phosphorous they stated that it 'was only fired at open unpopulated areas and only used for marking and signalling'. They also maintained that the IDF 'went out of its way to try and get humanitarian relief to Palestinian civilians' and that although extensive damage was caused to residential property 'much of the damage resulted from the necessities of war and Hamas's mode of operating'. Israel made a series of accusations against Hamas. It argued that the organisation used 'human shields' including children, to prevent attacks against launch sites and other military targets. It also claimed that the organisations located forces in civilian areas and fought from civilian buildings. It also accused the organisation of using 'ambulances and medical facilities as a cover for terrorist operations'. Finally Israel stated that it had set up robust systems for investigating any wrongdoing by its forces. Similar arguments regarding Israeli and Hamas conduct in the war were made by the British colonel Richard Kemp, the former commander of British forces in Afghanistan, when he testified before the United Nations Human Rights Council on the Goldstone report:

> During Operation Cast Lead, the Israeli Defence Forces did more to safeguard the rights of civilians in a combat zone than any other army in the history of warfare. Israel did so while facing an enemy that deliberately positioned its military capability behind the human shield of the civilian population .... The truth is that the IDF took extraordinary measures to give Gaza civilians notice of targeted areas, dropping over 2 million leaflets, and making over 100,000 phone calls. Many missions that could have taken out Hamas military capability were aborted to prevent civilian casualties. During the conflict, the IDF allowed huge amounts of humanitarian aid into Gaza. To deliver aid virtually into your enemy's hands is, to the military tactician, normally quite unthinkable. But the IDF took on those risks ... More than anything, the civilian casualties were a consequence of Hamas' way of fighting. Hamas deliberately tried to sacrifice their own civilians ... Israel had no choice apart from defending its people, to stop Hamas from attacking them with rockets. (*Jerusalem Post*, 31 January 2010)

These arguments have been criticised by the United Nations, human rights groups and international lawyers. They also raise the question of where the recipients of the 100,000 phone calls and the millions of leaflets would all go in a place as small as Gaza. United Nations officials stated during the conflict that insufficient humanitarian aid was getting through to the Gazan population, noting that 500,000 people lacked access to water (United Nations, 2009b). The organisation also noted that all aid had to be completely suspended for a period after Israeli forces killed a UN driver delivering humanitarian supplies (United Nations, 2009b). The arguments that Israel had no choice but to attack Gaza, that it was legally entitled to do so under Article 51 of the United Nations Charter, and that its actions conformed to international humanitarian law, were challenged by a group of 27 human rights lawyers and academics in a letter sent to the *Sunday Times* (11 January 2009). In it they stated that they 'categorically reject[ed]' Israel's contention that the attack on Gaza could be construed as 'an act of "self-defence" as recognised by Article 51'. This, they stated, was because of two factors. Firstly, they argued that the rocket attacks 'do not, in terms of scale and effect amount to an armed attack entitling Israel to rely on self-defence'. Secondly, they note that under 'international law self-defence is an act of last resort' and that since Israel had refused to renew the truce with Hamas it could not argue that it had exhausted all the other available options. This meant, the lawyers and academics said, that 'Israel's actions amount to aggression, not self-defence'. They also stated that 'its invasion and bombardment of Gaza amounts to collective punishment of Gaza's 1.5m inhabitants contrary to international humanitarian and human rights law' and that 'the blockade of humanitarian relief, the destruction of civilian infrastructure, and preventing access to basic necessities such as food and fuel, are prima facie war crimes'.

The arguments put forward by Israel and Colonel Kemp, that Israel had chosen its targets very carefully in order to minimise harm to civilians, and that the warnings given to Gaza residents to evacuate their houses meant that they had complied with international law, were critiqued in an article by Eyal Weizman on what he describes as the evolving pursuit of 'lawfare' (Weizman, 2009). Weizman suggests 'lawfare' can be seen in the way 'military lawyers in the midst of a campaign "legally [condition] the battlefield" by poring over target-maps and informing soldiers in what way they are entitled to kill civilians'. In this way, he argues, 'international humanitarian law becomes the ethical vocabulary for marking legitimate power and justifiable death'. In the case of the Gaza conflict Weizman points to the work of the International Law Division (IDL) in the Israeli Military Advocate's office and a statement from one of its employees that 'our goal was not to fetter the army, but to give it the tools to win in a lawful manner'. In the Gaza war the IDL were heavily involved in providing legal justifications for individual attacks such as the mass killing of policemen on the first day of the conflict (*Ha'aretz*, 7 May 2010). Weizman argues that the IDL also sought ways to provide legal cover for Israeli use of the 'Dahiyah Doctrine' in which the IDF would commit disproportionate attacks intended to devastate the civilian infrastructure. The terms of this doctrine had been laid out in an article that appeared in the Israeli press three months before the Gaza war, entitled 'IDF plans to use disproportionate force in next war':

> In an interview Friday with the daily Yedioth Ahronoth, Eisenkot presented his 'Dahiyah Doctrine,' under which the IDF would expand its destructive power beyond what it demonstrated two years ago against the Beirut suburb of Dahiyah, considered a Hezbullah stronghold. 'We will wield disproportionate power against every village from which shots are fired on Israel, and cause immense damage and destruction. From our perspective, these are military bases,' he said. 'This isn't a suggestion. This is a plan that has already been authorized.' Colonel (Res.) Gabriel Siboni recently authored a report through Tel Aviv University's Institute for National Security Studies backing Eisenkot's statements. The answer to rocket and missile threats from Syria, Lebanon and the Gaza Strip, he believes, is 'a disproportionate strike at the heart of the enemy's weak spot, in which efforts to hurt launch capability are secondary. As soon as the conflict breaks out, the IDF will have to operate in a rapid, determined, powerful and disproportionate way against the enemy's actions.' 'This strike has to be carried out as quickly as possible, through prioritizing strikes at its assets, rather than chasing after launch sites. Such a response is likely to be remembered by decision makers in Syria and Lebanon for many years, thus deepening deterrence,' he said. (*Ha'aretz*, 5 October 2010)

In order to provide legal cover for such attacks Weizman notes that the IDF employed warning devices in Gaza such as dropping bombs without explosives on houses (the 'knock on the door'), as a warning to residents to evacuate, just before destroying them in missile strikes. It also involved telephoning residents to warn them that a missile strike on their home was imminent. Such tactics could then be used to argue that any residents who were left behind were effectively 're-defined' as 'combatants' and/or 'human shields' and that their houses were now legitimate military targets:

An officer at the international-law division explained to Yotam Feldman [*Ha'aretz* journalist] the logic of these warnings: '*The people who go into a house despite a warning do not have to be taken into account in terms of injury to civilians, because they are voluntary human shields. From the legal point of view,* [once warned] *I do not have to show consideration for them. In the case of people who return to their home in order to protect it, they are taking part in the fighting.*' By giving residents the choice between death and expulsion, this military interpretation of international humanitarian law shifted people between legal designations – one phone-call turns 'non-combatants' into 'human shields', who can thus be defined as 'taking direct part in hostilities' and shot as 'legitimate targets'. The Israeli military's ability to warn people in Gaza about the impending destruction of their homes has also allowed it to define most buildings in Gaza as legitimate targets. [italics in original] (Weizman, 2009)

Reports from leading human rights groups including Amnesty International and Human Rights Watch were very critical of the way the war had been conducted by Israel and the Palestinians. Both organisations accused Palestinian groups of targeting civilians which is a war crime. Amnesty notes that Palestinian groups give a number of rationales for their attacks. These include the argument that they are a response to killings in Gaza or the West Bank, that they are a 'cry of protest' to the world over the occupation, that they are rarely lethal and 'that their main aim is to "disturb" life in Israel so long as Israel does not allow Palestinians to have a normal life', or that they are the only weapons available to them because they lack the precision-guided munitions used by the Israelis (Amnesty International, 2009: 73–4). However, Amnesty has stated that such arguments have no basis in international law:

All these arguments are inadmissible under international humanitarian law. Whether or not attacks actually result in civilian casualties, they are in violation of international law, which also prohibits attacks aimed at spreading terror among the civilian population. The patterns of attacks and statements by members and leaders of Palestinian groups also indicate that they have no qualms about launching attacks against civilians and that they in fact carry out such attacks intending to kill and injure Israeli civilians. Such attacks constitute war crimes. (Amnesty International, 2009: 74)

Both groups also accused Palestinian fighters of endangering Palestinian civilians by firing rockets from residential areas. Amnesty cited an occasion when a rocket was launched from a 'small patch of empty land some 50m from residential houses' (2009: 74). However Amnesty also claimed that it had 'seen no evidence that rockets were launched from residential houses or buildings while civilians were in these buildings' (2009: 75). Amnesty also refuted Israeli allegations that Palestinian groups used the civilian population as 'human shields'. The organisation stated that Israel had not provided evidence for these claims despite repeated requests. It also claimed that its own research did not find evidence of the practice:

Amnesty International, for its part, did not find evidence that Hamas or other Palestinian groups violated the laws of war to the extent repeatedly alleged by Israel. In particular, it found no evidence that Hamas or other fighters directed the movement of civilians to shield military objectives from attacks. Amnesty International delegates interviewed many Palestinians who complained about Hamas' conduct, and especially about Hamas' repression and attacks against their opponents, including killings, torture and arbitrary detentions but did not receive any accounts of Hamas fighters having used them as 'human shields'. In the cases investigated by Amnesty International of civilians killed in Israeli attacks, the deaths could not be explained as resulting from the presence of fighters shielding among civilians, as the Israel army generally contends. In all of the cases investigated by Amnesty International of families killed when their homes were bombed from the air by Israeli forces, for example, none of the houses struck was being used by armed groups for military activities. Similarly, in the cases of precision missiles or tank shells which killed civilians in their homes, no fighters were present in the houses that were struck and Amnesty International delegates found no indication that there had been any armed confrontations or other military activity in the immediate vicinity at the time of the attack. While the presence of Hamas and other fighters and weapons within civilian areas is not contested, this in itself is not conclusive evidence of intent to use civilians as 'human shields'. The presence of weapons in residential areas is likely, for instance, to be more the result of a growing gun culture in Gaza and the increasing internal tensions between Palestinian factions, which have led Hamas and Fatah, as well as some other groups, to keep weapons supplies close at hand to fight each other in recent years. (Amnesty International, 2009: 76–7)

Both Amnesty International and Human Rights Watch have argued that the majority of violations of international law during the conflict were carried out by the Israelis. A number of practices which qualify as war crimes were highlighted by both organisations. These included the indiscriminate use of heavy artillery in densely populated urban areas, the targeting of persons trying to convey civilian status using white flags, the killing of civilians with precision-guided munitions, the indiscriminate firing of white phosphorous over densely populated residential areas and the widespread and deliberate destruction of civilian infrastructure that had no military purpose. Both organisations also allege that members of the IDF used Palestinians, including Palestinian children, as 'human shields' 'including making them walk in front of armed soldiers; go into buildings to check for booby traps or gunmen; and inspect suspicious objects for explosives' (Amnesty International, 2009: 49). Similar allegations were also made by serving members of the IDF. 'Breaking the Silence' collected 54 testimonies from soldiers who served in the Gaza conflict. These stated that the Israelis did use Palestinians as 'human shields', that 'insane' firepower was employed and that 'permissive' rules of engagement enabled soldiers to 'act without moral restraint'. On its website the organisation states:

Among the 54 testimonies are stories revealing the use of 'accepted practices,' the destruction of hundreds of houses and mosques for no military purpose, the firing of phosphorous gas in the direction of populated areas, the killing of innocent victims with small arms, the destruction of private property, and most of all, a permissive atmosphere in the command structure that enabled soldiers to act without moral restrictions. The booklet compiles the testimonies of about 30 reserve and regular combat soldiers from various units that participated in the fighting. The testimonies demonstrate that the soldiers were not given directives stating the goal of the operation and, as one soldier testifies, 'there was not much said about the issue of innocent civilians.' Many soldiers said that they fought without seeing 'the enemy before their eyes.' 'You feel like an infantile little kid with a magnifying glass looking at ants, burning them,' one of the soldiers testified that 'a 20-year-old kid should not have to do these kinds of things to other people.' (Breaking the Silence, 2009)

The reports from human rights organisations appeared to anger the Israeli government. Binyamin Netanyahu's policy advisor, Ron Dermer was cited in the Israeli press as stating: 'We are going to dedicate time and manpower to combating these groups. We are not going to be sitting ducks in a pond for the human rights groups to shoot at us with impunity' (*Jerusalem Post*, 17 July 2009). Part of this counter-attack reportedly involved attempts to persuade the British, Dutch and Spanish governments to cut off funding to the organisation 'Breaking the Silence' (*Ha'aretz*, 2 August 2009). However, Human Rights Watch has alleged that the Israeli government has gone much further and accused it of attempting to discredit the organisation over its reporting of Gaza:

America's leading human rights organisation has accused Israel and its supporters of an 'organised campaign' of false allegations and misinformation, including 'extremely personal attacks' on its staff, in an attempt to discredit the group over its reports of war crimes in Gaza. Human Rights Watch (HRW) ties the campaign – which has included accusations that the group's reports on the Jewish state are written by 'anti-Israel ideologues' and that it has sought funds from Saudi Arabia – to a statement by a senior official in the Israeli prime minister's office in June pledging to 'dedicate time and manpower to combating' human rights organisations. The criticism began with Israeli pressure groups and rightwing blogs, but in recent weeks it has drawn the support of influential individuals such as Elie Wiesel, the Holocaust survivor and Nobel peace prize winner, and HRW's own founder, Robert Bernstein, who said the organisation's reports were 'helping those who wish to turn Israel into a pariah state'. He called on HRW to focus more on abuses by Arab governments. (*Guardian*, 13 November 2009)

Bernstein's accusations were made in the *New York Times* where he argued that Human Rights Watch had lost its 'critical perspective' on the Israel–Palestine conflict and used a methodology in its research which was critically flawed:

But how does Human Rights Watch know that these laws have been violated? In Gaza and elsewhere where there is no access to the battlefield or to the military and political leaders who make strategic decisions, it is extremely difficult to make definitive judgments about war crimes. Reporting often relies on witnesses whose stories cannot be verified and who may testify for political advantage or because they fear retaliation from their own rulers. (*New York Times*, 19 October 2009)

These allegations were refuted by Human Rights Watch, who argued that their methodology was robust and reliable:

It is not the case that Human Rights Watch had 'no access to the battlefield' after the Israeli operation in Gaza in January 2009. Although the Israeli government denied us access, our researchers entered Gaza via the border with Egypt and conducted extensive interviews with victims, eyewitnesses, United Nations officials, local authorities, and others. As in war zones around the world, we also visited attack sites, analyzed ballistics evidence, photographed wounds, and examined autopsy and other medical reports. (Human Rights Watch, 2009a)

2009: THE GOLDSTONE REPORT

Accusations of war crimes against Israel and Hamas were also made in the previously discussed Goldstone report. This document was more significant diplomatically than those produced by independent human rights groups because in it, Judge Goldstone recommended that the UN Security Council require both Israel and the administration in Gaza to investigate within six months the conduct of their forces during the war. If this was not completed satisfactorily Goldstone proposed that the International Criminal Court become involved. The Goldstone report accused Hamas of committing war crimes and possibly crimes against humanity. Its key offence was launching rockets into Israel. The report stated that using unguided munitions breached the 'fundamental principle of distinction' and 'where there is no intended military target and the rockets and mortars are launched into civilian areas, they constitute a deliberate attack against the civilian population' (United Nations, 2009: 365). The report also condemned internal repression by the Palestinian authorities in Gaza and the West Bank, particularly 'arbitrary arrests' and 'extra-judicial executions', and called on the Gaza authorities to release Gilad Shalit. But the report found no evidence for Israeli allegations that Hamas used the population as 'human shields' or that armed Palestinian groups 'engaged in combat in civilian dress' (United Nations, 2009a: 420).

However the report, like those produced by the major human rights groups, found that the overwhelming majority of the infringements of international law were carried out by Israel. The report claimed that Israel's blockade of Gaza constituted 'collective punishment' and was contrary to international law. It also stated that Israel had deliberately targeted civilians, tortured prisoners and employed phosphorous and flechette munitions in residential areas. It also accused Israeli forces of 'wantonly' and 'deliberately' destroying the civilian infrastructure, noting that in some cases, when strategic control of areas had been taken, D-9 armoured bulldozers were sent in to destroy residential homes, farms and agricultural land which had no military use. It concluded that Israel had engaged in 'a deliberately disproportionate attack designed to punish, humiliate and terrorize a civilian population, radically diminish its local economic capacity both to work and to provide for itself, and to force upon it an ever increasing sense of dependency and vulnerability' (United Nations, 2009a: 408).

International reactions to the conflict had varied. A number of countries were extremely critical of the Israeli attack particularly the non-aligned bloc of developing countries as well as South American and majority Muslim states. However the United States placed the blame on Hamas, and a number of other major states including Canada, Australia, Germany, Italy and the Czech Republic followed suit. The United States had used diplomatic pressure to block an attempt by the UN Security Council to pass a resolution calling for an immediate ceasefire on 3 January 2009 (*Guardian*, 4 January 2009). Press reports also indicated that American help for Israel extended beyond diplomatic support. An article from Reuters (9 January 2009) revealed that two weeks prior to the Israeli attack the United States had dispatched to Israel a 'very large quantity' of arms (5.8 million pounds of explosive weight). This delivery was said to be following on from a consignment of 'bunker buster' bombs which Israel took delivery of in early December and which were dropped on Gaza (Reuters, 9 January 2009).

In the wake of the war a major diplomatic battle broke out over the contents of the Goldstone report. Articles in the Israeli press claimed that there was concern that the report could be discussed by the United Nations Security Council and from there referred to the International Criminal Court in the Hague which might then issue arrest warrants for Israeli officials. To head off this possibility it was reported that Israel was embarking on a major 'diplomatic war':

Following the report's release, Netanyahu, Lieberman, President Shimon Peres and Defense Minister Ehud Barak will telephone many of their counterparts around the world. They will stress that the Goldstone report is one-sided, that it rewards terrorism and that it sets a precedent which will make it difficult for any country in the world to defend itself against terror. Israel's diplomatic efforts will focus on the five permanent members of the UN Security Council – the United States, Russia, China, Britain and France – but will also give priority to members of the European Union, because of their influence in the UN Human Rights Council in Geneva. The senior Israeli leaders will ask their counterparts to express disagreement with the report and to oppose any use of it as the basis for anti-Israel resolutions at other international institutions. 'It will be a long diplomatic and legal campaign,' said a senior Israeli staffer handling the Goldstone report. 'We will involve our friends around the world, especially the United States, to prevent Israel's isolation,' he said. (*Ha'aretz*, 15 September 2009)

A report in the Israeli press also claimed that pressure had been exerted on the Palestinian president Mahmoud Abbas and that Yuval Diskin, the head of the Israeli security service Sin Bet, had allegedly warned him that unless he asked for a deferral of the UN vote on the Goldstone report then 'Israel would turn the West Bank into a "second Gaza"' (*Ha'aretz*, 17 January 2010). The official Israeli response to the Goldstone document made a number of criticisms of the report. It argued that it 'ignored' Israel's 'right of self-defence', made 'unsubstantiated claims about its intent' and challenged 'Israel's democratic values and rule of law' (Israeli Ministry of Foreign Affairs, 2009c). More specifically, it argued that the mandate of the mission was one-sided in that it only examined Israeli behaviour and that officials who wrote the report were 'continuously accompanied by Hamas officials' during their visits to Gaza. It also stated that the mission had not screened out members who had 'clear political views on the issues under investigation', pointing out that one of the report's authors, the LSE academic Professor Christine Chinkin, had been a signatory of the *Sunday Times* letter (above) which had accused Israel of 'aggression not self-defence'. It also accused the report's authors of ignoring Hamas' use of 'human shields' as well as the 'deliberate terrorist strategy of operating in the heart of densely populated civilian areas which dictated the arena of battle'. The Israeli response also accused the Goldstone report of not taking into account 'Israel's extensive efforts, even in the midst of fighting, to maintain humanitarian standards'. The Israeli response also suggested that the report sought 'to absolve the Hamas of almost any wrongdoing' and objected to the fact that the word 'terrorist' was almost 'entirely absent' from the document.

The Goldstone report was passed by the United Nations Human Rights Council with 25 votes in favour, six against and five abstentions. It then was presented to the United Nations General Assembly where it passed with 114 in favour, 18 against with 44 abstentions. Despite strong lobbying from the European Jewish Congress, the European Parliament also voted to endorse the UN resolution though the vote here was much closer with 335 in favour, 267 against and 43 abstentions (*Jerusalem Post*, 3 November 2009). Richard Howitt, a spokesman for the 'Group for the Progressive Alliance of the Socialists and Democrats' in the EU Parliament who had helped draft the resolution, stated that 'International humanitarian law and international human rights law must be respected by all parties and under any circumstances in the conflict, and the EU has an obligation to protect and ensure the application of this principle' (*Jerusalem Post*, 3 November 2009). A very different reaction was taken by the United States, who voted against the resolutions passed by the two UN bodies. The United States Congress passed a resolution condemning the Goldstone report by 344 votes to 36. Resolution 687 stated that the Goldstone report 'denied the State of Israel the right to self-defence' and claimed that its findings reflected a 'pre-judged outcome'. It also argued that the 'report makes no mention of the relentless rocket and mortar attacks' by Palestinian armed groups into Israel and claims that Hamas shaped the report's findings by 'selecting and prescreening some of the witnesses'. These accusations were strongly denied by Judge Goldstone, and human rights groups were very critical of the stance taken by the United States and EU governments who refused to endorse the report. Human Rights Watch argued that this weakened the rule of law and undermined the ability to push for justice in other conflict areas such as the Congo and Darfur. Juliette de Rivero, the Geneva director of Human Rights Watch, stated that:

The US effort to dismiss the Goldstone report was downright shameful for an administration that claims to promote the rule of law and accountability for war crimes ... It was also deeply disappointing that key EU governments did not seize this valuable opportunity to demand justice for victims on both sides of the conflict. The report's detailed findings and its careful recommendations deserve support, not dismissal and silence. (Human Rights Watch, 2009)

THE SECOND NETANYAHU ADMINISTRATION

Three weeks after the end of the war Israeli voters went to the polls in new national elections. In a tightly fought contest Kadima led by Tzipi Livni emerged with 29 seats in the 120-seat Knesset. This put the party just ahead of Likud led by Binyamin Netanyahu who picked up 28 seats. However, right-wing parties had performed much better overall than those of the left, meaning that Netanyahu was in a better position to form a coalition than Livni. Labour, traditionally the key force in left-wing Israel politics and the party that had been the dominant political actor in Israel until the mid 1970s, had a disastrous election. It polled less than 10 per cent of those who voted. Other left parties, such as Meretz, did extremely badly whilst the proportion of Israel's Arab population who voted slumped. The factors behind the decline of the left in Israel's political system were subject to competing explanations from left and right. Israel Harel, a right-wing columnist, argued that Labour had lost votes because Ehud Barak lacked 'the courage to decisively defeat the terror of the Gaza Strip' during the war (*Ha'aretz*, 12 February 2009). He suggested Meretz had declined because they called for an early end to the war and accused the IDF of 'war crimes'. He also argued that the 'increase in oppositional activities among Israeli Arabs – which often exceed the bounds of legitimate expression of opinion' – had 'alienated voters from the left'. A very different explanation of the left's electoral decline was offered by Gideon Levy. Levy argued that much of its wane was due to its leader Ehud Barak's decision to declare that there was no partner for peace on the Palestinian side following the collapse of the Camp David peace process in 2000:

The Israeli left died in 2000. Since then its corpse has been lying around unburied until finally its death certificate was issued, signed, sealed and delivered on Tuesday. The hangman of 2000 was also the gravedigger of 2009: Defense Minister Ehud Barak. The man who succeeded in spreading the lie about there being no partner has reaped the fruit of his deeds in this election. The funeral was held two days ago [election day]. (*Ha'aretz*, 12 February 2009)

Robert Malley, director of the International Crisis Group and a former advisor to US president Bill Clinton, argued that what the election result highlighted was a complicated fragmentation in both Israeli and Palestinian polities which would make negotiating peace more difficult. 'In Israel, the fragmentation is across left and right, and inside the left and the right. The Palestinians are fragmented into Hamas and Fatah', argued Malley. 'That means it is structurally difficult for anyone to do anything because there is no unity of decision-making on any side. Fundamentals cannot change' (cited in O'Dwyer, 2009).

Whilst the left had a dreadful election the parties of the right enjoyed unprecedented success. One of the big winners on election night was Avigdor Lieberman's Yisrael Beytenu Party which won 15 seats making it the third largest party in the Knesset. Lieberman is a very controversial politician particularly amongst Israel's Arab minority. Fareed Zakaria, the editor of Newsweek International, notes that prior to the election Lieberman had 'proposed the effective expulsion of several hundred thousand Arab citizens by unilaterally redesignating some northern Israeli towns as parts of the Palestinian West Bank' and stripping the citizenship of 'several hundred thousand' more 'for failing to meet requirements such as loyalty oaths or mandatory military service' (*Newsweek*, 14 February 2009). Zakaria points out that even figures not associated with the Israeli left or peace camp such as the editor of the New Republic, Martin Peretz, have described Lieberman as a 'neo-fascist … a certified gangster … the Israeli equivalent of [Austria's] Jörg Haider' (cited in *Newsweek*, 14 February 2009).

On 20 February 2009 the Israeli president Shimon Peres invited Binyamin Netanyahu to try to form a coalition, and six weeks later Netanyahu succeeded in forming a government with a working majority in the Knesset. The new administration included Likud, Yisrael Beytenu, Shas, plus two smaller right-wing religious parties. Avigdor Lieberman was appointed foreign minister. Since all of the parties in the coalition were virulently opposed to key parameters of any likely peace agreement with the Palestinians, such as the division of Jerusalem or a withdrawal to the pre-1967 borders, it was widely assumed that little progress was imminent in the peace process. Nevertheless, during Prime Minister Netanyahu's first official visit to Washington in May 2009 he was pressed by Barack Obama to stop settlement building in the West Bank. During the visit Obama also reiterated his support for the creation of a Palestinian state.

On 4 June 2009 President Obama gave a major speech at Cairo University. The address was widely seen as an attempt to rebuild bridges with the Arab and Muslim populations in the Middle East who had been deeply alienated by George W. Bush's approach to the region. In his speech Obama restated his opposition to Israeli settlement building and expressed understanding for the plight of Palestinians enduring what he described as 'daily humiliations, large and small, that come with occupation' (*New York Times*, 4 June 2009). Obama pledged that Americans would 'not turn our backs on the legitimate Palestinian aspiration for dignity, opportunity and a state of their own'. Ten days later, in a speech widely seen as a response to Obama's Cairo address, Netanyahu for the first time endorsed the concept of a Palestinian state. However, Netanyahu's position was faraway from the long-standing international consensus on how to resolve the conflict embodied in the Geneva Accords. Netanyahu did not sketch out the territorial dimensions of the Palestinian state. He insisted Jerusalem remain as the unified capital of Israel and declared that all Palestinian refugees be settled in the future Palestinian state. He also stated that settlements would not be removed from the occupied territories. For Palestinians, Netanyahu's proposals were completely unacceptable. The PLO negotiator Saeb Erekat denied that Netanyahu had accepted a Palestinian state but had instead 'announced a series of conditions and qualifications that render a viable, independent and sovereign Palestinian state impossible' (*New York Times*, 14 June 2009).

In early September 2009 it was revealed that, despite American demands for a settlement freeze, the Netanyahu administration had approved the construction of hundreds of new housing units in the occupied West Bank (*The Times*, 5 September 2009). This drew condemnation from the Palestinian leaders who had been demanding a settlement freeze as a pre-condition for restarting peace negotiations. It also led to a rebuke from the Obama administration. Meanwhile the Palestinian president Mahmoud Abbas was reported to be seeking EU backing for a unilateral declaration of statehood (*Guardian*, 16 November 2009). However this had little support from the EU who were reportedly lukewarm on the idea, while America was certain to veto any move to take the proposal to the UN Security Council and Israel was completely opposed.

In March 2010 relations between America and Israel again became strained when the Israeli interior minister, Eli Yishai, announced the construction of new settlements in occupied East Jerusalem during a visit by the American vice-president Joe Biden. He condemned the move as 'precisely the kind of step that undermines the trust we need right now' (*The Times*, 9 March 2010). Later in the month it was reported that President Obama had snubbed Netanyahu during an official visit to the White House. Obama had reportedly been 'livid' over Israel's decision to announce the increase in settlement building during Biden's visit. 'The Prime Minister [Netanyauhu] leaves America disgraced, isolated and altogether weaker than when he came', the Israeli daily newspaper *Ha'aretz* commented (25 March 2010).

2010: THE ATTACK ON THE GAZA AID FLOTILLA

At the end of May 2010 the siege of Gaza was brought very dramatically to the attention of the world when Israeli commandos boarded a ship carrying international activists who were attempting to break Israel's blockade. During the operation, which was carried out in international waters, the Israeli soldiers shot and killed nine people and wounded a further 54. The ship on which the killings occurred, the *Mavi Marmara*, was part of a flotilla of eight ships which were carrying over 700 people from 36 countries. These included academics, journalists, novelists, NGO members, religious representatives and political activists. There were also elected parliamentarians from Germany, Kuwait, Israel, Ireland, Sweden, Greece, Southern Cyprus, Morocco, Yemen, Egypt and Algeria. The ships were carrying 10,000 tonnes of supplies for the Gaza population including medical equipment, food, textiles, construction materials and hardware such as hand tools, power generators and desalination units.

The Israeli ambassador to the United States Michael Oren defended the operation, stating that it was 'perfectly legal, perfectly humane – and very responsible' (*Daily Telegraph*, 2 June 2010). He maintained that 'Israel acted in accord with international law', adding that 'any state has the right to protect itself, certainly from a terrorist threat such as Hamas'. Oren also stated that America 'acted under similar international law when it fought the Germans and the Japanese in World War Two' (*Daily Telegraph*, 2 June 2010). In the official Israeli version of events their forces sent repeated warnings to those aboard the flotilla. These 'requested the ships to redirect toward Ashdod where they would be able to unload their aid material which would then be transferred over land after undergoing security inspections' (Israeli Ministry of Foreign Affairs, 2010). When these warnings were not heeded Israel landed soldiers on board from helicopters. When they landed they were attacked 'with live fire and light weaponry including knives and clubs' (Israeli Ministry of Foreign Affairs, 2010). Israel stated that two weapons were taken from their soldiers and used against them. In order to respond to this 'life-threatening and violent activity' it was said that naval forces first employed riot dispersal means, followed by 'live fire' (Israeli Ministry of Foreign Affairs, 2010). The Israelis also stated that following the takeover of the ship the injured were evacuated to hospital. The Israeli perspective presents their actions as wholly defensive and argues that it was those aboard the *Mavi Marmara* who initiated 'life-threatening' violence.

Those aboard the *Mavi Marmara* have argued that they refused to transfer the aid shipment to the Israelis to deliver because on two previous occasions when this occurred Israel failed to deliver the bulk of the aid. They also maintain that they told the Israeli Navy that the ship had been checked for weapons before it left Turkey and that they would be willing to submit to additional checks from a neutral body such as the United Nations or the International Committee of the Red Cross. The passengers on the *Mavi Marmara* also provide a very different account of events leading up to the killings. They stated that the Israelis first tried to board the vessel from the side using naval boats. Whilst this was occurring the Israeli forces launched stun and gas grenades and fired rubber bullets. They repelled this initial attempt to board by employing water cannon and cutting the grappling hooks that the Israeli forces had attached to their ship. Then Israeli helicopters arrived and lowered abseiling ropes in order to allow soldiers to descend onto the ship. Before soldiers could land it is said that Israeli forces starting firing rubber bullets and live ammunition, killing two people on the deck. Those on the *Mavi Marmara* point out that twelve people – including the ship's captain, one professor, three journalists, two lawyers and two MPs – all testified that Israeli forces began using live ammunition before the first soldier descended and that several of the testimonies were given in widely dispersed locations making it difficult for them to confer. Those aboard the *Mavi Marmara* admitted fighting with the Israeli troops who landed on the ship but argue that they were acting within international maritime law in trying to repel an illegal and violent assault. However, they denied using firearms and maintain that all of the guns that were taken from Israeli troops, bar one, were thrown overboard. The sole firearm that was retained was emptied of ammunition and kept as evidence that they had been attacked by armed troops. They further point out that Israel has failed to provide evidence that firearms were used against the Israeli soldiers and that it had seized all the film footage shot by those aboard the ship. After the Israeli troops took control of the ship it was alleged that they refused to provide medical care to the wounded resulting in the deaths of three of the injured, two of whom bled to death. There were also claims that many of those aboard the *Mavi Marmara* were subject to beatings following their transfer to Ashdod and that Israel has refused to return large quantities of cash and electrical equipment that it took from those on board.

The attack on the *Mavi Marmara* led to widespread international condemnation and on 2 June 2010 the United Nations Human Rights Council appointed a mission to examine what happened. The mission which was headed by Judge Karl T. Hudson-Phillips QC, a retired Judge of the International Criminal Court, released its report on 22 September 2010. The report stated that at the time of the incident there was 'overwhelming' evidence of a 'humanitarian crisis' in Gaza and that because of this the Israeli blockade was 'unlawful' (United Nations, 2010: 54). This meant that 'the action of the IDF in intercepting the Mavi Marmara in the circumstances and for the reasons given on the high sea was clearly unlawful' and that the action could not be justified 'under Article 51 of the United Nations Charter' (United Nations, 2010: 53). The report found that the *Mavi Marmara* had been subject to 'meticulous security checks' in Turkey prior to departure 'similar to those in airports before boarding' (United Nations, 2010: 21). The report stated that during the day prior to the boarding the passengers on board became aware that the Israeli forces would try to land on the ship and that 50 to 100 made plans to defend the ship. These passengers used hand tools to cut railings to use as weapons and tested the water hoses. There were also reports that just prior to the Israeli landing other passengers fashioned rudimentary weapons which the report argued confirmed its earlier finding that no weapons had been taken aboard. The report says that Israeli soldiers first tried to board using naval vessels and during these attempts employed smoke bombs, stun grenades, tear gas and paintball pellets. Plastic bullets 'may also have been used' but the mission declared itself 'not satisfied' that live ammunition was used at this stage (United Nations, 2010: 25). A few minutes later Israeli forces tried to land troops via helicopters and dropped smoke and stun grenades in order to try to clear a space for boarding. The mission 'concluded that live ammunition was used from the helicopter onto the top deck prior to the descent of the soldiers' (United Nations, 2010: 26). A fight broke out between the passengers and the first soldiers who landed which led to at least two soldiers being thrown to the bridge deck below where they were involved in struggles with more passengers. During this phase three soldiers were overpowered by passengers and taken below decks. Some passengers wanted to harm the soldiers but others ensured that they were protected and they were given medical treatment by doctors on board.

The report confirmed the account from those aboard the *Mavi Marmara* relating to the seizure and disposal of the weapons taken from Israeli soldiers. The passengers fought the soldiers 'using their fists, sticks, metal rods and knives' and that at least two passengers fired catapults at the helicopters. At least one of the soldiers 'was stabbed with a knife or other sharp object' (United Nations, 2010: 25). The passengers stated 'that their objective was to subdue and disarm the soldiers so that they could not harm anyone' (United Nations, 2010: 25). The report 'found no evidence to suggest that any of the passengers used firearms or that any firearms were taken on board the ship' and 'rejected' Israeli accounts alleging the use of firearms by passengers because they were 'so inconsistent and contradictory' (United Nations, 2010: 25). Whilst trying to secure the top deck Israeli forces fired paintballs, plastic bullets and live ammunition both from the helicopters above and from those who had already landed. During this part of the fighting four passengers were killed with live ammunition and a further 19 injured, 14 with gunshot wounds. The report found that the 'majority of gunshot wounds received by passengers were to their upper torsos in the head, thorax, abdomen and back' and that the 'vast majority' of the passengers on the upper deck where the Israeli troops landed sustained gunshot injuries (United Nations, 2010: 26). Israeli soldiers continued firing at those who were injured and forensic evidence showed that two passengers 'received wounds compatible with being shot at close range while lying on the ground' (United Nations, 2010: 26). Once the Israeli soldiers had secured the top deck they began moving downstairs to the bridge deck in order to take control of the ship. Israeli soldiers fired live ammunition from the top deck at the passengers below on the bridge deck and after they had moved to the bridge deck. This resulted in the deaths of at least a further four passengers. The mission found that 'none of the four passengers who were killed, including a photographer, who at the time of being shot was engaged in taking photographs and was shot by an Israeli soldier positioned on the top deck above, posed any threat to the Israeli forces' (United Nations, 2010: 27).

As the situation on the top decks deteriorated those holding the three Israeli soldiers below decks became very concerned that their continued detention threatened the security of all the passengers aboard the *Mavi Marmara* and a decision was made to release them on to a lower deck. Once released two jumped into the sea, where they were picked up by the Israeli navy, and the third was quickly joined by other soldiers from the decks above. The Israeli forces stated that the 'active phase' of their operation concluded at 05.17 when the soldiers had been released and they had full control of the ship. Following the takeover of the ship the Israeli forces refused to allow the wounded, some of whom had sustained gunshot wounds, to receive medical attention for 'up to two hours'. The authors also reported that many of the passengers reported being physically abused and treated in a humiliating manner.[55] The passengers were then transferred to Ashdod where they were pressured to sign official papers which stated that the 'signatory admitted to having entered Israel illegally and consented to deportation and be banned from re-entering Israel for a 10-year period' (United Nations, 2010: 41). Most passengers refused to sign the forms and some 'were beaten or physically abused for refusing to sign or for advising others not to sign' (United Nations, 2010: 41). After the passengers were processed at Ashdod the majority were taken to Ella Prison near Beersheba where a number complained of further beatings and most stated that they were refused legal or consular access. Following their detention in Ella Prison some passengers were taken by road to Jordan whilst the majority were taken to Ben Gurion airport. At the airport there were further reports of 'extreme and unprovoked violence' directed against passengers. The report concluded that the 'accounts were so consistent and vivid as to be beyond question' (United Nations, 2010: 43).

The conclusion was that during the storming of the *Mavi Marmara* Israeli forces had used a level of force that was 'disproportionate to the occasion' and demonstrated levels of 'totally unnecessary and incredible violence' which 'betrayed an unacceptable level of brutality' (United Nations, 2010: 53). It stated that 'although there may have been a justifiable belief of an immediate threat to life or serious injury of certain soldiers which would have justified the use of firearms against specific passengers ... less extreme means could have been employed in nearly all instances of the Israeli operation, since there was no imminent threat to soldiers' (United Nations, 2010: 36). The report also concluded that at least six of those killed by Israeli forces were summarily executed:

> The circumstances of the killing of at least six of the passengers were in a manner consistent with an extra-legal, arbitrary and summary execution. Furkan Doğan and İbrahim Bilgen were shot at near range while the victims were lying injured on the top deck. Cevdet Kiliçlar, Cengiz Akyüz, Cengiz Songür and Çetin Topçuoğlu were shot on the bridge deck while not participating in activities that represented a threat to any Israeli soldier. In these instances and possibly other killings on the Mavi Marmara, Israeli forces carried out extralegal, arbitrary and summary executions prohibited by international human rights law, specifically article 6 of the International Covenant on Civil and Political Rights. (United Nations, 2010: 37)

It was also noted that the passengers had been subjected to unlawful detention and torture both on the *Mavi Marmara* and other ships in the flotilla as well as during their time in Israel. On the ships this included references to the tightening of handcuffs in a manner which was 'deliberately used to cause pain and suffering to passengers' and that 'most passengers who requested that the handcuffs be loosened were ignored or it resulted in the handcuffs being further tightened' with the consequence that 'many were experiencing neurological damage up to three months after the events' (United Nations, 2010: 39–40). Whilst at the processing centre, prison and airport this referred to acts of 'physical violence and abuse' perpetrated against passengers (United Nations, 2010: 46). The report also concluded that Israel's seizure of passengers' property had been illegal and 'remains a continuing offence' (United Nations, 2010: 54).

Israel, which had refused to cooperate with the mission, accused the United Nations Human Rights Council as having a 'biased, politicized and extremist approach' (*Jerusalem Post*, 23 September 2010). Andy David, a spokesman for the Israeli Foreign Office, stated the 'Human Rights Council blamed Israel prior to the investigation and it is no surprise that they condemn after' (*Jerusalem Post*, 23 September 2010). This comment was in reference to the decision by the UN Human Rights Council to issue a resolution in June 2010 condemning the attack before it dispatched the mission. Israel is issuing its own report and has also stated that it is cooperating with another UN investigation under the chairmanship of the former Colombian president Alvaro Uribe and the former New Zealand prime minister Geoffrey Palmer. Uribe was a controversial choice as co-chair. The ex-Colombian president has been criticised by human rights groups for failing to investigate the activities of paramilitary death squads in his own country and a number of his political allies are under investigation for links to paramilitaries (Human Rights Watch, 2009c).

The *Mavi Marmara* killings damaged Israel's relationship with one of its key military allies, Turkey. The deaths also refocused international attention on the Gaza blockade and led to a number of countries, including the United States, arguing that the siege was untenable. This led to a slight easing in the blockade in early July 2010. It was reported that Israel was to allow in 'most consumer goods' but 'maintained its limits on many building materials, which it said could be used to manufacture weapons' (*Guardian*, 5 July 2010). However, this exclusion meant that Gazans would still be unable to rebuild the damage to housing and infrastructure inflicted by Israel in the 2008–09 war. The report also noted that there were 'no details in the announcement regarding the import of raw materials which Gazan economists say are essential to allow crippled businesses to recover' and that 'exports, also critical to the Gazan economy, were not mentioned'. Oxfam was cited as describing the move as 'a step in the right direction' but also warned that the restrictions on exports had to be lifted in order to allow Gazans to rebuild their economy. The organisation said that the blockade had to be 'fully lifted to enable Palestinians to engage in productive, dignified work. That would help restore hope in the future for Gazans and it would be an important step on the road to peace' (*Guardian*, 5 July 2010).

The following month it was announced that peace talks would recommence between Israel and the Palestinians in Washington in September 2010 under the auspices of President Obama. The Americans promised that all the most contentious final status issues would be on the table and that they would strive to complete a comprehensive peace agreement within a year. However, many remained deeply sceptical that any serious progress would be made when such a deep gulf existed between the two parties. There was also the issue of Hamas who the Obama administration, like its predecessor, had continued to ostracise. They dismissed the negotiations. Abdul Rahman Zidan, a former minister in the Hamas government, stated: 'Nothing positive will come out of these fruitless talks – we have tried this way several times. The Americans and the Israelis need talks – any talks – just for the feeling that there is a peace process. But for us, this is a negative, empty feeling because there is nothing on the table. It's a merry-go-round,' he said (*Guardian*, 20 August 2010).

A report in the journal *Foreign Policy* (30 June 2010) suggested that some of America's most senior military planners were also sceptical about the Obama administration's strategy towards groups like Hamas and Hezbullah. The article carried extended extracts from a report by CENTCOM, the American army's strategic command centre for the Middle East, East Africa and parts of Asia, which was entitled 'Managing Hizballah and Hamas'. The report, which was said to reflect the thinking of 'a significant number of senior officers at CENTCOM headquarters' as well as 'senior CENTCOM intelligence officers and analysts serving in the Middle East', questioned the wisdom of many of the administration's key policies (*Foreign Policy*, 30 June 2010). The CENTCOM report cited comments from former US peace negotiator Aaron David Miller that the two organisations were 'serious political players respected on the streets, in Arab capitals, and throughout the region. Destroying them was never really an option. Ignoring them may not be either.' It suggested that the American strategy of trying to build up Fatah's forces in the West Bank in order to suppress Hamas would fail in the absence of a negotiated peace deal between Israel and the Palestinians. A better strategy for dealing with groups like Hamas and Hezbullah might be to try to tie them into their respective political mainstreams:

> The U.S. role of assistance to an *integrated* Lebanese defense force that includes Hizballah; and the continued training of Palestinian security forces in a Palestinian entity that *includes* Hamas in its government, would be more effective than providing assistance to entities – the government of Lebanon and Fatah – that represent only a part of the Lebanese and Palestinian populace respectively. (emphasis in the original)

CENTCOM also suggested that Israel's siege of Gaza which kept 'the area on the verge of a perpetual humanitarian collapse' may actually 'be radicalizing more people, especially the young, increasing the number of potential recruits' for Hamas. Lifting the siege, it argues, and facilitating reconciliation between Hamas and Fatah would be 'the best hope for mainstreaming Hamas'. The report also argues that such a move, together with a decision by Hamas to renounce violence, would win 'widespread international support and deprive the Israelis of any legitimate justification to continue settlement building and delay statehood negotiations'.

Wider misgivings about American support for Israel were also brought into the public domain following the publication of an article titled 'Israel as a Strategic Liability?' by Anthony Cordesman (2010) of the influential Center for Strategic and International Studies. Cordesman argued that the approach of Israel to the Palestinians and their use of excessive military force was damaging American interests abroad.[56] Cordesman stated that America should not acquiesce in Israeli settlement building or its attempts to move Palestinians out of East Jerusalem. Instead, he argued that the US should make clear to Israel that 'it had obligations to the United States' and that it should 'show enough discretion to reflect the fact that it is a tertiary U.S. strategic interest in a complex and demanding world'. Commenting on Mr Cordesman's article, in the *New York Times* Helene Cooper noted that its 'dispassionate argument' had 'gained increased traction in Washington – both inside the Obama administration (including the Pentagon, White House and State Department) and outside, during forums, policy breakfasts, even a seder in Bethesda' (5 June 2010). Cooper pointed to recent statements by President Obama and General Petraeus, who oversees the American war in Afghanistan, that a failure to resolve the Israeli-Palestinian conflict was damaging US interests and threatening the lives of American soldiers. Such concerns were also reportedly expressed by Vice-President Joe Biden when he visited Israel in March 2010. Shimon Shiffer wrote in the Israeli daily *Yediot Ahronot*:

> People who heard what Biden said were stunned. 'This is starting to get dangerous for us,' Biden castigated his interlocutors. 'What you're doing here undermines the security of our troops who are fighting in Iraq, Afghanistan and Pakistan. That endangers us and it endangers regional peace.' The vice president told his Israeli hosts that since many people in the Muslim world perceived a connection between Israel's actions and US policy, any decision about construction that undermines Palestinian rights in East Jerusalem could have an impact on the personal safety of American troops fighting against Islamic terrorism. (11 March 2010, cited in Rozen, 2010)

Unease over Israel's policies towards the Palestinians and a conviction that the United States should be heavily involved in forcing a peace settlement is now apparently prevalent amongst America's Jewish population. Peter Beinart has suggested that there is a widening divide between the American Jewish establishment in the form of groups like AIPAC or the Anti-Defamation League, and ordinary Jewish Americans (*New York Review of Books*, 10 June 2010). Beinart notes that the establishment organisations have tended to support Israeli policies towards the Palestinians uncritically but that particularly younger Jewish Americans, with the exception of the orthodox and ultra-orthodox, were much more willing to criticise Israel's behaviour and were much more supportive of peace efforts. Such trends appear to be borne out in large-scale polling. Research carried out by J Street (2010), the Jewish American lobby group, found that by a '71–29 percent margin, American Jews support the United States "exerting pressure" on both the Israelis and the Arabs to make the necessary compromises to achieve peace'. The poll also found that '52–48 percent, still support an active role even if the United States were to publicly state its disagreements with only Israel' and that 'American Jews are evenly split on support for exerting pressure on only Israel'. This perhaps heralds potential changes in support for Israel amongst the population of its key ally and this in itself could be a major factor in the pressure for a just settlement.

Our intention in giving these histories was to illustrate the range of contested positions which exist over this conflict. In the chapters which follow we will show how the arguments of the different sides appeared on television news and how they were received and understood by different audiences.

2
Content Studies 2000–02[1]

INTRODUCTION: THE DISPUTED ORIGINS OF THE CONFLICT

Our content studies focus on TV news coverage of the second Palestinian intifada or uprising, following its outbreak in September 2000. We have already indicated in the histories above that the events leading up to this are complex and contested by different parties. We can see this if we look at key issues such as the origins and history of the Palestinian refugees. These people were displaced from their land when the Israeli state was formed in 1948. The account of how they were displaced varies and for many years Israel claimed that they had simply fled the fighting in 1948 (when the nascent state of Israel fought with its Arab neighbours) or they had been told to leave by their leaders. More recently, the Israeli historian Avi Shlaim has given a carefully documented account which suggests that many were forced to leave and the military offensive on civilian areas began in the period before the official outbreak of hostilities on 15 May 1948. He shows that the military forces of what was to become Israel had embarked on a new offensive strategy which involved destroying Arab villages and the forced removal of civilians. The intention was to clear the interior of the future Israeli state of what were seen as potentially hostile 'Arab elements'. As he writes:

> The novelty and audacity of the plan lay in the orders to capture Arab villages and cities, something [they] had never attempted before ... Palestinian society disintegrated under the impact of the Jewish military offensive that got underway in April, and the exodus of the Palestinians was set in motion ... by ordering the capture of Arab cities and the destruction of villages, it both permitted and justified the forcible expulsion of Arab civilians. (Shlaim, 2000: 30)

He also notes how the displacement of the Palestinians and its consequences were clearly acknowledged by Moshe Dayan, one of the most prominent of Israel's military leaders and politicians.

170

Speaking in 1955 at the funeral of an Israeli killed by Arab insurgents, Dayan commented:

> What cause have we to complain about their fierce hatred for us? For eight years now they sit in their refugee camps in Gaza, and before their eyes we turn into our homestead the land and villages in which they and their forefathers have lived. (quoted in Shlaim, 2000: 101)

The Palestinian view was indeed that they had been forced from their land and homes in 1948. They had then to live as refugees in countries such as Lebanon, Syria, Jordan and on the West Bank (of the Jordan river) and the Gaza Strip. There followed a series of conflicts and at times outright war between Israel and its Arab neighbours. The most significant of these conflicts was perhaps the 1967 Six Day War. In this, Israel occupied the West Bank and East Jerusalem (which had been under the control of Jordan), the Gaza Strip (which had been under the control of Egypt) and the Golan Heights (which were Syrian). This occupation brought many Palestinian refugees under Israeli military control and was bitterly contested. Jerusalem as a religious centre for both Muslims and Jews became a major point of conflict. The Israelis also built settlements in the newly occupied areas of Gaza and the West Bank and they exploited natural resources, in particular taking control of the vital resource of water. To occupy and exploit land in this fashion is widely seen as a violation of international law and for this reason newspapers in Britain such as the *Guardian* routinely refer to the Israeli settlements as 'illegal'. This has also been the view of the British government. In 1997 the Conservative Foreign Secretary Malcolm Rifkind referred to the building of a large settlement in occupied East Jerusalem as follows: 'The start of construction can do nothing but harm the peace process ... like all settlements this one will be illegal' (quoted in Shlaim, 2000: 582). As Avi Shlaim suggests, these settlements were about much more than simply building houses and farms. They were part of a systematic policy of exerting strategic and military control, which in this case involved 'surrounding the huge Greater Jerusalem area with two concentric circles of settlements with access roads and military positions' (2000: 582).

Within Israel there were divisions over the occupation and the settlement policies. Some argued that occupied land should be returned to the Palestinians in exchange for a final peace agreement.

But many Israelis defended the occupation arguing that they had religious claims (from the time of the Bible) on the land and Jerusalem. It was also argued that Israel's security needs could only be met by extending its borders as, for example, when Israel expropriated a part of Southern Lebanon in 1982/83 as a 'security zone'. This action had led to an extended conflict with Hezbullah guerrillas from Lebanon, and Israel eventually withdrew in 1999 after suffering serious losses. The conflict with the Palestinians in the occupied territories resulted in two major intifadas (or uprisings) in 1987 and 2000. In the period between these there was a series of American-led peace efforts, notably the Oslo agreements of 1993 and 1995, and the Wye Accords of 1998. These in practice gave the Palestinians some self-rule in parts of the West Bank and Gaza. But the Israeli army still controlled roads and access and could effectively seal off the Palestinian areas, thus exerting a stranglehold on economic movement. They also continued to control and exploit water supplies as well as keeping a large army and undercover police presence.

Despite the hostility which was generated by the occupation there is some evidence that by the time of the Wye Accords of 1998, most Palestinians still supported the peace process and many Israelis also accepted the principle of returning land in exchange for peace. But this was opposed by right-wing politicians in Israel who urged settlers to take more land even as Israeli troops were withdrawing from Palestinian areas under the Wye agreements. As Avi Shlaim writes:

> Some hard-line ministers publicly urged the Jewish settlers to grab more West Bank land to keep it out of Palestinian hands. The first stage of the Israeli troop withdrawal was matched by a renewed spurt of land confiscations for the purpose of building Jewish settlements and a network of roads between them ... In sharp contrast to Israeli backsliding, the Palestinians scrupulously adhered to the course charted at Wye. (Shlaim, 2000: 605)

In May 1999 Ehud Barak was elected as prime minister of Israel with a commitment to establishing peace. However, his election stimulated further occupations by Israel settlers. Under the headline 'Settlers Race for Land', the *Guardian* described the situation on the ground. It quoted the mayor of a Palestinian village as follows:

When the settlers brought their bulldozers we went down with our papers to prove it was our land. Then the Israeli soldiers arrived and just went mad. It was like a war here, they were throwing tear gas grenades and firing CS gas canisters and live ammunition into our houses. (*Guardian*, 25 May 1999)

The control of water was also crucial and another *Guardian* report (2 November 1998) showed that the pattern of settlement construction since the 1970s was along the ridges and edges of aquifers and that 'this strategic consideration was part of the Jewish pattern in populating the area'. This was a central issue for Palestinians since a third of their economy was agricultural and could not be sustained without water. The report also noted that 26 per cent of Palestinian houses had no water and each Israeli was consuming over three times as much water as a Palestinian.

Under Barak's leadership in Israel, the peace process continued through 2000 and he met with Yassar Arafat and President Clinton at Camp David in the US. But no agreement was reached and there was a growing frustration with the peace process. This reached a climax in September 2000 when the right-wing Israeli politician Ariel Sharon walked through the most holy Muslim places in Jerusalem. Sharon was a notorious figure for Palestinians and was blamed by many for the killing of refugees in Lebanon in 1982. His action in Jerusalem was seen as a statement of Israeli control and sovereignty, and it was followed by riots which grew into the second intifada.[2] Our study focuses initially on media coverage of these events (particularly television news) and the potential influence which this has had on public understanding of the Israeli-Palestinian conflict.

This study has two main dimensions. The first is the content analysis of BBC and ITV news and is the focus of this chapter. The purpose of this work is to analyse how the news presented the conflict and the different ways in which it was explained. The second is a substantial audience study using both focus groups and questionnaires, and is discussed in Chapter 3. In this we examine what TV audiences understood from what they had seen and their use of other sources of information such as formal education or direct experience of the conflict.

CONTENT ANALYSIS: METHODS

The media are central to the exercise of power in society. They can set agendas in the sense of highlighting some news stories and topics, but they can also severely limit the information with which we understand events in the world. The analysis of media content remains a prime concern. The method that the Glasgow University Media Group has developed to analyse the content of media texts is called *Thematic Analysis*. It is based on the assumption that in any contentious area there will be competing ways of describing events and their history. Ideas are linked to interests and these competing interests will seek to explain the world in ways which justify their own position. So ideology (by which we mean an interest-linked perspective) and the struggle for legitimacy go hand in hand. Part of our work has focused on the role of the media in these ideological struggles, and how the reporting of events can embody different ways of understanding which are linked to perspectives and interests. In our early work on television news content we analysed the public debate which existed at that time about the failings of the British economy. In the 1970s and 1980s, this was a matter of great concern as Britain was perceived to be falling behind the rest of the world's economies. In this public controversy the trade unions pointed to management mistakes in the organisation of industry and low levels of investment which meant that machines often broke down and production was much less efficient than that of competitors in other countries. In contrast, right-wing commentators (including the Conservative Party) preferred to point to the actions of the workforce and blamed strikes for the failings of the economy. This became a favourite theme of the Conservatives in the 1980s, in the early years of Margaret Thatcher's government (see Philo et al., 1995). We were interested in how the TV news reported such debates and the potential influence on public belief. The essence of our method was first to note each of the explanations and ways of understanding which were being put forward in public debate and the range of available evidence which could underpin different positions. We identified these from published materials such as books, reports, the press and TV and any other relevant sources. We then analysed the content of TV news programmes and showed how all of these different explanations were featured (or not). In practice we found that some explanations were given prominence in news headlines or interview programmes while others were downgraded or excluded. So for example, there were many headlines in the news about strikes and the problems these were allegedly causing, but none blaming management mistakes. If some explanations were present on the news and others were absent, then it seemed likely to us that this would affect what TV audiences understood and believed. Of course people might have access to other sources of information, for example if they had direct experience of working in a factory or if they read 'alternative' accounts which gave information which was not on the news. This might include the financial pages of newspapers, from which we derived much of our information.[3]

Using this method, we showed that the view that 'strikes were to blame' was clearly endorsed on the news while other explanations were downgraded or excluded. Sometimes the explanation would appear as a direct statement from a journalist, such as: 'It's the kind of strike which has done so much to contribute to the dire economic problems' (quoted in Philo et al., 1995: 10). But we also developed at this time the concept of the explanatory theme, by which we meant that an assumed explanation gave a pattern or structure to an area of coverage. For example, the explanatory theme that strikes were to blame underpinned the whole process of news reporting including going to a factory, interviewing workers, asking them about strikes and crucially *not* asking the management about investment policies or their own mistakes, and then perhaps listing in the bulletin other strikes or disputes which had occurred that week. The crucial point is that the pattern of the coverage and the subjects that it highlights can assume the explanation even without it being directly stated.

In analysing news coverage of the Israeli-Palestinian conflict we identified a number of areas where there were competing perspectives over how it was to be explained and understood. We have already indicated the disputes that exist over the history and origins of the conflict. Another area of controversy would be the motives of those involved – for example, are there deeply rooted causes for the intifada or are the Palestinians merely responding to incitement by mendacious leaders? We have examined other potentially contested areas such as who is portrayed as initiating violence and the reporting of casualties. Such accounts carry with them assumptions about cause, responsibility and consequences that connect directly to wider social values. For example, a story about children dying in conflict is not merely a disinterested account of the day's events. Such a story is implicitly linked to strongly held social values that children should not be killed by tanks or blown up by bombs and it is therefore likely to affect audience responses and judgements about the conflict. It is important to study how the inclusion or exclusion of certain types of descriptions or explanations and the use of emotive language (words such as 'murder' or 'atrocity') may influence public understanding. Journalists should strive to meet the crucial criteria of accuracy and balance, but it is always the case that the reporting of such events is infused by social values.

There are other social values that affect the structuring of news. These would include assumptions about hierarchy and status that affect how stories are chosen and told. For example, a news topic such as 'peace negotiations between world leaders' is chosen partly because peace is assumed to be important but also because 'world leaders' are given a special status and can command access to the media. So beyond the specific meanings and perspectives of a particular story, the construction of news is influenced by other value assumptions about who is seen as a legitimate authority and what status and deference is given to different speakers. This might affect how interviews are conducted – there is a difference between asking someone for a brief opinion in the street and the legitimacy and status which is implied by interviewing an 'expert' in a studio. It is also important to identify the manner in which journalists report the views of the different sides. Sometimes journalists go beyond simply reporting a view and directly endorse it. There is an important difference between stating that one side in the conflict '*claims* that there was a massacre' and saying directly 'this was a massacre'. We will discuss such issues later in conjunction with our main focus on how different perspectives and explanations are included or excluded and how some are highlighted and endorsed in news reports.

It is quite possible for the news to feature a range of perspectives and indeed it should do so if it is to meet the requirement of balance. We have often found, however, that some perspectives dominate in news stories. We have also found that sometimes a perspective that is highlighted in one bulletin can be undermined or contradicted by information that is given in another. To obtain some measure of the relative dominance of different accounts and perspectives we count their frequency and the manner in which they appear (for example, the number of appearances in headlines and the number of 'direct' and 'reported' statements from the different sides). We can illustrate this in relation to an actual case that we discuss in detail later in our results. This case is a news report that Hezbullah guerrillas from Lebanon had kidnapped three Israeli soldiers. ITV News had the headline: 'Trouble continues as Hezbullah take three Israeli soldiers prisoner' (7 October 2000). One side can therefore be seen as initiating the 'trouble'. This was commonly reported, but a small number of news programmes also reported that the Israelis had been holding Lebanese hostages for many years and that the kidnap was linked to this. If the audience has this information then it may alter how they understand the events and the judgements that they make. There are in effect two competing explanatory themes. The first implies that one side is a victim and the second shows that both sides have taken hostages.[4] The first of these themes actually dominated the news and this can be seen from its position in headlines and also the frequency of references to this way of seeing the events.

There is a further point to be made about our methods for analysing language. When we make numerical assessments of the presence of some explanations or the dominance of some types of description, we always attempt to keep as close as possible to the actual language used in the text. In other words, we count phrases, words or sentences that are actually used. We avoid employing a priori categories such as 'statements for' one side or 'statements against' and we do not attempt to group language within such categories. We are concerned that such methods can lead to the bundling together of a wide range of textual meanings into rather crude 'boxes'. We try to account for the range of subtlety of language, as it is used to convey a complex variety of meanings, and then to trace how these exact messages are received and understood by audiences.

In practice for this content analysis, we began by calculating the amount of coverage given to different subject areas, such as the depiction of violence or peace negotiations. We did this by counting lines of text from transcribed news programmes. We then engaged in a detailed examination of how the causes and origins of the conflict were represented. We followed this with a further analysis of how different perspectives were highlighted in headlines, interviews and in the routine reporting of events such as attacks, deaths and casualties. Much of our analysis deals with verbal text, but we have also looked at visual images and at how these were given meaning and context by the words that accompanied them. We may, for example, see a dramatic picture of riots and gunfire in streets, but not know much about why this is happening. The judgements that we form about it may depend upon the spoken description that accompanies the image.

This work was undertaken in conjunction with an analysis of audience understanding and reception of news, which we discuss below. It is important to combine such studies because research which rests on content analysis alone leaves the researchers in the position of having to assert what the audience would be likely to understand from the news. There are in fact wide variations between people in terms of how well they understand news items. We have argued elsewhere that when journalists construct news reports they assume levels of knowledge in viewers. But these levels of knowledge do not exist in all cases and many in the audience do not understand the causes of the events which are being shown (Glasgow University Media Group, 2002). In our present study it was apparent that the news sometimes offered explanations of the conflict which were brief and enigmatic. For example, a description of fighting in Jerusalem notes that 'The city's most holy place for Arabs and Jews became a battlefield ... on this the eve of the Jewish New Year it's the age-old problem that is setting the agenda' (ITV late News, 29 September 2000). Those who know something of Middle East politics could understand this reference to the 'age-old problem' as being the struggle between Israelis and Palestinians over the ownership of Jerusalem, where the Israeli occupation is opposed by the Palestinians. But those who do not have this knowledge may simply be mystified as to why the two sides were fighting. The difficulty is that what may seem obvious to the researcher or the journalist may not be so to all members of the audience. As we will show, in order to establish how the text is understood by different audiences, it is necessary to work directly with them.

As part of this study, we also contacted and interviewed journalists and news editors who had a close working knowledge of the conflict. It was not our intention to write a full production analysis but we used these contacts to check information, to give us background on specific stories and to explain where necessary how processes of news gathering actually operated in Israel and the occupied territories. As a further dimension to the study, some of these journalists also took part in the audience reception work and sat in on focus groups, contributing to discussions (see Chapter 3).

SAMPLES AND RESULTS

SAMPLE ONE: 28 SEPTEMBER TO 16 OCTOBER 2000

Our first major sample of news content focused on news coverage of the outbreak of the intifada in September 2000. For this we examined the lunchtime, early evening and late news bulletins for BBC1 and ITV (Channel Three). The focus was on these because they are on the most popular channels and attract a very substantial audience. We have analysed bulletins which featured the conflict between 28 September 2000, the first day of the intifada, and 16 October 2000, the date of an attempted peace summit in Egypt (a total of 91 bulletins[5]). We used the national press and other programmes such as Channel 4 News and BBC *Newsnight* for purposes of comparison. We also examined news items from outside this period to see whether trends in coverage that we had identified were sustained in subsequent news reporting. These were drawn from three other sample periods: 17 October 2001 to 13 December 2001, 2–9 March 2002 and 9–16 April 2002 (a total of 98 bulletins).

There were four main elements to our first content analysis, 28 September to 16th October 2000:

1. We examined the main areas of coverage in news programmes and produced a quantitative assessment of their relative prominence. As part of this we identified the explanations which were given of the causes of the conflict.
2. We examined interviews and made an assessment of who got on to speak and the circumstances in which they did so.
3. We analysed news headlines and how they might shape ways of understanding the conflict.
4. We analysed coverage of a series of events in which Israelis and Palestinians were injured or killed to illustrate how the actions and motives of different parties in the conflict were presented, and the language used to describe the two sides.

Areas of coverage

There were five broad areas of coverage which we identified. The first was images and descriptions of conflict and violence. The second area was the coverage of funerals of people who had died in the conflict. In practice these offered scenes of agitation and rage and were frequently linked to further violence or to the possibility of it. The third area was discussions of peace negotiations and the prospects for peace. The fourth area was the discussion of the tactics being employed by different parties in the conflict in response to changing events. These included political or military manoeuvres and also the every-day responses of ordinary citizens. Finally we identified reasons for the conflict and references to its history.

Violence

The coverage as a whole was permeated with images, descriptions and references to conflict and violence including riots, mobs, stone-throwing, stabbings, shootings, kidnapping, protests and military attacks. In our audience groups these were the images which overwhelmingly dominated memories of what they had seen on television. In our analysis, such coverage constituted 28 per cent of this sample (measured in lines of text). Reporting of violence and conflict normally contained very little explanation of the history and origins of the conflict. As in the following example which is simply a list of the day's conflicts:

> Well you join me on the Mount of Olives overlooking the old city of Jerusalem and it was down there on Haram al-Sharif, as the Muslims call it, the Temple Mount as known to the Jews, where the clashes broke out again this morning. If the cameraman could just move a little to my left you'll see that down there on the edge of the wall of the Old City there's a fire burning, that's an Israeli police station that was set alight by Palestinian demonstrators about an hour ago and the fire still seems to be raging. A little bit before that I was down in exactly that area when the most ferocious battle broke out as young Palestinian worshippers came off the Haram al-Sharif after the Friday prayers [*images of crowd rioting*]. They had rocks in their hands, they started throwing these rocks at Israeli policemen and soldiers who fired back and for the rest of us trapped in the middle it was just a question of finding a rock to hide behind because there was a lot of ammunition being fired. There were rubber bullets, rubber-coated bullets and we think also some live ammunition, and we understand that there are quite a number of injured, and according to Palestinians who were on the Temple Mount at the time, we believe that at least one person was killed. Inevitably this has led to further trouble elsewhere on the West Bank today. We're getting reports already of disturbances in Ramallah, in other parts of the West Bank some injuries. We all thought that perhaps today the situation was going to calm down after the efforts at a diplomatic level to restore calm after this crisis that has lasted a week now. But it seems as though this morning's episode in the Old City of Jerusalem has triggered yet another round of confrontation. (BBC1 lunchtime News, 6 October 2000)

The emphasis here is on 'hot' live action and the immediacy of the report rather than any explanation of the underlying causes of the events. One BBC journalist who had reported on this conflict told us that his own editor had said to him that they did not want 'explainers' – as he put it: 'It's all bang bang stuff.' The driving force behind such news is to hold the attention of as many viewers as possible, but in practice, as we will see, it simply leaves very many people confused. Here is another example from BBC1:

> The Palestinians have been warned to call off their uprising by tonight but this was their answer to the Israelis, a hail of rocks, in Ramallah in the West Bank [*images of Palestinian crowd, noise of gunfire*]. Young boys join in what is called the new intifada and sometimes women too. On this occasion the rioters are forced to retreat. They say they won't be threatened by Israel's ultimatums and deadlines. They feel they have little to lose by fighting and little to gain from the peace process now on the brink of collapse. They flaunt pictures of the Iraqi leader, Saddam Hussein; some call on him to attack Israel. In the meantime the Palestinians use their catapults and their slingshots. Bucketloads of ammunition are brought up to the front line, but many told me what they really want are guns, so they can turn this crisis into a war. (BBC1 late News, 9 October 2000)

There is a hint of an explanation here in the reference to the Palestinians belief that they have 'little to gain from the peace process', but then the moment passes and the commentary is back to 'catapults and slingshots', 'Bucketloads of ammunition', and the desire for guns. The escalation of the conflict is clearly important but viewers might also want to know why. There are sometimes brief references to causes in such coverage, but the bulk of it is taken up with dramatic pictures and commentary on the latest 'clashes', as in this account from ITV:

> Minutes after the praying finished the fighting resumed and today saw violence in Jerusalem itself. Hundreds of Palestinian youths attacking Israeli security forces [*shouting, gunshots*]. Running battles were fought in the alleyways that make up this historic place. There were calls for calm, there were calls for restraint, but yet again all have been ignored. This is an Israeli police station inside the Old City of Jerusalem, a part of the City of Peace, is on fire [*shouting*]. Israeli soldiers have been trapped in the burning building, firing outside to keep rioters at bay [*gunfire*]. Colleagues had to come to the rescue [*gunshots*]. Using his M16 rifle, one conscript blew open the front door. It took a few minutes but they got their people out. Several had been injured [*shouting*].

Jerusalem, and who controls it, is at the centre of the conflict, for a time today the Palestinian flag flew, a direct challenge to Israeli sovereignty. There has been trouble elsewhere, but it is the fighting in the Holy City that is of most significance. Today this was the Via Dolorosa [*gunshots*], the path that's said Christ walked to his crucifixion. It is also called 'The Way of Sorrows'. (ITV late News, 6 October 2000)

The reference to Jerusalem and to who controls it is typical, in that it is so brief that it will only make sense to those who already understand Middle Eastern politics. To those who have a more limited grasp it does sound as if it is simply two groups of people fighting for control of a holy city and who can put their flag up over it. Some in our audience groups did indeed see the conflict in these terms, as if it was just two groups of neighbours who somehow could not get on.

Funerals

Funerals were often linked to the fighting and the coverage of them frequently included powerful and emotionally charged images.[6] In this example there is the suggestion that the grief and passion lead to more violence and the 'holy war' over Jerusalem is again mentioned, but there is no discussion of how the conflict originated:

There is a huge turnout for each and every Palestinian funeral. These people regard their dead as martyrs killed in a religious war over Jerusalem and therefore worthy of being honoured. How long the fighting and killing goes on will be determined by them and appearing at each funeral are many more men prepared to die. This is one of several funerals taking place on the West Bank today and it is not only an outpouring of grief, it is a call to arms, a call for retaliation. (ITV early evening News, 2 October 2000)

The screen is filled with images of passion and rage but with little opportunity to understand how this situation has come about. Here are three examples from BBC News:

When they are not fighting, Palestinians are busy burying their dead ... funerals like this are focal points not only for grief, but also for Palestinian rage and resentment and the dead man's cousin greets the idea of a ceasefire with derision. (BBC1 late evening News, 3 October 2000)

In Nablus a 22-year-old was buried this morning his funeral like so many others attracted a large embittered crowd ... there's a funeral going on, the streets are full of heavily armed angry men and up on the mountains above us, Israeli snipers are watching. With emotions still raw it will take more than words to end this crisis. (BBC1 lunchtime News, 4 October 2000)

Last night Israeli soldiers and Palestinian gunmen exchanged fire in a part of Hebron. Such night-time gun battles are becoming commonplace [*images of Palestinian crowd chanting*] in Ramallah, another funeral and another focus for Palestinian anger. (BBC1 lunchtime News, 9 October 2000)

Such images are prominent in the memories of television viewers but, as we will see from our work with audiences, the relationships which underpin the conflict and its history are much less well understood.

Prospects for peace and negotiations

Discussions on the prospects for peace and meetings between key figures in the conflict were another major category of news content (the largest category, accounting for 33 per cent of this sample). There were a series of meetings of political leaders in this period, the first in Paris on 4 October 2000 when the Israelis and Palestinians met with the US Secretary of State. The UN Secretary-General, Kofi Annan, flew to Israel on 9 October, and there was a summit of world leaders including the US president in Egypt on 16 October 2000. The coverage of these was taken up mainly with the comings and goings of the key figures and reports on the lack of progress in negotiations for a peaceful resolution of the crisis:

There are few smiles on display at this summit and for good reason, for while the Israeli and Palestinian leaders talk amid the grandeur of Paris, they have left behind them on the West Bank and in Gaza mounting chaos and bitterness. The best hope is American mediation led by the US Secretary of State Madeleine Albright, who is seeking a ceasefire on the ground and then an accelerated timetable for peace negotiations. For now, all of that seems out of her grasp. (ITV early evening News, 4 October 2000)

And on the BBC the summit in Egypt was headlined as follows:

Middle East peace summit gets underway, but no sign of a breakthrough. While they try to end the bloodshed, the killing continues on the streets. (BBC1 early evening News, 16 October 2000)

A significant point to emerge from this coverage is the manner in which the United States is presented and how this presentation influences the understanding of audiences. At this time the US was featured as being extensively involved in peace moves. Thus on ITV we hear that the 'Americans are desperately trying to broker a meaningful and lasting ceasefire' (ITV early evening News, 3 October 2000) and a later headline tells us that there are 'More Middle East clashes as Clinton vows to step in' (ITV lunchtime News, 9 October 2000). On the BBC, President Clinton is referred to as having a long history of 'trying to bring permanent peace':

Never before has President Clinton flown into a summit where the stakes are so high and the outcome so uncertain. Today and tonight the man who has spent eight years trying to bring permanent peace to the Middle East has to salvage something from the past 18 days of violence. (BBC1 lunchtime News, 16 October 2000)

On ITV, in a discussion between two journalists, one explicitly refers to 'the even-handedness which has characterised American diplomacy in the Middle East'. The second takes up the point and comments:

Well, the administration had been under a great pressure, as indeed have both the presidential candidates, to take a more pro-Israeli line, both from the Israeli lobby here and the Jewish lobby here and also from certain sections of the media. I don't expect that that pressure will affect this administration's policy or even the next one, because the Americans have long maintained that the only way they have any influence in the Middle East is to be a relatively neutral, honest broker. (ITV early evening News, 12 October 2000)

Yet there were other comments on the news which apparently contradict this view. For example, this BBC1 report mentions the distrust which young Palestinians have of the US:

[visuals of fighting, stone throwing] ... a lethal game of cat and mouse in the narrow streets of Hebron. This is what the leaders in Paris are up against. The idea that Washington might act as honest broker depressed these young Palestinians. It was a similar picture all over the West Bank again today but the level of violence was significantly lower. After six days of this, people are getting tired, but in Gaza, Israel still wielded a big stick. Helicopters fired rockets killing at least one Palestinian. (BBC1 early evening News, 4 October 2000)

On ITV news we also hear that 'many [Palestinians] do not trust the Americans to be honest brokers when it comes to mediation' (late News, 4 October 2000). But that is all that we hear; there is no explanation given as to why this might be so. It would be difficult for viewers without specialist knowledge to make sense of this contradiction. One reason for the Palestinian response is that the US supplies $3 billion each year to Israel, a large part of which is spent on military equipment. In other words, the US arms one side in the conflict. Yet this is very rarely spoken of in news coverage. Other news in our sample showed pictures of Palestinians burning an American flag but again did not say why or give the information that the US was supplying weapons which were being used in the Israeli attacks. It was possible to find such information in news reports but it was very rare and was on the 'periphery' of television news, that is, late night on BBC2 or Channel 4 rather than on the mass audience programmes of BBC1 and ITV. This example is from Channel 4 News:

With two billion pounds of US money every year, much of it spent on arms, Israel has never been such a supreme regional power ... Palestinians look up and see American-supplied Apache helicopters, just as Hezbullah in Lebanon look south and see American-supplied missiles, tanks and artillery. (Channel 4 evening News, 13 October 2000)

Without such information it is difficult to understand the actions or rationale of some of those who are portrayed in television news stories. In our audience sample of young people we asked why Palestinians might be critical of the US and burn the American flag. Most did not know that the US supplied money and arms to Israel. Reporting on such issues is complicated for journalists by the closeness of Britain's relationship with the US. In the TV news bulletins we found very little criticism of US policy, and this became perhaps more of a taboo area after the attacks on the US on 11 September 2001, often referred to as '9/11'. The BBC Director-General famously apologised for the content of a *Question Time* programme broadcast live shortly after 9/11, where such criticism had been made. To explain in detail the rationale of those who oppose US policy is to court controversy. It is simpler to avoid explanations or to leave them to the margins of television and radio. The difficulty with this is that it leaves many viewers ill informed.

Tactics

This is a substantial area of news coverage in which journalists discuss the actions and responses of the different parties in the conflict to the latest events and likely future developments. This may include consideration of political or military tactics or the everyday responses of local populations to events, which accounted for 14 per cent of this sample. In this example, the BBC describes military tactics:

> Later, we saw the Israelis bringing in extra tanks on low-loaders to reinforce their positions here on the West Bank. So another display of extremely tough tactics by Israeli security forces here in Ramallah. They are on the highest state of alert, extra troops have been drafted in and leave has been cancelled in Jerusalem. Israeli security forces prevented all male Palestinians under the age of 45 from getting into the old city. (BBC1 early evening News, 13 October 2000)

Political moves are also reported such as a statement by Ehud Barak, the Israeli prime minister, that he intended to form a government of national emergency (BBC1 late News, 12 October 2000). On the same day Yasser Arafat was reported as ordering a general mobilisation of his people. There is also some discussion of how the Israelis intend to cope with the revolt in the long term and to 'restore' order. On ITV two journalists take up these issues:

> *Journalist 1*: So John, if there is no magic formula what might Israel do?
> *Journalist 2*: Well the Israeli prime minister, Mr Barak, has pledged to use all means to restore order. Over the weekend we saw him move more heavy armour, more tanks onto the West Bank. They are now positioned around the Palestinian towns and

villages where we have seen clashes over the past eleven days. It may be that the Israelis plan to surround these Palestinian areas to choke the life out of the revolt. (ITV late News, 9 October 2000)

The journalist concludes that the Palestinians would be likely to react violently to such a move. The theme is taken up again on the following day when the same journalist is asked again: 'What are the tactics of the Israeli government?'

> Their intention appears to be to stifle this revolt economically. The Palestinian Authority is effectively a scattering of Arab communities on the West Bank and the Israelis appear to be trying to cut off those communities from each other and from Israel proper. (ITV lunchtime News, 10 October 2000)

It is perfectly proper to discuss the tactics of the Israeli government. However, there is no critical consideration here of the nature of the 'order' which they wish to restore. From the point of view of the Palestinians it would consist of military control, which has involved large-scale arrest, imprisonment without trial, torture and extrajudicial killing. There is no extensive discussion by journalists on what 'tactics' the Palestinians might employ to end this.

Explanations of the conflict[7]

This is a key area for the analysis of public understanding of events and their causes. Our audience research showed that many people had little knowledge of the reasons of the conflict and its origins. To understand the origins of the crisis there are at least two sequences of historical events of which the audience would need to be aware. The first is that when Israel was created in 1948, a large number of Palestinians were displaced from their homes and became refugees. The second is that many of these people then went to live on the West Bank of the Jordan, in East Jerusalem and in Gaza, all of which were occupied by Israel in the war of 1967. The Palestinians subsequently lived under Israeli military control which they bitterly contested. There are of course many qualifications which each side would wish to make to these statements to explain and legitimise their own actions. But without a knowledge of these events, it is extremely difficult to understand the rationale of the different participants in the conflict or even where it was happening. This knowledge was not available on much of the news – indeed some bulletins would be likely to add to viewers' confusion.

When the intifada began in September 2000, some news reports seemed unclear that it was taking place in the occupied areas which were subject to military control. Instead it was sometimes described as taking place in 'Israel'. For example, some news programmes contained large visual backdrops saying 'Israel violence' when the events described took place in occupied East Jerusalem (ITV early evening News, 29 September 2000, and lunchtime News, 6 October 2000). A newscaster summarises the events by saying: 'Fighting over a sacred site in Israel' (ITV early evening News, 29 September 2000). The BBC also described the occupied Palestinian areas as 'Israel's West Bank' (early evening News, 2 October 2000). Later events in the Palestinian town of Ramallah were headlined on a BBC lunchtime news as 'Mob violence in Israel' (12 October 2000). ITV seemed unclear at times over whether Israel had sovereignty in East Jerusalem. It doesn't, and as a BBC Radio 4 journalist succinctly put it: 'just about every country apart from this one [Israel] believes that the occupation is illegal' (*Today*, 7 February 2002). A correspondent in the *Guardian* also noted that:

Under international law East Jerusalem has been occupied by Israel since 1967, which is why only two states – Costa Rica and El Salvador – recognise Jerusalem as the capital of Israel and maintain embassies there. (*Guardian*, 26 January 2001)

ITV, however, reported that at one point in the conflict Palestinians had raised their own flag, challenging 'Israeli sovereignty': 'Jerusalem and who controls it is at the centre of the conflict. For a time today the Palestinian flag flew, a direct challenge to Israeli sovereignty' (ITV late News, 6 October 2000). In a later bulletin, the significance of the Temple Mount in Jerusalem is described: 'For Muslims it is the third holiest place in the world. It is, however, also sacred to the Israelis and they have sovereignty over it and are not prepared to give that up' (ITV late News, 12 October 2000).

There are other ways in which the areas of the conflict were described, sometimes by giving the name of towns or by references, such as the 'Palestinian-ruled Gaza Strip' (BBC1 early evening News, 2 October 2000) or the 'Palestinian-controlled West Bank' (ITV early evening News, 2 October 2000).

The key point is that if journalists are unclear over which territories are occupied and how they are controlled and what this signifies to those involved, then it is not surprising if viewers are confused. Another key reason for confusion and the lack of understanding in the television audience was that explanations were rarely given on the news and when they were, journalists often spoke obliquely, almost in the form of shorthand. For the audience to understand the significance of what they were saying would require a level of background knowledge which was simply not present in most people. For example, in the news bulletin which featured the progress of peace talks a journalist made a series of very brief comments on the issues which under-pinned the conflict:

> The basic raw disagreements remain – *the future, for example of this city Jerusalem, the future of Jewish settlements and the returning refugees.* For all that, together with the anger and bitterness felt out in the West Bank then I think it's clear this crisis is not about to abate. (ITV early evening News, 16 October 2001 – our italics)

On the BBC, a journalist notes of the Palestinians that:

> Their anger is fuelled by a lethal combination of economic discontent, frustration with the peace process, religious passion and the desire to avenge the deaths of friends and loved ones. (BBC1 late News, 3 October 2000)

The above news reports raise some of the key issues which underpin the continuing conflict. Each requires to be sufficiently explained such that an audience may understand their significance. We can now look in detail at these and other 'explanatory' areas as they appear on the news to see what was actually available to viewers.

History and origins of the conflict on TV news.   In the bulletins which we transcribed from 28 September until 16 October 2000, there were over 3,500 lines of text in total. Just 17 lines referred to the history of the conflict. The BBC offered this account which appeared in just one bulletin on 10 October:

> So where is the past 50 years of Arab-Israeli conflict now leading? From the moment of birth the Jewish state of Israel has been fighting for land against Palestinians forced into exile. In 1967 Israel doubled its territory in the Six Day War. For Arabs this was the great setback. Ever since, Israel has been trading land for guarantees of peace from its neighbours. The last great effort

to secure total peace was launched in 1993. Seven years on it brought Bill Clinton and today's leaders to the brink of success at Camp David. But the division of land could not be agreed and today Israel's prime minister speaks of the peace process in the past tense. (BBC1 late News, 10 October 2000)

The journalist noted that: 'Ever since, Israel has been trading land for guarantees of peace.' This description of Israeli actions might be questioned. There were many press reports prior to this which showed how peace moves were actually accompanied by the expansion of Israeli settlements (see, for example, 'Land grab gathers pace in West Bank', *Guardian*, 8 January 1999). The BBC journalist does note that the Palestinians were 'forced into exile'. This is the only such reference in the whole period of this sample. We found a small number of references in other time periods, but they are apparently rare. In February 2002, for example, a BBC2 *Newsnight* presenter asked a Palestinian negotiator: 'Are you prepared to negotiate over the return of the Palestinians who were driven out of their homes in 1948?' (27 February 2002). In March 2002 a journalist on BBC1 mentioned in passing the 'Palestinians who were driven out or who fled when Israel was created in 1948' (BBC1 late News 26 March 2002). It is not surprising then that the great bulk of people in our audience sample did not know where the Palestinian refugees had come from and how they had become refugees. This has a crucial effect on how audiences can understand reports on issues such as the peace process. In the following example two journalists are discussing the prospects for negotiations and mention the issue of refugees without any further explanation. The first journalist asks what chance there is of a successful outcome, and the second replies:

> If both sides can now somehow come out of this, with some sort of ceasefire, some sort of end to the violence, then perhaps they can move on to final status talks, perhaps after that concerning Jerusalem, and perhaps the return of Palestinian refugees. It is a very big day indeed for the Middle East tomorrow. (BBC1 early evening News, 15 October 2000)

The references which journalists made to the history of peace negotiations were similarly brief. On ITV, a news presenter puts this question to a correspondent: 'You've been following this process now for about nine years since it began, is this in your view one of the bleaker moments?' His colleague replies:

> Well it's been a roller-coaster ride hasn't it, since the euphoria of the Madrid peace conference in '91, at the Oslo Accords and through to the shock of the Yitzak Rabin assassination, but what strikes me is how quickly it's all regressed. We are now hearing the same old tired debates ... (ITV early evening News, 16 October 2000)

The problem is once again that such a sequence of references to past events implies a level of knowledge which is simply not present in many viewers.

The cycle of violence. As the intifada developed journalists began to speak of it as having taken on a life of its own. The assumption here was that violence produced more violence in a self-perpetuating cycle:

> Five days of mayhem, the cycle of death and confrontation has acquired its own momentum. (BBC1 early evening News, 2 October 2000)

> The funeral of a murdered Jewish settler called Rabbi Hilal Leibermen. He'd been shot dead. But in this crisis violence begets more violence and today was no exception. Mourners from the settlement ... were heavily armed including the women. After the funeral service the Jewish settlers attacked Arab homes nearby. They were fired up with grief and bent on revenge. (BBC1 main (late evening) News, 11 October 2000)

ITV also pursued the themes of a constant cycle and a 'self-perpetuating tragedy':

> The cycle of violence is unbroken, the trouble spots are the same each day. (ITV early evening News, 4 October 2000)

> It has become a self-perpetuating tragedy. Each day starts with the funerals, but afterwards many Palestinian men make their way to the usual flashpoint to confront their enemy. Then there is the familiar exchange. Stones for rubber-coated bullets, stun grenades and tear-gas canisters. (ITV early evening News, 9 October 2000)

Israelis and Palestinians are on the brink of war tonight after a day of tit-for-tat violence in the Middle East. (ITV main (late evening) News, 12 October 2000)

There were over 50 lines of text where such explanations were directly given (approximately similar numbers for each channel) and many other references to 'response' and 'revenge'. Of course it is the case that violence can beget further violence and an escalation of the tactics which are used. But it is not possible to explain the genesis of major conflicts with such an analysis. The 'reasons' for the Second World War, for example, were not that Britain and Germany kept bombing each other. The origins of a conflict and the implications that these have for how it may be resolved cannot be understood simply by reporting day-to-day events and responses. As the BBC journalist Paul Adams commented to us: 'It's a constant procession of grief – it's covered as if it's a very large blood feud, and unless there's a large amount of blood, it's not covered' (Interview, 22 August 2003). Such an approach is unlikely to leave much room for the analysis of underlying causes.

Land, water and economic discontent.   The economic consequences of the Israeli occupation have been cited as a key factor in the Palestinian uprising. These were well known from very early in the intifada and indeed before it began. In October 2000 the *Guardian* reported that resources and land disparity were behind the unrest ('Poverty and Resentment Fuel Palestinian Fury', 14 October 2000). It quoted a report from the UN Development Programme that noted that: 'The Palestinians are still suffering from the legacy of the prolonged occupation, which has a striking impact on their deteriorating social and economic conditions.' The UN report also noted the impact of the 'expansion of the Israeli settlements and military infrastructure'. Other reports had described what this process looked like on the ground. In January 1999 the *Guardian* had cited a critical account from the Israeli group Peace Now on the development of settlements. The newspaper also reported a process by which Palestinian villages were razed, their land was then declared to be a 'nature reserve', and subsequently became housing for Israeli settlers (8 January 1999). This was a very extensive programme of settlement and military expansion which could hardly be missed by journalists. In May 2002 the Israeli human rights group B'Tselem reported that Israel had seized 42 per cent of the West Bank. The report noted that the mechanisms for this included seizure for 'military needs', declaration of land as 'abandoned assets' and the expropriation of land for 'public needs'. These mechanisms according to the report were generally supported by the Israeli high court, thus giving them a 'mask of legality'. As a result of this, the report concluded, Israel was operating a regime with two separate legal systems in the West Bank based on racial discrimination (*Guardian* 15 May 2002).

An obvious question arises: if these issues are so crucial then why is there so little about them on television news? In the period of our sample there were a tiny number of scattered references to the issue of land. The peace process was referred to, as we have seen, as failing because of a lack of agreement on 'the division of land' (BBC1 main News, 10 October 2000). Clashes in Jerusalem are referred to as being over 'hotly disputed territory' (ITV early evening News, 29 September 2000). The Gaza Strip was described as being 'a 30-mile-long finger of land that is home to a million Palestinians and a few thousand Jews'. This report does not discuss the implications of the military occupation for the Palestinians, but instead goes on to say 'in one place, Nezarim, Israeli soldiers protect around 400 of those settlers' (ITV early evening News, 3 October 2000). The Palestinian perspective on these issues is simply not explained in these news programmes. We are told, for example, that they are 'frustrated by the peace process' (BBC1 main News, 6 October 2000), and that the 'peace process has simply not delivered' (BBC1 late News, 2 October 2000). But to understand the significance of such statements requires some knowledge of the control of resources and what has actually happened under the military occupation.

As we have indicated, the control of water supplies by Israel is another crucial issue in the conflict. It is an interesting area for media analysis since it clearly has an extraordinary visual impact on the areas in which Palestinians and Israelis live. This is described in a report by Suzanne Goldenberg in the *Guardian*. She notes of the Gaza Strip that it is the most densely populated place on earth. As she writes:

1.1 million Palestinians live in a mere two-thirds of Gaza's 360 square kilometres, penned into wretched refugee camps or blocks of flats ... all are hemmed into the claustrophobic Strip by an electric fence on one side and the settlements on the other. Meanwhile 6,000 Jewish settlers and army installations occupy the rest – a full one-third of Gaza. That includes a fair chunk of the coastline and the underground aquifers in an area that is mostly sand dune and hard scrabble. (*Guardian*, 16 June 2001)

She then describes the visual difference that control of the water brings:

> The contrast between the communities could not be crueller. Inside the Jewish settlements, residents live in red-roofed bungalows, surrounded by well watered land. There are community centres, swimming pools and hot houses producing cherry tomatoes and lettuce. The Palestinian world outside is bone dry and dusty, narrow lanes crammed with donkey carts, children and push carts. (*Guardian*, 16 June 2001)

If a print journalist can describe a scene so vividly, then how did the ultimate visual medium of television portray it? In practice we found it was virtually absent from the coverage. Although TV journalists often went to settlements there were no comparisons made as above, linking the disparity of resources to the Israeli occupation. The issue of water was in fact barely mentioned. On ITV, there was a brief reference to it in this account of the issues that were frustrating a peace settlement:

> There is also the question of millions of Palestinian refugees that live in neighbouring countries or in impoverished camps. Will they ever be allowed to return home? And what will be the fate of Jewish settlers, the Israelis who now live on the West Bank, land the Palestinians say must be part of their future country? And there are other seemingly mundane issues like *access to water* which are so important in the Middle East and that are still eluding negotiators. (ITV early evening News, 2 October 2000 – our italics)

Such an account names a series of key issues but without explaining them. The audience could not understand from this, how the Palestinians became refugees or why they are impoverished. Water is said to be an important issue, but viewers would be unlikely to understand why. In the focus group interviews which we undertook for this study, less than 10 per cent knew that water was a key issue. In the period of this sample, the issue was not mentioned at all on BBC1. On BBC2 a journalist listed major issues for peace negotiations and commented that: 'last but not least [there would need to be] an agreement on water rights' (BBC2 *Newsnight*, 3 October 2000).

The occupation clearly had important effects on the economy and allocation of resources that were not explored on the news. There were a series of other consequences on social life, which were important factors in explaining the conflict.

The occupation: social consequences for Israelis and Palestinians. From the Israeli perspective security is a major concern, and their continued presence in the West Bank and Gaza has been justified on these grounds. From the Palestinian perspective a central issue is that they are living under Israeli military control. The effects of the occupation on the everyday life of the Palestinians is substantially absent from media coverage. Phrases such as 'military occupation' or 'military rule' are not normally used. Yet the conditions which the military presence has imposed on the Palestinians are a major factor in the unrest. In December 1998, the *Observer* reported a survey that had been published by B'Tselem, the Israeli human rights group. The survey was to mark the fiftieth anniversary of the Universal Declaration of Human Rights and B'Tselem observed: 'Apart perhaps, from the article prohibiting slavery, the State of Israel violates each and every one of the Declaration's provisions in its behaviour towards the Palestinians in the territories' (*Observer*, 13 December 1998).

B'Tselem found that the killing of Palestinians by Israeli settlers was rarely punished. It also reported that of the 1,000–1,500 Palestinian prisoners interrogated by the Israeli Shin Bet security services each year, 85 per cent were tortured.[8] This was in the period before the intifada and at this time Palestinian security forces were working extensively with Israel to arrest and detain dissidents and militants who were opposed to the agreements which had been reached between the Israelis and Arafat's administration. The *Observer* reported that the 13 different Palestinian security forces had modelled themselves on Shin Bet and that three-quarters of their detainees had been tortured (13 December 1998). At the same time there were reports that thousands of Palestinians remained in Israeli jails, some from the time of the previous intifada 1987 (*Guardian*, 7 November 1998).

To live under such rule had profound effects on the everyday lives of Palestinians. From their perspective, the Israelis had used the peace to extend their military and economic dominance. It became more difficult for Palestinians to travel as more settlements and roads between them were built for the use of Israelis. These involved the bulldozing of large areas of land and the development of extensive systems of checkpoints and military security. One of the journalists we interviewed for this study had been the head of a news agency in Jerusalem in the period before the 2000 intifada. He commented to us:

> My Palestinian neighbours could not go to the beach which you could practically see. They carry identity cards which tell everything about them. If an American viewer ever saw the extent to which the apartheid system is applied in the occupied territories – the pass laws make the South African system look benign. The Israelis say that [most] of the Palestinians are now under Palestinian Authority control. What they don't say is that they often can't even leave the town they are in.

He also commented that members of his Arab staff had been arrested and tortured by the Israelis. He made this criticism of TV news coverage of the conflict: 'They cover the day-to-day action but not the human inequities, the essential imbalances of the occupation, the day-to-day humiliations of the Palestinians' (interview, 10 June 2002).

Our own analysis of news content showed that the consequences to the Palestinians of living under military occupation were very rarely explored. There were occasional comments in the news that obliquely raised the issue. The BBC, for example, mentioned in a report that the Palestinians were 'tearing down security cameras', referring to these as 'hated symbols of Israeli authority' (BBC1 main News, 6 October 2000). Another report describes undercover police grabbing a demonstrator noting that 'these officers who never want to be identified, pretend to be Palestinians during a riot but when they spot a suspect they treat him with little mercy' (BBC1 early evening News, 13 October 2000). There are also occasional references to the occupation and occupied territories – as, for example, when a BBC journalist says of young Palestinians that 'they don't trust the Americans and after all, they say it's the occupation to blame' (BBC1 lunchtime News, 2 October 2000). It was clear from our audience studies that many people would not understand such a reference. Because the Israeli presence is not described as a military occupation and the significance of this is not explained, it was not clear what the word 'occupation' actually meant. Some understood it to mean simply that people were on the land (as in a bathroom being 'occupied').

There were two other occasions when news events were reported which could have been used to explain the nature of the occupation. On 13 October 2000, the Israelis were reported on BBC and ITV as stopping young Muslims from entering the Old City to pray. Also, as we have seen, on 9 and 10 October, ITV discussed how the Israelis had surrounded Palestinian areas to 'choke the life out of the revolt'. Both of these examples illustrate that the movement of Palestinians is subject to the wishes of the Israelis, but there was no commentary to indicate that movement could be routinely controlled, or discussion of this as a feature of the military occupation. The clearest statement on this issue came in a brief statement from a Palestinian who said that people are 'penned like chickens, they can't move freely' (BBC1 main News, 10 October 2000), but this comment is not taken up or developed by journalists.

There are two problems with coverage that does not explain the 'military' nature of the occupation and the consequences of this for the Palestinians. The first is that it is difficult for viewers to understand why the conflict is so intractable. It can appear simply as two communities who 'can't get on' and who are squabbling over the same areas of land. The second is that such coverage disadvantages the Palestinian perspective, as a key reason for their unrest and anger is left unexplained. Some observers have commented on their own surprise when viewing the conflict at first-hand. They noted how this revealed the limits of their previous understanding of the accounts that were prevalent in the media. For example, a businessman wrote as follows in the *Guardian*:

> I have had business interests in the Middle East for many years, I often travel to Israel and the West Bank and I'm in contact with journalists, aid workers and UN officials there. I can state categorically that all those whom I have met, who have come to work on the West Bank with an open mind, or even, like me, with some prejudice in favour of Israel, leave with disgust and rage at Israeli brutality, racism and hypocrisy. Some are Jewish. It is experience on the spot that leads them to this perception.

He also commented how even a newspaper such as the *Guardian* 'seems never to address adequately the justice [or the tragedy] of the Palestinian position, or the frightening racism that seems to me to be at the core of Israeli arguments and actions' (letter, *Guardian*, 29

March 2001). Another correspondent discusses the role of the Israeli
settlements in this system of control and also notes the absence of
such analysis in media coverage:

> A few days ago the BBC showed aerial film of a settlement. I
> was surprised by how unfamiliar it was to see one. I realised
> that few if any pictures are normally shown of settlements –
> their sheer scale, their facilities and their monopoly of the water
> supply. Nor is there any detailed map of their distribution ...
> nothing prepared me for the shock of the prevalence and scale
> of the settlements when I visited the occupied territories. It is as
> though every other hilltop in Devon and Cornwall was taken over
> by a Milton Keynes-like town and occupied ... looking down
> triumphantly over the indigenous locals corralled in the valleys
> below. (Letter, *Guardian*, 26 May 2001)

The issue that this raises is that the settlements have a key military
and strategic function in the occupation. The point of being situated
on the top of hills is that this offers a commanding position. At
the time of the signing of the Wye Accords (supposedly a land for
security agreement), Ariel Sharon, who was then the Israeli Foreign
Minister, urged settlers in the West Bank to 'grab the hilltops'
(*Guardian*, 8 January 1999). Yet when the BBC visits a settlement
at the beginning of the intifada, the journalist stresses that it is
'intensely vulnerable, high on a hill'. There are no comments on
how it functions in the occupation:

> One regular target for Palestinian gunmen is the Jewish settlement
> of Passagot. It's *intensely vulnerable, high on a hill,* surrounded
> on all sides by Palestinian territory. Even a children's nursery
> had a bullet fired through the window. The settlers know they
> are in mortal danger. A dozen babies have been evacuated just a
> few minutes earlier to the settlement's bomb shelter. Settlers say
> Palestinians are trying to force them out. (BBC1 late News, 5
> October 2000 – our italics)

The settlers are then interviewed but there are no questions on what
the conflict is actually about:

> *Settler*: Well they want us out of here. They're shooting at us
> hoping that we'll pick up and leave.
> *Journalist*: Do you have any intention of leaving?

Settler: No, no.
Journalist: Some people would say you're crazy staying here with so many bullets flying.
Settler: No, not crazy, we have our ideas and our ideals and we'll stick up for them and it's important to us. (BBC1 late News, 5 October 2000)

The journalist then comments without explanation that 'This place looks more like a fortress than a settlement' – which seems to miss the key argument that this is indeed what many settlements are. It is of course the case that some settlements are more exposed than others, but as Avi Shlaim notes, their overall impact is to exert a strategic and military control as well as to command land and water resources. It is this analysis which is missing from news which focuses on vulnerability and the 'threat' to settlers, and in reports which present the Palestinians and Israelis as simply two warring communities. The key issue that remains unexplained is the structural division of society – one group is effectively controlling the lives of the other (with some resistance). This point of view is not put to the settlers and they are not asked if they think it is right that Palestinians have lost their land so that settlements can be developed. In the following example from ITV the initial emphasis is again on Israel 'defending' and 'protecting' the 'small Jewish enclaves', while the Arabs are referred to as 'continuing their onslaught'. The reporter does note that the Palestinians regard the settlements as a 'symbol of the Israeli occupation'. But without an explanation of what this occupation is and what it signifies for the Palestinians there is no clear rationale for their action other than that they are 'driven by hatred'. The report begins with a studio introduction that contrasts the peace talks with the ongoing violence:

Newscaster: And even while those talks were on, the violence between Palestinians and Israeli security forces continued for the seventh day in a row. Among six Palestinians reported killed today was a boy of nine.
Journalist: The cycle of violence is unbroken, the trouble spots are the same each day. The Israeli army has again been defending the small Jewish enclaves on the West Bank and the Gaza Strip – pockets in the midst of Palestinian towns and villages … here 400 people are protected by around a thousand soldiers. Some Israelis believe such little Alamos should be defended at all costs. The Arabs of course feel very differently and today *driven on by*

hatred continued their onslaught and there's not much sign of conciliation here. These Palestinians regard the Jewish settlement here in Hebron as an affront, a symbol of the Israeli occupation that has not been brought to an end by the political process. (ITV main News, 4 October 2000 – our italics)

The official Israeli view is that the settlements are simply Jewish communities under threat from 'terrorists' and 'mobs', as in this report: 'Israeli soldiers are accused of using excessive force in response to the violence but insist they're only defending their communities from the stone-throwing mobs' (ITV lunchtime News, 4 October 2000).

This view of the settlements as essentially vulnerable and under 'threat' is clearly developed in other news accounts where journalists spend time following the lives and concerns of the settlers. The following report, which is from before the outbreak of the intifada, explored the worries which settlers have about the peace process. The initial focus is again on children's safety:

Machabi Lutz is worried about his children's safety. The Lutz family live in the settlement of Bet Al on land which Israel captured in the 1967 war because they feel this is the heartland of the Jewish people. Now they are disgusted that the prime minister they voted for is transferring more territory to the Palestinians. (BBC1 early evening News, 23 October 1998)

There is then an interview with the settler's wife:

Interviewee: This agreement endangers us more than we were endangered before. We're worried because we've seen friends of ours killed and the murderers run away – it takes them two minutes to flee into the autonomy areas and now there are going to be more of these areas and we are very scared and we are very disappointed.

The only reference to Palestinian views is a comment that 'the Palestinians here say Israeli settlers are trying to take their land'. There is no evidence given as to whether or not this claim is true. An Israeli peace activist is then interviewed who says that he does not want his grandchildren to die for nothing. The journalist then comments that these 'Israeli leftists believe their country will never have peace until the Palestinians have justice'. There is no explanation of what this justice would consist of or why the Palestinians need it. The report then returns to the settlers:

> Tonight in Jerusalem, the Jewish religion's most holy place, Mrs Chanie Lutz and other residents of the settlement of Bet Al went to pray for God's help. The settlers now plan a sustained campaign against the Washington agreement. (BBC1 early evening News, 23 October 1998)

There are no critical questions addressed to the settlers here on their role in the military occupation, on the control of land and water or indeed on accusations that settlers have killed Palestinians. In a later report in February 2002 a BBC Radio 4 journalist produces a 'diary' from Israel and the occupied areas. He also spent time with the settlers and travelled to work with them. This account was published on the BBC website:

> It did feel odd sitting in the front seat of their Mazda, flak-jacketed and helmeted with an M16 rifle jammed up against my leg, while Suzie [the settler's wife] looked after little Liam in his car seat behind me. It can't be much fun risking your life every time you drive to the office. This couple have paid heavily for their convictions. (*Tel Aviv Diary*, Radio 4 – BBC website, 7 February 2002)

A very different image of some settlers was given in a report by the Israeli human rights group, B'Tselem which discusses attacks by settlers against Palestinians:

> Among the settlers' actions against the Palestinians are setting up roadblocks to disrupt normal Palestinian life, shooting at rooftop water heaters, burning cars, smashing windows, destroying crops and uprooting trees, and harassing merchants and owners of stalls in the market. (B'Tselem, 2003d)

They also state that the purpose of some of the settlers' violence is 'to force Palestinians to leave their homes or land, so that the perpetrators can take control over Palestinian land.' They describe the difficulties in gathering crops:

> During the olive-picking season, in which many Palestinians are at work in the olive groves, violent groups of settlers increase

their attacks on Palestinians. In these attacks, settlers fire at olive pickers, killing and wounding them, steal their crop, and destroy their trees. (B'Tselem, 2003d)

A further report by Amnesty International on the deaths of children on both sides in the conflict notes the difference in response of the Israeli Army and describes the following attack:

> On 19 July 2001, Diya Marwan Tmeizi, a baby of almost four months from the village of Idna (near Hebron), was killed when the car he was travelling in with his family on their way home from the wedding of relatives, was shot at by Israeli settlers. Two other family members were also killed in the attack and five were wounded including, two year old Amira. The attack happened not far from the Tarqumiya roadblock, but the soldiers manning the roadblock did not stop the killer's car when it fled. (Amnesty International, 2002b)

As early as 1994, Israel Shahak reviewed a series of accounts in the Israeli press about the relations between settlers and Palestinians and the responses of the army. Quoting a report in *Ha'olam Ha'ze* he notes that 'Beating the Arabs, or humiliating them otherwise or vandalising their property before the very eyes of the army soldiers is not regarded as a 'sufficient reason' for arresting a settler'. He describes another report in *Kol Ha'ir* by a journalist who has travelled on a bus with religious settlers:

> 'On the way,' he reports, 'the religious youths from Kiryat Arba kept themselves busy slinging stones at Arab passersby, explaining their behaviour by saying, 'We are the settlers, aren't we?' (Shahak, 1994)

The journalist describes graffiti at the entrance to Kiryat Arba reading, 'Only a sucker doesn't kill an Arab'. (Shahak, 1994)

These accounts contrast with the tv news images of settlers in our samples where there was a tendency to present them as worried members of small, vulnerable communities. It is a partial account which can disguise the very deep levels of racism which exist in some parts of Israeli society as well as the key role of the settlements in the occupation, i.e. that they are involved in the imposition of economic and military control and their own position is guaranteed by the Israeli army. To present settlers and Palestinians as simply two communities who can't get on, misses the point that one group is supported by an occupying military force, while the other is living under its control. Palestinians and settlers certainly do shoot at each other but the consequences for the two communities are very different. As B'Tselem has noted:

> The Israeli authorities employ an undeclared policy of leniency and compromise toward Israeli civilians who harm Palestinians.... This policy is in total contrast to the rigid policy of law enforcement and punishment where Palestinians harm Israelis. Towns and villages in the area of the incident are routinely placed under curfew...and intensive searches and arrests are made. (B'Tselem, 2003e)

The curfew system referred to is applied to Palestinians but not settlers, and can result in thousands of people being confined to their homes for 24 hours a day forbidden to leave even for medical help or schooling.

As we have indicated, what is missing from many news accounts is the structural imbalances of this society. Without such explanation it is difficult to understand the depth of hostility and the intractability of the violence. Conflicts can appear simply as a 'cycle' in which one death leads to more attacks or as unexplained friction between communities. In the following report settlers are described as attacking 'Arab homes' after the funeral of a Jewish settler:

> In this crisis violence begets more violence and today was no exception. Mourners ... were heavily armed, including the women. After the funeral service the Jewish settlers attacked Arab homes nearby. They were fired up with grief and bent on revenge. (BBC1 late News, 11 October 2000)

In the next example, we are told that the presence of pockets of Jewish settlements in Palestinian towns is a source of friction, but were not told why this is so:

> Violence in the West Bank too ... rioters attacked a Jewish religious outpost. The presence of small pockets of Jewish settlements in the midst of Palestinian towns is a constant source of friction. It was a similar story in Bethlehem. (BBC1 early evening News, 1 October 2000)

But the causes of 'friction' are not hard to find. In 1994, the Society of Saint Yves, the Catholic Legal Resource Centre for Human Rights, submitted a report to the high court in Israel. It noted that in East Jerusalem (which was occupied) 86 per cent of the land had been made 'unavailable for use by Arabs'. It also commented that the Arabs whose homes have been demolished for Jewish settlements often 'come from the lowest economic strata of their community' and now 'live in makeshift hovels, doubled and tripled up with other families, or even in tents and caves' (cited Chomsky, 1999: 547). But without such knowledge, Israelis and Palestinians can appear simply to be bad neighbours. As in this report:

> Violence spills over into Jerusalem itself. Here where Israeli and Palestinians live in close proximity, sometimes across the same street, the potential for friction is great. In Nablus [a 22-year-old] was buried this morning ... (BBC1 lunchtime News, 4 October 2000)

This news report on ITV comments on 'neighbours fighting' within Israel: 'Arabs and Jews took to the streets of Nazareth. The Israeli army were in the middle, preventing a huge street fight between neighbours' (ITV main News, 9 October 2000). There are qualifications which should be made to this analysis. As we will see, some reports did refer briefly to the intifada as a 'popular uprising', which does imply resistance, though what it was resistance to, and why, was less clear. There was also sympathetic coverage in this sample period of the deaths of Palestinian children. To this extent the consequences of the conflict for Palestinians were reported, but what remained unexplored was the nature of the military occupation and the distorted relationships it produced between the occupiers and the subject population.

Religion.   There is a strong focus in news reporting on religious differences as a central explanation for the unrest. There are a large number of references to 'sacred' and 'holy' places from the first days of the intifada when Ariel Sharon is reported as 'visiting one of Islam's holiest sites in Jerusalem' and 'sparking off' the violence (BBC1 main News, 30 September 2000). The initial fighting was described as 'centred on a shrine sacred both to Muslims and Jews' (ITV early evening News, 29 September 2000). The BBC reported that:

This was the holiest site in Jerusalem today. Palestinians tried to force the Israeli police out. The response came with live ammunition. At least four people died, over a hundred and fifty were injured – and many of these people had come here to pray. There was outrage amongst Palestinians that this could happen here, outside the third most sacred site in Islam of all places. (BBC1 late News, 29 October 2000)

On the following day we hear:

Rioters attacked a Jewish religious outpost … It was a similar story in Bethlehem. Behind the fortress is a place called Rachel's Tomb, religious Jews wanting to pray there today thought better of it. (BBC1 early evening News, 1 October 2000)

The references to religion and religious conflict run through the news accounts, particularly in the first days of the intifada. We are told that the Palestinians regard their dead as 'martyrs killed in a religious war over Jerusalem' (ITV early evening News, 2 October 2000), and on BBC that 'once again blood has been spilt in a place that is sacred to both Muslims and Jews' (BBC1 late News, 6 October 2000). There are also very explicit statements by journalists which explained the source of the violence as being religion. In this account from the BBC, the arguments over 'sacred ground' are presented as 'almost the last real barrier to peace':

This magnificent vista is the source of the violence and almost the last real barrier to peace. It's a corner of the Old City of Jerusalem, sacred ground to Muslims and Jews alike and Israelis have sole control of this ground, but how is it to be shared? Jews call it the Temple Mount and it is flanked by the Western or Wailing Wall. The most sacred place of the Jewish religion, directly above it the Al-Aqsa mosque which for Muslims ranks behind only Mecca and Medina in spiritual significance, and within it the Dome of the Rock. It's here according to the Koran that the Prophet Mohammed ascended to heaven. (BBC1 late News, 3 October 2000)

A report on ITV also highlights the key importance of religion and the holy sites. It also includes a rather optimistic view of how the Palestinians 'enjoy self-rule':

So the entire Middle East process has now come down to the most contentious issue of all, who controls Jerusalem's holy sites? Thanks to the peace process the Palestinians enjoy self rule in the Gaza Strip and over large swathes of the West Bank. But in the heart of Jerusalem no compromise seems possible. The Temple Mount is the site of the holy Al-Aqsa mosque crucial to Palestinian and Islamic identity, but the area is also bordered by the Western Wall which Jews all over the world see as the focus of their faith. (ITV early evening News, 2 October 2000)

The level of hostility and the explosion of anger might suggest that the Palestinians bitterly resent the military occupation, in spite of their having some local autonomy. The reasons for this, which we outlined above, were not explored on the news. This is important, because to reduce the conflict to 'religion' and to 'fighting over holy sites' can be misleading. To see it in these terms can lead to simplistic solutions such as advocating religious 'tolerance' between communities. Of course this is an admirable objective, but the problem is that such an explanation and solution miss out other key factors which are producing the conflict. As many commentators have noted, religious tensions are often underpinned by other social and economic problems (see, for example, 'Poverty and Resentment Fuel Palestinian Fury', Guardian, 14 October 2000). In times of great stress, populations often turn to religion or spiritual ideas which can become the focus of struggle. There are many historical examples of this and it is especially so when the conflict is unequal or particularly desperate. Religious ideas can of course be a motive in their own right, but violent and fearful struggles often intensify religious commitment. The crucial point in relation to the Israeli-Palestinian conflict is that by neglecting the social and economic factors, journalists sometimes presented it simply as a religious struggle. This apparently affected the belief of some audience members who were unaware of the deep social and economic divisions and how they may have related to the unrest.

Israeli perspectives on security needs, terrorism and incitement.   These areas relate primarily to Israeli rationales for their own actions and the legitimacy or necessity of the occupation. While the Palestinians see themselves as resisting an illegal military presence, the Israeli perspective focuses on what they see as the vulnerability of their own nation. As Nomi Chazan, a member of the Israeli Knesset, has commented, 'we are trapped in two narratives which both sides believe are incompatible: the Palestinian struggle for national liberation against Israeli occupation, [and] Israel's continued struggle to survive' (*Observer* 18 August 2002). This sense that the Israelis have of being under threat is well expressed in the following report from the BBC. It is from the early days of the intifada and mentions the kidnapping of Israeli soldiers on the border with Lebanon as well as the conflict with the Palestinians:

[The Israelis] say from their point of view that they feel as if they are under threat, as if they are under attack from all sides. They say, and they truly believe, that it was a concerted effort on the side of the Islamic militants in Lebanon to attack Israel when they took the three soldiers hostage yesterday, and there were also some stone-throwing incidents up here on the border from where I'm speaking. And the Israelis also feel as if they are under attack from the Palestinians, they blame all the violence on them. (BBC1 early evening News, 8 October 2000)

Israeli security concerns and fears over terrorism are commonly reported in news coverage and this appears to be a well established historical pattern in TV reporting. A study of news coverage of peace negotiations in the period before the intifada shows that these security concerns were given a strong prominence, sometimes to the exclusion of other issues such as the nature of the occupation and its impact on Palestinian beliefs and action.[9] In the following example, a journalist is asked about the main obstacles to peace, and his reply focuses on the issues that concern the Israelis:

Newscaster: What are the main obstacles to peace?
Journalist: Well I *just mentioned security arrangements, and those are the key issues* and in a sense the key obstacles. It's quite clear now that the Israelis are committed to pulling back from a further 13 per cent of the West Bank but only if the Palestinians can convince them that they are able to offer new written cast-iron security commitments, better than anything they have offered in the past. *There are key issues like the Israelis wanting* the extradition of more than 30 Palestinian Islamic militants to Israel for trial. For example they want to make sure that illegal weapons held by Palestinians in the West Bank and Gaza are confiscated. Those are specific detailed issues the Israelis want the Palestinians to deliver and they want American intelligence to be involved to

verify Palestinian compliance. (BBC1 early evening News, 18 October 1998 – our italics)

At the time of the intifada there were also references to Israeli fears: for example, the comment that 'what is increasingly worrying the Israelis is the prospect of some kind of terrorist attack' (ITV early evening News, 13 October 2000). And on the BBC the same day: 'But what the Israeli security forces really fear now is a new wave of terrorist bombings by Palestinian extremists' (BBC1 late News, 13 October 2000).

The Israelis are also described as feeling 'besieged', as in this report:

And in the meantime Israeli troops are still on high alert. We visited this space in Gaza where snipers are on the look out for Palestinian gunmen who frequently open fire on them. The troops here showed us a network of breeze block tunnels they use to protect themselves. *Many Israelis feel besieged at the moment* by a Palestinian uprising they didn't expect. (BBC1 main News, 10 October 2000 – our italics)

The above report is made without irony and there is no comment that the soldiers are actually imposing a military occupation upon the Palestinians. The paradox would also not be apparent to many viewers since the occupation and its routine effects on the lives of the Palestinians were not explored on the news. This raises a very significant point, that in the absence of such discussion new developments in Israeli tactics can be presented as 'security' requirements (from the point of view of Israel) rather than as an extension of military control or the occupation (which is how the Palestinians see it).[10] Thus when Palestinians were prevented from entering the Al-Aqsa mosque the reason was reported as being because 'security forces' were 'afraid of a riot' (BBC1 late News, 13 October 2000). The Palestinians were shown as being angry at this treatment, but key elements of the reason for this anger are missing from the coverage. This absence also made it easier for the Israelis to present their account of the cause of the unrest. Rather than it being seen as a popular uprising against a military occupation, they suggested that the main cause was 'incitement' by Arab leaders and particularly by Yasser Arafat. We will discuss this further below.

Yasser Arafat and Ariel Sharon: the instigation of violence.   In the early days of the intifada both Yasser Arafat and Ariel Sharon were accused of having a role in causing or promoting the violence. The intifada was reported as having been 'sparked off' by the famous walk which Sharon made through Muslim holy places accompanied by hundreds of armed policemen. This was widely seen as a deliberate provocation and as an assertion of Israeli sovereignty. Sharon was already a notorious figure for the Palestinians. They blamed him for the killing of refugees at the Sabra and Shatila refugee camps in Lebanon in 1982. Before that in the 1950s he had commanded a unit that launched punitive raids against Jordan and Egypt. It was reported that 'in one of them at Qibya, scores of civilians were massacred'. In the early 1970s 'he was responsible for a brutal crackdown on Palestinian resistance activities in the Gaza Strip' (*Guardian,* 14 October 2000). This information on Sharon's history was not given on TV news. His walk was initially reported on the BBC as follows:

> This man, Israel's right-winger Ariel Sharon, visited the religious compound yesterday and that started the trouble. He wants Israel alone to have sovereignty over the holy sites, an idea that's unthinkable to Palestinians. None of this will help the search for compromise. (BBC1 main News, 29 September 2000)

ITV did not report that day on the role of Sharon in its early evening or late bulletins, but noted that 'Israelis and Palestinians are blaming each other for the street violence that has followed today's events in Jerusalem, when the city's most holy places for both Arabs and Jews, became a battlefield' (ITV late News, 29 September 2000).

ITV news actually reports the role of Sharon rather less than the BBC. In this reference on 30 September, Sharon is not actually named: 'Arabs here are outraged at what happened on the disputed site, and they are blaming the disturbances on a visit to the holy compound on Thursday by a hard-line Israeli politician' (ITV early evening News, 30 September 2000). In the late News of that day the oblique reference to Sharon has gone altogether:

> Palestinian leaders had called a one-day general strike in memory of the people killed yesterday during rioting on Jerusalem's Temple Mount. However, the Israelis have accused the Palestinian security forces of not doing enough to quell the violence and they say

Arab leaders have been guilty of incitement. (ITV late News, 30 September 2000)

The Israeli view is given here but there is nothing on the role of Sharon or his history. Without this it is not easy to understand why the Palestinians were so angry. Two days later ITV reported that 'The violence [was] sparked off by a provocative visit by right-wing Israeli politicians to a Muslim holy site' (ITV lunchtime News, 2 October 2000). And later that evening Sharon is actually named:

> It was the visit of Ariel Sharon, the hard-line Israeli politician, to Jerusalem's Temple Mount that appears to have triggered the wave of violence. It is a site holy to Jews and Muslims, and Palestinians judged it to be a deliberately provocative gesture. Sharon claimed it was the opposite.
> *Ariel Sharon*: 'I came here with the message of peace. I believe that we can live together with the Palestinians.'
> But his presence started days of rioting and armed clashes. (ITV early evening News, 2 October 2000)

Why his presence should so enrage the Palestinians is not clear from these accounts. The same problem occurs with the BBC coverage, though they are more forthright in naming Ariel Sharon and in pointing to the consequences of his actions:

> The violence was sparked off three days ago when the right-wing politician Ariel Sharon visited one of Islam's holiest sites in Jerusalem. (BBC1 late News, 30 September 2000)

> It all began with a gesture of calculated provocation by Israel's right-wing leader Ariel Sharon. Surrounded by hundreds of armed policemen, Mr Sharon paraded in front of a Muslim holy site in Jerusalem.
> *Ariel Sharon*: 'I came here with the message of peace.'
> But it was no such thing. At a time when the future is at stake, Mr Sharon was appealing to Israeli hard-liners. The consequences were immediate and inevitable. (BBC1 early evening News, 2 October 2000)

The BBC makes clear its view on the intention of Sharon and he is termed a 'right-wing enemy of the peace process': 'Ariel Sharon, right-wing enemy of the peace process, knew exactly what he was doing when he very publicly walked the ground last week' (BBC1 late News, 3 October 2000). Later we hear:

> It's just two weeks since the visit to Jerusalem's holy site by Israel's opposition leader Ariel Sharon touched off the wave of unrest which has ripped up the Middle East peace process. Mr Sharon has been a long-standing opponent of conceding territory to Palestinians and now he's being offered a place in a coalition cabinet. (BBC1 lunchtime News, 13 October 2000)

Sharon's role is clearly stated in these references. But as with the ITV news, it is not clear *why* what he did is of such significance to Palestinians. Without an account of the occupation and Sharon's history it is not likely to be.

There was also extensive reporting on the role of Arafat in the intifada. The Israeli view was that he was responsible for inciting street violence. This is a view that was frequently reported and persistently put forward by interviewees. But some journalists who were witnessing the events tended to discount the explanation. They suggested that the intifada was 'a popular uprising' over which Arafat had little control. Some commentators at the time had noted the difficulties that such an uprising created for Arafat. In the period before the intifada, he had co-operated extensively with the Israelis to suppress dissidents and those opposed to the agreements that he had reached. The Palestinian Authority was accused of repression, the use of torture and of corruption. At the same time, its co-operation with the Israelis was seen as resulting in their taking more land and water. As Edward Said wrote two years before the intifada:

> Arafat and company have now completely delivered themselves to the Israeli and US intelligence apparatus, thereby putting an end to anything even resembling a democratic and independent Palestinian national life. And this, by the way, has been sacrificed to the survival of Arafat and his coterie of advisers, hangers-on, and security chief, for whom the idea of Palestinian civil society with an independent judiciary and legislative body is a silly inconvenience to be disposed of like the land they have given up with scarcely a look back. (*Guardian*, 7 November 1998)

When the intifada began, the Israeli journalist Amira Hass described the difficulty of Arafat's position:

Seven years after the Oslo Accord all Palestinians feel betrayed, because they are still living under occupation ... When six Palestinians were killed by close-range bullets at the mosque by Israeli police, the anger which swept everybody contained all other angers, of seven years and longer. This time Arafat could not dream of checking the spreading anger with his security forces. After all, it was about al-Aqsa. All his credibility would have been lost. (*Guardian*, 3 October 2000)

The important point made here is that the 'message' of the intifada was meant 'not only for Israel but for Arafat too'. This suggests that the problem for Arafat was that if he opposed a mass popular uprising, he might be in danger of being swept away by it. Without such background information it is difficult to understand the position of Arafat or the anger of the Palestinians. ITV News did feature a comment from a Palestinian referring to Arafat as 'useless', but it is not made clear why he thought this:

This man was also shot during rioting yesterday, he has a bullet lodged in his chest. I asked him about the peace efforts being made today in Paris
Palestinian: 'Yasser Arafat the chairman is useless. Palestinian Authority is useless. We do not need them any more.'
So who if anyone is in control? The Palestinian security forces did manage to curb some of the trouble today, the death rate is down but there were still plenty of battlegrounds. (ITV early evening News, 4 October 2000)

None the less, both BBC and ITV News did question the view that Arafat could simply 'rein in' the protesters. Journalists on the ground who were witnessing the events were openly critical of the Israeli view:

Israel believes Yasser Arafat wants the violence to continue but it's doubtful whether the Palestinian leader could simply tell these young men to stop. (BBC1 lunchtime News, 2 October 2000)

Even if Mr Arafat agrees to stop the uprising, there are question marks over whether he can, whether it has spun beyond his control. (BBC1 late News, 9 October 2000)

ITV News also reports that 'this is not a campaign being waged by two armies, it is a popular people's uprising'. They also note that: 'The so-called ceasefire was never endorsed by ordinary Palestinians, for whom this remains a full-scale revolt. For the moment it seems, these people cannot be reined in' (ITV late News, 3 October 2000). There is a paradox here. Notwithstanding the clearly expressed comments that the intifada is a 'popular uprising', the view that Arafat is to blame actually takes precedence in the BBC's coverage (as measured by the amount of text which features it). This is because the Israelis used their superior media and public relations output, including the use of interviews to press the message. Their views on this were not challenged by the interviewers. This is particularly noticeable on the BBC where there was over twice as much coverage blaming Arafat as against that which criticised this view. On ITV News, which carried fewer interviews, the positions were more evenly expressed. There was also more coverage blaming Arafat than Sharon for instigating the violence. As we will see in this and later samples, the role of Sharon in instigating the conflict largely disappears, but there is a continued focus on Arafat. The Israeli view is given in reported statements such as the following from a BBC journalist:

I mean what we've been hearing for instance today from the Israeli prime minister Ehud Barak is all sorts of accusations and charges against Yasser Arafat the Palestinian leader. Mr Barak is saying that it is up to the Palestinians to end the violence, that they instigated it, that the Palestinian police have egged on and encouraged the crowds of stone-throwers and petrol-bombers by using ammunition themselves. Palestinian police brought the obvious response from the Israelis. Countering that, of course, Yasser Arafat condemned Israeli action of using gun-ships against civilians, the use of what he regards as excessive force. (BBC1 lunchtime News, 4 October 2000)

There is some sense of balance here in that 'both sides' are represented, but what is missing in the charges and counter-charges is any analysis of the nature of the conflict or its origins and history. The view that Arafat is to blame is highlighted in this BBC headline: 'Israel gives Arafat an ultimatum: stop the violence or no more peace talks' (BBC1 late News, 7 October 2000). The programme includes a direct statement from Barak:

Journalist: Israel has accused Yasser Arafat's Palestinian Authority of failing to protect [a Jewish religious shrine]. In his toughest warning yet, the prime minister told Yasser Arafat to stop the violence.

Ehud Barak: If we will not see an end to the violence within the next two days we will read it as a deliberate decision of Chairman Arafat to put an end to the peace process at this stage. (BBC1 main News, 7 October 2000)

In the following interview we can also see how Arafat is blamed for the violence without any challenge to this position from the interviewer:

Journalist: The Palestinians want a wide-ranging international inquiry into what has happened over the last two weeks, the Israeli government is less keen on that, why?

Interviewee: (former Israeli government minister): The most important thing is to get calm restored. Unfortunately, we were in the best part of negotiations, very advanced, and Mr Arafat had not got wholly what he wanted, turned the tables, went to the streets, creating so much violence, deaths and injuries ... Why did he move to the street rather than go on negotiating with us?

Journalist: Mr Barak when he came to power staked his whole prime ministership on finding peace ... it looks now as if he is on the brink of failure, doesn't it?

Interviewee: Yes it does unfortunately ... I remember now the last days of Camp David, President Clinton desperate telling Arafat 'It is the last opportunity, take it, it is a wonderful offer', and he decided not to and he preferred violence. It is a pity.

Journalist: Now obviously the summit is still going on ... but if it were to fail ... what do you think are the consequences not just here but for the region?

Interviewee: Consequences are bad, and the future will be much more gloomy. I'm afraid we may see more violence. We will have to defend ourselves. We see the gathering of Saddam Hussein and Yasser Arafat telling everybody 'We have to exterminate Israel'. We see the Iranians helping with the kidnapping of people and using their language. We see the extremists in the street, the Muslim extremism and I think it is bad. We have to defend ourselves. I would rather have a positive conclusion than a bad one.

Journalist: We will have to leave it there. Thank you for joining us. (BBC1 lunchtime News, 16 October 2000)

There are a number of key points that emerge from this analysis. First, Ariel Sharon was presented on the news as having sparked the intifada through a deliberate provocation of the Palestinians, though there was little information given as to why they would see it as such. Second, there was actually more coverage of the Israeli view that Arafat was promoting the violence than of the role of Sharon. Third, this was in spite of the fact that journalists on the ground were reporting that the intifada was a popular uprising and were questioning whether Arafat *could* control it. Fourth, the reason for the prominence of the view that 'Arafat is to blame' was that the Israelis used their commanding position in TV interviews and in the supply of statements to the media. We will discuss the issues raised by interviews and headlines in the next section.

Interviews and headlines

These are key areas for understanding how some viewpoints are highlighted or developed in the flow of news coverage while others are downgraded or lost. In our analysis of interviews, we found important differences in the manner in which Israelis and Palestinians were presented. The Israelis had twice as much time to speak (as measured by lines of text).[11] Another major difference was in the way in which the two sides appeared. Israelis were more likely to be interviewed in calm and relaxed surroundings. We saw this for example in the above interview with the Israeli former cabinet minister. Shortly before this there is a brief comment included from a Palestinian. It is actually a couple of snatched sentences given while in the middle of the noise of a protest march: 'We want peace, every day we want peace but what we can do now, they shooting the kids and the people. We want peace. We need it more than them' (BBC1 lunchtime News, 16 October 2000). This is followed by a brief interview with an Israeli in a street and then the longer, more relaxed interview with the Israeli former cabinet minister. There are clear differences between these types of interview and it may be beneficial to express views at length in a calm atmosphere with all the implied status that it entails. These are all issues in the production of television programmes and involve decisions made by broadcasters about how the different sides will be presented. We asked a very experienced Middle East correspondent for the BBC to explain why these differences between Israelis and Palestinians occurred. He made two important points. The first is that the Israelis have a very well organised media and public relations operation; the second is that the Israelis limit what the Palestinians are able to do because of the impositions of their military occupation. As he commented:

> The way you sound is terribly important for credibility. If you are in an absolutely sound studio setting, you have more credibility. If you are on a scratchy telephone line you are at a disadvantage. The reason the Palestinians suffer is their limited facilities – the Israelis have more money to spend and spend it on a sophisticated Western style of media communications and links. The second point is that the occupation limits Palestinians' freedom of access to the media. Ninety-nine per cent of the media is based in Jerusalem. If you have a Palestinian minister and you want him to come to a studio in Jerusalem then he can't or it will take him hours because of the restrictions [on the movement] of the Palestinians on the roads. (Interview, 26 August 2002)

He also noted that the difficulties of movement applied to media teams trying to reach Palestinian areas could affect coverage. This cannot be an acceptable situation for a publicly accountable broadcasting corporation that is committed to impartiality. Broadcasters cannot absolve themselves from the requirement for balance by accepting a status quo in which one side can ensure that it receives more favourable treatment by imposing restrictions on the other. The broadcasters really have to devote the necessary resources to make sure that both sides are properly represented. It should also be clearly indicated to viewers where the difficulties that Palestinians have in making their case result from the actions of the Israelis. For example, if a Palestinian is speaking down a scratchy telephone because of the limitations of movement imposed by military rule, then viewers should be told that this is so. To avoid doing this is to legitimise a structural imbalance.

Headlines

The purpose of headlines is to attract viewers' attention and to focus on the key themes of a bulletin. For the purposes of this part of our study we analysed 67 headlines from bulletins on BBC1 and ITV News between 30 September 2000 and 16 October 2000. We found that some headlines offer a relatively neutral account of events such as the progress of negotiations or the arrival and departure of politicians or comments that the conflict is continuing, as in the following examples:

Chaos in the Middle East ahead of emergency peace talks tomorrow. (ITV early evening News, 3 October 2000)

A Middle East summit on Monday, but the fighting goes on. (ITV early evening News, 14 October 2000)

Clashes continue as leaders prepare for Middle East summit. (ITV late News, 15 October 2000)

Fighting rages on the West Bank as peace talks begin. (ITV early evening News, 16 October 2000)

The Middle East, more violence as the peace talks now reach a delicate stage. (BBC1 early evening News, 10 October 2000)

Tensions remain high as world leaders gather for Israeli and Palestinian peace talks. (BBC1 early evening News, 15 October 2000)

The Israeli and Palestinians leaders prepare for tomorrow's crucial peace talks. There is hope for the end of immediate violence but not of a lasting breakthrough. (BBC1 main News, 15 October 2000)

Urgent diplomacy tonight to try to bring Israel and the Palestinians together. America warns that if violence continues other nations could be sucked in. (BBC1 main News, 10 October 2000)

We say that these are relatively neutral in that they do not clearly endorse one side or the other in the conflict. None the less, they do contain value assumptions and judgements – for example, that peace may be found in the comings and goings of world leaders and that their priority is to urgently secure peace, rather than to pursue more narrowly defined concerns such as national interests or political support at home. We have already noted the military aid that Israel receives from the US and how the Palestinians perceive this. Some might see a contradiction in attempts to 'end bloodshed' while continuing to supply weapons to one side. But there is no hint of such thoughts in a headline such as this:

Middle East peace summit gets underway, but no sign of a breakthrough. While they try to end the bloodshed the killing continues on the streets. (BBC1 late News, 16 October 2000)

Other headlines can offer a relatively straightforward account of events, even though the event itself may be controversial. For example, statements that 'Israel has moved in tanks' or that 'Palestinians have been killed' or that 'A suicide bomber has killed Israelis' are relatively neutral as long as the actions of both sides are reported impartially. This impartiality is lost, however, if the actions of one side were reported differently from the other – for example, if killings by one side were under-reported while those of the other side were highlighted. We did actually find some differences in the reporting of Palestinian deaths between BBC and ITV News at the beginning of the intifada. In this period those who died were overwhelmingly Palestinian but this was not always made clear in news headlines. The BBC was more likely than ITV to indicate Palestinian deaths and to give specific numbers, as in the following examples:

At least twelve Palestinians have been shot dead in clashes with Israeli forces. Another 300 are injured in the worst fighting for four years. (BBC1 early evening News, 10 September 2000)

Fifteen Palestinians are killed in clashes with the Israeli army. At least 300 are injured in the worst fighting for four years. (BBC1 late News, 30 September 2000)

Israeli forces kill eleven more Palestinians on a fourth day of bloodshed. (BBC1 late News, 1 October 2000)

Two Palestinians are reported to have been killed and dozens injured after clashes with Israeli forces using anti-tank missiles and helicopter gunships. (BBC1 early evening News, 3 October 2000)

ITV was more likely to say simply that there had been 'more deaths' or 'more killings' or to give numbers without saying who had died:

Four die in violence at sacred shrine in Jerusalem. (ITV late News, 29 September 2000)

Four dead as Palestinian protests continue. (ITV early evening News, 30 September 2000)

At least a dozen dead as Palestinian protests continue. (ITV late News, 30 September 2000)

Four die in gunfights between Palestinians and Israelis. (ITV early evening News, 1 October 2000)

Nearly 30 are killed in Palestinian-Israeli gun battles. (ITV late News, 1 October 2000)

More die as Middle East violence spirals out of control. (ITV early evening News, 2 October 2000)

More die as Middle East erupts into all-out violence. (ITV late News, 2 October 2000)

More killings as ceasefire fails. (ITV late News, 3 October 2000)

More deaths in Mid-East clashes despite peace talks. (ITV early evening News, 4 October 2000)

Israelis kill ten during Palestinian day of rage. (ITV late News, 6 October 2000)

The ITV News made it clear in the text of the bulletins that the deaths were Palestinian, but the lack of clarity in the headlines is noteworthy. When two Israeli soldiers were killed, the ITV News gave the headline 'Swift retaliation after Israeli soldiers are lynched' (ITV early evening News, 12 October 2000).

There is a third category of headlines that are clearly prejudicial in that they employ the assumptions and ways of understanding the conflict of one side to the exclusion of the other. We can see this in the reporting of what was termed an 'Israeli peace deadline' on 7 October 2000, in which Israel gave Yasser Arafat an ultimatum to 'stop the violence'. As we have seen, from the perspective of the Israelis, the main cause of the intifada was incitement by Arab leaders, but for the Palestinians the cause was the continued military occupation and the violence that this did to their lives. Thus when the Israelis are reported as imposing 'peace deadlines' or demanding 'an end to violence', such language is likely to be regarded as meaningless by the Palestinians and they reject the assumptions that it contains. From their perspective, the world would not be 'peaceful' just because they stopped resisting the Israelis. They were also very critical of assumptions that it is they who need to stop the violence. Between 29 September and 9 October, around 90 people were reported to have been killed, nearly all of whom were Palestinians, while hundreds more had been shot and wounded. The Palestinians and indeed other commentators also believed that it was Israelis who had provoked the trouble with the intention of ending the peace process. The important point is that the Palestinians did not acknowledge or accept the 'normality' which the Israeli government was trying to impose. For them, the 'peace deadline' was merely another threat from Israel. This is clear from Palestinian comments in the text of some bulletins but it is absent as a view from the headlines. Thus in a BBC bulletin on 8 October we hear that 'already senior Palestinian officials have said that they are not going to respond to Israeli threats'. In the same bulletin the journalist attempts to lay out the views of both sides:

> ... and the Israelis also feel as if they are under attack from the Palestinians, they blame all the violence on them. Of course, there are two sides to the story, and we've all seen the awful images over the last ten days of how fierce the Israeli response has been. (BBC1 early evening News, 8 October 2000)

This may be contrasted with the following headlines that do not express both sides and report only the Israeli position:

> Israel gives Arafat an ultimatum: *stop the violence* or no more peace talks. (BBC1 main News, 7 October 2000 – our italics)

> Israel threatens to go in harder if Palestinian attacks don't stop. Palestinians are told they've seen nothing yet, but won't back down. (BBC1 early evening News, 8 October 2000)

> Israel threatens to go in harder if Palestinian attacks don't stop. (BBC1 late News, 8 October 2000)

> A peace process on a knife-edge as Israel's ultimatum to Arafat runs out. (BBC1 main News, 9 October 2000)

> Israel crisis: Prime Minister delivers ultimatum to Arafat. (ITV early evening News, 8 October 2000)

> Israel prepares for attack as *deadline to end violence* approaches. (ITV main News, 8 October 2000 – our italics)

> Israeli peace deadline passes with no end to violence. (ITV main News, 9 October 2000)

It would have been quite possible for these headlines to be balanced by including the Palestinian view. For example, the news could have said: 'The Israelis say they are imposing a peace deadline to end violence, but Palestinians say it is the Israelis who have done most of the killing.'

We found other problems in headlines dealing with Israeli 'security operations'. On 13 October it was reported that 'in Jerusalem, Israeli security forces prevented all male Palestinians under the age of 45 from getting in to the Old City' (BBC1 lunchtime News). In this operation, the Palestinians were prevented from entering the Al-Aqsa mosque and had to pray in the street. They were reported to be 'seething with anger'. From the Israeli perspective, this was indeed a security operation designed to prevent riots and to ensure the safety of their own people. From the Palestinian perspective it is seen as an extension of Israeli military rule, but this perspective is absent from the headlines:

> Israel mounts a massive security operation as Palestinians gather in Jerusalem. (BBC1 lunchtime News, 13 October 2000)

> Israeli clamp down struggles to stop simmering Middle East violence. (ITV main News, 13 October 2000)

Here again we can see that the headlines could have included the Palestinian perspective. For example, the news might have said: 'Israel mounts a massive security operation, but Palestinians say it's more military rule.'

It is certainly the case that the Israeli authorities saw themselves as under attack. Some headlines followed this perspective, reporting, for example, on the kidnapping of three Israeli soldiers by Hezbullah guerrillas from Lebanon. On 7 October the BBC reported that

> three Israeli soldiers have been kidnapped during fighting on the Lebanese border. The guerrilla group Hezbullah say they are responsible. Israeli warplanes have since attacked Hezbullah targets in Southern Lebanon. (BBC1 early evening News, 7 October 2000)

There is very little history given of the Lebanese conflict and consequently the kidnapping may have the appearance of being an unprovoked act. Two days later, however, the BBC did report that 'Hezbullah guerrillas are holding three soldiers and hope to swap them for Lebanese civilians being held as bargaining chips by Israel' (BBC lunchtime News, 9 October 2000). A report in the *Guardian* expands on this, noting that 'There are international efforts to get the three soldiers back safely probably by trading Lebanese who have been held hostage in Israeli jails for years' (9

October 2000). The information that the Israelis had been holding Lebanese hostages was given on two BBC1 bulletins (lunchtime and early evening News, 9 October 2000) but not on four other bulletins on BBC1 which reported the Hezbullah kidnap (early evening and late News, 7 October 2000; early evening News, 8 October 2000, and lunchtime News, 10 October 2000). ITV News reported the Hezbullah kidnap on five bulletins without saying that Israel had been holding hostages. We can also see that the headlines for this story relate to the actions of Hezbullah rather than to those of Israel. It is Hezbullah who are apparently the source of the 'trouble':

Trouble continues as Hezbullah take three Israeli soldiers prisoner. (ITV early evening News, 7 October 2000)

Hezbullah kidnap three Israeli soldiers after the wave of violence spreads. (BBC1 early evening News, 7 October 2000)

There were very few headlines that could be said to express the Palestinian perspective. The following two highlight Palestinian losses and the desire to retaliate:

As Palestinians bury their dead, there will be a Middle East summit. (BBC1 early evening News, 14 October 2000)

Palestinians want their dead avenged but there will be a summit on Monday. (BBC1 late News, 14 October 2000)

Overall, there is a stronger tendency in the headlines to highlight Israeli statements, actions or perspectives. Palestinian views are featured but tend to be buried deep in the text of news bulletins. There is no obvious reason why they could not have been included in headlines and it is hard to avoid the conclusion that one view of the conflict is being prioritised.

Casualties and deaths: case studies

We will look here in detail at how violence, casualties and deaths on both sides of the conflict were reported.[12] As we have noted, in this sample period (28 September to 16 October 2000) the deaths and casualties were overwhelmingly Palestinian. The BBC reported four days after Ariel Sharon's walk through the Muslim holy places that 35 Palestinians had been killed and hundreds injured. By 16 October it was reported that 100 people had died, all but seven of whom were Palestinians/Arabs (ITV lunchtime News, 16 October 2000).

It is clear that Palestinian/Arab deaths were far greater than those of Israeli armed forces or settlers, apparently by a ratio of around 13:1.[13] Yet when we analysed news content, we found that deaths and casualties of Israeli armed forces/settlers received about a third of the coverage allocated to this area.[14] While the Israelis received less in absolute terms at this point, these figures still represent a disproportionate emphasis upon them, relative to actual numbers of deaths and injuries. This imbalance continued in programmes from our later samples of news, to the point where there was actually more coverage of Israeli casualties, even though in real terms Palestinians were still experiencing much higher losses. As we will see, we also found differences in the language used to describe deaths on both sides, with certain words such as 'murder', 'atrocity', 'lynching', 'savage killing' and 'slaughter', being used by journalists to describe Israeli deaths rather than those of Palestinians.

However, some Palestinian deaths, particularly those of children, were treated with great sympathy. Reporting on the death of twelve-year-old Mohammed al-Durrah, a BBC journalist comments that 'there was a sickening gloom at his mother's house today' (BBC1 main News, 1 October 2000). Another BBC report focuses on the deaths of Palestinian children. The newscaster notes:

> The world has been shocked by the number of Palestinian children killed and injured in the last two weeks of fighting. At least 26 of the 100 or so people killed were children. The Palestinians claim that the Israeli army is deliberately shooting to kill. The Israelis say the Palestinians are using children to get the world's sympathy. (BBC1 main News, 13 October 2000)

The imbalance between the two sides is specifically referred to as a 'controversial and uneven pairing'. A journalist reports directly from a hospital and cites the comments of doctors that shots were deliberately aimed at the upper body 'and a quarter of those killed have been children. Doctors here believe these shots were carefully aimed at the upper body, in order to kill.' Later in the report there was a statement from an Israeli spokesperson:

> No one should be so naive to think this happens only because the children and something terrible happened on the way. It is a brutal and cynical way of using the image that the more casualties they have the more you are right.

The journalist then discounts this by reporting a mother's comments and noting that another Palestinian boy was shot with a satchel on his back:

> But Mohammed wasn't sent to the protest by anyone. He has never been to a rally in his life, his mother told me, he wasn't the type. Another Palestinian boy was shot this week with a satchel on his back. (BBC1 main News, 13 October 2000)

There were also criticisms made of the level of force being used by the Israelis. As a journalist commented in another bulletin: 'The Israelis call this restraint but only about six of their men were wounded, compared to more than 300 Palestinians' (BBC1 early evening News, 30 September 2000). Later, on ITV it was reported that Israeli soldiers were 'showing absolutely no restraint, firing live ammunition into crowds from 20 metres' (ITV early evening News, 20 October 2000). Sometimes the references are more muted, as in these comments:

> Serious questions are being asked about the use of live ammunition. (ITV early evening News 2 October 2000)
>
> ... Israel's lethal brand of policing. (BBC2 late News, 3 October 2000)
>
> Israel still wielded a big stick – helicopters fired rockets killing at least one Palestinian. (BBC1 early evening News, 4 October 2000)
>
> So another display of really tough tactics by the Israeli security forces. (BBC1 main News, 13 October 2000)

More severe criticisms emerged from within Israel itself when, for example, Shimon Peres, the Israeli foreign minister, was reported in October 2001 as trying to 'rein in' the Israeli army. It was clearly stated that elements of the army were trying to 'wreck' a ceasefire:

> Aides of Mr Peres have accused the army of damaging Israel's image, and seeking to wreck the ceasefire he brokered last week with the Palestinian leader, Yasser Arafat, by opening fire on stone-throwing protestors. (*Guardian*, 2 October 2001)

The newspaper went on to report that:

> Seventeen Palestinians have been killed since last week's truce ... two of them were shot dead on their way to work on Sunday

when a convoy of Palestinian taxis came under fire from Israeli soldiers at an unmarked roadblock … there are growing signs of disquiet with the army's operations in the West Bank and Gaza – including the use of live fire against unarmed protestors and 'surprise' checkpoints in the West Bank at which the two Palestinian labourers were killed. (*Guardian* 2 October 2001)

However, it was not suggested on television news at the time of our sample that the actions of the army might be linked to a political agenda (that is, to stop the peace process). But as we have noted above, the view put forward by the Israeli government at the time, that Yasser Arafat was encouraging violence for political ends, was in fact reported and discussed on TV news. There were also clear differences in the way in which deaths were reported for both sides. Although the Israeli army was reported as firing live ammunition into crowds, words such as 'murder' and 'atrocity' were not used by television journalists in our samples to describe the deaths of Palestinians.[15] Some emotive language was used in reporting Palestinian deaths. For example, a Palestinian is said to have 'died in the most horrific circumstances' when his mutilated and burnt body is reported to have been found. But it is noteworthy that this brief report appears only on the BBC and then the circumstances of the death are reported as a 'claim' made by Palestinians:

> Outside a morgue in Ramallah, his children are grieving their father, it is claimed he was kidnapped by Israelis tortured and beaten to death. The children asked to go in and see their father's corpse, they are told they should remember him as he was because Isaam Joda was mutilated. Inside the morgue doctors examining the body say he was burnt with cigarettes and an iron before he died. (BBC1 main News, 10 October 2000)

In the same bulletin, the BBC also reports the death of an Israeli settler, Rabbi Leiberman. This death and the subsequent funeral service receives about twice as much coverage as that of the Palestinian. It is described as a 'savage, cold-blooded killing' and there is no use of the word 'claim' in referring to its circumstances. The account, which, according to press reports, came from the Israeli authorities, is simply endorsed and reported by the journalist:

> And there is grief too in this Jewish settlement. Children are in mourning on both sides of the divide, this family has also lost

a husband and a father. Rabbi Leiberman was kidnapped and shot dead as he tried to get to a Jewish shrine being ransacked by Palestinians.

This is followed by an interview with an Israeli:

This is the way it is going at the moment, it shows that there is no way we could live together. Because the Arabs don't want to, not because we don't want to, because the Arabs don't want to. We've given them every chance to be able to live together and they don't want to accept it.

The journalist then continues:

Rabbi Leiberman's body was found here in a cave. This was a savage cold-blooded killing in a remote and isolated area and the tragedy is that even if there's a lasting deal to end this crisis it may not be enough to prevent random acts of sectarian violence like this one. (BBC1 main News, 10 October 2000)

There are two points to be made here. The first is on language. On the same day that these stories appeared, the BBC had also reported that 'almost one hundred people have died in the past twelve days, almost all of them Palestinians' (BBC1 early evening News, 10 October 2000). Despite the very large number of Palestinians who had died, words such as 'savage cold-blooded killing' had not been used to describe their deaths. The second point is that there are differences in the way in which statements from Palestinian and Israeli sources are treated. In practice this means that Israeli definitions and the use of specific emotive words can become the 'normal' language of news. We can see this in the reporting of the death of the twelve-year-old Palestinian boy, Mohammed al-Durrah, on 30 September 2000. This death was widely reported and was presented as a tragedy. The boy was reported to have 'wept with fear as his father tried to shade him' (BBC1 main News, 30 September 2000), and that they 'cowered terrified in no-man's land' (ITV early evening News, 2 October 2000).

But it is clear that there are competing explanations of the circumstances surrounding the death. The Palestinians regarded it as a deliberate killing. This view appears very infrequently. On one BBC bulletin the boy's parents are interviewed. The journalist begins by reporting the views of the boy's mother:

'This was an outrage', she said 'and I want the whole world to know how it happened. Miraculously his father survived but his body is punctured with eight bullet holes. "They shot at us until they hit us", he told me, and I saw the man who did it – the Israeli soldier. The Israelis haven't admitted responsibility.' (BBC1 main News, 1 October 2000)

The Israeli view was that the boy was caught unintentionally in crossfire and that they had not seen him. It is quite clear from other bulletins that this view predominates and is sometimes endorsed by journalists, while the view that the boy and his father were deliberately targeted is absent. We can see this in the following examples:

Newscaster: Palestinians have been mourning the death of a twelve-year-old boy *killed in the crossfire*.
Journalist: The Palestinian death toll is rising steadily, among them a twelve-year-old boy, Mohammed al-Durrah, who, with his father, got *caught in the crossfire*. Israeli soldiers should open fire only when their lives are in danger but they killed the child who clearly posed no threat whatsoever. (ITV early evening News, 1 October 2000 – our italics)

The worst clashes have been in Jerusalem, the Gaza Strip and the West Bank, where a twelve-year-old boy was *killed in the crossfire*. (ITV main News 1 October 2000 – our italics)

One death more than any other has inflamed Palestinian passions, that of this twelve-year-old boy filmed over the weekend, cowering with his father before he was shot and killed. (BBC1 main News, 2 October 2000)

... the fatal shooting by Israeli soldiers at the weekend of twelve-year-old Mohammed al-Durrah as he cowered with his father. Israel says the boy was *caught unintentionally in crossfire*. (ITV lunchtime News, 2 October 2000 – our italics)
Newscaster: Children were again caught up in the clashes today in a repeat of the scenes in which a twelve-year-old Palestinian boy was shot and killed yesterday.
Journalist: The Israelis are fully aware of the worldwide abhorrence at the death of twelve-year-old Mohammed al-Durrah, who, with his father, got pinned down during a *gun battle*. For 45 minutes they cowered terrified in no-man's land, but eventually the Israelis

killed the boy. *They said afterwards they hadn't seen him.* (ITV early evening News, 2 October 2000 – our italics)

Journalist: Twelve-year-old Mohammed al-Durrah with his father pinned down during a *gun battle*. For 45 minutes they cowered terrified. But then the Israelis killed the boy. *They said afterwards they hadn't seen him* ...
President Clinton: 'It was a heartbreaking thing to see a child like that *caught in a crossfire*.' (ITV main News, 2 October 2000)

Journalist: Nearby I met the mother of twelve-year-old Mohammed al-Durrah, the Palestinian boy killed on Saturday *in the middle of a ferocious gun battle*. Mohammad's last moments alive were captured on film, his father telling him not to be afraid, a few seconds later he was shot dead. (BBC1 main News, 3 October 2000 – our italics)

It is clear that the journalists are sympathetic and do say that it was the Israelis who killed the boy, but it is the Israeli explanation of this event which is most frequently referenced. These patterns in the use of language and the adoption of 'official' Israeli definitions are also shown in the news coverage of a sequence of deaths in October 2000 in which Israeli soldiers and Israeli Arabs were reported as having been killed by angry crowds.

Between 8 and 11 October 2000, there were a series of reports in the press and on television of attacks on Israeli Arabs by Jewish Israelis, in Tel Aviv, Tiberius, Jaffa and Nazareth. Israeli Arabs make up 20 per cent of the population of Israel.[16] Many believe that they are treated as second-class citizens within Israel and in the early days of the intifada they had been reported as protesting/rioting in 'support for their Palestinian cousins' (BBC1 early evening News, 1 October 2000). On 10 October 2000, the *Guardian* reported an attack on the Arab community in Nazareth as follows:

In Nazareth, in the heart of Israel, hundreds of Jewish extremists attacked an Israeli/Arab neighbourhood overnight. When the police arrived they fired rubber bullets at the local Arabs – not their assailants, killing two men. (*Guardian*, 10 October 2000)

On the same day, the *Independent* reported attacks in Tel Aviv and Jaffa: 'in the seaside community of Bat Yam, just south of Tel Aviv, two Israeli Arabs were stabbed'. They also reported that 'in nearby Jaffa, three Arab-owned apartments were burned' and that some Jews were chanting 'death to the Arabs' (*Independent*, 10 October 2000). On the following day the *Guardian* reported that 'mosques and Arab businesses in Tel Aviv were besieged by Jewish mobs in a night of mayhem', and that 'on two consecutive nights this week, Jewish mobs attacked the two-hundred-year-old Hassan Bek mosque in central Tel Aviv' and that those who did it were screaming 'death to Arabs' (*Guardian*, 11 October 2000). On the same day the *Independent* reported that:

> A Jewish mob wrecked one of Israel's most famous restaurants and tried to kill its Arab waiters by blocking them inside and torching the place … outside a young man gazed happily at the mess. 'We want to cut all the Arabs throats; we want to kill them all' he said. (*Independent*, 11 October 2000)

In all, thirteen Israeli/Arabs were reported to have been killed in these events. The *Guardian* reported that the clashes in Nazareth had been described as a pogrom by an Israeli peace group:

> … what is happening in Nazareth today is a pogrom, bearing all the hallmarks which were well known to Jews in tsarist Russia, that is collusion between the racist attackers and police. (*Guardian*, 10 October 2000).

The television news reporting of these events was rather muted by comparison. The following references were made within our sample:

> Some Israeli civilians are taking matters into their own hands. Last night a Jewish mob attacked a mosque in the city of Tiberius. It seemed to be an act of revenge, following a Palestinian assault on a Jewish holy shrine on the West Bank. (BBC1 early evening News, 8 October 2000)

> Some Israelis are taking it upon themselves to respond. In Tiberius on Saturday night a Jewish mob attacked a mosque and beat up Arabs. It seemed to be an act of revenge following a Palestinian assault on a Jewish shrine on the West Bank. Tonight Jews are again attacking Arabs, in the northern city of Nazareth. (BBC1 main News, 8 October 2000)

> Inside Israel itself Jews have taken to the streets to show their anger. This is a mosque being attacked in Tiberius last night. (ITV main News, 8 October 2000)

A second Israeli Arab was killed in Nazareth and a Jewish settler died near Nablus in the West Bank. (BBC1 lunchtime News, 9 October 2000)

As the national mood in Israel darkens, these were the rare scenes in Tel Aviv, it may be far removed from the West Bank but even here the conflict is spilling out onto the streets. Two Israeli Arabs were stabbed and Arab homes were set alight as Jews staged running battles with the police. (ITV lunchtime News, 10 October 2000)

Passions on all sides are still running high. Even in Tel Aviv violence has now hit the streets. These were angry Jews last night looking for Arab victims. (ITV early evening News, 10 October 2000)

Overnight violence flared again inside Israel. In Acre, Israeli Arabs clashed with the police. (BBC1 lunchtime News, 11 October 2000)

On the following day, two Israeli soldiers were reported on TV news to have been killed by a crowd of Palestinians. According to these reports, four Israeli soldiers in a civilian car were arrested by Palestinian police in Ramallah. The Israelis stated that they were simply reservists who had taken a wrong turning into the town. The Palestinians believed them to be part of the Israeli undercover units. A crowd gathered outside the police station where they were being held. Some of these Palestinians gained access to the station, where two of the soldiers were then killed and the body of one of these was thrown from a window. The other two soldiers who had survived were later handed over to the Israeli authorities.

There are three points to be made about the TV news coverage of these events. The first is that the deaths of the two Israeli soldiers receive over five times as much coverage as that of the 13 Arabs who had been killed in 'mob' violence. Second, the deaths of the Israeli soldiers are highlighted in the coverage, receiving headlines such as 'Swift retaliation after Israeli soldiers are lynched' (ITV early evening News, 12 October 2000). Third, there is a very clear difference in the language used to describe the two sets of events. For example, 'lynch-mob' is not used in relation to the Arab deaths. We can see these very sharp differences in the structure and tone of coverage if we consider the following accounts from our sample of the deaths of the Israeli soldiers. In this BBC News from 12 October 2000, a 'frenzied mob' is reported as 'baying for their blood':

A *frenzied mob* of Palestinians besieging the police station in Ramallah. It was here that several Israeli soldiers had been arrested by Palestinian police and the mob were *baying for their blood*. Eventually they burst into the police station surging through the gates and clambering into the windows. Israel says the soldiers inside were just reservists who lost their way. The Palestinians insist they were members of a plain-clothes undercover unit. Whatever the truth, two of them were about to die. With cameras filming from the outside, young Palestinians could be seen in this window *savagely beating and stabbing soldiers to death*. Victory signs to indicate the deed had been done. The *frenzied crowd could hardly contain their glee*, especially when one of the bodies was thrown down to them from the window. Israel was outraged and promised vengeance. It was almost immediate. Just after noon prayers, Israeli helicopter gunships swarmed over Ramallah. People ran for their lives for they knew what was coming. They had incurred the wrath of Israel.

From a nearby rooftop we watched wave after wave of rockets rain down on Ramallah. First target, the police station where the soldiers had been *so barbarically killed*. (BBC1 main News, 12 October 2000 – our italics)

There are a number of words which were used specifically to describe the deaths of the Israeli soldiers, such as 'atrocity', 'murder' and, as we have seen, 'lynch-mob' and 'barbarically killed'. None of these were used in our samples for Arab/Palestinian deaths. The following examples are all from the first day on which the deaths of the two soldiers were reported:

The [Israeli] attack is precise and repeated. Rocket after rocket slams into the police station destroying the very rooms where the *murders* took place ... Israel said it would take drastic action and it has, for the brutal *murder* of its soldiers this morning it has now traded a direct assault on the heart of the Palestinian city ... The Israelis are saying these are symbolic, if you like, pinprick attacks against, first of all the scene of this morning's *atrocity*. (BBC1 early evening News, 12 October 2000 – our italics)

Palestinian police seized four Israeli soldiers and took them to a police station, but two were apparently *lynched by a mob*. (ITV lunchtime News 12 October 2000 – our italics)

This was the trigger [for Israeli attacks]. The *murder* of two Israeli soldiers inside a Palestinian police station in Ramallah. The Palestinian security forces could not keep a *lynch-mob* of their own people at bay. In a first-floor room the soldiers were beaten and stabbed to death. Their bodies were later dumped out of this window. (ITV early evening News, 12 October 2000 – our italics)

There is also some discussion of the implications of the killings and a journalist refers to the Israeli view that they are a justification to 'abandon restraint':

On Monday night Ehud Barak had withdrawn his ultimatum and threat of a crackdown but clearly he felt that the brutal killing of the two soldiers here was a step too far – *justification for abandoning restraint*. (ITV early evening New, 12 October 2000 – our italics)

Some might question the uncritical use of the word 'restraint' – since, as the previous bulletin had noted, 'the violence has left about one hundred people, mainly Palestinians dead' (ITV lunchtime News, 12 October 2000). It is also noteworthy that while the Israeli attacks after the killing of the soldiers are consistently referred to as a 'retaliation' and 'a response', the same links are not made to Palestinian actions. In other words, the killing of the soldiers is not routinely described as a response to the large number of Palestinian deaths. In analysing such points we are not seeking to justify or legitimise any killings in the conflict. But as we will see, such linkages in the structure of coverage are very important in how viewers understand the origins and causes of violence.

The language of 'lynching', 'brutal murder' and 'slaughter' continues over the days which follow:

This is the Ramallah police station where two Israeli soldiers were *brutally murdered*. (BBC1 lunchtime News, 13 October 2000 – our italics)

Today they buried one of the Israeli soldiers who was beaten and stabbed to death by a mob of Palestinians and whose *murder* triggered a wave of Israeli reprisals. (BBC1 late News, 13 October 2000 – our italics)

On this BBC bulletin we are then given details of the personal and tragic circumstances of the victim. We are told that 'he married his sweetheart only last week. She is expecting his baby.' The Palestinians are then said to 'show no sign of remorse':

> In Ramallah Palestinians have been marching past the police station where the two soldiers died such horrific deaths. It has now been reduced to a pile of rubble by Israeli gunships. But these Palestinians show no sign of remorse. Instead they chant Islamic revolutionary slogans and protest about the Israeli attacks on their town. (BBC1 late News, 13 October 2000)

On the same day ITV news describes the deaths of the soldiers using words such as 'brutal slaying' and 'slaughter' (ITV lunchtime News, 13 October 2000). A later bulletin also notes that 'It was here yesterday with the mob violence that the Israeli-Palestinian conflict reached its lowest moment, exposing a raw and brutal enmity' (ITV late News, 13 October 2000).

It is perhaps significant that the 'lowest moment' in the conflict is seen as the mob violence which killed Israeli soldiers rather than the killings of Israeli Arabs or other Palestinian deaths. People on both sides of the conflict suffered terrible fates, but there were some clear differences in the manner in which these were described on the news. These differences in the use of language to describe deaths and killings are part of a much wider pattern in which some views, explanations and ways of understanding the conflict are given prominence. It may of course be argued that news which is balanced and impartial should not endorse any perspective but should report the views of both sides. However, we did find many departures from this principle, both in the sense that Israeli views were sometimes endorsed and highlighted, and that Palestinian/Arab perspectives were more likely to be downgraded or simply absent. In the section which follows we will examine a series of later samples of news coverage to identify possible similarities or changes in the patterns of coverage to which we have pointed so far.

ADDITIONAL CONTENT SAMPLES: OCTOBER–DECEMBER 2001, MARCH–APRIL 2002

Here, we analyse a series of additional content samples of TV news using the same methods as above. The purpose is to examine whether the trends which we have identified thus far are continued in later coverage. There were a number of specific areas of news content which we wished to identify and analyse for purposes of comparison with the earlier samples. These included news on the origins and history of the conflict, the reasons for the fighting, the rationales of the two sides, descriptions of motives and coverage of casualties. We chose these additional samples of news from periods where there was extensive media coverage of the conflict and analysed early evening and late bulletins from BBC1 and ITV. The sample dates from which the bulletins came were 17 October to 13 December 2001 (47 bulletins), 2–9 March 2002 (21 bulletins) and 9–16 April 2002 (30 bulletins). We also wished to identify any new themes or issues which had emerged in these periods. These later samples came after the events of the 9/11 attack on the US, which changed the international climate in which acts of violence and 'terrorism' were discussed. Within Israel, Ariel Sharon, the right-wing politician who had played such a role at the outset of the intifada, was now prime minister. There were also changes in the manner in which the Israeli-Palestinian conflict was fought. In 2001, the Israelis had begun a series of military incursions into areas which had been under local Palestinian administration, and some Palestinian groups were engaging in the extensive use of suicide bombs. The incursions were reported as involving attacks on refugee camps and the demolition of Palestinian homes as part of a new plan announced by Ariel Sharon to deal with the revolt against the Israeli occupation. As we have noted, this was a period of extensive settlement and military development in the occupied areas and it was reported that the Israeli army had 'uprooted thousands of olive trees and vast tracts of farmland in Gaza' (*Guardian*, 12 April 2001). In our analysis of news content above we noted the dominance of Israeli perspectives and how this in part reflected the success of their public relations output. In on-screen appearances/interviews, Israelis had twice as much coverage as Palestinians. To develop this analysis further in these samples, we analysed all reported statements as well as interviews. We counted all the coverage given to statements from each side and found that the Israeli dominance was sustained, notably in BBC coverage.[17]

In our first sample, we found that there was very little coverage of the history and origins of the conflict or discussion of the nature of the relationship between the two sides – that one was subject to military control by the other. The same was true of our later samples – we found nothing on the history and origins of the conflict. As before, there was extensive coverage of the violence and there was sympathy expressed for those caught up in it, but very little analysis of its nature and causes. We did, however, find that such issues were discussed more directly in other media and interestingly within Israel itself. In March 2002, Michael Ben-Yair, the Israeli Attorney General between 1993 and 1996, wrote in the Israeli newspaper *Ha'aretz*:

> The intifada is the Palestinian people's war of national liberation. We enthusiastically chose to become a colonialist society, ignoring international treaties, expropriating lands, transferring settlers from Israel to the occupied territories, engaging in theft and finding justification for all these activities ... we established an apartheid regime. (quoted in the *Observer*, 31 March 2002)

Because such perspectives on the history and nature of the conflict were substantially absent from TV news, the practical effect was to remove the rationale for Palestinian action. Much of the news implicitly assumed the status quo – as if trouble and violence 'started' with the Palestinians launching an attack to which the Israelis 'responded'. The lack of commentary on the nature of the occupation is clearly one dimension to this. Another is that there is little discussion of the possibility that actions by some Israeli groups might be designed to provoke a Palestinian response. We did, however, find that this was a subject taken up in the Israeli press. For example, in November 2001 the *Guardian* reported that Israeli newspapers were being very critical of the assassination policy pursued by Ariel Sharon's government. In November 2001 the military commander of Hamas in the West Bank had been killed shortly before the arrival of two US peace envoys. This, said the Israeli commentators, had increased the threat of suicide bombing. As one noted in Israel's largest daily paper, *Yediot Ahronot*:

> Whoever gave the green light for the assassination operation knew full well they are actually breaking, with a single blow, the gentleman's agreement between Hamas and the Palestinian Authority of refraining in the coming days from perpetrating terror attacks.

The Israeli paper also criticised the army for planting an explosive device which had killed five Palestinian children, noting that

> The act of revenge now hovering in the air has complete legitimacy, both on the Palestinian street and in the Palestinian Authority, in

the light of the deaths of five children by an Israeli Army bomb. (quoted in the *Guardian*, 26 November 2001)

Other Israeli commentators have suggested that the policy of 'targeted killings' by the Israelis was being used to provoke the Palestinians. A spokesman from Courage to Refuse, an organisation of dissenters from the Israeli Army, commented that:

> Any suicide attack within Israel, deplorable as it is, is used by Sharon as a pretext for inflicting ever-increasing misery on the 3.5 million inhabitants of Palestine. And if suicide attacks are not forthcoming, you can count on Sharon to provoke them with his so-called 'targeted killings'. (*Guardian*, 5 July 2002)

It has also been argued that the reason for such 'provocation' is that some powerful political and military groups did not want a peace with the Palestinians, which involved an independent Palestinian state. They would prefer a completely subordinate Palestinian population or another diaspora in which Palestinians move into other countries. The Israeli peace activist Uri Avneri has commented on Ariel Sharon that

> From the day he took power, his agenda has been to erase the Oslo accords and dismantle the Palestinian Authority and its armed forces. He believes that ultimately the Palestinians will flee, as they did in 1948, or agree to be herded into a few isolated bantustans. (quoted in the *Guardian*, 11 January 2002)

David Hirst makes a similar point in an extended analysis of the Middle East crisis:

> Ostensibly [Ariel Sharon] wants to return to the peace process. In reality he never did. For this was a war, which he and like-minded soldiers and politicians long anticipated; and once he got this war he did everything to fuel and perpetuate it. It was never a secret: he always opposed the Oslo Accord, and the historic compromise it involves, a Palestinian state on 22 per cent of original Palestine. From the outset, this was his war to destroy any idea of Palestinian self-determination on any portion of Palestinian land, and any legitimate institution in power to bring it about. (*Guardian*, 22 February 2002)

It can be seen that from a Palestinian perspective, the issue is not simply that the Israeli authorities may be acting 'first' in the sequence of violence, it is also that the Israeli 'response' is less about catching 'terrorists' than about destroying the possibility of a Palestinian state. The Israeli historian Avi Shlaim has argued that Ariel Sharon pursued this objective by linking his own actions to the American 'war against terror':

> Ever the opportunist, Sharon was quick to jump on the bandwagon of America's "war against terror" in the aftermath of September 11. Under this banner Sharon has embarked on a sinister attempt to destroy the infrastructure of a future Palestinian state. His real agenda is to subvert what remains of the Oslo Accords, to smash the Palestinians into the ground and to extinguish hope for independence and statehood. (*Observer*, 14 April 2002)

As we will see, the news coverage in our samples was not normally informed by such perspectives. It tended rather to focus on the narrow reporting of violent events within a framework of Palestinian 'action' and Israeli 'retaliation'.

SAMPLE TWO: OCTOBER–DECEMBER 2001

Motives, retaliation and response

In analysing what we call the rationales of action, it is not our intention to legitimise or justify any killings. It is clear that people from both sides in this conflict met terrible fates. But in explaining the construction and development of public understanding, it is important to show any differences that exist in descriptions of the motives of different parties and in the consequences of their actions. As we have indicated, there are very distinct and different perspectives, which exist on the nature of this conflict and the motives of those involved. The Israeli authorities and much of the Israeli population see the issue in terms of their security and indeed the survival of the state in the face of threats from terrorists and hostile neighbours. They present their own actions as a response or retaliation to attacks. In contrast, the Palestinians see themselves as resisting or responding to a brutal military occupation by people who have taken their land, water and homes and who are denying them the possibility of their own state. Our analysis suggests that the news framework and presentational structure, which was most frequently used in reporting events, tended to favour the Israeli perspective.

In this sample we found that Israelis were said to be 'retaliating' or in some way responding to what had been done to them about six times as often as the Palestinians.[18] This was a period of very intense conflict, including Israeli incursions into Palestinian towns and villages, suicide-bombs and other attacks. In summarising the period on BBC *News 24*, a journalist commented that: 'This cycle of violence began six weeks ago when an Israeli cabinet minister was shot' (BBC1, *News 24*, 2 December 2001). This is also how the Israelis presented the sequence of events. The Palestinians, however, regarded the killing of the Israeli minister as a 'response' to the assassination of one of their political leaders. The *Independent* described the sequence as follows:

> The most notorious assassination came at the end of August when Israeli helicopters hovering over the West Bank town of Ramallah fired two missiles through the office windows of the leader of the Popular Front for the Liberation of Palestine, Abu Ali Mustafa, 64, decapitating him as he sat in his swivel chair. As the leader of an established PLO faction, who according to Palestinians, was a politician rather than a member of the PFLP's military wing – he was the most senior figure to be picked off by the Israelis. Seven weeks later the PFLP sought revenge by infiltrating a Jerusalem hotel and assassinating Israel's tourism minister, Rehavem Ze'evi, whose support for ethnically cleansing the West Bank and Gaza of Arabs had long made him an enemy of the Palestinians. (*Independent*, 9 November 2001)

The Israelis frequently referred to the killing of their own minister and gave it as their reason for the incursions/attacks on Palestinian towns and villages. The news then commonly reported this view without commenting on the Palestinian perspective on the sequence of events:

> Israel has been under intense pressure from the Americans to pull out of Palestinian areas it occupied last week *following the killing of the* Israeli tourism minister. (BBC1 late News, 26 October 2001 – our italics)

A tribute to the minister assassinated one week ago today, Ariel Sharon says he has now captured some of the men involved, the reason he gave for his incursions into the West Bank. (BBC1 late News, 24 October 2001)

The assassination of an Israeli cabinet minister *led to the reoccupation* of Palestinian areas. (BBC *News 24*, 3 November 2001 – our italics)

Israeli forces have withdrawn from the town of Ramallah. Ramallah was one of six Palestinian towns which were occupied *after the killing of an Israeli cabinet minister.* (BBC Radio 4, 7 November 2001 – our italics)

The Israeli incursions/attacks were reported to have resulted in the deaths of 79 Palestinians in three weeks and other casualties plus the extensive destruction of homes and property (*Guardian*, 8 November 2001). Yet the pattern is persistent, that Palestinian attacks are rarely referred to on TV news as a 'response' or 'retaliation' to Israeli action. This structure can be seen clearly in the reports of a Palestinian attack and an Israeli 'retaliation':

Ten people have been killed and 30 injured after Palestinian gunmen opened fire on an Israeli bus travelling to a Jewish settlement in the West Bank. The bus was attacked as it approached Immanuel, north of Jerusalem. Tonight, *Israeli warplanes have retaliated* with air strikes against Palestinian targets in Gaza and Nablus. (BBC1 main News, 12 December 2001 – our italics)

Ten Israeli settlers were killed and up to 30 wounded in an attack by the Palestinian terrorist group, Hamas, on a bus in the West Bank. *Israel responded with air raids* on the West Bank and Gaza. (ITV main News, 12 December 2001 – our italics)

There is a much smaller number of references from journalists to the possibility of Palestinian counter-attacks and future action, as in the following reports:

The Israeli cabinet is meeting tonight and are planning more tough action but the lesson from the past is that Israeli strikes are met by Palestinian counter-attacks. The future is already written here and it holds a lot more blood. (BBC1 main News, 12 December 2001)

The bitter experience of the past 15 months suggests that the Palestinians will not regard this strike as a salutary lesson, but as a provocation. (ITV main News, 4 December 2001)

The BBC also describes how the actions of both sides are generating more hatred. A report notes that Israeli tanks have moved in on the headquarters of Yasser Arafat 'following the latest attacks on Jewish settlers'. A journalist then goes on to describe the attitudes on both sides:

> If Arafat falls, his successors could be more extreme – the UN warning of chaos. Israel isn't listening; it's consumed by rage and grief. This woman, burying her husband today, one of ten people killed near a Jewish settlement last night by men Arafat did not jail. Israel now punishing innocent Palestinians. We found troops stopping May, her sister Rena, and sick mother from driving to their home. Israel generating more hate. (BBC1 early evening News, 13 December 2001)

Such references suggest that one reason for the continuing violence is its self-perpetuating nature – that it is a cycle of 'tit-for-tat' action. We saw this explanation in the first weeks of the intifada. There is, however, an apparent move in this later period towards the Israeli perspective that it is Palestinian action which is driving this cycle. The assumption is revealed in an extraordinary exchange between a journalist and an MP interviewed on Radio 4 about his recent visit to Egypt. The MP is asked: 'What can the Egyptians do to stop the suicide bombers – because that in the end is what is cranking up the violence at present?' The MP then replies: 'Well that is one view, the Israeli view' (Radio 4, 5.00 p.m. News, 1 April 2002). One consequence of the adoption of this view by journalists was that of the dominant pattern of action–retaliation which we have described. This was especially so in the headlines and in the introductory phrases of news stories. On 1 and 2 December 2001, there were reports of suicide-bomb attacks in Israel which killed 25 people and left hundreds injured. On 3 and 4 December, the BBC News reported Israeli attacks on Palestinian areas as follows:

> *Headline*: No mercy – the Israelis *hammer the Palestinians after the weekend bombs*. The West Bank and Gaza under attack tonight, a moment of truth says Israel.

Israel *has hit back* with maximum force against Palestinians after the bomb attacks at the weekend which left 25 dead and hundreds injured.

Israel's *payback* to Yasser Arafat – at sunset Apache helicopters move in ...

Palestinians claim two were killed during Israel's *retaliation*.

Sum up: Israeli missiles have pounded Gaza city and the headquarters of Yasser Arafat, the Palestinian leader, *after the bomb attacks of the* weekend which left 25 dead and hundreds injured. The Israeli cabinet meeting in emergency session this afternoon said the attacks were a clear message to Mr Arafat to deal decisively with the problem of Palestinian terrorism. (BBC1 early evening News, 3 December 2001 – our italics)

Headline: Second day of *Israeli's retribution* – Palestinian targets are hammered again.

It's the second day of raids *in retaliation* for the Palestinian suicide-bomb attacks in Israel over the weekend.

Two people were killed and many injured. This is all part of Israel's *furious response* to the weekend's suicide bombings, which killed so many Israelis.

Interview question: We're into the second day of *retaliation*, is there any end in sight to this series of attacks that we've seen? (BBC1 early evening News, 4 December 2001 – our italics)

On ITV news it was reported that

Israel gave the Palestinian Authority another humiliating reminder of its military power today with more attacks *in response* to the weekend's suicide-bombings.

Sum up: Israel launched more attacks *in response* to the suicide bombings of the weekend. (ITV main News, 4 December 2001 – our italics)

This is a pattern which was apparently used quite extensively. The following are from programmes outside our main samples:

Dozens of Palestinians and Israelis have been killed in a relentless round of suicide-bombings and *Israeli counter-attacks*. (BBC2 *Newsnight*, 10.30 p.m., 13 December 2001 – our italics)

The Israelis had carried out this demolition *in retaliation for* the murder of four soldiers. (Channel 4 News, 7.00 p.m., 10 January 2002 – our italics)

Five Palestinians have been killed when the Israeli army launched new attacks on the Gaza Strip *in retaliation for* recent acts of terrorism. (Radio 4, 7.30 a.m., 6 March 2002 – our italics)

Such formulaic reporting excludes at least two key 'alternative' perspectives on the motivations of those involved in the conflict: (1) that Palestinians may be seen as resisting or responding to Israeli military control and the occupation as well as reacting to specific events such as attacks and assassinations; (2) that Israeli actions may be designed to destroy the possibility of a Palestinian state as well as to attack the 'terrorist infrastructure'. At one point the BBC does touch on the future of the Palestinian Authority, which is responsible for the local administration of the Palestinian areas. On 13 December 2001 there was a report on Israeli attacks on the Authority's buildings in Gaza and the West Bank. Israelis are said to be 'smashing [Arafat's] institutions one by one, bulldozing his territory into rubble ...'. A UN Middle East envoy says on camera, 'if the Palestinian Authority crashes, then Oslo is over' (meaning that the peace process is over). But what is the rationale for the destruction of these institutions? We do not hear the view that Sharon has always been against the Oslo agreement or the suggestion that he has provoked Palestinian action to make sure that it fails. Following the comments of the UN envoy, we hear only that 'Israelis say it's over already, they are consumed by rage and by grief' (BBC1 late News, 13 December 2001). This does not mean that the rage and grief are not genuine, but to see the destruction of the potential Palestinian state simply as a 'grief-stricken response' is only one view of what this conflict is about.

Arafat and Sharon

Our research suggests that the Israeli perspective is highlighted in terms of causes, motives and preferred outcomes. The Israelis present themselves as confronted by an unreasoning terror – the preferred solution is therefore simply to catch the terrorists. Within this way of understanding the conflict, the only problem is that Arafat will not co-operate sufficiently in arresting the 'extremists'. There is no comparable criticism of Sharon on television news at this time. In our earlier sample from the first weeks of the intifada, he had been referred to as a 'right-wing enemy of the peace process' and his role at the inception of the intifada had been discussed. By the time of this sample, however, Sharon was prime minister of Israel, and criticism of him is more muted. In contrast, the view that Arafat is to blame is more extensively featured and pursued on the news. In the wake of the suicide-bombs of 1 and 2 December 2001, Sharon was able to develop his account of Arafat's responsibility and to do so with some help from journalists who reiterated his views:

> *Newscaster*: And within the past minutes the Israeli prime minister, Ariel Sharon, has addressed the nation on television. He said that Israel had been dragged into a war of terror. He said that Yasser Arafat was the biggest obstacle to peace in the Middle East.
> *Ariel Sharon*: Arafat is responsible for everything that is happening here. Arafat chose a strategic decision; he chose a terrorism strategy. He chose to try and achieve political achievements through murder by killing innocent civilians. Arafat chose the way of terror.

We are then given more detail on these views by the correspondent in Israel:

> Well the prime minister has been speaking on television as you say, saying that Israel is going to use new methods and old in the fight against terrorism, insisting that it will not be stopped by the militants who *he says are trying to drive the Israelis out of their land*. He's also claiming basically as we had suspected that the Americans had effectively given him carte blanche. He's been saying that George Bush told him that the United States and Israel stand together side by side in the war against terrorism. (BBC1 early evening News, 3 December 2001 – our italics)

There are no comments here by the journalist on international law, on the legality of the occupation, on Sharon's policies, or questioning the issue of who has been driven from what land. On the following evening, the Israeli views are developed further:

> *Journalist*: For months, Israelis have said that he must do more to crack down on Palestinian militants. Now, they argue, his failure makes him personally responsible for this weekend's acts of terrorism.

Israeli spokesman: Yasser Arafat can't have it both ways. He can't be a statesman and give harbour to the PFLP, to Hamas, to Islamic Jihad.

Journalist: The bombs were the worst suicide attacks for years, but part of a terrible pattern. Before long, Hamas activists had released a video of one of the suicide-bombers. Arafat seemed unable or unwilling to stop it. His Palestinian police did then swoop in to arrest more than 100 suspected militants. But for the Israelis it was too little, too late ... (BBC1 early evening News, 4 December 2001)

The Israeli view is also reported on ITV news:

Israel has warned that its military will resume the bombardment of Arafat's power base unless he proves he can control the extremists among his people. (ITV early evening News, 6 December 2001)

The Israelis continue to take matters into their own hands because they believe Yasser Arafat is simply not doing enough to rein in the Palestinian extremists. (ITV early evening News, 10 December 2001)

On 6 December 2001, ITV news interviewed Arafat. There was no criticism of Sharon or his policies in this, and little on the history or nature of the Israeli military occupation other than to report Arafat's comments that the Israeli measures were 'humiliating' him and his people. The main focus of the interview was on Arafat's attitude to 'terrorism' and on the 'crackdown' which he was supposed to be pursuing on 'terrorist activities'. The interview ends with the journalist equating the success of this with being committed to 'peace':

The general verdict on Yasser Arafat's crackdown appears to be so far so good, but the Palestinian leader will have to do much more in the days ahead to convince the sceptics that he is, as he said tonight, truly committed to peace. (ITV late News, 6 December 2001)

There is no commentary here on what the Israelis might have to do in order to be seen as 'committed to peace'. On the following day BBC news interviews Yasser Arafat and focuses on Israel's claim that 'Yasser Arafat isn't doing enough to arrest militants'. Before speaking with Arafat, the BBC is taken through the backstreets of Gaza to meet members of Hamas. The point they are making is that 'Yasser Arafat says it's a struggle to hunt down the extremists of Hamas, but it didn't take us long to find them.' The reporter notes that 'the men who believe in suicide-bombings are all senior militants, the kind Arafat has promised to arrest'. We hear that these men do not expect to be rounded up any time soon and one states that Arafat 'can't stop us resisting the Israeli occupation'. The subsequent interview with Arafat then focuses on whether he will make arrests, as in this interview exchange:

> *Journalist*: There are many still out on the streets. We ourselves found one of the men on Israel's wanted list.
> *Yasser Arafat*: I arrested now 70, what they are asking beside who I had arrested before.
> *Journalist*: Will you arrest them all?

The journalist then notes finally, 'those excuses not good enough for the Israelis' (BBC1 late News, 7 December 2001). There is nothing here on the role of Sharon or the Israelis in the continuing violence. But without this it is very difficult to understand the perspective or the motivations of the Palestinians. The journalist goes on to note the difficulties which Arafat has in arresting the wanted men. The problem is apparently that they enjoy wide popular support:

> The extremists are heroes to many Palestinians, more popular every time they kill. Few want to see them behind bars, so Yasser Arafat is trapped between the wrath of Israel and the wrath of his own people. (BBC1 late News, 7 December 2001)

We can see why viewers might be confused by such coverage or have difficulty in understanding why the violence is so intractable. ITV news asks in one, more critical, bulletin: 'What is driving this succession of bombings by Islamic terrorist groups and can Yasser Arafat or anyone else stop the perpetrators?' The answer it gives is as follows:

> The majority of Palestinians now back the hard-line groups. They're demanding Israel leaves territory in the West Bank and Gaza Strip that was promised to their people in a peace deal. (ITV late News, 3 December 2001)

The question was an important one to ask, but the above answer shows the problems which we identified earlier. There is nothing to indicate the relationship which exists between the two sides. It sounds rather like an argument over a piece of land, which is how some viewers understood it. In the same bulletin, there are then two brief comments from Middle East experts, who indicate that Arafat cannot control Hamas and Islamic Jihad because they are opposed to him, but there is little to explain why all these events are occurring. Viewers might also ask what is the sense of using a word such as 'extremist' if it is the majority position? Why would 'ordinary' Palestinians support such action? One BBC News programme in our sample had attempted to answer some of these questions by going to interview the family of a suicide-bomber. The action of the bomber is referred to as 'a reply to Ariel Sharon's devastating air strikes' and the bomber's family is described:

> We found the bomber's family in their modest house near Bethlehem, not militants or gunmen, just ordinary people, but such is the hatred now between the two sides that they wished more blood had been spilled. (BBC1 late News, 5 December 2001)

This report is noteworthy in that it attempts to situate suicide-bombing in the context of Palestinian society. It makes the point that the bomber was a 'quiet family man' who was 46 years old:

> Relatives showed me a picture of the bomber, not the typical young militant but a quiet family man of 46. 'He got up at four this morning', his wife Fatima said, 'prayed and read the Koran. He told me to look after our sons and our daughters, and he said goodbye.' (BBC1 late News, 5 December 2001)

One explanation of such an action, suggested in the report, is that it is part of the cycle of violence – of constant attack and counter-attack. But the report leaves open the issue of why this cycle continues. The only clue to this is given in a reference to 'political progress':

> Suicide-bombings are a source of pride and Palestinians say they won't stop without *political progress*. However many militants Yasser Arafat puts behind bars, others are waiting to take their place. (BBC1 late News, 5 December 2001 – our italics)

This is the limit of the presentation of the Palestinian perspective. The phrase 'political progress' is used to cover the whole relationship of the Palestinians to the Israelis – the loss of homes, land and water, the occupation and military rule. The phrase equates to those in our first sample of news where Palestinian actions were explained by references to 'frustrations with the peace process'. Such phrases act as a form of euphemism, and effectively avoid raising some of the more controversial aspects of this conflict. There has, however, been criticism that such interviews are conducted at all. Some pro-Israel groups have argued that to discuss the motives and personal histories of suicide bombers is to 'sanitise' them or give them legitimacy (see, for example, Phillips, 2003). But it is clear that to understand the conflict requires an analysis of motivations and historical causes. This does not imply approval of violent actions. Indeed, the consequences of such actions were made perfectly clear on television news, as can be seen in the very graphic accounts that were given of the aftermath of suicide-bombings and other killings.

Terrorists, gunmen and defenders: words and perspectives

The choice of a word to describe a social action can have a crucial influence on how the action is understood and the legitimacy which is granted to it. This is in part the traditional debate about the difference between calling someone a 'terrorist' or a 'freedom fighter'. In describing the Israeli-Palestinian conflict, journalists are obviously aware of how different words relate to different perspectives. In this example from ITV news, a journalist identifies the two viewpoints:

> The Palestinian people regard these gunmen as the defenders of Bethlehem. However, Israel views them as terrorists who should be arrested by Yasser Arafat's police force. (ITV early evening News, 24 October 2001)

There is nothing in the commentary to explain why the two sides would see their world so differently or the nature of the relationship between them. It is, however, an attempt to distinguish two ways of speaking about the participants. But although the journalist is consciously presenting the Palestinian view, his sentence still uses the word 'gunmen'. In our culture, this word has very negative connotations – it is usually used to describe armed bank robbers or those involved in other criminal activity, and is also used interchangeably with the word 'terrorist'. We can consider an actual example of its use in a different political context. In the following case a report from the *Daily Telegraph* about Northern Ireland discusses a proposed amnesty as part of the peace process. The headline for the report is: 'Amnesty for *Gunmen* still on the Run' (our italics). The first line of the report then reads: '*Terrorists* who are still at large and wanted for offences ... will be given an amnesty' (*Daily Telegraph*, 25 October 2001). In a report from the Israeli-Palestinian conflict, ITV news also uses the words interchangeably. This report is about the deaths of five Palestinian children killed by an Israeli bomb, which was apparently triggered as they walked to school. We are told initially that 'Israel is investigating whether a bomb meant for *terrorists* may have been to blame' (our italics). A few lines later in the report we hear 'Such a bomb would have been intended for Palestinian *gunmen*' (ITV early evening News, 23 November 2001 – our italics).

It is clear from our work that negative words such as 'terrorists' and 'gunmen' were typically applied to Palestinian actors rather than to Israelis. We also found a number of examples in periods before our samples, which apparently indicates a long-term trend – for example, 'a Palestinian terrorist hurled two grenades into a bus queue' (BBC1 early evening News, 19 October 1998), and 'tougher Palestinian measures against Islamic terrorists' (BBC2 *Newsnight*, 23 October 1998). We have already seen how the word 'terrorist' was used in Israeli criticism of Arafat. There were a number of other references to Israeli views on terrorism in our sample, such as:

[Ariel Sharon] used every opportunity he could to attack the Arabs as terrorists, and to make it clear that there would be absolutely no room for compromise at all until all the terrorist problem was solved. (BBC1 early evening News, 1 November 2001)

For them [the Israelis], it is their war against terrorism. (BBC1 early evening News, 4 December 2001)

[Ariel Sharon] said that Israel had been dragged into a war on terror. (BBC1 early evening News, 6 December 2001)

The Israeli army says the intended target was a known Islamic terrorist. (BBC1 early evening News, 10 December 2001)

There were also references to the views of the US government, which in practice tended to reinforce the Israeli perspective, as in the following examples:

President Bush: Once again I call upon Chairman Arafat to make maximum efforts to *end terrorism* against Israel. (BBC1 late News, 7 March 2002 – our italics)
Colin Powell: As we have responded to terrorism we know that Israel has the right *to respond to terrorism*. (ITV early evening News, 12 April 2002 – our italics)[19]

There are also occasions when journalists endorse the use of the word 'terrorist' by using it directly in their own speech without attributing it as part of a reported statement:

Israel unleashed its pent-up anger against Palestinians today after a weekend of deadly suicide-bombings by Islamic *terrorists*. (ITV late News, 3 December 2001 – our italics.)

Ten Israeli settlers were killed and up to 30 wounded this evening in an attack by the Palestinian *terrorist* group, Hamas, on a bus in the West Bank. (ITV late News, 12 December 2001 – our italics)

Journalist: The Americans know that they can hardly tell the Israelis that they cannot use all the means at their disposal to go after *terrorists*, when of course that's exactly what the Americans are doing in Afghanistan. (BBC1 late News, 2 December 2001)

The Israeli army launched new attacks in the Gaza Strip in retaliation for recent acts of *terrorism*. (BBC Radio 4, 7.30 a.m., 6 March 2002 – our italics)

Five Israelis were killed in attacks by Palestinian *terrorists*. (ITV late News, 5 March 2002)

[The Jenin refugee camp in the West Bank] the target of Israel's most determined efforts to *root out potential terrorists*. (BBC1 early evening News, 12 April 2002 – our italics)

Headline: Deadlock still on the West Bank. Israel stays *until the terrorists are beaten*. (BBC1 late News, 14 April 2002 – our italics)

Interview question: If Arafat can't arrest members of Hamas, can't arrest the *terrorists* … (BBC2 *Newsnight*, 9 August 2001 – our italics)

He [Israeli reservist] had to search hundreds of Palestinian homes, *rooting out terrorists*. (BBC1 Breakfast News, 8.30 a.m., 11 June 2002 – our italics)

There is one occasion in our sample when a BBC reporter refers to the Israelis as 'state terrorists', while reporting the views of President Assad of Syria. The British prime minister, Tony Blair, was visiting the country shortly before travelling to Israel. The journalist notes that 'Tomorrow's hosts are the very same people that today's hosts regard as bloody state terrorists, and of course the Israelis think much the same thing of the Syrians, the Palestinians and others.' He also notes that 'Syria's President Assad ... regards Palestinian suicide-bombers and assassins as freedom fighters' (BBC1 late News, 30 October 2001). Journalists are unlikely to take their lead from the president of Syria, given the nature of the Syrian regime, but this is hardly a reason for not representing the Palestinian perspective in other news coverage. There are many people apart from the president of Syria who view the conflict very differently from the perspective offered by the Israeli authorities. As Max Hastings has pointed out, writing in the *Daily Mail*:

It may be argued that Israeli action represents a rival terrorism, rather than a counter-terrorism. Yet the Israelis have been largely successful in persuading the Bush administration that Palestinian suicide bombers represent a common foe, in the same league as the September 11 hijackers. To most outsiders, however, it is plain that what is happening in Israel and the West Bank must be addressed primarily as a political issue, rather than a military one. (Hastings, 2002)

The key point is that the use of a label such as 'terrorist' can actually obscure the proper consideration of causes and possible solutions. On the news, confusions over how people are described are symptomatic of a larger problem in explaining the motivations of those involved and the history and the nature of the conflict. The sheer number of terms used to describe Palestinians does seem to indicate this. Israeli forces were described as 'soldiers', 'troops', and in one case 'brothers in arms', but were most frequently referred to as 'the Israelis'.[20] Words applied to Palestinians included 'activists', 'followers [of Hamas]', 'guerrillas', 'militants', 'extremists', 'assailants', 'gunmen', 'bombers', 'terrorists', 'killers', 'assassins', 'fundamentalist groups', 'attackers', 'self-styled Palestinian martyrs' and 'fanatics'.

As far as the Palestinians are concerned, such labels can obscure what for them is central, that this conflict is a war of national liberation against what they see as a brutal military occupation.

This is a long way from the perspective that the key issue is to 'catch the terrorists'. It does seem that there is a reluctance or an inability in TV news to talk about the nature of the occupation and Israeli military control and a reluctance to discuss these issues as motives for Palestinian action. This is not to say that there is no sympathy expressed by journalists for Palestinians, or indeed for those who are presented as the 'innocent victims' on both sides of the conflict. The issue of casualties and victims is an important area of coverage in terms of potential impacts on public understanding, and we turn to this now.

Victims and casualties of the conflict

We noted in our first sample that there was sympathy expressed for victims and especially for children who were injured or killed. In this sample, such casualties now included Israeli children because of the growing use of the tactic of suicide-bombing. There was also sympathy expressed for those who were displaced by this new phase of the conflict. This BBC bulletin describes an Israeli military incursion into Bethlehem and the effect on those who lived there. It begins with a description of a march by church leaders, calling for the troops to go, and comments that the protesters are walking 'straight into a battleground'. It then describes a family trying to escape the danger:

> The disruption caused by Israeli troops is what lined the road to Bethlehem today ... Outside a brother and sister reunited, Esa told me he slipped into Bethlehem behind the march to get his sister and her children away from danger ... Their ordeal wasn't over yet, we followed as they set off with their car, but then a warning from down the street, it wasn't safe. As they ran back to the church more gunfire but in the end this one family did get out, leaving this behind. (BBC1 late News, 23 October 2001)

The image of victims caught up in violence beyond their control is continued in this description of a suicide-bombing by the same journalist:

> Another night of death in Israel. Emergency workers sift through the wreckage left behind by one more Palestinian suicide-bomber. More families who will grieve, more damage to America's bid for a truce. The wounded being brought in, passengers who had just been trying to get home, like this woman who stared the bomber

in the face, but saw no hint of what he had in mind. (BBC1 late News, 31 October 2001)

When children are involved, the theme of their innocence as victims can be very powerfully expressed, as in the next three examples. The first is from when five children were killed by an Israeli bomb on the way to school, the second is a description of suicide-bomb attacks on 1 and 2 December, and the third is of Israeli 'retribution' after these attacks:

> Yet more child victims of the lethal stalemate bedevilling the Holy Land. The young innocents this time were five Palestinian boys, all from the same extended family. The youngest just seven, two were ten years old, the other two 14. (ITV early evening News, 23 November 2001)

> At the hospital, more families in mourning, Israel is bleeding … The terror began last night in downtown Jerusalem, the victims were the young teenagers, maimed and killed on the street's pedestrian mall. Two suicide-bombers had struck, causing carnage. (BBC1 late News, 2 December 2001)

> The bombs were aimed at a Palestinian security base, but the base is close to a school. Dozens of children were on the streets. Two people were killed and many injured … Yet again the innocent are caught at the centre of the conflict. (BBC1 early evening News, 4 December 2001)

In the following example, a BBC journalist describes the effects of a suicide-bomb detonated on a bus:

> Yet another deadly strike and a return to chaos and carnage … Israeli soldiers and civilians on board had little chance. They were caught in a hail of metal; explosives had been packed with nuts and bolts. Those not killed were injured – in Haifa's hospital, the agonising wait to find out who lived and who died. (BBC1 early evening News, 10 April 2002)

A young girl had been terribly injured in the blast. The journalist translates the mother's words:

> 'She used to be a beautiful girl,' her mother says, 'now she is burned, her hair is gone. I wish I'd taken a picture of her before

this happened.' Long after the blast, the mobile phones of the victims were still ringing – family and friends hoping to hear voices that are gone forever. (BBC1 early evening News, 10 April 2002)

However, we did note in our earlier sample that there were some differences in the manner in which the casualties on each side were reported. To explore this further here, we will compare the reporting of two incidents which occurred on 10 and 12 December 2001. The first was an attack by Israeli helicopters using missiles in Hebron, which killed two Palestinian children. The second was an attack by Palestinians on a bus carrying Israeli settlers, cars and a military vehicle, in which ten people were reported to have been killed. In both cases there is an emphasis on the suffering of the casualties and the involvement of children:

> Israeli helicopters on a mission to kill. Smoke rising after they fired their missiles. Israel trying to kill a leading militant, but while he was sitting in traffic on a busy street. This, the wreckage left behind by the botched assassination. The target, Mohammed Satr, is expected to recover but Israel's missiles killed a boy called Sha'adi and a child still in nappies, Puram, who was only three. (BBC1 late News, 10 December 2001)

> A journey home that ended in death. Bus number 189 ambushed as it neared a Jewish settlement. The attack, brutal and sophisticated, first a roadside bomb just off the bus, then gunmen firing on the passengers as they tried to flee. Flares lighting up the hillside as troops chased the attackers, one was killed at the scene. Shocked survivors rushed to hospital, ultra-orthodox Jews who live on occupied Palestinian land. They'd taken their children out to celebrate a Jewish holiday. This father managed to escape with his baby. '*It was a massacre*', Israel said, promising a severe response. (BBC1 late News, 12 December 2001 – our italics)

There were, however, differences in the reporting of these two events which relate to systematic patterns in news coverage. The first is the difference in the words used to describe them. The Palestinian action is referred to as 'a horrific attack' (BBC1 early evening News, 12 December 2001). In a later news on ITV, the Israeli description of this event as a 'massacre' is taken up and used by journalists when describing a subsequent Israeli action:

The trigger for the Israeli offensive *was a massacre on the West Bank*. Funerals took place today for ten Israelis shot dead when Hamas gunmen ambushed a bus. (ITV early evening News, 13 December 2001 – our italics)

This statement again illustrates the point noted above that Israeli actions are frequently presented as a response, in this case as being 'triggered' by the Palestinian 'massacre'. There is no similar link made in the case of the bus attack by the Palestinians. There is no reference to the Israeli missile strike of two days before, or to any other Israeli attacks. A third point of difference is that in discussing the missile strike, the Israelis' rationale for their action is very clearly expressed. We are told the following:

The Israelis say the intended target was a known Islamic terrorist. (BBC1 late News, 10 December 2001)

The intended target, a member of Islamic Jihad, survived the strike, although he was among nine people injured. A suicide attack that wounded eight Israelis today brought orders for more military action against the Palestinians. (ITV early evening News, 10 December 2001)

The Israelis continue to take matters into their own hands because they believe Yasser Arafat is simply not doing enough to rein in the Palestinian extremists. (ITV early evening News, 10 December 2001)

The journalists do not always sound happy about the Israeli rationales that are given, but they were none the less included:

Israel says the main target here was planning further attacks. Maybe so, we have only Israel's word for that, but whatever his crimes may be, innocent lives have been taken. (BBC1 late News, 10 December 2001)

Today's missile strike may have prevented an impending suicide attack, but children were killed in the process. (ITV early evening News, 10 December 2001)

There is no comparable inclusion or discussion of the reasons for Palestinian action. This does not mean that the Israelis escape without criticism – an Israeli spokesman is interviewed and asked: 'Is it acceptable for Israel, a democracy, to kill two children?' (BBC1 late News, 10 December 2001).[21] But the fact remains that it is the Israeli rationales that are routinely present in the coverage, both in the form of reported statements and in interviews with their spokespeople.[22]

These differences between the coverage of the two sides are partly a result of Israel's very developed public relations output and its practised ability to supply information and speakers to the media. We also found in other news stories that the Israelis were able to affect the structure and content of coverage by placing limits on the movements of journalists. This particularly affected TV reporting, since cameras were sometimes not allowed into 'sensitive' areas. We can see this more clearly if we look in detail at the reporting of an Israeli incursion into the village of Beit Rima in October 2001. The BBC report begins with an account of the deaths of Palestinians, followed immediately by an Israeli statement:

> At least nine Palestinians were killed after Israeli tanks, helicopters and ground troops forced their way into Beit Rima, a village north of Ramallah. The Israelis say they arrested two people over the assassination last week of the Israeli tourism minister. (BBC1 late News, 24 October 2001)

The report then gives two versions of the events and the journalist notes the limits on what they were allowed to see. There was then a brief interview with an Israeli soldier:

> The dead of Beit Rima, Israel sent them back for burial. It says there was a gun battle in the village. Palestinians say a bloodbath. Israeli tanks still prowling the outskirts of Beit Rima today, that's all we were allowed to see, but we found these soldiers on their way out, brothers in arms embracing, some faces still blackened from combat, all proud of their part in the assault, but not saying much.
> *Journalist*: Well what was it like last night?
> *Israeli soldier*: Intense, it was intense. (BBC1 late News, 24 October 2001)

There are two accounts of what has happened. There is no evidence offered as to which is correct, and the journalist notes that it is impossible to take the camera in. The problem is outlined in the report:

One soldier stopped ... maybe thanking God for his survival. Israel hasn't lost any troops in the past six days, but the Palestinians say they have more than 40 dead. But these Israeli soldiers have just come out of the village, having finished their mission, but they are making sure we can't go inside. Beit Rima was sealed by the army when it began its operation and it remains sealed still. So, it's impossible for us to take our camera in, speak to the villagers and get their accounts of what happened. (BBC1 late News, 24 October 2001)

The journalist also notes that the material which they are showing was recorded by the Israeli army and supplied to the BBC:

The first pictures from inside Beit Rima, the Israeli army apparently helping the wounded, though Palestinians claim they kept ambulances out for hours. It was the army which recorded this material and supplied it to us. (BBC1 late News, 24 October 2001)

ITV news on the same night also notes the limits on movement imposed by the Israeli forces and is left, as with the BBC, in the position of simply reporting the statements of both sides:

At least six more Palestinians died today in fierce fighting on the West Bank after Israeli forces moved into the village of Beit Rima. Troops sealed off the village, preventing ambulances and reporters from entering. The Palestinians accused them of carrying out a massacre, but the Israelis insisted they were hunting for the killers of Israeli cabinet minister, Rehavam Ze'evi. (ITV late News, 24 October 2001)

On the following day, the media gained access to Beit Rima. The BBC showed pictures of demolished houses and reported local people as saying 'it was a night of hell'. A local Palestinian and relatives of a wanted man are spoken to amidst the rubble of their homes. There is no doubt that this bulletin shows the consequences of the war on the Palestinians, but there is no questioning of Israeli claims which are reported as follows:

'We'll have to bring out mats', Amallah told me 'and sleep on the rubble tonight.' Everything is gone. Beit Rima was in mourning today, Israeli sources say the troops didn't find the man they wanted most. He's free but the five policemen are dead. *Israel claims there was a gunfight.* They're going now to bury the dead. *Whatever the truth of what happened here,* Israel is claiming the heavy assault on this village as a military victory. (BBC1 main News, 25 October 2001 – our italics)

The use of the phrase 'Israel claims' may imply a note of doubt, but later reports in the press give a much more critical account. The *Guardian* reported that at least five Palestinians were killed in the first moments of the assault. These were policemen and other local militia working for the Palestinian Authority. The *Guardian* quoted the director of emergency services for the Palestinian Health Ministry as saying 'They did not have time to put on their shoes.' It also commented on the scale of the operation:

> For a village the size of Beit Rima, just four thousand people, the scale of the Israeli operation was astonishing. Witnesses say as many as thirty tanks and army vehicles drove in under covering machine gunfire from helicopters in the dark early hours of Wednesday. (*Guardian*, 26 October 2001)

Interestingly, a journalist from the *Observer* also interviewed Israeli troops leaving the village but used their account to explicitly criticise the official Israeli version of events. As their reporter notes:

> One thing seems certain. The Palestinian account of a lethal ambush on Beit Rima launched without warning by a massively superior force equipped with tanks, helicopters and elite combat troops against half a dozen men, is given credence by the stories of the assault troops of the Nahal Brigade, who attacked them. (Observer, 28 October 2001)

The *Observer* report in some way parallels the BBC's description of the troops leaving the village:

> We met them at dusk on Wednesday walking out of the village, two lines of young Israeli soldiers, heavily armed, their faces blacked up for night fighting. Reaching the Israeli checkpoint that blocked the entry of reporters into the village, they hugged and cheered each other. (*Observer*, 28 October 2001)

The newspaper journalist then makes two specific points: (1) that resistance had been light, contrary to Israeli claims, and (2) according to Palestinians, some people were killed while they slept:

> What had they done? we asked. 'We killed some Arab terrorists', the young men replied. It was, they told us an, 'easy operation' despite some Israeli injuries. Combat, they added, had been short – resistance light after the first assault by the undercover soldiers. This contradicted the claims of army spokesmen that the gunmen had been killed during 'fierce fighting'. Was the fighting fierce? we asked. They laughed and shook their heads. It was not fierce say Palestinians because some of those who died were executed as they slept. (*Observer*, 28 October 2001)

The *Observer* report also notes disquiet in the Israeli press about the raid on Beit Rima. It quotes a report in *Ha'aretz* that the raid on Beit Rima was planned two weeks before the killing of the Israeli cabinet minister. The *Observer* report also notes that a distinguishing feature of the village is that it is easily cut off at the end of a solitary road, and makes the following point:

> The suspicion that is emerging is that Beit Rima was selected for no other reason than it was an easy target for Israeli forces to make a lethal demonstration. Next time – the warning is explicit – it will be the Palestinian state, not just a village, which will be the target. (*Observer*, 28 October 2001)

Some of these differences between the TV and press coverage arose because of the difficulties experience by TV journalists in the limited time which they have and in the restrictions that can be put upon the movement of cameras and equipment. But it is also clear that some press accounts speak much more directly about the effects of what Palestinians experience as the military occupation and clearly articulate the view that Israeli policy is directed against the whole Palestinian population. As the *Observer* notes:

> The military operations against six Palestinian cities in the past week became a vast reprisal raid against the entire Palestinian people. In Ramallah and in Bethlehem, in Tul Karm, Jenin, Qalqilya and Beit Rima, it is ordinary civilians who are being given a brutal lesson in the exigencies of the overwhelming nature

of Israeli military power and being punished simply for existing. (*Observer*, 28 October 2001)

This account differs sharply from that given later by a BBC journalist who summarised the sequence of events. In this BBC account, there is no mention of the possible Israeli motive being to 'mount a lethal demonstration' or the Palestinians being 'punished for existing'. This report simply repeats the Israeli view that they moved in 'to catch the gunman':

> This current cycle of violence may be beyond control. It began six weeks ago, an Israeli cabinet minister, a right-winger, was shot dead in Jerusalem. That day, Israeli forces moved into Palestinian areas to catch the gunman (BBC1 late News, 2 December 2001)

As we have seen, while there is extended criticism and commentary in television news on the policy and actions of Arafat, there was nothing in this sample which offered a comparable critique of Ariel Sharon or his policies. The main focus of the television account is to present the conflict as between two warring parties caught in a cycle of violence. This cycle is shown as propelled mainly by Palestinian action, and a key issue is whether Arafat will be able to stop this and 'catch the extremists'. The result of this tragic cycle as portrayed on television news is that innocent civilians suffer. Within this account, as we have indicated, there were also clear differences in the manner in which the casualties of both sides were featured. It was Israeli casualties who were described by TV journalists using words such as 'atrocity', 'murder' and 'horrific attack'.

In our earlier samples we had also found an emphasis on Israeli casualties in terms of the amount of coverage which was devoted to them. In this sample from October to December 2001 we found that there was significantly more coverage of Israeli casualties than Palestinian.[23] To investigate this further we took an additional sample from March 2002.

SAMPLE THREE: MARCH 2002

Coverage of casualties

This sample ran from 2 March to 9 March and included a total of 21 bulletins (ITV: 11 and BBC1: 10). This was a period of relatively high casualties on both sides. On 9 March 2002 the BBC reported that 'for the Palestinians it's already the bloodiest week of this conflict: 140 dead, one-tenth of the casualties since the uprising began' (BBC1 late News, 9 March 2002). Israeli deaths were just under one-third of this number. When we analysed the text of the news bulletins, we found that there was actually more coverage of Israeli deaths and casualties, than of Palestinian' (120.25 lines covering Israeli deaths and casualties, compared to 46 lines covering Palestinian deaths and casualties).[24] We can see this pattern in the following examples. The first is headlined as a story about Israeli 'hitting back' at the Palestinians:

> *Headline*: Avenging their dead, Israel hits back against the Palestinians. The West Bank under attack. Tanks and warplanes hit Palestinian targets. (BBC1 late News, 3 March 2002)

The story which follows then focuses very largely on the casualties of the Israeli side. There was a sharp contrast between the non-specific language of 'tanks and warplanes hit Palestinian targets' and the very detailed account given of Israeli deaths and injuries. The report goes on as follows:

> Good evening. Israel's prime minister Ariel Sharon is facing mounting pressure to stop the escalation of violence in the conflict with the Palestinians. More than 20 Israelis have been killed in the past 24 hours. Israel has retaliated with a renewed offensive against Palestinian targets. Tonight the Israeli security cabinet is holding an emergency meeting to discuss its strategy.
> *Journalist (in Israel)*: Behind the barbed wire, the dead lined up in a row. Ten Israelis killed this morning at this lonely checkpoint. Seven of them soldiers. A Palestinian sniper shot them one by one. And just a few hours later this – burying last night's victims. Nine Israelis killed in a suicide bombing. This is the final farewell for an entire family. Here they were in life, Shlomo and Nechmad and their daughters Larin and Sheraz. Ambulances full of young victims last night. 'Evening the score', Palestinian militants said, after Israel's push into refugee camps killed more than 20. So revenge was taken on babies like Shimon. Today his grandmother Hannah was at his bedside. She wants tougher action against the Palestinians. (BBC1 late News, 3 March 2002)

As we have seen above, the deaths of children tend to be treated with special sympathy. On the following day, the BBC reported on an Israeli attack:

Among the dead, a doctor in his ambulance and five children killed after school. Three taken from this family leaving Hafaz behind – today he lost his mother, his sister and his two brothers. 'Poor children', their Aunt Najah told us, 'What were they guilty of?' she wants to know. Here on the right, the children's father, a militant called Hussein Abu Quik. Israeli security sources say he was the target but he's alive, clutching this photo of a family that's gone. (BBC1 late News 4 March 2002)

On ITV News, the report is introduced as follows:

Israeli missiles destroy a Palestinian security building in Bethlehem tonight causing explosions that could be heard in Jerusalem six miles away. But what has angered the Palestinians more is the death of five children, among 16 Palestinians killed on the West Bank today. (ITV late News 4 March 2002)

But overall there is a continued emphasis on Israeli deaths and injuries, both in terms of the amount of coverage which they receive and the consistently detailed accounts which are given of them.

On 8 March 2002 it was reported that more than 40 Palestinians died when Israel launched raids by land, sea and air on the West Bank and Gaza (BBC *News 24*, 7.00 p.m., 8 March 2002). On the BBC main news that night, the headline is: 'More than 40 dead in the Middle East on the intifada's bloodiest day.' The news item then initially mentions the casualties on both sides:

The bloody violence in the Middle East reached a new level of intensity today. More than 50 people have been killed in less than 36 hours, making this the worst day since the start of the Palestinian intifada 17 months ago. The total number stands at more than 1,300. The killing accelerated last May with the Palestinians suffering the highest casualties, but the number of Israeli civilians dead has been rising too [*bar graph on screen showing number of deaths*]. (BBC1 late News, 8 March 2002)

The item then continues with a report from a journalist in the Middle East, which focuses very largely on Israeli casualties:

Journalist: The bloodiest day yet began with 19-year-old Mohammed Farhad. He's dead now but death came only after he had killed five young Israelis and injured many more. It was mayhem, Farhad acted alone, infiltrating a Jewish settlement before using his assault rifle and grenade to maximum effect. The victims were religious students, young men being groomed to become officers in the Israeli army. Most of the casualties were hit as they sat together during Bible studies. Today the Jewish settlers who live on this occupied Palestinian land were retracing the steps of the attacker. After cutting the perimeter wire, he raced up the sandbank. At the top there was nothing between him and the settlement school. The killing only stopped when he too was gunned down. It is this kind of incident which incenses Israeli public opinion and guarantees a massive and bloody response. Standing here amid all of this, international diplomacy seems frankly irrelevant. The violence on the ground has reached a new level of intensity and in many ways, it feels that it's beyond the control of the politicians. And so the Israelis are determined to continue their crushing assault against the Palestinians. This is the West Bank city of Tulkarem, the population of some 20,000 is under a second day of Israeli military occupation. The fighting here and in the Gaza Strip means that today alone the Palestinians are counting by their dead by the dozen. The deadliest 24 hours in all these months of conflict. (BBC1 late News, 8 March 2002)

The report then goes on to give the Israeli rationale for their actions:

Journalist: Tonight there is no question about the Israelis' ability to inflict pain. They continue to insist that this is their war against terrorism, that they are rounding up extremists. But the bitter experience here is that even all of this cannot stop the Palestinian attacks, which have provoked such furious retaliation. (BBC1 late News, 8 March 2002)

Here again we see that it is the Palestinians who 'attack' and the Israelis who 'retaliate'. The Israeli intention is given as being to round up 'extremists' and the only criticism of this strategy is whether it will work to stop Palestinian attacks.

Motivation and rationales for action: March 2002

Much of the coverage in this sample follows the well established patterns which we have already identified. Israeli 'retaliation' continues to be a persistent theme, as we can see in the following examples:

> Israel has *retaliated* with a renewed offensive. (BBC1 late News, 3 March 2002 – our italics)

> Predictably, the Israelis launched fierce military *reprisals*. (ITV late News, 3 March 2002 – our italics)

> Headline: Blood for blood; Palestinian suicide attacks *trigger* more Israeli raids. (BBC1 late News, 5 March 2002 – our italics)

Such patterns have clear implications for the manner in which the rationale and motives of the two sides are presented. There are very clear differences in the manner in which the actions of both sides are described. On 4 March, BBC1 reports on the deaths of Palestinian children in a family. A mother, sister and two brothers were killed when Israel attempted an attack on a Palestinian 'militant'. This Israeli rationale is given and the dead are referred to as having been 'killed in a wave of reprisals for the deaths of more than 20 Israelis over the weekend' (BBC1 late News, 4 March 2002). On the following day the BBC lunchtime News reports Palestinian attacks which have killed Israelis, but there is no reference here to past Israeli action. The headline speaks of murder: 'The killing goes on in Israel. Nine more are murdered in twelve hours' (BBC1 lunchtime News, 5 March 2002).

There are also references to other themes which we have seen before, such as the cycle of violence in which both sides are referred to as being involved in a constant sequence of attacks, as in these references: 'Bloodshed here always guaranteed more bloodshed' (BBC1 late News, 4 March 2002) and 'There have been more violent revenge attacks by both Palestinians and Israelis' (BBC1 late News, 5 March 2002). There are occasional references by journalists on the ground to the Palestinian 'response' and, in this example from ITV, to a 'strike back':

> After a week that had seen scores of Palestinians killed in towns and refugee camps across the West Bank and the Gaza Strip, it was the strike back that all had feared and in the end none could prevent. (ITV late News, 9 March 2002)

But this view does not appear in the headline and overall, there is an emphasis on Palestinian action and Israeli 'retaliation'. In this sample there are over three times as many references describing the Israelis as 'responding' as the Palestinians.[25] There are other respects in which this sample follows previous patterns of news content. There is almost nothing on the origins or history of the conflict. There is little analysis of the role of Ariel Sharon or his policies. There are brief references from interviewees, such as 'He promised the Israelis that he will make peace and he made war' (BBC1 late News, 3 March 2002) and 'I hold Mr Sharon solely responsible for the escalation of violence' (BBC1 lunchtime News, 5 March 2002). In our earlier sample of the first days of the intifada Ariel Sharon had been referred to by a BBC journalist as a 'right-wing enemy of the peace process' (BBC1 late News, 3 October 2000). His role in the outbreak of the intifada was also described, but by the time of this sample, Sharon was prime minister of Israel and such commentary from journalists had disappeared. Indeed, one BBC journalist, while referring to his attacks on the Palestinian areas, noted that there was 'still no sign that Mr Sharon can bomb the Palestinians back to the negotiating table' (BBC1 lunchtime News, 5 March 2002). Such a comment implies quite clearly that Ariel Sharon's purpose is to negotiate and it is the Palestinians who are somehow holding the process up.

We have indicated that the Israeli perspective was simply assumed in some accounts by journalists. There was also what sometimes appeared to be an identification with the Israelis. On 8 March 2002, when five Israeli military students were reported to have been killed at a settlement in occupied territory, they were described as 'preparing to defend their country'. The commentary on ITV News was as follows:

> Here four other teenagers were preparing to defend their country at a military training camp when they were killed. The Palestinian gunman caused panic by throwing several grenades before opening fire and students were gunned down as they tried to escape the flames. But there was no remorse from the gunman's father, who said he was proud of his son. That attack only reinforced Israeli determination to drive further into the towns and camps where Palestinians live – *ripping up roads around Bethlehem as part of the ongoing fight against terror*. (ITV early evening News, 8 March 2002 – our italics)

There are dreadful deaths on both sides in this conflict, but it is clear that there are differences in how the actions and motives of each side are described. The above commentary refers to 'Israeli determination' in the 'fight against terror'. We do not hear of the Palestinians or their actions being described in this fashion. There are no commentaries such as 'the Israeli attacks have reinforced the determination of Palestinian fighters to defend their land against Israeli terror'. There are other examples to which we can point. We do not hear of Palestinian attacks as sending 'a tough message to the Israelis to end military rule'. But an Israeli attack with bombs and missiles was described on BBC Radio 4 as 'the Israelis are sending the toughest possible message to the Palestinians' (6.00 p.m., 19 May 2001). In TV news there is sometimes an assertion of Israeli action and its rationale which is not present for the Palestinians. On 7 March 2002, the BBC described Israeli incursions into locally controlled Palestinian areas with these words:

> The Israelis have vowed to hit the Palestinians hard and that's exactly what they're doing ... The commanders insist this is an anti-terror mission – the Israeli army is in good spirits, its political leaders determined to press on with the offensive. (BBC1 late News, 7 March 2002)

It is unlikely that an attack by Palestinians would be presented in this way.

The example below from ITV News offered a different perspective, suggesting that both sides were equally aggressive and that both justified their actions as 'legitimate defence':

> Mr Sharon has predicted that the current army offensive will be both aggressive and continue, but so too is the campaign being waged by Palestinian militants ... Neither the Israelis nor the Palestinians accept any of the blame for this situation. Instead both sides justify their actions as legitimate defence. (ITV early evening News, 6 March 2002)

This suggestion of an 'equivalence' between the two sides is of course one possible perspective on the conflict. It does not, however, say anything about the origins or history of the conflict or that one side is subjecting the other to military occupation, or international opinion on the legality of this.

We have suggested that the Israeli perspective tends to predominate in news accounts, but it does not do so exclusively. As we have noted, journalists do show the effects of the war and the suffering it causes for both sides. In the above BBC report, the journalist notes that 'the Palestinians are facing desperate times' (BBC1 late News, 7 March 2002). In the following ITV News, a journalist describes the terrifying experience of waiting for bombs to fall:

> Israeli air raids have become a daily hazard for the Palestinians of the overcrowded Gaza Strip. The sight of warplanes overhead may be familiar, but it is none the less a terrifying experience to be on the ground waiting for the bombs and missiles to land. (ITV early evening News, 6 March 2002)

The news also shows how Israelis feel 'vulnerable' and 'threatened' as, in the following example. In addition it illustrates the emphasis on Israeli casualties, to which we have already pointed. Although the headline for this story is about Israeli attacks on Palestinian areas and the report notes that there is violence across Israel and the Palestinian territories, the bulk of the text features events in Israel:

> It feels like war on all fronts. A day of bewildering, widespread violence across Israel and the Palestinian territories; a day of bloodshed and death. During morning rush hour a Palestinian suicide attack in the northern town of Rapullah – one Israeli killed, many injured. At about the same time near Jerusalem, an Israeli woman was shot dead in her car as she drove to work, and all of this came hours after yet another Palestinian gun attack, this time in a Tel Aviv restaurant. Three more Israelis died here. *It's all left many Israelis feeling threatened and vulnerable*, especially the Jewish settlers, who live on land regarded by the outside world as occupied Palestinian territory. Many are frightened, but determined they will not be driven out. (BBC1 late News, 5 March 2002)

A female settler is then interviewed:

> Even though I'm scared, I still go out on the streets and I send my kids to school and I go shopping and I continue my daily life. But I do ... the fear is getting worse.

The report then mentions the 'Israeli response' to Palestinian attacks:

> An Israeli response to Palestinian attacks has been predictable. Panic in Nablus and destruction in Bethlehem. Devastating,

yes, still no sign though that the Palestinians can be bombed back to the negotiating table. (BBC1 late News, 5 March 2002 – our italics)

The BBC1 early evening news on the same night had featured an interview with a different settler, but again made the point about settlers being 'frightened but determined to stay'. This report also included an interview with a Palestinian and did in some respects feature the views of both sides. The report was introduced with the words 'the Jewish settlements in the West Bank are blamed by many for provoking the fighting'. A journalist in the Middle East then describes the settlement, referring to it as a 'Jewish neighbourhood in the outskirts of Jerusalem'. He then notes that its families are 'deeply religious' and have the 'unshakeable belief that this is their land by the will of God'. The views of the outside world are mentioned and a settler then speaks on camera:

> *Journalist*: They know that the outside world regards this as an illegal settlement built on occupied Palestinian territory. But for the people here that is irrelevant. Many are frightened but determined to stay.
> *Male settler*: Sometimes I think I just want to go back to my family. I came here and I am by myself and all my family is back in New York but then I love this country so much and I feel it is such a beautiful country that I just will not leave.
> *Journalist*: From his apartment balcony, Seth Clayman has a clear view of neighbouring Arab villages. He remembers when there was a peace, even co-operation between the communities and even in these violent times he has hope for the future.
> *Male settler*: There is a lot of room for everyone. I guess if we can get along – it is not beyond our reach. Not beyond our reach.

The journalist then goes on to note that there are Palestinian flats and apartments just a few metres away from the Israeli homes and that a fence has been built between the two sides, which he refers to as 'a physical symbol of the hatred and distrust which now separates these two neighbouring communities'. He then comments on how the Palestinians view the settlements, and a Palestinian teacher appears briefly on camera:

> For many Palestinians, the Jewish settlements are clearly visible from their homes. On this side of the divide the settlements are

a gross provocation, a symbol of occupation and repression. Mohammed is a teacher and a bitter man. 'The land they live on was my grandfather's and now it's mine', he says. 'They took it in ways God only knows and when someone takes our land that is death for us.' There is much anger here and that promises still more violence. (BBC1 early evening News, 5 March 2002)

This report offers an image of a frightened but friendly settler who wants peace and co-operation. The Palestinians, we are told, see the settlements as a symbol of occupation and repression. But since the nature of the occupation and its history are barely discussed on the news, viewers might well ask, 'What repression?' It is not surprising if many are puzzled over the relationship between the settlers and the Palestinians. There is no mention in this BBC report of the religious settlers as described in the Amnesty International and B'Tselem reports, noted above. These referred to a series of attacks, attempts to take Palestinian land and to how 'violent groups of settlers...fire at olive pickers, killing and wounding them, steal their crops and destroy their trees (B'Tselem, 2003d). The point is that from the Palestinian perspective and indeed for some Israelis the settlements are a key factor in exerting military and economic control. It is not hard to explain the Palestinian position. As they see it, when Israel was created, they were driven from their homes and had to live as refugees. The Israelis then took over the land that they had moved to and they have had to live under variations of Israeli economic and military control ever since. Without the knowledge of such perspectives and their links to motivation, it can be very difficult to understand why the conflict is so intractable. The question which must be asked about TV news journalism is why it has such difficulty in explaining the Palestinian perspective, when it can so readily feature that of the Israelis.

SAMPLE FOUR: JENIN, APRIL 2002

On 29 March 2002, the Israeli army launched a new offensive on locally controlled Palestinian areas, including Jenin, Nablus and Bethlehem. These conflicts, and particularly the attack on Jenin, attracted widespread media coverage and were the subject of bitter controversy. This focused on the conduct of the Israeli forces and also on the manner in which their actions were reported. There were claims that Palestinians had been 'massacred' and then counter-accusations that the media were reproducing propaganda and a distortion the truth. The access which journalists had to Jenin was severely controlled by the Israeli authorities while the fighting was in progress. This raised further questions about how journalists should cover a conflict in which one side could restrict the flow of information by virtue of its military dominance. To shed some light on these issues and on how TV news did actually cover Jenin, we took a further sample of 30 early evening and late news bulletins from BBC1 and ITV News between 9 April and 16 April 2002.

Restrictions on coverage and effects on news content

Both BBC1 and ITV News made it clear that there were severe restrictions on their reporting. As the BBC noted on 11 April:

> Israel has been very careful to keep the international media out. Today is the first opportunity that we've had to have even a limited freedom to go around and talk to people and ask them to tell us their stories. And there is no way we can prove what they're saying is true. (BBC1 early evening News).

ITV also noted the intimidation of journalists in enforcing these limits:

> When they saw us filming, the Israelis made clear they didn't like it. We're just on the edge of the Jenin refugee camp, taking some cover, as Israeli snipers have been firing warning shots over our heads. (ITV late News, 11 April 2002).

When the restrictions were briefly lifted, the TV news included critical reports on Israeli actions. But as this BBC bulletin notes, the journalists cannot pursue the stories or verify them, and before they can film very much, the Israeli army 'ushers them away':

> Itadel is grieving for her husband Mohammed. She claims he was killed by soldiers as he tended his sheep. This boy told us he saw Mohammed being shot once, then left to bleed to death. His word against the army's. It denies killing innocent civilians. The relatives are struggling home to mourn now, it's only an hour since the dead man was shot. Israel says its troops are here to crush the militants, to stop the suicide-bombers but Palestinians in Jenin say civilians are paying a high price. A whole city being punished for what the militants have done. Before we could film

too many more scenes like this, the army ushered us away. (BBC1 early evening News, 11 April 2002)

One consequence of the inability to pursue stories was that journalists were frequently reduced simply to repeating the claims and counter-claims of both sides, as in these examples:

For now, there are two conflicting accounts. The Palestinians call it a massacre, a war crime. They say that many hundreds of Palestinians in the camp have been killed, including many civilians ... But Israel's version is very different. It says no massacre, no mass graves and no cover-up ... and it says that the attack on Jenin is part of Israel's legitimate war against terror. (BBC1 early evening News, 12 April 2002)

The Palestinians accuse the Israelis of a massacre here and of bulldozing bodies under the rubble. The Israelis, who continue to patrol the streets of Jenin in strength, deny that. (ITV early evening News, 12 April 2002)

Channel 4 News apparently gained better access by going into Jenin by a back route, travelling through olive groves. Lindsey Hilsum described to us how they were able to do this, because they were led by a guide who had military experience. Their report raised some additional issues such as allegations of looting by Israeli troops and the use of a Palestinian as a human shield. They carried this interview:

Journalist: Like many others, Ali Abu Sereh was initially imprisoned in his house but then the soldiers decided they had a better use for him.
Interviewee: [caption: 'Ali Abu Sereh, teacher']: After two days they took me with them, I had to go knock on my neighbours' doors, so that the soldiers could enter the houses, each time a door was opened, they would rush in. They searched five or six houses while I was with them. Whenever I entered they would make me lay on the floor and tie me up until they had finished the search, but when I was knocking on the door of one house, another Israeli patrol shot me.
Journalist: A mistake presumably, he says they left him on the street. The next morning a neighbour rescued him, but it was five days before they were able to get him to hospital, which is

why his wound has gone septic. (Channel 4 News, 7.00 p.m., 11 April 2002)

There were other areas in which Channel 4 News differed significantly from BBC1 and ITV News. The following extracts from interviews show that it raised very clearly the issues of the legality of Israel's action and also asked whether the Palestinians could be seen as resisting 'terror' imposed by Israel. The first interview is with Mark Sofer, the Israeli ambassador to Ireland:

> *Journalist/presenter*: Ambassador, what you have surely shown us is that violence begets violence. The terror that you are visiting upon the refugees in the Palestinian camps, gunmen there may be in there, they regard as resistance, you regard them as terrorists. Its one man's terrorist and another man's resistance.
> *Mark Sofer [caption: 'Israeli Government Spokesman']*: When I ask you if placing a bomb in a synagogue, or blowing yourself up next to little babies in pram and their mothers is anything but terror, is that resistance? The terror has affected us even prior to the '67 war, prior to the fact that the time that we were actually in the territories, it affected us during the peace process itself in the 1996 and 1997 period, it's affecting us today, terrorism and peace cannot exist.
> *Journalist/presenter*: Ambassador, I must ask you the same question in return. When you sent massive hardware, tanks, into refugee camps, where again there are babies in prams, and you fire your shells into areas in which there are women and children living, let alone gunmen, who regard themselves as resisters, what can you expect? (Channel 4 News, 7.00 p.m., 10 April 2002)

On the following night the same journalist interviewed Gideon Meir, introduced as a spokesman for the Israeli government:

> *Gideon Meir*: We must understand this was a war, this was a war against terror.
> *Journalist/presenter*: But there has clearly been terror on both sides. And I mean, you have also got to expect that if you are illegally in someone else's territory, they are going to resist and that is what happened. (Channel 4 News, 7.00 p.m., 11 April 2002)

We might ask why such arguments are clearly made on Channel 4 News, but not on BBC1 or ITV News. There does seem to be a reluctance to raise such issues. This, together with the limits imposed on coverage, can give a very constrained view of the conflict. We have already noted how Israeli casualties are disproportionately covered relative to actual numbers of deaths and injuries.[26] We discussed the issue of the restrictions of coverage imposed by the Israeli military with three very senior journalists: Paul Adams and Tim Llewellyn, who had both covered the Israeli-Palestinian conflict for the BBC, and Lindsey Hilsum from Channel 4 News. Paul Adams suggested that it might have been better, if possible, to have gone into Jenin with mini-cameras. In fact, it does seem that there were journalists who were present in Jenin during the attack. Marie Colvin from the *Sunday Times* described to us how she was there when the assault started and then had to stay because it was too dangerous to leave. Another suggestion made in these discussions was that there were now sufficient numbers of young journalists who would be prepared to take the risk of living for extended periods in the occupied territories. This would in some way reverse the imbalance of having the bulk of the journalistic community based in Israel. The difficulty would be in getting the newsrooms in London to use such reports from the occupied territories. As we have seen, there seems to be even less interest in featuring informed accounts of the nature and origins of the conflict.

TV News and propaganda

At the time of the attack on Jenin, Palestinians described it as a massacre by the Israelis and claimed that hundreds of people had been killed. The Israelis, on 12 April 2002, gave the figure as 100 dead and more injured (BBC1 early evening News, 12 April 2002). They later revised this figure and a UN report published on 1 August 2002 gave the figure of 52 confirmed Palestinian dead, of whom between 14 and 22 were civilians (the Israelis gave the figure of 14, Human Rights Watch gave it as 22). In part, the variations in these figures emerge from the confusion which normally characterises reporting of war and disasters. However, in the case of Jenin, it was argued by some that the claims of a massacre of hundreds of people were part of a propaganda effort by the Palestinians to discredit the Israelis. It was also suggested that the BBC had reported the Palestinian claims as 'fact'. Thus Stephen Pollard, writing in the *Guardian*, criticised both the original BBC coverage of Jenin as well as a later BBC2 news item on the UN report when it was published:

Newsnight's coverage of the UN report into Jenin was typical. The BBC had faithfully reported the Palestinian claims of a massacre as fact. So how would they deal with an inquiry which confirmed that there was no massacre? Easy: change the attack. The opening film by David Sells signed off with this impartial thought, which summed up the tone of his report: 'What happened in Jenin was no massacre but it was appalling in its own right'. (*Guardian*, 24 September 2002)

The first of these arguments that Palestinian claims had been reported 'as fact' seems clearly to be incorrect. In the extensive body of coverage which we have analysed, the BBC did not endorse the Palestinian view but merely reported it. It is also clear that at the time of Jenin, Palestinian claims were very directly questioned, as in this exchange between two BBC journalists:

Newscaster: A lot of claims are being made by the Palestinians, how can we be sure those claims are genuine?
Journalist: I think at this point the simple answer is, we can't.
(BBC1 early evening News, 11 April 2002)

Journalists seem to have been quite scrupulous in this. Lindsey Hilsum, for example, from Channel 4 News, told us that she very carefully avoided employing the word 'massacre' in her reports. It is important to distinguish between two types of statements – those which simply report a source and those which endorse or assume a perspective. In this case, the difference is between a journalist stating that 'Palestinians call it a massacre' and a direct statement such as 'there was a massacre'. We saw above that when a bus carrying settlers, a military vehicle and cars were reported to have been attacked by Palestinians, the killing of ten people was described by the Israeli authorities as a 'massacre'. The description was then taken up and endorsed in this reference on ITV News: 'The trigger for the Israeli offensive was a massacre on the West Bank' (ITV early evening News, 13 December 2001).

Although the BBC apparently avoided using the word 'massacre' to describe Palestinian deaths in Jenin, soon after they did endorse its use, in this headline about a bombing: 'Arafat warns his people after the latest massacre of Israelis' (BBC1 early evening News, 8 May 2002). Another suicide-bomber at the time of Jenin, who killed six people, was described as a 'mass murderer'. In this BBC report, '[She] made herself a martyr and mass murderer in yesterday's suicide attack in Jerusalem' (BBC1 early evening News, 13 April 2002).

We found no evidence that the BBC unduly accepted Palestinian claims. There were, however, occasions where they clearly endorsed Israeli perspectives. Consider these two descriptions from the BBC and ITV of the aforementioned suicide-bomber and her origin in Jenin. On ITV we hear that 'The bomber was a woman from the *beleaguered* Palestinian town of Jenin' (ITV early evening News, 12 April 2002 – our italics). In this description she comes from a 'beleaguered' place which is under attack. In the BBC's description, however, Jenin is the place where the Israelis are making 'determined efforts' to 'root out terrorists': 'The suicide-bomber is believed to have come from the Jenin refugee camp in the West Bank, the target of Israel's most determined efforts to root out potential terrorists' (BBC1 early evening News, 12 April 2002).

The second claim made by Stephen Pollard is that the BBC misreported the conclusions of the UN report. The quote from David Sells, which he criticises, does, however, include a clear statement that there was 'no massacre' and it is not greatly different from the commentary on the UN report which appeared in other media. The *Daily Telegraph*, for example, is a newspaper which is often thought of as being sympathetic to Israel. It stated that:

> A United Nations report on the April 'battle of Jenin' has dismissed claims that Israel massacred hundreds of civilians but it cited copious evidence that the army violated international law by using human shields, failing to protect civilians, shooting at ambulances and denying medical aid to the wounded. (*Daily Telegraph*, 2 August 2002)

Other press reports gave further accounts of civilian deaths. The *Independent* noted the cases of

> Fadwa Jamma, a Palestinian nurse who was shot through the heart while trying to tend a wounded man ... fourteen-year-old Faris Zeben, who was shot dead by an Israeli tank when he went shopping for groceries when the curfew was lifted ... Afaf Desuqi, who was killed when Israeli soldiers blew open the door of her house as she tried to open it for them ... Kemal Zughayer, shot dead as he tried to wheel himself up the road in his wheelchair. (*Independent*, 2 August 2002)

The *Guardian* noted that 'the civilian toll in Nablus was perhaps double that in Jenin', and quoted the UN report as revealing that 497 Palestinians were killed and 1,500 wounded in the period of the Israeli actions between 1 March and 7 May 2002. It also noted that during the same period there had been 16 bombings and suicide attacks in Israel in which more than 100 people were killed and scores wounded (*Guardian*, 2 August 2002). A report by Amnesty International in November 2002 noted the case of a 38-year-old severely disabled man who was in a house in Jenin which Israeli soldiers were preparing to demolish. According to the Amnesty report, his family showed the soldiers the man's ID, indicating his disabilities. The soldiers refused to help and the house was then bulldozed with the man 'trapped inside', killing him, despite appeals from his family (*Guardian*, 4 November 2002). It seems to us distasteful to argue over whether 'enough' civilians were killed in Jenin or elsewhere to justify the use of a word such as 'massacre'. As we have seen, it was in fact used to describe the killings of smaller numbers of Israelis than of Palestinians who died in Jenin. However, the key point is that journalists should report such killings by either side and should make it clear when international law is violated. Both the UN report and another report by Amnesty International in fact pointed to the illegality of the actions of both sides. Amnesty particularly highlighted the killing of children, noting that 'Israel had killed 250 Palestinian youngsters since the beginning of the Palestinian uprising in September 2000' and that 'Palestinian groups had killed 72 Israeli children in "direct and indiscriminate" attacks' (*The Times*, 1 October 2002).

As we have seen, in practice on TV news the coverage of deaths and casualties had a very disproportionate emphasis on those of Israel and different language was sometimes employed by journalists to describe these. There is no evidence from our analysis to suggest that Palestinian views were given preferential treatment on the BBC. The opposite is really the case.[27] This is part of a consistent pattern on TV news in which Israeli perspectives tended to be highlighted and sometimes endorsed by journalists. The next chapter examines possible relationships between such structures in news content and the development of public belief and understanding of the conflict.

3
Audience Studies 2001–02[1]

INTRODUCTION

Television news remains the main source of information on world events for a large majority of the population. A recent study by the Independent Television Commission of viewing habits found that in 2002, 79 per cent of the population regarded television news as their main source of world news (ITC, 2003). We have shown above the patterns of explanation which exist in news coverage and the manner in which some perspectives on the conflict are dominant. We will now explore the possible links between these structures in news content and the nature of audience belief. This will cover issues such as the role of visual imagery and how the inclusion or exclusion of different types of explanation may influence audience understanding. We will also examine the manner in which the structuring of reports may influence belief, for example, that one side in the conflict is often presented as initiating action while the other 'responds'. We also analyse links between audience understanding of stories and the effect of this on levels of interest – if people do not understand, do they simply switch off? Another key area is to examine how it might be possible to increase audience comprehension in this very complex area of news output.

SAMPLES AND METHOD

For this work we used both questionnaire and focus group techniques. The focus groups consisted of seven to eight people on average, who engaged in activities and discussion with a single moderator. They were selected on the basis of income, age and gender. Thus they included ten groups of middle-class and low-income men and women (aged around 25–50), plus one group of elderly people (aged over 65) and three further groups of young people aged 17–23, who were students. This was a total of 100 people. A list of the groups is given below. As far as is possible we selected 'normally occurring' groups, that is, people who would meet and speak with each other in the normal course of their lives. Thus some groups were drawn from parents at a school in London, and were local residents; others met for social activities, such as a group of women who went to dance classes together; others worked together, such as groups of teachers, cleaners and office workers, and some groups included family members.

Participants in focus groups

1. Low income male and female cleaners/janitors, Glasgow (six people).
2. Low-income females, residents, Hammersmith, London (five people).
3. Low-income males, residents, Hammersmith, London (ten people).
4. Middle-class males, residents, St Albans (four people).
5. Middle-class females, office workers, Glasgow (four people).
6. Middle-class females, dance class, Paisley (eleven people).
7. Middle-class males, residents, Glasgow (four people).
8. Middle-class male and female teachers, Paisley (six people).
9. Middle-class females, residents, Hammersmith, London (six people).
10. Middle-class males, residents, Hammersmith, London (eight people).
11. Young male and female students, Glasgow (ten people).
12. Young male and female students, Glasgow (eleven people).
13. Young male and female students, Glasgow (five people).
14. Elderly/retired males and females, Glasgow (ten people).

This project was designed with the help of journalists and broadcasting professionals. One of its key features was that we invited journalists to sit in on focus groups, to take part in the discussions and to raise issues as they wished. Those who took part in the study included George Alagiah and Brian Hanrahan of the BBC, and Tim Llewellyn, a former BBC Middle East correspondent; Lindsey Hilsum from Channel 4 News; Ken Loach, independent film-maker, and Adrian Monck and Gaye Flashman from Channel Five News. Others who helped and gave advice and comments include John Humphrys, Sian Kevill, Fran Unsworth, Sue Inglish, Evan Davis, Paul Adams and Nik Gowing from the BBC; John Underwood from Clear Communications; Alex Graham from Wall to Wall Television and Sandy Ross and Paul McKinney from Scottish Television.

We also had a specific interest in the responses of young people since there is a considerable contemporary debate on their usage of news and on whether this relates to how well they are informed on politics and world affairs and to their level of interest in these. Part of the work for the focus groups involved the detailed discussion of a series of questions about the Israeli-Palestinian conflict. We developed an abbreviated version of these and asked them in questionnaire form to two separate groups of British students (one of 300, the other 280) aged between 17 and 23. These two groups were asked the same questions one year apart, in October 2001 and October 2002. For purposes of comparison we also asked the same questions to two groups of students from Germany and the United States (114 from Germany who were High School students aged 16–18, and 49 from the US who were Journalism/Communications students aged 20–21). Thus our total sample was 100 in focus groups and 743 who answered the questionnaire.

FOCUS GROUP METHODS AND QUESTIONS ASKED

A key feature of this work was to identify the nature and sources of audience belief. The media are a key source of information, so one dimension of the study was to analyse how people respond to messages and to examine the conditions under which they accepted or rejected what they heard or saw. At the beginning of each focus group, the moderator explained to those present that they would be asked questions about the conflict, but it was also stressed that this was not a 'quiz'. The group were told that we were only interested in what each person knows and understands and that it did not matter to us if their answers were 'right' or 'wrong'. We are studying the judgements they have made about the information they have received and the processes by which beliefs are formed. It is an important part of this method to explain very carefully what we are doing and to establish a level of trust with the participants so that they are not afraid to say what they are actually thinking.

The method and sequence of activities in the focus groups were as follows. First, we asked nine questions about the conflict and sources of information which had been used. Each member of the groups gave written answers to these questions:

1. What comes into your mind when you hear the words 'Israeli-Palestinian conflict?' It might be a picture, it might be something someone has said, it might be something you have read or seen,

or even somewhere you went on holiday – but what comes into your head?

2a. What is the source of what came into you head when you heard 'Israeli-Palestinian conflict'?

2b. Are there any other sources which you have ever used to find out information about that particular conflict?

For questions 3 and 4 the groups were read a phrase from television news which used the words 'occupied' and 'settlers'. The phrase was 'the settlers who have made their homes in occupied territory' (BBC1 early evening News, 9 February 2001). They were then asked:

3. Who is occupying the occupied territories?

4. What nationality are the settlers?

5. In the period since the intifada began (September 2000), which side would you say has had the most casualties? Is it a lot more Israelis, a few more Israelis, about the same for each side, a few more Palestinians or a lot more Palestinians?

6. Why are they fighting? What is the conflict about?

7. There have been a number of wars in that region since the Second World War which involved Israel. Can you name any of them and give dates?

8. What land or countries were occupied in these conflicts?

9. Do you know of any United Nations resolutions or any criticisms that have been made by the UN about the actions of anyone in the conflict?

Following this, we then gave each group member a set of 16 photographs that were taken from TV news coverage. The photographs showed the main areas of reporting as revealed in our content analysis. They included images of fighting, stone-throwing, the aftermath of a suicide-bombing and pictures of past peace talks and negotiations (for example, of Yasser Arafat meeting President Clinton and Ehud Barak). The group members were then asked to imagine that they were journalists and to write a brief news story using the pictures as a stimulus. The purpose of this was to examine whether they were able to reproduce news language and the explanations of the conflict which were prominent in news accounts. This was then followed by a discussion about the pictures they had used and their understanding of them. For example, one picture featured a group of Palestinians burning an American flag. We asked the group members what they understood from this and what the motive for this action might be. An important element of this procedure was to establish what information group members were taking from news accounts and whether they believed what they were told. Some people who were well informed about the conflict could write very good versions of the news but were also quite critical of it, so the ability to reproduce a news programme is not the same as actually believing the news. However, the news writing exercise and the questions provided an excellent starting point for extended discussions about what the group members did understand and believe about the reasons for the conflict and the manner in which they were informed.

After the news writing exercise, the moderator initiated a further discussion by going through each of the questions and asking in detail about how the group members had arrived at their answers. In practice the participants often joined in spontaneously to offer their own personal histories and accounts of how they had come to understand the conflict. This then led to a more extended discussion on the origins and causes of the conflict. The moderator then raised other specific issues such as whether the group had heard of the Palestinian refugees or knew their history. They were also asked about how they 'saw' the conflict, for example, as 'religious' or 'economic' or simply as a dispute between bad neighbours. How did they see the 'trouble' as starting, and had they heard of other issues such as disputes over water and how it was controlled?

Finally we discussed the general issue of how understanding related to levels of interest. In the group sessions, many questions were addressed to the moderator and to the journalist present by group members who simply wanted to know more and to increase their own understanding. We will discuss this further in our results section, but it was clear that a major reason for viewers 'turning off' from the news was simply that they had little understanding of what they were watching.

QUALITATIVE AND QUANTITATIVE APPROACHES

'Qualitative' methods imply a concentration on processes of meaning and understanding. There are several advantages in using the qualitative techniques of focus group work (so called because they offer a higher qualitative integrity of data). The first is that they enable the investigator to check that the respondents have really understood the questions and that the answers given do reflect what is actually believed. A second advantage is that the detailed discussion often throws up other related issues which can be pursued. For example, when we asked questions about the reasons for the conflict, a frequent response was that it was over 'land'. But we did not realise until the discussions that some people understood this to mean that it was a form of border dispute in which two countries fought over a piece of land which separated them. Another advantage of such discussions is that, as people hear more arguments and information with which they are unfamiliar, it is possible to see how beliefs are modified and develop. A further very important element of the focus group approach is that it enables a rapport or level of trust to develop between those taking part and the moderator, so that people become less guarded and more prepared to say what they really believe. It takes time for people to think carefully about the origins of their own understanding and to be clear about what they are being asked to do. We can see this if we consider an actual exchange of views in a focus group. In this example, the moderator asks about the issue of who is seen to be 'starting' the violence and how this is shown on the news. The difficulty with this for the group was that some of them were sympathetic to the Palestinians. As it turned out they did think that the news presented the Israelis as responding to Palestinian 'action'. But they were reluctant to acknowledge this because they themselves rejected this way of seeing the conflict. It took some time to separate their beliefs about what was 'really' happening from what they were 'seeing' on the news. The moderator began by asking if the news gave the impression of one side starting the fighting while the other 'retaliates':

> *First speaker*: It depends what you call fighting because they are depriving them of the things they are depriving them of and that's an aggressive act in itself.
> *Moderator*: But do you get the sense that one side is starting the actual …
> *First speaker*: Yeah, the Israelis.
> *Moderator*: You get the sense that the Israelis are firing the guns first …
> *First speaker*: Not firing the guns but they're doing things that are leaving the Palestinians thinking they have no choice.
> *Moderator*: I just wonder if from the news you get the sense that one side is starting it and the other side retaliates …
> *First speaker*: Usually what we see on the news is the Palestinians doing something and the Israelis overreacting.

Moderator: How many people think it comes across as the Palestinians doing something like a suicide-bomb and the Israelis retaliate? [*No response*]
Nobody sees this thing about retaliation? Because a minute ago you were saying you did see it as the Palestinians starting it and the Israelis retaliating.
First speaker: But you're assuming that I trust what I see on the news.
Moderator: No, I'm not saying do you believe it, that's separate. I'm saying do you think it comes across as that?
First speaker: Maybe to other people, yeah.
Moderator: Let me make that point again, I'm asking you does it come across as that – whether you believe it or not is another matter – does it come across as one side doing something and then the other side retaliating? How many people think that? I'm not talking about whether you believe it or not. Before, you said it did come across as that.
First speaker: Well that's obviously what we are led to believe and what most people believe.
Moderator: I'm not sure that it is.
Second speaker: In reality, you could have half a brain like me, but you wouldn't believe it – you could see the falsehoods in it.
Moderator: That's a separate question – whether you believe it or not, I'm only interested in what you think the news is saying.
First speaker: It does seem the way they report it on the news.
Second speaker: It's being portrayed that way, yes.
First speaker: It does seem that the Israelis are retaliating to something the Palestinians did.
Third speaker: Yes.
Moderator: How many people think that? [*General nods*] How many, one, two, three, four ... eight. (Low-income group, London)

Establishing what people do actually believe can take time. As the first speaker commented after this exchange: 'I just think we're a lot of paranoid people.'

Another advantage of the focus group discussion is that participants can reproduce the everyday speech and interaction with each other in which they might 'normally' discuss TV or what they have seen or read about current events. This can show how the assumptions of cause and the relationships presented in the media become part of everyday speech. For example, in the following exchange one participant explains why he thinks most casualties are Israeli, and then a second person spontaneously introduces the 'retaliation' theme which he expresses with the words 'getting their own back':

> *First speaker*: Because of the indiscriminate attacks. It seems like there's been more Palestinian attacks.
> *Second speaker*: But if you watch the news you know that they always get their own back. (Middle-class male group, St Albans)

The focus group can also be combined with other qualitative techniques such as the personal interview, in which participants may be spoken with individually after the main session, to clarify specific points and to enable people to say anything which they were reluctant to comment on in the context of a group. This is important in areas of great personal sensitivity, for example, where we have investigated issues such as media coverage of child abuse or mental distress. The disadvantage of focus groups is the amount of time and resources they consume to establish such a high level of qualitative integrity of data. The corresponding advantage of questionnaire methods is that they enable very large numbers of people to give replies relatively quickly. Such quantitative techniques can give a snapshot of what people know or believe at any one time. But to examine in detail the processes by which such beliefs are formed really requires qualitative approaches such as the focus group.

THE QUESTIONNAIRES

We gave an abbreviated version of the questions which we used with the focus groups to our two groups of British students. The questions were:

1. When you hear the words 'Israeli-Palestinian conflict', what comes into your mind? What do you see in your head?
2a. What is the source of what you have just thought of, where did it come from?
2b. Are there any other sources which you have used to find out information about this conflict?

The same phrase from TV news ('the settlers who have made their homes in occupied territory') was read to them as with the focus groups. They were then asked:

3. Who is occupying the occupied territories?
4. What nationality are the settlers?
5. Since the beginning of the intifada, which side has had the most casualties? Is it a lot more Israelis, a few more Israelis, about the same for each, a few more Palestinians or a lot more Palestinians?
6. Where did the Palestinian refugees come from? How did they become refugees?
7. TV news has shown pictures of Palestinians burning the US flag, why would Palestinians do this?

We also took two groups of seven to eight students from this main sample and met them separately to discuss their answers, in a similar way to a normal focus group. The intention was to identify any problems which might have existed in answering the questions.

We also gave the same questionnaire to groups of American and German students, since we had a specific interest in the knowledge which young people had of world and political events. For the same reason we asked a series of additional questions which were not about the Israeli-Palestinian conflict. These questions related to a range of historical and contemporary events. The British, American and German students all gave answers to these. Some related to wars such as the Second World War and Vietnam, others to the history of the Soviet Union and the slave labour camps about which Solzhenitsyn wrote. We also asked about US interventions in Latin America: Nicaragua, where a private army was financed by the Reagan administration, and Guatemala, where the US was involved in the so-called 'dirty war'. The questions were as follows:

8. What were the Gulags in the Soviet Union?
9. In the Vietnam War how many casualties were there on each side, was it a lot more Americans, a few more Americans, about the same, a few more Vietnamese or a lot more Vietnamese?
10. Who were the Contras in Nicaragua?
11. In 1999 President Clinton made a public apology in Guatemala – why?
12. In the Second World War, which country of the Allies defeated the most German divisions?

These questions also offered an interesting point of comparison with the Israeli-Palestinian conflict, since many of the subjects to which they related were not covered at all in recent news reporting.

Others such as the Second World War and the Vietnam War have been featured in fictional accounts such as Hollywood films and made-for-TV dramas. It was therefore interesting to examine any differences in knowledge or understanding which might emerge from these variations in media output. The replies to these questions and a fuller account of this part of the research are given in Appendix 3.

RESULTS

The replies to the questionnaires and the responses and discussion in the focus groups fell into seven categories. These were:

1. Memories, images and associations that group members had of the conflict.
2. The sources of information used.
3. The origins, history and causes of the conflict.
4. The news writing exercise.
5. Beliefs about casualties.
6. Cultural identification and empathy.
7. Understanding and interest in news.

We will discuss each of these in turn.

MEMORIES, IMAGES AND ASSOCIATIONS

The first question was on what came into people's minds when they heard the words 'Israeli-Palestinian conflict'. The responses over-whelmingly referred to images of war, conflict and violence, such as 'war, death, children dying'; 'bombings, people dying'; 'gunmen, suicide-bombers' and 'children throwing stones at Israeli soldiers'. In our two large samples of British students 71 per cent and 79 per cent of them gave such answers (for the German students 82 per cent and US students 74 per cent) and for the focus groups it was 75 per cent. Others named general issues such as 'religious conflict' or political figures, and a few cited personal experiences. A detailed breakdown of the responses is given in Appendices 1 and 2. There was one very noticeable difference between the British students interviewed in 2001 and the second group a year later in 2002. In 2001, 2 per cent of the first group named suicide-bombings, but this rose to 24 per cent in the second group a year later, which may be a result of the increased emphasis on Israeli casualties which we noted in our content analysis.

SOURCES OF INFORMATION USED

The participants mostly linked their answers for question 1 to TV news as the key source. For the two groups of British students, 82 per cent and 85 per cent cited the news, while for the focus groups the figure was 84 per cent. This corresponds with other research, including the findings of the ITC 2002 study (ITC, 2003) we cited above. For the German and American students the figures were lower at 61 per cent and 58 per cent respectively. The American students were more likely than the British to cite newspapers as a source, but this probably reflects the fact that they were studying media and journalism. Other sources included books, journals, radio, personal experiences and the comments of other people. Peace rallies appeared as a source in the British sample of 2002. For more information on the use of sources see Appendices 1 and 2.

In the focus groups middle-class males and professional groups tended to be the best informed about the conflict and also to cite the widest range of sources. It was also apparent that where people were well informed, the main sources were often not TV news. Middle-class males tended to be heavy consumers of news, but this consumption was indicative of a high level of interest which was being fed by other sources such as books, the quality press or further study in higher education. In fact such groups could be rather disparaging of TV news as a source. As one participant commented:

> There is no depth to it – television news more or less covers anything superficially. I think we are dumbing down. Someone has told the BBC that the average person has an attention span of less than two minutes and that is rubbish but they are buying into it. More and more it's 'How can we keep them watching – whether we are giving information or not?' I certainly wouldn't rely on BBC television news for anything I thought was really important. (Middle-class male group, Glasgow)

The statement on attention span seemed to be confirmed by George Alagiah from the BBC who commented in another focus group that

> In depth it takes a long time, but we're constantly being told that the attention span of our average viewer is about 20 seconds and if we don't grab people – and we've looked at the figures – the

number of people who shift channels around in my programme now at six o'clock, there's a movement of about 3 million people in that first minute, coming in and out. (At low-income male group, London)

None the less, for many viewers, TV news was still a key source of information about events in the conflict. The news apparently affected beliefs even amongst those who watched very little or claimed to be non-watchers. In the following example a woman comments on how she avoids the news:

I don't ever watch the news. They are normally not particularly happy incidents that have gone on in the world throughout the day, so I avoid it. (Middle-class female group, London)

But her written answers had apparently been affected by the news, which became clear as they were discussed:

Moderator: [As reasons for the conflict] you had territory and religion.
Female speaker: It vaguely came from listening to the news when I was doing something else.
Moderator: It sort of seeped in?
Female speaker: While doing something else, yes. (Middle-class female group, London)

There was also some concern expressed in the groups as to the quality of the information and explanations given on the news. Some believed they were not being given the whole story:

First speaker: There's too many gaps, if you are being shown a partial picture, you are obviously not being shown a whole picture ... they are showing you what they want you to see, and it shows that they are showing you what they want you to see, what we are seeing is what we are being fed.
Second speaker: They never really tell you the in-depth reasons about it – 'This guy went into bomb a pizza restaurant' – why? 'The Israelis are going to attack' – why?
First speaker: What pushes them to that extreme? (Low-income male group, London)

One reason for this criticism of television news was that the first speaker had alternative sources of information which offered a different version of events. This focus group took place in a very busy multi-ethnic part of London. The first speaker commented on how he had met people with direct experience of events that he had seen reported on television:

[I was] meeting people who were refugees who were actually in the country and [them] saying 'You're watching this on the news but I was actually there on the day this took place.' (Low-income male group, London)

As we will see, such access to alternative accounts had a strong influence on the beliefs of some participants about the nature of the Israeli-Palestinian conflict and its causes.

ORIGINS, HISTORY AND CAUSES OF THE CONFLICT

Most of the participants in this research had little idea of the history or origins of the conflict. In the large sample groups of British students in 2001, 4 per cent wrote that the Palestinians had been forced from their homes on the formation of Israel. In 2002 the figure was 8 per cent (for the German and American students the figure was 26 per cent and 19 per cent respectively – see Appendices 1 and 2). For the British students there were an additional 14 per cent in 2001 and 22 per cent in 2002 who suggested that the Palestinians had in some way lost their homes because of Israel, or who mentioned the occupation as a factor – they used words such as 'kicked out', 'deported', 'evicted' or 'excluded'. The majority simply did not know or made general references to the problems of refugees, such as 'driven out by fear of war and hunger' or 'through armed conflict, bombing'. It was also clear from the focus groups that most people had very little detailed knowledge. The British students were studying social sciences, arts and history at university and the focus groups contained a strong representation of middle-class males/professionals who are high consumers of news. Even so, in the focus groups as a whole just 19 per cent mentioned the formation of Israel in relation to the Palestinian refugees and most could not name any wars in the region. The level of public knowledge as a whole is probably even lower than this.

The majority also had no knowledge of the link between the wars of 1948 and 1967 – that Palestinians who were displaced from what became Israel in 1948 moved to areas such as Gaza, the West Bank of the Jordan and East Jerusalem and were then subject to military occupation after 1967. In the focus groups, the moderator was sometimes asked by the participants about the origins of the conflict. In response they were given a very brief account of the events of 1948 and 1967, based on the work of the Israeli historian Avi Shlaim (2000), and sometimes helped by the comments of journalists who were present. Although the account given was extremely brief, it could have a very dramatic effect on the understanding of group members as this exchange indicates:

Moderator: Would it help you when you are watching the news, if you knew that history?
First speaker: Yes.
Second speaker: A lot more.
Third speaker: Absolutely.
Second speaker: If they did refer more to the history, the whole thing would mean a hell of a lot more for a lot of people.
First speaker: That's right, we need to know more.
Third speaker: It's so fragmented and vague, I mean to try and explain it to my children, I found it difficult – I'm not the sharpest tool in the box anyway, but having said that, on what I was given by the media, a great deal of it was blank, and you just filled in the blanks that I didn't have a clue about – 1948? Was there a war in 1948? Well now I know there was. (Low-income male group, London).

Lindsey Hilsum from Channel 4 News put the question directly to a group of middle-class women as to whether they would like more background information:

Lindsey Hilsum: I want to know whether you want to know more about it or not. Would you like there to be more background information on the Middle East or do you think there's plenty … ?
First speaker: Yeah I absolutely agree with that. I always think if only they'd give just us the quick potted history of what brought us to this point. Sometimes when the Israeli-Palestinian conflict kicks off again I become really interested and I follow it day by day to see what's going up, who's retaliating and what's happening with the suicide-bombers. But I think, God, if anybody just turned on their television or their radio now, they wouldn't have a hope in hell of following what was happening.

Lindsey Hilsum: Yes.
First speaker: You want somebody to say, this is all because in 1948, that happened and that happened.
Lindsey Hilsum: A sort of 'New readers start here' ...
First speaker: Yes, yes, something like that. (Middle-class female group, London)

Tim Llewellyn, a former BBC Middle East correspondent, then goes on to describe how he has sometimes found it hard to follow news which is outside his area of expertise:

Tim Llewellyn: I know a lot about the Middle East, but I was watching BBC World the other night, which is supposed to be better on foreign coverage ... I was amazed to see, I remember one story was about presidential elections in Brazil. Now I watched very closely on this, I don't know much about Brazil, I knew there were elections, but I haven't been following it in the newspaper – what the background is, who's running for office and why. I thought [the item] was dreadful. You were given no background information, it was extremely glib, it took a lot for granted, it took a lot of knowledge for granted on the part of the viewer.
First speaker: Yes, that's right.
Moderator: Is that a feeling that you quite often have, that you don't feel you've got enough background knowledge to actually understand what's going on?
First speaker: Yes.
Second speaker: Definitely, with home news and American news you're very conscious and you do know, but even with European news you don't get that much – in the Bosnia war there wasn't a great lot of background. (Middle-class female group, London)

One BBC journalist actually told us that he had been instructed not to do 'explainers' by his own editor. As he put it: 'It's all bang bang stuff.' In another focus group, one participant specifically raised the issue of how the news is dominated by images of atrocity and horror to the exclusion of material on background and origins:

First speaker: One of the problems with most of the news is that you get the atrocity, the horror but it's the background that is the key bit. *Newsnight* does go some way to filling one in a bit on that but I'm pretty ignorant of it really and that's the more

important, more interesting, important stuff, the background, the origins rather than the latest [action].
Second speaker: I'm drawn to background and overview articles rather than the latest bus being blown up.
Moderator: Is that a general feeling, that there is too much emphasis on immediate action and image?
Third speaker: I think that characterises all news coverage.
Moderator: That is your view?
Third speaker: Yes, absolutely. (Middle-class male group, London)

Yet as the first speaker also pointed out, there is clearly an important role for powerful images since they may have a strong emotional influence and can affect the commitment to watch a particular story:

When that boy and his dad were shot by Israeli soldiers, unfortunately the British TV cut the pictures, but even so it's still fairly shocking and that re-energised, reawakened my interest. Just because that brought it home to me as a parent. If I was in that situation with my son ... that did make me realise just what it must be like. (Middle-class male group, London)

There were some other reservations expressed in this and other groups as to how much historical detail could be included in news and whether longer historical accounts should be shown in dedicated current affairs programmes. A small number of people indicated that they were not interested in the subject or were just too busy – 'it goes in one ear and out the other', as one participant said. Another questioned whether audiences would want more in-depth accounts (middle-class males, London), but overall there was a strong feeling in the groups that it was difficult to understand the present without some knowledge of the past. As a young male from Glasgow put it:

I've not heard any historical context from the news at all. They don't tell us that – they don't say – they leave it on the short scale. 'This fighting was due to yesterday's fighting, which was due to the day before.' But they don't go back to all that, I don't know anything about that [history]. The reporter will say 'The Israelis fired into a Palestinian refugee camp today in response to a Palestinian suicide-bomber yesterday', but they won't say why the Palestinians are fighting or why the Israelis are fighting – it doesn't go back any length of time. (Student group, Glasgow)

The lack of historical knowledge made it very difficult for people to understand key elements of the conflict. For example, some had written that 'land' was an issue but there was a great deal of confusion over what this meant. Another participant described how his understanding included no sense of the Palestinian case that land had been taken from them:

> The impression I got was that the Palestinians had lived around that area and now they were trying to come back and get some more land for themselves – I didn't realise they had been actually driven out, I just thought they didn't want to live as part of Israel and that the places they were living in, they decided they wanted to make self-governed – I didn't realise they had been driven out of places in wars previously. (Student group, Glasgow)

Some people saw the conflict as a dispute between two countries or peoples, who had a strip of land between them that they both wanted, as in this exchange:

> *Moderator*: How did this land conflict come about?
> *Male speaker*: They are right next to each other and they are trying to get a bit more off each other.
> *Moderator*: Do you see it as two countries, two groups and two countries and they are both fighting over this bit of contested land?
> *Male speaker*: That is it, yes.
> *Moderator*: So something in the middle of it all?
> *Male speaker*: It is like the border and they are trying to take a bit off each other. (Low-income group, Glasgow)

The same point is made in another group:

> I didn't realise – I didn't know all the geography of Palestine being occupied. I thought there was Palestine, then there was Israel and then there was the border in between that they were fighting over. (Office workers, female, Glasgow)

Another sees the conflict as a 'nice piece of land' that they are both fighting over, without any sense that land has been taken:

> *Female speaker*: I just thought it was disputed land, I wasn't under the impression that the Israeli borders had changed or that they

had taken land from other people. I just had the impression that it was a nice piece of land that both, to put it simplistically, that they were fighting over and I thought, it was more a Palestinian aggression than it was Israeli aggression
Moderator: Did anyone else see it this way?
Answers: Yes, yes [five out of ten people in this group assented]. (Student group, Glasgow)

There were similar problems in understanding terms such as 'occupied territories'. Because many in the groups did not understand that Palestinians had been subject to military occupation after 1967, there was some confusion over what the word 'occupied' meant.

The nature of the occupation and limits to understanding

In our questions we had asked, 'Who is occupying the occupied territories and what nationality are the settlers?' In our main samples of British students only 9 per cent in 2001 and 11 per cent in 2002 knew that the Israelis were occupying and that the settlers were Israeli. In the first of these samples there were actually more people who believed that the Palestinians were occupying the territories and that the settlers were Palestinian. In the German and US groups there were more people who knew the correct answer to both questions (26 per cent of the German students and 29 per cent of the American students). In the focus groups the figure was 39 per cent. The figure for the American students probably overstates the level of knowledge amongst young Americans since these were journalism and media students and some had done projects on the Israeli-Palestinian issue. Even so, there was a good deal of confusion amongst them. For example, over half of those who had written that the Palestinians became refugees on the formation of Israel or were 'forced from their homes by Israel' also thought that the Palestinians occupied the occupied territories. We found similar confusion in the British focus groups over who was occupying and what this signified. One woman from a London group commented on her reply as follows: 'I put "not sure", then I thought it was the Jews, then I thought maybe it was the Palestinians moving into Jewish occupied territory' (low-income female group, London).

Given that so many did not know that there was a military occupation, it is not surprising that the consequences of it for the Palestinians were little understood. Even in groups that were comparatively well informed, such as middle-class males in Glasgow, there was little knowledge of economic consequences such as those caused by the Israeli control of water. In the focus group sample as a whole only 9 per cent were aware of this issue. There was little understanding of areas such as human rights – only two people in all the focus groups raised these as an issue. Even in groups that tended to be sympathetic with the Palestinians (such as low-income males in London) there was some surprise when they heard that there were pass laws and identity cards which restricted movement. There was almost no knowledge of the large number of UN resolutions which have been passed, either those relating to the legality of the occupation or to human rights abuses in the territories. These absences in public knowledge very closely parallel the absence of such information on the TV news. The issue of what people were not told was sometimes raised in the groups. In this exchange, Brian Hanrahan from the BBC asks whether reporters are seen to be taking sides in the conflict:

> *Brian Hanrahan*: Do you think the reporter is telling you to believe one side rather than the other?
> *Female speaker*: I don't think it is always just the reporters telling you what side to believe. There's information that you get and also a lot of information that you don't get, so in that sense I feel what I'm being given is quite limited or selective. (Low-income female group, London)

This participant then speaks about the limited coverage of dissent within Israel. She describes how she had seen a very small article about this issue and compares it with very large headlines on other subjects:

> I remember seeing in the newspaper a tiny little article and it was about some young students in the Jewish army who refused to fight: 'This isn't fair' [they said] and they refused. They were supposed to be forcing some Palestinians out of some territory and they refused to do it and they put down their arms ... but it was only like a tiny little piece of information, so in that way, when you get a small piece of information, a tiny article and it's further down the newspaper it's very, very easy to miss. I feel as though in other [subjects] you get big headlines and even those are choosing. (Low-income female group, London)

The perception audiences had of Israeli settlers in the occupied territories was also significant. On the news as we have seen, the settlers were presented as vulnerable and under attack. Yet as we noted above, the settlements have a key role in the occupation. As the Israeli historian Avi Shlaim (2000) put it, they were part of a policy of exerting strategic and military control. Many were built on hilltops to give them a commanding position with the explicit encouragement of Ariel Sharon. Established settlements were strongly fortified and their occupants were often heavily armed. One of the very few people in the focus groups who knew this actually wrote that 'the word "settler" is a euphemism' (male teacher, Paisley). But it was more common to see the issue in the terms adopted by the news. The 'occupied territories' were not seen as having been subject to military occupation and the settlements were not understood as being part of this. The army was there simply to keep the Palestinians back:

> *Moderator*: Do you get the impression watching the news that it is a military occupation by Israel?
> *Male speaker*: A military occupation? No, it's to give the Israelis land to work on, to live on and the army backs them up and keeps back the Palestinians in my opinion. (Middle-class male group, Glasgow)

Another participant described his impression of TV news:

> I think you sometimes get the impression from the news that these are people who happen to want to live there … and the military backup is in pursuit of their peaceful wish to just go and live there, and I think that's the impression I get from the news, rather than that it is a military occupation. (Teachers group, Paisley)

With this perception of the conflict it is not hard to see how the Palestinians appear as the aggressors. As a Glasgow student put it:

> I had no idea why they were fighting, I just thought it was the Palestinians trying to claim more land. I didn't know it was kind of like back [had a history]. I knew it was disputed but I didn't know the Israelis had taken land.

Two other students from Glasgow described the influence on their beliefs of seeing a documentary by John Pilger, which showed the power and reach of the settlements:[2]

First speaker (male): The all-Jewish roads, I'd not seen that before. *Second speaker (female)*: It made it look much more like an invasion and not just a bunch of poor benighted people trying to find somewhere to live.

Even people who were sympathetic to the Palestinians had absorbed the message of the settlers as small embattled communities. A middle-class male from Glasgow described his surprise when he heard that the settlements controlled over 40 per cent of the West Bank:

I had absolutely no idea it was that percentage – I was gobsmacked when I heard it. I saw them as small, embattled and surrounded by hostile Palestinians – that's entirely thanks to watching the television news.

And there were other areas where the absence of explanation made it difficult to understand the motives of those involved.

The United States, Israel and the Palestinians

We asked the participants why the Palestinians might wish to burn the American flag. Some thought it might be for religious reasons or because of extreme support for Islamist opponents of the US. A middle-class woman in London wrote that it was 'to show support for Taliban hijackers'. But there was also considerable confusion over the relationship between Israel and the US. In the two British groups of students, just over a third wrote that the US gave 'support' or military/monetary aid to Israel (37 per cent and 38 per cent). For the Germans, the figure was 69 per cent and for the American students, 46 per cent (see Appendices 1 and 2). In the focus groups 34 per cent of the participants knew of support or military/monetary aid. There were also a number of comments that the US was 'not welcome' (office workers, Glasgow), that they were 'sticking their noses in' (low-income group, Glasgow), and that the US was seen as 'interfering with the situation' (Paisley teachers). In a group of middle-class women in London it was said that the Palestinians had 'lost faith in American intervention', but none of these women knew that the US supplies arms and money to Israel. There was also a sense that the US was involved in brokering between the two sides, but why they might not be trusted in this was, for most people, very unclear. What was missing from many people's understanding were more direct explanations for Palestinian hostility, such as that the armaments being used to attack them were paid for by the US. There was a clear feeling in the groups that such information should be given. Even those people who were concerned about how much explanation could be included in news programmes said that this was 'the least' they should be told (middle-class males, London).

Without any understanding of the origins or history of the conflict or the rationales of those involved, the dispute could be seen simply as an argument between 'bad neighbours' or just an undifferentiated mess of inexplicable violence: 'We don't actually listen to what's going on, it's all kind of like shock value, "Oh my goodness, look at all the nightmares with what is happening over there".' (student group, Glasgow). A middle-class woman in London described it as 'a big mish-mash area'. A woman from Glasgow suggested that the fighting would stop 'if they kept their children in the house and stopped them throwing stones'. Others thought that there were probably deep reasons for the conflict but that they just did not know what they were. A minority were comparatively well informed, often by sources other than TV news. We can see this mixture of responses in a typical student group of ten people which met in Glasgow. In this group five saw it as a fight over land between 'conflicting neighbours'. None of them had heard of the economic issue of water and none had any idea that the occupation was widely seen as illegal. Two members of this group knew that the US gave aid and money to Israel and one of these knew that the US also supplied them with arms. We have already commented on the lack of historical knowledge of members of this group who did not know that Israel had taken any land. This lack of knowledge of origins and causes had another important effect on some participants in this and other groups, in that the conflict and fighting was seen as being initiated by the Palestinians.

Response and Retaliation: Who Starts the Violence?

We showed in our content analysis of TV news that a consistent pattern existed which emphasised Palestinian action and Israeli response and retaliation. This apparently affected how some people saw the conflict and how they allocated 'blame' for the violence. As one student from the above focus group commented:

Female speaker: You always think of the Palestinians as being really aggressive because of the stories you hear on the news. I always put the blame on them in my own head.

Moderator: Is it presented as if the Palestinians somehow start it and then the Israelis follow on?
Female speaker: Exactly, I always think the Israelis are fighting back against the bombings that have been done to them. (Student group, Glasgow)

Another student answering a questionnaire believed that 'a lot more Israelis' had been killed than Palestinians and wrote that 'The Palestinians trigger every incident which makes the Israelis retaliate.' The news presentation of Palestinian action and Israeli response was clearly seen within the groups, as in these comments:

First speaker: They [the Palestinians] killed that minister earlier in the year and that sparked reprisals ...
Second speaker: There was bombing today of the Palestinian areas and the linkage was made absolutely with that bombing by the Palestinians. (Middle-class male group, St Albans)

The second of these speakers commented of the Israelis 'they are so vulnerable'. But another speaker in the same group questioned the relationship as portrayed on the news: 'You hear it is always the Israelis holding back a bit and then they do the reprisal, but it has been going on so many years it could be anyone starting it.' In another group, a middle-class male from Glasgow offered this critical view of TV news:

The Palestinians are always regarded as terrorists, Israel is the ideal state which is being attacked by the terrorists ... if it wasn't for the Palestinians and their suicide-bombs, the thing would run perfectly well.

There were often mixed views within the groups. For example, in the group of women from Paisley, three stated that they did see the Israelis as 'responding' to what was done to them by the Palestinians, but then a fourth women used the phrase 'retaliate' while speaking and then paused, saying that she was surprised at herself as she did not see the Israeli actions as justified.

Another participant raised a further important point. He argued that although the structure and language of news might favour the Israelis, the visual images of Israeli dominance may lead viewers to criticise them:

The reporting of the Palestinians, of the atrocity of the car bombs, of suicide-bombings by Hamas, is clearly reported as being a dreadfully wrong thing and an atrocity. I think the reporting of the Israeli army in the Palestinian territories is not so clearly put across as Israel are in the wrong, but just the repetition, the sheer volume of images of Israeli dominance in Palestinian territories puts across the idea that Israel is wrong in that context. (Middle-class male group, London)

Another person from the same group thought that the news was biased against Israel exactly because it did show images of boys throwing stones against soldiers and tanks. He thought that these would necessarily prejudice the viewer against Israel: 'How anybody could think that the images of tanks smashing down buildings, of Israeli soldiers armed against boys throwing stones is sympathetic to the Israelis defies logic.' This does raise an interesting question which the moderator noted, which is that if such events are occurring in the conflict, then what would constitute 'bias' on the part of the broadcasters? Would it be to show the images or to avoid transmitting them, so that audiences could *not* see them? Another speaker in the group raised a more crucial point, that images alone are unlikely to convince an audience on the legitimacy of either side in a dispute. As he pointed out, in the case of Northern Ireland, British audiences became accustomed to seeing young people throwing stones at troops, but it did not follow that the audience sympathised with the stone-throwers. As he said: 'We generally believed that the British Army and the British government was right.' In the same way, in the Gulf War of 1991, the Iraqi army was clearly the 'underdog' in terms of military power but audiences in the West did not identify with the cause of Saddam Hussein. In the Israeli-Palestinian conflict, Israel argued that Palestinian children were being deliberately exploited by mendacious leaders and had been incited to attack the troops. For people who believe this, it might well affect how they perceive the actions of the Israeli army and the causes of the violence. In a Glasgow group, some participants had accepted the TV account of the sequence of the violence and concluded that the problem could be resolved if the children stayed in their houses and did not throw stones:

Moderator: Did you ever see one side as starting the trouble and then the other one … ?
First speaker (female): All the wee guys with all the wee bricks.

Moderator: All the wee guys with the wee bricks?
First speaker: They are usually the ones that are usually standing there flinging them and then the army comes in.
Moderator: They start it?
First speaker: Yes, and then the army comes in.
Moderator: OK, anybody else have that image, that it started with the people throwing the stones and bricks and then the others retaliate?
First speaker: I think it starts that way. They fling the bricks and then they start flinging them and before you know it a fight breaks out.
Moderator: When you watch that do you ever think that they oughtn't to be throwing the bricks in the first place?
First speaker: Yes.
Moderator: You do think that?
Second speaker (Male): Yes.
Moderator: You have that feeling?
First speaker: Oh aye, if they went into the house and never minded, there wouldn't be any fighting. It wouldn't be so bad.
(Low-income group, Glasgow)

The important point here is that the image of inequality in the conflict does not necessarily result in the audience identifying with one side or the other. It might be that there are some images from war and conflict that are so grotesque that it would be difficult to find any way of justifying them. But as can be seen, the bulk of what we are shown is contested in terms of what it is to mean and signify about the actions of the two sides. In this country much of what the TV news audience hears is dominated by the official Israeli perspective and this does seem to have had some effect on audience beliefs. There was little knowledge of alternative accounts of the origins or causes of the conflict which might have been used in questioning such a perspective. The key source of what was known about the conflict was very often the television news. As we will see next, group members sometimes showed a remarkable ability to reproduce what they have seen.

THE NEWS WRITING EXERCISE

For the news writing exercise, each member of the focus groups was given a set of 16 photographs which were taken from TV news footage of the conflict. They were then asked to write a short news item using the pictures as a stimulus. They were not constrained to focusing on these pictures but in practice could write anything they wished. As a method this was designed to show what audiences have retained from news programmes. The pictures they were given included the aftermath of a suicide-bombing, an image of a dead Israeli soldier being pushed from a window, groups of Israelis rioting, a Palestinian boy being sheltered by his father as he was shot, and other images of stone-throwing, Palestinians in masks with guns and Israeli tanks. There were also pictures of prominent leaders and of peace negotiations showing Ehud Barak, Yasser Arafat and Bill Clinton, and a picture of Palestinians burning the American flag.

We found in this, as with other research using the same method, that many participants had a remarkable ability to reproduce both the content and structure of news bulletins. These are examples of 'news items' written by participants:

In response to yesterday's attack on the settlers' camp at Yashmin, Israeli tanks again battered [Palestinian] refugee camps. The Israeli tanks destroyed seven buildings. Palestinian sources reported 14 casualties including four children. The Israeli commander denied that any Palestinian civilians had been involved. Palestinian crowds stoned Israeli soldiers through the night. During the day a suicide-bomber blew himself up. This was the first such attack outside the occupied territories for some months. The Israeli Premier said that the Israeli army would continue to take a hard and aggressive line while attacks on Israeli citizens continued. (Middle-class male, London)

Here in the Middle East guerrilla warfare rules. As you can see from our pictures the streets are a war-zone. Young men as young as twelve are involved in brutal slayings. Tanks and heavy artillery patrol at the West Bank and young men are seen in victorious mood as each tank hits its target. Yasser Arafat meets with President Clinton to try to find a solution but as this meeting takes place, Palestinians are seen burning the American flag in an act of defiance. (Low-income male, Glasgow)

Yasser Arafat, head of the PLO, is still being bombarded by artillery and heavy shelling by the Israeli army today. Arafat has been under siege in his compound for ten days now with no signs of a let-up from the Israelis. Ariel Sharon is insisting that the four men wanted for "terrorist activities" who are still in

Yasser Arafat's compound give themselves up or the bombing will continue. Meanwhile in Gaza itself the stone-throwers are still on the streets with a determination that will not end until their leader is free. (Low-income female, London)

Not all showed such high levels of ability in writing the news. Some were vague over who was doing what and why it was significant:

The conflict between Israel and Palestine has been very violent, lots of guns and tanks. It has been caused by one of the parties invading land owned by the others. This land is currently unused but still does not belong to them. Leaders have tried deals to bring the fighting to an end but they have been futile. The fighting continues; it is the people themselves that are involved not just armies. (Young female student, Glasgow)

Another participant gave this account of the outbreak of the intifada:

Yasser Arafat has tried to get peace for his people for years. He has met Bill Clinton so that they can speak about what is happening. This time a leader went onto holy ground that he should not have been near and sparked more fighting. (Low-income female, Glasgow)

One of the reasons for the 'vagueness' amongst viewers is perhaps that the news itself is unspecific. We noted above in our content analysis that in reports of the onset of the intifada, Ariel Sharon was not named in many news bulletins and the significance of him as a figure to the Palestinians was not explained. Another participant in a Glasgow focus group made an important point about the nature of news reporting. She argued that the news effectively conveyed a series of emotional sequences (such as violence and its innocent victims) which characterised war reporting. As she comments, although the news had not conveyed 'the facts' to her she could still write the 'emotional' story:

When I wrote about the pictures, I could have been writing about any war because obviously the facts have not been communicated to me there on the news, but the emotion of it all has, so I wrote about it in an emotional way. So it's like emotional reportage rather than factual reportage. (Female office worker, Glasgow)

This is the news she had written:

> Looking back over the Arab-Israeli conflict, moments of hope have
> emerged from the despairing gloom, only to be overshadowed by
> the ongoing bloodiness of the conflict. Hands have been shaken,
> alliances/agreements made, but lurking behind the politicians'
> gestures are more scenes of violence, townships being destroyed,
> innocent victims hiding behind their protectors – all being shot
> to pieces. Rebel forces are burying their dead as martyrs to their
> cause; meanwhile US influence is being rejected as unwelcome
> interference in a domestic conflict which is not theirs. (As above,
> female office worker, Glasgow)

Another participant from the group of elderly people also saw
the images as representing the desolation and fear of war: 'These
pictures represent the horror of warfare. Desolation, fear, hatred
and two intractable leaders' (elderly male, Glasgow).

A lack of knowledge about events and why they happened was
apparently no bar to being able to write the news. This became
very apparent in the next example. Here a student noted that he
was interested in the news on the Israeli-Palestinian conflict and
watched items on it. He was able to produce a very competent and
quite plausible news programme. Yet he is the same student who
was quoted above as saying that he, 'just thought the Palestinians
wanted to get some more land for themselves' and 'didn't realise
they had been driven out of places in wars previously'. He had
no knowledge of the origins of the conflict and misunderstood its
causes, yet he could still write the following 'news':

> There is still much fighting close to the Israeli border with
> Palestinian territories with innocent children known to be
> among the victims. Yasser Arafat will not demand less than full
> control over the West Bank and Gaza and the Muslim quarter
> of Jerusalem but the Israelis are no longer willing to negotiate
> since the change of government. Despite the efforts of the US and
> Clinton in particular, what progress has been made was soon lost
> when Barak left office, replaced by the more hard-line Sharon.
> Hezbullah remain a threat to Israel which Palestine seems unable
> to control or unwilling to, as Israel claims. Both sides seem intent
> on attacking, with each attack causing more damage than the
> last – Israel has used the most advanced planes in its air force

while there are repeated warnings of more suicide-bombers being ready to strike. (Young male student, Glasgow)

This is a clear account of some of the key themes in news content – of innocent children as victims, the threat to Israel from Hezbullah and suicide-bombing and Israel's use of advanced weaponry. Other participants reproduced in their stories the structure of TV news accounts – notably the sequence of Palestinian action and Israeli response to which we have pointed in our content analysis. In the first example below, the cause of Palestinian discontent is vague, the Palestinians then act by coming out in mass protests and riots and the Israeli army 'retaliates and fires':

> President Bush meets Arafat and new Israeli PM to encourage talks to find a peaceful solution. *Something sparks discontent/ aggression toward Israel government* and Palestinians come out in mass protest with riots on the streets. *Israeli army retaliates* and fires on Palestinians. (Female office worker, Glasgow – our italics)

In the following examples the sequence is simply of Palestinian action and Israeli response:

> A new, more hard-line leader has come to power in Israel *who has retaliated with* force on attacks by the Palestinians on Israel. (Young male student, Glasgow – our italics)

> There has been continuing conflict between the Israeli authorities and the Palestinians on the West Bank over borders and security. Bomb outrages and atrocities have been swiftly followed by *government reaction* from Israeli tanks. (Male teacher, Paisley – our italics)

> Palestinian snipers and suicide-bombers attacked Israeli targets and the Israeli army *retaliated with tanks*. (Female teacher, Paisley – our italics)

> Today on the West Bank the conflict between the Israelis and Palestinians was renewed as Arafat supporters burned the American flag *and Israelis responded*. (Middle-class female, Paisley – our italics)

> *In response* to Palestinian attacks on Israeli settlements, coupled with suicide-bombings in Israel, Israeli forces have destroyed large amounts of Palestinian homes. (Middle-class male, London – our italics)

One participant wrote that both sides were 'retaliating' to each other; another mentioned the 'cycle of violence', and two mentioned that Palestinians were responding/retaliating to Israeli action. But it is noteworthy that the common theme of Palestinian action and Israeli response had a significant effect on how some people remembered events. The picture of a young Palestinian boy being sheltered by his father was used in some of the stories. The boy's death occurred in the first days of the intifada. In the following 'news stories' this death is linked to the killings of Israelis by Palestinians, including that of the soldier thrown from the window of a police station and that of a newly-wed couple killed in a suicide-bombing. These events actually happened after the death of the Palestinian boy, but the use of the action-retaliation formula effectively reverses the sequence of events so the Israelis are seen as responding to something that has been done to them:

> An Israeli soldier was taken hostage and thrown to his death by Palestinians on the rampage. The scene was witnessed live on TV by a shocked nation who took to the streets to protest ... the Israeli people vowed to revenge this act and in the fighting that followed a ten-year-old Palestinian boy was shot dead in his father's arms. (Female teacher, Paisley)

> A young boy was killed as his father helplessly tried to shield him from Israeli bullets. The Israeli onslaught came as a direct retaliation to a newly-wed Israeli couple being killed by a Palestinian suicide-bomber in the latest Palestinian terrorist attack. (Middle-class female, London)

Many of the 'news stories' repeat the familiar themes of violence, confrontation and death. Some specific instances such as the deaths of the Israeli soldiers are described using the words 'mob' and 'lynching', as in the actual news:

> The violence continues – two Israeli soldiers were captured by a Palestinian mob, beaten then killed and their bodies defiled. (Middle-class male, Glasgow)

> The most heinous act to date was the lynching of Israeli policemen in Ramallah. (Middle-class male, Glasgow)

There were no stories written about the killing of Arabs by 'mobs' in Israel, although we had included the pictures of 'angry'

Israeli crowds that had been briefly shown on TV news. As we have seen, the story of the young Palestinian boy being sheltered by his father was featured in the participants' 'news stories'. As we noted in the content analysis, the Palestinian view was that he had been deliberately killed, but this was very rarely featured. The Israeli statement that he had been 'caught in crossfire' was more commonly reported. This language is used in a number of the groups' 'news stories':

> Today there was yet another casualty of the Israeli-Palestinian conflict. A young boy was *caught in the crossfire* as Israeli troops opened fire in the West Bank. (Middle-class female, London – our italics)

> Israeli soldiers return fire and a father and son are *caught in crossfire* – the boy is fatally wounded. (Middle-class male, Glasgow – our italics)

> The fatal shooting of an eleven-year-old Palestinian boy *caught in the middle of another clash* between the Israeli army and Palestinians liberation extremists raised tension in the current intifada campaign against Israel. (Middle-class male, London – our italics)

> The American flag has been publicly burned by the Palestinians following the death of a young child who had been *cornered in crossfire* between the Jewish soldiers and Palestinians in Jerusalem. (Middle-class female, Paisley – our italics)

Audience members appear to have absorbed both the language and the structure of news accounts, although it does not follow that they always believe what they are told. To investigate this further, we asked specific questions about casualties.

We showed in our content analysis in Chapter 2 that there is sometimes a difference in the language employed in television news to describe casualties from the two sides, and also that there was an emphasis on Israeli casualties in terms of the amount of coverage they received. We will now examine how this might affect audience understanding and beliefs.

BELIEFS ABOUT CASUALTIES

We asked the participants: 'Which side has had the most casualties? Is it a lot more Israelis, a few more Israelis, about the same for each, a few more Palestinians or a lot more Palestinians?' In the period of our analysis the Palestinians had a casualty rate which was in fact much higher than that of the Israelis, (with a ratio of 2–3:1 in terms of deaths). Yet, if we look at the sample of British students from 2002, just 35 per cent knew that the Palestinians had significantly more casualties, while 43 per cent stated that there were more Israeli casualties or that the figures were the same for each side (for the German students the figures were respectively 24 per cent and 51 per cent, and for the US students, 18 per cent and 47 per cent).

In the focus groups we found that 42 per cent of the participants believed either that Israel had the most casualties or that the numbers were about equal. The key factor in the first of these beliefs appeared to be the extensive coverage of attacks on Israelis and in particular of suicide-bombings:

I couldn't remember any figures, but then I thought it was the one, I remembered it was the suicide-bombers. They are the ones who go in and take maybe a whole busload and I thought it would be more Israelis. I don't remember anything showing me the amount of Palestinians who have been killed – I don't remember that, but when it's something about Israelis being killed that has more effect on me – maybe there's more publicity about that. (Middle-class female, Paisley)

Because of the indiscriminate attacks – it seems like there's been more Palestinian attacks. (Middle-class male, St Albans)

The view of Israeli casualties was also linked to the perception about the Palestinians as being 'more hostile':

Moderator: Who thought that the Israelis had the most casualties, what made you think that?
Male speaker: I just assumed the Palestinians were hurting [them] and they had a bigger army and they were trying to wade in there to Israel ...
Moderator: What are the images in your head that gave you that idea then?
Male speaker: Just seeing people in Israel getting shot in the streets and getting thrown out windows and things like that. It seemed as if it was the Palestinians that were taking over. (Low-income group, Glasgow)

Female speaker: I thought the Palestinians were being quite hostile and that was basically the only theory behind it. I heard the word Palestinian more on the news, I think, I assumed. (Student group, Glasgow)

Some people stated simply that they had seen more coverage of Israeli casualties: 'I thought I'd heard more about Israeli casualties on the news' (female student, Glasgow). One speaker believed the casualties were about equal, but commented that 'Usually the images you see are wounded Israelis. They show Palestinians but not as often or as powerfully' (male student, Glasgow). Another student commented on how she had 'picked up' her view that most casualties were Israeli: 'It must have been something I picked up from watching the news – you are surrounded by the media and you're not consciously taking it in but you do take it in and get a perspective' (female student, Glasgow).

There was another key factor in the formation of belief which related to the manner in which news accounts were structured. The presentation of violence as a constant sequence of attacks by each side had led some people to believe that casualties would be about equal. A participant from a group of elderly people commented that he thought the casualties were the same because 'first of all it would be some of the Israelis being killed then it would be the Arabs being killed'. A student also noted that 'you hear stories about Israel bombing camps and stories about suicide-bombers in Israel' and this had led him to believe that the casualties were 'roughly the same'. The phrase 'tit for tat' which had been used on the news was used by some participants in explaining their beliefs:

Moderator: Why did you see [casualties] as even?
Female speaker: Because usually it is a case of you go in and shoot somebody and then the next thing somebody else is dead on the other side – it is usually a tit for tat. (Low-income group, Glasgow)

It's always portrayed as tit for tat – I believed that the numbers are about level. (Male student, Glasgow)

The strong influence of TV imagery is very apparent. In the following exchange the first speaker says that there are more Palestinian casualties, but thinks there is not much difference between those of the two sides and cites the frequency of attacks on Israelis. The second speaker believes that there were 5,000 Israeli casualties and 1,000 Palestinian casualties, and then directly relates this to what she has seen on television:

> *First speaker*: I would have thought more Palestinians within the past two years. I wouldn't have thought it was that many more. There's been quite a lot of attacks that have involved a lot of Israelis – you know big groups, buses, restaurants, and so on, so I would imagine there's not that much difference …
>
> *Second speaker*: Well basically on the news coverage they do always seem to make the Palestinians out to be the ones who are the suicide-bombers, so it's like, I would imagine it's going to be more casualties on the Israeli side, but it is purely from television, that's where I'm getting my info from, that's how it's been portrayed to me on television. (Low-income female group, London)

In the group of teachers from Paisley, it was thought that the news did feature more Israeli casualties, but they used logic to deduce that there would be more Palestinian casualties. They focused on the imbalances in weaponry and differences in the manner in which casualties were inflicted:

> *First speaker (male)*: Mine was the Palestinians suffer more casualties at all levels of severity. The nature, the way the casualties are inflicted is different. They … the big news story of a suicide-bomber usually happens to the Israelis and Jews in Tel Aviv. Whereas the kind of reprisals and shootings of the military actions against people in the West Bank is ongoing all the time virtually.
>
> *Moderator*: So what was your view about how many were on each side?
>
> *First speaker*: I think the Palestinians suffered most casualties. I'm not entirely certain about that … the impression the news gives you is there is higher Jewish casualties.
>
> *Moderator*: The impression the news gives you is there are higher Jewish casualties?
>
> *Second speaker (male)*: It certainly seems to get mentioned more – any Jewish casualties …
>
> *Moderator*: Is that …
>
> *Third speaker (male)*: You hear more of the Israeli atrocities.

Fourth speaker (female): Again by virtue of the nature of the Palestinians, I always seem to see them throwing stones, with Israelis with weapons and from that I would assume. (Teachers group, Paisley)

One of this group mentioned the 'brutality' of Israeli retaliation as a factor in his belief, but the most common reason given for seeing most casualties as Palestinian was simply the disparity in the military capacity of the two sides:

Images of tanks pounding Palestine – it just seemed to make more sense ... mainly just from that one image – that if they're using heavy artillery, then it is probably going to cause more casualties. (Male student group, Glasgow)

They show that the Palestinians are young boys with sticks and stones trying to fight the Israelis with their guns and tanks. If that's all they've got to fight with, presumably they are killed more often than someone with a gun. (Middle-class female group, Paisley)

They are much less armed, one side is fighting with stones ... Yasser Arafat headquarters – the Israelis were just like crushing everything. (Low-income male group, London)

Very few people in the groups cited any specific information from TV news on relative casualty figures. Some people had information from alternative sources, such as newspapers, leaflets, documentaries and the Internet. But an important factor seemed to be the logical deductions which were made. These were sometimes extended to take in other areas such as care of the wounded – the assumption here was that the Israelis had more funds and therefore more of their people would survive:

The Israelis have more money and they can take better care of people who are injured. (Low-income male group, London)

When you do see something like the suicide-bombers and what happens in Israel because of that, Israeli casualties, I'm always amazed at the number of ambulances and the support system that's rushing to deal with that crisis, and whenever you see the other end of it, the Palestinian casualties, they are there on their own with nothing. I get the feeling there isn't the backup system in Palestine to deal with those casualties that there is in Israel. (Middle-class female group, London)

There were some people in the groups who had connections with Israel either through friends or through having stayed there. Two of these stated that most casualties were Palestinian but at the same time said that there was more 'fuss' made about these casualties on the TV news or that Palestinian deaths were treated with more sympathy. It may be that they simply watched different bulletins from those in our samples, but their view is not supported by the material which we analysed. An alternative explanation might be that they were sympathetic to Israel and that coverage of Palestinian casualties in some way upset or contradicted their preferred view. They were comparatively well informed about events in the conflict and any sympathies which they had did not affect their judgement about the number of casualties. Interestingly, as we have seen above, viewers who were informed by the TV news and had apparently no great interest in the area were more likely to believe that the casualties were about equal or that most had been sustained by Israel.

CULTURAL IDENTIFICATION AND EMPATHY

Identification can be conditional on personal relationships – for example, contacts with friends or on cultural or family history. One student told us how she had attended an Arab school and how this had affected her understanding of the conflict. Such cultural histories can also affect the 'facts' and versions of causes of disputes which are heard by the individual. It was also made clear to us that for some members of the Jewish community, memories of the Holocaust had a powerful influence on how the Israeli-Palestinian conflict was seen. In a one-to-one discussion outside the groups, a Jewish woman described her experience of visiting Auschwitz and the appalling sight of piles of children's shoes. She then said that 'Sharon is a thug', but commented that there are times when someone like that is needed. The conflict was seen through the prism of the Holocaust – as she said, 'We cannot go quietly into the gas chambers again.'

Another woman in a focus group expressed her view that the history of the Jewish people had affected how the Israeli-Palestinian conflict was understood. She saw Israeli actions as being motivated by fear and thought that public perceptions were influenced by feelings of guilt:

> I felt that [the Israelis] had tried to enlarge their area, but I could understand because there is a lot of fear from the Israeli point of view. They feel very frightened where they are, and also, because of the past history of the Jewish people, we feel quite guilty as well. (Middle-class female group, Paisley)

It is also possible for audiences to identify at a more general cultural level – for example, to see one side of the conflict as being 'people like us' with manners, customs and lifestyles which are readily understood and recognised. As one participant from London put it:

> It's much easier for those of us in the West to imagine that a car bomb in the middle of a city is a tremendously terrifying thing ... when you see a car bomb go off in the middle of a sophisticated city, the experience is much closer to one we can 'imagine'. (Middle-class male group, London)

An additional factor to which this speaker pointed was that London had experienced being attacked during the IRA campaigns and he and another participant described being close to bombs when they went off. The issue of cultural identification was raised by other participants – Israel was referred to as 'an island of democracy' in the Middle East (middle-class male, London). At the same time, some aspects of Muslim culture were seen as strange and difficult to identify with. A female participant, who was actually quite sympathetic to the Palestinians, gave her own rather mixed feelings on this:

> I feel there are lots of images I have of Muslim women that I find it very hard to see them beyond my own sort of white Western perspective because they're all covered up. And when you hear them mourning – because I know that my voice goes 'What's that noise?' and I know that that must be my Western culture that makes me think [that], but it does come across as alien to me, and I'm aware that it is my perspective, but that doesn't make me get any closer, if you know what I mean. (Low-income female group, London)

These comments then stimulated a further discussion between Brian Hanrahan from the BBC and the film-maker Ken Loach who were present in this group. They focused on the issue of whether journalists should intervene to help audiences 'see through' cultural difference by appealing to more universal values;[3] for example, concern for human suffering or loss – and should this be done in the name of balance?

> *Ken Loach*: That seems a very reasonable response that people do empathise with situations that match their own. Do you consciously try to counteract that effect when you are interviewing people who don't speak English or who are speaking Arabic or some language we don't understand. Is there an attempt to re-balance that and should there be?
>
> *Brian Hanrahan*: Erm, no.
>
> *Ken Loach*: Should there be, do you think if we are even-handed to both sides?
>
> *Brian Hanrahan*: Re-balance in the sense of trying to deliberately skew the scales so that you feel more sympathy for this person, no; re-balance if you mean, do we try and present that person in their own, so that their argument or their background comes across clearly?, yes. I certainly wouldn't try if there was someone who looked alien, was in an alien culture in an alien setting, I wouldn't try to do something that made them seem more like us, because I would feel that I was then intervening too much.
>
> *Ken Loach*: It's a question more of not to skew it, but to elucidate it …
>
> *Brian Hanrahan*: I'd certainly try.
>
> *Ken Loach*: … in a way that the audience would identify with the person because of their motherhood or because of their plight which is universal, so that you are not distracted by the veil …
>
> *Brian Hanrahan*: We would go looking for common themes so you could understand, 'this is a mother', 'this is a teacher'. (At low-income female group, London)

The predominant response in the groups was that in practice people did 'see through' cultural difference and they spoke in terms of universals. As one woman put it, 'suffering is suffering'. There were also references to other values such as a concern with the abuse of power and the perception of the Palestinians as the 'underdog'. One young male participant commented on how the Israelis had 'built up' their country – while the Palestinian areas were 'not very good'. The Israeli towns were Westernised, with discos – but this did not affect how he identified with the two sides. As he put it, 'I would support the Palestinians, I'd support the underdogs' (low-income male group, London). As we have already noted, visual imagery of the Palestinians as the underdog does not necessarily produce a sympathetic response. A key factor is how such imagery is contextualised through explanations of cause and how these affect understanding of the legitimacy and rationale of the two sides. In the above case, the speaker had also been influenced by Palestinians he had met, who had been giving out leaflets at the local shopping precinct.

We also found cases in the groups where the visual imagery of war was simply too much for some people and they said that they turned away. Ken Loach explored this response and asked why they would not feel empathy with those involved:

> *Ken Loach*: Obviously everyone here is very caring and thoughtful in general in the way that we are talking about it, and yet I was very struck by what you said, when you said 'I can't bear to watch it.' Now sometimes you'll see pictures of mothers and their dead children and grandparents with children who have died or sons who have died and you as parents, daughters or whatever, I would think that you would, all things being equal, you would identify with that person's suffering. What is it that stops you, stopping in front of the television and saying: 'I absolutely understand what that person is going through, I have a sense of what that person is going through', because if news is to work that is what sharing a story is. What is it that stops you feeling that empathy? (Low-income female group, London)

One speaker replies that such images may be 'emotionally exhausting'. And then Ken Loach asks: 'Is it also to do with feeling you have no control, no say in it?' To which a female participant replies: 'Oh yes, because there is a thing that nothing is going to change, there are so many of those images, it's depressing and futile' (low-income female group, London).

One dimension in this sense of powerlessness is the lack of understanding about why the events are occurring. As we have found in this and other research, the world can appear to people as an inexplicable mess. Of course a greater understanding does not necessarily mean that something can be easily done by viewers to solve the problem. But in principle, to see events as having causes can be a first step towards understanding the possibilities for change, and to engaging with what is shown and to having opinions about it. As another participant put it:

> There is definitely an absence of explanation which causes an absence of feeling because I can quite easily sit and I say I feel no way about it whatsoever. Because I haven't been there it's got nothing to do with me whatsoever, so I have a lack of feeling about it. But I also have a lack of understanding about it – maybe if I knew a lot more about it, I'd have more feeling and more opinions on it. (Low-income male group, London)

There was a strong feeling in the groups that the news should explain origins and causes and that journalists should speak more directly to viewers about was happening and why. The participants in the groups did not want news that was in any way biased or inaccurate, but the desire for clear, straightforward accounts was very apparent. It was also the case that when viewers did understand the significance and relevance of what they were watching, then this could strongly affect their level of interest in the news.

UNDERSTANDING AND INTEREST IN NEWS

We asked the participants in the focus groups whether, when watching the news, they felt that journalists assumed a level of knowledge or understanding which they did not have. A clear majority assented to this. Not all agreed – the middle-class males were more likely to say they understood the news very well. But for many there was a problem and examples were given of how the lack of understanding impacted on the interest which viewers had on the news:

> Every time it comes on [the Israeli-Palestinian conflict] it never actually explains it so I don't see the point in watching it – I just turn it off and go and make a cup of tea or something. I don't like watching it when I don't really understand what's going on. (Female student, Glasgow)

> It's like the Kosovo conflict, I don't want to watch it, I don't understand it – I switch it off. (Middle-class female group, Paisley)

Others pointed to their feeling of complete incomprehension:

> It is all mumble-jumble and you don't understand. (Low-income male group, Glasgow)

> I hear them waffling on and it's all so quick and he knows what he's talking about but I just don't have a clue what they're going on about ... you could be sitting there listening to it but it's going to have less interest to you if you don't understand it. (Middle-class male group, St Albans)

Another problem which some participants identified was that explanations may have been given at the beginning of a story, on the first day of being reported. But since they frequently came into stories 'halfway through' a cycle of events, they could not understand what was happening:

> *Moderator*: Do you ever have the feeling that the journalist expects you to have a background knowledge that you don't actually have?
> *Female speaker*: Yes definitely, there's loads of times when like, there's just the background stuff that I don't really know anything about.
> *Male speaker*: I think it's more of a case that they assume, kind of, it's part of an ongoing story. They assume that you've been there from the start and that you've constantly watched. (Student group, Glasgow)

In another group the same point is made:

> It's not like I watch BBC News every day. You might miss a couple of weeks of news; you might miss some developments happening. And it's not like *Newsround*, where they tell you why they are fighting, over what, what's happened recently. They assume that you actually know more – over the last three years of watching it. (Male student, Glasgow)

There was some concern in the groups as to whether the news could sustain long explanations. Yet we found in practice that a relatively small amount of new information could substantially improve understanding. In this exchange, the moderator mentioned the confusion over the phrase 'occupied territory' and had previously explained what it meant:

> *Moderator*: If they use words such as 'occupied territory' it's not clear from that phrase who is occupying what.
> *Female speaker*: By adding just a couple of words they could make that clear. (Middle-class female group, London)

In another group it was apparent that a relatively straightforward piece of information, such as that the Israelis controlled water supplies and how this affected Palestinian agriculture, had a strong effect on how a participant understood the intractability of the conflict: 'What was really important for me today was learning about the water because that's a real power point isn't it?' (low-income female group, London).

We found clear links between understanding and levels of interest, as in this exchange:

> *Moderator*: Is there a link between you turning off and not being interested and that you don't actually quite understand what is going on?
> *First speaker*: Sometimes if you are not up to speed …
> *Second speaker*: Sometimes things are more human and more real if you do understand the things that are behind it.
> *Moderator*: I see you nodding [*to third woman who has previously said she does not watch the news*] …
> *Lindsey Hilsum*: [*To the same person*] Is there anything that would make you more interested in the news?
> *Third speaker*: I can understand what you are saying and I think that is probably one of the things if I was to turn on the news, if I was forced to for whatever reason, it would help if I actually knew what I was listening to, if I understood where they were coming from. So take this war, I don't know how it started, I don't know the background behind it, so I'm actually listening in effect to gibberish, so that would make a difference. (Middle-class female group, London)

This also came across strongly in the following exchange from a student group. There was a very strong feeling within the group that their interest was linked to understanding, and the point was also made that the explanations should be contained within news programming:

Moderator: So when they talk about 'Palestinian refugees' and 'occupied territories' it really doesn't mean anything to you? Would you have found the news more interesting if you had understood those things?

First speaker (female): Yes.

Second speaker (male): Possibly, I wouldn't have switched off if I'd known the historical context. I would probably have had an emotional tie to it and got into it a bit more.

First speaker: It wouldn't have been just random facts, 'cos that's what it feels like, just random facts with no context at all really. And it's much preferable to see a short slot on the news, because obviously a documentary lasts half an hour or an hour and you don't want to watch all that.

Third speaker (female): It would change my perception of it, I would understand it. (Student group, Glasgow)

A clear majority in the groups as a whole stated that their interest increased when they understood more. This was very marked in the responses of group members to discussions in which they took part. Some became extremely interested and stayed behind to ask extensive questions. In two groups it was suggested that they might meet again as informal discussion groups. Other participants told us subsequently that they had spoken for long periods with friends about the issues that were raised, and others told us that they would now watch the news with more interest. This was not true of everyone. A minority said that they understood the news or that they preferred it as it was or that they thought the subject matter of news was intrinsically boring and it would not make any difference if they understood it more. But for the bulk of the people in this study the relationship between understanding and interest in news was very marked. This did suggest the need for change in the current structure and content of news programmes to address the problem that so many people are apparently not well informed by the news services which they see as their primary source of information.

4
Why Does it Happen?[1]

FACTORS IN PRODUCTION?

We look here at key factors which affect the production and structuring of news accounts in this area. As we have seen, there is in general a dearth of in-depth, analytic and explanatory material included in news reports. Journalists in our focus groups pointed to the problems in producing a constant flow of news items and to pressures of time. Newsroom discussions do not focus very often on issues of audience comprehension or the overall effect of news programming on public understanding. As Adrian Monck pointed out to us, the main concern of news producers is often the logistics of how to get the job done in the time available. As he noted, there are a limited number of ways in which news stories are currently told. These include the standard news package with video inserts, or a studio discussion or a live piece to camera by an expert journalist. As he put it, which format is used and what goes into the story is often dominated by the pressure to deliver a sequence of programmes lasting exactly 24 minutes and 36 seconds (timed to the second). He believed that it was now very important for journalists and broadcasters to reorient their concerns and think about how news output could be restructured to improve its capacity to inform. Others also pointed to factors in the current organisation of news programming which limit the ability of journalists to explain and analyse. One participant in the focus groups was a professional photographer and he commented that

> Part of the problem is just the way the news medium works nowadays – where you are geared up to having constant 24 hour news and you get the feeling that some of the journalists on the spot are spending more time in front of a camera because they have to do 15 different TV news programmes and four different radio programmes, than they are actually finding out what's happening in the story, and that means we do not get as much analysis, as much colour, as much depth in what's going

319

on. You get moment-by-moment repetition. (Middle-class male group, London)

Lindsey Hilsum also noted the pressures of time but linked this to the specific difficulties of covering the Israeli-Palestinian conflict, with its long complex history in which explanations are intensely contested:

> There are two problems … how far back do you go is one and the other is with a conflict like this, nearly every single fact is disputed … I think, 'Oh God, the Palestinians say this and the Israelis say that' and I have to, as a journalist, make a judgement and I say this is what happened and it's quite clear and there are other things where I wasn't there and I didn't see it with my own eyes. I know it's a question of interpretation so I have to say what both sides think and I think sometimes that stops us from giving the background we should be giving, because I think 'Well, bloody hell, I've only three minutes to do this piece in and I'm going to spent a minute going through the arguments.' (Middle-class female group, London)

But, as she notes, the journalists should be giving the context, and our study suggests that the removal of it has important consequences. As we have indicated, the absence of key elements of Palestinian history makes it difficult to understand their perspective. Their actions could appear without context and in consequence they may be seen as 'initiating' the trouble. In contrast, when the Israelis acted, the news often gave an explanation which could legitimise what they were doing. Israeli views on terrorism and the rationale for their actions were clearly included on the news, and Israelis were more frequently quoted and featured than Palestinians. One reason for this disparity was the more efficient public relations machine which the Israelis operated to supply information to journalists. At the same time it was sometimes difficult for journalists to obtain information from the Palestinian side about current events. We interviewed a US journalist who had headed a Jerusalem-based news agency in the period before the intifada. As he noted, most journalists actually lived in Israel and were regularly supplied with information:

> Nearly all [the journalists] lived in Israel or West Jerusalem, rather than in Palestinian areas. The Israelis were very nice to them. They speak their languages, they dress like us, for the most part

they act like us. They press the right buttons. The other thing is the Israeli efficiency, 'You want these documents, I'll get them for you', miles of statistics![2] (Interview, June 2002)

He believed the Palestinian operation was far less effective:

Palestinian spokesmen are their own worst enemy. They often come across as boorish, the message is often incoherent. Official Palestine does have a method problem. They miss the essential points. Arafat is a one man show, he is almost always incoherent. (Interview, June 2002)

He also noted the difference in that the Israeli approach was essentially proactive while the Palestinians were essentially reactive:

Palestinians don't have a clear public relations approach. They [Palestinians] start from a reactive approach. I get 75–100 emails a day from official Israeli sources and organisations which support [Israel] (about 15 per cent from government, the rest lobbyists and supporters). I get perhaps five a week from Palestinian sources. (Interview, June 2002)

In contrast, some British Zionists with whom we spoke took the view that there were weaknesses in Israeli press and public relations, particularly in the Israeli Defence Forces (IDF). Joy Wolfe from the Women's International Zionist Organisation commented on the 'inexperience' of the IDF team who have 'very poor communication equipment and not even a proper English-speaking translator who can put out a decent and accurate press release' (23 October 2003). Overall, however, it does seem from our research that the Israelis achieved much more space for their views than the Palestinians (as shown, for example, in the relative amounts of reported statements/interviews).

British journalist Robert Fisk has also described how the regular supply of information and well organised public relations can set agendas in news:

The journalists' narrative of events is built around the last thing someone has said and the last thing, given the constraints of time and the rolling news machine that they have heard on the agency wire. So what you would find on television in the last few weeks is that every time an Israeli statement was made, it was pushed across at the Palestinians. So the Israelis would say: 'Can Arafat control the violence?' and instead of the television reporters saying: 'Well that's interesting, but can the Israelis control their own people?' the question was simply taken up as an Israeli question and became part of the news agenda. There seemed to be no real understanding that the job of the reporter is to analyse what's really happening, not simply to pick up on the rolling news machine, the last statement by one of the sides. And given the fact that the Israelis have a very smooth machine operating for the media, invariably what happened is, it was Israel's voice that came across through the mouths of the reporters, rather than [having] people who were really making enquiries into both sides and what both people were doing. (*The Message*, BBC Radio 4, 20 October 2000)

It has often been noted that it is easier for journalists to accept the routine supply of information than to undertake the difficult, expensive and sometimes dangerous path of generating independent material. Journalists who were working in the occupied territories complained of extensive intimidation and it has been suggested that this has worsened as the intifada gathered momentum. The veteran BBC correspondent Keith Graves has written in the *Guardian* that

When I was first based in the Middle East as a BBC correspondent thirty years ago, Israel was rightly proud of its position as the only country in the region where journalists could report freely. Not anymore. Under the Sharon government intimidation of reporters deemed 'unfriendly' to Israel is routine and sanctioned by the government. (*Guardian*, 12 July 2003)

Organisations such as the Foreign Press Association (FPA) in Jerusalem and Reporters Sans Frontiers have accused the Israelis of deliberately targeting gunfire at journalists, noting that eight had been wounded (*The Observer*, 17 June 2001).[3] A recent programme on Channel 4 television gave a detailed account by journalists of what they regarded as the deliberate killing of a colleague by Israeli security forces, when he had been filming the bulldozing of Palestinian homes.[4]

The Palestinian Authority has also made attempts to limit unfavourable coverage by, for example, trying to control what is filmed. But it seems clear that, overall, Israel's public relations and system of information supply is more sophisticated and well resourced. There are also powerful lobbies which support them in the US and to some extent in Britain. The *Independent*, for example, has reported that 'the Israeli embassy in London has mounted a huge drive to influence the British media'. The paper quoted the embassy's press secretary as saying that

> London is a world centre of media and the embassy here works night and day to try to influence that media. And, in many subtle ways, I think we don't do a half bad job, if I may say so … We have newspapers that write consistently in a manner that supports and understands Israel's situation and its challenges. And we have had influence on the BBC as well. (*Independent*, 21 September 2001)

The *Observer* has also written of the intensity of this campaign, noting that:

> A new front is opening in the intifada. Faced with increasing international criticism of its handling of the Palestinian uprising, the Israeli government of Ariel Sharon and its allies in the powerful and influential pro-Israeli lobby, have stepped up their efforts against international media reporting of the current crisis. News organisations that fall foul of Israel are accused of being pro-Palestinian at best, and at worst anti-Semitic. (*Observer*, 17 June 2001)

Journalists spoke to us of the personal criticism and 'flak' which they had received. Lindsey Hilsum from Channel 4 News commented on 'the number of emails that I receive saying that I'm anti-Semitic because I've written something they don't like about Israel' (in focus group: middle-class females, London).

The *Observer* also noted the organised nature of letter writing campaigns:

> For many years, pro-Israel organisations have organised letter-writing campaigns to protest against articles and programmes they dislike. With the development of email, this activity has grown enormously. Websites … target individual journalists and provide ready-written letters of complaint for subscribers to send out. (*Observer*, 17 June 2001)

Pro-Israel groups often argue that both 'bias' in the media and physical attacks upon Israel are at root caused by anti-Semitism. There is certainly evidence of anti-Semitism in the speeches of some Muslim clerics and in the Arab media.[5] The Israelis have occasionally pointed to this as part of making their own case. We spoke in some detail about this with Nachman Shai, who was a key Israeli spokesman in the early period of the intifada. He was also Director General of the Ministry of Science, Culture and Sport and had been chief spokesperson for the IDF at the time of the Gulf War. His view was that Israel tended to avoid using anti-Semitism as an argument. He also noted that it was more significant as an issue to Jews living outside Israel: 'Anti-Semitism doesn't have the same significance to Israelis as to non-Israelis, since we are not exposed to it in our everyday life' (interview, 15 August 2003).

There was another very important issue which affected the contemporary development of Israeli public relations. After the events of 9/11 and the attack on the US, Israel had stressed its role as part of the 'war against terror'. This had much more 'general' connotations in terms of presenting Israel as one part of the Western Alliance. As Nachman Shai commented:

> We selected the first [war on terror] instead of the second [anti-Semitism] because we are part of the Western world. We very much played the first argument. It worked better with governments, they gave us more support. It's like if you've run out of arguments, you're stuck with anti-Semitism. The first one is based on common interests. (Interview, 15 August 2003)

We might note that for Israel to present itself as part of a general 'war on terror' against those who dislike Western values also has the advantage of drawing attention away from specific actions by Israel which have contributed to the origins and development of the Middle East conflict. However, a final comment from Nachman Shai was on the quality of international media coverage, including that of Britain. He regarded it as having improved and cited the effect of suicide-bombings on how the conflict was seen:

> It has gradually become more balanced than in the beginning – the media are now seeing more of the complicated issues than at the beginning, because of the indiscriminate violence of the suicide-bombers against the Israeli population. (Interview, 15 August 2003)

The essence of what Nachman Shai is saying is that the Israelis have stressed their role in the general 'war on terror' rather than the issue of anti-Semitism, and also that the coverage of suicide-bombing has improved the 'balance' of coverage, from the Israeli perspective. This is strikingly different from the arguments of pro-Israeli commentators in Britain who have stressed anti-Semitism and attacked media coverage.

CLAIMS THAT THE MEDIA ARE BIASED AGAINST ISRAEL

The *Observer* also pointed to the influence of lobby groups such as the Conservative Friends of Israel which invites senior journalists to lunches at the House of Commons. It commented that 'for those working for organisations perceived as being biased against Israel these can be uncomfortable affairs'. Such lobby groups often assert that the media is biased against Israel. The Conservative MP Gillian Shephard is quoted as saying:

> Let's not forget that Israel feels under siege. And it literally is. That is what drives the feeling of ultra-sensitivity. They feel that there is bias and there is a conspiracy against them. There is a perception that Israelis are portrayed as instigating the problems and that the historical context of the threat against Israel is forgotten. There is a feeling too that Israel – which is a tiny island of democracy amid much less democratic neighbours – never gets enough credit for what it has achieved. (*Observer*, 17 June 2001)

As we have seen, our study does not support the view that Israel is portrayed unfairly. Yet Gillian Shephard points to the deep sense of persecution which some in the wider Jewish community still apparently feel at the hands of the media. In February 2003, for example, Melanie Phillips wrote in the *Jewish Chronicle* of a conference on anti-Semitism and the discussions and evidence which were presented at it. The recurring theme, she notes, was 'a nexus of anti-Jewish hatred between fanatical Islamists on the one hand and the British and European media on the other'. She argues that

> Europe has waited for fifty years for a way to blame the Jews for their own destruction. So instead of addressing genocidal Muslim anti-Semitism, the Europeans have seized upon a narrative which paints the Jews as Nazis and the Palestinians as the new Jews. (Phillips, 2003)

She notes how the conference 'was told about the way the British media describes Israel's "death squads", "killing-fields" and "executioners" while sanitising Palestinian human bombs as "gentle", "religious" and "kind"' (Phillips, 2003). While it is clearly true that vicious anti-Semitism exists in some Islamic groups and elsewhere, this description of the British media does not accord with what we have found. We were also puzzled by what some people in our focus groups believed about TV news. There is an interesting phenomenon well documented in psychological studies whereby a strong commitment can lead to an inability to see information that contests the preferred view or violates a preferred expectation. We did find in our study at least one case where a person found it difficult literally to see what was in front of him. The great majority of those in our audience groups did not process information in this way, but in this case the participant stated that the news was biased against Israel and that the photographs he had used in the news writing exercise were also 'pro-Palestinian'. We pointed out that they had been carefully chosen. They did in fact include a picture of the aftermath of a suicide-bombing, which showed an Israeli ambulance with the Star of David on the side. They also included the image of a dead Israeli soldier being thrown from the window of a Palestinian police station. But the participant focused his attention very largely on an image of an Israeli tank in a Palestinian area and expressed his concern about what people would think of this.

Overall, the results of our study suggest that it was Israeli perspectives which predominated in TV news and this is in part the result of a very well developed system of lobbying and public relations. Another key factor affecting media coverage is the very close political and communication links which exist between the US and Britain.

THE US CONNECTION

Our content analysis showed that speakers from the US were frequently featured on TV news and that they commonly endorsed or supported Israeli positions. There was no comparable referencing of the governments of other nations who were more critical of Israel.[6] Given the significance of the US as the world's sole remaining superpower and its relationship with Britain, it is not surprising that the views of its politicians would be featured but none the less it had a significant effect on the balance of TV news coverage. There is some evidence to suggest that the perspectives on the Middle

East adopted by US politicians are strongly influenced by pro-Israel lobbies. A recent Radio 4 programme looked in detail at this and noted how the pro-Israel groups now included the Christian Right:

> *Journalist*: It's time to revive one of the oldest stereotypes in American politics, the power of the Jewish lobby. Today, it's not the Jewish lobby which counts, it's the pro-Israel and the difference is crucial. Two of the most formidable organisational networks in America, the Jewish Establishment and the Christian Right have joined forces. Together, they can penetrate deep into the body politic. (*A Lobby to Reckon With*, BBC Radio 4, 7 May 2002)

The programme visited the Cornerstone Church in San Antonio, Texas, 'a stadium-sized arena' with 10,000 worshippers, whose services are broadcast to millions of homes. The pastor's sermon is heard:

> God entered into an eternal covenant with Abraham, Isaac and Jacob that the nation of Israel would belong to the Jewish people for ever, and forever means 2002, 3002, 4002, forever is forever. Jerusalem is the eternal capital of the Jewish state. (*A Lobby to Reckon With*, BBC Radio 4, 7 May 2002)

The programme also pointed out the strength of Jewish American activism and the role of AIPAC (the American Israel Public Affairs Committee). It was also stated that there are smaller Jewish groups in the US who are opposed to Israel's current policies, but the influence of AIPAC is very noteworthy:

> *Journalist*: AIPAC's power has become the stuff of Washington legend. *Fortune* magazine consistently puts it in the top five special interest groups. No other foreign policy based lobby group gets into the top 25. (*A Lobby to Reckon With*, BBC Radio 4, 7 May 2002)

The programme also interviewed J.J. Goldberg, an American author who has written on AIPAC and other pro-Israel groups. He comments on how the influence of 'political action committees' has developed through the financing of the opponents of those who speak against Israel:

AIPAC has a lot of influence on foreign policy, they work hard to make sure that America endorses pretty much Israel's view of the world and of the Middle East. They do it partly by convincing, partly by implied threats. AIPAC does not raise money for candidates but there are Jewish PACs (Political Action Committees) that raise campaign funds for candidates. Four or five times over the last twenty years, these PACs have gone after members of Congress who voted in ways that AIPAC didn't like. They have flooded their opponents with money and enabled them to beat the incumbents. Sent a message that if you really go against AIPAC, you'd better know where you're next dollar is coming from. So that, as I've been told by a number of congressional aides over the last few years, if the congressman doesn't vote against Arafat they'll pay a price. If they do vote against Arafat, there's no price to be paid. There's no percentage for the member of Congress to stand up for peace, for compromise. Nobody is going to reward them, they'll be punished. (*A Lobby to Reckon With*, BBC Radio 4, 7 May 2002)

As the BBC programme notes, the strength of the lobby was shown at the annual conference of AIPAC which featured the attendance of half the US Senate and half the members of the lower house. It has also been argued that media coverage in the US is strongly influenced by the pro-Israel lobby. Michael Massing, writing in *The Nation*, noted that the activities of AIPAC are rarely analysed in the American media:

Journalists are often loathe to write about the influence of organised Jewry. Throughout the Arab world, the 'Jewish lobby' is seen as the root of all evil in the Middle East, and many reporters and editors – especially Jewish ones – worry about feeding such stereotypes. (*The Nation*, 10 June 2002)

But he also comments that the main obstacle to covering such groups is fear:

Jewish organisations are quick to detect bias in the coverage of the Middle East and quick to complain about it ... As the *Forward* observed in late April, 'rooting out perceived anti-Israel in the media has become for many American Jews the most direct and emotional outlet for connecting with the conflict six thousand miles away.' Recently an estimated one thousand subscribers

to the *Los Angeles Times* suspended home delivery for a day
to protest what they considered the paper's pro-Palestinian
coverage. The *Chicago Tribune*, the *Minneapolis Star Tribune*,
the *Philadelphia Enquirer* and the *Miami Herald* have all been
hit by similar protests. (*The Nation*, 10 June 2002)

Massing asks whether such protests have an effect and considers
the experience of the *New York Times*. On 6 May 2002 the paper
had run two photographs of a pro-Israel parade in Manhattan:

> Both showed the parade in the background and anti-Israel
> protesters prominently in the foreground. The paper, which for
> weeks has been threatened with a boycott by Jewish readers,
> was deluged with protests. On May the seventh the *Times* ran an
> abject apology. That caused much consternation in the newsroom,
> with some reporters and editors feeling that the paper had buckled
> before an influential constituency. 'It's very intimidating', said
> a correspondent at another large daily who is familiar with the
> incident. Newspapers, he added, are 'afraid' of organisations like
> AIPAC and the President's Conference. 'The pressure from these
> groups is relentless. Editors would just as soon not touch them.'
> (*The Nation*, 10 June 2002)

Ted Turner, the founder of CNN also famously ignited an
international controversy by saying that both the Israelis and the
Palestinians were engaged in 'terrorism'. As the *Guardian* reported:

> After the Turner interview appeared ... there were calls for the
> cable and satellite operators [in Israel] to pull CNN from their
> output. One of the main satellite operators in Israel, Yes, added
> CNN's arch-rival Fox News – perceived to be sympathetic to
> Israel – to its package of channels. CNN clearly had some talking
> to do, and its most senior editorial executive got himself on the
> first flight out of Atlanta when he read Turner's comments. Eason
> Jordan, chief news executive at CNN spent the next week or so
> on a whirlwind damage-limitation exercise [in the Middle East].
> (*Guardian*, 1 July 2002)

The *Guardian* also noted that Fox News had 'endeared itself' to the
conservative right in its approach to the Middle East conflict: 'It now
refers, for example, to Palestinian suicide bombers as "homicide-

bombers". In Israel, it is held up as a model of "objective" reporting'
(*Guardian*, 1 July 2002).

Fox is part of Rupert Murdoch's organisation which has extensive
media interests in Britain, owning, for example, the *Sun, The
Times,* the *Sunday Times* and the *News of the World.* Sam Kiley, a
correspondent for *The Times,* resigned in September 2001, blaming
its allegedly pro-Israeli censorship of his reporting. He spoke of
Rupert Murdoch's close friendship with Ariel Sharon and heavy
investment in Israel. Writing in the London *Evening Standard*, he
commented that

> *The Times* foreign editor and other middle managers flew into
> hysterical terror every time a pro-Israel lobbying group wrote
> in with a quibble or complaint and then usually took their
> side against their own correspondent ... I was told I should
> not refer to 'assassinations' of Israel's opponents, nor to 'extra-
> judicial killings or executions'. (Quoted in the *Guardian*,
> 5 September 2001)

The *Guardian* also reported Kiley as saying that

> Murdoch executives were so scared of irritating the media mogul
> that when [Kiley] interviewed the Israeli army unit responsible
> for killing a twelve-year-old Palestinian boy, he was asked to
> file the piece without mentioning the dead child. (*Guardian*, 5
> September 2001)

The *Daily Telegraph* has also been the subject of disputes over
its Middle East coverage. The proprietor of the Telegraph group,
Conrad Black, is strongly supportive of Israel and journalists
complained that this was affecting editorial policy. In March 2001,
The *Guardian* reported that:

> Three prominent writers – all of them past contributors to Mr
> Black's Telegraph group have signed a letter to the *Spectator*
> accusing him of abusing his responsibilities as a proprietor.
> Such is the vehemence with which Mr Black has expounded his
> pro-Israeli held view, they say, no editor or reporter would dare
> write frankly about the Palestinian perspective. (*Guardian*, 16
> March 2001)

On the same day in the *Guardian*, William Dalrymple, one of the authors of the letter, wrote:

> A press baron is an immensely powerful figure. With that power, comes responsibilities, and those responsibilities are abused when he makes it clear that certain areas are off-limits to legitimate enquiry, and that careers will suffer if those limits are crossed. (*Guardian*, 16 March 2001)

The pressures of organised public relations, lobbying and systematic criticism together with the privileging of Israeli perspectives by political and public figures, can affect the climate within which journalists operate. There is no total control and there are areas of the media where the debate is relatively open. But these factors go some way to explaining why journalists sometimes have difficulty in giving a clear account of the Palestinian perspective, while they can apparently more easily facilitate that of the Israelis.

5
Conclusions on the 2000–02
Content and Audience Samples[1]

One of the key issues to emerge from this research is that for many viewers, their level of interest in news related very directly to their level of understanding of what they were watching. We found strong increases in interest when people understood more about the history, origins and causes of events. A parallel phenomenon was that incomprehension led to detachment and increased the sense of powerlessness some people felt when watching terrible events with which they could not engage or relate to. There was a strong demand for clear direct explanations from journalists which cut through 'waffle' and 'spin' and which explained why these events were happening.

We also examined the conditions under which some viewers did engage with news stories or identify with the people who were being represented. There was some evidence of identification with the Israelis as being 'people like us', who have similar customs or who were 'democratic', and some people with Arab connections or friends identified with the Palestinians. A much more widespread identification in our audience samples came with what were seen as common or universal values. These included a concern with human suffering or with value judgements on, for example, oppression or the use of power. But how such values were applied by viewers could depend very much on the manner in which events were explained and understood. Some group members had argued that images of tanks against poorly armed Palestinians would necessarily result in an identification with the 'underdog'. But it was also pointed out that in other circumstances such as Northern Ireland, images of troops versus crowds of stone-throwers did not result in audiences identifying 'against' the soldiers. The crucial issue is whether the use of force is understood to be legitimate and in this sense TV news did have an important role in establishing how what was seen was to be evaluated. The Israelis could be seen as 'bullies' or their actions could be understood as emanating from their own 'vulnerability'. The image of a Palestinian fighter in a mask with a gun might be seen as a fearful icon of terrorism or as symbolising heroic resistance against an illegal occupation – the mask might appear as sinister or simply as a necessary precaution against arrest. The key issue is what we know and understand of the relationships which underpin events and the manner in which such images are contextualised when they are shown. It is in this contextualisation that the partisan nature of much TV news is revealed. As we indicated, to understand the origins of the Israeli-Palestinian conflict requires a knowledge of at least two key historical events. The first is that when Israel was established in 1948, large numbers of Palestinians were displaced from their homes and land. Both sides have given their own account of this and have sought to legitimise and explain their own actions. But even if we leave aside the accounts of Palestinians, it is clear that some eminent Israeli historians have given documented descriptions of how Palestinian society collapsed under deliberate military attacks. A second key issue is that after 1967, Palestinians in the occupied territories lived under various forms of military control in which they were ultimately subject to the power of Israel. The land, water and economic resources of these territories were then extensively exploited by Israel. Again, both sides give their own accounts of the legitimacy of this. Some Israelis and the Christian Right in the US might, for example, argue that the land was given to the Jews thousands of years ago by God, so it all belongs to the Israelis anyway. But it is clear that the fact of the military occupation and its consequences is crucial to an understanding of the rationale of Palestinian action. Television news has largely denied its audiences an account of these relationships and their origins, and in doing so has both confused viewers and reduced the understanding of the actions of those involved. Many in our audience samples did not even understand that there was a military occupation or that it was widely seen as illegal. There was very little knowledge of the conditions of the occupation or its effects on the Palestinian economy. There is a great difference between understanding the Palestinian view that they are fighting a war of national liberation against an occupying power and seeing the conflict as a border dispute between two countries that happen to want the same piece of land (which is how many people did see it). We also found that the attitudes of those in our audience groups could change sharply when they did learn more about the origins of the conflict. One female participant had commented in a focus group that the fighting would stop if the parents just kept their children in and stopped them throwing stones. When she heard in the discussion that Palestinians had lost their homes, she said 'If you knew, you'd be flinging bricks yourself' (low-income group, Glasgow). The absence of the Palestinian rationale also meant that on the news they were frequently presented as 'starting' the trouble while the Israelis 'retaliated'. This had a measurable impact on audience understanding and even extended to participants reversing in their memories the sequence of actual historical events (so the Palestinians were seen to do the first action and Israelis responded).

In contrast, Israeli views such as their need to defend themselves against terrorism were very well represented on the news. Israeli perspectives were more frequently featured in headlines and were often highlighted to the exclusion of alternatives. A frequency count of the coverage given to interviews and reported statements also showed the Israeli dominance.[2] Journalists sometimes adopted the language of Israeli statements and used it as their own direct speech in news reports. On controversial issues such as the Israeli settlements in occupied territory, there was a tendency to present these as 'vulnerable' and under attack without indicating that many are heavily fortified and play a key military and strategic role. This had a clear effect on how some audiences members saw them, including people who were sympathetic to the Palestinians (for example, one described his surprise when he had heard how much land the settlements controlled). There were other areas where the news was apparently partisan. Through the period of our work, Palestinians consistently incurred the highest number of casualties. The number killed was greater than that of Israelis by a ratio of 2–3:1. But on the news there was an emphasis on Israeli casualties both in the amount of coverage they received and in the language used to describe them. One of our samples was of a week when Palestinians incurred the highest number of casualties since the intifada had begun, yet there was more coverage of Israeli casualties. In our samples of news content, words such as 'mass murder', 'savage cold-blooded killing' and 'lynching' were used by journalists to describe Israeli deaths but not those of Palestinians/Arabs. The word 'terrorist' was used to describe Palestinians, but when an Israeli group was reported as trying to bomb a Palestinian school, they were referred to as 'extremists' or 'vigilantes' (ITV main News and BBC1 lunchtime News, 5 March 2002).

As we have also indicated, the level of pressure, lobbying and public relations which exists in this area is likely to affect the media climate in both Britain and the US. This has important implications for the clarity and impartiality of the information which is received by mass publics. Of course, there is propaganda on both sides. The BBC correspondent Paul Adams discussed this with us and commented on the arguments put forward by the Palestinians and Israelis at the time of Jenin. The Israelis had sought to present themselves as engaging in targeted operations against terrorists. But the Palestinians wanted to present the inhabitants as civilians under attack and thus argued that the Israeli actions constituted a 'massacre'. As Paul Adams commented: 'The argument disappears into sterile debate about what is a massacre.' What is missing is the view that this is an uneven war and that 'It is a war of national liberation – a periodic guerrilla war, sometimes using violent means, in which a population is trying to throw off an occupying force' (interview, 9 August 2002).

We have seen that this 'war' has sometimes drawn on other elements such as anti-Semitism and amongst some, an intense rejection of Western culture. But it seems unlikely that the bulk of the world's populations are intrinsically 'fanatical'. In the past, historical compromises have been possible to resolve the most intractable of conflicts. But a key factor in moving towards this is that judgements about how it might be resolved require clear and accurate information and the perspectives of those involved have to be properly understood. The dust-storms of propaganda, which are created by those seeking to defend their 'own side', will in the end do nothing more than prolong the conflict and the agony that the people of the Middle East are having to endure.

6
News Content and Competing Explanations of the 2008/09 Gaza Attack

This is a case study of news coverage of the Israeli attack on Gaza between 27 December 2008 and 17 January 2009. It expands upon our earlier findings on the coverage of the second intifada which appear above. The sample of news content is very substantial and enables us to make comparisons with the trends which we identified in this earlier work. The areas on which we will focus are as before: news on the origins of the conflict, the motivations and rationales of the two sides, and coverage of casualties. We use the same methodological approach, which we term thematic analysis. This is a method for understanding how meaning is conveyed in texts by examining how they are organised around and include (or exclude) key thematic explanations.[1] The method also includes the examination of production processes within institutions such as broadcasting and the press, as well as the inputs of public relations and the sources used by journalists, and how all of these can affect the shaping and transmission of messages. Finally the method also extends to the study of reception processes. Here the purpose is to show the conditions under which the structures of understanding that are built into the news text (relating, for example, to cause and effect or motives of key actors) are accepted, rejected or in other ways interpreted by audiences.

The first step in our content analysis is to identify the range of explanations and perspectives which are linked to the different sides in a conflict. We have given these in detail in the extended history which forms the first chapter of this book. A brief summary here clarifies the range of views which are available before we go on to show how they were featured in actual new texts. In this case, the essence of the Israeli position was that they were forced to respond to unwarranted rocket attacks by the Palestinian group Hamas, which had taken control of Gaza. The motivation for the attacks were found in Islamic extremism and terrorism. Israel was part of the free world, while Hamas was not. It was central to this message that the reasons for the conflict were not found to be the military occupation by Israel from 1967 or the war in 1948 and the creation of Israel. The Israeli narrative begins rather in 2005 with their pull out from Gaza. Their argument is that the Palestinians, instead of building a new state, voted instead for Hamas and the conflict, because their primary interest is in killing Jews. Chris McGreal, writing in the *Observer*, summarised the key elements of the Israeli position:

> In briefings in Jerusalem and London, Brussels and New York, the same core messages were repeated: that Israel had no choice but to attack in response to the barrage of Hamas rockets; that the coming attack would be on 'the infrastructure of terror' in Gaza and the targets principally Hamas fighters; that civilians would die, but it was because Hamas hides its fighters and weapons factories among ordinary people. (McGreal, 2009a: 2)

The message was promoted via the National Information Directorate of Israel, which was set up early in 2008. Yarden Vatikai, its head, commented on it that:

> The hasbara (explanation) apparatus needed a body that would co-ordinate its agencies, co-ordinate the messages and become a platform for co-operation between all the agencies that deal with communication relations and public diplomacy. (*Guardian*, 2 January 2009)

As Rachel Shabi notes, writing in the *Guardian*, this body had 'for months been concerned with formulating plans and role-playing to ensure that government officials deliver a clear unified message to the world's press' (2009: 16). This was a highly developed system of public relations which paralleled in its planning, the military operation. As McGreal notes, the intention of the Information Directorate was to focus attention on the 8,500 rockets fired from Gaza and the 20 civilians who were killed, 'rather than the punishing blockade of Gaza and the 1,700 Palestinians killed in Israeli military attacks' in the three years following the withdrawal (2009a: 2). A further element of the Israeli message was to argue, as Shabi notes, that Hamas and the Palestinians were responsible for the ending of the six-month ceasefire which had existed from June 2008.

Hamas had also appointed a public relations consultant, but had nothing to match the sophistication or range of the Israeli operation. The latter included, for example, a multi-lingual media centre to brief foreign journalists which was opened in the Israeli town of Sderot, which had received many rocket attacks. The Israelis apparently believed that they had done very well with this approach. It was reported after the attack on Gaza that a foreign ministry assessment of eight hours of international broadcast media showed they had 58 minutes of air time, compared to 19 minutes for the Palestinians (*Guardian*, 2 January 2009).

From the perspective of Hamas and the Palestinians, the causes of the conflict were very different. Their narrative focused on the loss of homes and land to Israel, its military occupation of Palestinian land, and the siege of Gaza. The last of these meant that the official border crossings into Gaza from Israel and Egypt were severely restricted and the population relied on tunnels dug through to Egypt.[2] These were unauthorised but functioned allegedly on the basis of copious bribes. Writing in the *Guardian*, Toni O'Loughlin describes the development of the blockade:

> Having built a wall around Gaza before disengagement, Israel then imposed a progressively tighter blockade, by barring Gazan labourers from entering Israel in late 2005, then by banning Gazan commercial trade in 2006, and finally, in mid-2007, by squeezing humanitarian aid. (O'Loughlin, 2008: 7)

The consequences on the living conditions of the people were dramatic. The Liberal Democratic MP, Sarah Teather visited Gaza nine months before the Israeli attack. She spoke of her experiences on the BBC Radio 4 programme, *Any Questions*:

> I was absolutely appalled by the conditions there. Really terrible. The level of poverty is unimaginable. You see as you first go into Gaza, the area in the north of Gaza has been bombed to nothingness. It is wasteland and then as you drive into the city the first thing that hits you is the smell of sewage because it lies in raw lakes on the north side of the city and we went to visit people's homes that are as good as slums. They are huts that people are crammed into and you cannot rebuild these homes (even though) the UN has the money to rebuild. Because of the siege on Gaza, Israel won't allow construction materials to go across the border. (9 January 2009)

As we have seen, Israel regards Hamas as a terrorist group, who have killed civilians through suicide bombing and rocket fire. These are clearly designated as war crimes. But Palestinians regard Israel as state terrorists, and a report by Amnesty International in the aftermath of the Gaza attack accused both sides of war crimes (Amnesty International, 2009).[3]

It has also been argued strongly that Hamas would have halted the rocket fire in exchange for the lifting of the blockade. Chris McGreal of the *Guardian* notes the comments of Ephraim Halevy, the former head of the Mossad Intelligence Service. Halevy stated in the Israeli press that the 'government in Jerusalem could have stopped the rocket attacks long ago by lifting its siege of Gaza'. But Israel's key interest was in undermining Hamas in favour of its rival Fatah, seen as a more amenable partner in negotiations (McGreal, 2009b: 1). Johann Hari in the *Independent* adds to this by quoting Yuval Diskin, then head of the Israeli security service, Shin Bet. He is reported as telling the Israeli Cabinet on 23 December that Hamas would continue the truce but wanted an end to the blockade and an Israeli ceasefire on the West Bank. The Cabinet, with an election looming and wishing to appear tough, is said to have rejected the terms. Hari also cites Ephraim Halevy's comments on Hamas, specifically that in practice they would accept a compromise for peace and a state based on the 1967 borders (2008: 2). Writing in *The Times*, William Sieghart also points to the pragmatic nature of Hamas. He notes its highly qualified political leadership and that it relies too much on secular votes to have an ultimate goal of 'Islamising Palestinian society' (2008: 2).[4] Whether it does or not, Hamas were the winners of the Palestinian elections of 2006 and have therefore, some authority as a governing body. Finally, Hamas and the Palestinians of Gaza would certainly reject the view that it was they who broke the ceasefire. They point to an Israeli incursion in November 2008 in which six Palestinians were killed. Writing in the *Observer*, Chris McGreal notes that 'even during the cease-fire, Israel killed 22 people in Gaza, including 2 children and a woman' (2009a: 4).

There are other areas of controversy and divided opinion about the attack on Gaza which often related to specific events, such as the deaths of civilians and the justifications and explanations which were offered at the time. We will discuss these further in our content analysis. But the major explanatory themes outlined here relate to the causes of the conflict and underpin broader ways in which it is contextualised. Crucially, as we will show, they have important impacts on audience understanding.

SAMPLE AND METHODS

For this sample we recorded and transcribed BBC1 and ITV (channel 3) early evening and main news programmes from the first day of the conflict, 27 December 2008, until the announcement by Israel of a ceasefire on 17 January 2009. Over 4,000 lines of text were analysed using the thematic approach which we have discussed in Chapter 2. We focused on statements reported from different sides, defending or explaining their position and on areas such as civilian casualties, plus public demonstrations and protests which raised questions on the legitimacy of action in the conflict. We were interested in issues that potentially divided opinion rather than areas such as reports on troop movements, the arrivals and departures of world politicians or speculation of how long the conflict might last. We grouped statements for analysis into the following categories:

1. Israeli and Palestinian explanatory statements on the causes of the conflict.
2. Other Israeli and Palestinian statements, e.g. on military claims or appeals for peace/reconciliation.
3. Other comments on causes.
4. Histories of the conflict/rockets/blockade.
5. Additional criticisms of the Israeli attack on Gaza and defences of the Israeli action.
6. Defences of Hamas/Palestinian action.
7. Additional criticism of Israel and Hamas (saying that both were to blame).
8. Protests and demonstrations.
9. Israeli and Palestinian casualties/suffering.

The number of statements in each category is given in tabulated form in Appendix 3. We will discuss them here in two broad groups which are, first, statements about cause, criticism and defence of action (categories 1–8), and second, coverage of Israeli and Palestinian casualties and suffering (category 9).

CAUSE, CRITICISM AND DEFENCE OF ACTION

The most striking feature of the news texts in these areas is the dominance of the Israeli perspective, in relation to the causes of the conflict. We can illustrate this initially through a quantitative analysis. The news bulletins which we examined were transcribed and the numbers which we give here relate to the lines of text on specific explanations (a full list of these is given in Appendix 3). We can see on the BBC for example, that the themes of 'ending the rockets', the 'need for security' and to 'stop the smuggling of weapons' received a total of 316.5 lines of text. Others such as the need to 'hit Hamas' and that 'Hamas and terrorists are to blame' received 62 lines. The total for Israeli explanatory statements on the BBC is 421.25. This compares with a much lower total for Hamas/Palestinian explanations of just 126.25. There is another important point to make here which is that the bulk of the Palestinian accounts do not explain their case beyond saying that they will resist. They are mostly declamatory statements saying for example that 'Gaza is a graveyard for Israel' or that 'Israel will face a dark destiny' (68.5 lines). These may have a function in terms of rallying supporters but as we will see they do little to inform wider audiences about the nature of the conflict. Crucially, many of the core elements of the Palestinian rationale for their actions are very sparsely represented. There are just 14.25 lines referring to the occupation and only 10.5 on the ending of the siege/blockade. The same pattern occurs in ITV's coverage with over 302 lines relating to Israeli explanatory statements and just 78 for Hamas/Palestinian. Here again the core elements of the Palestinian case on the causes of the conflict rarely appear. As we will see, there are other areas where the Palestinians receive more extensive coverage such as in the showing of casualties. The absence of explanations on cause is critical since it can have profound impact on audience belief and judgements.

In practice the importance of the Israeli dominance of such accounts is that key moments in the reporting of events are accompanied by a coherent statement which contextualises and has the potential to legitimise Israeli action. Crucially, these explanations then act as organising principles for the structuring of coverage – they become explanatory themes. We can see this by examining specific examples of news text. The opening lines of the BBC early evening news on the first day of the bombing contain a clear statement from Israel that the air strikes are 'in response' to missile attacks, while from Hamas we hear that they 'have vowed revenge':

Newscaster: Israeli war planes have carried out a wave of attacks on the Gaza Strip in one of the bloodiest days of the conflict. Palestinian officials say more than 200 people have been killed in the raids. *Israel says the air strikes were in response to missile attacks on its country* and now is the time to fight. The targets were security compounds belonging to Hamas, the militant group that controls Gaza. *They vowed revenge.* (BBC1 early evening News, 27 December 2008 – our italics)

Later, a BBC correspondent notes that a big question is whether the rocket attacks will stop. Otherwise there will be more 'retaliation':

Newscaster: But there are big questions now about what happens next. Will this stop the rockets coming into Israel? *Otherwise it's going to be a matter of more and more retaliation.* What about civilians in Gaza? (BBC1 early evening News, 27 December 2008 – our italics)

In the following example, the story opens with an account of the campaign and into this is inserted the Israeli rationale:

Newscaster: There have been intensive clashes between Israeli ground forces and Palestinian fighters as Israel steps up its offensive against militants *who have been firing rockets into the south of the country.* (BBC1 early evening News, 4 January 2009 – our italics)

These examples follow very much the pattern which we have seen elsewhere in this volume, where Israeli actions appear as a 'response' to problems initiated by the Palestinians. The Israeli narrative is followed in other ways: In the first of the examples above, the targets are referred to as 'security compounds'. They are said to belong to Hamas, described as 'the militant group that controls Gaza'. This is the perspective of Israel and others who are critical of Hamas. It takes no account of the fact that Hamas won the Palestinian elections and in that sense had a degree of democratically given authority. The 'security compounds' described here were police stations, which in international law may be classed as civilian. This is a point on which the *Guardian* commented at the time:

The targets were not the training camps of Hamas' military wing, which were empty when the jets struck, but rather police stations. The raids were intended to destroy the infrastructure on which Hamas builds its administrative as much as its military hold over Gaza. But that means killing police-men not just the militants who assemble and fire the rockets. Presumably it also means targeting judges, officials, and doctors too. (*Guardian* editorial, 29 December 2008)

The BBC news however, classes the targets as military. After referring to a police station, it states 'there were civilian casualties too' and says there were homes and families near to 'every military target':

> More than 100 tonnes of bombs were dropped, Israel said, on dozens of targets. This was one, a Gaza city police station. A badly injured man recites the Muslim prayer for those about to die. The Gaza police chief himself was also killed. *There were many civilian casualties too* including children. Gaza is one of the most crowded places on earth, every military target has homes and families close by. (BBC1 early evening News, 27 December 2008 – our italics)

We found in our audience studies that some people drew a clear distinction between Hamas and the Palestinians and were unaware that Hamas had won the elections of 2006. This perspective was assumed in headlines and commentaries which presented the Israeli attack as being directed only at Hamas, and this is certainly how Israel wished it to be seen. Consider the following examples:

> The bombardment continues on Hamas targets. (BBC1 early evening News headline, 31 December 2008)

> The offensive against Hamas enters its second week. (BBC1 early evening News, 3 January 2009)

> Israeli ground forces enter Gaza in the second phase of their offensive against Hamas. (BBC1 late News, 3 January 2009)

> Israel said it will continue its assault on Gaza until Hamas puts down its rockets. (ITV early evening News headline, 28 December 2008)

> Israel shows no sign of letting up in its onslaught against Hamas. (ITV early evening News, 5 January 2009)

> Day 10 of Israel's assault on the Gaza strip and its Hamas fighters is coming to end. (ITV late News, 5 January 2009)

The Israeli perspective on the purpose of the attack and the claim that it was not directed at civilians was sometimes contested. A journalist on the BBC, for example, comments that:

> After inflicting so much pain and death, Israel still says that Gaza's civilians are not its enemy. That's something that the Gazans and millions of others in the Middle East do not believe. (BBC1 late News, 17 January 2009)

From the Palestinian side, it was argued that a key purpose of the Israeli action was to weaken support for Hamas. There were many who believed that to do so involved killing and terrorising people in the civilian population.[5] But such a view was rarely expressed on the news. The dominant explanation for the attack was that it was to stop the firing of rockets by Hamas. The offer that Hamas was said to have made, to halt this is in exchange for lifting the blockade (which Israel had rejected), was almost completely absent from the coverage. So the news perpetuated a one-sided view of the causes of the conflict, by highlighting the issue of the rockets without reporting the Hamas offer and by missing the alternative Palestinian view on the purpose of the attack. There is a prominence accorded to the Israeli perspective on the causes of the conflict which is not given to that of the Palestinians. The Israeli account is repeated by journalists with force and clarity. In this example it is incorporated into a discussion of public opinion in Israel:

> Public opinion (could turn) against a long battle in Gaza *even if that is what is needed to rid them of the menace of rocket attacks.* (ITV early evening News, 5 January 2009 – our italics)

As the Israeli operation began, ITV interviewed a CNN journalist who describes the Israelis as saying how 'sick and tired' they are of the rocket attacks:

> *Newscaster*: Well earlier I spoke to (a CNN journalist) in Jerusalem and first asked her why Israel had acted now and with such force. *CNN Journalist*: Well Israel is saying that it was just sick and tired of the rockets that Hamas and Palestinian militant groups were firing from Gaza into neighbouring Israeli towns. And certainly they are saying that enough is enough. (ITV main News, 27 December 2008)

There is nothing wrong with journalists expressing very clearly the views of one side. But the question for BBC and ITV news is whether they are doing it for both sides – at least if they wish to sustain their claims to be giving a balanced account. In the above example, the journalists discuss why Israel is acting, but there is no question on why Hamas and the Palestinians are firing rockets. There is nowhere in the thousands of words which we have analysed where a journalist says that the firing at Israel is because Hamas or other Palestinians say they are 'sick and tired of Israeli military control'. Journalists do not report that the rockets will be fired 'even if that's what it takes to end the menace of the siege' or for Palestinians 'to get their homes and land back'. When it comes to the Israeli views, journalists may have no problem in endorsing them. For example, a BBC journalist comments that:

> Israel feels itself surrounded by enemies, *with reason*. (BBC1 early evening News, 8 January 2009 – our italics.)

Would the BBC feel able to endorse the Palestinian view in this way? We have not found a commentary noting that 'Palestinians feel themselves to be subject to a brutal military occupation, with reason'. In another example, a BBC journalist comments that 'the reason' for the Israeli offensive is to defend Sderot, an Israeli town close to the border:

> Safeguarding places like this town is the reason why Israel has been blockading and is now attacking Gaza. (BBC1 early evening News, 31 December 2008)

This is contentious since, as we have seen, some including the ex-head of the Israeli intelligence service have argued that the rocket attacks could have been stopped 'long ago' by lifting the siege of Gaza (McGreal, 2009b: 1). But more to the point, the official Israeli view is simply stated as a fact. Palestinian views on the cause of the conflict are not endorsed in this way. The legitimacy accorded to the Israelis means that their perspective can become incorporated into the normal language of journalism. The perspective is explicitly endorsed. In the following example, a journalist speaks of 'contraband' being smuggled into Gaza by Egypt:

The (Israeli) military has been targeting tunnels used to smuggle contraband from Egypt. (ITV early evening News, 5 January 2009)

But what to the Israelis is 'contraband', may be to the other side, necessary supplies. This may include weapons since by the Hamas/Palestinian definition they are fighting a legitimate struggle against Israel. And because Hamas was elected they can be seen by Palestinians as representing them in that struggle. Journalists are sometimes unwilling to acknowledge this and, as we have seen, maintain the division between Hamas on one side and the Palestinians of Gaza on the other. Thus a journalist speaks of Hamas smuggling weapons while 'the people' smuggled food. It makes little sense since Hamas as the controlling authority is likely to have a role in the bringing in of all materials. The main point is that such a comment sustains the division between Hamas and 'the people':

The main target (of the Israelis) is this thin strip of land between Egypt and Gaza beneath which Hamas had smuggled their weapons and the people had smuggled their food. (BBC1 main News, 17 January 2009)

We are not arguing that all Palestinians in Gaza support Hamas or believe in a military solution. Our point here is that a key perspective is missing. As the BBC journalist Paul Adams commented elsewhere in this volume, what is absent is the view that the Palestinians are a people in a war of national liberation, trying to throw off an occupying force. The reasons for this are largely not explained or developed as themes in the news coverage which we examine here. In the following example, even the notion of their actions as 'resistance' is questioned. As the attack on Gaza ended, the BBC1 main news began with an account of the Israelis claiming victory and a speech by their Prime Minister explaining the rationale for their actions:

Newscaster: Israel calls a halt to its military offensive in Gaza. The unilateral ceasefire ends their 22-day campaign with Israel claiming victory.
Israeli Prime Minister (in vision with translation): Rocket factories have been destroyed, the smuggling routes using the tunnels have been bombed. Their ability to move weapons inside Gaza has been damaged.

The newscaster then mentions the response of Hamas:

> *Newscaster*: Hamas responds by promising to continue *what they call* their resistance. (BBC1 main News headlines, 17 January 2009)

The BBC would not say of the Israelis that they are terminating 'what they call' their attempt to stop the rocket fire.[6]

In other coverage on ITV there is a commentary on the first Israeli soldier to die in the conflict, the impact on his family and how they are convinced the invasion is right:

> *ITV Correspondent*: For a mother, it is the unbearable loss of her only son, but the smiling face (of this) 22 year old *symbolises Israel's sacrifice*, he was the first soldier to die when they invaded Gaza, no-one knows how many more there will be.
>
> *Soldier's sister*: In our private level it is not worth it, but in a global vision, this is the price.
>
> *ITV Correspondent*: But his mother and three sisters are convinced the invasion is right.
>
> *Soldier's sister*: We've a little land to live and we want to live here in peace and protect ourselves and we all believe that. (ITV main News, 6 January 2009 – our italics)

The correspondent comments that 'they know they are often condemned by the outside world but this time they are determined to ignore the criticisms until they have completed the job' (ITV main News, 6 January 2009). Could we imagine such a moving profile for a young Palestinian fighter, saying that he symbolised Palestine's sacrifice? The nearest in this sample is in another commentary from ITV. It is reported that a Norwegian doctor in a Palestinian hospital says he is there because he says 'the Palestinians are his friends and heroes' (ITV early evening News, 9 January 2009). The difference is instructive since the comment is attributed and there is no explanation to what the heroism relates to. But Palestinian fighters of Hamas can be referred to as 'fanatics', as in these examples also from ITV:

> *ITV Correspondent*: Israeli soldiers battle the fanatical Islamic fighters of Hamas. (ITV main News, 3 January 2009)

And on another occasion on the death of a Hamas leader:

> *ITV Correspondent*: The despair of the Palestinians has produced a generation of fanatics – one fanatic is dead, another fanatic will now doubtless step forward to take his place. (ITV early evening News, 1 January 2009)

The 'resistance fighters' of one side are to the other 'fanatics'. But such crude labelling does little to explain the conflict, its origin or possible solutions.

EXPLANATORY THEMES

The numerical frequency, the prominence and the legitimacy accorded to Israeli accounts are important in understanding how the news works to explain and contextualise events from a particular perspective. But there is another important factor, which is that this perspective is used to structure and develop news accounts. It becomes an organising principle which affects the allocation of resources for the production of strands of news – an explanatory theme. For example, the following ITV bulletin includes in its headlines images of damage in Israel from rocket attacks. The presenter says over these:

> *Newscaster*: And this is why we speak to Israelis who have lived under the threat of Hamas rockets for years. (ITV early evening News, 5 January 2009)

This news also includes an extensive commentary on Palestinian casualties, which we will discuss later. But the point here is that the Israeli rationale for the attack on Gaza is illustrated by sending a journalist to do an extensive series of interviews with Israelis. We are told that ITV's correspondent 'has been to meet the people living under threat from Hamas'. The report begins over images of a distressed woman:

> This time she's escaped with her life but the latest rocket attack on southern Israel leaves an elderly lady deeply traumatised. (ITV early evening News, 5 January 2009)

We are shown the remains of rockets that have been fired and introduced to a soldier who was one of the first Israeli casualties.

There are statements from him, his mother and his sister and then from the Israeli president. This news package ends with more images and commentary on rocket damage, footage of an Israeli soldier's funeral and finally the comment which we noted above about 'what is needed to rid them of the menace of rocket attacks' (ITV early evening News, 5 January 2009).

The BBC also includes extensive commentary on rockets and the damage which they have caused. We will examine one such account in detail as it illustrates well the manner in which the two perspectives on the causes of the conflict are presented. This bulletin is from 7 January and it includes in its first part a brief reference to what are called the demands of Hamas:

> *Journalist*: In Beirut, Osama Hamdan laid out the demands of Hamas. He said they wanted an immediate end to the Israeli aggression, a pull back of Israeli troops and equipment and the opening of all openings into the Gaza strip. Any proposal without all that is a waste of effort, he said. (BBC1 early evening News, 7 January 2009)

The last of these, 'the opening of all openings' would be counted by us as a reference to the siege, yet in practice it is almost meaningless as an explanation of Palestinian action unless the viewer already knows about the blockade, its consequences and why they oppose it. The news also reports that Israel is letting in aid convoys and has suspended the military operation for three hours to allow this. There are comments from a BBC correspondent on Israel's conditions for a ceasefire agreement and we are told that:

> Israel wants the border secured to stop Hamas smuggling weapons in through tunnels. (BBC1 early evening News, 7 January 2009)

This is Israel's view and can scarcely be seen as a reference to the siege from the point of view of the Palestinians. The correspondent then says more about Israel's aims, that it wants to weaken Hamas so it can't claim victory and that this might take 'more time than Israel has left in the campaign and too many lives'. These comments function as a prelude to a very long presentation on the rockets. The newscaster introduces it with the above comments on the Hamas/ Palestinian view on the blockade. This amounted to the couple of phrases which we have indicated. And then it is time to hear once again about what the Israelis think:

Newscaster: So as (our correspondent) was saying Hamas wants an end to the blockading of its territory, but what about Israel? It wants a stop to Hamas rocket attacks and to prevent the group from re-arming, they say that's the only way to lift the constant fear in which many Israelis live. (BBC1 early evening News, 7 January 2009)

This is followed by the extended commentary on the rockets from the BBC's security correspondent, on what type they are, 'how dangerous they are', and 'can they be stopped?':

Security Correspondent: Well the success or failure of any ceasefire is going to depend largely on the issue of Gaza's rockets which Israel says must stop. Compared to Israel's twenty-first-century firepower they are crude and inaccurate but they are effective as a psychological weapon against Israel's southern population. So how dangerous are they and can they be stopped? There are two broad types of rocket; this is one of them, the Al-Qassam. Palestinian militants put them together in back street workshops producing up to ten a day. In the past they've launched them out in the open, often bringing immediate Israeli retaliation. So now they fire them by wires running underground. The rockets aimed at Israeli towns carry a small warhead and no guidance. Then there's the Kakushka or Grad similar to this weapon used by Hezbollah fighters in Lebanon. With a longer range and bigger warhead the Israelis fear that they could one day hit Tel-Aviv. (BBC1 early evening News, 7 January 2009)

Then we hear again about the number of Israelis 'under threat' and there is a brief comparison with Palestinian casualties:

Security Correspondent: As the range of these weapons has increased so too has the numbers of Israelis living within target range. Nearly a million people now lie under threat from Gaza. Although the numbers killed are dwarfed by Palestinian casualties from Israeli reprisals. (BBC1 early evening News, 7 January 2009)

The Palestinian casualties are said to have come from Israeli 'reprisals' and here again is the formula that Israeli action is a retaliation to a problem initiated by the Palestinians. The security correspondent continues with more on the target range of the rockets, which leads to a further piece from another BBC correspondent in the Israeli town of Sderot:

> *Security Correspondent*: Towns like Ashkelon have long been in target range of Gaza's rockets but recently Beersheba, 40 kilometres away, has also come under fire. Sderot with a population of 20,000 Israelis remains a favoured target. Our correspondent was there today:
> *BBC Correspondent*: There have been many more rocket attacks here over the last couple of weeks but people in Sderot see that as a necessary evil. They believe that the military campaign against Gaza must be prosecuted to its conclusion if they are to bring an end to what for them has been eight years of rocket attacks. Also in Sderot today was visiting Israeli opposition leader Benjamin Netanyahu. He found himself having to take cover during a rocket alert. (BBC1 early evening News, 7 January 2009)

Then it is back to the security correspondent and more on the rockets. We hear how the Israelis say they come through the tunnels and what they want done about it:

> *BBC Security Correspondent*: Last year over 3,000 rockets and mortar shells landed in Israel, double the total for 2007. So where are the munitions coming from? Through tunnels like these say the Israelis, dug beneath the Egyptian border. There are said to be hundreds, possibly thousands of them and *Israel wants them blocked*. The smuggling tunnels that fan out from the border town of Rafah form a sophisticated underground supply network. It's almost as if there were two Gaza Strips, one above ground and one below. *Blowing up Palestinian rocket launchers or the tunnels that supply them is not going to satisfy Israel*. Whatever deal is reached it wants to end the rocket threat from Gaza permanently. But just about every analyst I've spoken to says that is unrealistic even with international monitors. Two years on from the Lebanon war for example Hezbollah now has more rockets than ever. So as negotiations for a ceasefire continue, *Israel will be looking for whatever guarantees it can get that the rocket threat from Gaza will at least be minimised*. (BBC1 early evening News, 7 January 2009 – our italics)

Finally, the item returns to the first correspondent on the Israeli/ Gaza border. He is asked about the shape of a possible peace deal and he outlines what each side wants. First we hear the Israeli position:

> *BBC Correspondent*: Israel's conception as you've been hearing is one that stops rocket fire and stops Hamas' ability to rearm itself, in other words to bring weapons in mainly through the tunnels, they say from Egypt into Gaza. Israel essentially wants to break Hamas as a military formation. (BBC1 early evening News, 7 January 2009)

As we have seen, this viewpoint has been exhaustedly explained and pursued through a number of news segments. The correspondent then speaks of the kind of ceasefire that Hamas wants:

> *BBC Correspondent*: Hamas has a different conception. Hamas says that the kind of ceasefire that it would like to have is one where Israel stops firing and pulls its troops out straight away and its equipment and also one in which the crossings between Gaza and Israel and Gaza and Egypt are opened up. (BBC1 early evening News, 7 January 2009)

The last of these comments on the opening of the crossings is again a reference to the siege, but this has not been explained or pursued as a theme in any way.[7] Yet it is a crucial part of the Hamas/Palestinian arguments on the cause of the crisis.

THE FRAGMENTED PALESTINIAN CASE

There were limits on foreign journalists entering Gaza, but there were many other information sources and people with direct experience who could have explained the consequences of the Israeli blockade. We saw above, the comments of the Liberal Democrat MP Sarah Teather and her graphic account of the bombed wasteland in the north of Gaza, the lakes of raw sewage and the problems of building because of the blocking of materials. There is almost no discussion of these conditions and how they might relate to the firing of rockets in any of our sample of BBC and ITN news bulletins.[8] But on the night before the BBC bulletin which we quoted extensively above, Channel 4 News had a telephone interview with a Hamas spokesman in Gaza. He speaks of the effects of the Israeli blockade, of how it produces the 'smuggling' and how if the crossings were open they could export and import normally:

We want to open the crossings in Gaza ... if you open the crossings between Gaza and Israel, we can export and import, we don't need smuggling, but you can't let these people die slowly – we have people who are the victims of the blockade and the embargo in Gaza. (Channel 4 News, 7 p.m., 6 January 2009)

A key absence in terms of explaining the Hamas/Palestinian position is the offer referred to above, by which the rockets would be stopped in exchange for a lifting of the siege. There is no discussion in our sample of the comments attributed to Ephraim Halevy, the former head of Mossad or of Yuval Diskin, the head of the Israeli security service. There is only the briefest mention that such debate was taking place. On 31 December 2008, a BBC correspondent makes this passing reference:

The human suffering in Gaza and reports that Hamas is offering a ceasefire if Israel lifts its siege, are increasing international pressure on the Israelis which they continue to ignore. (BBC1 early evening and main News, 31 December 2008)

This compares with literally hundreds of references in our sample to the rockets as the rationale for Israeli action. The point about the Hamas/Palestinian offer of a ceasefire is made with more force on Channel 4 News in an interview with the Palestinian politician, Moustafa Barghouti. He is asked:

Channel 4 Correspondent: You would agree with Israel on one thing which is surely that Hamas need to stop firing Gazan missiles into Israel?

And he replies:

Moustafa Barghouti: Hamas agrees with that too. They say today, their leader has showed an article saying he's ready for a ceasefire; he's ready to stop that if the Israelis also stop and lift the embargo on Gaza. (Channel 4 News, 7 p.m., 6 January 2009)

He then goes on to make the point that it was Israel who broke the ceasefire in November 2008 by conducting attacks which killed six Palestinians:

Moustafa Barghouti: There is a misleading lie that has spread all over the world media, as if it was the Palestinians who broke the ceasefire. This is a lie. Israel broke the ceasefire by re-establishing the embargo and siege on Gaza and Israel broke the ceasefire back in November when they conducted several attacks that took the lives of six Palestinians. (Channel 4 News, 7 p.m., 6 January 2009)

This last point barely appears in our sample of BBC and ITV bulletins. The nearest to it is in a history of the conflict given on BBC1. But this does not state clearly the view that Israel broke the ceasefire, saying instead that 'the ceasefire broke down' and there is no reference to the killing of six Palestinians:

BBC Correspondent: In November (2008) the ceasefire broke down. Israel bombed a tunnel they said Hamas would use to attack its soldiers. After days of mounting tension, Hamas fired a barrage of rockets into southern Israel. (BBC1 early evening News, 5 January 2009)

There is also a reference on 9 January on the BBC in which a correspondent says, 'when it comes to ceasefires, Hamas believes Israel can't be trusted'. This is followed by a rather unclear statement from a Hamas spokesman and then a very clear one from the BBC correspondent explaining the Israeli position:

Osama Hamdan: We had already a ceasefire for six months and the Israelis did not respect that, they did not accept to play their terms so they demonstrate they did not give a new chance for the ceasefire.
BBC Correspondent: And so Hamas launched more rockets from Gaza. This was an alert in the Israeli town of Ashdod north of the Gaza Strip. Israel says the rocket attacks prove the UN resolution calling for a ceasefire would not be respected by what it called, the Palestinian murder organisations. Israel's thinking about a ceasefire seems to be determined by its two main stated objectives for this war. The first is to do as much damage to the military wing of Hamas that either it won't be able to fire rockets into Israel or that it will be too scared. The second objective is to stop Hamas smuggling weapons into the Gaza Strip to re-arm after all this is over. (BBC1 main News, 9 January 2009)

The Palestinian view on the breaking of the ceasefire and the siege does appear, but as confused, scattered moments and oblique references. Crucially it is not explored or clearly explained on BBC and ITV news. The contrary perspective, that Hamas and Palestinian groups were responsible for the onset of violence, occurs as a consistent and clearly stated theme in news reports. It is very strongly put by speakers from the US and Israel, as in these examples:

> *BBC Correspondent*: Israel says it's targeting the Islamist movement, here. President Bush in his weekly radio address has blamed the Islamic movement for what has been happening in Gaza:
> *President Bush*: This recent outburst of violence was instigated by Hamas. A Palestinian group supported by Iran and Syria which calls for Israel's destruction. Eighteen months ago Hamas took over the Gaza Strip in a coup and since then has imported thousands of guns and rockets and ordinance. (BBC1 early evening News, 3 January 2009)

> *Ehud Barak (Israeli Defence Minister)*: So far the Israeli Defence Forces have dealt unprecedented heavy blows to Hamas, in order to complete their mission, will now launch the ground operation. We are peace seekers; we have restrained ourselves for a long time but now is the time to do what needs to be done. (BBC1 main News, 3 January 2009)

> *Tzipi Livni (Israeli Foreign Minister)*: We have no other alternative. The only way around, the other way is to have our citizens being killed daily by Hamas on a daily basis. (BBC1 early evening News, 31 December 2008)

> *President Bush*: Hamas decided to use Gaza to launch rockets to kill innocent Israelis. Israel has obviously decided to protect herself and her people. (BBC1 main News, 5 January 2009)

> *Tzipi Livni (Israeli Foreign Minister)*: We are trying to target Hamas which hide amongst civilians, they don't care and they really don't care about what is going to happen to the citizens of Gaza. They are responsible to the situation in Gaza, Israel wants to live in peace in the region but we cannot because Hamas is targeting our civilians from civil population centres in Gaza. (ITV early evening News, 29 December 2008)

Other references are sometimes accompanied by brief quotes from Hamas/Palestinian sources to offer a form of balance. But this is illusory at least as far as offering an alternative explanation, since as we have indicated these comments are declarations about victory or that Israel will face a 'black destiny'. They add nothing of explanations of cause or responsibility for the onset of violence:

> *ITV newscaster*: Mr Bush said that Hamas must turn away from terror, but they've warned Israel faces a black destiny if it launches a ground invasion.
> Good afternoon. The blame for the violence devastating Gaza was laid squarely at the feet of Hamas by President Bush today. He said the Hamas attacks on Israel were an act of terror that has caused the conflict. (ITV early evening News, 3 January 2009)

> *Tzipi Livni (Israeli Foreign Minister)*: I can understand the eagerness of the international community to see the region calm. This is our dream as well. This is what we are looking for. Unfortunately, there are those who cannot accept the idea of living in peace in this region.
> *BBC Correspondent*: From his hiding place in Gaza the senior Hamas leader Mahmoud Zahar sent out a message. He told Palestinians they were paying a tax for resisting Israel and that victory would come. (BBC1 main News, 5 January 2009)

In a further example, an ITV correspondent states on the early evening news that Hamas has 'become an impediment to the peace process' (in the main news which follows it is referred to as an 'absolute impediment'). The statement is coupled with a clip from a press conference given by President Bush:

> *President Bush*: I know people are saying let's have a ceasefire and those are noble ambitions but any ceasefire must have the conditions in it so that Hamas does not use Gaza as a place from which to launch rockets.
> *ITV Correspondent*: The Americans would dearly like to see the defeat of Hamas in Gaza and there are two reasons for that. *Hamas has become an impediment to the peace process* and secondly Hamas is backed by the Iranians. (ITV early evening News, 5 January 2009 – our italics)

The BBC offers a different view by showing an interview which they recorded the previous year with a senior Hamas spokesman, who names the occupation as the problem and suggests they would accept a two state solution:

> *BBC Correspondent*: Last year one of (Hamas') leaders told the BBC how co-existence with Israel might be possible.
> *Khaled Neshaal (words translated)*: We could accept a state based on the 67 borders, he says, but Israel insists on continuing its occupation of our land, so we have no choice but to resist. (BBC1 main News, 9 January 2009)

This interview appears only once in our sample and it is followed immediately by a statement from an Israeli spokesman, denying that Hamas would accept such a state, but nonetheless it does offer a different perspective from that portrayed so routinely elsewhere.[9] It also shows that it is possible to feature alternative accounts, even though access to Gaza was physically limited. Overall there are very few coherent statements of the Palestinian case on the origins of the crisis, the occupation or on the loss of their lands. There are less than five of the last of these in the whole sample. One is from Ehab al-Hussein of the Hamas interior ministry:[10]

> *Ehab al-Hussein*: The Israelis are doing this because they want us to give up but we will not give up, we will stay to say that we want our lands back, but we need a move from the world. (BBC1 early evening News, 28 December 2008)

The BBC has just 14 lines on the occupation, and ITV even fewer. The bulk of the BBC references come in a description of how Israel has brought in increased 'security restrictions' in Jerusalem, because of the Gaza conflict. We are told that 'Palestinian men had to prove they were over 50 to get into the old city to pray', and that

> Israel says these restrictions were security necessities, but they deepen a Palestinian conviction that Israel wants to dismantle their religious and national identity. (BBC1 main News, 2 January 2009)

There is a description of the actions of Palestinian and Israeli police:

> The Israelis kept Palestinian protesters at a distance at the main checkpoint between Jerusalem and the West Bank town of

Ramallah. On the far side of the clouds of tear gas, Palestinian police stopped all but a few young men from getting too close. (BBC1 main News, 2 January 2009)

This in itself is confusing unless the viewer already knows what the occupation is, the significance of checkpoints and the relation, for example, between Israeli and Palestinian police. Those with a detailed knowledge of the situation may understand, but our interviews repeatedly show that most audience members have a vague and limited knowledge of the occupation – or even who the occupiers are. The journalist concludes:

On days like this you can really feel the occupation and the strength of opposition to it. (BBC1 main News, 2 January 2009)

This might be correct, but there is very little here and almost nothing in the rest of the sample to explain the key issues to which the Palestinians say they object – such as the taking of land and water by Israel, extra-judicial killing, the curfews, the economic control plus mass arrests and imprisonment. Without this perspective, it is difficult to understand what the 'strong opposition' is actually opposing.

PROTESTS AND DEMONSTRATIONS

In this period there were a large number of demonstrations and protests reported, most of which were in favour of the Palestinians, but there was one in support of Israel on 11 January 2009. They were said on the news to be taking place in many different countries as well as in the UK. In this example, a report of demonstrations is linked to a statement from Israel:

BBC Newscaster: After eight days of air strikes, the Israeli government says the ground offensive will not be short or easy. The actions spark protests across Europe, with angry demonstrations outside Israel's embassy in London. (BBC1 main News headline, 3 January 2009)

There are reports about demonstrations on 28 and 29 December 2008 and on 3, 4, 10, 11 and 15 January 2009. This is a considerable amount of coverage with over 190 lines of text. It could have provided a space for discussing or at least featuring some of the issues which underlay the conflict and which were missing elsewhere. But in practice any form of explanation was very sparse. Protests in the UK are reported as being 'against the violence in Gaza' (BBC1 early evening News, 3 January 2009), 'in protest at Israel's actions in Gaza' (BBC1 main News, 3 January 2009) and 'against Israel's bombing of Gaza' (ITV early evening News, 10 January 2009). Rallies are reported to have taken place in London and Manchester 'to express solidarity with Israel' and these are said to follow 'yesterday's demonstrations against the military offensive' (BBC1 early evening News, 11 January 2009). ITV included a report from Iran, where a student leader says that Hamas will win and people would give their lives against Israel (ITV early evening News, 15 January 2009). In another report, there is a sentence from the comedian Alexei Sayle, saying that:

> The people of Gaza are stuck, they cannot move in an area the size of Shepherds Bush. They cannot move and for 40 years, thousand-ton bombs, rockets, shells from the sea have been landing on them. (ITV early evening News, 3 January 2009)

There are also comments that Israel should conform to international law and that their 'response' should be proportionate (BBC1 main News, 3 January 2009). But none of this goes very far in explaining what the conflict is about, how it started or why it is continuing. Meanwhile, as we have seen, the Israeli case is being put very efficiently via other forms of public relations activity. In practice, a very clear statement of the Israeli perspective could appear alongside a rather vague call, attributed to protestors that Israel should 'stop the bloodshed':

> *Newscaster*: Bush points the finger of blame. The outgoing American president says Hamas is responsible for the violence in Gaza as thousands across Britain call on Israel to stop the bloodshed. (ITV early evening News headline, 3 January 2009)

Much of the coverage of the protests has no explanation of any sort – to the point where it would be difficult to tell from the news commentary whether the protestors are more critical of one side than the other:

> *Newscaster*: Demonstrations against the violence in Gaza have been taking place in the Middle East and within the UK. Up to 10,000 protesters gathered in London and marched towards

Trafalgar Square. In Manchester, 2,000 marched. There were hundreds more in Edinburgh, Glasgow and Portsmouth and elsewhere around the country. (BBC1 early evening News, 3 January 2009)

BBC Newscaster: Here an estimated 20,000 people marched through London to protest against the violence in Gaza. It was one of a number of protests taking place across Europe and the Middle East.
Protestor: There are a lot of Jews here, there are a lot Israelis here as well and they are people who, like the rest of us, think this is a terrible, terrible situation that has bad implications for everybody.
BBC Correspondent: An estimated 20,000 people joined the march as it wound its way through west London. They were simply here to show that they cared. (BBC1 main News, 10 January 2009)

The journalist contrasts such good intentions with the violent actions of a few demonstrators:

The organisers had appealed for restraint; there were some who didn't listen. In the packed streets of west London, they smashed windows and turned their anger on police lines. (BBC1 main News, 10 January 2009)

Such violence can then dominate coverage and a central focus becomes the conduct of the demonstrators themselves. Clashes or 'confrontations' can very rapidly become the news angle and the point of the demonstration recedes ever further:

Newscaster: Well here several thousand people are marching in London in support of the Palestinians. The largely peaceful demonstration stopped at the Israeli embassy, where a small number of demonstrators have been clashing with police in the last hour. Let's get the very latest from our correspondent.
BBC Correspondent: Well there is indeed a stand-off here with police; you can see behind me mounted police, police on foot in riot gear trying to clear the road. There have been a number of incidents of damage on the far side of the road, just across the road there, a smashed window of a Starbucks store, a crash barrier was thrown through that earlier. Around 15,000 people, we don't know the exact numbers of the demonstration. The Stop

the War Coalition asking for peaceful protest, marshalling this affair very carefully, they hoped this wouldn't happen. I think one should stress that it is a minority and the number of arrests this afternoon given the numbers has been very, very low. This is a very difficult situation for police, there's not really anywhere for this crowd to go and I could see this continuing for a little while yet until they can disperse. But at the moment a very tense situation, a changing mood to what we've seen throughout the afternoon. (BBC1 early evening News, 10 January 2009)

The media are drawn to violence and disruption, and their response is so predictable that in practice it would be possible for a small group to reorient the news for their own purposes. For example, a demonstration of 30,000 people may be organised to promote or publicise a particular cause. A group of 50 people who disagree with it have then only to form themselves into a small cohort who are noisy and throw bricks at an embassy or the premises of a global coffee chain. They will then capture much of the media coverage, irrespective of what the rest of the 30,000 people think. We are not pointing to particular cases where this has occurred, but those who produce media coverage should be aware of how easily their own news values can produce an absence of rational debate.

Without explanation it is difficult for audiences to understand the origins and causes of conflicts. News journalism by itself provides very little of such analysis. Our study shows that the Israelis reacted to this by supplying the media with clear accounts of the reasons for the conflict, who was to blame and the negative motivations of their opponents. The success of their public relations campaign is evident. But the very existence of such an extensive operation should have triggered a response from journalists to make sure that the views of both sides were heard. This is especially so in a situation where there were physical limits being put on the movement of journalists by Israel. Actually these limits should have made little difference in terms of the featuring of key explanations, since to show the rationales of both sides does not require access to Gaza. It is not difficult to explain the Hamas/Palestinian case. At the heart of the conflict, from the Palestinian perspective, is their perception of themselves as a people who were forced from their homes and land when Israel was created and now live under military and economic subjugation which they are trying to throw off. These ideas are not hard to grasp and they do not take long to say. The news found time to explain and feature the Israeli case on the causes of the conflict in hundreds of lines of text. Yet the Palestinian view, where it exists, is more likely to occur in fragments and one-off lines. The dots are simply not joined up by journalists to offer a consistent account of Palestinian rationales or motivation.

It is not our role here to defend Hamas and the Palestinians. We are well aware that Hamas has been accused of war crimes and violations of international law. But so too has Israel and it is not the job of academics or television journalists to promote one side or the other. For journalists the main concern should be to report what happens, to explain why and to indicate the perspectives of the different parties in the conflict. If they do not do this, then the consequences on public understanding can be very powerful and one role of our research is to demonstrate such impacts where they occur. Thus far, we have shown the dominance of the Israeli perspective in the presentation of the origins and causes of the conflict and the motivations and rationales of those involved. We can now move to news coverage of casualties, which is an important area and one in which there is much more criticism and scrutiny of the Israeli action.

COVERAGE OF ISRAELI AND PALESTINIAN CASUALTIES

One of the key points to emerge from this part of our study is that media coverage cannot be properly understood in terms of a crude notion of bias. The patterns of meaning in news reports are complex and should not be explained with the simplistic assertion that the journalists are in favour of one side rather than the other. We have seen many criticisms featured of Hamas and the Palestinians. But there are a number of areas in which the conduct of Israel and occasionally the West are also criticised. A BBC correspondent makes the point that the Western politicians involved in the peace process 'have move or less ignored Gaza, they've supported the blockade and the international isolation of Hamas' (BBC1 early evening News, 31 December 2008). It was also suggested that the Israeli action would have the effect of increasing hatred and extremism in the region. This view was expressed very clearly in an interview with the leader of Syria (BBC1 early evening News, 14 January 2009). There are additional explanations given of Israel's motives, such as that it wished to 'restore the deterrent power' of its army (BBC1 early evening News, 29 December 2008). These references are relatively sparse, but in the area of harm to civilians the conduct of both sides is subject to more sustained criticism. The coverage of casualties is very extensive. On the BBC, there are just over 300 lines devoted to those of the Palestinians, and on ITV the figure is over 450. For the BBC this represents about five times the amount given to Israeli casualties and for ITV over seven times. But since the number killed on the Palestinian side was around 100 times that of the Israelis, the amount of coverage given is not proportional to the harm inflicted. In these terms it can be seen that there is a disproportionate representation of Israeli casualties. Also, as we have seen above, the news on both BBC and ITV explores extensively the effect of the rockets on Israeli civilians. But there is also a very intense and critical focus on the effects of Israel's attack on the population of Gaza. The issue of civilian casualties and their inevitability in such an operation is raised very early in the news. In this example a report on the killing of five sisters from a Palestinian family is followed by an Israeli claim about the avoidance of civilian casualties. This however is then effectively dismissed by the journalist, citing the UN:

> *BBC Correspondent*: Mourners braved Gaza's deadly streets to bury five sisters from (this) family. They were killed by an Israeli attack while they were sleeping last night. Israel talks about pinpoint strikes avoiding civilians, but the UN said this is what happens when massive force is used in Gaza's overcrowded densely packed refugee camps. (BBC1 early evening News, 29 December 2008)

And on ITV, an Israeli statement that casualties are exaggerated is immediately undermined by a direct statement from the journalist:

> *ITV Correspondent*: An Israeli government minister has accused the Palestinians of exaggerating the number of their civilian casualties, but at Gaza's main hospital wounded civilians are coming in thick and fast. (ITV early evening News, 1 January 2009)

The journalist then goes on to criticise video evidence supplied by Israel:

> *ITV Correspondent*: Israel wants to show that the air strikes are surgical. Earlier this week it released this video of what it said were Hamas militants and a truck load of rockets being destroyed. Eight people died but there is now evidence that they may have been civilians and that the bombing may have been

a terrible mistake. (A witness) says that the truck was moving oxygen cylinders from his workshop and the dead were all his relatives. (ITV early evening News, 1 January 2009)

This is followed by an Israeli statement that Hamas is attempting to manipulate the media. It is interesting that the word 'mistake' is used in relation to Israeli actions, but this later falls out of use as the tone of criticism hardens, in relation to the deaths of civilians in the conflict. On 8 January, ITV headlines show the criticisms made by the UN and the Red Cross, and the accusation that Israel is breaching international law:

ITV Correspondent: I'm on the Israeli border with Gaza as aid agencies condemn Israel's onslaught. The UN has suspended all operations here after the death of one of its workers. And the normally neutral International Red Cross says it has found starving children surrounded by corpses and accuses Israel of breaching international law. (ITV early evening News, 8 January 2009)

This story is developed by interviewing a representative of the Red Cross, who explains the breach of law, followed by a graphic account of the events:

This three-year-old boy is one of the survivors of that attack, which killed at least twelve members of his family. Near him in hospital, (were) his cousins. According to the Red Cross, one of the teams found these children starving and too weak to stand amid the bodies of their dead relatives in a ruined house. Israeli soldiers nearby have done nothing to help them. (The boy) remembers he was at kindergarten when the Israelis started shooting and he went back home. But back at home, according to his aunt, there was carnage. (ITV early evening News, 8 January 2009)

This is followed by an interview with the children's aunt:

Children's aunt (translation): As we were stepping out on the doorstep, the rockets came down on us like rain. The first shell killed one of the men.

The journalist notes that the district has come under fierce Israeli attack, but it is a Hamas stronghold and that the 'Israelis have reportedly used hard tactics to protect their own soldiers'. There is then a further description of the events in which the term 'house of horror' is used and the criticisms made by the Red Cross are repeated:

> *ITV Correspondent*: The family's home was hit by shells which killed 30 people and left the survivors in what has been called a house of horror. Israeli soldiers prevented ambulances from reaching the area. This, says the Red Cross, was unacceptable conduct. (ITV early evening News, 8 January 2009)

There is a statement included from Israel saying that their army works with aid organisations to give civilian assistance and that serious allegations will be investigated. But there follows immediately a further potential criticism raised by the journalist:

> In spite of the mounting toll of civilian casualties, Israel is still firing heavy guns into Gaza. (ITV early evening News, 8 January 2009)

In other coverage there are interviews with medical personnel in hospitals, who criticise in the strongest language. A Norwegian doctor, for example, comments on the death of two boys:

> These injuries are not survivable injuries, *this is murder*, this is a child. (BBC1 early evening News, 2 January 2009 – our italics)

Another interviewer describes the effects of white phosphorous:

> *BBC Correspondent*: The local hospital here is full of civilian casualties. Most have glass wounds but today we met (this patient), his body blistered by phosphorous which doctors are unable to control.
> *Doctor*: That kind of burn, progressive tissue damage. Even after the burn occurs its damage continues.
> *BBC Journalist*: So it is eating his flesh?
> *Doctor*: Yes it is eating his flesh up.
> *BBC Journalist*: By day the dead are brought to the mortuary, they queue for the bodies. The youngest overcome with grief, sons who have lost fathers. (BBC1 early evening News, 17 January 2009)

The words 'horror' and 'terror' are used in headlines about Israeli actions:

> *Newscaster*: Inside Gaza, an eyewitness account of the terror of the bombings from the heart of the conflict. (ITV main News headline, 16 January 2009)

> *Newscaster*: Horror on the streets of Gaza. At least 40 people die as schools come under attack. The UN-controlled buildings were sheltering civilians taking refuge from the Israeli assault. Tonight no sanctuary in Gaza, dozens were killed in the very place they were supposed to find safety. (ITV early evening News headline, 6 January 2009)

After another attack on a UN school, the UN refugee agency in Gaza is reported as calling for a war crimes investigation (BBC1 early evening News, 17 January 2009). There is a substantial body of critical commentary on these news programmes (over 240 lines on the BBC and over 300 on ITV). Israel replies to these with a series of specific arguments, saying for example that buildings were being used by terrorists or that Hamas is hiding amongst civilians. These run in conjunction with the comments on rockets, the need for security and other explanations which we discussed above.

There are two important points to make here about the coverage of civilian casualties. The first is that journalists are very critical and quite outspoken in relation to these, and this level of criticism certainly extends to Israel's actions in the attack on Gaza. The second point is that when these criticisms appear, they are normally accompanied by defences of Israel and/or the Israeli account of the causes of the conflict. The following example illustrates this juxtaposition. The BBC correspondent is initially quite dismissive of the Israeli statement that they are trying not to hurt civilians:

> *BBC Correspondent*: The message from Israel is that it is interested in a ceasefire but not yet. That means no respite for Gaza civilians. Israel says it tries not to hurt them and says it is the fault of Hamas. *Try telling that to the people in Gaza's overwhelmed hospitals.* This is what happens when a modern army uses heavy weapons in a place packed with young families. (BBC1 main News, 5 January 2009 – our italics)

There is a description of a packed hospital with doctors describing patients dying as they wait for surgery. But this is then followed by an extensive exposition of the Israeli rationale, and their arguments on the need to protect their people:

> *BBC Correspondent*: Israel wants to keep on fighting until it has destroyed Hamas' capacity to hit its soldiers and civilians. It says any ceasefire must include a way for Hamas to stop from re-arming itself. That's the reason why Israel has also been bombing the tunnels that run between Egypt and Gaza. Hamas rockets are still hitting Israel. Israel argues that any country in the world would do what it's doing to protect its people. (BBC1 main News, 5 January 2009)

There is then an interview with Tzipi Livni, the Israeli Foreign Minister. The message on the news overall is that it is the Palestinians in Gaza who start the problem, that it is they who need to be disarmed, and that the Israelis respond but with terrible consequences for civilians. Because the Israeli account of cause is not challenged, the focus of criticism is on the manner in which the Israelis have conducted their 'response'. So an argument develops into whether it is 'disproportionate' or 'excessive'. Thus, on 29 December, the BBC reports a UN statement:

> *Newscaster*: A war to the bitter end, the Israelis insist they are justified in attacking the Gaza Strip, but after a third day of action the UN says the Israeli response is excessive and calls for a ceasefire. (BBC1 main News headline, 29 December 2008)

In another example, an ITV correspondent, while interviewing Tony Blair, asked if he condemns 'Israel's disproportionate use of force' (ITV early evening News, 6 January 2009). The Israeli arguments are couched within these assumptions. Their reply to accusations on this is that they have no alternative:

> *BBC Correspondent*: Israel says it has no alternative.
> *Shimon Peres, Israeli President*: No country on earth would take 80–90 missiles a day. Some people are talking about it being proportionate, what is proportion? Thirty missiles instead of 80 missiles? (BBC1 main News, 4 January 2009)

Shimon Peres is able to argue this way in a context in which his account of cause is not being challenged with the view that it was the Israelis who broke the ceasefire and that the rockets could have been stopped by lifting the blockade. When journalists present the story, in effect they balance the Israeli account of the reasons for their attack on the one hand with its consequences for Palestinian civilians on the other. The images of the latter are indeed terrible, but they are explained as being the result of a conflict which the Palestinians are shown as having started. This, as we will see, can have profound consequences on audience understanding.

7
Audience Understanding of the Israeli-Palestinian Conflict and the Gaza Attack 2008/09

SAMPLE AND METHOD

This chapter is based on new audience research which we have conducted since the publication of the first edition of this book. For that, we had questioned two large groups of young people in higher education in 2001 and 2002, and undertaken a series of focus groups. The results are reproduced above in Chapter 3. For the new research we continued to question similar groups of young people in subsequent years, in 2004, 2005, 2008, 2009 and 2010. Each year, the sample was new, but they were all as before, aged between 17 and 23, and in higher education. The total number in these new samples was 641. Our purpose in this was to track possible changes in belief and understanding of the conflict over an extended time period. We asked the same questions in 2004–09 as we had done in 2001 and 2002. We reproduce them here:

1. What comes to your mind when you hear the words 'Israeli-Palestine conflict'?
2a. Source?
2b. What additional sources have you used?
3. Who occupy the occupied territories?
4. What nationality are the settlers?
5. Which side has had the most casualties? Is it a lot more Israelis, a few more Israelis, about the same for each side, a few more Palestinians, or a lot more Palestinians?
6. Where did the Palestinian refugees come from? How did they become refugees?
7. TV news has shown pictures of the Palestinians burning the American flag – why would Palestinians do this?

In 2008–09 we asked an additional question to examine understanding of the occupation. In 2006 the BBC had published a report, commissioned by its own Board of Governors, into the impartiality of its coverage. As we noted above, one conclusion of this had been that 'there was little reporting of the difficulties facing Palestinians in their daily lives' and of 'the disparity in the Israeli and Palestinian experience, reflecting the fact that one side is in control and the other lives under occupation' (Thomas, 2006: 6–7 cited above). To investigate audience beliefs on this we asked in 2008 and 2009 an additional question on curfews imposed by the Israelis in the occupied territories. These had attracted criticism from human rights groups because of their impact on the economy and the daily lives of people. Palestinians had been confined to their houses for very extended time periods and allowed out for only a few hours a week to get food (B'Tselem, 2002). In 2008, the *Guardian* carried a detailed commentary about the imposition of a curfew following demonstrations against the Israelis' 'separation wall':

> After four days, the village of Nilin is not a pretty sight. Torched cars lie strewn on the sides of the road, bedroom windows sport gaping bullet holes, and debris is scattered the length and breadth of the town … 'look what they did to me!' screamed an elderly grandmother, hoisting up her robes to display the raw wounds inflicted by soldiers who had thrown her against a stone wall during a raid … This psychological trauma is just as bad, with parents talking of children terrified to sleep in their family homes convinced that the soldiers will come back … the fact that the army had to resort to imposing a curfew demonstrates that they are succeeding in disrupting and delaying the day-to-day construction of the barrier. (Freedman, 2008)

The additional question which we asked was:

8. Were you aware that Palestinians could be subject to strict curfews?

The remaining questions were asked in context of the attack on Gaza between December 2008 and January 2009. The questions were put in 2009 to a group of 128 young people in higher education who answered them in addition to questions 1–8, as above. We recruited six focus groups to whom the new questions on Gaza were addressed for purposes of discussion. We also conducted some individual interviews to follow up specific points. There were an average of six to seven people in each focus group (total 40). The composition of five of the groups was of the same age and background as the main sample (i.e. 17–23 and in higher education) plus a further group of seven people aged 25–45 who were in work. This part of the research is qualitative. The intention is not to make exact generalisations across whole populations. Our purpose is rather to analyse the processes by which individuals make judgements when for example they view graphic images of casualties. We were interested in how audiences allocated responsibility and blame between the two sides and whether the viewing of such images was a central determinant, or if there were other mediating factors which conditioned audience reaction. How, for example, might it be possible that judgements about responsibility could move away from the side that was actually doing the killing? The focus groups were useful in that they helped us to understand the judgements that had underpinned the responses given in the larger samples.

The first three of the new questions related to knowledge of specific events in the period before the attack on Gaza. A point which the Israelis and their supporters have often stressed is that Israel withdrew its settlers from Gaza in 2005 and this has been presented as a move towards peace. But as the Israeli historian Avi Shlaim (2009) has pointed out, although 8,000 people had been withdrawn from Gaza in the following year 12,000 Israelis settled in the occupied West Bank.

So, for questions 9 and 10 we asked how many people knew that each of these movements had taken place. In 2006, Hamas had emerged as the winner in the Palestinian elections. For question 11, we asked how many people knew this. We have found in our research that knowledge of such historic events can have important effects on audience understanding and the report for the BBC Governors had specifically pointed to 'an absence of historical background' as a problem in news coverage (Thomas, 2006: 6).

Television news tends to focus on specific events such as a bombing or an explosion, but beliefs about the precursors of such moments and the history of such action which leads to them can be decisive in how they are interpreted. So would, for example, the showing of large numbers of Palestinian casualties lead to a negative judgement of Israeli actions or would such judgements be tempered by beliefs about the reasons for the conflict and how the violence was initiated? To examine this we asked for question number 12:

12. In the Gaza conflict many pictures were shown of civilians, women and children killed in Gaza. When you see these, whose fault do you think it is?

This question raised the key issue of how audiences understood the underlying reasons for violence and how it was initiated. One dimension of this was who had broken the ceasefire which had been in place between June and December 2008. We asked this as question 13. It was apparent as we processed the replies to this question and discussed it in focus groups that there was some confusion over how the ceasefire had ended. To investigate this further we then asked another sample of 108 people in 2010, two specific questions on the issue. They were again young people in higher education, aged 17–23. The questions were:

14. Did you think the cause (for the breakdown of the ceasefire) was rockets at Israel?
15. Did you know that Israel had attacked and killed six Palestinians in November 2008?

Finally, there were also issues raised in the focus groups relating to the numbers of casualties in the Gaza conflict and the conditions of people living in Gaza under the Israeli siege. We will discuss the responses to these below.

RESULTS

The first of the questions we asked related to memories and what came to people's minds when they heard the words 'Israeli-Palestinian conflict'. In our new samples, as before, the TV news was the key source of these. The later samples from 2004–09 also showed the same emphasis on images of violence, war and conflict. But there were some changes, which show the power of media to highlight specific aspects of the conflict. For example, 'suicide bombing' had been the first thing that came to mind for 24 per cent of the young British people in 2002. By 2004 and 2005, this had fallen to 9 per cent and by 2008 and 2009 to 1 per cent. As we saw in our first study, the media coverage of such killings had led some audience members to believe that Israel had the most casualties. But by the time of the Gaza attack in December 2008 to January 2009, the focus of media coverage was more clearly on Palestinian casualties. The number who believed that there were 'a lot more

Palestinian casualties' moves from 29 per cent in 2004 to 48 per cent in 2009. The data for this was collected just after the attack on Gaza. But the responses also show that the number of people with knowledge of issues underlying the conflict remains very low. Only about one-third of the sample know that it is the Israelis who are occupying the occupied territories and these are students studying social science in higher education. There is little difference between 2004 (31 per cent) and 2009 (34 per cent) with a dip in 2008 (22 per cent). Only one-fifth know both that the Israelis occupy the occupied territories and that the settlers are Israeli. Less than 10 per cent relate the existence of Palestinian refugees to the loss of homes on the formation of Israel. The perception that Palestinians are critical of America because it gives 'military and monetary' support to Israel, remains relatively unchanged from 2002.

We also asked a question about Palestinians being subject to curfews. This was in the context of the criticism that had been made of news coverage, that it did not adequately show the nature of the military occupation by Israel and 'the difficulties faced by Palestinians in their daily lives' (Thomas, 2006: 6–7). In our sample, there was very little knowledge that strict curfews could exist. In 2009 just 24 per cent knew this and in 2008 the figure was 19 per cent. We discussed this issue in the focus groups and it was apparent that even where people said that they knew, there could still be a very vague understanding of what they signified. Some, for example, saw curfews as positive, with connotations of the Second World War in Britain. As one put it:

> When I think of curfews, I think of the Second World War, when you were not allowed to go out at night time. You had to keep your lights off and stuff like that. (Student 2009)

Another thought they were about stopping robberies:

> I knew there were curfews but thought it meant people had to be home by a certain time of night because of robbing or things like that. (Student 2009)

Still another mixed the idea of control with protecting the civilian population:

> The purpose of curfews was; to keep people under control or stop civilians getting in the way of bombs maybe. I've no idea. (Student 2009)

So although the word 'curfew' is sometimes used in relation to the conflict, the implications of it from the point of view of the Palestinian side may not be understood. This is because journalists have often avoided the task of explaining what the occupation actually means to the Palestinians and how it impacts on their lives.

At the time of the Gaza attack, there had been a number of protests and demonstrations in British universities. Some group members suggested that these were counterproductive as they apparently did not like being shouted at by people chanting slogans. But others said that the issue of the conflict had been raised and that people were discussing it. So the protests were potentially a source of new knowledge. In the groups, it was interesting to note how attitudes sometimes changed as the discussion progressed and included new information on, for example, the occupation and curfews. One group began with a participant giving a familiar view of why the conflict continued – that it is somehow just what people have got used to doing. As we noted in our first study, news coverage which does not explain underlying causes can foster the view that the conflicting sides are simply 'bad neighbours' or are involved in an endless series of tit for tat attacks. As this participant expressed:

> They are fighting because that's what their grandfathers did, but they will carry on fighting *even if they are equal*, because they will still carry on fighting because that's what their ancestors did and that's what they know how to do. (Student 2009 – our italics)

There is little sense here that the two sides are unequal and that one is controlling the other through military rule. But as new information emerges in the group on this, some attitudes begin to alter. The above participant is asked whether knowledge of curfews and how strict they could be, made any difference:

> *Participant 1*: A little yeah. If I had to live through that I would fight back and would be probably pretty pissed off as well.

This stimulates comments from other group members:

> *Participant 3*: I don't think the extent of input ... it is not usually publicised. It's not what's on the front page. Usually you are hearing about specific incidents, attacks and bombings.
> *Participant 2*: I think if you heard that, you would have sort of a different perspective. Maybe you would know what's going on,

we would better know. I think what's portrayed in the news is not accurate enough. I don't have a good perspective of what's going on. If you would hear that, you would look at it in a different light.

Participant 4: I think now I can understand why the protestors and now I see why they felt so strongly about it because I didn't realise how bad it was at all.

Moderator: So it would definitely make a difference to hear more about what?

Participant 4: About how awful the conditions are for the people like the curfews and things like that. I just didn't know that. I think there will be a lot of people that are just completely oblivious to it, they just don't have a clue of what's going on. (Student group 5, 2009)

The absence of information which can explain Palestinian responses and actions can affect public belief and attitudes to the conflict. But as we have seen, there is no shortage of information in the news which explains Israeli perspectives and which functions to legitimise their actions.

QUESTIONS AND REPLIES ON THE GAZA ATTACK

The remaining questions related specifically to the attack between December 2008 and January 2009. We asked first about the history of Gaza in the period leading up to this. For question 9 we asked respondents if they knew that in 2005, Israel had withdrawn 8,000 people from Gaza? Question 10 asked if they knew that in the following year another 12,000 had moved to the West Bank? Most did not know about either of these movements but it is interesting that more than twice as many knew of the first (25 per cent), than of the second (10 per cent). Question 11 showed that again only a minority (30 per cent) knew that Hamas had been elected to be the majority group in the Palestinian Parliament. The issue was discussed in the focus groups and some expressed surprise that they had not heard this reported on television:

Participant 1: I do not know what 'Hamas' stand for but just that they are always involved in conflicts. I hear of this mainly on the TV news but it is not clear to me what the whole story is.

Participant 2: Images of carnage and suicide bombings spring to mind when Hamas is mentioned on the news ...

Participant 4: Is it maybe because maybe the UK are more sympathetic to Israel, as they seem to be in cahoots with the West? *Participant 2*: Most people do not recognise Hamas are elected. *Participant 5*: I did not know until the recent conflict but had to read it in a book. It was not on any of the news I watched. *Participant 1*: I watched the news quite a bit during the recent conflict and never once heard a report mention Hamas were democratically elected. I had the impression they were a terrorist group from watching on the BBC. *Participant 6*: Me too. I cannot believe they are elected. I feel ignorant for not knowing that. (In-work group, 2009)

The message that Hamas were 'terrorists' had come across very clearly to some. As another participant, a student, put it:

From what I've seen in headlines, Hamas was like a terrorist group. As far as I knew, it was just like they changed the word Taliban for Hamas and it was only last week that I found out that Hamas had been democratically elected. It does change your perspective on it. (Student 2009)

There is no mention in any of these groups of the alternative perspective that Hamas might be seen as pragmatic, or of offers which they have made which might lead to peace or a reduction of conflict. This brings us to the last of the questions which relate to the issue of who is seen as responsible for the onset of violence in December 2009, and who is blamed when people see the tragic images of the conflict. Question 12 asked:

In the Gaza conflict many pictures were shown of civilians, women and children killed in Gaza. When you see these, whose fault do you think it is?

In answering this, 29 per cent blamed Israel and 11 per cent, Hamas and the Palestinians. The majority, 52 per cent, blamed both equally. It should be remembered that these figures are based on the views of students studying social science, just after the attack on Gaza, at a time when university campuses featured a great deal of protest against the Israeli actions. This might have been expected to have increased support for Palestinians, yet the figures show that when looking at the images, 63 per cent either blame the Palestinians or blame both sides equally. Our next task was to unpack these beliefs and to understand how they were constituted. A key issue is the apparent success of the Israelis in establishing a link between the breaking down or ending of the ceasefire and the firing of rockets by Palestinians. Question 13 asked:

> Before the conflict of December 2008 to January 2009, there was a ceasefire. Who broke it?

In answering this 44 per cent stated that it was Hamas and the Palestinians, while 36 per cent replied that it was Israel. The following year, in 2010, we asked more specific questions to another group of over 100 students. They were asked how many believed the ceasefire had been broken because of rockets fired at Israel and how many had heard of the Israeli attack and the killing of six Palestinians in November 2008. Of 104 replies, 45 per cent answered yes to the first while the figure for the second was just 20 per cent. We explored this in the focus groups and again found a strong current of belief relating the onset of violence in December 2008 to rocket fire:

> I was pretty sure that it was the Palestinians who started the conflict with the rocket attacks because I've seen it on TV. Every report on TV I seem to remember it being that the Israelis were responding to the Palestinian rocket attacks and not so much the other way around. (Student 2009)

> I thought the rockets were catalytic for their thing most recently. (Student 2009)

And in still another group, these responses were given when asked who broke the ceasefire:

> *Participant 4*: Hamas as they fired missiles.
> *Participant 3*: Yeah, I thought that too as Hamas fired missiles into an Israeli village.
> *Participant 2*: I did that too.
> *Participant 6*: Hamas rocket attacks.
> *Participant 1*: I wrote that too. (Student group 4, 2009)

And in the group of those in full-time work, when asked about the ceasefire:

> *Participant 2*: Wasn't it Hamas that broke the ceasefire?
> *Participant 3*: I think so, I think it was Hamas.

Participant 4: Me too, I think it was a suicide bomb.
Participant 5: I think it was Hamas as I seen on the news that Hamas were firing rocket launchers. (In-work group 6, 2009)

Since the Palestinians are seen as initiating the violence, it follows that Israel is 'retaliating' or 'responding'. This is very much the pattern which we identified in news coverage and on which we wrote in the first edition of this volume. We can see in the following comment from a respondent, how the belief that the Palestinians have a grievance is tempered by the assumption that they are somehow starting the violence, to which the Israelis 'retaliate':

I definitely think that the Palestinians have a grievance against Israel. They do have a right because of what Israel has done to try to break free from that oppression so I can understand why they're doing that but then again if you're asking who is to blame for the casualties exclusively, then people firing rockets maybe have to take part of the blame for that because *if they hadn't fired the rockets then maybe Israel maybe wouldn't have retaliated* and went in so heavy handed. (Student 2009 – our italics)

The logic of this, as we noted in our analysis of news content, leads to the argument on whether the Israeli 'response' was 'disproportionate'. The discussion in the following group show very clearly the success of the Israelis in establishing key elements of their perspective and the effect of these being relayed uncritically in media accounts. There are a sequence of assumptions which can become part of commonly held beliefs about responsibility. These are that the Palestinians have started the violence through rocket fire, it is Hamas that is inflexible and wants to destroy Israel, and therefore 'Hamas cannot blame Israel for Palestinian casualties':

Moderator: Who was to blame for the current conflict?
Participant 1: Hamas weren't willing to renew the ceasefire as they were firing rockets and *didn't want to compromise* as they wanted to destroy the state of Israel but they would effectively need to compromise. But I also think it's *hard to get over the scale of destruction of the retaliation*.
Moderator: You think Israel retaliated to Hamas?
Participant 1: Yeah but I think it's difficult to separate. Israel clearly are separated this occasion, *as they were retaliating*.

Participant 2: The images shown just made me feel sad, but I didn't feel anything in particular about cause or blame.

Moderator: Had you heard about rockets being fired into Israel?

Participant 3: Yeah, but I just thought *they can't have expected Israel to have retaliated any other way*. The scale of Israel's retaliation was too much though, it seems like Israel are trying to destroy the people, it seems to have went beyond political.

Participant 4: Yeah, if Hamas had fired rockets at a school then *they must expect Israel to respond*. So *Hamas cannot blame Israel for Palestinian casualties as they are only retaliating* to what they started.

Participant 5: I find it hard to remove this context from the historical context in which I would blame Israel, but in this conflict they are both to blame. Hamas still wants to destroy the Israeli state, so it is more complex now and more compromise is needed to achieve a goal of securing a Palestinian state.

Participant 6: *Israel's responses are massively disproportionate*. (Student group 4, 2009 – our italics)

There is a sense amongst some that the disparity between the power of each side is 'unfair'. But what is missing from most of this audience is the Palestinian perspective, that, for example Palestinians have been subject to continuous killings even during the ceasefire. The Israeli historian Avi Shlaim, has noted that in the three years after the withdrawal from Gaza, eleven Israelis were killed by rocket fire. But he goes on to comment that 'in 2005–7 alone, the IDF killed 1,290 Palestinians including 222 children' (Shlaim, 2009: 4). We asked all the members of the focus groups if they had heard these figures and were aware of the scale and disparity of the killing. Less than a quarter said that they were. In these groups, no one recalled or mentioned the view that Israel could have had a ceasefire if it lifted the blockade. Knowledge of the siege was mostly very limited. We read to the groups the description of the conditions under which Palestinians lived, which had been given by Sarah Teather, including the reference to 'lakes of sewage' (quoted in Chapter 6). Again, less than one-quarter of those in the groups knew of this. The key point is that the gaps in audience knowledge very closely parallel the absences in news reporting. On the other hand, many elements of what is assumed to be true are exactly the points which were highlighted in Israeli public relations and reported uncritically on the news. Crucially, this can affect how audiences apportion blame and responsibility and also influence how the images of civilian casualties were interpreted. One participant who was in full-time work expressed this as follows:

> When I saw the pictures of the dead children, it was dreadful, I was in tears but it didn't make me feel that the Palestinians and Hamas were right … I think the Palestinians haven't taken the chance to work towards a peaceful solution. Hamas were offered the chance to sit down and talk and they haven't taken it and they called an end to the last ceasefire. (In work 2009)

This participant cited BBC Radio 4 as the key source of information on these issues and was very surprised to hear the view that the rockets could have been stopped by lifting the siege. The key point to be made here is that the ability to control understanding of relations of cause and effect as well the history of events, gives the power to influence how new actions will be understood. This can ameliorate audience perceptions of even the grimmest outcomes and reduce the allocation of blame to those who perpetrate them.

8
Attack on the Gaza Flotilla, 2010

As we were finishing the research for this book in May 2010, an Israeli attack took place on a flotilla trying to break the siege of Gaza. The media coverage of this assault had some features in common with that of the attack on Gaza, which we have described in the previous chapter. We therefore decided to include some comments on it here. We took a sample of early evening and main news bulletins from BBC1 and ITV plus two lunchtime (BBC and ITV) bulletins on the first day from 31 May until 6 June 2010, which featured the news story (eleven on the BBC, and seven on the ITV news). We also examined news programmes from Channel 4 plus newspaper reports between the same dates, for purposes of comparison. Using the same method as above, we analysed the information and perspectives which were present or absent. There are three main areas on which we will comment. First, the criticisms which were made of Israel and the explanations which were offered relating to the responsibility for the outbreak of violence and also for the deaths of nine activists. Second, the presentation of the siege of Gaza; and, third, how this was related to the legitimacy and rationales for action of each side. In this case, as with the attack on Gaza, there were very substantial criticisms made of the Israeli action. The news breaks on the 31 May 2010 and ITV reports it as follows:

> *Headline*: At least ten people are killed as Israeli commandos storm an aid ship bound for Gaza. (ITV lunchtime News, 31 May 2010)

There are reports of widespread criticism of the action with Israel said to be guilty of 'state terrorism':

> *Journalist*: The Turkish Prime Minister said Israel was guilty of state terrorism. (BBC1 late News, 31 May 2010)

Journalist: News of the raid sparked angry protests across the Middle East with Turkey's leaders calling it state terrorism. (ITV late News, 31 May 2010)

The UN Security Council is said to be meeting in emergency session and the breadth of the criticism and protest is made clear:

Journalist: Turkey, Israel's biggest Muslim ally, has had enough, the US is furious. (ITV main News, 1 June 2010)

Journalist: Outrage on the streets as governments around the world lined up to demand explanations from Israel. These were the scenes in the Middle East. There were angry protests across Europe too, this was Paris this afternoon and this was central London, as the British government joined a growing chorus of condemnation deploring the loss of life. (BBC1 late News, 31 May 2010)

The implications for the peace process are also raised and the Palestinian president is quoted as saying how Palestinians routinely face state terrorism:

Journalist: Peace negotiations with the normally conciliatory Palestinian President, Mahmoud Abbas, are looking even more difficult. He's called the raid a massacre and a war crime. Palestinians, he said in Bethlehem, face state terrorism from Israel every day. (BBC1 main News, 2 June 2010)

The Israeli response to the criticism was, as one journalist put it, that their 'public relations operation has gone into overdrive trying to explain what happened' (ITV main News, 31 May 2010). The essence of the Israeli strategy was to close down communications from the flotilla, to take hundreds of peace activists and hold them incommunicado in Israel and then to issue their own edited footage of what had happened, complete with captions to direct audience understanding. These captions contained statements such as 'Soldiers being hit with metal rod'. Antony Lerman, writing in the *Guardian* website on 4 June 2010, commented on the success of the Israeli approach:

What the world has been watching since (the attack) is either edited video shot by the Israelis or other videos shot by the activists, confiscated by the Israelis and subsequently edited and made available through Israeli sources. In an operation reminiscent of the first week or so of the Israeli offensive against Gaza in winter 2008–2009, the Israeli PR machine succeeded in getting the major news outlets to focus on its version of events and to use the Israeli authorities' discourse for a crucial 48 hours. (Lerman, 2010)

The Israeli position was that the killings occurred because they were forced to act in self-defence. As Binyamin Netanyahu, the Israeli Prime Minister, put it:

Binyamin Netanyahu: They deliberately attacked the first soldiers who came on the ship. They were mobbed, they were clubbed, they were beaten, stabbed, there was even a report of gunfire, and our soldiers had to defend themselves, defend their lives, or they would have been killed. (BBC1 main News, 31 May 2010)

This account was contested by the activists on the flotilla. They stated that the first attack on the main ship, *Mavi Marmara*, had come from naval boats and an attempted boarding from the side, which had been repelled. Haneen Zuabi, a Palestinian member of the Israeli Knesset, was quoted in the *Guardian* on 3 June 2010:

Zuabi said that naval boats surrounded the *Mavi Marmara* and fired on it before soldiers abseiled aboard from a helicopter. (*Guardian*, 3 June 2010)

The point is reiterated by Hassan Ghani, a British journalist who was also on board the *Mavi Marmara*:

He told how the Israelis had first fired grenades on to the boat as some of its passengers were at morning prayers. And he went on to describe how soldiers first tried to board the vessel from the side, before dropping down on to it from helicopters … 'they began by throwing stun grenades onto the deck of the ship when people were in the middle of morning prayers. Then they began using rubber bullets, they tried to come aboard the ship from the side. People repelled the commandos with water cannons they had set up on the side of the ship. Then the Israelis used helicopters to drop people onto the roof.' (*Independent*, 4 June 2010)

This witness describes how soldiers came down 'with machine guns and tasers and firing rubber bullets'. The Israeli authorities were reported as denying that shots were fired from helicopters (Channel 4 main evening News, 6 June 2010). But a further account from Osama Qashoo, who was also on board, states on Channel 4 News that there were two soldiers on the door of the helicopters, shooting down, while another descended on the rope:

> There are two soldiers on the door of the helicopters who will be shooting down, and the other soldier will be taking the rope and going down. My friend was taking pictures of these soldiers, he was shot like here. He was shot like here, between his eyes. (Channel 4 main evening News, 6 June 2010)

The account given by the activists was that they were reacting to violence which was started by the Israelis. As Osama Qashoo put it, 'the self-defence that we took is basically nothing but self-defence' (Channel 4 main evening News, 6 June 2010). This is an almost mirror opposite of what the Israelis were arguing. We can now look at how ITV and BBC television news responded to these two perspectives.

ITV was fairly circumspect about the Israeli claims. On its lunchtime news on 31 May 2010, as the story was breaking, the two perspectives are reported side by side:

> *Newscaster*: Israel insists its forces were attacked first. Activists say the troops came on board firing. (ITV lunchtime News, 31 May 2010)

By that evening, Israel has released its edited version of events and the news begins with the Israeli defence:

> *Headline*: Israel defends its commando raid on a Gaza aid convoy but expresses regret for the deaths of nine civilians. Israel's prime minister insists his troops were fighting for their lives but the international community has been swift to condemn the strike. Plus, protests in the Middle East and beyond as demonstrators show their anger over the Israeli raid.
> *Newscaster*: Good evening. Israel has responded to a deluge of international anger tonight over the killing of nine activists on an aid convoy to Gaza. The Israeli army has released video which it says proves that their soldiers were forced to defend themselves

after coming under attack as they tried to board the aid ships. (ITV main News, 31 May 2010)

On the following night, the two positions are very clearly juxtaposed, with 'state terror' being put first:

Headline: An act of state terror or an act of self-defence? (ITV early evening News, 1 June 2010)

The Israeli action is referred to as 'its deadly operation' and 'the Israeli army pictures' are described as showing 'how commandos stormed the Turkish ship, and ran into resistance from activists armed with sticks and knives'. The Israeli edited footage is shown and is accompanied by this qualification:

Journalist: The vital minutes when the troops opened fire have not been released and most of the potential witnesses are in Israeli detention. (ITV early evening News, 1 June 2010)

On the main news that night we are told that 'today some protestors disputed Israel's version of events' and they include on this news the testimony of Hasan Nowarah who is reported as having seen 'the start of the assault':

Out of the blue all I could hear was screaming and bullets all over the place and on top of the Turkish ship the helicopters, they are dropping soldiers and all you can see is screaming and fires and bullets. At the same time they started using bombs, sound bombs and tear gas. (ITV main News, 1 June 2010)

Both BBC and ITV news made quite extensive use of the Israeli edited footage. But the BBC news is more problematic since in its description of the events and their sequence, it highlights and at times clearly adopts the Israeli perspective. The lunchtime news does not include the activist statement that troops came on board firing as ITV did in its headline. But the Israeli view that they 'have accused the activists of starting the violence' is clearly put. We hear that those on board dispute it and that it has been called an act of piracy but the sequence of events is not challenged (BBC1 lunchtime News, 31 May 2010). On the early evening news it is reported that 'people on board the stormed vessel say the Israelis fired first' (BBC1, 31 May 2010). But in the main news later that night this statement is left out and the news reporting moves towards clear identification with the Israeli account of events. On the evening of 31 May 2010, this account is given of the commandos abseiling from helicopters, speaking of how each Israeli 'was set upon as he came down the rope':

> *Journalist*: In the hours before dawn, in international waters, the Israeli navy closed in on the ships that were heading for Gaza, issuing a warning:
>
> *Israeli naval officer*: (Voice on film.) The Gaza area coastal region and Gaza harbour are closed to all maritime traffic.
>
> *Journalist*: On the ships the protestors put on their life jackets *and when Israeli naval commando's abseiled down from the helicopters, some of them were waiting. Each man was set upon as he came down the rope.* The Israeli military released these night-vision pictures complete with captions. They didn't expect this kind of resistance. 'Be careful, they're fighting over there,' one of them yells on the radio. (Caption on IDF footage reads: 'Soldiers being hit with metal poles and chairs'.) One of the commandos was thrown off the top deck. (Caption reads: 'Demonstrators throwing soldiers off board'.) Here, protestors seem to be beating someone on the ground. (Caption reads: 'Soldiers being hit with metal rods'.) 'They're finishing him off,' one of the Israelis shouts. It's not clear when they opened fire. The Israelis say their men were under orders to use their weapons only if their lives were in danger. (BBC1 main News, 31 May 2010 – our italics)

There is then a statement from the Israeli prime minister making the point very strongly that the Israeli soldiers were acting in self-defence. The journalist then goes on to contrast the planning of non-violent protest with the 'rough reception' given to the Israelis. There is apparently 'no doubt' about this. The commentary then moves directly into the framework of explanation which we have seen above with the attack on Gaza. The question becomes whether the Israeli 'response' to what was being done to them was 'proportionate':

> *Journalist*: This was planned as a non-violent protest *but there's no doubt that the Israelis had a rough reception.* The question is whether *their deadly response* was in proportion to the dangers they faced. (BBC1 main News, 31 May 2010 – our italics)

The following night, on the early evening news the Israeli perspective is repeated, with further showing of the edited footage and claims that the violence began after the soldiers had abseiled down:

> *Journalist*: (Over IDF edited footage with captions.) Israel released its own dramatic pictures of the raid showing, it says, soldiers under attack. The Israeli government said it was a clear case of self-defence because the commandos were set upon as they were inspecting the ships. (Caption on footage reads: 'Soldiers being hit with metal poles and chairs'.) Israel later released this edited footage of a soldier involved in the raid. He says that every man who abseiled down was jumped upon, beaten and lynched by three or four protestors. (BBC1 early evening News, 1 June 2010)

The journalist reports criticism of Israel but apparently assumes that the sequence of events given by the Israelis is correct:

> *Journalist*: Israel had warned the flotilla of six ships that it would stop it with force if necessary, but the deaths of ten activists *as Israeli commandos dropped from helicopters and later opened fire* has been widely criticised. (BBC1 early evening News, 1 June 2010 – our italics)

In the late BBC news that evening, there is a repetition of the Israeli claims with footage of Binyamin Netanyahu visiting wounded servicemen. One of these describes how Israeli weapons had been turned on them by the protestors. There is also a statement from Ehud Barack, the Israeli defence minister. As with the ITV news, the BBC journalist notes that the Israelis have chosen 'not to show the moment when the commandos opened fire, killing nine people' (BBC1 main News, 1 June 2010). There is also a juxtaposition in the headline for this bulletin, of the two positions:

> *Headline*: The Israelis are accused of carrying out a bloody massacre, but they claim it was self-defence. (BBC1 main News, 1 June 2010)

But there is no attempt here to highlight the criticisms of the Israeli sequence of events or to discuss how the violence is initiated.[1] This continues even as these criticisms become more apparent, when activists are released. We are told for example on 3 June 2010 by a BBC journalist, now in Turkey, that the Israeli version 'that its men opened fire in self-defence is utterly rejected here'. There is a description included from an activist of the killings but again no commentary on how the violence was initiated. Then on 5 June 2010, another Gaza bound aid ship, the *Rachel Corrie*, is reported to have been intercepted. This event was then used by the Israelis to argue that because there was no violence on that occasion, then what had happened before was not their fault. The BBC1 coverage gives an extensive account of this position, noting that 'it's very different from last Monday' and then to illustrate the point, cuts once again to Israeli edited footage which apparently shows protestors holding or firing catapults:

> *Journalist*: (Over IDF footage of the *Rachel Corrie* from above.) From high in the air, an Israeli helicopter spots the *Rachel Corrie* heading for Gaza. Down below the Israeli navy orders the ship to divert. (Caption: 'The captain asks all of the passengers to sit'.) This Israeli military video shows what happens next. (Caption changes to: 'The soldiers board the ship'.) As commandos go aboard the ship the activists sit down, offering no resistance. Moments later the ship is under Israeli control.
> *Shahar Arieli (Israeli Foreign Ministry)*: Soldiers of the IDF boarded the ship in complete agreement and in a peaceful way. That was after several times the ship was notified by the Israeli navy that the equipment can be, that we invite them to dock in Ashdod.
> *Journalist*: (Over IDF edited footage of earlier attack on *Mavi Marmara*.) It's very different from last Monday when commandos from the same unit stormed a Turkish ship in the same waters. (Cuts to colour footage in which a protestor apparently fires a handheld catapult and another is clearly shown holding a catapult.) In the ensuing melee nine activists were shot dead. (BBC1 main News, 5 June 2010)

But by this time, there is a growing commentary pointing to evidence which is critical of the Israeli account. On the same day as the above, the *Guardian* had published the autopsy results on the bodies of those killed earlier in the week. It reported that they were 'peppered with 9mm bullets, many fired at close range'. Five of the people were reported to have been shot either in the back of the head or the back (*Guardian*, 5 June 2010). The BBC programme above did not report this and neither did any other BBC news in our sample. But the main news does find space the following day to report on pictures from a Turkish newspaper, showing Israeli soldiers 'disarmed and beaten':

> *Journalist*: Meanwhile these photographs have been released today by a Turkish newspaper. They show Israeli commandos being disarmed and beaten on board the Turkish ship the *Mavi Marmara* last Monday. These photos will only intensify the dispute over Israel's bloody assault that left nine Turkish activists dead. (BBC1 main News, 6 June 2010)

This contrasts with accounts given elsewhere. Channel 4 News, for example, reported the autopsy results on 5 June 2010. In the same bulletin, a journalist described the attack with the phrase, 'nine Turkish activists were killed when Israeli commandos boarded, guns blazing last Monday' (Channel 4 main News, 5 June 2010). On that first day, Channel 4 had reported that 'pro-Palestinian activists claim the commandos came on board shooting' (Channel 4 main News, 31 May 2010). On the following day they also interviewed Haneen Zoabi, from the Israeli Knesset, who states:

> *Haneen Zoabi*: I saw 14 Israeli ships approaching the *Mavi Marmara* ship and a helicopter. At the same time when they were close to the ship they started shooting at the ship. They started to shoot, maybe not all of them, I saw at least two. They started to shoot before the helicopter approached. (Channel 4 main News, 1 June 2010)

The BBC did feature severe criticisms of Israel including those relating to the killing of the activists and the mistreatment of others. But they did not highlight or often even include accounts of the causes and sequence of the violence which critiqued the Israeli view that its soldiers were acting only in self-defence. In some commentaries, journalists came close to assuming the Israeli perspective. There was a particular problem with the use of the edited footage of the boarding of the *Mavi Marmara*. This was employed very extensively in news coverage and shown ten times across six BBC bulletins (eleven by ITV). Let us imagine a different situation in which a controversial event occurred on the West Bank. Would the TV news routinely employ footage supplied by the Palestinians, with captions saying for example, 'Israeli soldiers shoot unarmed civilians'? Would they do so if the Israelis were denying the validity of the footage or the sequence of events? The use of Israeli edited material in this case is indicative of the legitimacy accorded to them, rather than to Palestinian sources.

In September 2010, the UN Human Rights Council published a report on the attack. This reached a number of significant conclusions. It stated that the Israeli blockade was 'unlawful', it reported that the Israeli forces had used torture and that at least six of the passengers had been subjected to 'extra-legal, arbitrary and summary executions' (for example being shot at close range while lying injured). It also noted that live ammunition was used from the helicopter onto the top deck prior to the descent of the soldiers (United Nations, 2010: 54, 27). The response of the main TV channels to this report was very largely to ignore it. ITV made a twelve-second reference as follows:

> *Journalist*: A UN investigation into an aid flotilla heading to Gaza last May says Israeli forces used 'incredible violence'. Nine people died in the attack. (ITV main News, 22 September 2010)

The BBC lunchtime, early evening and main news did not cover it. On BBC *News 24* there was a one and a half minute piece, which reported that Israel had used 'disproportionate force', had 'violated international law' and displayed 'unacceptable levels of brutality' (22 September 2010). This news has a very small audience compared to the main terrestrial news programmes. A good part of the one and a half minutes is taken up with Israel's response, saying the report is 'biased'. This news does not include the statements on torture or extra-judicial killings, but it does manage to feature a large subtitle across the screen saying 'Stun Grenade Thrown at Soldiers'. As we have indicated above, a typical response from the broadcasters when faced with material which is likely to generate problems is simply to leave it out. But given the extent to which the BBC in particular, had highlighted and endorsed the Israeli view of events in the raid, the exclusion of this alternative account is extraordinary. It is difficult in the face of this to see how the BBC can sustain a claim to be offering balanced reporting.

It should also be said that there was a tone in some of the reporting of the original attack which suggested that the problem in such killings was the diplomatic fallout and that they were a public relations disaster for Israel:

> *Journalist*: Israel was already feeling the diplomatic fallout of the assassination in a Dubai hotel of a Hamas leader, forged British

passports used for the operation. Now the deadly storming of the aid flotilla is being seen both as a political and PR disaster. (BBC1 main News, 31 May 2010)

This contrasts with these comments from an ITV journalist on the same night. They also mention the damage to Israel's reputation but are clear about the tragic nature of the incident and stress the consequences in terms of possible future violence:

Journalist: Israel's public relations operation has gone into overdrive trying to explain what happened. But there's no doubt this is a major and tragic international incident that will damage Israel's reputation and may spark further violent confrontation. (ITV main News, 31 May 2010)

Certainly if the situation were reversed and it was nine Israelis that had been killed, it is unlikely that it would be discussed in terms of the implications for Palestinian public relations. But there were other aspects of this story which opened up more critical accounts, particularly in relation to reporting of the Israeli blockade.

THE BLOCKADE

As we saw in Chapter 6, in the coverage of the attack on Gaza in December 2008 to January 2009, there was very little coverage of the impact of the siege on Palestinians and how it related to their actions. The attack on the flotilla produced some important changes. As one journalist remarked:

A week ago, most people around the world had probably forgotten there was a blockade on Gaza, but tonight it is again headline news. (BBC1 main News, 5 June 2010)

This is a little disingenuous since the news itself has some responsibility for setting such agendas. The Palestinians had clearly not forgotten and there have been many attempts over the previous years to break the blockade and bring support to the inhabitants of Gaza. The news makers decided when such activity was to be on the agenda. It was only when the Israelis attacked, nine activists were killed and there were injuries to both sides that the story is defined as headline news. It is a tragic cost, but it did have the effect of propelling the siege and its effects on the Palestinians into the news.

The attack itself offers the news value of 'drama' and the statements of 'primary definers' such as world politicians again have the effect of amplifying the story. The political landscape momentarily changes, the powerful speak and the news responds to that. One result is that detailed accounts were given suggesting that the siege was irrational and untenable. In this example, a commentary from a journalist is linked to a statement from Hillary Clinton:

> *Journalist*: Gazans face strict limits on what reaches them through the border. It's both an economic squeeze and a political one. A satellite image shows the crossing points into Gaza which were opened three years ago, including one at Rafa controlled by Egypt. But in stages, three Israeli crossings have now been closed completely. So what does Israel allow to reach Gazans? It can seem odd or even arbitrary. Israel refuses to publish lists but an Israeli humanitarian organisation, Gisha, gave these examples last month. Some fresh fruit was allowed in, but canned fruit was banned. By contrast, frozen meat was permitted, but fresh meat prohibited. Cinnamon got through but coriander was stopped. Animal feed was allowed, but not goats or cattle. Most countries back a UN resolution which calls for the blockade to be lifted and tonight Washington increased the pressure.
> *Hillary Clinton*: The situation in Gaza is unsustainable and unacceptable. (BBC1 main News, 1 June 2010)

In the same bulletin another journalist tells us that the UN and many others see the blockade as a 'collective punishment against the people of Gaza'. Many countries, we are told, including Britain, are saying it needs to end. The difficulty is apparently that they know 'the minute that the blockade is lifted, Hamas will declare a huge victory and it will strengthen them' (BBC1 early evening News, 1 June 2010). What is not said in any of this coverage is how the continuing existence of the blockade affects the rationale for Palestinian action and how they see their struggle against Israel and its continuing military occupation. But the news does find space to explain the Israeli rationale for imposing the blockade, such as to stop the firing of rockets and 'arms smuggling':

> *Journalist*: Israel says the flotilla was trying to break a blockade which is in force to prevent arms smuggling to Gaza. (BBC1 main News, 31 May 2010)

Newscaster: (Speaking to journalist in Jerusalem.) I guess we need to remember that Israel always says the reason it has a blockade is because it's trying to prevent attacks from Gaza. (BBC1 main News, 1 June 2010)

Journalist: Gaza, where last year Israel killed 1,700 Palestinians in a brutal assault to stop militants firing rockets. (ITV main News, 1 June 2010)

Journalist: Israel believes it's the only way to prevent repeated attacks by Hamas. (ITV early evening News, 1 June 2010)

There is no mention here of offers of a ceasefire by Hamas and the Palestinians as a way of halting attacks, or the words of Ephraim Halevy of Mossad, that the attacks could have been stopped 'long ago by lifting (the) siege of Gaza' (cited in Chapter 6). We are told why the Israelis want the blockade, but not the Palestinian rationale and why they have been attacking the Israelis. The news does carry criticism of Israel and can express sympathy for the plight of the Palestinian people. But what is missing is the perspective which shows the Palestinians as a people who are trying to get back their homes and land and to actively throw off a military occupation.

9
Conclusions

Our findings in the new research for this volume in some respects echo those of the earlier studies. While the broadcast media give a clear account of the Israeli perspective on this conflict, many journalists and especially in the BBC still find great difficulty in doing the same for the Palestinians. This is in spite of the report, originally commissioned by the BBC Governors, which made clear the weaknesses in the BBC's approach to presenting the history of the conflict and the nature of the military occupation imposed by Israel on the Palestinians. Some might wonder if BBC journalists will ever run out of euphemisms for describing this. In July 2010, it was reported that the Israeli Prime Minister, Netanyahu was to meet President Obama in Washington. Their last meeting had apparently been soured by a dispute over 'building'. On BBC Radio 4 at 6 a.m. we heard:

> *Newscaster*: Their last meeting ended in disagreement over Israeli building in East Jerusalem. (*Today*, BBC Radio 4, 6 a.m., 6 July 2010)

And half an hour later we heard:

> The issue of building in East Jerusalem soured their last meeting. (*Today*, BBC Radio 4, 6.30 a.m., 6 July 2010)

This vague description conveys very little of what is at stake. Actually what the Israelis were doing was putting houses for their own people in a city which they had taken by force. It does not take long to say this. The BBC has no problem in describing Palestinians as using force. For example, in an earlier item on *Today*, at the time of the flotilla attack, a journalist describes how the purpose of the blockade is to undermine Hamas. He notes that 'Hamas forcibly took control of Gaza' (BBC Radio 4, 1 June 2010). There is no mention that they had won the Palestinian elections. Neither is it mentioned that Hamas came to power in circumstances in which the US was allegedly promoting by force the supremacy of its own favoured party, Fatah, that had lost the Palestinian elections. We are not asking for journalists to favour one group or the other, but only to give an accurate account of the perspectives of each side. To offer such selective reporting and to leave out crucial information does not do this. We have seen how other broadcasters such as Channel 4 News have apparently much less of a problem with this. So the question remains, why is some BBC news still so partial? In Chapter 4 we answered this in part by pointing to the power of Israeli public relations, to effective lobbying and to the political and commercial links between Britain, the US and Israel. Since we wrote that for the first edition of this book, there have been further studies of the Israeli lobby in both the US and Britain and its impact on American foreign policy (see for example Mearsheimer and Walt, 2008). The Channel 4 programme, *Dispatches*, also produced an extended account in 2009 of the impact of pro-Israel lobbying on British political life and the media. It noted the close relationship between lobby groups and political parties in the Westminster Parliament:

> So how does the lobby work? Money plays a big part. Millions of pounds in donations from businessmen and others into the bank accounts of politicians and political parties. The Conservative Friends of Israel is one of Westminster's most active lobbying groups. It claims that its members include 80 per cent of all Conservative members of Parliament ... Aside from raising cash some of the pro-Israeli lobbies in Parliament pay for and arrange trips to Israel. They have sent almost as many MPs and candidates on trips to Israel as have been made by all MPs to the United States and Europe combined over the last eight years. ('Inside Britain's Israel Lobby', *Dispatches*, Channel 4, 16 November 2009)

In addition, the programme indicated the historical relationship between the Israel lobby and the Labour Party and links to Tony Blair:

> It was under Tony Blair that the Israel lobby first acquired real influence in government. Former chairman of Labour Friends of Israel, John Mendelsson boasted, 'Zionism is pervasive in New Labour' ... it is automatic that Blair will come to Labour Friends of Israel meetings. Today Mendelsson is Labour's chief fundraiser. ('Inside Britain's Israel Lobby', *Dispatches*, Channel 4, 16 November 2009)

There was also an indication of a climate of anxiety amongst some politicians, which paralleled that which we had been told existed in areas of the media. The presenter of the programme describes conversations with two Conservative MPs:

> One Tory MP privately taunted me to make a programme about the pro-Israeli lobby. He said 'you don't have the guts, it's the biggest lobby in Westminster and it's a big story'. But when I went back to this courageous individual and said 'Hey come on television and tell us about it', he ran a mile. One Tory front bencher was so paranoid that he insisted I didn't just turn off my mobile phone, but take out the battery in case we were being bugged. ('Inside Britain's Israel Lobby', *Dispatches*, Channel 4, 16 November 2009)

The programme was criticised by pro-Israeli writers and groups, saying that it promoted anti-Semitism and 'lacked context'. As Jonathan Boyd wrote in the *Guardian*:

> Apparently, according to Channel 4's *Dispatches* programme on Monday night, there are some wealthy Jews out there bent on influencing British government policy on Israel. What a shocking finding. I wonder what they will uncover next? Lobbyists trying to influence government health policy perhaps? Pressure groups seeking to change government policy on the war in Iraq? Business leaders trying to alter government thinking on economic policy?
>
> Aside from the shoddy research and the barely concealed anti-Semitic undertones (the idea of a shady, morally repugnant 'cabal' of Jews seeking to control the world is a classic antisemitic myth) it was this lack of context that was most disturbing about the programme ...
>
> But then, context is always the problem. There was no effort throughout the programme to contextualise operation Cast Lead in Gaza. There was no mention of the Israeli government's withdrawal from Gaza in 2005, and the fact that, subsequently, Hamas had used the territory to launch countless randomly targeted missile attacks on Israeli towns and villages. (Boyd, 2009)

Although, if the programme had given as 'context' the Israeli view on the withdrawal from Gaza, it would also, on grounds of balance have been required to give the Palestinian view on, for example, the siege and occupation (a point not acknowledged by this author). The link between criticising pro-Israeli groups and anti-Semitism has also been contested. It is certainly not accepted by all Jewish people. The programme made a clear distinction, as we have, between Israel, its lobbying activity and Jewish people as a whole. It noted that many did not feel themselves or their views to be well represented by the pro-Israel lobbies. Rabbi David Goldberg of the Liberal Jewish Synagogue was interviewed and describes Israel in the occupied territories as 'an apartheid state':

> In the occupied territories, Israel is an apartheid state, there is no two ways about it ... when settlers are governed by Israeli law and Palestinians are governed by military law, you are talking about apartheid. ('Inside Britain's Israel Lobby', *Dispatches*, Channel 4, 16 November 2009)

The debate on the influence of Israel and pro-Israeli groups on media coverage raises an important question for public broadcasting. If the BBC is not providing a balanced account of the range of views in the conflict, then is this properly representing the public interest and, more simply, is this what the public want? We commissioned a study of public opinion relating to these issues in 2008. This was the year of what Israel termed its 'birthday' of 60 years since the setting up of the state. It was also of course the anniversary of what the Palestinians saw as the great disaster, when they were forced from their homes and land. Israel's public relations machine and superior resources meant that they were once again allowed to set the agenda. On BBC news, they could take the headlines and the Palestinian perspective came as a sort of afterthought. In a poll conducted by YouGov, a sample of 2,086 UK adults were asked whether they thought that more coverage should be given to the Israeli point of view, or more to the Palestinians, or equal for both. Nearly twice as many people thought that the Palestinians should have the most as compared with Israelis, but the bulk of the replies (72 per cent) were that both should have the same. Only 5 per cent thought that the Israeli perspective should have the most coverage. This does suggest that the downgrading of Palestinian views is not supported or desired by the public as a whole.

It is also apparent from our own audience research in this volume that there is still a great deal of confusion about the origins and causes of the conflict. But some elements of audience understanding have altered over the last eight years, largely as a result of changes in media coverage. In our samples, the number of people who believed that Palestinians had many more casualties than the Israelis, has moved from 8 per cent in 2001 to 48 per cent in 2009. It is in the area of the reasons for the fighting that the Israeli perspective has been allowed by broadcasters to achieve and sustain a prominence. The Palestinian view is often simply absent and this has clear impacts on audience belief. In 2009, two-thirds of our sample still did not know who was occupying the occupied territories. There was little understanding of how such an occupation actually affected the lives of Palestinians. When Gaza was attacked in December 2008, more than twice the number in our sample attributed this onset of violence to the actions of Palestinians in firing rockets than knew the Palestinian account that it was the Israelis that had broken the ceasefire. The broadcasters had shown many images of the suffering of Palestinians, but had 'balanced' these with the Israeli account of the causes of the conflict. The result for some audience members was the belief that the Palestinians and Hamas had brought the suffering on themselves. This is of course what many Israelis and their supporters suggest, but the population as a whole should have a news service which presents both sides of the argument on what has caused the violence. The broadcasters and notably the BBC must invest resources and have the confidence to ensure that the different perspectives on the conflict are accurately and fairly reported.

As academics, our role is to analyse how the struggle is presented, the impacts of this on public belief and crucially how the shaping of public debate may affect the possibility of resolving the conflict. But we are also aware that academic work such as ours is not neutral in its consequences. If we show that the Palestinian view is downgraded, then this raises issues for journalists about what they should be doing to make sure that both sides are properly represented. After the first edition of this volume we were asked what did the Israelis think of our work? We replied that we thought they had understood its lessons very thoroughly. Their public relations campaigns have been modelled on the principles that we and others like us have outlined to ensure the clear communication of a message. But it is not helpful for wider public understanding if only one side learns this and journalists go along with the presentation of a partial account of the conflict and its causes. The effect of presenting propaganda is in the end to prolong the violence, but a proper understanding of its causes, is a major step in the move towards peace.

Appendix 1
Answers to Questions on the Israeli-Palestinian Conflict by Student Groups 2001–02

1. What comes into your mind when you hear the words 'Israeli-Palestinian conflict'?

Response	British sample 2001 (%)	British sample 2002 (%)	German sample 2002 (%)	American sample 2002 (%)
War/violence/fighting	69	55	60	46
Suicide-bombings	2	24	22	20
Conflict over land	4	1	2	4
Religious conflict	11	8	12	12
Personalities: Arafat, Sharon, Bush	2	3	–	8
Muslims/Arabs	1	–	1	2
Environment: sand, sun, etc.	1	1	–	–
Flags: Israeli, etc./maps	1	–	–	–
Poverty	4	–	2	–
World Trade Center: Bin Laden,	4	1	1	6
Saddam Hussein	–	2	–	2
Emotional statement: injustice, tragedy etc.	–	5	–	–
No response	1	–	–	–

2a. Source of images.

Response	British sample 2001 (%)	British sample 2002 (%)	German sample 2002 (%)	American sample 2002 (%)
Television news	82	85	61	58
Newspapers	13	9	8	27
General media	2	–	–	11
Documentaries	–	1	–	–
Internet	1	–	4	–
Personal experience	1	–	1	–
Indirect experience (friends/relatives)	–	1	2	–
Books/journals	1	–	–	4
Radio	–	1	4	–
Peace rallies	–	2	–	–
No source identified	–	1	20	–

2b. What additional sources have you used?

Response	British sample 2001 (%)	British sample 2002 (%)	German sample 2002 (%)	American sample 2002 (%)
Television news	6	7	17	23
Newspapers	48	47	18	39
Documentaries	1	3	–	–
Internet	3	5	–	1
Personal experience	1	1	–	–
Indirect experience (friends/relatives)	5	7	3	1
Books/journals	4	2	–	5
Radio	6	2	2	6
Peace rallies	–	2	–	–
University course/school	–	–	–	4
No source identified	26	24	60	21

3. Who occupy the occupied territories?

Response	British sample 2001 (%)	British sample 2002 (%)	German sample 2002 (%)	American sample 2002 (%)
Israelis	19	29	47	39
Palestinians	15	16	26	43
Don't know/other	66	55	27	18

British sample 2001

Within the 19 per cent (57) who stated Israelis, 1 per cent (4) specified Israeli army/soldiers; 15 per cent (45) thought that the Palestinians occupied the occupied territories. Of the 66 per cent (198) who noted an alternative answer:

- 15 per cent (45) stated refugees
- 11 per cent (33) simply stated army/military/soldiers:
  - military of some kind
  - US army (4)
  - foreign soldiers
  - invading army
  - troops from somewhere
- 14 per cent (42) 'other' answers included asylum seekers, Afghans, white South African farmers, Afrikaners, terrorists and Iraqis and Macedonians
- 26 per cent (78) did not offer an answer

British sample 2002

Within the 29 per cent (81) who stated Israelis, 5 per cent (15) specified Israeli army/soldiers; 16 per cent (46) thought that the Palestinians occupied the occupied territories. Of the 55 per cent (153) who noted an alternative answer:

- 9 per cent (26) stated refugees
- 8 per cent (22) stated army/military/soldiers
- 3 per cent (8) thought US armed forces or UN
- 11 per cent (31) 'other' answers included white South Africans (5), gypsies and Iraqis
- 24 per cent (66) did not offer an answer.

4. What nationality are the settlers?

Response	British sample 2001 (%)	British sample 2002 (%)	German sample 2002 (%)	American sample 2002 (%)
Israeli	20	35	44	55
Palestinian	29	38	27	22
Don't know/other	51	27	29	23

British sample 2001

20 per cent (61) noted the Israelis as being the settlers; 29 per cent (88) that the Palestinians were the settlers.

Of the remaining 51 per cent (151) the majority did not offer an answer. However, the following were suggested: Zimbabwean, Pakistani (3), mixed Races/nationalities (7), Asian/Indian (2), the Taliban (2), Iranian (2), Afghani (11) Albanians, Kurds (2), Dutch South Africans, Kosovan refugees (2), Croatians, Americans (3).

British sample 2002

35 per cent (98) noted the Israelis as being the settlers; 38 per cent (107) that the Palestinians were the settlers.

Of the remaining 27 per cent (75) the majority (59) did not offer an answer. However, the remaining participants suggested the following: Africans (white farmers), Afghanis (2), Americans (5) (they thought US forces were the occupiers), Asians (2), South Africans (2), Dutch, Turks, Iraqis, and 4 thought both the Palestinians and Israelis were the settlers.

Summary of questions 3 and 4

Response	British sample 2001 (%)	British sample 2002 (%)	German sample 2002 (%)	American sample 2002 (%)
The Israelis occupy the occupied territories and the settlers are Israeli.	9	11	26	29

The Palestinians are the settlers and occupy the occupied territories	11	8	12	12
The Israelis occupy the occupied territories but the Palestinians are the settlers	11	19	12	18
The Palestinians occupy the occupied territories but the Israelis are the settlers	6	9	8	23
The remaining participants answered either Q3 or Q4 or neither question	63	53	42	18

5. Which side has had the most casualties? Is it a lot more Israelis, a few more Israelis, about the same for each side, a few more Palestinians or a lot more Palestinians?

Response	British sample 2001 (%)	British sample 2002 (%)	German sample 2002 (%)	American sample 2002 (%)
A lot more Palestinians	8	35	24	18
A few more Palestinians	32	21	12	31
A lot more Israelis	2	6	9	8
A few more Israelis	9	14	7	27
About same on each side	22	23	35	12
No response/limited answer	27	1	13	4

6. Where did the Palestinian refugees come from? How did they become refugees?

Response	British sample 2001 (%)	British sample 2002 (%)	German sample 2002 (%)	American sample 2002 (%)
Displaced from homes on the formation of Israel	4	8	26	19
Forced from homes by Israel/occupation	14	22	3	16
Don't know/general references to refugees/war	82	70	71	65

British sample 2001

Of the 14 per cent (43) who wrote that the Palestinians were forced from their homes by Israel, a small number, 5 per cent (16) of participants used the term 'occupation', and a further 2 per cent (7) of participants noted that it was a military occupation. One participant stated 'when Israel extended to the East/Gaza Strip'. The remaining 7 per cent (21) used the following phrases: 'displaced', 'seized', 'taken', 'pushed out/off', 'forced out' (10) and 'conflict caused dispersion'.

82 per cent (246) either did not know or referred generally to war/conflict and the problems of refugees. Of these 30 per cent (91) referred generally to war and conflict in terms such as:

- fight between the two governments
- through armed conflict (bombing)
- fleeing from oppressive regime
- running away from war
- driven out by fear of war and hunger
- they fled from somewhere because they were Muslim
- Palestinians became refugees as they were trying to escape war/poverty in their own country

The remaining 20 per cent (58) referred to war and conflict in terms of Afghanistan, Iraq, Kosovo 'war torn regions', '[Came from] other Middle Eastern countries affected by war'. Three participants thought the refugees were Afghani and one thought they were Jews from Europe; 32 per cent (97) gave no answer.

British sample 2002

Of the 22 per cent (61) who wrote that the Palestinians were forced from their homes by Israel/occupation, 7 per cent (19) of participants referred to this in terms of the 'occupation', and a further 5 per cent (15) of participants described it as a military occupation. The remaining 10 per cent (27) used the following phrases: 'displaced', 'evicted' 'kicked out', 'taken over' (7) , 'pushed out/off', 'forced out' (9), 'deported'; 'excluded'.

70 per cent (196) either did not know or referred generally to war/conflict and the problems of refugees. Of these, 22 per cent (62) referred to war and conflict in a similar way to the 2001 sample; for example:

- homes ruined by war
- they're fleeing homes because of war
- refugees through war, left their country to seek a better lifestyle
- to escape the war zones
- driven away by conflict

48 per cent (134) gave no answer.

7. TV news has shown pictures of the Palestinians burning the American flag – why would Palestinians do this?

Response	British sample 2001 (%)	British sample 2002 (%)	German sample 2002 (%)	American sample 2002 (%)
Military/monetary support for Israel	13	15	9	8
Support for Israel (unspecified)	24	23	60	38
Alternative response/no response	63	62	31	54

British sample 2001

Of the 13 per cent who stated that the US was supplying Israel with military/monetary aid, 7 per cent (23) noted that the US also supplied Israel with arms and 6 per cent (19) noted monetary aid. Two of this number suggested the extent of the financial support:

- US gives $3 billion foreign aid to Israel each year. Over 40 per cent of US foreign aid ... [to] Israel, 16th richest nation in the world.
- $5 billion of US 'Aid' used a year by the Israelis against the Palestinians.

In this sample 24 per cent (71) were non-specific about US support for Israel and used terms which do not directly imply military/monetary support:

- Americans seen to be helpful towards Israelis
- Americans operate a pro-Israeli, anti-Palestinian policy
- The US has had a large part to play in the peace process and Palestinians view input as very pro-Israel and biased
- America totally biased in conflict towards Israel (3)
- US has strong connections with Israel (2)
- America is allied to Israel (2)
- The Americans sympathise with the Israelis (3)
- America favouring Israel
- America siding with Israel (12)
- American support of Israeli policy in the 'homeland'
- Americans support and protect their enemies [Israelis]
- America is a supporter of Israel (3)
- US support of Israel, anti-capitalist
- US supported the Jewish in their campaign against Palestine

Of the 63 per cent (187) who offered 'Alternative response/no Response':

- 15 per cent (44) stated the reason as being that the Palestinians oppose US intervention/interference/trying to take charge; 'Resent American intervention in what they see as their business'; 'They hate Americans for trying to take over and interfering'
- 6 per cent (17) thought the Palestinians burned the American flag because the US has not supported them or become involved/intervened in finding a solution to the conflict, 'not helping their economy and debts', 'American refusal to provide arms to Palestinians', 'America withdrew from peace talks', 'America stopped aid'
- 22 per cent (65) stated dislike/disrespect/hatred of US and ideals/way of life/power in the world.
- 7 per cent (21) noted support for the Taliban, 'Osama bin Laden supporters', religious differences, anti-Bush sentiment over proposal to attack Saddam Hussein, support of Iraq in first Gulf War , 'American occupancy of Holy Land'
- 8 per cent (25) noted anti-capitalist sentiment
- 5 per cent (15) did not offer a response

British sample 2002

Of the 15 per cent (42) who stated that the US was supplying Israel with military/ monetary aid, 13 per cent (37) stated that the US also supplied Israel with arms and 2 per cent (5) stated monetary aid. One in this sample suggested the extent of the financial support: 'US gives Israel $3 billion military aid a year and supports the occupation'.

In this sample 23 per cent (65) were non-specific about US support for Israel and used terms which do not directly imply military/monetary support:

- US has a big Jewish population and tends to side with the Israelis
- Americans side with Jewish (9)
- US sympathetic towards Israelis (2)
- US is pro-Israeli ... they [Palestinians] believe they are anti-Muslim
- US prejudice in favour of Israel
- They see US as an ally of Israel (2)
- The 'special relationship' and continued support of Israel
- America favours the Israelis in this conflict
- The US comes down on the side of the Israelis
- US are friends with Israel
- US sticking up for Israel
- US supportive of Israel
- US supports Israel over conflict; more lenient to Israel because of strong lobbying in US from Jewish groups
- US supporting Israel and they hate all things Western
- US supports Israelis ... way of life [US] totally against their religion
- US supports Israeli government

Of the 62 per cent (173) who offered 'Alternative response/no response':

- 7 per cent (21) because the Palestinians oppose US intervention/interference/ trying to take charge/US dictate and responsible for the conflict
- 15 per cent (41) thought the Palestinians burned the American flag because the US has not supported them [Palestinians] or because they had become involved/intervened in finding a solution to the conflict
- 13 per cent (37) simply stated dislike/disrespect/hatred of US and ideals/way of life/power in the world
- 13 per cent (36) of this number some noted support for the Taliban, 'celebrate World Trade Center "bombing"', US support for the Palestinians, anti-Bush sentiment over proposal to attack Saddam Hussein
- 9 per cent (25) noted anti-capitalist sentiment
- 5 per cent (13) did not offer a response

American sample 2002

Of the 8 per cent who stated that the US was supplying Israel with military/monetary aid, 4 per cent noted that the US also supplied Israel with arms and 4 per cent noted monetary aid.

In this sample 38 per cent were non–specific about US support for Israel and used terms which did not directly imply military/monetary support:

- The US allies itself with Israel (6 per cent)

- America sides with Israel (14 per cent)
- US was too involved and supports Israel

Of the 54 per cent who offered 'Alternative response/no response':

- 17 per cent stated dislike/disrespect/hatred of US and ideals/way of life/power in the world:
  - because they are Muslim and against US ideals
  - US is evil and treating them unfairly
  - they don't like democracy or all our [US] freedoms
- 35 per cent because the Palestinians oppose US intervention/interference/trying to takes charge/US dictate and responsible for the conflict because they introduced the immigrants:
  - US trying to interfere and help fix the problem
  - [Palestinians] detest pro-Israeli bias in peace-making diplomatic efforts
  - Palestinians think it is not the US's business to be involved, they [US] are merely an interference
  - they don't like how the Americans want the conflict resolved and their interference
  - dislike the West's intrusion into their lives
- one participant noted anti-capitalist sentiment
- 2 per cent did not offer a response

German sample 2002

Of the 9 per cent who stated that the US was supplying Israel with military/monetary aid, 8 per cent noted that the US also supplied Israel with arms and 1 per cent noted monetary aid.

In this Sample 60 per cent were non-specific about US support for Israel and used terms which did not directly imply military/monetary support:

- political support for Sharon (2)
- friend of Israel
- solidarity with Israel (2)
- US allied with Israel (3)
- US sided with Israel (7)
- US supports Israel (44)
- because the US helped to form the Israeli State (9)

Of the 31 per cent who offered 'Alternative response/no response':

- 11 per cent stated dislike/disrespect/hatred of US and ideals/way of life/power in the world:
  - Palestinians don't want to be supported by American way of life
  - betrayed of their rights by American government
  - do not agree on US's political system
  - hate America and their mentality
- 6 per cent stated it was because they [Palestinians] object to American interference:
  - US is involving itself in the whole conflict
  - don't want the US to try and solve this conflict
- 14 per cent did not offer a response

Appendix 1 (*continued*)
Answers to Questions on the Israeli-Palestinian Conflict by Student Groups 2004, 2005, 2008, 2009

1. What comes into your mind when you hear the words 'Israeli-Palestinian conflict'?

Response	British sample 2004 (%)	British sample 2005 (%)	British sample 2008 (%)	British sample 2009 (%)
War/violence/fighting	62	59	70	75
Suicide-bombing	9	9	1	1
Conflict over land	1	1	–	1
Religious conflict	2	3	5	1
Personalities: Arafat, Sharon, Bush	4	4	2	2
Muslims/Arabs	–	–	–	2
Environment: sand, sun, etc.	6	2	5	7
Flags/maps	3	–	3	1
Emotional statement: tragedy, etc.	2	2	–	2
Poverty	1	–	–	–
News	2	3	–	–
Countries/places	4	–	2	6
Protests	1	–	2	–
Debate/discussion/argument	1	–	–	–
Wall/segregation	1	3	2	–
Car bombs/terrorism	–	9	2	–
History	–	–	2	–
Civilians/people	1	3	4	1
Star/grey image	–	2	–	1

2a. Source of images

Response	British sample 2004 (%)	British sample 2005 (%)	British sample 2008 (%)	British sample 2009 (%)
Television news	79	48	76	52
Newspapers	10	14	9	11
General media	6	28	7	25
Documentaries	–	1	–	2
Internet	–	3	1	2
Personal experience	–	–	–	–

Indirect experience (friends/relatives)	–	1	2	–
Books/journals	1	2	–	–
Radio	1	–	–	2
University/school	1	1	1	–
Peace rallies	–	–	–	1
Government	–	–	–	2
No response given	2	2	4	3

2b. What additional sources have you used?

Response	British sample 2004 (%)	British sample 2005 (%)	British sample 2008 (%)	British sample 2009 (%)
Television news	10	2	2	9
General media	3	–	3	2
Newspapers	38	25	19	21
Documentaries	1	–	2	1
Internet	7	8	26	22
Personal experience	1	–	–	–
Indirect experience (friends/relatives)	4	4	8	13
Books/journals	3	3	2	2
Radio	1	2	1	2
Peace rallies	1	1	–	2
University course/school	2	1	2	3
No response given	29	54	35	23

3. Who occupy the occupied territories?

Response	British sample 2004 (%)	British sample 2005 (%)	British sample 2008 (%)	British sample 2009 (%)
Israelis	31	30	25	36
Palestinians	12	20	12	18
Soldiers/army	8	13	15	3
The settlers	12	4	4	9
Refugees	5	9	5	4
Americans	–	3	–	–
Civilians	2	–	1	–
Occupiers	2	–	–	–
Asylum seekers	–	1	2	–
Other answers included: immigrants, those invading the Israelis, normal people, cattle, tramps	12	6	12	9
No response given	16	14	24	21

4. What nationality are the settlers?

Response	British sample 2004 (%)	British sample 2005 (%)	British sample 2008 (%)	British sample 2009 (%)
Israeli	39	38	26	36
Palestinian	30	32	19	18
Palestinians and Israelis	2	2	–	2
Russian	–	–	–	1
Afghan	1	–	–	–
European	–	1	–	–
American	–	2	7	1
Asian	1	1	1	1
British	–	–	2	2
Any nationality	–	1	2	3
Eastern/Western	1	–	1	1
Iraqi	–	1	–	1
Jewish	–	1	–	–
Islam	–	2	–	–
Polish	–	–	2	–
Lebanese	–	–	2	–
Spanish	–	–	2	–
Middle East	–	–	2	1
Irish	–	–	1	–
Muslim	–	–	1	–
From all over came to be 'American'	–	–	1	–
Bosnian	–	–	1	–
African	–	–	1	–
Eastern European	–	–	1	–
Foreign	–	–	–	1
No response	26	19	28	32

Summary of questions 3 and 4

Response	British sample 2004 (%)	British sample 2005 (%)	British sample 2008 (%)	British sample 2009 (%)
The Israelis occupy the occupied territories *and* the settlers are Israeli	21	22	13	22
The Palestinians occupy the occupied territories *and* the settlers are Palestinian	4	14	4	9
The Israelis occupy the occupied territories *but* the settlers are Palestinian	4	9	8	8
The Palestinians occupy the occupied territories *but* the settlers are Israelis	4	1	6	3
The remaining participants answered either Q3 *or* Q4 or neither question	67	54	69	58

5. Which side has had the most casualties? Is it a lot more Israelis, a few more Israelis, about the same for each side, a few more Palestinians, or a lot more Palestinians?

Response	British sample 2004 (%)	British sample 2005 (%)	British sample 2008 (%)	British sample 2009 (%)
A lot more Palestinians	29	32	37	48
A few more Palestinians	21	16	25	16
A lot more Israelis	4	8	5	6
A few more Israelis	14	16	9	10
About the same on each side	24	27	20	16
No response	8	1	4	4

6. Where did the Palestinian refugees come from? How did they become refugees?

Response	British sample 2004 (%)	British sample 2005 (%)	British sample 2008 (%)	British sample 2009 (%)
Displaced from homes on the formation of Israel	7	3	8	6
Forced from homes by Israel/occupation	21	22	16	15
General references to refugees/war	44	22	55	53
No response	28	53	21	26

7. TV news has shown pictures of the Palestinians burning the American flag – why would Palestinians do this?

Response	British sample 2004 (%)	British sample 2005 (%)	British sample 2008 (%)	British sample 2009 (%)
Military/monetary support for Israel	18	11	15	18
Support for Israel (unspecified)	12	32	8	26
Alternative response such as: oil, US at war with them, reject US help as want to stay the way they are and not improve the country/No response	70	57	77	56

8. Were you aware that Palestinians could be subject to strict curfews?

Response	British sample 2008 (%)	British sample 2009 (%)
Yes	19	24
No	81	73
No response given	–	2

9. Did you know that in 2005 Israel had withdrawn 8,000 people from Gaza?

Response	British sample 2009 (%)
Yes	25
No	72
No response given	3

10. Did you know that in the following year another 12,000 moved into the West Bank?

Response	British sample 2009 (%)
Yes	10
No	88
No response given	2

11. In 2006, the Palestinian group Hamas was elected to become the majority group in the Palestinian Parliament – for the West Bank and Gaza. Did you know this?

Response	British sample 2009 (%)
Yes	30
No	67
No response given	3

12. In the Gaza conflict many pictures were shown of civilians, women and children killed in Gaza. When you see these, whose fault do you think it is?

Response	British sample 2009 (%)
Hamas/Palestinians	11
Israel	29
Equal	52
No response	8

13. Before the conflict of December 2008 to January 2009, there was a ceasefire – who broke it?

Response	British sample 2009 (%)
Hamas/Palestinians	44
Israel	36
No response given	20

Appendix 2
Answers to Questions on the Israeli-Palestinian Conflict by Focus Groups 2001–02

1. What comes into your mind when you hear the words 'Israeli-Palestinian conflict'?

Response	Student groups (26)	Elderly/ retired (10)	Low-income groups (21)	Middle-class male groups (16)	Middle-class female groups (21)	Middle-class mixed (6)
Conflict, war/violence	15	8	12	10	13	5
Suicide-bombings	4	–	4	2	2	–
Conflict over land	–	–	–	–	1	–
Religious conflict	4	–	2	1	1	1
Personalities: Arafat, Sharon, Bush	1	1	1	1	1	–
Non-specific: simply stated, Muslims/Arabs	–	–	–	–	–	–
Environment: sand, sun, etc.	1	–	–	–	–	–
Flags: Israeli, etc./maps	–	–	1	1	–	–
Poverty	–	–	–	–	–	–
World Trade Center: Bin Laden	–	–	–	1	–	–
Emotional statement: injustice, tragedy, etc.	–	–	1	–	3	–
No response	1	1	–	–	–	–

2a. Source of images.

Response	Student groups (26)	Elderly/ retired (10)	Low-income groups (21)	Middle-class male groups (16)	Middle-class female groups (21)	Middle-class mixed (6)
Television news	22	7	15	9	18	5
Newspapers	1	1	2	4	3	–
General media	1	–	2	2	–	1
Documentaries	–	–	–	–	–	–
Books/magazines	–	–	1	1	–	–
Personal experience	–	–	–	–	–	–
Indirect experience (friends/relatives)	1	–	1	–	–	–
Radio	–	1	–	–	–	–
Internet	–	–	–	–	–	–
Peace rallies	–	–	–	–	–	–
No source identified	1	1	–	–	–	–

413

2b. What additional sources have you used?

Response	Student groups (26)	Elderly/ retired (10)	Low-income groups (21)	Middle-class male groups (16)	Middle-class female groups (21)	Middle-class mixed (6)
Television news	–	2	4	1	3	–
Newspapers	12	1	5	7	15	–
Documentaries	2	–	1	–	–	1
Internet	2	–	–	2	1	–
Books/journals	1	–	–	1	1	–
Personal experience	–	–	1	2	–	1
Indirect experience: (friends/relatives)	2	–	1	2	–	2
Radio	–	–	–	1	1	2
Peace Rallies	–	–	–	–	–	–
No source identified	7	7	9	–	–	–

Student groups

Two stated indirect experience as being: 'sister over in Israel'; 'Jewish friend who has lived in Israel'. Of the two participants who stated documentaries as a secondary source of images/information, one specified *Blue Peter* documentaries. One participant noted BBC Online as a secondary source.

Low-income groups

One participant stated personal experience as being: 'visit to region – talking to the people'. One participant stated indirect experience as being: 'Arabic friends'.

Middle-class male groups

Two participants stated personal experience as being: 'have visited the region several times'; 'visited Israel, personal emails from contacts'. Two participants stated indirect experience as being: 'a friend in the army with some knowledge of the area'; 'verbal first-hand stories told to me' 'other photographers' experiences ... photo essays from Palestine/Israel'. A further two participants noted in addition to their responses: 'Dad visited recently'; 'talked to people of the states involved'. Two participants who noted Internet specified BBC Online News and Guardian Online.

Middle-class female groups

The majority of participants in this group used newspapers as a secondary source of images/information. One participant noted *Time* magazine as a secondary source of images/information. Two participants who stated newspapers as a secondary source noted that they only read them occasionally.

Middle-class mixed group (teachers)

One participant stated personal experience as being: 'been to Israel and West Bank a number of times (had an MA in Middle Eastern Studies)'. Two participants stated indirect experience as being: 'brother-in-law from the Middle East'; 'corresponded with a missionary teacher in Tabetha school in Israel (Church of Scotland school)'. Two participants who noted the radio as a source of information referred to the BBC World Service.

3. Who occupy the occupied territories?

Response	Student groups (26)	Elderly/ retired (10)	Low-income groups (21)	Middle-class male groups (16)	Middle-class female groups (21)	Middle-class mixed (6)
Israeli	6	9	7	15	9	4
Palestinian	5	–	7	1	7	1
Don't know/other	15	1	7	–	5	1

4. What nationality are the settlers?

Response	Student groups (26)	Elderly/ retired (10)	Low-income groups (21)	Middle-class male groups (16)	Middle-class female groups (21)	Middle-class mixed (6)
Israeli	6	6	7	13	6	4
Palestinian	5	2	7	2	8	1
Don't know/other	15	2	7	1	7	1

Summary of questions 3 and 4

Response	Student groups (26)	Elderly/ retired (10)	Low-income groups (21)	Middle-class male groups (16)	Middle-class female groups (21)	Middle-class mixed (6)
Those who understood that the Israelis occupy the territories, and that the settlers are Israeli	4	6	5	13	7	4
Those who think the Palestinians are the settlers and occupy the occupied territories	2	–	3	1	7	1
Those who stated that the Israelis occupy the occupied territories but that the Palestinians are the settlers	2	2	1	1	1	–
Those who stated that the Palestinians occupy the occupied territories but that the Israelis are the settlers	1	–	2	–	–	–
Answered either Q3 or Q4 or neither question	17	2	10	1	6	1

5. Which side has had the most casualties? Is it a lot more Israelis, a few more Israelis, about the same for each side, a few more Palestinians or a lot more Palestinians?

Response	Student groups (26)	Elderly/ retired (10)	Low-income groups (21)	Middle-class male groups (16)	Middle-class female groups (21)	Middle-class mixed (6)
More Palestinians	8	5	10	13	9	5
More Israelis	5	–	5	2	4	–
About the same on each side	8	3	6	1	7	1
No response/limited answer	5	2	–	–	1	–

6. Why are they fighting? What is the conflict about?

Response	Student groups (26)	Elderly/ retired (10)	Low-income groups (21)	Middle-class male groups (16)	Middle-class female groups (21)	Middle-class mixed (6)
Palestinians displaced from homes on the formation of Israel	4	–	2	6	4	3
Palestinians forced from home by Israeli occupation	1	3	1	4	2	–
Dispute over land	15	5	11	5	11	2
Religious dispute	3	–	5	1	2	1
Other/don't know	3	2	2	–	2	–

7. Can you name any of the wars involving Israel since the Second World War?

Response	Student groups (26)	Elderly/ retired (10)	Low-income groups (21)	Middle-class male groups (16)	Middle-class female groups (21)	Middle-class mixed (6)
4 wars identified	–	–	–	2	–	2
3 wars identified	–	–	–	3	–	–
2 wars identified	2	2	1	6	1	1
1 war identified	3	5	2	5	3	2
No response/other	21	3	18	–	17	1

8. What countries were occupied during these wars?

Response	Student groups (26)	Elderly/ retired (10)	Low-income groups (21)	Middle-class male groups (16)	Middle-class female groups (21)	Middle-class mixed (6)
4 countries identified	–	–	–	6	–	1
3 countries identified	2	–	–	3	–	3
2 countries identified	3	2	–	3	–	2
1 country identified	–	3	1	1	1	–
No response/other	21	5	20	3	20	2

9. Do you know of United Nations resolutions or criticisms made by the UN of the actions of anyone in the conflict?

Response	Student groups (26)	Elderly/ retired (10)	Low-income groups (21)	Middle-class male groups (16)	Middle-class female groups (21)	Middle-class mixed (6)
4 or more resolutions	–	–	–	–	–	–
3 resolutions	–	–	–	–	–	–
2 resolutions	–	–	–	1	–	–
1 resolutions	3	–	1	4	–	2
No response	23	10	20	11	21	4

10. Can you explain the image of the American flag being burnt?

Response	Student groups (26)	Elderly/ retired (10)	Low-income groups (21)	Middle-class male groups (16)	Middle-class female groups (21)	Middle-class mixed (6)
Military/monetary support for Israel	3	1	–	10	3	1
Support for Israel (unspecified)	–	3	5	5	1	2
Alternative response/ No response	23	6	16	1	17	3

11. Are you aware of any issues regarding water in the area?

Response	Student groups (26)	Elderly/ retired (10)	Low-income groups (21)	Middle-class male groups (16)	Middle-class female groups (21)	Middle-class mixed (6)
Aware of the significance of water	–	–	–	7	1	1
Some awareness of the significance of water	–	–	–	–	–	–
Not aware of the significance of water	26	10	21	9	20	5

Middle-class male groups

Seven participants had an understanding of the significance of water, for example:

- Israel uses the water supply in the West Bank ... while siphoning off large amounts for its settlers in occupied territories
- Israel controls the infrastructure of the occupied territories and so controls the supply of water necessary for the irrigation of crops in Palestinian territories
- have read Palestinian families having water cut off for hours each day ... Israeli settlements, people swimming in pools. Water is being used as a weapon by Israel
- Israel monopolising water supply for agriculture and domestic supply
- Arab states believe Israel is taking more than its agreed share from mutual sources
- Israel accused of cutting off water supplies

One participant referred to water as being significant during discussion session.

Middle-class female groups

One participant referred to water during discussion session.

Middle-class mixed group

One participant referred to water.

Appendix 3
Gaza Study, Content Analysis
Language Counts

BBC

Other Palestinian Statements

Military claims	2.25
Peace/ceasefire prospects/could co-exist/must be ceasefire	10.5
Complaints about world response	2.0
Coping with attack/siege	20.5
Total	*35.25*

Additional Criticisms of Israeli Attack on Gaza

Condemned/blamed for civilian casualties/suffering/strikes 'not surgical'/mistakes/massacre/atrocities/murder/ terror/Israel must stop bombing	95.5
Disproportionate/excessive	26.25
Israel must conform to/is breaking/is behaving above international law	40.5
Types of weapons/phosphorus	9.5
There is a humanitarian crisis	4.75
Israeli army (IDF) false claims on targets	3.75
Israeli ground invasion will destabilise the Middle East	6.5
Action will radicalise young Muslims/action will not break Islamist nationalist ideas	45.5
Barring journalists	3.75
US/Bush statements unhelpful/unbalanced	4.75
Defying demands for a ceasefire/reject ceasefire	3.75
Total	*244.5*

Defence of Israeli Action

Buildings in 'terrorist' use	21.75
Leaflets/phoned and warned	12.75
Hamas hide among civilians/use humans as shields	8.75
Israel deny violating the Geneva Convention	8.5
Apology	4.25
Protect civilians/civilians not the enemy	3.25
Feel bad/don't sleep	3.0
No humanitarian crisis	2.25
Ceasefire 'unrealistic'/premature	1.25
Security necessities of occupation	1.25
Medical aid/supplies to help casualties	1.0
Will investigate	0.75
Total	*68.75*

Defence of Palestinian/Hamas Action

Palestinians are 'friends and heroes'/we're with you	2.0
Buildings not in 'terrorist' use	0.25
Tunnels a lifeline (not just weapon)	3.0
Right to resist	1.5
Total	6.75

Protests/Demonstrations (for Israel)

For Israel – UK	
Support of military operations	5.0
Total	5.0

Protests/Demonstrations (against Israel)

Against Israel – UK	
No explanation	44
Against ground offensive	0.75
Against Israeli action/in Gaza	11.5
End action	1.0
Against military offensive	2.0
Response is disproportionate	2.75
Israel must conform to international law	2.0
Want to raise awareness/support Gaza	2.0
Against Israel – Other Countries	
No explanation	5.0
Against Israeli action in Gaza	3.75
About Israeli elections	1.75
Horror at Israel	7.5
Against Israel – General	
No explanation	1.5
'Disproportionate'	4.5
Against Israel – Palestinians	
No explanation	9.75
Protests against Gaza violence	
No explanation	13.25
Total	*113*

Other Causes

Israel restore deterrent power	15.0
Israeli elections	11.75
Absence of Hamas from negotiation/no discussion of Gaza	8.5
Diplomatic end game intensifies fighting	7.25
New US administration	3.75
End of ceasefire	1.25
Israel wants to make Palestinians blame Hamas	1.0
Total	*48.5*

Israeli Casualties/Suffering

Civilian	32.25
Non-civilian	13.25
Non-specified	12.75
Total	*58.25*

Palestinian Casualties/Suffering

Civilian	207.0
Non-civilian	33.0
Non-specified	66
Total	*306*

Israeli damage	11.0
Palestinian damage	21.0
History of conflict/rockets/blockade	21.0
Additional criticisms of Israel and Hamas (both to blame)	3.25

ITV

Israeli Explanatory Themes

End rockets/security	160.0
Stop smuggling weapons	26.0
Hit Hamas/militants/terrorists/Hamas are terrorists/to blame	54.5
Hamas initiated recent violence/impediment to peace/ no commitment to ceasefire/reject new ceasefire	21.25
Keep Iran out of Gaza/linked to Iran	13.75
War on terror	1.0
Need to defend Israel/time to fight	26.25
Total	*302.75*

Palestinian Explanatory Themes

Land/refugees	–
Occupation	1.0
Israel must withdraw troops from Gaza	7.25
End siege/blockade	12.25
Open borders/crossings/allow freedom of movement	5.75
Retaliate/resist/Israel will face dark destiny/Gaza is a graveyard/victory will come/day of rage/now legitimate to kill Israeli children/Israel broke ceasefire	51.75
Total	78.0

Other Israeli Statements

Peace/ceasefire prospects	11.0
Clarifications of limits of action	12.5
Military claims	8.0
Appeals for reconciliation	2.0
Will not be deterred by Israeli casualties	2.5
Rejects capture claims	1.0
Know where Hamas is	6.25
No second front	2.5
Critic of British journalism	1.25
Total	47.0

Other Palestinian Statements

Military claims/captured soldiers	3.0
Peace prospects	2.5
Complaints about world response	1.5
What has been targeted by Israel	0.5
Total	7.5

Additional Criticisms of Israeli Attack on Gaza

Condemned/blamed for civilian casualties/suffering/strikes 'not surgical'/mistakes/atrocities/murder/terror	140.5
Disproportionate/excessive	29.25
Israel must conform to/is breaking/is behaving above international law	61.5
Types of weapons/phosphorus	12.25
There is a humanitarian crisis	11.25
Israeli army (IDF) false claims on targets	17.0
Israeli ground invasion will destabilise the Middle East	6.75
Action will radicalise young Muslims/action will not break Islamist nationalist ideas	2.0

Barring journalists	12.5
US/Bush comments unhelpful/unbalanced	1.75
Defying demands for ceasefire	22.0
Deep concern	0.75
Contradictory statements	8.0
Total	*325.5*

Defence of Israeli Action

Buildings in 'terrorist' use	26.5
Leaflets/phoned and warned	3.0
Hamas hide among civilians/use humans as shields	14.25
Israel deny violating the Geneva Convention/Hamas broke international law	2.25
Apology	2.0
Protect civilians/civilians not the enemy	16.0
No humanitarian crisis	7.5
Ceasefire 'unrealistic'/premature	8.5
Medical aid/supplies to help casualties	25.5
Will investigate	2.25
Hamas/Palestinian militants to blame	21.0
Hamas manipulate the media	3.0
Total	*131.75*

Defence of Palestinian/Hamas Action

Palestinians are 'friends and heroes'/we're with you	8.5
'Must launch holy war against the Israelis in Gaza'	1.75
Not supplied by Iran (weapons for Hamas)	0.75
Total	*11.0*

Protest/Demonstrations

Against Israel – UK

No explanation	11.0
Stop the bloodshed	2.0
Against Israeli action	18.0
Halt bombing	3.5
Against Israel's bombing of Gaza	17.75

Against Israel – Other Countries

Against Israeli action	2.0
Halt bombing	5.0
Attack on Gaza	8.0

Against Israel – General

No explanation	2.75
Against Israel's bombing of Gaza	1.5

Against Israel – Palestinians

No explanation	1.0
Retaliate	5.0

Against Israel – Israeli Arabs

Against the war	1.0
Total	78.5

Other Causes

Israel restore deterrent power	1.25
End of ceasefire	1.0
Despair has produced 'generation of fanatics'	1.25
Total	3.5

Israeli Casualties/Suffering

Civilian	27.5
Non-civilian	16.5
Non-specified	16.75
Total	60.75

Palestinian Casualties/Suffering

Civilian	336.5
Non-civilian	28.0
Non-specified	87.25
Total	451.75

Israeli damage	12.75
Palestinian damage	22.0

History of conflict/rockets/blockade	–

Additional criticisms of Israel and Hamas	2.0
(both to blame)	6.0

Appendix 4
Black Holes of History: Public Understanding and the Shaping of Our Past

In March 1999, President Clinton made a public apology in Guatemala. It was an extraordinary event and we asked a group of 280 young people why he might have done this. We were engaged in a study of what people knew about the history of their world and this was one of a series of questions which we put to groups of students. Very few of them knew why Clinton had apologised. Three per cent wrote correctly that it was because of US involvement in 'dirty wars' in support of right-wing regimes; 10 per cent believed he was apologising for the Monica Lewinsky affair, a subject which people knew much more about; the majority simply did not know. Yet Clinton's apology was remarkable. It followed the publication of a report by an independent commission which concluded that the US was responsible for most of the human rights abuses during a 36-year-old civil war in which 200,000 people died. Clinton was reported as saying:

> It is important that I state clearly that support for military forces or intelligence Units which engaged in violent and widespread repression of the kind described in the report was wrong. (quoted in the *Guardian*, 12 March 1999)

At the same time the US government declassified documents which showed the US had 'initiated and sustained a murderous war conducted by Guatemalan security forces against civilians suspected of aiding left-wing guerrilla movements' (*Guardian*, 12 March 1999). The documents revealed that the US set up a safe house in the presidential palace in Guatemala City which became the headquarters for the 'dirty war'. A state department cable from October 1967 showed that security operations included 'kidnapping, torture and summary execution'. Twenty-five years later, a CIA cable confirmed that civilian villages were targeted because of the army's belief that the Maya Indian inhabitants were aiding guerrillas. As the *Guardian* also reported:

> A report released this month by the Guatemala Truth Commission confirmed that entire communities were massacred. It said children were killed, abducted, forcibly recruited as soldiers, illegally adopted and sexually abused. Foetuses were cut from their mothers' wombs and young children were smashed against walls or thrown alive into pits. (*Guardian*, 12 March 1999)

Such events are intensely controversial and their history is often contested. Yet in this case the source was the US president and the documentary proof came from the US government itself. We put the same question to a group of 49 American journalism and media students and to another group of 114 high school students from Germany. In these samples 8 per cent of those from the US knew the correct answer and 4 per cent of the Germans, but the great majority did not know or thought it was related to Monica Lewinsky.

The United States has been involved in many 'dirty wars' in Latin America and there have been extensive accusations of human rights abuses. Right-wing military regimes were supported in countries such as Brazil while some elected regimes were attacked or displaced as in Nicaragua and Chile. In another question we asked: 'Who were the Contras in Nicaragua?' These were the private army financed by the US in the 1980s to attack the left-wing Sandinista government. The great majority of the students had not heard of them. We also found that the abuses of the Soviet communist system had apparently vanished into a similar black hole. We asked: 'What were the Gulags in the Soviet Union?' These were the slave labour camps which were established under Stalin's regime and which Solzhenitsyn wrote of in his books, *The First Circle* and *The Gulag Archipelago*. Five per cent of the British students and 8 per cent of the Americans knew what they were. The German students were better informed and 30 per cent gave the correct answer.

Popular history is likely to be shaped by the priorities and interests of those who produce it. In controversial areas it may serve to legitimise past actions or to celebrate them. This is expressed in the phrase 'history is written by the victors'. When beliefs about historical events do exist they are likely to have been coloured by the cultural struggles which characterize the writing of history and its popular construction. Beliefs about a major conflict such as the Second World War can also vary between different societies. This is partly because history is told from the side and perspectives of those involved. We are taught about the famous battles that involved 'our' soldiers and watch popular films and TV programmes about them. But such memories were also affected by a second level of cultural struggle which developed after the war. This was the Cold War between East and West, which provided another filter for our perception. In the Second World War, the Soviet Union was allied with the United States and Britain in a common struggle against fascism. But after the war, the West and East were divided as ideological enemies. This meant that the contribution of the Soviet Union to the winning of the Second World War was not only neglected but was actually obliterated in some popular accounts. We can look, for example, at the manner in which anniversaries of the war were conducted. The fortieth anniversary of D-Day was on 6 June 1984. The early 1980s was a period in which the American Right had become dominant under President Reagan. This signalled an intensification of the Cold War, an intention to increase defence expenditure and extensive rhetoric on the 'evil empire' of the Soviet Union. When President Reagan attended the D-Day ceremonies in Europe, the commemoration of what was actually a joint struggle against the Nazis was turned into a straightforward attack on the Soviet Union. This is an extract from President Reagan's speech that was shown on British television news:

> The Soviet troops that came to the centre of this continent did not leave when peace came. They are still there, uninvited, unwanted, unyielding almost 40 years after the war. (ITN/Channel 4 News, 6 June 1984)

The effect was to remove consideration of the role of the Soviet armies in the actual war. This was discussed at the time by an 'alternative' weekly news programme made by Channel 4, under the title *Diverse Reports* (27 June 1984). Its role was to highlight issues that were missing from other news programmes. It produced a feature on the D-Day story and began by pointing to gaps in national news coverage.

For example, the programme showed a report by ITN/Channel 4 News that stated: 'The Union Jack rose under the Queen's proud and watchful eye, to join the flags of all the nations who fought and defeated Hitler' (7.00 p.m., 6 June 1984). The programme commented 'not quite all; the Soviet flag was missing' (*Diverse Reports*, 27 June 1984). The programme then went on to describe the decisive role of the Soviet Union in the combat. It noted that the Battle of Stalingrad in 1943 was a key defeat for the Nazis in which they lost an elite army of a quarter of a million men. This was followed by the Battle of Kursk Bulge which was reported to be the biggest tank battle of all time. The German army was again routed and a significant proportion of its ground armour destroyed. D-Day was still a year away. By 1945 the Western allies had defeated 170 German divisions; the Soviets had defeated 607. The Soviet losses were enormous, with an estimated 20 million dead (compared to around 1 million for the Western forces).

Ten years after Reagan's speech, President Clinton came to Europe for the fiftieth anniversary of the D-Day celebrations. By then the Soviet bloc had collapsed, but the US president's speech still highlighted the role of the Allies and spoke of them as 'beginning to end' the war: 'Here the miracle of liberation began ... the forces of democracy landed ... on beaches such as these an army landed from the sea to begin to end a war' (BBC1 5.45 p.m., 6 June 1994). We asked the students the question: 'In the Second World War, which Allied country defeated the most German divisions?' Just 18 per cent of the American students and 29 per cent of the British gave the answer as the Soviet Union (65 per cent of the American students and 48 per cent of the British put Britain or the US). Interestingly, the German students were better informed and 73 per cent named the Soviet Union.

We also asked about the war in Vietnam, which the Americans eventually withdrew from in 1975. It is believed that the US dropped 3 million tons of explosives in this war which would have been more than the total tonnage dropped by the US and Britain in the Second World War (including the atomic bombs). In Vietnam, just under 60,000 Americans were killed. Vietnamese deaths were estimated at over 2 million. The question we put to the students was: 'In the Vietnam War, how many casualties were there on each side. Was it a lot more Americans, a few more Americans, about the same for each side, a few more Vietnamese or a lot more Vietnamese?' To this, 37 per cent of the US students replied that it was more Americans or that the numbers were about equal. The same percentage replied that it was 'a lot more Vietnamese'. The remainder thought it was 'a few more Vietnamese' or did not know. For the British, 34 per cent though it was 'a lot more Vietnamese' and for the German students it was 36 per cent. In our popular culture, US films have portrayed American forces as involved in heroic and bloody action against a deadly enemy. They do not typically discuss the millions of Vietnamese – mostly civilians – who were killed or injured. When the British students were told of the actual casualties, an audible gasp came from them. What is clear is that many of these young people, including the Americans, had no idea of the scale of death which had been imposed on Vietnam. In conclusion, it is clear that a limited knowledge of history can produce great confusion about past conflicts and, as we have seen elsewhere in this volume, about the origins of those which are still with us. Another very obvious issue to emerge from this part of our study is the difference in levels of knowledge between the students of different countries. The German students were from a high school and were being asked (and were answering) the questions in English. Yet in many questions a higher proportion gave correct answers compared with older British and American students who were at universities. This perhaps reflects in part the fact that in Germany, history and political studies are compulsory subjects until the age of 17. It is a matter of real concern if young people understand so little of the world in which they live and their judgements are shaped by the distorted history they are given. The democracy and human rights which some in the world enjoy are still fragile and subject to challenge. They were fought for under the slogan 'Knowledge is Power'.

The tables below give a fuller account of these results.

What were the Gulags in the Soviet Union? (as a percentage)

Response	British sample 2001	British sample 2002	German sample 2002	American sample 2002
Slave labour/prison camps	7	5	30	8
Other answers				
Rebels/terrorists	6	10	6	2
The army	1	6	3	2
Secret police	1	4	2	4
Working class	–	2	–	–
No answer given	85	73	59	84

In the Vietnam War how many casualties were there on each side? Was it a lot more Americans, a few more Americans, about the same for each side, a few more Vietnamese or a lot more Vietnamese?

Response	British sample 2001	British sample 2002	German sample 2002	American sample 2002
A lot more Vietnamese	21	34	36	37
A few more Vietnamese	31	32	14	14
About equal numbers	7	6	3	11
A few more Americans	10	11	3	6
A lot more Americans	8	16	9	20
No answer given	23	1	35	12

Who were the Contras in Nicaragua?

Response	British sample 2001	British sample 2002	German sample 2002	American sample 2002
Anti-communist 'freedom fighters' funded by Reagan, trained by the CIA, to overthrow Sandinista government	1	1	–	6

Freedom fighters/ rebels/guerrillas	11 (4% stated freedom fighters, 7% guerrillas)	10 (1% stated freedom fighters, 8% rebels against government)	2 (Rebels)	16 (Rebels, guerrillas)
Other answers (For example, drug lords, political group, army, local tribal people, communist group, dictatorship in country, farmers, peacekeepers, secret police, drugs	10	9	7	12
No answer given	78	80	91	66

In 1999 President Clinton made a public apology in Guatemala – why?

Response	*British sample 2001*	*British sample 2002*	*German sample 2002*	*American sample 2002*
US gave support to a brutal military regime under which there was much abuse of human rights	4	3	4	8
Because he lied about affair with Monica Lewinsky	1	10	11	6
US military action against/accidental bombing	9	10	3	–
America using country for nuclear testing	1	–	–	–
Other answers (slavery, regime change, exploited them, etc)	6	8	–	18
No answer given	79	69	82	68

British sample 2001

4 per cent (12) showed some understanding of US involvement in Guatemala:

- the USA backed a dictatorship
- American sanctions and military presence which caused many deaths – domino theory
- the US supported a military regime and there was much abuse of human rights
- America supported an oppressive regime
- human rights violations in the country whilst under American guardianship
- American interference in a conflict there
- America had a large interference in Latin American countries over fruit companies
- American intervention, slaughtered lots of people
- atrocities in Cold War
- American war atrocities, war crimes
- US oppression of socialism
- American war crimes

The following are the 'other' answers (6 per cent) (17):

- US involvement in slavery: 'For the US using them as slaves in the past' (4)
- America financed Contra rebels
- for not letting the Cubans into America/revolutionary movement against the government
- gave aid to their opponents
- sanctions against their country and inhabiting their land
- for deserting them when they needed help
- for being campaigners to change political regime (4)
- the US quelled fighting, Guatemala wanted independence
- financial backing in the conflict went to rebel group to fight America's war for them
- because the Americans exploited them (2)

British sample 2002

3 per cent (8) showed some understanding of US involvement in Guatemala:

- the US installed a brutal dictatorship in the 1950s to protect United Fruit
- for US supporting the military dictatorship in that country
- US responsibility, involvement in loss of life there
- for 'involving' them in a conflict which killed many of their people
- for casualties due to US intervention
- admitting to atrocities committed by US in the country
- in the 1960s the US government brought down the democratically elected regime through subterfuge
- for trying to control their country with military presence

The following are the 'other' answers, (8 per cent) (21):

- for American history of mistreating the people there
- for American sanctions on Cuba
- Cuban missile crisis and American attitude to Cuba
- trade embargoes (3)
- lack of American support to the country in order to fight the guerrillas
- for enforcing regime change
- for loss of life during Vietnam conflict (2)
- for not helping the government avoid a military coup
- for not helping them with money and aid to the country/caused death of people by not assisting with aid (5)
- Americans using force during Cold War
- for Guatemalans being slaves/slave labour (3)
- supporting opposition

German sample

4 per cent showed some understanding of US involvement in Guatemala:

- because America contributed heavily to the civil war with weapons and undermined peace

- US troops invaded and tried to help a government and civilians died
- because of the US trade unification of whole American continent

American sample

Nine people gave the following comments:

- US involvement in their country's government affairs
- some conflict in which US became involved and it went bad
- for what happened in civil war – US failure to involve themselves in the genocide
- for loss of life in the revolution and US failure to assist
- failed to put down an uprising that threatened US investments in the banana industry
- ownership of the Panama Canal
- for US attack on country to put down an uprising that threatened US investments in the banana industry
- economic neglect (2)

In the Second World War, which Allied country defeated the most German divisions?

Response	British sample 2001	British sample 2002	German sample 2002	American sample 2002
Soviet Union	32	29	73	18
Other answers	68	71	27	82
Britain	31	31	6	49
US	16	17	16	16
France	9	16	2	10
No answer given	12	7	3	7

Appendix 5
Responses on History Questions
2004–09

These are the replies of UK students studying social science in higher education, collected between 2004 and 2009. They are the same sample groups which we used for the new Israel-Palestine studies above. The figures give little cheer to those worried about how much young citizens know about the world in which they live or its history. The replies for the period as a whole show that less than one in five know what the Gulags were in the Soviet Union. The history of Latin America and its relations with the US, remain a blank to most. In 2005, just 1 per cent thought that President Clinton might have apologised to Guatemala because the US gave support to a brutal military regime. But 19 per cent thought the apology was about Monica Lewinsky. We might blame the Cold War and nationalism for the fact that, in 2008, just 26 per cent knew that the Soviet Union had defeated the most German divisions in the Second World War. But how could it be that the same number of students, at the top of higher education, actually believed that the answer was France? Surely the most rudimentary discussion in school of such a major event as the Second World War would have quickly revealed that this could not have been the answer. For this to occur suggests a very narrow focus by students on fragmented moments of whatever is to be learned, and little beyond this. We would need another book to discuss the impact of league tables and the professional delivery by teachers of limited parcels of knowledge designed for success in the exam system. But it is clearly time to move beyond such fragmented learning and to think again about what constitutes education. The responses are given in more detail below.

What were the Gulags in the Soviet Union?

Response	British sample 2004 (%)	British sample 2005 (%)	British sample 2008 (%)	British sample 2009 (%)
Slave labour/prison camps	10	11	18	18
Land owners killed by Stalin	–	1	–	1
Rebels	2	–	–	1
Opposition to Soviet rule/Communist rule/prisoners of war	3	3	4	2
The army/soldiers/secret police/police	4	2	9	10
Working class/middle class/peasantry	–	2	3	2
Political group/government/ leaders/royalty	2	–	5	3
Spies	1	–	–	–
Headwear	2	–	–	–
People in the black market	1	–	–	–

People from Eastern Europe	1	–	–	–
A weapon	1	–	–	–
People	1	–	1	–
Ghettos	–	–	1	–
Russians	–	–	1	–
Mock courts	–	–	1	–
Hooligans	–	–	1	–
Fundamentalists	–	–	1	–
Women who like to cook Russian food	–	–	1	–
Terrorists	3		2	
Ethnic minority group	–	–	–	1
Groups of countries	–	–	–	3
Chinese	–	1	–	–
No response given	69	79	52	60

In the Vietnam War how many casualties were there on each side? Was it a lot more Americans, a few more Americans, about the same for each side, a few more Vietnamese or a lot more Vietnamese?

Response	British sample 2004 (%)	British sample 2005 (%)	British sample 2008 (%)	British sample 2009 (%)
A lot more Vietnamese	39	35	28	40
A few more Vietnamese	39	41	45	40
About equal numbers	5	5	8	5
A few more Americans	7	13	12	7
A lot more Americans	7	6	6	5
No response given	4	–	1	3

Who were the Contras in Nicaragua?

Response	British sample 2004 (%)	British sample 2005 (%)	British sample 2008 (%)	British sample 2009 (%)
Anti-communist 'freedom fighters' funded by Reagan, trained by the CIA, to overthrow Sandinista government	4	1	3	5
Freedom fighters/rebels/guerrillas	17	11	5	7
Other answers included: terrorists, natives, tribe, other nationalities e.g. Mexicans, people, army/ military/police, drug lords	13	8	19	8
No response given	66	80	73	80

In 1999 President Clinton made a public apology in Guatemala – why?

Response	British sample 2004 (%)	British sample 2005 (%)	British sample 2008 (%)	British sample 2009 (%)
US gave support to a brutal regime under which there was much abuse of human rights	4	1	9	1
Because he lied about his affair with Monica Lewinsky	3	19	5	10
US military action against/accidental bombing	8	4	8	6
US using country for nuclear testing	–	–	–	–
References to war/war or bombing of other countries	3	4	2	–
General bad treatment by the US	20	4	8	8
Inexplicit statements of failures by the President	2	2	3	1
False imprisonment of terror suspects/treatment of prisoners at Guantanamo Bay	–	6	2	7
Acknowledging deaths which had been denied	–	–	–	1
No response given	56	58	58	62
Other answers included: cutting down rainforests, third world debt, trade sanctions, to make Americans look good, Rwandan genocide, and America did not help	4	2	5	4

In the Second World War, which Allied country defeated the most German divisions?

Response	British sample 2004 (%)	British sample 2005 (%)	British sample 2008 (%)	British sample 2009 (%)
Soviet Union	27	25	26	34
Britain	30	15	17	20
US	14	28	15	25
France	16	17	26	14
Poland	–	–	1	–
Allies	–	–	1	–
Spain	–	–	1	–
Australia	1	–	–	–
Austria	1	–	–	–
Netherlands	1	–	–	–
Jamaica	–	1	–	–
Canada	–	1	–	–

China	–	1	–	–
Japan	–	1	–	–
Sweden	–	1	–	–
Italy	–	1	–	–
No response given	10	9	13	6

Notes

1. For a discussion of issues in popular culture and audience response, including the active audience, resistance and post-modern accounts see Philo and Miller (2001). For discourse analysis and discussion of media group methods in relation to the work of Norman Fairclough and Teun van Dijk see Philo (2007). Much of our work is also available in the Glasgow University Media Group website.

CHAPTER 1: HISTORIES OF THE CONFLICT

1. In a letter dated 24 October 1915 McMahon laid out the areas that Britain planned to grant independence: 'The two districts of Mersina and Alexandretta and portions of Syria lying west of the districts of Damascus, Homs, Hama and Aleppo cannot be said to be purely Arab, and should be excluded from the limits demanded. With the above modification, and without prejudice to our existing treaties with Arab chiefs we accept those limits. As for the regions lying within those frontiers wherein Britain is free to act without detriment to the interests of her ally, France, I am empowered in the name of the Government of Great Britain to give the following assurances and make the following reply to your letter: (1) Subject to the above modifications, Great Britain is prepared to recognize and support the independence of the Arabs in all the regions within the limits demanded by the Sharif of Mecca' (letter cited in Ingrams, 1972: 2)
2. According to the British census of 1922 the total population of Palestine was 752,048, comprised of 83,790 Jews, 589,177 Muslims and 71,464 Christians (United Nations, 1945).
3. In a memorandum to Lord Curzon on 11 August 1919, Balfour wrote: 'the contradiction between the letters of the Covenant and the policy of the Allies is even more flagrant in the case of the "independent nation" of Palestine than in that of the "independent nation" of Syria. For in Palestine we do not propose even to go through the form of consulting the wishes of the present inhabitants of the country, though the American [King-Crane] Commission has been going through the form of asking what they are' (British Government, Foreign Office, 1919b, cited in Ingrams, 1972: 73).
4. The Revisionist movement was a political rival of Ben-Gurion's Labour movement. It espoused a more militant attitude towards the Arabs and a more liberal economic policy. Much of their support came from Polish immigrants in the 1920s and 1930s. The Revisionists laid claim to all of Palestine and Transjordan and argued that conflict with the Arabs was inevitable. Their military wing Betar was formed in the 1920s. Some Betar members split away in the 1930s to form the Irgun paramilitary group who fought the British mandatory authorities in the 1940s. The Revisionist movement later provided much of the constituency for the Herut and Likud parties.

5. The Oxford historian Albert Hourani described the Joan Peters book as 'ludicrous and worthless' in the *Observer*. Ian and David Gilmour described it as 'preposterous' in the *London Review of Books*. *Time Out* described it as a 'piece of disinformation roughly the size and weight of a dried cowpat', whilst the chair of the Philosophy department at the Hebrew University, Avishai Margalit, condemned Peters' 'web of deceit' (reviews cited in Finkelstein, 2001: 45–6). McCarthy argues that unrecorded Arab immigration into Palestine during the Mandate period was 'small' and that for it to 'have had a significant effect on the ethnic composition of Palestine it would have had to have been immense'. He concludes that the 'argument that Arab immigration somehow made up a large part of the Palestinian Arab population is thus statistically untenable' (1990: 34). For a discussion of the effects of improvements in sanitation and hygiene on population increase in Palestine see Friedlander and Goldscheider (1979).

6. Gilbert claims that in 1943 the British authorities at Churchill's behest relaxed the bar on Jewish immigration into Palestine by allowing 'any refugee who could get by rail or sea, out of the Balkans to Istambul [to] proceed to Palestine regardless of existing quotas' (1999: 115). He estimates that several thousand took this route.

7. The US Secretary of State, James Byrnes, wrote to the British Foreign Secretary, Lord Halifax, arguing that American Jewry was not interested in the plight of the refugees in Europe, their main concern was that Jews 'ought to have a country to call their own'. Harold Beeley in the British Foreign Office complained that 'the Zionists have been deplorably successful in selling the idea that even after the Allied victory immigration to Palestine represented for many Jews "their only hope of survival"' (both cited in Ovendale, 1999: 94).

8. The pressure to open up Palestine to the Jewish refugees worried the British who feared the impact on public order. Ovendale (1999) claims that the US War Department had estimated that it would have to send 300,000 troops to Palestine to keep the peace if the area was opened to Jewish immigration. He also suggests that the US State Department was also concerned that an Arab backlash would strengthen Russian influence in a vital geostrategic area and recommended that the British colonial Empire be maintained intact.

9. For a comprehensive overview of the case put forward by the Arab delegates see the Official Records of the General Assembly, Second Session, Ad Hoc Committee on the Palestine Question, pp. 276–9, cited in UN (1990).

10. The Philippines, Haiti, and Colombia all spoke out against the partition resolution, but at the last minute changed their position with the Philippines and Haiti supporting the resolution and Colombia abstaining.

11. A number of delegates, including Lebanese representatives, claimed during debates at the UN that representatives from the US and USSR had used bribes and threats of economic sanctions in order to coerce smaller states to vote for the partition of Palestine (Official Records of the General Assembly, Second Session, Plenary Meetings, vol. II, 124th meeting: 1310).

12. For an overview of the concept of transfer in Zionist thinking see Masalha (1992). This perspective is challenged by Karsh (2000).

13. In 1959 the Palestinian historian Walid Khalidi went through the official records of Arab governments as well as Arab newspapers and the radio monitoring reports of the BBC and CIA and could find no evidence of broadcasts urging Palestinians to flee. This research was also independently corroborated by the

Irish scholar Erskine Childers in 1961. For an overview and discussion of the controversy see Hitchens and Said (1988). Some historians, such as Gilbert (1999), argue that many Arabs left voluntarily prior to the arrival of the Arab armies in May 1948 without mentioning the impact of the alleged broadcasts.

14. This position is supported by Shlaim who points to an array of underlying political and geopolitical rivalries which were camouflaged by claims that the Arab states were acting to defend the Palestinians in the spirit of pan-Arab unity: 'Dynastic rivalries played a major part in shaping Arab approaches to Palestine. King Abdullah of Transjordan was driven by a long-standing ambition to make himself the master of Greater Syria which included, in addition to Transjordan, Syria, Lebanon, and Palestine. King Faruq saw Abdullah's ambition as a direct threat to Egypt's leadership in the Arab world. The rulers of Syria and Lebanon saw in King Abdullah a threat to the independence of their countries and they also suspected him of being in cahoots with the enemy. Each Arab state was moved by its own dynastic or national interests. Arab rulers were as concerned with curbing each other as they were in fighting the common enemy. Under these circumstances it was virtually impossible to reach any real consensus on the means and ends of the Arab intervention in Palestine. Consequently, far from confronting a single enemy with a clear purpose and a clear plan of action, the Yishuv faced a loose coalition consisting of the Arab League, independent Arab states, irregular Palestinian forces, and an assortment of volunteers. The Arab coalition was one of the most divided, disorganized, and ramshackle coalitions in the entire history of warfare' (Shlaim, 2005).

15. Shlaim suggests that Ben-Gurion was very keen for Israel to develop its own nuclear weapons and the supply of French nuclear technology was a significant factor in encouraging Israel to join the French and British in their attack on Egypt. Recently discovered British government files also reveal that Britain played an important role in facilitating Israel's development of nuclear weapons by supplying Israel with heavy water (*Guardian*, 4 August 2005).

16. This controversial incident has been the subject of much debate. The Israeli authorities have always maintained that it was a 'tragic case of misidentification'. Bregman (2003: 120–2) notes that others have suggested that it was deliberately undertaken to prevent the *Liberty* from detecting Israeli troop concentrations massing in Galilee as part of the next day's attack on the Golan Heights. He argues that recently declassified tapes of conversations between air-force personnel support the conclusion that the attack on the American ship was deliberate.

17. Yitzak Rabin remarked after Israel's victory that 'I do not believe that Nasser wanted war. The two divisions that he sent into Sinai on May 14 would not have been enough to unleash an offensive against Israel. He knew it and we knew it' (*Le Monde*, 29 February 1968, cited in Hirst, 1977: 211). In a 1982 speech at the National Defense College, Menachem Begin stated that 'The Egyptian Army concentrations in the Sinai do not prove that Nasser was really about to attack us. We must be honest with ourselves. We decided to attack him' (*New York Times*, 21 August 1982).

18. Menachem Begin claimed that, in the penultimate Ministerial Committee on Defense prior to the war, military leaders 'had no doubt of victory' and 'expressed their belief not only in the strength of the army but also in its ability to rout the enemy' (Begin, cited in Finkelstein, 2001: 135). The former Commander of the Israeli Air Force, Ezer Weizmann, has claimed in relation to

the 1967 war that 'there was no threat of destruction' to the State of Israel but that the war was justified so that Israel could 'exist according to the scale, spirit and quality she now embodies' (*Ha'aretz*, 29 March 1972, cited in Chomsky, 1999: 100).

19. Norman Finkelstein (2001) alleges that Marshall Tito of Yugoslavia put forward a peace plan involving a full Israeli withdrawal from the occupied territories in exchange for 'full demilitarisation and other security guarantees in the evacuated territories, as well as an end to the call for an Arab state of Palestine'. He alleges that this proposal was accepted by both Egypt and Jordan but rejected by Israel as 'one-sided'.

20. The British representative Lord Caradon denied any ambiguity in the interpretation of Resolution 242 claiming that 'in our resolution we stated the principle of the "withdrawal of Israeli armed forces from territories occupied in the recent conflict" and in the preamble emphasised the "the inadmissibility of the acquisition of territory by war". In our view the wording of the provisions is clear.' The French delegate emphasised that 'on the point which the French delegation has always stressed as being essential – the question of the withdrawal of the occupation forces – the resolution which has been adopted, if we refer to the French text which is equally authentic with the English, leaves no room for any ambiguity, since it speaks of withdrawal "des territoires occupes", which indisputably corresponds to the expression "occupied territories"'. The Indian representative asserted that 'the principle of the inadmissibility of territorial acquisition by force is absolutely fundamental to our approach' and 'it is our understanding that the draft resolution, if approved by the Council, will commit it to the application of the principle of total withdrawal of Israeli forces from all of the territories – I repeat, all the territories – occupied by Israel as a result of the conflict which began on 5 June 1967' (all cited in Finkelstein, 2001: 146).

21. Finkelstein points to the memoirs of the American diplomat Dean Rusk who claimed that the United States favoured omitting the definite article in the withdrawal clause because 'we thought the Israeli border along the West Bank could be "rationalised", certain anomalies could easily be straightened out with some exchanges of territory, making a more sensible border for all parties' (Rusk, 1991: 388–9, cited in Finkelstein, 2001: 148). However, he stressed that 'we never contemplated any significant grant of territory to Israel as a result of the June 1967 war. On that point we and the Israelis to this day remain sharply divided' (Rusk, 1991: 388–9, cited in Finkelstein, 2001: 148).

22. See for instance Efrain Karsh, 'What Occupation?', *Commentary*, July 2002, or Max Singer, 'Right is Might', *Jerusalem Post*, 29 June 1997.

23. Chomsky points to an article by Yedidia Segal in the 3 September 1982 issue of *Nekudah*, the journal of the religious West Bank settlers, which stated that 'those among us who call for a humanistic attitude towards our [Arab] neighbours are reading the Halacha [religious law] selectively and are avoiding specific commandments'. Segal argues that the gentiles are 'a people like a donkey' and that the scriptures insist that 'conquered' peoples must 'serve' their Jewish masters and must be kept 'degraded and low' and 'must not raise their heads in Israel but must be conquered beneath their hand ... with complete submission'. 'There is no relation', Segal insists, 'between the law of Israel and atheistic modern humanism.' He cites Maimonides that 'in a divinely-commanded war [such as the 1982 Lebanon invasion] one must destroy kill and eliminate men,

women and children', there being 'no place for any humanistic considerations' (cited in Chomsky, 1999: 123–4).

24. United Nations General Assembly Resolution 54/37 adopted 1 December 1999.

25. Hirst claims that 'In Israel's Arab schools children have always had to see their own Arab culture, history and religion through Israeli eyes: they saw it deliberately mocked and falsified. Arab history became little more than a series of revolutions, murders, feuds and plunderings, whilst everything in the Jewish past was ennobled and glorified. It was always the Arabs in decline they learned about, never in their greatness; the heroes of the past, the Prophet, the Caliph Harun al-Rashid and Saladin, got perfunctory mention. In four years of secondary education Arab children had 384 periods of Jewish history as against only 32 of their own. The study of Old Testament was compulsory, while the Muslim and Christian religions were not taught at all' (1977: 238).

26. For instance, General Assembly Resolution 53/56 passed 3 December 1998 by 151 votes to 2, Resolution 52/67 passed 10 December 1997 by 151 to 2, Resolution 51/134 passed 13 December 1996 by 149 votes to 2, Resolution 49/36C passed 9 December 1994 by 145 votes to 2, Resolution 47/70D passed 14 December 1992 by 142 votes to 2.

27. In the late 1970s a *Sunday Times* report (19 June 1977) found that torture was so widespread and systematic that 'it appears to be sanctioned at some level as deliberate policy' perhaps 'to persuade Arabs in the occupied territories that it is least painful to behave passively'. More recently Amnesty International has issued annual reports cataloguing the use of torture by the Israeli authorities (e.g. Amnesty International, 2001a, 2000a, 1999b, 1998, 1997). A report (Amnesty International, 1999a) entitled 'Flouting UN Obligations in the Name of Security' concluded that Israeli 'interrogation methods, such as violent shaking, or hooding and shackling detainees to low chairs with loud music playing, constituted torture or cruel, inhuman or degrading treatment or punishment and thus contravened Article 1 of the Convention against Torture' and that torture is 'officially authorized at the highest level and indeed effectively legalized'. In the same report it was noted that the 1,600 Palestinians detained by Israeli security forces in 1998 were 'routinely tortured or ill-treated during interrogation'. The *Independent* journalist Robert Fisk has produced a number of reports from the Israeli-controlled Khiam detention centre in Southern Lebanon detailing the use of electric shock torture applied to the genitals (*Independent*, 20 May 2000). A BBC *Correspondent* documentary (4 November 2000) also reported from Khiam, claiming that torture had also been used against children and pregnant women, and that prisoners had been tortured to death, in what Amnesty International described as 'war crimes'.

28. The use of 'administrative detention' involved detaining Palestinians for long periods without trial or legal recourse. In the 1970s Hirst alleges that many Palestinians suspected of involvement with opposition movements were interned in camps in the desert: 'At its worst it meant the establishment of veritable concentration camps buried in remote corners of the Sinai desert. Nakhl, Abu Zu'aiman, Kusseimah were the names of places where whole families were kept in isolation from the outside world. They were there because relatives of theirs were suspected, no more, of working for the resistance. Crowded into tents surrounded by barbed wire, they were denied radios, newspapers or the most basic amenities from their homes, which were frequently destroyed during their captivity. Women and children would be put in one camp, male relatives

of "wanted persons" – brother, nephews, cousins – in another' (1977: 248). By 1980 the Israeli daily *Ha'aretz* estimated the number of security prisoners or detainees passing through Israeli jails since 1967 at close to 200,000 people or 20 per cent of the population, leading to a situation of 'horrendous overcrowding' and 'appalling human suffering and corruption' (8 August 1980, cited in Chomsky, 1999: 128). For more recent reports on detention without trial see Amnesty International (1999a).

29. Collective punishment could involve curfews where the local population is not allowed out for more than an hour or two a day for weeks or months at a time, schools are closed and there is no employment. Israel has justified the use of curfews on the basis that confining the Palestinian population to their homes for long periods prevents militants from attacking Jews. The use of collective punishment is illegal under international law and Israel has drawn repeated censure from the United Nations: 'The United Nations Commission on Human Rights calls upon Israel to cease immediately its policy of enforcing collective punishments, such as demolition of houses and closure of the Palestinian territory, measures which constitute flagrant violations of international law and international humanitarian law, endanger the lives of Palestinians and also constitute a major obstacle in the way of peace' (United Nations, 1999). A report by the Israeli journalist Aharon Bachar in the Israeli daily *Yediot Ahronot* described a meeting where Labour Alignment leaders presented Menachem Begin with 'detailed accounts of terrorist acts [against Arabs] in the conquered territories'. They described the collective punishment in the town of Halhul where: 'The men were taken from their houses beginning at midnight, in pyjamas, in the cold. The notables and other men were concentrated in the square of the mosque and held there until morning. Meanwhile men of the border guards broke into houses beating people with shouts and curses. During the many hours that hundreds of people were kept in the mosque square, they were ordered to urinate and excrete on one another and also to sing Hatikva [Jewish National Anthem] and to call out "Long Live the State of Israel". Several times people were beaten and ordered to crawl on the ground. Some were even ordered to lick the earth. At the same time four trucks were commandeered and at daybreak, the inhabitants were loaded onto the trucks, about 100 in each truck, and taken like sheep to the Administration headquarters in Hebron' (3 December 1982, cited in Chomsky, 1999: 131). The report further alleged that prisoners were beaten, tortured and humiliated and that settlers were permitted into prisons to take part in the beatings. For more recent reports on collective punishments see Amnesty International (2001b, 2001c) or Human Rights Watch (1996).

30. Hirst cites evidence from the Israeli League for Civil and Human Rights, that searches 'were often carried with great brutality and violence'. During night-time raids, Hirst claims that it was a 'regular practice to ... carry men off to prison without any good reason, beat them up and torture them' (1977: 249).

31. The suspicion that the concept of the 'Democratic State of Palestine' was not sincere was reinforced by the fact that the Palestinian National Council failed to produce an amendment to the Palestinian National Charter which would have specified that all the Jews in Palestine (not just those after a specified date such as 1917 or 1948) would have been entitled to Palestinian citizenship (Hirst, 1977).

32. After 1967 there were numerous diplomatic efforts to break the deadlock, all of which were fruitless. King Hussein issued a six-point peace plan in early 1969 at the National Press Club in Washington. Speaking officially in conjunction with Egypt's Nasser, Hussein offered a comprehensive peace treaty and recognition of Israel in exchange for 'the withdrawal of its armed forces from all territories occupied in the June 1967 war, and the implementation of all the other provisions of the Security Council Resolution (242)', adding that 'Israel may have either peace or territory – but she can never have both' (*Washington Report on Middle East Affairs*, 2 April 1984). This proposal was rejected by Israel. In December 1969 the American Secretary of State William Rogers put forward another peace agreement based on UN Resolution 242, specifying that Israel would return to the pre-1967 borders (with minor border modifications) and a solution to the Palestinian refugee problem would have to be found, in exchange for a comprehensive peace treaty. The proposals were rejected by the Israeli cabinet who declared that 'if these proposals were carried out, Israel's security and peace would be in grave danger. Israel will not be sacrificed to by any power policy, and will reject any attempt to impose a forced solution upon it' (cited in Shlaim, 2000: 291). In 1971 the Swedish diplomat Dr Gunnar Jarring reported that Egypt had offered Israel a full peace treaty based on Resolution 242, with the stipulation that Israel also had to withdraw from the Sinai and Gaza Strip, settle the refugee problem in line with UN resolutions, and establish a UN force to keep the peace. Israel's reply, though positive, insisted that 'Israel will not return to the pre-5 June 1967 lines' (Shlaim, 2000: 300). This, Shlaim suggests, doomed the Jarring Initiative (2000). It also drew repeated criticism from the United Nations. The Jarring Initiative was followed by attempts at achieving an interim solution which Shlaim suggests floundered on Israel's refusal to accept a timetable for a permanent settlement, and its desire for territorial revisionism. There followed in 1972 and 1973 a number of openly annexationist pronouncements by Israeli leaders. Moshe Dayan told *Time* magazine in July 1973 'there is no more Palestine. Finished', and in an April 1973 interview he talked of 'a new state of Israel with broad frontiers, strong and solid, with the authority of the Israeli government extending from the Jordan to the Suez Canal' (both cited in Shlaim, 2000: 316). Shlaim suggests that this, together with the later publication of the Galilee document detailing a large expansion of settlement building in the occupied territories, left Sadat little choice but to use force to try to regain the Sinai.

33. Boyle (2002) argues that when the Israeli forces started advancing, the Soviets had considered inserting their own force into the conflict leading the Americans to raise their nuclear alert to Def Con Three, the highest state of preparedness. He claims that in the face of this the Soviets backed down but that the world had come perilously close to a nuclear confrontation between the superpowers. Three Israeli and American analysts have also claimed that Israel threatened to use nuclear weapons against Egypt and in fact prepared to do so at the beginning of the 1973 war. This was in order to force America to provide a large consignment of conventional weapons, which was forthcoming (Perlmutter, Handel and Bar-Joseph, 1982).

34. In March 1977 the Palestinian National Council called for an 'independent national state' in Palestine and an Arab-Israeli peace conference. Prime Minister Rabin's reply was that 'the only place the Israelis could meet the Palestinian guerillas was on the field of battle' (*New York Times*, 21 March 1977). In

1977, the PLO leaked a 'peace plan' in Beirut which stated that the (explicitly rejectionist) Palestinian National Covenant would not serve as the basis for inter-state relations and that any progression beyond a two-state solution 'would be achieved by peaceful means' (*Manchester Guardian Weekly*, 7 August 1977). Tillman claims that, in November 1978, Yasser Arafat in requesting a dialogue with American representatives issued the following statement: 'The PLO will accept an independent Palestinian state consisting of the West Bank and Gaza, with connecting corridor, and in that circumstance will renounce any and all violent means to enlarge the territory of the state. I would reserve the right, of course, to use non-violent means, that is to say diplomatic and democratic means, to bring about the eventual unification of all Palestine ... we will give de facto recognition to the State of Israel' (Tillman, 1982: 215–18). In April 1981, after PLO acceptance of the Soviet peace plan, the PLO representative Issam Sartawi declared that 'from this it follows that the PLO has formally conceded to Israel, in the most unequivocal manner, the right to exist on a reciprocal basis'. A week later Sartawi issued a joint statement with the former Israel general Mattityahu Peled: 'the PLO has made its willingness to accept and recognize the state of Israel on the basis of mutual recognition of each nation's legitimate right of self-determination crystal clear in various resolutions since 1977' (all references cited in Chomsky, 1999: 68–78).

35. Testimony of Dr Chris Giannou before the House Sub-committee on Europe and the Middle East, 13/7/1982 (cited in Chomsky, 1999: 229).

36. For other reports on ill-treatment of detainees see *Der Spiegel*, 14 March 1983; *Haolam Haze*, 15 December 1982; or *The Times*, 18 March 1983.

37. On the subject of Palestinian weaponry see Ze'ev Schiff (*Ha'aretz*, 18 July 1982) or Hirsh Goodman (*Jerusalem Post*, 9 July 1982) who suggested the Palestinian 'army' and weapons posed no significant threat to Israel and that many of the claims regarding the scale of weaponry were exaggerated. With regard to ceasefire violations the *Christian Science Monitor* (18 March 1982) reported that the PLO had observed the ceasefire despite many Israeli provocations. The Abu Nidal group who attempted to assassinate the Israeli ambassador were sworn enemies of the PLO leadership and had previously tried to assassinate Yasser Arafat. All above references cited in Chomsky (1999: 210).

38. All extracts taken from *Do Not Say That You Did Not Know*, a report by the Israeli Committee for solidarity with Bir Zeit, 5 June 1982, cited in Chomsky (1999: 60).

39. See for instance Report of the Special Committee to Investigate Israeli Practices Affecting the Human Rights of the Population of the Occupied Territories, A/RES/38/79, 15 December 1983, or Special Committee to Investigate Israeli Practices Affecting the Human Rights of the Population of the Occupied Territories, A/RES/39/95, 14 December 1984, or UN Commission on Human Rights: Question of the violation of human rights in the occupied Arab territories, including Palestine, E/CN.4/RES/1985/1, 19 February 1985.

40. A B'Tselem (Israeli human rights group) report on the treatment of children detained by Israeli forces found that 'illegal violence against minors ... many [of whom] are innocent of any crime ... occurs on a large scale'. It found that violence directed against minors, including 'slapping, punching, kicking, hair pulling, beatings with clubs or with iron rods, pushing into walls and onto floors', was 'very common'. It also detailed more severe forms of ill-treatment: 'Beating the detainee as he is suspended in a closed sack covering the head and

tied around the knees; tying the detainee in a twisted position to an outdoor pipe with hands behind the back for hours and, sometimes, in the rain, at night, and during the hot daytime hours; confining the detainee, sometimes for a few days, in the "lock-up" – a dark, smelly and suffocating cell one and a half by one and a half meters [five by five feet]; placing the detainee, sometimes for many hours, in the "closet" – a narrow cell the height of a person in which one can stand but not move; and depositing the tied-up detainee for many hours in the "grave" – a kind of box, closed by a door from the top, with only enough room to crouch and no toilet.' The Israeli daily *Hotam* (1 April 1988) reported the beating of a ten year old during an army interrogation who was left 'looking like a steak', noting that soldiers 'weren't bothered' when they later found out that the boy was a deaf mute and mentally retarded. Reporting on the treatment of Palestinians as young as 14 arrested 'on suspicion of stone throwing' the Israeli daily *Hadashot* (24 February 1992) cited the testimony of an insider at the Hebron detention centre: 'What happened there ... was plain horror: they would break their clubs on the prisoners' bodies, hit them in the genitals, tie a prisoner up on the cold floor and play soccer with him – literally kick and roll him around. Then they'd give him electric shocks, using the generator of a field telephone, and then push him out to stand for hours in the cold and rain ... They would crush the prisoners ... turning them into lumps of meat.' All above reports cited in Finkelstein (1996: 47–9).

41. For other references on Hezbullah's influence on Hamas see *Ha'aretz* (21 April 1994) or *Nida' al-Watan* (15 November 1996).

42. Amongst others the poet Mahmoud Darwish, the PLO's Lebanon representative Shafiq al-Hut (both of whom resigned from the PLO executive committee in protest), the leader of the Palestinian negotiating team and Gaza Red Crescent Society, Haidar Abd al-Shafi, the Palestinian negotiator as well as other prominent Fatah and PLO officials

43. Hezbullah, which also run a network of social services, claim they are trying to protect the local population, many of whom have been expelled from their home by Israel's proxy force the South Lebanon. Human rights groups have condemned the expulsions as 'war crimes' and demanded that they stop (Human Rights Watch, 1999). The organisation has also condemned both Israel and Hezbullah for targeting civilians.

44. The day before the agreement was signed Human Rights Watch (1998) urged the United States and Israel not to pressure the Palestinian Authority to expand its security crackdown without all sides making a clear commitment to safeguard human rights. Human Rights Watch pointed out that the 'Palestinian Authority's human rights record is already deplorable', and that the 'U.S. doesn't condemn these violations now – will the U.S. condemn violations once it is formally part of the process that creates them?' The Israeli human rights group B'Tselem published a report a month after the signing, pointing to 'mass arbitrary arrests by both the Palestinian Authority and Israel' and alleging that 'the agreement merely pays lip service to human rights, with no intention by any of the parties – Israel, the Palestinian National Authority or the United States – to hold the sides accountable for human rights violations'.

45. Barak claimed that he would not allow the Syrians to reach the waters of Lake Tiberias (where Israel draws much of its water), the Syrians claimed that Barak was trying to lure them into an 'Arafat-style agreement, normalize relations, curb Hezbullah and then we might withdraw'.

46. See for instance Conal Urquhart's article 'Israeli soldiers tell of indiscriminate killings by army and a culture of impunity' (*Guardian*, 6 September 2005).
47. See Amnesty International (2007b), B'Tselem (2009a) or Human Rights Watch (2007a).
48. See for example 'Offering Video, Israel Answers Critics on War' (*New York Times*, 5 December 2006) or Israeli Ministry of Foreign Affairs (2006a).
49. See for example 'Our aim is to win – nothing is safe, Israeli chiefs declare' (*The Times*, 14 July 2006), 'IAF continues attack on Lebanon' (*Jerusalem Post*, 17 July 2006), 'High-ranking officer: Halutz ordered retaliation policy' (*Jerusalem Post*, 24 July 2006) or 'Israel vowing to rout Hezbullah' (*New York Times*, 15 July 2006).
50. Britain's stance which appeared to be dictated by Tony Blair was intensely controversial and aroused strong opposition within the parliamentary Labour party who later suggested that it was a significant factor in speeding up the prime minister's departure.
51. According to Human Rights Watch (2008a) the estimated 1 million unexploded bomblets 'have severely damaged the economy by turning agricultural land into de facto minefields and interfering with the harvesting of tobacco, citrus, banana, and olive crops'. A later report by Reuters (27 November 2008) claimed that in the two years since the end of the war 40 Lebanese had been killed by exploded Israeli cluster munitions and a further 270 wounded.
52. For the Israeli accusations regarding the alleged use of human shields see Israeli Ministry of Foreign Affairs (2009b) or the article entitled 'Hezbullah's Human Shields' by Alan Dershowitz (*National Post*, 1 August 2006).
53. See Weiner and Bell (2008) or Israeli Ministry of Foreign Affairs (2010).
54. A report by Amos Harel in *Ha'aretz* (24 October 2006) discussed the results of a 'secret, two year investigation by the defense establishment' which found that 'there has been rampant illegal construction in dozens of settlements and in many cases involving privately owned Palestinian properties'. The results of the study, which according to 'security sources' were described as 'political and diplomatic dynamite', indicated that the public information that was given out regarding settlement building was inaccurate because 'a number of key officials in the Civil Administration actively [were] deleting information from the data base out of ideological allegiance with the settlers'.
55. 'In the process of being detained, or while kneeling on the outer decks for several hours, there was physical abuse of passengers by the Israeli forces, including kicking and punching and being hit with the butts of rifles. One foreign correspondent, on board in his professional capacity, was thrown on the ground and kicked and beaten before being handcuffed … The manner in which plastic handcuffs were attached to the wrists of passengers caused severe pain and discomfort. There was widespread misuse of the handcuffs by the Israeli soldiers who tightened the plastic handcuffs to an extent that caused pain, swelling, a loss of blood circulation in the hands and the loss of sensitivity in their hands and fingers. Most passengers who requested that the handcuffs be loosened were ignored or it resulted in the handcuffs being further tightened. A number of passengers are still experiencing medical problems related to the handcuffing three months later and forensic reports confirm that at least fifty-four passengers had received injuries, transversal abrasions and bruises, as a result of handcuffing on board the Mavi Marmara' (United Nations, 2010: 37).
56. This perspective was also expressed in Mearsheimer and Walt (2008).

CHAPTER 2: CONTENT STUDIES 2000–02

1. Originally published in the 2004 edition.
2. Ariel Sharon was subsequently elected as Prime Minister of Israel in January 2001.
3. Thus we quoted a report in the *Financial Times* which noted that 'Shop stewards tell hair-raising stories about managerial failings, and point at the moment to constant assembly track hold-ups caused by non-availability of supplier component parts' (quoted in Philo et al., 1995: 12).
4. The three soldiers were later reported to have been killed either during or shortly after the abduction (www.ujl.org). On 10 November 2003, it was reported that the Israeli government had approved an agreement with Hezbullah to swap hundreds of Palestinian and Lebanese prisoners in exchange for a captured Israeli businessman and the bodies of the servicemen.
5. There were a small number of news items or parts of them which were lost through machine failure or because of sudden changes in programme times. This would not affect our overall conclusions on trends in coverage because the losses were random and news items tended to be repeated with slight variations throughout each day.
6. As a percentage of the coverage they accounted for 1.5 per cent, as measured in lines of text.
7. Of the explanations given, 6.5 per cent of the coverage in this sample described the allocation of blame by one side or the other (including discussions on the roles of Arafat and Sharon). The conflict was explained as a 'cycle of violence' in 2 per cent of the sample (61 lines). Religion was referred to as a cause in 2 per cent of the coverage (80.5 lines). Land, water and economic discontent were referred to in 18 lines (0.5 per cent). Israeli perspectives on security needs were 3 per cent (104.5 lines). The 'occupation' as a cause was 1 per cent (37.25 lines). The remaining text was taken up with studio links (3.5 per cent) and references to associated events, such as the effect of the conflict on oil prices (3 per cent). There were 17.5 lines on the history and origins of the conflict.
8. The use of torture by Israeli forces was outlawed by the Israeli high court in 1999. But after the start of the intifada in October 2000 there were reports that it was again being widely used (*Guardian*, 13 June 2002).
9. See Mike Berry's PhD thesis (Berry, 2004).
10. A similar problem arose when the Israelis constructed what they termed their 'security fence' in 2003. The Palestinians rejected this term, seeing the construction as a new attempt by the Israelis to take more land. It was also referred to by some Palestinian groups as an 'apartheid' wall. The BBC and other media sometimes chose to use the Israeli definition. When BBC Online was questioned over this, the following remarkable reply was given: 'Thank you for your email. We feel we are right to use the term "security fence" as this is what Israel is calling it' (BBC News Online, 8 August 2003). Although, as the BBC notes, they have published the views of those who are critical of the fence, this does not address the problem of the adoption by journalists of the language and explanatory definitions of one side. It should be possible for journalists to include both views. We found this example from ITV news where this was done: 'This is the Israeli response to the assassination: the checking of all Palestinians driving into the West Bank. *The Israelis call this a*

security precaution, but there is chaos here and the Palestinians call it collective punishment' (ITV early evening News, 17 October 2001 – our italics).

11. For interviews and on-screen appearances, as expressed in lines of text, the figures were: Israeli – 105.5, Palestinian – 52.25.

12. Such measures require decisions about what is to be included or excluded from counts, which have to be consistent across all the samples. For this count we included: time, date, place; who or what inflicted the casualties; descriptions of who was killed/injured as given by the reporters and eye-witnesses' accounts/ statements by families or others; treatment by emergency services; funerals and mourning and specific references to the events, for example, 'the killing of the soldiers'. We also included estimates of casualties over time, for example, numbers of deaths since the beginning of the intifada. We did not include damage to property rather than people (such as bomb damage to shops); non-specific references to suicide-bombings or attacks, for example, 'Yasser Arafat is under pressure to control the suicide bombers' or claims and counter-claims of killings or massacres, which cancelled each other out (that is, when both sides were represented saying the opposite of each other at the same time). We also excluded from this count general commentaries on the wider ramifications of military action or bombings on world opinion or the peace process.

13. The disparity in deaths and casualties continued through the conflict, though not at the level of the first two weeks. In December 2000, the Israeli human rights group B' Tselem reported that between 29 September and 2 December 2000, 231 Palestinians had been killed and 29 Israelis, while nearly 10,000 Palestinians had been injured and 362 Israelis, (B'Tselem, 2000).

14. As expressed in lines of text, the figures were: Israelis/Jews – 92.5 lines, Palestinians/Arabs – 195.75.

15. The word 'massacre' was used on one occasion but not in relation to events in the intifada. While interviewing a Palestinian who had been injured, an ITV journalist notes: 'Six years ago he took twelve bullets when a Jewish fanatic carried out a massacre'. (ITV early evening News, 4 October 2000).

16. The *Independent* described their position in Israeli society as follows: 'Israel's one million Arabs form a fifth of the population. They are waiters and factory workers, a cheap labour pool that serves a growing consumer society, slogging on, despite civil rights violations and prejudice' (11December 2000).

17. In the sample from October–December 2001 the figures (all measured as lines of text) were: on BBC1 – Israeli 140.75 and Palestinian 53.25, on ITV – Israeli 36 and Palestinian 35.5. In the sample from March 2002 the figures were: on BBC1 – Israeli 22.25 and Palestinian 9, on ITV – Israeli 15 and Palestinian 6. In the sample from April 2002 the figures were: on BBC1 – Israeli 89.25 and Palestinian 50.25, on ITV – Israeli 64.5 and Palestinian 35.5. Taken together the figures were: for the BBC1 – Israeli 252.25 and Palestinian 112.5, and for ITV – Israeli 115.5 and Palestinian 77.

18. Measured in terms of the references, the figures were: Israeli 41 and Palestinian 7. For Sample Three (March 2002) the figures were Israeli 28 and Palestinian 9 (both BBC1 and ITV together).

19. The link between the actions of Israel and the 'global war on terror' being pursued by the US was challenged in an ITN bulletin which we noted above as having posed some critical questions about the conflict. A journalist asked rhetorically: 'Does this have any connection to the wider global war on terror? … the majority of Israelis certainly believe so, but most of the world considers

it a decades old problem with no direct link to Osama bin Laden or his terrorist network' (ITV late News, 3 December 2001). Such referencing of 'world opinion' which is critical of Israeli perspectives is comparatively rare in our samples. US opinion is much more frequently referenced. Indeed, statements from US politicians far outweigh even those from Britain. In the coverage from 2001 and 2002, for example, there were 66 US and 33 British statements (both BBC1 and ITV together). The figures for each channel are: BBC1 – US 34 and British 19, and ITV – US 32 and British 14. In the following example from a later ITV bulletin 'world opinion' is simply equated with that of the US: 'The presence in Jerusalem today of New York mayor Giuliani is further evidence that for now it's the Israelis *who have the world's sympathy*' (ITV main News, 9 December 2001 – our italics).

20. On 5 March 2002, BBC and ITV carried a report that a bomb had been planted at a Palestinian school and this was attributed to 'Jewish extremists' and 'Jewish vigilantes' (ITV main News) and to 'Jewish extremists' (BBC1 lunchtime News). The word 'terrorist' was not used to describe them but was used in the ITV bulletin to describe Palestinians.

21. An Israeli minister was also challenged by the BBC journalist in the report of the five Palestinian children killed on their way to school. The minister states that 'civilians are not there', and the journalist replies: 'Minister, I stood there yesterday, this is an area where children pass to go to school, this is an area where people cultivate. I have stood there and I have seen it. Now is it appropriate that a roadside bomb should be planted in this place?' (BBC1 late News, 23 November 2001).

22. As we have indicated above, Israeli statements substantially outnumber those from Palestinians on the BBC in this sample. For on-screen comments and reported statements, measured as lines of text, the figures were: Israeli 140.75 and Palestinian 53.25.

23. As measured as lines of text, both BBC1 and ITV: Israeli 152.75 and Palestinian 102.75. Individually the figures were: BBC1 – Israeli 94 and Palestinian 64.5, and ITV – Israeli 58.75 and Palestinian 38.25.

24. The breakdown of these figures was: BBC1 – Israelis 61.25 and Palestinians 21.25, and ITV – Israelis 59 and Palestinians 24.75.

25. The figures were: Israeli 28 and Palestinian 9 (both BBC1 and ITV together).

26. In this sample the figures for the coverage of both sides' casualties were: Israeli 128 and Palestinian 117.25 (both BBC1 and ITV together, measured as lines of text). The BBC had an equal amount of coverage for each side, for ITV the figures were: Israeli 44.75 and Palestinian 34.

27. We counted the on-screen appearances/interviews and reported statements in this period. The Israeli dominance was again apparent – the figures were: Israeli 153.75 and Palestinian 85.75 (measured as lines of text, both BBC and ITV together).

CHAPTER 3: AUDIENCE STUDIES 2001–02

1. Originally published in the 2004 edition.
2. *Palestine is Still the Issue* – ITV broadcast, 16 September 2002.
3. Such values are not 'universal' in the sense that everyone believes in or subscribes to them. They are universal in as much as they have the potential to traverse

cultural difference, but they do not always do so. They may be contested by other cultural and political values such as racism. A white colonialist, for example, might not think that the 'value' of universal freedom should be applied to black people.

CHAPTER 4: WHY DOES IT HAPPEN?

1. Originally published in the 2004 edition.
2. Relationships became more fraught after the outbreak of the intifada. Journalists accused the Israeli armed forces of deliberate intimidation. We were also told that it was especially difficult for journalists whose work was actually seen in Israel (notably CNN and the BBC). One journalist was said to have taken her name from the door where she lived because of the amount of hate-mail she received. Journalists who are based in Israel tend to live in West Jerusalem. Those who are passing through on short-term assignments often stay in the American Colony hotel in East Jerusalem – a place which Melanie Phillips suggests is often used successfully by Palestinians to establish contacts (*Jewish Chronicle*, 31 October 2003). She also complains that because of a mixture of arrogance and despair the Israelis are not sufficiently committed to their public presentation. She says they take the view that Jews 'are no longer prepared to justify their own existence'. Yet paradoxically she also notes that the Israeli government press office and other ministry spokesmen deluge journalists with information and offers of help (*Jewish Chronicle*, 31 October 2003) The consequence of what she sees as Israel's public relations failure is that those who support Israel are left to run a gauntlet of 'lies and vilification'. Both sides often accuse the other of lying. Joy Wolfe commented to us on 'all the lies' by Palestinians in the portrayal of Jenin. But we also had two very senior journalists saying to us independently that, 'the Israelis lie and lie' and 'the Israelis lie all the time' (August 2003). Other journalists have criticised the quality of Palestinian accounts. What emerges from all this is that both sides complain about the quality of their own public relations and about the actions of the other side, but Israel and its supporters do have a comparatively well-resourced system and their views are well featured on TV news.
3. The Israelis also accused the Palestinians of intimidating journalists, but the FPA was reported to have disputed this and to have laid the blame on the Israelis (*Observer*, 17 June 2001).
4. *The Killing Zone*, Channel 4, 18 May 2003.
5. See, for example, a recent article by David Aaronovitch noting that 'The amount of anti-Semitic literature, journalism and television in Arab countries is voluminous ... what on earth is the blood libel doing in a column in a respected Egyptian mass daily paper, *Al-Ahram*, in a book by the Syrian defence minister and in broadcast sermons from various Palestinian mosques?' (Aaronovitch, 2003).
6. As we have indicated above, in our samples from 2001 and 2002 there was a very strong dominance of reported statements and interviews/on-screen appearances from US politicians, outnumbering even those from Britain (66 US and 33 British).

CHAPTER 5: CONCLUSIONS ON THE 2000–02 CONTENT AND AUDIENCE SAMPLES

1. Originally published in the 2004 edition.
2. In the 2001 and 2002 samples, the figures were: Israeli 367.75 and Palestinian 189.5 (both BBC1 and ITV, measured as lines of text).

CHAPTER 6: NEWS CONTENT AND COMPETING EXPLANATIONS OF THE 2008/09 GAZA ATTACK

1. It differs from much of discourse analysis because it views these 'explanatory themes' as ideologies and examines their generation and development in wider processes of class and political conflict. As such it looks beyond the immediate text and 'preferring strategies' within it. For more on the difference between the Glasgow approach and discourse analysis see Philo (2007).
2. Writing in the *London Review of Books*, Nicholas Pelham notes that around 80 per cent of Gaza's imports come through the tunnels, and that 'almost everyone has an interest in the tunnel economy: Egyptians, from the top dynasts to the lowliest guards, pocket copious baksheesh for letting the traffic through; Hamas gets a handsome cut; Israel can use the existence of the tunnels as an excuse (not the only one) to try to palm responsibility for Gaza onto Egypt; and ordinary Gazans can find food in the shop and a little relief from the siege' (2009). But as he notes, while the tunnel economy had brought wealth to some, four out of five Gazans live in poverty and 20,000 war victims were still displaced.
3. The BBC News Online account of the report refers to it as saying 'Israel committed war crimes and carried out reckless attacks and acts of wanton destruction in its Gaza offensive' and that the report 'also calls rocket attacks by Palestinian militants war crimes' (BBC News Online, 2 July 2009). Amnesty was also reported in February 2009, to have new evidence that Hamas forces perpetrated a 'campaign of abductions, deliberate and unlawful killings, torture and death threats against those they accuse of "collaborating" with Israel, as well as opponents and critics'. The evidence was said to corroborate witness accounts given to the *Guardian* and an investigation by the Palestinian Centre for Human Rights (McCarthy, 2009a: 31).
4. Subsequent to the attack on Gaza between December 2008 and January 2009, however, it was reported in the *Guardian* that there were attempts by Hamas to make Palestinian society more Islamist (McCarthy, 2009b: 24).
5. This was also seen by many to be the purpose of the blockade, as a form of collective punishment imposed with increasing stringency after Hamas became the governing body of Gaza. For this reason journalists at Al Jazeera, the Arab television service, were told in their guidelines that when referring to the embargo or sanctions, they should say 'the embargo against the Palestinians and not the embargo against the Palestinian government of Hamas'. The guidelines go on to say that 'the embargo is not confined to the government, everybody is affected in Palestine' (Al Jazeera internal guidelines cited in Barkho, 2010).
6. ITV in contrast simply reports that 'Hamas says their resistance will continue and they fired more rockets tonight' (ITV main News, 17 January 2009). On 11 January ITV began their main news with the headline, 'Defiant. Palestinian fighters tell us they are confident of victory against Israel's bombardment of

Gaza' (ITV main News, 11 January 2009). But as with the BBC, the causes of the conflict and the rationale for the Palestinian actions remain largely unexplored.

7.   There is another comment from the point of view of the Palestinians, to the use of the tunnels and the siege, on the BBC main news of the same day. This comes after three comments on the smuggling of weapons. The BBC journalist then notes: 'but besides weapons they smuggle essential fuel, electricity, even livestock for civilians and after 18 months under siege the Palestinians say these tunnels are their lifeline' (BBC1 main News, 7 January 2009). There is however no commentary here on the consequences of the siege, its reasons from the Palestinian perspective or of the report of the offer to stop firing rockets if it is lifted.

8.   There is an oblique reference to the effects of the siege in a brief history of the conflict given on BBC1. After mentioning the six-month ceasefire which began in June 2008, the journalist comments: 'the result, Hamas rocket attacks into Israel dropped sharply yet they did not stop completely. In return, Israel's blockade of Gaza was eased, the flow of some essential goods to the people of Gaza increased but UN relief workers complained they could still not refill their warehouses and the economy could not recover' (BBC1 early evening news, 5 January 2009). On ITV there is a report on 7 January about Israel allowing aid during a three-hour ceasefire in response to international pressure. It quotes the UN as saying that 1 million people are without electricity and two-thirds don't have access to running water. But it is not clear whether these conditions relate to the immediate conflict. The words 'blockade' and 'siege' are not mentioned. In these examples from BBC and ITV, there is no link made between the siege and the firing of rockets or to the report of the Hamas offer to stop these in exchange for a lifting of the siege.

9.   The view of Hamas as absolutely inflexible occurs later in coverage of the attack on the aid flotilla to Gaza in May 2010. An ITV journalist comments that, 'Hamas is an independent Palestinian entity that is totally opposed to the existence of the state of Israel and still trying to take military measures against it' (ITV early evening News, 31 May 2010).

10.   Another brief reference is made by a BBC journalist who notes that in Gaza thousands have been made homeless and that 'this isn't a new experience, many Gazan families who are refugees from the land that became Israel in 1948' (BBC1 main News, 12 January 2009).

CHAPTER 8: ATTACK ON THE GAZA FLOTILLA, 2010

1.   The BBC does include comments from activists which could possibly have been developed to offer an alternative account. For example on 1 June, Hasan Nowarah is featured momentarily saying 'As they come into our boat, they were pushing everybody and they were running around and they are hitting us with the backs of their guns' (BBC1 main News, 1 June 2010). But it remains as a fragment unconnected to any critique of the sequence which the Israelis gave to argue that they were acting in self-defence.

References

Aaronovitch, D. (2003) 'The New Anti-Semitism', *Observer*, 22 June.

Aham, A. (1923) *Am Scheideweg* (Berlin).

Amnesty International (1996a) 'Israel/Lebanon Unlawful Killings during Operation Grapes of Wrath'. AI Index: MDE 15/042/1996.

—— (1996b) 'Israel/Lebanon: Amnesty International Demands Effective Protection for Civilians, Calls for Proper Enquiry into Killings by Israel'. AI Index: MDE 15/049/1996.

—— (1997) 'Annual Report 1997 Israel and the Occupied Territories'. AI Index: POL 10/001/1997.

—— (1998) 'Annual Report 1998 Israel and the Occupied Territories'. AI Index: POL 10/001/1998.

—— (1999a) 'Israel: Flouting UN Obligations in the Name of Security. Oral Statement to the UN Commission on Human Rights on Israel and the Occupied Territories'. AI Index: MDE 15/034/1999.

—— (1999b) 'Annual Report 1999 Israel and the Occupied Territories'. AI Index: POL 10/001/1999.

—— (1999c) 'Israel and the Occupied Territories: Demolition and Dispossession: the Destruction of Palestinian Homes'. AI Index: MDE 15/059/1999.

—— (2000a) 'Annual Report 2000 Israel and the Occupied Territories'. AI Index: POL 10/001/00.

—— (2000b) 'Israel and the Occupied Territories: Excessive Use of Lethal Force'. AI Index: MDE 15/041/2000.

—— (2001a) 'Annual Report 2001 Israel and the Occupied Territories'. AI Index: POL 10/001/2001.

—— (2001b) 'Israel/OT: The International Community Must Act to End Israel's Policy of Closures and House Demolitions'. AI Index: MDE 15/066/2001.

—— (2001c) 'Israel/OT: Committee Against Torture Says Israel's Policy of Closures and Demolitions of Palestinian Homes May Amount to Cruel Inhuman or Degrading Treatment'. AI Index: MDE 15/105/2001.

—— (2001d) 'Israel/OT: Annual Report'. AI Index: POL 10/001/2001.

—— (2001e) 'Israel/OT/Palestinian Authority: Amnesty International Condemns Bombing of Discotheque'. AI Index: MDE 15/049/2001.

—— (2002a) 'Without Distinction: Attacks on Civilians by Palestinian Armed Groups'. AI Index: MDE 02/003/2002.

—— (2002b) 'Israel and the Occupied Territories: Shielded from Scrutiny: IDF Violations in Jenin and Nablus'. AI Index: MDE 15/149/2002.

—— (2006a) 'Israel/Occupied Territories: Deliberate Attacks a War Crime'. AI Index: MDE 15/061/2006.

—— (2006b) 'Israel/Lebanon: Under Fire: Hezbullah's Attacks on Northern Israel'. AI Index: MDE 02/025/2006.

—— (2006c) 'Lebanon: Deliberate Destruction or "Collateral Damage"? Israeli Attacks on Civilian Infrastructure'. AI Index: MDE 18/007/2006.

—— (2007a) 'Occupied Palestinian Territories: Torn Apart by Factional Strife'. AI Index: MDE 21/020/2007.

—— (2007b) 'Israel/OPT: Civilians in the Line of Fire in Gaza and Sderot'. AI Index: MDE 15/040/2007.

—— (2008a) 'Gaza Blockade – Collective Punishment'. AI Index: MDE 15/021/2008.

—— (2008b) 'Israel/OPT Immediate Access to Humanitarian Workers and Observers Essential' [Internet] Available from <http://www.amnesty.org/en/news-and-updates/news/israelopt-immediate-access-humanitarian-workers-and-observers-essential-20081231> [Accessed 8 September 2010].

—— (2009) 'Israel/Gaza. Operation "Cast Lead": 22 Days of Death and Destruction'. AI Index: MDE 15/015/2009.

Aronson, G. (1998) 'Palestinian Leadership Fails to Understand the Importance of Settlements', *Report on Israeli Settlements in the Occupied Territories*, July/August.

—— (2001) 'Deconstructing the Taba Talks', *Report on Israeli Settlements in the Occupied Territories*, March/April.

—— (2003) 'Sharon Government's Separation Plan Defines Palestinian Borders', *Report on Israeli Settlements in the Occupied Territories*, July/August.

Bard, M. (2003) *Myths and Facts Online Israel and Lebanon* [Internet] Available from <http://www.us-israel.org/jsource/myths/mf11.html [Accessed 6 September 2003].

Barkho, L. (2010) *News from the BBC, CNN and Al-Jazeera – How The Broadcasters Cover the Middle East*, Hampton Press Communication Series (Hampton Press: Cresskill NJ).

Bauer, Y. (1970) *Flight and Rescue: Brichah* (New York: Random House).

BBC Trust (2009) [Internet] Available from <www.bbc.co.uk/bbctrust/our_work/complaints_appeals/index.shtml> [Accessed 30 September 2010].

Beilin, Y. (1985) *Mehiro Shel Ihud* (in Hebrew) (Revivim).

Benhorin, Y. (2006) 'Hamas: Ceasefire for Return to 1967 Border' [Internet] Available from <http://www.ynetnews.com/articles/0,7340,L-3207845,00.html> [Accessed 8 June 2010].

Berry, M. (2004) 'Television and the Israeli-Palestinian Conflict', PhD thesis, University of Glasgow.

Bohm, A. (1935) *Die Zionistische Bewegung* (Berlin).

Boyd, J. (2009) 'Antisemitism and the Reported World', *Guardian*, Comment is Free, 18 November.

Boyle, W.J. (2002) *The Two O'Clock War: The 1973 Yom Kippur Conflict and the Airlift that Saved Israel* (New York: St Martin's Press).

Breaking the Silence (2009) 'A New Booklet by "Breaking the Silence"' [Internet] Available from <http://www.shovrimshtika.org/oferet/news_item_e.asp?id=1> [Accessed 1 October 2010].

Bregman, A. (2003) *A History of Israel* (Basingstoke: Palgrave Macmillan).

British Government (1919a) Public Record Office. Foreign Office No. 800/215.

—— (1919b) Public Record Office. Foreign Office No. 371/4183.

—— (1930) 'Palestine: Report on Immigration, Land Settlement and Development' – Cmd. 3686.

—— (1939) 'Report of a Committee on Correspondence between Sir Henry McMahon and the Sherif of Mecca', Parliamentary Papers – Cmd. 5974.

—— (1947) 'The Political History of Palestine under the British Administration' (Memorandum to the United Nations Special Committee on Palestine), Jerusalem.

B'Tselem (2000) *Illusions of Restraint*, Report, December.

—— (2002) *Lethal Curfew – the Use of Live Ammunition to Enforce a Curfew*, Report, October.

—— (2003a) *Casualty Statistics 1987–2003* [Internet] Available from <http://www. btselem.org/English/Statistics/Total_Casualties.asp> [Accessed 6 September 2003].

—— (2003b) *Fatalities in the Al-Aqsa Intifada, Data by Month* [Internet] Available from <http://www.btselem.org/English/Statistics/Al_Aqsa_Fatalities_Tables.asp> [Accessed 6 September 2003].

—— (2003c) *Behind the Barrier: Human Rights Violation as a Result of Israel's Separation Barrier*, Position Paper, April.

—— (2003d) *Violence of Settlers Against Palestinians* [Internet] Available from <http://www.btselem.org/English/Settler_Violence/Index.asp> [Accessed 6 September 2003].

—— (2003e) *Handling of Complaints of Settler Violence* [Internet] Available from <http://www.btselem.org/English/Settler_Violence/Law_Enforcement.asp> [Accessed 6 September 2003].

—— (2009a) *Attacks on Israeli Civilians by Palestinians* [Internet] Available from <http://www.btselem.org/english/Israeli_Civilians/Qassam_missiles.asp> [Accessed 19 August 2010].

—— (2009b) *One Year since Operation Cast Lead, Still No Accountability* [Internet] Available from <http://www.btselem.org/English/Gaza_Strip/20091227_A_year_to_Castlead_Operation.asp> [Accessed 7 September 2010].

—— (2009c) *B'Tselem's Investigation of Fatalities in Operation Cast Lead* [Internet] Available from <http://www.btselem.org/Download/20090909_Cast_Lead_Fatalities_Eng.pdf> [Accessed 7 September 2010].

—— (2010a) *Fatality Statistics* [Internet] Available from <http://www.btselem.org/English/Statistics/Index.asp> [Accessed 20 August 2010].

—— (2010b) *Israeli Civilians Killed by Palestinians in Israel, 29.9.2000–30.11.2010* [Internet] Available from <http://www.btselem.org/English/statistics/Casualties_Data.asp?Category=6&region=ISRAEL> [Accessed 12 December 2010].

—— (2010c) *Palestinians Killed by Israeli Security Forces in the Gaza Strip, 29.9.2000–26.12.2008* [Internet] Available from <http://www.btselem.org/english/statistics/Casualties_Data.asp?Category=1&region=GAZA&sD=29&sM=09&sY=2000&eD=26&eM=12&eY=2008&filterby=event&oferet_stat=before> [Accessed 12 December 2010].

—— (2010d) *Palestinians Killed by Palestinians in the Gaza Strip, 29.9.2000–26.12.2008* [Internet] Available from <http://www.btselem.org/english/statistics/Casualties_Data.asp?Category=23&region=GAZA&sD=29&sM=09&sY=2000&eD=26&eM=12&eY=2008&filterby=event&oferet_stat=before> [Accessed 12 December 2010].

Cattan, H. (1973) *Palestine and International Law* (London: Longman).

Childers, E. (1976) 'The Wordless Wish: From Citizens to Refugees', in *The Palestinian Issue in Middle East Peace Efforts*, hearings from before the Committee on International Relations, House of Representatives, September, October, November 1975 (US Government Printing Office).

Chomsky, N. (1992) *Deterring Democracy* (London: Vintage Books).

—— (1999) *The Fateful Triangle: The United States, Israel and the Palestinians* (London: Pluto Press).

Cockburn, A. and Cockburn, L. (1991) *Dangerous Liaison: The Inside Story of the US-Israeli Covert Relationship* (New York: HarperCollins).

Cohn-Sherbok, D. (2001) 'A Jewish Perspective', in D. Cohen-Sherbok and D. El-Alami (eds) *The Palestinian-Israeli Conflict: A Beginner's Guide* (Oxford: One World Publications).

Cordesman, A. (2010) 'Israel as a Strategic Liability?' Center for Strategic and International Studies [Internet] Available from <http://csis.org/publication/israel-strategic-liability> [Accessed 27 September 2010].

Crum, B.C. (1947) *Behind the Silken Curtain* (New York: Simon & Schuster)

Dodd, P. and Barakat, H. (1968) *River Without Bridges* (Beirut: Institute for Palestine Studies).

Eban, A. (1977) *An Autobiography* (New York: Random House).

—— (1992) *Personal Witness: Israel through my Eyes* (New York: Putnam Publishing).

Eddy, W. (1954) *F.D.R. Meets Ibn Saud* (New York: American Friends of the Middle East).

Feingold, H.L. (1970) *The Politics of Rescue* (New Brunswick: Rutgers University Press).

Finkelstein, N.G. (1996) *The Rise and Fall of Palestine: A Personal Account of the Intifada Years* (Minneapolis: University of Minnesota Press).

—— (2001) *Image and Reality of the Israel-Palestine Conflict* (London: Verso).

Fisch, H. (1982) *The Zionism of Zion* (in Hebrew) (Tel-Aviv: Zmora Bitan).

Fisk, R. (2001) *Pity the Nation* (Oxford: Oxford University Press).

Flapan, S. (1987) *The Birth of Israel: Myths and Realities* (New York: Pantheon Books).

Foundation for Middle East Peace (1997) 'Settler Population 1972–97' [Internet] Available from <http://www.fmep.org/charts/chart9811_1.gif [Accessed 6 September 2003].

Freedman, S. (2008) 'The Village Defying Israel's Wall', *Guardian*, Comment is Free, 11 July.

Friedlander, D. and Goldscheider, C. (1979) *The Population of Israel* (New York: Columbia University Press).

Gabbay, R. (1959) *A Political Study of the Arab-Jewish Conflict: The Arab Refugee Problem* (Geneva: Librairie E. Droz).

Gilbert, M. (1999) *Israel: A History* (London: Black Swan Books).

Glasgow Media Group (2002) 'Media Coverage of the Developing World: Audience Understandings and Interest'. This has been published in an extended version as Philo (2002).

GlobalSecurity (2009) 'Hamas Rockets' [Internet] Available from <http://www.globalsecurity.org/military/world/para/hamas-qassam.htm> [Accessed 6 September 2010].

Gush Shalom (1998) *Who is Violating the Agreements?* [Internet] Available from <http://www.gush-shalom.org/archives/oslo.html> [Accessed 6 September 2003].

—— (2003) *Barak's Generous Offers* [Internet] Available from <http://www.gush-shalom.org/generous/generous.html> [Accessed 6 September 2003].

Hari, J. (2008) 'The True Story Behind this War is Not the One Israel is Telling', *Independent*, 29 December.

Harris, W.W. (1980) *Taking Root: Israeli Settlements in the West Bank, the Golan and the Gaza-Sinai 1967–1980* (Chichester: Research Studies Press).

Hastings, M. (2002) 'The Disturbing Truth about a War on Terror', *Daily Mail*, 28 October.

Heller, Y. (1985) *The Struggle for the State: Zionist Diplomacy of the Years 1936–48* (in Hebrew) (Jerusalem: Jewish Agency Protocols).

Herzl, T. (1960) *The Complete Diaries of Theodor Herzl* (New York: Herzl Press and Thomas Yoseloff).

Hirst, D. (1977) *The Gun and the Olive Branch* (London: Faber & Faber).

Hitchens, C. and Said, E. (1988) *Blaming the Victims* (London: Verso).

Human Rights Watch (1996) 'Israel's Closure of the West Bank and Gaza Strip', July, vol. 8, no. 3 (E).

—— (1998) 'Security Pact May Encourage Human Rights Violations'. Press Release: New York, 22 October.

—— (1999) *Israel/Lebanon, Persona Non Grata: The Expulsion of Civilians from Israeli-Occupied Lebanon* [Internet] Available from <http://www.hrw.org/reports/1999/lebanon/Isrlb997.htm> [Accessed January 2004].

—— (2007a) 'Indiscriminate Fire', July, vol. 19, no. 1 (E).

—— (2007b) *Why They Died* [Internet] Available from <http://www.hrw.org/en/node/10734/section/5> [Accessed 25 August 2010].

—— (2007c) *Civilians under Assault* [Internet] Available from <http://www.hrw.org/en/node/10758/section/3> [Accessed 25 August 2010].

—— (2008a) *Flooding South Lebanon* [Internet] Available from <http://www.hrw.org/en/node/62428/section/4> [Accessed 25 August 2010].

—— (2008b) 'Israel/Gaza: Israeli Blockade Unlawful Despite Gaza Border Breach' [Internet] Available from <http://www.hrw.org/en/news/2008/01/25/israelgaza-israeli-blockade-unlawful-despite-gaza-border-breach> [Accessed 29 August 2010].

—— (2009a) 'Why We Report on Open Societies' [Internet] Available from <http://www.hrw.org/en/news/2009/10/20/why-we-report-open-societies> [Accessed 25 August 2010].

—— (2009b) 'UN: US, EU Undermine Justice for Gaza Conflict' [Internet] Available from <http://www.hrw.org/en/news/2009/09/30/un-us-eu-undermine-justice-gaza-conflict> [Accessed 25 August 2010].

—— (2009c) 'Colombia: Obama Should Press Uribe on Rights' [Internet] Available from <http://www.hrw.org/en/news/2009/06/26/colombia-obama-should-press-uribe-rights> [Accessed 12 December 2010].

Hunter, J. (1996) *Israeli Foreign Policy: South Africa and Central America* (Boston: South End Press).

Independent Television Commission (2003) *The Public's View* (London: ITC).

Ingrams, D. (1972) *Palestine Papers 1917–1922, Seeds of Conflict* (London: John Murray).

Intelligence and Terrorism Information Center (2008) *Implementing the Lull Arrangement* [Internet] Available from <http://www.terrorism-info.org.il/malam_multimedia/English/eng_n/html/lull_290608e.htm> [Accessed 4 September 2010].

—— (2009) *Summary of Rocket Fire and Mortar Shelling in 2008* [Internet] Available from <http://www.terrorism-info.org.il/malam_multimedia/English/eng_n/pdf/ipc_e007.pdf> [Accessed 4 September 2010].

International Crisis Group (2009) 'End the War in Gaza', Middle East Briefing 26 [Internet] Available from <http://www.crisisgroup.org/~/media/files/middle%20east%20north%20africa/israel%20palestine/b26_ending_the_war_in_gaza.ashx> [Accessed 5 September 2010].

Israeli Defence Forces (2003) *Israeli Civilians Killed/Wounded on the Lebanese Border 1985–99* [Internet] Available from <http://www.idf.il/english/statistics/civilian.stm> [Accessed 5 September 2003].

Israeli Ministry of Foreign Affairs (1996) *Israel's Settlements: Their Conformity with International Law* [Internet] Available from <http://www.israel.org/mfa/go.asp?MFAH0dgj0> [Accessed 5 September 2003].

—— (1999) *Suicide and Other Bombing Attacks Inside Israel Since the Declaration of Principles, September 1993* [Internet] Available from <http://www.mfa.gov.il/mfa/go.asp?MFAH0i5d0> [Accessed 5 September 2003].

—— (2004) *The Cabinet Resolution Regarding the Disengagement Plan*, 6 June [Internet] Available from <http://www.mfa.gov.il/MFA/Peace+Process/Reference+Documents/Revised+Disengagement+Plan+6-June-2004.htm> [Accessed 5 February 2006].

—— (2006a) *Responding to Hizbullah Attacks from Lebanon: Issues of Proportionality*, 25 July [Internet] Available from <http://www.mfa.gov.il/MFA/Government/Law/Legal+Issues+and+Rulings/Responding+to+Hizbullah+attacks+from+Lebanon-+Issues+of+proportionality+July+2006.htm> [Accessed 25 August 2010].

—— (2006b) *The Second Lebanon War* [Internet] Available from <http://www.mfa.gov.il/MFA/Terrorism-+Obstacle+to+Peace/Terrorism+from+Lebanon-+Hizbullah/Hizbullah+attack+in+northern+Israel+and+Israels+response+12-Jul-2006.htm> [Accessed 25 August 2010].

—— (2006c) *Hizbullah's Exploitation of Lebanese Population Centers and Civilians: Photographic Evidence* [Internet] Available from <http://www.mfa.gov.il/MFA/MFAArchive/2000_2009/2006/Operation%20Change%20of%20Direction%20Video%20Clips> [Accessed 25 August 2010].

—— (2008) *One Month of Calm Along the Israel-Gaza Border*, 27 July [Internet] Available from <http://www.mfa.gov.il/MFA/Terrorism-+Obstacle+to+Peace/Hamas+war+against+Israel/One+month+of+calm+in+Gaza+28-Jul-2008.htm> [Accessed 25 August 2010].

—— (2009a) *Operation Cast Lead: Israel Strikes Back Against Hamas Terror in Gaza*, 19 July [Internet] Available from <http://www.mfa.gov.il/MFA/Terrorism-+Obstacle+to+Peace/Hamas+war+against+Israel/Israel_strikes_back_against_Hamas_terror_infrastructure_Gaza_27-Dec-2008.htm> [Accessed 25 August 2010].

—— (2009b) *FAQ: The Operation in Gaza – Factual and Legal Aspects* [Internet] Available from <http://www.mfa.gov.il/MFA/Terrorism-+Obstacle+to+Peace/Terrorism+and+Islamic+Fundamentalism-/Operation_in_Gaza-Factual_and_Legal_Aspects.htm> [Accessed 25 August 2010].

—— (2009c) *Israel's Analysis and Comments on the Gaza Fact-Finding Mission Report* [Internet] Available from <http://www.mfa.gov.il/MFA/Terrorism-+Obstacle+to+Peace/Hamas+war+against+Israel/Israel_analysis_comments_Goldstone_Mission_15-Sep-2009.htm> [Accessed 25 August 2010].

—— (2010) *MFA Legal Expert Sarah Weiss Maudi on the Legal Aspects of Gaza Aid*, 26 May 2010. [Internet] Available from <http://www.mfa.gov.il/MFA/HumanitarianAid/Palestinians/Legal_aspects_Gaza_aid_26-May-2010.htm> [Accessed 25 August 2010].

J Street (2010) 'NEW POLL: American Jews Continue to Support Obama Push for Two-State Solution, Back Strong U.S. Engagement' [Internet] Available from <http://www.jstreet.org/blog/?p=937> [Accessed 26 September 2010].

Kapeliouk, A. (1984) *Sabra and Shatila: Inquiry into a Massacre* (Belmont, MA: Association of Arab-American University Graduates).

Karsh, E. (2000) *Fabricating Israeli History: The 'New Historians'* (London: Frank Cass).

—— (2002) 'What Occupation?', *Commentary*, July.

Khalidi, W. (1971) *From Haven to Conquest: Zionism and the Palestinian Problem Until 1948* (Munich: KG SaurVerlag).

—— (1988) 'Plan Dalet: Master Plan for the Conquest of Palestine', *Journal of Palestine Studies*, Autumn 1988.

Kimmerling (1983) *Zionism and Territory: The Socio-Territorial Dimension of Zionist Politics* (Berkeley: University of California Regents).

Laqueur, W. and Rubin, B. (1984) *The Israel-Arab Reader* (New York: Facts on File/Viking Penguin).

Lebanon Higher Relief Council (2006) *Rebuilding Lebanon Together 100 Days After* [Internet] Available from <http://www.rebuildlebanon.gov.lb/images_Gallery/Rebuilding%20Lebanon%20Together-4.pdf> [Accessed 26 August 2010].

Lilienthal, A. (1978) *The Zionist Connection* (New York: Dodd, Mead & Co.).

Linowitz, S. (1957) 'The Legal Basis for the State of Israel', *American Bar Association Journal*, vol. 43.

Lorch, N. (1961) *The Edge of the Sword: Israel's War of Independence, 1947–1949* (New York: Putnam).

Loughborough University Communication Research Centre (2006) *The BBC's Reporting of the Israeli/Palestinian Conflict, August 1st 2005–January 31st 2006*, Loughborough University. (Published as an appendix to the *Report of the Independent Panel for the BBC Governors on Impartiality of BBC Coverage of the Israeli/Palestinian Conflict*, Thomas, Q. 2006).

Lurman, A. (2010) 'Israeli PR Machine Won Gaza Flotilla Media Battle', *Guardian*, Comment is Free, 4 June.

Lustick, I. (1980) *Arabs in the Jewish State: Israel's Control of a National Minority* (New York: University of Texas Press).

Masalha, N. (1992) *Expulsion of the Palestinians: The Concept of 'Transfer' in Zionist Political Thought* (Beirut: Institute for Palestinian Studies).

—— (1999) 'The 1967 Palestinian Exodus', in G. Karmi and E. Cotran (eds) *The Palestinian Exodus 1948–1998* (London: Garnet Publishing).

Mayhew, C. (1973) *Crossroads to Israel* (Bloomington, IN: Indiana University Press).

McCarthy, J. (1990) *The Population of Palestine* (New York: Columbia University Press).

McCarthy, R. (2009a) 'Hamas Murder Campaign in Gaza Exposed', *Guardian*, 14 February.

—— (2009b) 'Shifting Sands: Hamas Police Patrol the Beaches in Move to Enforce Conservative Dress Code', *Guardian*, 19 October.

McGreal, C. (2009a) 'Why Israel Went to War in Gaza', *Observer*, 4 January.

—— (2009b) 'Israel Incursion into Gaza Replays Well-Worn Foot Print', *Guardian* analysis, 4 January [Internet] Available from <http://www.guardian.co.uk/world/2009/jan/04/israel-gaza-invasion-troops-hamas> [Accessed 12 December 2010].

Mearsheimer, J.J. and Walt, S.M. (2008) *The Israel Lobby and US Foreign Policy* (London: Penguin).

Mendel, Y. (2008) 'How to Become an Israeli Journalist', *London Review of Books*, 6 March.

Mishal, S. and Sela, A. (2000) *The Palestinian Hamas: Vision, Violence and Coexistence* (New York: Columbia University Press).

Morris, B. (1989) *The Birth of the Palestinian Refugee Problem* (London: Cambridge University Press).

——— (1992) *Israel's Secret Wars: A History of Israel's Intelligence Services* (London: Futura Publications).

——— (1997) *Israel's Border Wars, 1949–1956 Arab Infiltration, Israeli Retaliation, and the Countdown to the Suez War* (Oxford: Oxford University Press).

——— (2001) *Righteous Victims: A History of the Zionist-Arab Conflict* (New York: Vintage Books).

Nasrallah, H. (2006) Press Conference, *Al Manar*, 12 July. Translated by Mideastwire.com. *Law* [Internet] Available from <http://web.archive.org/web/20061113080502/http://www.upc.org.uk/hasann12jul06.html> [Accessed 24 August 2010].

Neff, D. (1985) *Warriors for Jerusalem* (New York: Smithmark Publishing).

Netanyahu, B. (2000) *A Durable Peace: Israel and its Place Among the Nations.* (New York: Warner Books).

O'Dwyer, T. (2009) 'Israel: How Things Fell Apart' [Internet] Available from <http://www.opendemocracy.net/article/israel-how-things-fell-apart> [Accessed 10 September 2010].

O'Loughlin, T. (2008) 'Israel Builds PR Campaign to Lay Blame on Hamas', *Guardian*, 29 December.

Ovendale, R. (1999) *The Origins of the Arab-Israeli Wars* (Harlow: Pearson).

Palestinian Centre for Human Rights (2009) *Gaza Casualty Statistics* [Internet] Available from <http://www.pchrgaza.org/files/PressR/English/2008/list.pdf> [Accessed 24 August 2010].

Pappe, I. (1999) 'Were They Expelled? The History, Historiography and Relevance of the Palestinian Refugee Problem', in G. Karmi and E. Cotran (eds) *The Palestinian Exodus 1948–1998* (Reading: Garnet Publishing).

Pelham, N. (2009) 'Diary', *London Review of Books*, 22 October.

Perlmutter, A., Handel, M. and Bar-Joseph, U. (1982) *Two Minutes over Baghdad* (London: Vallentine Mitchell).

Peters, J. (1984) *From Time Immemorial: The Origins of the Arab-Jewish Conflict over Palestine* (New York: HarperCollins).

Phillips, M. (2003) 'New Threat, but Left with Their Blinkers On', *Jewish Chronicle*, 28 February.

Philo, G. (2002) 'Television News and Audience Understanding of War, Conflict and Disaster', *Journalism Studies*, vol. 3, no. 2. London: Routledge.

——— (2007) 'Can Discourse Analysis Successfully Explain the Content of Media and Journalistic Practice?' *Journalism Studies*, vol. 8, no. 2.

Philo, G., Hewitt, J. and Beharrell, P. (1995) 'And Now They Are Out Again: Industrial News', in G. Philo (ed.) *Glasgow Media Group Reader*, Vol. 2 (London: Routledge).

Philo, G. and Miller, D. (2001) *Market Killing* (London: Pearson Education).

Pundak, R. (2001) 'From Oslo to Taba: What Went Wrong?' *Survival*, vol. 43, no. 3.

Randal, J. (1983) *The Tragedy of Lebanon: Christian Warlords, Israeli Adventurers and American Bunglers* (London: Chatto & Windus/The Hogarth Press).

Rozen, L. (2010) 'What Biden Told Netanyahu Behind Closed Doors: "This is starting to get dangerous for us"', *Politico*, 11 March [Internet] Available from <http://www.politico.com/blogs/laurarozen/0310/What_Biden_told_Netanyahu_

behind_closed_doors_This_is_starting_to_get_dangerous_for_us.html?showall> [Accessed 26 September 2010].

Rubin, U. (2006) 'Hizballah's Rocket Campaign Against Northern Israel: A Preliminary Report', *Jerusalem Issue Brief*, vol. 6, no. 10.

Rusk, D. (1991) *As I Saw It* (New York: Penguin USA).

Sachar, H.M. (1977) *A History of Israel: From the Rise of Zionism to Our Time* (Oxford: Blackwell).

Segev, T. (1993) *The Seventh Million: The Israelis and the Holocaust* (New York: Hill and Wang).

—— (2001) *One Palestine, Complete. Jews and Arabs Under the British Mandate* (London: Abacus).

Shabi, R. (2009) 'Special Spin Body Gets Media on Message, says Israel', *Guardian*, 2 January.

Shafir, G. (1999) 'Zionism and Colonialism', in I. Pappe (ed.) *The Israel/Palestine Question* (New York: Routledge).

Shahak, I. (1994) 'Israel's State-Assisted Terrorism: "Settlers" as Armed Combatants', *Washington Report on Middle East Affairs*, February/March.

—— (1995) *Analysis of Israeli Policies: The Priority of the Ideological Factor.* Report no. 154. 12 May.

Shahak, I. and Mezvinsky, N. (1999) *Jewish Fundamentalism in Israel* (London: Pluto Press).

Shlaim, A. (2000) *The Iron Wall: Israel and the Arab World* (London: Penguin Press).

—— (2001) 'Israel and the Arab Coalition in 1948', in E. Rogan and A. Shlaim (eds) *The War for Palestine: Rewriting the History of 1948* (Cambridge: Cambridge University Press).

—— (2009) 'Israel and Gaza: Rhetoric and Reality' [Internet] Available from <http://www.opendemocracy.net/article/israel-and-gaza-rhetoric-and-reality> [Accessed 15 September 2010].

Shonfeld, M. (1977) *The Holocaust Victims Accuse: Documents and Testimony on Jewish War Criminals, Part I* (Brooklyn: Neturei Karta of USA).

Sieghart, W. (2008) 'We Must Adjust Our Distorted Image of Hamas', *The Times*, 31 December.

Singer, M. (1977) 'Right is Might', *Jerusalem Post*, 29 June.

Thomas, Q. (2006) *Report of the Independent Panel for the BBC Governors on Impartiality of BBC Coverage of the Israeli/Palestinian Conflict*, London: BBC.

Tillman, S. (1982) *The United States in the Middle East: Interests and Obstacles* (Bloomington: IN: University of Indiana Press).

UNICEF (2006) *The Humanitarian Challenge in Lebanon* [Internet] Available from <http://www.unicef.org/emerg/index_35274.html> [Accessed 1 September 2010].

United Nations (1945) League of Nations. 'The Mandate System. Origin Applications Principles'. 30 April 1945. LoN/1945.VI.A.1.

—— (1967) General Assembly Fifth Emergency Session, 5 July.

—— (1988) 'Report of the Special Committee to Investigate Israeli Practices Affecting the Human Rights of the Population of the Occupied Territories'. Resolution 43/58A, passed 6 December.

—— (1990) 'The Origins and Evolution of the Palestine Problem 1917–1988' [Internet] Available from <http://domino.un.org/UNISPAL.NSF/561c6ee353d740fb8525607d00581829/aeac80e740c782e4852561150071fdb0!OpenDocument> [Accessed 6 September 2003].

—— (1994) Commission on Human Rights. 'Question of the Violation of Human Rights in the Occupied Arab Territories, Including Palestine'. E/CN.4/RES/1994/3 (A+B)E/1994/24E/CN.4/1994/132, 18 February.

—— (1996) 'UN Report on Israel's Bombing of the United Nations Compound at Qana, Lebanon'. S1996/337, 7 May.

—— (1997) 'Illegal Israeli Actions in Occupied East Jerusalem and the Rest of the Occupied Palestinian Territory'. Resolution A/RES/ES-10/2, passed 25 April.

—— (1999) Commission on Human Rights. 'Question of the Violation of Human Rights in the Occupied Arab Territories, Including Palestine'. E/CN.4/RES/1999/5, 23 April.

—— (2007) 'The Closure of the Gaza Strip: The Economic and Humanitarian Consequences' [Internet] Available from <http://unispal.un.org/pdfs/GSclosure.pdf> [Accessed 29 August 2010].

—— (2009a) 'Report of the United Nations Fact-Finding Mission on the Gaza Conflict' [Internet] Available from <http://www2.ohchr.org/english/bodies/hrcouncil/specialsession/9/docs/UNFFMGC_Report.pdf> [Accessed 30 September 2010].

—— (2009b) 'Gaza: UN Official Reports Horrific Hospital Scenes of Casualties' [Internet] Available from <http://www.un.org/apps/news/story.asp?NewsID=29520&Cr=gaza&Cr1=unrwa> [Accessed 29 August 2010].

—— (2010) 'Report of the United Nations Fact-Finding Mission to Investigate Violations of International Law, Including Humanitarian and Human Rights Law, Resulting from the Israeli Attacks on the Flotilla of Ships Carrying Humanitarian Assistance' [Internet] Available from <http://www2.ohchr.org/english/bodies/hrcouncil/docs/15session/A.HRC.15.21_en.pdf> [Accessed 12 December 2010].

Usher, G. (2006) 'The Wall and the Dismemberment of Palestine', *Race & Class*, 47: 9–30.

Weiner, J.R. and Bell, A. (2008) *International Law and the Fighting in Gaza*, Jerusalem Center for Public Affairs [Internet] Available from <http://www.jcpa.org/text/puzzle1.pdf> [Accessed 3 September 2010].

Weisgal, M. (1944) *Chaim Weizmann* (New York: Dial Press).

Weizman, E. (2009) 'Lawfare in Gaza: Legislative Attack' [Internet] Available from <http://www.opendemocracy.net/article/legislative-attack> [Accessed 15 September 2010].

Yisraeli, D. (1974) *The Palestine Problem in German Politics* (Bar Ilan University: Ramat Gan).

Index

Compiled by Sue Carlton